'Each essay offers a critically insightful examination of a particular author or work, and the coverage of the region is admirable in terms of both geographical spread and literary genre ... This collection of articles, carefully grouped around specific themes and the authors who invoke them, is an important contribution to the study of modern Arabic literature.'

ROGER ALLEN

'One of the best, most illuminating, exhaustive, and up-to-date [works on] the subject in any language, including Arabic ... The breadth of this book, covering Arabic literature from the Mashriq to the Maghrib, is matched by its depth and erudition, and its balance of theory and close-reading of key texts is admirable ... It is an immensely valuable book, extraordinarily intelligent in its conception and design and its rigor, vigour and scholarship.'

SABRY HAFEZ

Arabic Literature

Postmodern Perspectives

Edited by

Angelika Neuwirth
Andreas Pflitsch
Barbara Winckler

SAQI

ISBN: 978-0-86356-694-3

First published as *Arabische Literatur, postmodern* by edition text + kritik, Munich

Copyright © edition text + kritik, 2004

This English edition published by Saqi, 2010

© Saqi, 2010

A full CIP record for this book is available from the British Library.
A full CIP record for this book is available from the Library of Congress.

Printed and bound by CPI Mackays, Chatham, ME5 8TD

SAQI
26 Westbourne Grove, London W2 5RH, UK
2398 Doswell Avenue, Saint Paul, Minnesota, 55108, US
Verdun, Beirut, Lebanon
www.saqibooks.com

Contents

PREFACE   9

INTRODUCTION

Postmodernism   13
Facets of a Figure of Thought
Ines Kappert

The End of Illusions   25
On Arab Postmodernism
Andreas Pflitsch

PART ONE: MEMORY

Introduction   41
Angelika Neuwirth

The Divinity of the Profane   65
Representations of the Divine in the Poetry of Adonis
Stefan Weidner

Days of Amber, City of Saffron   76
Edwar al-Kharrat Remembers and Writes an Unintended Autobiography
Andreas Pflitsch

On the Necessity of Writing the Present   87
Elias Khoury and the "Birth of the Novel" in Lebanon
Sonja Mejcher-Atassi

Historical Memory in Times of Decline   97
Saadallah Wannous and Rereading History
Friederike Pannewick

Linguistic Temptations and Erotic Unveilings   110
Rashid al-Daif on Language, Love, War, and Martyrdom
Angelika Neuwirth

Memories for the Future: Abdelrahman Munif   134
Susanne Enderwitz

Authenticity as Counter-Strategy: Fighting Sadat's "Open Door" Politics   146
Gamal al-Ghitani and *The Epistle of Insights into the Destinies*
Stephan Guth

"This reality is deplorable"   158
The Egypt of Sonallah Ibrahim: Between Media Representation and
Experienced Everyday Reality
Andrea Haist

Hebrew Bible and Arabic Poetry   171
Reclaiming Palestine as a Homeland Made of Words: Mahmoud Darwish
Angelika Neuwirth

Traditions and Counter-Traditions in the Land of the Bible   197
Emile Habibi's De-Mythologizing of History
Angelika Neuwirth

The Poet of the Arabic Short Story: Zakariyya Tamir   220
Ulrike Stehli-Werbeck

PART TWO: POLYGAMY OF PLACE

Introduction   233
Andreas Pflitsch

"From the Orient to the Occident it is just a reflection"   243
The Mirror-Worlds of Habib Tengour
Regina Keil-Sagawe

"I dream in no man's land": Anton Shammas   259
Christian Szyska

Exile at Home   272
Samir Naqqash – Prophecy as Poetics
Osman Hajjar

Reading the Ruins   287
Repressed Memory and Multiple Identity in the Work of Sélim Nassib
Christian Junge

British-Lebanese Identity Fallacies   302
Tony Hanania and a Malady Called Homesickness
Andreas Pflitsch

The Forbidden Paradise   311
How Etel Adnan Learnt to Paint in Arabic
Sonja Mejcher-Atassi

"So we are called Lebanese"   321
Rabih Alameddine on the Unbearable Lightness of Being
Nowhere at Home
Andreas Pflitsch

The Desert as Homeland and Metaphor   331
Reflections on the Novels of the Tuareg Writer Ibrahim al-Koni
Hartmut Fähndrich

A Surrealist Trip to Paradise and Back   342
The Iraqi Author Abdalqadir al-Janabi
Sibylla Krainick

PART THREE: GENDER TRANSGRESSIONS

Introduction   361
Barbara Winckler

Changing the Sexes between Utopia and Heterotopia   369
Tahar Ben Jelloun's *The Sand Child* and *The Sacred Night*
Roland Spiller

Androgyny as Metaphor   382
Hoda Barakat and *The Stone of Laughter*
Barbara Winckler

Transgression as Program   397
On the Novels of Rachid Boudjedra
Doris Ruhe

An Egyptian Don Quixote?   410
Salah Abd al-Sabur's Rethinking of the Majnun-Layla Paradigm
Angelika Neuwirth

On Writing in the "Language of the Enemy"   429
Assia Djebar and the Buried Voices of Algerian History
Barbara Winckler

I Write, Therefore I Am   444
Metafiction as Self-Assertion in Mustafa Dhikri's *Much Ado About a Gothic Labyrinth*
Christian Junge

Transgressions, or the Logic of the Body   461
Mohamed Choukri's Work: A Fusing of Eros, Logos and Politics
Özkan Ezli

A New Trojan War?   471
Vénus Khoury-Ghata on Sexuality and War
Monika Moster-Eichberger

Beyond Autobiography   484
Under the Sign of Destruction: the First-Person Narrator
in Alia Mamdouh's novel *Naphtalene*
Verena Klemm

CONTRIBUTORS   497

INDEX   499

Preface

Right up to the present day, modern Arabic literature has led a niche existence; the quest for the audience it deserves is far from over even now. International disinterest in literature is in stark contrast to the keen attention that is paid to the Arab states in political newscasts and reports, which continue to be dominated by the unresolved Middle East conflict and the precarious situation in Iraq. Although the award of the Nobel Prize for Literature to Naguib Mahfouz in 1988 placed him on the map of world literature, the expectations of Western readers continue to be shaped by a desire for the exotic. Picturesque Oriental scenarios and ancient traditions are not merely implicit; they are avidly consumed. This perspective fails to recognize the quality and diversity of Arabic literature which – along with other world literatures – reflects our (post-)modern condition without denying its own tradition. Moreover, such an attitude obstructs any true cultural dialogue. Thus a very different outlook is long overdue: to finally see Arabic literature as what it undoubtedly is – an important contribution to contemporary culture worldwide.

Organized around the central themes of memory, identity and gender, each of which is discussed in an introductory essay, this volume introduces the work of twenty-nine pivotal authors from the Arab world, from Morocco and Algeria via Egypt and Palestine through to Iraq, who write in Arabic, English, French and Hebrew.

An extended and updated version of a volume published in German under the title of *Arabische Literatur, postmodern* in 2004, the present publication would not have been possible without the generous financial support provided by the German Research Foundation (DFG) and the Free University of Berlin. We are equally indebted to Paul Bowman (Berlin) who translated most of the texts and saw to it that all the articles were put into their final form. And last but not least, we would like to thank Saqi Books for accepting the manuscript and realizing its print.

Angelika Neuwirth, Andreas Pflitsch, Barbara Winckler

Introduction

Postmodernism
Facets of a Figure of Thought

Ines Kappert

Once passionately debated, postmodernism is now regarded somewhat more calmly. Only a few years ago it was still highly controversial in the Western world, the theme on everyone's lips. Architecture was postmodern where it combined colorful, playful turrets and oriels with reflective glass facades, displaying a breathtaking disinterest in the rigorous forms of classical modernism such as those of the Bauhaus. Novels were postmodern when they pilfered from other works, sampled texts in the style of pop music, nonchalantly skipped over the boundaries between genres, and brashly rejected the dominating position of the author as the origin or "vanishing point" of a text.

Accordingly and unfailingly, Umberto Eco's *The Name of the Rose* (1980) was taken as the stellar reference point for postmodernism in literature. His delight in using pastiche merged with mirthful playfulness in an ironic reproduction that included the staging of clashes between the incongruous. Hypertext and hyperspace as miniscule universes of the eclectic became symbols of an epoch that was declared to be new and whose beginnings were dated back to the 1960s. The aspiration typically pinned to so-called modernism, namely to create something unprecedented that surpassed existing works, was considered elitist and therefore undesirable. Instead of a coming age envisioned in works of art; instead of progress and emancipation obtained through the process of dialectical negation; focus now switched to paradoxical figures like the "contemporaneity of the non-contemporaneous", to "dynamic standstill" – and the "end of the grand narratives". Anything seemed possible, precisely because the belief in miracles had ebbed away. "Come here, shooting star", writes Rainald Goetz in his five-volume *Geschichte der Gegenwart*, encapsulating the astronomical demand, so typical of the outgoing twentieth century, for endless consumerism in the here and now.

In his 1984 essay *Postmodernism, or the Cultural Logic of Late Capitalism*, a pivotal text in the definition of postmodernism, the American literary theorist Fredric Jameson takes postmodern architecture and its particular staging of space as the starting point:

... this latest mutation in space – postmodern hyperspace – has finally succeeded in transcending the capacities of the individual human body to locate

itself, to organize its immediate surroundings perceptually, and cognitively to map its position in a mappable external world.

Jameson explains his observation that hyperspace, which is to say the nucleus of postmodernism, deprives the individual of coherent orientation in a fundamental sense by analyzing a gigantic hotel designed by John Portman in 1977. The Bonaventure Hotel in Los Angeles comprises five many-storied towers congregated closely together, the facades made entirely of reflective glass. The buildings form an interconnecting ensemble of shopping mall, hotel, cinema complex, and small parkways, i.e. they form a giant and multi-defined space, meaning that they are less an extension than a miniature imitation of the city itself. The entrances are withdrawn and understated, an aspect Jameson underlines; so too the exits: they are barely visible and difficult to find. The characteristics of postmodern hyperspaces are thus not solely limited to eclectic styles and functions; integral is a closing-off from the outside world. Once one has entered these mini-cities, the outside world recedes and time seems no longer to advance linearly but rather to turn in a circle. Future and past subsequently appear to be equally present; here too the same definition applies as that given by Rainald Goetz for the law of the pop novel: "the time form of absolute present tense." It is precisely this kind of de-historicizing that in turn determines the individual's difficulty in identifying his/her location. According to Jameson and other theorists of postmodernism, when combined with the manicured multiculturalism that is aligned to a mixture of styles and epochs and driven by commercial branding, it causes the individual to feel engulfed, at times losing any sense of self. This totalization of capitalist space, which foresees no escape, assimilates and swallows the individual by offering as few orientation markers as possible in terms of time, space, and culture, redressing the swirling confusion by pegging out as many orientation markers for consumerism as possible. Once he has entered, or perhaps more accurately, been sucked in, the prospective consumer could be anywhere on the globe, which thus becomes very small and very large at once.

The loss of exterior, or the decomposition of truth into a thousand splinters

From a retrospective – and thus composed – perspective, postmodernism has lost the idea of an exterior, which is ultimately a cipher for utopia. This not only has a multifaceted impact on the consumerist and motional behavior of the individual, but on the idea of truth, of the human aptitude for action, and the concept of the subject; in other words an instance authorized to say "I". As a form of critique, postmodernism aims at devoutly metaphysical constructs, eschatology or theologies of history: only the here and now counts. The sacred has served its time and the divine plan has turned out to be a blank page. Whoever wants nevertheless to continue to believe believes in the cosmic forces emanating from vividly colored stones, their belief is esoteric.

Conversely, the one absolute and transcendent truth sought by art, philosophy and religion is unattainable. Hence there is a need to recognize that the limits of what is knowable, the determination of which is critique in the Kantian sense, and the experience of finitude set together the horizon of the conceivable. As Michel Foucault writes in *A Preface to Transgression*:

> By denying us the limit of the Limitless, the death of God leads to an experience in which nothing may again announce the exteriority of being, and consequently to an experience which is *interior* and *sovereign*. But such an experience, for which the death of God is an explosive reality, discloses as its own secret and clarification, its intrinsic finitude, the limitless reign of Limit, and the emptiness of those excesses in which it spends itself and where it is found wanting.

Dependent on context, truth is now defined only in terms of how a cause or an idea emerges and becomes "right", meaning that instead of an absolute we have a relational or relative truth. Due to its finiteness truth pluralizes; postmodernism therefore speaks of truths. While this insight is by no means new, the nonchalant way in which it is accepted and then exploited in some quarters most certainly is. There is no trace of mourning or anguish evinced by a sense of transcendental homelessness, but rather revelry and joy in ironic play, a lust to transgress and violate laws and boundaries without gravitating to or reoccupying a center.

This new operation along surfaces is in turn supremely conducive to a popular end-time climate, as represented by Paul Virilio. Instead of serving the revolution, one now assumes the exciting position of observer, looking on as a limitedly sustainable world dwindles away: things occur. The factitious sun rises or the world sinks. Wars flicker on television screens; they appear, at least in the West, to be virtual. Sentences chain themselves together. Language speaks itself. For this, it does not necessarily need a human subject capable of commanding history. This was the conviction of the French philosopher Jean-François Lyotard, who introduced the concept "postmodern" into contemporary philosophy at the end of the 1970s. His report on the condition of knowledge, *The Postmodern Condition* (1979), remains a key reference point despite the intervening years of controversy. For his own part, Lyotard came to consider the term "postmodern" to be somewhat "unfortunate" and seven years after his path-breaking report he advocated seeing postmodernism not as a coherent philosophical concept but primarily as a "disposition or rather a state of mind."

The controversy about a new attitude and sensibility

In summary, this new attitude and sensibility is characterized by an often attested-to disorientation, an extensive profanation, a critique of modernism's alleged elitism, including its totalistic tendencies, a positive reevaluation of enjoyment based on consumerism, and the loss of faith in the liberating power of utopia. Diehard postmodernists have come to accept the disenchantment of the world; capitalism seems as all-embracing as it is invincible, while the collapse of its counter model, the Soviet Union, now appears to us as the belated realization that a dream had long since petered out, betrayed into becoming a nightmare. Symptomatic of this fading of utopian aspirations is the corresponding global rise of commercial entertainment culture, which from musicals and Hollywood movies through to TV soap operas addresses and attracts all population strata.

One could of course dismiss postmodernism as a cheap gaudy product of the culture industry, or assign it a place in the inexorably expanding field of society's obsession with the spectacle, and so consider it to be long past its sell-by date. That would probably be legitimate. After all, in the catchphrase competition to find a term encapsulating the attitude and sensibility of the present age, "postmodern" has long been supplanted by "globalization". This would, however, mean scrapping any attempt to close in on the reason that postmodernism, both as sensibility and aesthetic concept, sparked such controversy and debate, leaving a mark on contemporary thought that is still very much discernible today.

To take Lyotard as an example, it is patently clear that disappointment at the failure of a leftwing utopia deeply affected the generation of 1968. In France, "Sartre's errors", meaning his misjudgment of Stalinism and disillusionment with the authoritarian postcolonial governments in former French colonies, were the background to turning away from a political engagement that strove to bring about revolution. In the case of Germany, in addition to the failure of the '68 movement, the crisis of the welfare state and the failure of the peace movement in the 1980s are usually cited as founts of such disappointment.

No longer interested in class conflict and no longer fundamentally critical of capitalism, analytical attention now turns to the spectacles and linguistic games within society. This shift in direction is by no means uncontested. The normalization of the loss of utopia, the disappearance of the author, the erasure of a historical subject, the radical profanation of the realm of ideas, and the delight in a new superficiality: for around thirty years, these trends and their critical observation were the fabric of which outrage was spun in Western feuilletons and the academia of the industrialized states. One need only recall the almost titanic – and at times spiteful – encounters between Lyotard, Derrida and Habermas, not to mention the attempts to mediate by theorists like Manfred Frank, exemplified by his *What is Neostructuralism?*, 1983.

Debate as to the direction of feminist thought was no less heated. The postmodernist critique of the one truth, multiculturalism, and the entry of popular culture into theory and academic disciplines ushered in a paradigmatic shift: women's studies became gender studies. Emblematic of this transition is the continuing controversy surrounding Judith Butler's critique of the universalism of women's studies, first articulated in *Gender Trouble* (1990). The majority of the second-wave feminist movement, which had formed out of the 1968 movement, were (and in part still are) up in arms at the American philosopher's claim that feminist theory had implicitly reproduced the hierarchies between white and non-white, between rich and poor. According to Butler, this stems from the perspective taken: feminist theories only regard the problematic from the position of white middle-class women, while simultaneously abstracting this particularity into the status of all women. What is worse, in blending out their dominant position as white and relatively wealthy in global terms, it is this figure that is universalized as a victim, which amounts to nothing less than the dislodgement of non-white women from any genuine representation. For Butler, only by pluralizing the feminist subject, recognizing the essential difference between non-white and white women, and taking leave of the dictate of heterosexuality; accompanied by a simultaneous openness towards what it means to be female, black, or colored as well as lesbian, gay, or transsexual: in short by bidding farewell to an entirely positively contoured concept of femininity as celebrated by the so-called difference feminism of a Hélène Cixous or Julia Kristeva; only then could one speak of feminist theory reclaiming its status as a critique of society. This realignment would entail, however, the relativization of the idea that gender alone determines the position of the individual in the social and patriarchal structured vertical hierarchy. Categories like class and race are just as important. This also means that the feminist subject can be male, gay and black. Blanket classifications of men as a homogenous set of offending culprits and thus the abstract idea of the patriarch are assailed as being ideological and myopic.

Along with the mushrooming of "temples of consumerism", an increasing acceptance of homosexuality and transsexuality, the rise of hip hop and the self-confident presence of blacks in popular culture are all hallmarks of postmodernism. The primacy of white masculinity as the foundation of a sovereign subject is called into question and on this point, at the very least, the 1968 generation has been outstripped on its own leftist flank. A critique disclosing how the drawbacks of the current economic dynamic are placed on the working population, the bedrock of our gleeful consumerism, has more or less fallen by the wayside: they are the subject of relatively little analytical attention. The pact between broad sections of society with the spectacle, with pop culture, and with facile enjoyment should not be seen in isolation, though: it is inextricably bound to the strengthening of an anti-elitist, postcolonial, feminist and queer perspective; a perspective that denounces the grand narratives of potential progress and the emancipation of "man" as idealistic and paternalistic. Moreover, it is bound to the extrusion of the "non-solvent" from public discourse.

But none of this provides sufficient explanation for the massive show of resistance from large parts of the 1968 generation and hermeneutically schooled thinkers against postmodernist thinking: its ideas of relative truth claims; its supplanting of the allegiance to truth with a love of play and difference; and its acceptance of a world that is basically arbitrary and unreliable – but not without its amusing aspects. So what was at stake in this standoff? And what is the state of play today?

To find our bearings in this thicket, I shall undertake what I have hitherto avoided in the effort to recall and delineate these often extremely confusing debates: a distinction needs to be drawn between postmodernism as a label for a critical-hedonistic sensibility and outlook in (as Marxists would put it) "late capitalism", and the theoretical approach of "post-structuralism", pivotal in philosophy since the end of the 1960s.

The excision of the revolution

The paradox of the subject being thrown back upon a fragmented self, so heatedly debated in the postmodernist age, and the waning of the imaginative power to envision that life could be radically different obviously has grave repercussions for the cardinal narrative strategies and philosophical reflections in circulation. When utopian thinking suddenly appears anachronistic, when – from a Western perspective – one's own life-world becomes total, breaking out of encrusted structures and given circumstances seems almost a hopeless endeavor, while the imaginative invention of something completely new appears idealistic, if not naïve. What remains, in the view of many post-structuralists, is to trace and tap into the force that is generated by displacements and the proliferation of differences and variations within the inevitable repetition of traditional epistemes and their necessary representation through language. In his 1966 essay "Structure, Sign and Play in the Discourse of Human Sciences", Jacques Derrida writes:

> There is no sense in doing without the concepts of metaphysics in order to shake metaphysics. We have no language – no syntax and no lexicon – which is foreign to this history; we can pronounce not a single destructive proposition

which has not already had to slip into the form, the logic, and the implicit propositions of precisely what it seeks to contest.

Critique thus always entails at least a partial recreation or restoration of what it criticizes.

Derrida describes this simultaneity with his famous strategic concept of *deconstruction*, pivotal for literary theory and studies. This conceptual term draws together the two movements of destruction and construction, mutually preclusive in a binary logic, and so designates them as inseparable moves in a process. This aspect needs to be reiterated: in this approach critique is always bound to what is criticized and is therefore not the sacrosanct realm of a single critic. Something new, a new way of thinking, can only be evoked by supplementing something already given, a supplement that shifts the weighting in this given field. The *supplement* does not erase an established meaning of a concept, but rather inscribes itself into an already existing field of meaning. It writes over or crosses out without ever replacing what has been negated. In this way, a trace of another meaning, a different way of thinking, always adheres to or abides in each newly supplemented concept or approach. Like footprints in damp sand, an illustrative metaphor favored by Derrida, they mark a vanished presence as being present.

These supplements, which circumvent and thus undermine an already existing prescriptive signification, are possible because language, by virtue of the absence of an all-controlling center, is an open system. Language continually extrapolates itself and qua incessant differential movements initiates and generates meaning. For as long as a word, a sentence – or in short, "language" – transports a meaning, then movement is in play.

> If totalization no longer has any meaning, it is not because the infiniteness of a field cannot be covered by a finite glance or a finite discourse, but because the nature of the field – that is, language and a finite language – excludes totalization. The field is in effect that of play, that is to say, a field of infinite substitutions only because it is finite ... because instead of being an inexhaustible field, as in the classical hypothesis, instead of being too large, there is something missing from it: a center which arrests and grounds the play of substitutions.

Here Derrida advocates undermining dichotomous logic built on rigid opposites: in his view, which is typically post-structuralist, there is an unceasing play of meaning within the confines of a finite language. The field is not arbitrarily extendable, yet the movement of signification never finds an end. This is because it feeds on the movement of pluralizing differences, a movement which eludes the rigid opposition between subject and object, the one versus the other. It is for this reason that post-structuralist thinking is at once anti-authoritarian and anti-revolutionary. There is no longer a sole authority, elevated above all else, capable of deciding on what is good and right, capable of sealing a seamless break with tradition.

The narrowing of the spaces for thinking to the given and the shifting of this pre-given does not necessarily lead to the view that the postmodern is the best of all possible worlds. The path of critical analysis no longer leads via the reference to a transcendental instance – a God in the sense of a center that guarantees and authenticates truth, even though it is elusive in its eternal withdrawal. Instead, the critical gaze is directed downwards, to discover the world in its diversity and thousand-fold splitters of difference. The watchword of all post-structuralists is this: admit the proliferating multiplicity of small differences; search for the incommensurable; and end black-and-white thinking grounded in dichotomies. Deviations, ruptures, differences in all their permutations – all seem to agree despite specific variations – are no longer to be embraced or colonized by the binary code of one versus the other. Difference is at last to be released from the one-way street of binary opposition. Accordingly, rigid juxtapositions, assumed to be irreducible and of absolute necessity, are rejected; for instance those of truth and lie, reason and madness, man and woman.

The critique leveled at an absolute truth is fundamental for both postmodern and post-structuralist thinking. It is for good reason that Nietzsche is a source for Lyotard, Derrida, Foucault, and Deleuze and Guattari. In "On Truth and Lie in an Extra-moral Sense" (1873), Nietzsche stated:

> What, then, is truth? A mobile army of metaphors, metonyms, and anthropo-morphisms – in short, a sum of human relations which have been enhanced, transposed, and embellished poetically and rhetorically, and which after long use seem firm, canonical, and obligatory to a people: truths are illusions about which one has forgotten that this is what they are; metaphors which are worn out and without sensuous power ...

The relative freedom to be discovered resides in this movement of shifting and displacing, transferring and transposing, in the interstices of non-identity, in deferring the hierarchical and binary, in *différance*, to refer to the term Derrida brings into play to contour this ceaseless conceptual labor. Meanings and contents are ever in motion and so elude and undermine themselves in their transference. There is no center to concentrate and stabilize them; and once there is no longer any secure "vanishing point", then the hermeneutic circle cannot be drawn to a close. Signification, so the post-structuralists affirm, arises through the differences in meaning between words themselves: that "tree" does not mean "house" is the source of semantics. Language, defined as the endless work of transposing meaning to concepts and vice versa – see Saussure – simply does not allow for standstill. But this does not mean that interpretation, for example of a novel, also defies conclusion. As long as one works in the medium of language, there is no antidote against one's own refutability. Saussure and Nietzsche shake hands and provide the leg-up for a philosophical direction which works with emphatically visual figures of thought: the torn thread of Ariadne; the wild proliferation of roots (rhizome); lines of flight; implosions; the fold; and differential systems on the same level, the thousand plateaus.

The rhizome and the map as new philosophical categories

In their rampant meandering, thinking and writing between philosophy and literature, the philosopher Gilles Deleuze and the psychiatrist Félix Guattari far outstrip their contemporaries. It is their aim to inaugurate a new rhizome-like thinking that simultaneously produces a new vision of the world, namely in the sense of a circuit layout or map. "The book as an image of the world is in any case utterly boring", they state in their book *A Thousand Plateaus. Capitalism and Schizophrenia* (1980).

Their premise is that diversity is not simply there to be found and recorded, but must first be produced; the thinking capable of such productivity must deny hierarchization, instead networking itself anarchically by working simultaneously in all of the dimensions as its disposal. "A system of this kind could be called a rhizome ... Bulbs and tubers are rhizomes." Explaining the concept, they go on to draw a crucial distinction. The rhizome is all about "principles of connection and heterogeneity: any point of a rhizome can be connected to anything other, and must be. This is very different from the tree or root, which plots a point, fixes an order." This is similar to the aforementioned image of the map or layout plan, which Jameson also explains as typical of postmodern thinking and its task to map. Here, though, these "maps" are thought of as being mobile in themselves, as in incessant flux. Deleuze and Guattari are fully devoted to the experimenting force of becoming. Transformation, adaptation, and retransformation, re-appropriation ("reterritorialization") and appropriation ("deterritorialization") are interconnected; this chain of opposed processes of becoming is defined spatially or territorially. Entities that in "classical thinking" have nothing to do with one another, for example an orchid and a wasp, are related to one another, generating a new visual figure of thought which oscillates between fauna and flora.

> How could movements of deterritorialization and processes of reterritori-
> alization not be relative, always connected, caught up in one another? The
> orchid deterritorializes by forming an image, a tracing of a wasp; but the wasp

reterritorializes on that image. The wasp is nevertheless deterritorialized, becoming a piece in the orchid's reproductive apparatus. But it reterritorializes the orchid by transporting its pollen. Wasp and orchid as heterogeneous parts form a rhizome.

Postmodern social criticism: the critical affirmation and the critique of the critical affirmation

After this brief digression into the realm of the sometimes-turbulent production of post-structuralist theory, we now need to turn our attention to the postmodernist novel and its production. Here, too, images and imaginative spaces play a key role in their palimpsest-like overlapping. The dissolution of history into a visual space, the *sampling* of surfaces and superficialities and the inner thoughts of contemporary consumers are some of the themes embraced by Western postmodernist novels. Frequently they reproduce the colorful world of consumer goods – at times ironically, at others without fracturing – by focusing on rather ordinary individuals. As in philosophy, systematic transversal and transgression of boundaries between genres and epochs take place on the textual level. Just as Deleuze and Guattari produce writing that crosses the border to literature, the postmodern novel assimilates other types of texts like advertising copy, pop songs or protocols. The *listing* and seemingly objective logging of details advance into traits of postmodernist narration.

A peculiarly postmodernist way of formulating social criticism is often tied to this narrative strategy. The main reproach leveled at postmodernist and post-structuralist thinking is that it is apolitical. This is to a large extent true, but there are at least two specifically postmodernist figures of social criticism. Highly censorious of contemporary power constellations and injustices, they do formulate a critique of capitalism, albeit – and this is their specificity – without concomitantly postulating the possibility of a different world order. The outcome is the figure of critical affirmation, particularly favored by subcultures in the 1980s.

The American author Bret Easton Ellis, whose novels created a furor in the early 1990s, draws on this figure. In *American Psycho* (1991) he celebrates the violence underpinning a postmodern life that strives incessantly to embody a perfect image. What is particularly postmodernist about his novels is that they formulate a radical critique of consumer capitalism without ever giving the slightest intimation of an alternative. Neither the author nor his characters signal any vision of another world. His five-hundred-page epic, in which the extremely vain son of a yuppie Patrick Bateman pursues his hobby, serial killing, at night, ends with "This is not an exit": we could add "from the terroristic empire of consumerism."

In this novel we encounter the typical elements of Western postmodernist thinking circling around themselves: the loss of exteriority and thus of utopian thought; the integration of pop culture; the obsessive preoccupation with the world of consumerism; and the lust to reproduce the appallingly wonderful world of consumer brands and items in language, while at the same time radically criticizing it. On the authorial side, the loss of any idea of redemption – that is, the lack of a vision for overcoming the given, a transcendental trajectory – is articulated in the detailed and eager recording of (commodity) fetishism and the violent excesses of his characters. From a position of immanence, Ellis meticulously shows how the capitalist world persistently perverts itself. "And yet" – so we may perhaps paraphrase the attitude behind this otherwise bleak view – "we have only this world and we like it." The paradoxical principle of affirmative critique, widespread in the subcultures at the end of the 1980s, thus finds its most consequential blossoming in Ellis's work, resulting in itself becoming a mass consumable.

Around ten years later, this paradoxical figure of critique itself becomes the object of sustained critique, continuing to work with postmodernist narrative strategies. The postmodern "screw" turns again, so to speak. Epitomizing this "turn" is the work of David Foster Wallace, whose cold playful sarcasm maneuvers this strategy into a deadlock that exposes its vacuous underbelly. The enlightened self-realization celebrated by Ellis and others, which because of its self-congratulatory complacency is unwilling to consider the need of self-correction, is ingeniously exposed by Wallace. In *Brief Interviews with Hideous Men* (1999), he complements "classical" short stories with fictional interview protocols imitating those usually taken by therapists or social counselors. Accordingly, they furnish formalized interior views of persons who in some way – it is never clearly stated how – have attracted the attention of society, allowing insights into the profane everyday of a globalized Western world. Essentially, Wallace produces delicate discourse analyses of currently circulating and standardized forms of self-description and self-legitimation. And it is in this "keeping in mind" that his social criticism crystallizes. His stories narrate threshold situations, when angst tips into aggression, or self-criticism into idiotic chauvinism; they also narrate a specific self-critical rhetoric, the prime feature of which is in fact to exclude self-correction and any attempt at change.

The protagonists in the work of both Wallace and Ellis are only concerned with themselves and they live for nothing else. It is this aggressive narcissism and the loss of any exterior perspective that the otherwise so divergent anti-heros share with one another. And it is the brazen cynicism of their creators, also greatly different from each other, which reveals to the reader that expelling the countenance of the other, to use Levinas's term, and repelling the possibility of thinking that things could be different not only reproduces the violence underpinning society, but is in itself a violent act. Making this perceptible is the merit of both Ellis and Wallace; overall it is an insight in which the very possibility resides in thinking and writing that is concerned with grasping and representing plurality and diversity, working with postmodernist strategies against postmodernism itself up until today.

WORKS CITED

Judith Butler: *Gender Trouble. Feminism and the Subversion of Identity*, New York: Routledge 1990

Gilles Deleuze, Félix Guattari: "Introduction: Rhizome," in: *Mille plateaux*, Paris: Minuit 1980

Jacques Derrida: *L'écriture et la différence*, Paris: Seuil 1967

Umberto Eco: *Il nome della rosa*, Milan: Bompiani 1980

Bret Easton Ellis: *American Psycho*, New York: Vintage Contemporaries 1991

Michel Foucault: *Language, Counter-memory, Practice. Selected Essays and Interviews*, ed. Donald F. Bouchard, trans. Donald F. Bouchard and Sherry Simon, Ithaca: Cornell University Press 1977

Manfred Frank: *Was ist Neostrukturalismus?*, Frankfurt/M.: Suhrkamp 1983

Rainald Goetz: *Geschichte der Gegenwart*, 5 vols., Frankfurt/M.: Suhrkamp 1998–2000

Fredric Jameson: *Postmodernism, or, the Cultural Logic of Late Capitalism*, Durham: Duke University Press 1984

Jean-François Lyotard: *La condition postmoderne. Rapport sur le savoir*, Paris: Minuit 1979

Friedrich Wilhelm Nietzsche: "Über Wahrheit und Lüge im außermoralischen Sinne" [1873], in: Friedrich Nietzsche: *Werke. Kritische Gesamtausgabe, vol. III. 2*: Nachgelassene Schriften 1870-1973, Berlin, New York: de Gruyter 1973

David Foster Wallace: *Brief Interviews with Hideous Men*, Boston: Little, Brown 1999

The End of Illusions
On Arab Postmodernism

Andreas Pflitsch

Postmodernism has – to couch it in a paradox – long become un-modern. "A time has namely dawned," declares the Ukrainian author Yuri Andrukhovych, "when amongst us only the lazy and the dead fail to criticize postmodernism." Today it is fashionable to repudiate postmodernism, to take a condescending stance towards it. Know-it-alls and trendsetters have long broken camp; only the smoldering ashes remain. While *postmodernism* provokes nothing more than a weary yawn in the West, the debate about *modernity* is raging in the Arab world. It seems that there can be no question of postmodernism there. There are two main reasons that the adjectives "Arab" and "postmodern" are so difficult to fit together. First, literature in the Arab world is produced in very different social conditions; second, its predominant image in the West is of a backward, traditional society striving to keep up with modernity.

The situation is somewhat reminiscent of the anecdote about the drunken man who in the middle of the night looks for his keys under a streetlamp. A passerby stops to help him and after searching futilely for a while he is moved to ask if the man is sure that he has lost the keys here. No, he answers, in fact he suspects that he lost the keys somewhere else entirely. But there it is far too dark to look. This disarming logic corresponds to the insistence with which the West explains the problems of the contemporary Arab world as stemming from the domineering role played by Islam, while simultaneously asserting an essential incompatibility between Islam and modernity. Everything that lies within the cone of light cast by this premise radiates as self-evident; the remainder, in the cover of darkness, is studiously overlooked. This has allowed an assumption to gain the status of a tenet that is today hardly called into question: that Islam is a fundamentally backward, even medieval religion, which positions the societies it shapes as nothing less than the ideal counterbalance to modernity. This misjudgment takes on thoroughly tragic dimensions in that it forms the basis both for Western claims to monopolize modernity and for its strict rejection by radical Islamists. The intellectual deadlock that marks the beginning of the twenty-first century, becoming ever more rigid in the context of the "clash of civilizations", leads frequently to an absurd involuntary alignment between Islamists and Eurocentrics. When Western commentators claim that democracy is not only alien to Islam but will remain so forever because these represent contradictory value systems, they adopt an Islamist argumentation and so stab the forces of reform in the back. The apparently fundamentally opposed parties prove strikingly kindred in their basic assumption that the Arab world is incapable of Enlightenment. The proponents of modern Islam come under attack from both sides.

Furthermore, the relationship between the West and the rest of the world recalls the race between the hare and the tortoise: the non-Western hare can try as hard as it wants; the Western tortoise will always be waiting at the finish line, nice and relaxed, to call out with its own distinctive self-assurance and superiority: "I'm already here!" There is no obvious escape: Europe not only produces Eurocentrism but also delivers the critique of the same. Accordingly, postmodernism is at once a counter or corrective movement to modernity and its very product. The Algerian philosopher Mohammed Arkoun proceeds from the assumption that modernity is *nolens volens* universally valid and no longer negotiable:

> The space and time within which collective perceptions have formed, self-understanding been formulated, formative world pictures originated, they have been essentially shaped and monopolized by Western reason, codified in a scientific discourse that the West has conducted, organized, and demarked externally since the eighteenth century.

The strangely paradoxical mélange emerging here, comprising a modernity that is indubitable and universal and a modernity that is specifically Western, points to the double game played by modernity. Like the tortoise of the fable, it exists twice: as a universal principle and a specific system. On the one hand, the concept of "modernity" acts as a synonym for a historical epoch and the contemporary age; on the other it stands for the social, cultural, political and economic development of a particular region that we designate as "the West" or Europe. At one point it designates the epoch, only to signify a programmatic project. Through the continuous confounding and commingling of the two notions of "modernity", an imbalance arises that necessarily leads to misunderstanding. The definition of modernity as the social system developed in the West and the claim that said system exists solely in the West is therefore a stark tautology.

The notion of what constitutes postmodernism varies according to the concept of "modernity" employed. Generally speaking there are two views. One starts from the claim that modernity, jaded and ruined, has been supplanted by a completely new epoch. The other runs counter to this, claiming that postmodernism is part of modernity, at once originating from and outgrowing it, but not essentially and fundamentally directed against its progenitor. As Peter Sloterdijk put it, modernity "must acquiesce to having its very own questions directed once more against itself." Metaphorically speaking, the latter view sees postmodernism standing on the shoulders of a giant – modernity – while the former pictures postmodernism sliding in to tackle the giant from behind, felling it and taking its place. No matter whether we regard postmodernism as having supplanted modernity or building on it, both views see in postmodernism an attempt to extricate thought from the premises and tenets of modernity, to escape the sense of self-assured contentment in its inner core, and to dare to take a look from the outside. Once grasped in this sense, of a radicalization of the reflectivity that is a distinctive feature of modernity itself, renouncing a concept of postmodernism would – even today – mean surrendering to a frivolous trivialization of this shift in paradigm.

Abiding by this definition immediately reveals the unique explosiveness of enquiring into what might constitute a non-Western postmodernism. Precisely identifying the commonalities and differences would ultimately entail re-approaching the question of the universality of modernity (and postmodernism). Perhaps it is this detour which would allow us more clearly to delineate and separate the two "moderns", modernity as a universal principle and modernity as a specific "Western" mould.

Literature and politics

It nonetheless sounds somewhat adventurous to speak of Arab postmodernism. Moreover: are not Enlightenment, democracy, and human rights infinitely more urgent and pressing than the search for Arab postmodernism? In light of the crisis-ridden present, with its wars and extreme acts of violence, it seems to be downright obscene. Is talk of postmodernism not ultimately a dangerous and cynical form of "living on the edge", on the crater of an active volcano?

That this is not merely a specialty of a barbaric "Third World" was pointed out by Heinrich Böll in his Frankfurt poetic lectures of 1963–64. With reference to German postwar literature, he asserted that "Any avant-gardism, any recourse to revolutionary literary forms" was at that time "ridiculous", for "it is senseless to want to provoke the bourgeois public when it no longer exists." Following this logic, in 1983 Peter Handke warned the readers of his journal *Phantasien der Wiederholung* always to keep in mind the conditions under which the text originated: "Attention: everything here is written in a time of peace, and under the aegis of peace." It is imperative to take into account the social conditions in which literature is produced, and the conditions in which literature is created in the Arab world are fundamentally different from those with which we are familiar.

Arab states today cover a broad spectrum of political systems and are on very different levels economically; their literary histories also vary greatly. But there is also much common ground: life in all Arab countries is determined by social injustice; there is a distinct lack of civic freedoms; economic malaise plagues broad sections of the population even in nominally rich states; and democratic political culture is conspicuous by its absence. All of these factors impact on literature and the intellectual climate. Whether in monarchies like Morocco, Jordan, and Saudi Arabia, or in one-party systems like Algeria, Egypt, and Syria, no pluralistic civil society has emerged in any Arab state up to the present day. Autocratic state leadership, whose iron grip on power stands in peculiar contrast to Western perceptions of chronic instability in the Middle East, has severely hampered the opposition. Since the 1980s Islamist groups have supplanted the Marxist opposition movements that were predominant from the 1950s through to the 1970s. This constellation had grave consequences for writers and intellectuals: there is hardly a renowned author who has not spent at least one spell in prison. Repression and censorship are part and parcel of an Arab writer's everyday working context. Exile is often the only alternative.

Is the postmodernist eschewing of responsibility, which modernity at once promised and imposed on writers and intellectuals, a step in the wrong direction? The long history of commitment characteristic of modern Arab literature does in fact appear to indicate a heavy political onus on Arab writing that runs contrary to postmodern *laissez-faire*. At the same time, the issue of engaged literature holds the key to understanding Arab postmodernism and delineating what is perhaps its most salient difference to Western postmodernism. Generally speaking, even authors who are not avowedly political never completely deny the political moment in their work. An author like Abdelrahman Munif, who never saw himself as a political writer, emphasized in an interview in 1990: "In countries where there is no freedom of expression, no political parties are tolerated, where there is perhaps not even a constitution, intellectuals must, or indeed anyone who can express themselves, must resist." The majority of the authors discussed in this present volume would most certainly uphold the political claims of their literature in these terms. In contrast to the engagement of classical modernism, however, the political movement of contemporary Arab literature resides on a completely different level.

The continuing discrepancy – or non-contemporaneity – between the Western and the Arab way of dealing with the relationship of politics and literature was made glaringly obvious in a discussion between Alain Robbe-Grillet, one of the most renowned representatives of the French *nouveau roman*, and the Palestinian author Jabra Ibrahim Jabra at a literature festival in Baghdad in 1988. Robbe-Grillet could not conceal his amusement about an Iraqi literature professor who demanded a commitment to social issues from literature. "We've moved on from this," he remarked, "we've finally overcome this foolish delusion." Jabra defended the professor, making it abundantly clear that in illiberal societies such as those that exist in Arab countries one simply could not indulge in the luxury afforded to writers in the West; that is to achieve such a degree of distance in art and literature that they are decoupled entirely from society and social conditions. Two years later, the Egyptian authors Sonallah Ibrahim and Ibrahim Aslan argued along similar lines in a discussion with the French Nobel laureate Claude Simon, another exponent of the *nouveau roman*. Simon had divorced the personal nature of literature from politics, thus provoking rebuke from his Egyptian colleagues, who adhered to literature's political claims.

In the mid-twentieth century, literary engagement was the all-determining concept in the discourse of literary criticism, in the Arab world and elsewhere. The Egyptian writer and sometime education minister Taha Husayn adopted the concept from Jean Paul Sartre as early as 1947 and introduced it into the Arab debate. In the 1950s, but above all in the 1960s, a period of extreme politicization worldwide, the proper nuances and parameters of political commitment in literature were the subject of hefty debate. Those authors who believed that the true home of Arab literature was in the Soviet doctrine of socialist realism called for the exploitation of the revolutionary potential of literature. In the opposing camp were the less strident adherents of literary engagement, authors who defended the freedom of art. It is crucial to gaining an understanding of this debate, which went on for years and was conducted mainly in influential Beirut literary journals, to realize that engagement was posited as a necessity and hardly ever called into question. The principal spark kindling controversy was the means of this commitment; at issue was not *whether* literature should be committed to social and political causes but *how* it was to undertake this mission. This – if a cautious generalization may be permitted – has remained the case until the present day.

That a profoundly political seam may be entwined with postmodernist aesthetics is evident in most of the work presented in this volume. The postmodernist moment is not, however, simply décor draped over a literature that remains in the clutches of outdated notions of commitment. On the contrary: the postmodernist skepticism voiced in these works against any claims of absoluteness and one-dimensional explanations, amidst the clamor of Middle East political ideologies on the one hand and religious self-assurance on the other, is highly political.

Two dates stand for a far-reaching shift in how Arab writers have broached the issue of political commitment: 1967 and 1975. The crushing defeat suffered by the Arab states at the hands of Israel in the June War of 1967 was far more than a military catastrophe; it marks a caesura that cleaves Arab cultural history in the twentieth century into a before and after. With the ideological edifice of Nasserism collapsing like a house of cards and the era of a new dawn and belief in progress and development coming to an abrupt end, it was not only Egyptian society that was propelled into a state of shocked rigidity. There was hardly a single Arab author whose belief in progress was not profoundly shaken and who was not suddenly deprived of any ideological orientation: in short, who had not begun to doubt the tenets of modernity. The undaunted belief in a better future, the hallmark of Nasserism at its prime, gave way to profound skepticism and deep-seated mistrust. The mood of a new dawn and the euphoria that anything could be done – frequently enough allied to megalomania and fantasies of absolute empowerment – gave way to a bludgeoning hangover and anguish. At once Nasserism was nothing more than a pompous ideology. The king was naked. Words had lost their innocence. Literature would never be the same again.

The Lebanese civil war that broke out in April 1975 and would drag on until 1990 had a similar impact on literature to the defeat of 1967. Here, too, dreams were shattered and language lost its innocence. The Lebanese author Rashid al-Daif expressed the wreckage thus: the reality one could describe no longer exists. In line with this, Elias Khoury consequentially dispensed with anything unequivocal in his novels. Much remains inconclusive; narrative strands come to nothing and peter out. Frequently the narrator intervenes and queries what has just been claimed: "This is what could have happened, but perhaps things were completely different, who knows for sure?" Khoury has emphasized the crucial importance of the civil war to Lebanese literature, claiming that it simply did not exist prior to the conflict. Before the war, only "Egyptian novels" had been written in Lebanon. Literary realism, as practiced by the Egyptian Noble laureate Naguib Mahfouz, had served its time. Postmodern Arab authors are therefore "post-Mahfouzian" authors, as Edward Said once put it.

After 1967 and 1975 it was not necessarily the political claims of Arabic literature that changed but rather the form of political intervention: the nature of political literature altered drastically. Authors like Rashid al-Daif or the Palestinian Emile Habibi have shifted the focus of their skepticism to language itself. Instead of paying back the official ideologies in kind and coining their own rallying cries and slogans, they have embarked on a search for a new, ideally untainted language. Cautiously, al-Daif is endeavoring to relearn a sincere manner of speaking and writing, to liberate Arabic from the ballast of the political slogans of the 1960s and 1970s, while Habibi is at pains to disclose the firmly established myths in the Holy Land. "There are Palestinian poets," he has taunted, mocking the mendaciousness of a large section of the self-appointed combative literature, "who let the sabers flourish in their verses but are unable to slaughter a chicken."

Irrespective of the changing political, religious or social objectives they pursue, the Israeli writer Amos Oz has defined a fanatic as someone who forces others to change. This compulsion as the essential element of fanaticism is alien to literature. Even if it wanted to be, literature cannot be fanatical. Most certainly it is capable of lying – and as fiction it even makes the lie socially acceptable – it can have a poisonous effect; it can promote short-fused reactions or truncate thought; it can persuade, lull or agitate. Literature can be biased, invoke evil, and betray values: in short, literature is neither powerless nor innocent – but literature cannot force anyone to do anything.

On the contrary: inherent to literature is the power to counter fanaticism, to be its antidote, not by prescribing ready-made solutions or helping to distinguish right from wrong but rather as a modus of thinking and perception that scrutinizes everything postulated as definitive and exclusive. To expect a patent remedy from literature in the form of directives for constructive action would clearly be misplaced. But in its unique open character, defying definitive completion and furnishing multiple perspectives, literature may be able to show a way that is superior to short-term measures combating symptoms instead of causes. Literature could, to call once again on Amos Oz, achieve "a partial and limited immunity against fanaticism." It is postmodern literature, says the American author and critic Raymond Federman, which "negates all forms of dualism." This dualism is a "double-headed monster that has imposed a system of values, ethical and aesthetic values, on us for centuries" and, one may add, has been strengthened rather than abated under the auspices of modernity with its simplification of diversity. In an essay bearing the wonderful title *How to debate with fundamentalists without losing your mind. A guide to subversive thinking*, the philosopher Hubert Schleichert pointed out that the closed systems of ideology and religious certainty are not receptive to argumentation: "The goal of enlighteners should not be to 'refute' fanatics but to ensure that their fervent outpourings no longer arouse interest because the public has become immune." The rationale behind this tact: "Ideologies are not refuted or defeated; they become obsolete, are ignored, are considered boring, and then forgotten."

Cultural heritage and tradition

The relationship between (indigenous) tradition and (Western) modernity has been a key – if not *the* key – theme of modern Arabic literature ever since its emergence in the nineteenth century. From the very outset Arab authors have elaborated positions vis-à-vis the West. The frequently simple, one could also say ignorant, appraisals circulating in the West stand in crass contradiction to this discussion taking place in the Arab world: on the West and modernity; on progress and tradition; on so-called Western values and the values of the indigenous religious tradition. The spectrum of views expressed is broad. One conviction is that the relationship of Islam to modernity is akin to that of water to fire and that the sole solution resides in abolishing or at least disempowering religion in the Arab world. Without an unequivocal commitment to modernity, which could never be genuine without taking leave of obstructive and debilitating traditions, the looming threat is, according to the drastic formulation of the Syrian Sadiq al-Azm, one of the most eminent contemporary Arab philosophers, "self-consignment to the rubbish tip of history." At the opposite end of the spectrum is the position that Arabs or Muslims have in fact distanced themselves so far from their traditions that a connection to progress and development is now only made possible by adhering to their own identity; consciously and proudly tapping into and modifying – to be understood in the sense of "modernizing" – indigenous cultural and social traditions.

Both views are evident in modern literature. Apologetic tones, cultural self-assertion, and the search for identity determine their form and thematic in large part. The mindset that sees Arab-Islamic culture as a whole in crisis, with the region in economic decline, politically weak if not incapacitated, and culturally witnessing – at best – the final convulsions of decadent epigonism, has managed to maintain its dominance, even in this overstated form. But this applies not only to the Western view; it also informs the Arab evaluation. Orientation on the West and its military and technological achievements appeared obvious and necessary if this decline was to be arrested. The West was set as the standard that had to be emulated. This mindset is replicated in the historiography of literature: the once thriving Arabic literature, along with classical Arabic poetry, lost its vitality from the thirteenth century onwards and became mired in stagnation and decadence. According to the trajectory of this perspective, nothing remarkable was produced for more than half a millennium, until European modernism entered the scene in the nineteenth century, breathing new life into an Arabic literature prostrate in a state of torpor. Modern prose and theater, for example, were seen from the very beginning as adaptations from the West and the novel was long tainted with the stigma of being an imported genre alien to the indigenous literary tradition. This view was not least put forward by Western Oriental studies.

Arab authors of the younger generation are the first to grasp the possibilities of breaking out of this rigid dichotomy between tradition and modernity, between the "indigenous" and the "alien", and thereby creatively revaluing their cultural and literary heritage. In this volume Stephan Guth takes the example of Gamal al-Ghitani to show that borrowing from the genres of classical Arabic literature also entails their infraction, cracking open a seam in the style and content for ironic play that turns medieval edification and light fiction into an engaged "literature that provokes through its internal tensions" in late twentieth-century Egypt. Recourse to the traditional forms of literary heritage is thus a move that takes a step back from the certainties of modernity, a detachment that is a particular form of its overcoming and hence postmodernist. Besides al-Ghitani, Edwar al-Kharrat and Elias Khoury, several other authors who creatively draw on Arab literary tradition and subversively exploit its dormant potential are discussed in this volume.

Atavism is as alien to them as the thoughtless imitation of Western fashions. The conceptual triad of tradition–modernism–postmodernism designates in the Arab context less the historical succession of epochs than coexisting approaches to the world which, although rival, can mutually complement and enrich one another. Many of the authors discussed here achieve the detachment from modernism that is characteristic for postmodernism by taking a new look at tradition. Genres of classical Arabic literature are appropriated, for example by the Algerian author Habib Tengour, without succumbing to the danger of nostalgic longing and idealizing a "Golden Age". The unprejudiced view backwards allows astounding parallels to emerge, for instance the status afforded the fragment, which, as Regina Keil-Sagawe shows in this volume, "pre-Socratics and Romantics alike appreciate, and which corresponds equally to the 'molecular structure' of Arabic poetry and the oral Maghreb narrative tradition."

With its interlaced stories, cyclical narrative structures, and parallel variants of stories resembling one another, the *Thousand and One Nights* became a source of inspiration for the self-referential texts of postmodernist Arab authors like Elias Khoury or Edwar al-Kharrat. Both authors position themselves in this tradition of classical Arab storytelling. In Jorge Luis Borges, a precursor and early innovator of postmodern literary strategies who drew attention to the peculiar narrative structures of the *Thousand and One Nights* as early as the 1930s, they have found a principal witness:

> In analogy to the encompassing frame story, one story tends to bear within itself other stories of no lesser dimension: scenes within the scene, as in the tragedy of Hamlet; dreamlike enhancements. The vestibules merge into the mirrors, the mask is behind the face, and no-one knows who the real person is and who their copy.

This exceptional structure triggers, for Borges, a "strange, almost endless effect" to which a "kind of swindle is peculiar." The incessantly self-referential stories of the *Thousand and One Nights* may be read as a rhizomic text due to their network-like connections; a thoroughly postmodernist text form that dissolves the centered perspective and thus matches the heterogeneity of reality. The rhizome, the rampantly proliferating rootstock, stands for the open, the non-linear. Botho Strauß is thinking along the same lines when he counters the (modern) "taut thread" with (postmodern) "braids":

> It is our endeavor to straighten the world, and this wherever we recognize the merest part of it. This is the equivalent of falling back on the simple when in crisis, as if it were closer to human nature than the complex, which is ultimately

considered a superfluous entanglement, although a braid promises greater stability than the taut thread.

A difficult reception

In his Lebanese travelogue *Das Tier, das weint* (2004), Michael Kleeberg scrutinized images frequently branded so deep in consciousness that we barely perceive their presence. Lebanese, Arabs, Orientals – time and again he has to admit his own puzzlement that they are not in fact that different. The author's father becomes the medium of tabooed, deep-seated – and long-established – phantasms. At a short encounter between the Lebanese poet Abbas Beydoun, Kleeberg's guest in the exchange project "East-West Divan" staged by the Institute for Advanced Study in Berlin, and his father, the son (over-) interprets the latter's reactions.

> I read into the short, muted look of my father: the intellectual superiority of the civilized European over the analphabetic camel driver from the Orient, the moral superiority of the modern Western Christian, a subject serving democracy and capitalism, over the fanatical, Islamic crypto-terrorist and butcher from a Stone Age culture of hate and envy, for whose criminal congeners we build mosques here from our tax money, so that they will succeed where in his day Prince Eugene and soon George W. Bush had denied their ilk, namely to steamroll over us, far worse than socialism was ever capable of.

9/11 is not the beginning of putting to the test themes like the multicultural society, the coexistence of cultures, or the universality of human rights. Islamic terrorism and the rejoining "war on terror" threaten, in an ever-intensifying process of mutual distrust, to lead to worldwide paranoia. For some time now we have been living, as Rüdiger Safranski has put it, "in a hysterical agitated society where the existential power of judgment is suspended. No one can distinguish anymore between real threats and non-threats." Can literature contribute to tempering the hysteria on both sides and reactivating and sharpening our power of judgment?

How really different are we? Where do the possibilities for encounter reside? Where do the limits of understanding lie? Indeed, are there any limits? Where is contemporary Arabic literature to be positioned between the poles of a local, tradition-bound "third world" phenomenon and a global (in a postmodernist sense) world literature? Which authors are canonical? The goal of this book is not to present an all-encompassing overview of contemporary Arabic literature. If the authors selected seem representative, then this was unintentional and purely coincidental. Instead of organizing a representative or encyclopedic collection based on whatever seemingly cogent criteria, we have compiled insights on exceptional protagonists in the Arab literature scene, examining authors and works which are of interest and stand out. That a selection based on these premises is of its very nature extremely subjective goes without saying. That some of the most interesting and finest authors in the Arab world are represented is more of a positive side effect and was not the actual starting point of our work. And for this reason the reverse conclusion has just as little efficacy: any author not dealt with in the following pages is not necessarily insignificant.

But the issue of representation may be located on another level as well. This not only concerns whether an important author or poet has been passed over, distorting the overall picture. Of far more fundamental importance is the question of the significance and relevance of the literature presented here for Arab society. What is the sense of examining the heady heights of literature from societies such as Iraq, Syria, or even indeed Egypt, where the prevailing social and political climate would seem to ridicule poetical subtleties and the refined complexity of postmodernist narratives? As justified as this objection is, as worthy of consideration the fact that literature reaches only the tiniest of elites may be, these are aspects which are valid for every literature and all societies. The differences are of degree, not in principle. In other words, one is just as unlikely to be able to discuss the gender thematic in the work of Tahar Ben Jelloun at the market in Cairo as the most recent prose by Botho Strauß at a market in Stuttgart. On the other hand though, it can happen in the Middle East that a taxi driver recites a verse by the Palestinian Mahmoud Darwish, whereas in Germany even die-hard lovers of literature and regular readers of the feuilletons in the *Frankfurter Allgemeine Zeitung* will hardly be capable of quoting even a single line by Durs Grünbein or Hans Magnus Enzensberger.

Doubts about the representative character of his guests assailed Michael Kleeberg in Lebanon as well. At a soiree in Beirut it suddenly occurs to him that there is something fallacious about the harmony they share:

> It now seems to me that a decisive gap in what I experienced during my travels was how I never met anyone with whom communicating would have been severely hampered by unbridgeable differences, and also people who aren't intellectuals, that I never visited slum areas or a ghetto like Chatila. No 'authenticity' outside the slim elite of educated intellectuals.

Are all the discussions on culture and literature not merely verbal Potemkin villages, shams where a harmony is simulated that has no basis in reality? Is the whole trip ultimately nothing other than a sanctimonious event because potential encounters with problems are factored out from the very outset? Kleeberg goes on to draw a parallel to the time he spent with Beydoun in Germany, in the autumn of 2002:

> Mind you, in Berlin I didn't take Abbas to visit shelters for asylum-seekers or

to the meetings of NPD thugs, we didn't travel out to Marzahn, and I didn't send him to the prefab high-rises to meet the people who have lost out with the fall of communism, or the Stasi officers ... I myself *know* nothing firsthand about these milieus, and I automatically presume my local friends would have access to *their* opponents and antipodes ...

The expectations held by Western audiences still stand in the way of an unprejudiced reception of Arabic literature. European and Western reception of modern Arab literature remains steadfastly oriented on exotic allures, the quaint embellishments of veiled women and palm-grove aesthetics. Poverty, backwardness and patriarchic social order, suppressed women and a population suffering under war and rampant violence appeal in turn to the conscience of bleeding heart liberals. The shudder at the tyrannical, a whisk of "third world" Romanticism, and unacknowledged longing for the alleged simplicity and languid tempo of Oriental life – or more precisely for what the West projects as being Oriental life – determine the taste of the broad public, and publishing houses are only too willing to pander. A glance at the cover designs for translations of Arab fiction available on the German market is revealing enough: the temptation to illustrate the cover with a camel and/or idyllic palm scene is seldom resisted, even if the novel in question is set amongst the urban petit bourgeoisie.

This shrouding of Arabic literature in clichéd exoticism not only brazenly disregards its diversity and quality; it also prevents any serious cultural exchange. No matter whether it is a sympathetic trivialization or a malicious prejudice, whenever the voices from the Arab world are not listened to – let alone taken seriously – this is negligent and outright dangerous in an age of a menacing, or, more precisely, conjured, "clash of civilizations". It is simple arrogance when public opinion in Europe stridently asserts the incongruity of Islam and modernity while at the same time sparing itself the effort of taking a closer look at the extremely richly faceted debate on this issue. To demand from others only that they fit in and integrate into the context of cultural globalization while wantonly persisting in self-righteousness is narrow-minded. The richness of contemporary Arabic literature belies the incessantly repeated view that the Orient is backward in itself, has a need to catch up across the board, and must measure its progress vis-à-vis the West. The West also has a debt to pay in globalization if this process is ever to become more than a euphemism for neo-colonial economic exploitation or neo-imperial power politics. This lies in a willingness to listen; a willingness to enter into a serious dialogue that goes beyond the street fairs with folk dances and kebabs; in other words beyond the usual multicultural, self-soothing rituals of societies otherwise petrified in what they think is their national culture. Contemporary

Arab literature needs to be taken seriously, dragged out of the exotic corner, and viewed on a par with contemporary world literatures.

WORKS CITED

Yuri Andrukhovych (= Juri Andruchowytsch): *Das letzte Territorium*, Frankfurt/M.: Suhrkamp 2003

Mohammed Arkoun: "'Westliche' Vernunft kontra 'islamische' Vernunft? Versuch einer kritischen Annäherung", in: Michael Lüders (ed.), *Der Islam im Aufbruch? Perspektiven der arabischen Welt*, Munich: Piper 1992, pp. 261–74

Sadiq al-Azm: *Unbehagen in der Moderne. Aufklärung im Islam*, Frankfurt/M.: Fischer 1993

Heinrich Böll: *Frankfurter Vorlesungen*, Munich: Deutscher Taschenbuch Verlag 1968

Jorge Luis Borges: *Siete noches*, Buenos Aires: Emeces 1980

Raymond Federman: *Surfiction. Der Weg der Literatur. Hamburger Poetik-Lektionen*, Frankfurt/M.: Suhrkamp 1992

Emile Habibi, Yoram Kaniuk: *La terre des deux promesses*, Arles: Actes Sud 1996

Peter Handke: *Phantasien der Wiederholung*, Frankfurt/M.: Suhrkamp 1983

Michael Kleeberg: *Das Tier, das weint. Libanesisches Reisetagebuch*, Munich: Deutsche Verlags-Anstalt 2004

Abdalrahman Munif: "Eine Brücke schaffen zwischen 'Innen und Außen'", in: *INAMO* 4 (1995), pp. 43–5

Amos Oz: *Wie man Fanatiker kuriert*, Frankfurt/M.: Suhrkamp 2004

Rüdiger Safranski: *Wieviel Globalisierung verträgt der Mensch?*, Munich, Vienna: Hanser 2003

Hubert Schleichert: *Wie man mit Fundamentalisten diskutiert, ohne den Verstand zu verlieren. Anleitung zum subversiven Denken*, Munich: Beck 1997

Peter Sloterdijk: *Kopernikanische Mobilmachung und ptolemäische Abrüstung*, Frankfurt/M.: Suhrkamp 1987

Botho Strauß: *Beginnlosigkeit. Reflexionen über Fleck und Linie*, Munich, Vienna: Hanser 1992

Part One

Memory

Introduction

Angelika Neuwirth

We live in an age in which, as never before, memory has become a factor of public debate. Memory is invoked to heal, to accuse, or to justify. It is now an essential component in forging individual and collective identity and provides a setting for both conflict and identification.

What Paul Antze and Michael Lambek identified as a dominant force in the Europe of the 1980s and 1990s – the overwhelming new experience of an intimate connection between memory and identity, until then only perceived latently – has its correlate in the realm of Arab culture, even if here it is somewhat less conspicuous. While in Europe developments of world historical dimensions triggered a reawakened interest in history and more or less forcibly imposed the return of memory – first the recollection and remembrance of the Holocaust in the 1970s that jabbed into the collective consciousness, then the re-emergence of long hidden cultural identities in Eastern Europe after the collapse of the East–West divide – in the core region of the Arab world, it was a seemingly local event that dealt an unprecedented blow to self-confidence, instigating a discourse concerned with historical memory. Although lasting only a few days, the June War of 1967 against Israel laid bare in painful vividness the shocking "backwardness" of the Arab world. This humiliating realization inflicted damage on far more than political power interests: the defeat shattered the dream of pan-Arab greatness. The prime loser was the Egyptian President Nasser, who had hurled Egypt into modernity and sought to revolutionize the Middle East; the only Arab politician of recent history who had envisioned the possibility of Arab unity.

Reactions to the defeat in the Arab world can be taken as exemplary for the impact of trauma and shock as anchors for historical memory. As with collective traumata elsewhere, the reverberations through the Arab world led to a "crisis of representation" in art and literature. A sense of how momentous this event would prove to be in the future can be gleaned from Jan Assmann's insight:

> The past as such is incapable of preserving itself in collective memory. It is perpetually organized by the changing frames of reference of an advancing present. Even the new can appear only in the form of a reconstructed past. Traditions can only be replaced by traditions, the past by the past. (...) Collective memory therefore operates in both directions: backward and

forward. Memory not only reconstructs the past, it also organizes the experience of the present and future.

The shock impact of the event can hardly be overestimated. For Palestinians, with the Israeli occupation of the West Bank and the Gaza Strip now completely divorced from the Arab world and placed under Israeli suzerainty, the defeat went down in history as the parallel event to the devastating catastrophe of 1948. The defeat was given the name *al-naksa* (setback), echoing *al-nakba* (catastrophe), the term used to describe the fall of Palestine.

The Syrian political philosopher Sadiq al-Azm condemned this expression as a euphemism that brushes over the comprehensive nature of this defeat. In a book published a year later, *A Self-Critique in the Wake of the Defeat*, he assigns blame to the Arabs themselves; they were incapable of critically assessing their situation due to their enslavement to authority. Al-Azm lays bare repressed problems and witheringly criticizes the frailties of an intoxicated nationalism aligned to a persistent backwardness of the masses. Less direct and more enciphered, this rejection of the prevailing self-assured and assertive thinking – the euphoria of recently achieved independence still resonated in most Arab states – was also expressed in literature.

For example: Egypt

Egypt, more than any other country, was gripped by a wave of intellectual self-criticism after the June defeat. The misjudgment of regional power relations was just the tip of an iceberg: it was increasingly obvious that all sorts of proclaimed certainties, hitherto accepted uncritically, were proving to be delusions. In the Nasser era Egypt was the hub of the Arab world, the stronghold of revolutionary movements; suddenly a single military venture sufficed to undo recent achievements and plunge the country back into renewed dependence on the West. This turn of fortune did not catch everyone by surprise, however: Egyptian literary figures such as Sonallah Ibrahim (b. 1937) and Gamal al-Ghitani (b. 1945) had articulated the unfounded basis of nationalist rhetoric in their novels years before the dénouement of Nasserism. Among the critics, the renowned caricaturist and dramatist Salah Jahin (1930–86) had been equally vocal and prescient. The defeat itself triggered hefty reactions in literature: Amal Dunqul (1940–83) expressed his rancor in his poems, while Ahmad Fuad Najm, performing together with the blind singer-songwriter al-Shaykh Imam, created satires on ideology. The literary critic Ghali Shukri proclaimed the end of an entire generation of writers and intellectuals; targeting not least the prolific novelist Yusuf Idris, who had been strongly influenced by the ideology of the Nasser era. Only a short time later, in the 1970s, a veritable "literature of the alienated" began to emerge, wherein nausea, disgust and *qalaq* (angst) became dominant themes.

But events would not only be mirrored in the medium of literature; they were to change literature and thus language itself fundamentally. The tense relationship between language, the writer, and the world, characteristic of the phase of individual emancipation in the postcolonial context, was exacerbated for Egyptian intellectuals by the political pressure that weighed heavily on them during the Nasser era. The critic Nagi Naguib spoke at the time of a feeling of "having missed out", a sense of lacking opportunities to participate that seemed inherent to the situation of the "floating intelligentsia" in the so-called Third World.

This discrepancy in the relationship to reality finds one of its clearest expressions in the work of Salah Abd al-Sabur (1931–81). Starting from the insight into this problematic, the dramatist and poet was one of the first to pursue in his literary work what Sadiq al-Azm had postulated: the demythologization of political thinking through the rigorous settling of accounts with an ancient tradition of thought that was deeply rooted in cultural memory. In a drama written shortly after the June War, *Layla and the Majnun*, Abd al-Sabur deconstructs what is probably the most powerful Near Eastern allegory on the relationship the writer/intellectual has to society. It is a fable that elevates the intellectual into a messianic figure, the sole legitimate spokesman of his society, while the society itself is judged immature and dependent. Until then, the widespread typecasting of the intellectual as *majnun* (possessed/obsessed, passionate) and the connection drawn to the early Islamic poet Majnun – so named because of his passionate love of Layla, which ended in madness – had led to a downgrading of reality in favor of political dreams. Majnun's greatness lay in his disdain of reality; in his capacity of sublimating loss; in his willingness to substitute the beloved denied him with an ideal image; and in his ability to translate anguished sorrow and madness into art.

Critique of myths: the Majnun-Layla syndrome

This recourse to a specific literary topos – disseminated most notably through the *ghazal*, a form of love poem that exerted a powerful influence over all regions of the Islamic world for a number of centuries – is not the result of a continuous reception of the ancient Arabic love poem, but rather a strategic device introduced by poets of the postcolonial age who were influenced by English poetry. The configuration of the homeland with her sole legitimate partner, the idealistic, obsessive poet, had only been established as a poetical device a few decades before, in the 1940s, by the Pakistani poet Faiz Ahmad Faiz (1911–84). Faiz, who was deeply rooted in the *ghazal* tradition, dissolved the configuration of the *ghazal* from its actual context wherein a poetically sensitive young man extols a young woman or a male partner and transposed it into a new scenario featuring a poet inspired by the struggle for freedom who praises an ideal beloved, the homeland. This shift from the individual to the collective was accommodated by an earlier allegorical re-reading of the *ghazal*: in pre-modern times the mystical tradition of the Islamic world had recast the poet's beloved as an abstract persona, the divine "thou". The further shifting of the lover's yearning onto the national "we" is an innovation of modernism.

In modernist Arab poetry the figure of the poet who assumes the role of the mythical lover of a cosmic "other", the land, or a collective "other", the homeland, emerged in 1958 in perhaps the most influential poem yet written in modern Arabic literature: "Hymn to Rain" (1958) by the Iraqi Badr Shakir al-Sayyab (1926–64), who is rooted in the same *ghazal* tradition. In this poem, the beloved is the Iraqi homeland, the lover the poet himself. From al-Sayyab the spark strikes the Palestinian poet Mahmoud Darwish (1942–2008), who eight years later refashions the famous poem into a work that received no less acclaim, "A Lover from Palestine" (1966), transferring the allegory to his own relationship to his cosmic beloved, the Land of Palestine.

To understand this development, which appears surprising at first glance, it suffices to recall the basis of a *ghazal* poet's self-conception: an experience of the real world as desolate wasteland, dominated by the suffering felt at the existential loss of belonging, at the remoteness of the beloved, and an insatiable thirst for reunification with the beloved "thou"; a consciousness through which the modernist poet, inspired by T. S. Eliot, empathizes strongly with Majnun. But above all, it is the triple disposition of passion, possession by an ideal, and poetic vocation that converges into a field of tension. Creativity springs from a self-imposed emotional imbalance. And yet it is Abd al-Sabur – an intellectual who counted for a long time among committed socialist writers – who is the first to demolish the Majnun paradigm in literature, shortly after the June War.

His drama *Layla and the Majnun* unhinges the Majnun paradigm at precisely the point that was previously regarded as its strength: the contempt for reality. Majnun's steadfast devotion to a timeless ideal image of the lost beloved exacts a price: the outright rejection of, or at the very least a disdain for, the real partner figure. The modern intellectual stylized as Majnun in Abd al-Sabur's portrayal is similarly uncompromising towards his real partner, whether this is conceived collectively as the homeland, or in individual terms as the modern woman: entrapped in the ideal, he despises a society that seeks pleasure and enjoyment, regarding it "as a whore", while his love of a woman embracing life suffers from the continual suspicion of her infidelity, her betrayal of his ideal of perfection.

With his rigorous critique, Abd al-Sabur not only counters the mythical transfiguration of the patriarchal system; he also deconstructs an important element of Arab nationalist thought by revealing the archetypical character projected by nationalist intellectuals to be long out of date. The continuing significance of the Majnun-Layla paradigm to modern perception is shown by a number of poems, dramas, and novels, some of which are addressed in this volume. Not dissimilar to the role of the classical tragedy of antiquity in contemporary Europe, the *ghazal* continues to assert its presence in today's Middle East. It does, admittedly, figure ever less as an object of literary enjoyment; conversely, it has become the target of a rethinking that manifests itself in a rigorous and constructive critique of myths and is indispensable for social renewal.

Critique of representation: the "new sensibility"

However important Abd al-Sabur's work may be, the genuine and lasting renewal of Egyptian-Arab literature came from another source. It was above all the authors of the "new sensibility", a literary trend that emerged in the early 1960s as an attempt to overcome the dominant realism, who asserted a new understanding of reality in Egypt, one that was profoundly infused with grave doubts and disappointment over prevailing social conditions. The most important figure in this group is undoubtedly the novelist and critic Edwar al-Kharrat (b. 1926). Until this point in time Arab literature was characterized by an optimistic belief in the mimetic representability of reality, as reflected in the work of the great Naguib Mahfouz. The authors of the younger generation cast doubt on the possibility of its immediate, undistorted depiction. Conscious of the principles and implications of textuality, they emphasize the referentiality of their texts. For this reason they draw a diametrically opposed conclusion from the defeat of 1967 to the Islamists, about whom al-Kharrat has remarked:

> In 1967 every trace of the liberal, democratic corpus of thought borrowed from the West vanished completely, being replaced by the Islamic philosophy of the Muslim Brothers, their rejection of the West and their turn towards traditional, mimetic faith.

Collective projection of a mythical past to assert a political ideal on the one hand; individual deconstruction of objective reality as a means of re-securing personal memories on the other: these are two synchronous manifestations of Egyptian thought of the time. In the context of "postcolonial literature", al-Kharrat's work represents an attempt to write Arab literature by means of reviving the indigenous cultural heritage and literary tradition: Arab literature that is post-Mahfouzian and at the same time more than simply "Western literature" in Arabic.

In the meantime the "new sensibility" exerts a profound influence on the writing strategies of young Egyptian authors, many of whom, such as Mustafa Dhikri, were born after the June War and have gone on to create their own short-prose genre, the "narrative poem"; literary snapshots in which the emotional and the rational, the real and the surreal intermingle. Thanks to the dwindling impact of nationalist dogmas, recent literature has liberated itself from their grand narratives and thus their exhortative appeal. Resistance to the forgetting of ideals long fought for – manifest in the social injustice occurring as a result of Sadat's policy of opening the economy to the West's free enterprise system – is continued by combative authors like Gamal al-Ghitani and Sonallah Ibrahim. All the same, this commitment has shifted its locus from a direct accusation to inner spheres and ultimately into language itself.

Two competing memories of exile: Palestine/Israel

With his depiction of the symbolic occupation of Palestine by Christian memory, *La Topographie légendaire des évangiles en terre sainte*, Maurice Halbwachs memorably demonstrated that Palestine/Israel is a *lieu de mémoire* (site of memory) *par excellence*. The sacred landscapes of the Jewish, Christian, and Islamic religious communities have existed here side by side ever since the twelfth century or even earlier; with them competing memories of the same land. The conflict between divergent visions of memory was initiated by the missionary movements of the nineteenth century, which by virtue of Biblical testimony redefined the territory as a "Holy Land" belonging solely to Jews and Christians. The conflict then became politically virulent in the early twentieth century with the progressive occupation and settlement of land by European Zionists, while the Palestinian Arab population, predominantly Muslim, was marginalized, regarded as being without history and incapable of civilization. This increasingly conspicuous imbalance, with the expulsion and flight of the great majority of the Palestinian population triggered in 1948 by the hostilities and the founding of the state of Israel, eventually led to the irreversible dominance of the immigrants, and concomitantly the prevalence of Jewish memory over that of the remaining Arab inhabitants.

Memory in the Palestinian context is therefore always exile memory. Paradoxically, the fate of Palestinian exile supplants that of Jewish exile. Both forms of exile memory, though separated by a historical time lapse, not only stand in correlation to one another in the second half of the twentieth century but also affect one another in multiple ways in political discourse, so that their representations, their literary reflexes, mirror one another in many respects. If from a Zionist viewpoint Jewish exile finally came to an end with the establishment of the state of Israel, this territorial recapture of the mythically defined place of origin is by no means the only option of a "Jewish homecoming". As the Israeli literary scholar Sidra DeKoven has stated, it can assume other forms as well:

> In the modern Jewish experience, 'home' has been overdetermined by the ideology and enactment of a collective repatriation in Israel, while at the same time, for Jews of European extraction, at least, even an imagined return to native grounds has been preempted by devastation. The simultaneous efface-ment of Jewish homelands in Europe and the creation of a central Homeland in Palestine form the primary master narrative of contemporary Jewish cul-ture, while two other grammars of homecoming compete for legitimacy in a minor key: in the one America emerges as a different kind of homeland. (...) The other and most antinomian, of the alternatives explored by (European) Jewish writers in the second half of the twentieth century, is an affirmation and reconfiguration of exile as a kind of literary privilege.

For Palestinians the options are narrower: since 1948 they have been denied the first option, the full territorial "return to their homeland", even if they had remained in Israel. Given the exclusive territorial claims realized by Jewish Israelis over the land, even their own physical presence translates into an exilic situation, one that is characterized not just by a lack of legal protection and an uncertain future but most notably by the lack of any official recognition of their real relationship to the land. Once the role of the "original land dwellers", so important in Zionism, was adopted as an exclusive claim by the dominant majority, the Palestinians became perceivable only as aliens, as intruders – paradoxically not dissimilar to the situation in individual epochs of Jewish exile which Zionism placed under a taboo.

There remain two other options: of these, immigration to the free but alien world of America or Europe is unattainable for most and is generally not desired. Exterritorial exile in the Arab world is the most common state of affairs since the refugee exodus of 1948, bringing about, however, the dire consequence that the majority of exiles are confined, mostly without any rights, to refugee camps. Now that the long-cherished vision of regaining the land has vanished and hopes for the establishment of a state guaranteeing security and legal protection have been dashed time and time again, DeKoven's third option, that of searching for the homeland in the virtual space of memory and text, has become increasingly relevant. This is a retreat into a kind of self-circumscribing that borders on resignation and can only be conveyed by poets and writers. It is all the more remarkable in that it is precisely the "inscribed fatherland", a perception initially articulated by European-Jewish authors, that appears to mark out the only practicable path into an uncertain future for many intellectual Palestinians at present. It is elaborated most prominently in Mahmoud Darwish's more recent poems.

The path leading to this insight, which crystallized in confrontation with Israeli culture, was long. A protracted process was necessary before the Palestinians in Israel regained orientation. Only after they had negotiated this process of concurrent "Palestinianization" and "Israelization" did the "Arabs in Israel" perceive the vital function of the combative debate between cultures and the struggle over conflicting memories. In this process, poetry played a key role.

Continuing a longstanding Arab tradition, poetry in the Arab world still claims not merely to reflect or question the direction of public opinion but indeed to be a decisive factor in its formation. In Palestine the poem functions as evidence that the marginalized group's culture is equally as valuable as that of the dominant majority; it is a document testifying to their capacity as a collective to claim to be firmly anchored historically and spatially in a contested land. An artwork of language, sculpted through its aesthetic code, indebted and committed to historical artistic models, the poem transports cultural memory; by virtue of its evocative form it is already "semiotized". Very much as Roland Barthes claimed of classical European poetry and verse drama, the rhythmically structured Arabic poem is "a strongly mythical system, since it imposes on the meaning one extra 'signified', which is regularity".

In Israel and likewise for Palestinians living in the West Bank, who are also without state sovereignty, modern poetry became a kind of second, unofficial, even subversive cultural and educational resource, a fount of shared knowledge that families and friends drew on when they got together. The latest poems were eagerly awaited, the printed or hectographed material collected and at times hidden from raids by the authorities. A 2001 survey of post-*nakba* poetry presents about a hundred poets. Mahmoud Darwish emerged as the most prominent Palestinian poet as early as the 1960s, dominating the scene until his death in 2008.

Only in recent years has the autobiography established itself as a medium of similar status. Here Jabra Ibrahim Jabra (1920–94), exiled poet and novelist, stands out. His Bethlehem memoir, *The First Well,* continued in his Baghdad memoir, *Princesses' Street,* is rivaled only by that of his compatriot, the celebrated poetess Fadwa Tuqan (1917–2003), who portrayed her youth in Nablus in *A Mountainous Journey* (1985), a memoir continued in *An Even More Difficult Journey* (1993). Meanwhile, the sheer number of Palestinian autobiographies which have been published, and continue to be written, points to what Susanne Enderwitz has termed a "uniquely Palestinian path", wherein writers do not give an account of their lives primarily for personal reasons, but employ their memory of events to appeal to the conscience of the Western world and gain recognition for their cause.

The challenge of Israel

To gauge the significance of the construction of collective memory consummated in Palestinian poetry, it must be realized – and continually kept in mind – that the process takes place in a land where the dominant Israeli population intensively nurtures its own cultural memory. The pertinent Hebrew word here is *zikkaron*; it refers to the maintenance and preservation of the memory of a past reconstructed as the history of salvation, a figure of thought that has always played an essential role in the Jewish life-world. Already, in antiquity, the historical texts of the Hebrew Bible had crystallized into a grand drama of divine acts impacting on Israel, played out successively as election, exodus, settlement, exile and promised salvation; a drama that in the Diaspora was actualized ever anew into a central figure of memory for the collective in both synagogue liturgy as well as theological reflection. The continuing influence exerted by the reception of this "drama" has remained – as the historian Daniel Krochmalnik demonstrated in 1989 – unquestioned in the modern, partially secularized state of Israel:

> Although today ordinary Jewish historical consciousness is generally lacking in religious reference points, the messianological pattern is still active, even amongst religiously oblivious Jews. More than ever secular Jews are reliant on disclosing the sense of their puzzling history, and the messianological evidence that self-evidently emerges from the Holocaust and the founding of the state of Israel, appears to completely satisfy this search for meaning (...). For contemporary Jewish 'end-of-days' consciousness, the sacrosanct conviction is characteristic that the state of Israel is not only a sanctuary for persecuted Jews from across the globe – here the messianological motif of the ingathering of the exiled joins in – but also that in the figure of the state of Israel the whole of Jewish history has reached its goal.

This setting of priorities, assigning the *temporal* dimension of Jewish history a far greater significance than the *space* of Palestine (which, paradoxically, had not been determined by Jewish presence for the large part of its history), has led to a situation where the Arab population is only reluctantly perceived as "Palestinians", genuine inhabitants of Palestine; until very recently they were classified ethnically as "Arabs" and so as aliens. Concurrently, the land was stripped of its non-Jewish history, the material traces of the still remembered past erased in favor of a reconstruction of ancient history, and a modern landscape cult was pandered to.

As a result, archaeology became a main stage of this struggle, with the discipline, as the Israeli archaeologist Ariella Azoulay has attested, serving as a means to inscribe and represent Israel's deed of ownership over the land. This has been a continuous practice since the beginnings of the Zionist movement, realized through remembrance and forgetting, settlement activities, cartography and archaeological sites, as well as the planning and configuration of new landscapes. To quote from the survey on post-Zionist debates by Laurence Silberstein:

> In Zionist discourse and in Israeli culture, sites have been represented as passive places that lie around covered by dust. When the dust is removed, "authentic" documents/objects are revealed. Zionism, regarding such sites as evidence of Jewish continuity in the land, has removed all traces of the power struggles and conflict that had transformed them into zones of memory. It has represented cultural objects, which are the products of willful and intentional power practices as 'natural'.

In Israeli society the establishment and control of historical places as *lieux de mémoire* were and remain a politically explosive issue. By simultaneously pursuing strategies of forgetting and remembrance: by wiping out Arab villages, erasing their names and erecting "authentic" Jewish sites in their place; and not least by replacing Arabic names for the land with Biblical and modern Hebrew ones, the Zionist founders of the state have reconstructed the past of the land and attempted to suggest a continuous Jewish presence. This tendency was intensified by developments after the June War, when, with the occupation of the West Bank, the core sites of Jewish ancient history came under Israeli control. In 1991 the historian Dan Diner wrote:

> Now the particularist religious self-understanding comes much more to the fore, precisely through those sites regarded as holy, above all the eastern part of the city of Jerusalem. That is to say that Israeli self-understanding is increasingly de-secularizing itself. It is penetrating ever deeper into what we describe as political theology. Or in short: the myth of Eretz Israel, the Land of Israel and its biblical-historical legitimacy is increasingly supplanting the secular self-legitimacy reflected in the concept of the state of Israel or – in Hebrew terms – Medinat Israel. This antithesis begins to exert an effect from 1967 onwards and runs through society, vitiating the internal formation of self-understanding, or reshaping it.

First, then, the land itself was reshaped through state measures into an artificially created *lieu de mémoire* before; second, the act of remembrance as such explicitly assumed the rank of an indispensable collective obligation. In the consciousness of modern Israelis, *zikkaron*, embedded in Zionist practice from the very outset, has gained an additional meaning since the 1960s: it stands – once more relating to Jewish historical time and not the history of the geographical space – primarily for the remembrance of persecution in recent history, even though for a long time the public perception of the Holocaust in Israel was controversial.

The overwhelming presence of this Jewish memory also furnishes an explanation of how the Palestinians have formed a culture of memory in a short span of time, a culture that in its form is very distinct from that of its rival. Yet with the term *dhakira* (remembrance), the Palestinian discourse on memory, established by Mahmoud Darwish, clearly positions itself in relation to the Jewish concept of *zikkaron*.

A Palestinian response

Around the time of the June War the voices of the Palestinian minority in Israel became more audible and their subversive potential recognizable. These voices were for a long time, despite efforts by left-liberal Israeli literary figures to mediate, perceived as potential threats to peace; attacks on the official Zionist image. Since the rise of a "post-Zionist" Israeli discourse in the 1990s, they have gained recognition amongst some intellectuals as constructive contributions. In the state of Israel – Israeli critics admit this – the situation of the Palestinians could be described as that of a subordinated "colonized group", representing a prime example of what the cultural philosopher Homi K. Bhabha has defined as "marginalized minorities".

In Bhabha's view, such groups make the national space recognizable as a contested space of action, where representations of normality created by the authoritarian state actually cause disorientation and confusion amongst members of minorities. Minority authors problematize the majority perception of a monumental historical remembrance and the all-embracing totality of society as well as the homogeneity of cultural experience. Writing from positions on the margin of society, these writers detect ambivalences, irresolvable by interpretation, which structure the purported uniformity of historical time.

To put an end to their incapacitation, they must present their own "counter text" vis-à-vis the public self-representation of the dominant majority, that is, render visible the concealed forms of their self-assertion. In this context Rachel Feldhay Brenner speaks of a "hidden transcript":

> Zionism furnishes a good example of an ideologically imposed unity. It created the powerful myth of a collective of "new Jews" who imagined themselves as reborn in the supposedly empty homeland of Israel, and posited the Zionist pioneer in opposition to both the parasitic powerless Diaspora Jews and the backward, irrelevant Palestinian Arab. Speaking the authoritative voice of revolution and redemption, the Zionist ethos effectively silenced all dissenting voices. (...) To offset colonization an avenue must be found (...) for a public declaration of the hidden transcript. Hidden transcripts are the "infrapolitics

of subordinate groups" since they register the defiance that the subordinate practice in secret, out of the view of the dominant power.

Palestinian critics have in fact contributed a great deal to problematizing the hegemonic Zionist representation of Israeli culture. In the first instance poetry – namely that of Mahmoud Darwish – has opposed the Biblical "inscription" of the land.

Darwish's early masterpiece "A Lover from Palestine", a poem about a beloved "Palestine", embarks on this work of recreating memory and de-narrating exile. What this key text establishes is a new self-image of the poet who gives himself up to the beloved – in this, no different to the classical *ghazal* poet's self-abandonment to the divine beloved – but ends in a triumphal mood. The poet's *ghurba* (exile) seems to be overcome with the poetic recuperation of the land. Still, his poetic sacrifice of his innermost self attests his *Weltverlust* (loss of world): his renunciation of a normal life; of an attachment to anything other than the homeland. A covenant has been concluded between the poet and the collective of his homeland.

Shortly after writing this poem, Darwish turned to another vision. Throughout the 1970s until 1982 he wrote militant poetry, forging a paradigm of Arab memory to counter that of Jewish history employed to legitimate Israeli ownership of the land. Relying on popular memory rather than historical documents, he created the ideal of the *fida'i* (resistance fighter). While the image of the fighter, deeply rooted in Arab collective memory, was already pivotal to the poetry of the 1930s, it was Darwish who wove the figure of the heroic, self-sacrificing fighter into a veritable myth, conferring on him the messianic role of the leader on the path to freedom. This myth, which was to serve as the foil for a host of poems Darwish wrote in the 1970s, links the affinity between land and people to the ideal of self-sacrifice:

> We have what is lacking in you: a homeland bleeding out a people
> Who bleed out a homeland.

The sacrifice the fighter brings forges *dhakira*; it is an act of collective self-assertion. Here an activism receptive to the heroic Arab tradition is channeled into a force generating memory, confronting the *zikkaron* idea based on Biblical history.

It should be noted, however, that Darwish would later disclaim the powerful myth he had created. During his sojourn in Paris, where he found another exile after the expulsion of the Palestinian activists from Beirut in 1982, his poetry changed substantially. The Israeli invasion of 1982 had created a new reality in many aspects. The war against Lebanon with its high death toll among civilians aroused sizable intellectual opposition inside Israel. Leftist groups not only demonstrated in the streets but also resumed and intensified their contacts with Palestinian writers and poets. Israeli poets like Dahlia Rabikovitch went so far as to publish Hebrew poems in the vein of Jewish prayers lamenting the Arab victims of the Beirut invasion, thus transferring a literary medium of commemoration from the Jewish community to individuals of the "other side". In the years following, Israeli intellectuals started to show intensive interest in Darwish's work, substantial parts of which were translated into Hebrew. His work in these years would go an essential step beyond his earlier poetry: not only did it level the antagonism between the two cultures to form an equilibrium of forces; it succeeded in deconstructing the antagonism altogether. This deconstruction of myth was again achieved with continuous reference to paradigms of thought established in the Hebrew Bible. Darwish now shifted his attention from the historical texts of Genesis and Exodus, to the poetic and erotic Songs of Songs.

That not just poets but also novelists and essayists play an important role here is not surprising given the closer connection their genres have to social reality. Visions and ideals of Palestinian poetry, however, underlie their works like a hidden subtext; it seems that for its part prose offers a reflective and often critical answer in response. Poetry has in turn received fresh impulses from the fragmenting of encrusted ideological positions achieved in prose works, impulses which have loomed large since the 1980s.

The narrative work of Emile Habibi (1923–96), particularly his novel *The Secret Life of Saeed, the Ill-Fated Pessoptimist* (1974), had a groundbreaking effect on the relationship of both national groups to their land. Habibi held up a mirror to both societies, revealing the grotesque character of their obsessions, subservient to the projection mechanism of analogous distorting images of the respective "other". Habibi is one of the few writers in the Arab world who succeeded in extracting laughter from those existential problems that create angst in the works of his contemporaries Ghassan Kanafani (1936–72) and Jabra Ibrahim Jabra. Biblically founded claims raised in Israeli everyday practice are reduced to absurdity by the ironic replacement of the "official" reference texts with their Biblical counter-traditions, such as the promise of the land to Abraham and his offspring, which is unmasked as problematic by the countertradition of the expulsion of Abraham's first son, Ishmael, and his mother from the land. The real people living in the land are presented in their ethnic hybridity and variedly mixed origins, contrary to every cultural myth of purity. Distorted perceptions are exposed through recourse to classical poetry, the Qur'an and narrative literature, a move that simultaneously divests the old texts of their museum-like earnestness. Avant-garde in its literary strategies and unreservedly de-mythologizing in its critique of ideologies, this work confronts two master narratives at once, two dominant myths: the Biblical drama of salvation recast in secularized form in Israel and the Palestinian martyr ideal. It was awarded the Israeli State Prize for Literature in 1992.

Habibi configures the idea of an "exile in the homeland itself", a self-perception that consciously projects the situation of exile Jews before the Holocaust into present-day Israel/Palestine. As early as 1972 he opposed the conventional Zionist condemnation of *galut*, used to designate the pre-state living conditions of Jews, demanding the acknowledgement of an exilic status for the Palestinians and the freedom to approach their situation with the same emotions as the diasporic Jews, with "a genuine longing for the land". This idea of an exilic *modus vivendi* would first be discussed in its full relevance ten years later with the deconstruction, above all by the Post-Zionist critic Amnon Raz-Krakotzkin, of the Zionist concept of *shelilat ha-galut* (negation of exile). A concept of *galut* as an "incomplete presence" that can be lived out in the homeland itself, discarded in Zionism but revived in more recent times, would, believed post-Zionist thinkers, admit both the denied Jewish past as well as the denied Palestinian past to memory.

With his novel *Arabesques*, written in Hebrew, Habibi's younger literary colleague Anton Shammas (b. 1950) took an even farther-reaching step in the direction of a "Hebrew national literature", not necessarily the sole domain of Jews but able to accommodate Palestinian memories as well. In *Arabesques* Shammas created a kind of Galilean saga, a novel set predominantly in pre-state Palestine, including the villages of the coastal area which in 1948 would be evacuated and converted into Israeli settlement territory. The autobiographical narrator/protagonist is an Arab novelist who writes in Hebrew and is taking part in the annual writing program of the University of Iowa. His use of Hebrew, and moreover his mastery of the language evident in his fiction, arouses hostility in another program participant, the Jewish-Israeli writer, Yehoshua Bar-On. The fictional conflict foreshadows the panicked reaction by Jewish-Israeli writers and critics to the publication of *Arabesques*; they would malign Shammas for writing his novel in what they assumed to be an exclusively Jewish language. Earlier, Shammas had been urged by one of his leftist Israeli colleagues, A.B. Yehoshua, to leave Israel for the Palestinian territories. Shortly after the publication of *Arabesques* he did indeed leave the country and has since settled in the United States. Gil Zahava Hochberg has pointed out that "while Shammas stresses the fact that Hebrew – as an Israeli language – belongs to all Israelis, Yehoshua and other Jewish critics argue that Hebrew remains, even as a national language, first and foremost a Jewish cultural territory."

Shammas also contextualizes his novel within the Arab heritage, presenting a playful variation of the Majnun-Layla paradigm to subvert the serious politicized reading so widespread since the early poetry of Mahmoud Darwish. The poet/writer in Shammas's case is not a suffering Majnun but is finally united with the beloved, however imaginary that union is to be viewed. Thus, in Shammas's novel, not only is the writer's existential Arab *ghurba* ironically subverted by his consummation of

Layla's love, but equally his Jewish *galut* is, by dint of his writing Hebrew literature, "negated". Not unlike Habibi, Shammas may therefore be credited with an ironic inversion of the Zionist dogma of *shelilat ha-galut*.

This outcome does not extinguish the notion of exile altogether: exile does remain real, but as in Mahmoud Darwish's early poems it is the exile of the land itself, precisely, the West Bank and its people; a belonging which Shammas' Israeli-Arab narrator does not partake in. In contrast to Darwish's early vision, Shammas pins his hopes on the "redemption" of the Palestinian remnants in Israel: it will come about through the Hebrew language, though he has no similar "redemption" to offer to Palestinians outside that enclave, who remain "in exile".

To present the portrait of the rural and urban Palestinian past, closely related as it was to that of neighboring Lebanon, in a Hebrew language novel rich in Israeli Jewish intertextual evocations was a daring venture. While much acclaimed by international critics, it was furiously rejected by Israeli writers. Shammas was virtually expelled from the Israeli literary scene and eventually chose to emigrate to the United States – his case reveals all too clearly the potential brisance this problem holds.

The clash of "linguistic memories", as attested in the case of Anton Shammas and other Arab-Israeli writers, has been analyzed by the Israeli scholar Reuven Snir:

> The figure of a Russian babushka which Shammas appropriates to describe the Palestinian minority in Israel, clearly represents the problematic situation of these writers: they comprise an exceptional minority (Hebrew writers) within a minority (Jews) in the Arab world in addition to the problematic condition of the Palestinian minority within the Arab majority. In their native environment, they are unique in their conscious aesthetic preference for Hebrew literature while in Hebrew literature they are unique not only in their being outsiders, but mainly because their activity in it is made possible precisely by their being representatives of a minority. (...) However, in the shadow of the vast cultural distance between the majority and the minority and the lack of true cultural interaction, there are no, as Shammas himself puts it, "crossing circles" between the Hebrew literature and the Arab one. The culture of the majority has not succeeded in imposing itself on the culture of the minority, moreover it has even pushed it to prove its particular identity and to look for its roots, even if imaginary. The high status of the Arabic language in Arab culture and religious heritage, especially among Muslims, makes it undesirable to write in a language that is considered inferior.

Focusing on these complex developments among Palestinian intellectuals in Israel makes it easy to forget that Palestinians are not limited to the "remnants" of their nation in the homeland. Edward Said, always aware of the range of Palestinian exile, justifiably juxtaposes the authors of the homeland with two exilic authors who have exemplarily explored the concept and experience of exile, Ghassan Kanafani in Lebanon and Jabra Ibrahim Jabra in Iraq:

> Exile is thus the fundamental condition of Palestinian life, the source of what is both over- and underdeveloped about it, the energy for what is best, say, in the components of its remarkable literature (Emile Habibi's *Pessoptimist*, the novels of Ghassan Kanafani, and Jabra, the poetry of Rashid Husayn, Fadwa Tuqan, Samih al-Qasim and Mahmoud Darwish, and the work of numerous essayists, historians, theoreticians and memoirists) and in its extraordinary network of communication, associations and extended families.

He then alerts us to "pre-literary", social anchors of memory:

> Every Palestinian has no state as a Palestinian even though he is "of" without belonging "to", a state in which at present he resides. There are Lebanese Palestinians and American Palestinians, just as there are Jordanian, Syrian and West Bank Palestinians ... they still identify themselves as being from Shafa 'Amr, or Jerusalem or Tiberias. These claims are almost meaningless except as they add to a genealogy and paradoxically Palestinian presence that sets itself against the logic of history and geography. For Palestinians have a sense of detail and reality through using the patterns of an acutely concrete space-time conflation. The pattern begins in Palestine with some real but partly mythologized spot of land, a house, a region, a village, perhaps only an employer, then it moves out to take in the disappearance of a collective national identity even while remaining inside the old Palestine, the birth of concrete exile, always, always a head-on – later a more subtle – collision with laws designed specially for the Palestinians finally some recent sense of revived hope, pride in Palestinian achievements.

To express this highly complex experience of both loss and belonging perhaps demands a hermeneutic tool that transcends the limits of textual representation. There is hardly a more congenial artistic expression of that ambiguity than the images conveyed by Palestinian cinema. The work of one of the most prominent filmmakers, Michel Khleifi, has been described by Nurith Gertz and George Khleifi as sending a double message. On the one hand, his films revive what has been lost "as if it is fully present, rather than a representation in memory of something that has already passed and is gone". On the other hand, the cinematic gaze, with its focus on the particulars of reality, presents an attempt to overcome loss and regain control over reality, in terms of time and space. It is an endeavor to proceed from dream to reality, without obliterating either.

Subdued reactions: Syria

Although present in Syrian political consciousness prior to the June War, the Palestine conflict came to the fore as a pan-Arab problem with the Israeli capture of Syrian and Egyptian territory in 1967. The reasons for defeat, stemming from Syrian society itself, and the resultant psychological crisis were subsequently addressed in literature. With his subversive play *Gala Evening for the Fifth of June*, written in 1968, the dramatist Saadallah Wannous (1941–97) was the first to explore the situation critically. Not only in terms of its openly articulated social criticism but also by virtue of its techniques, featuring apparently improvised staging and the inclusion of a stage director terrified of censorship authorities amongst the protagonists, this drama transgressed conventional boundaries. Wannous founded a project of "theater of politicization" that aimed at waking up and galvanizing the people, at opening their eyes, and stimulating dialogue. The intention of a play or dramatic dialogue was to induce them to reflect on their fate as a collective. This was also the direction taken by Muhammad al-Maghut (1924–2007) in his satirical poems and dramas, which bring together artistic experimentation and public appeal.

Nizar Qabbani (1923–98) was another poetical voice to spring a surprise in the wake of the June War. Renowned as a love poet, he switched genres to produce a furious poem mercilessly exposing the political circumstances responsible for defeat. The celebrated poet won over the public, his work fuelling popular rage against the political leadership of the countries involved in the war. He would go on to create a comparable philippic marking another important historical event, the announcement of the ill-fated Oslo peace accords. Like its forerunner, this poem was more a document of his powerful eloquence, his ability to lend expression to the collective bitterness felt at dashed hopes, than a self-critical incursion into conventional thinking that could have aroused doubts as to the pertinence of traditional poetic forms.

Apart from Wannous's theater reform and Maghut's satires, a renewal comparable to developments in Egypt and Israel-Palestine is not discernible in the domestic Syrian literary scene. After his own troubled experience as an exile, Hanna Mina (b. 1924), often mentioned in the same breath as Naguib Mahfouz and probably Syrian's most important novelist, has evaded a direct confrontation with contemporary Syria by setting most of his novels in distant times and remote lands and clinging to realistic models.

The political and intellectual climate reigning in Syria in these years explains why experimental literature was written in exile. Yusuf al-Khal (1918–87) was a Syrian poet who, upon his return from the United States to settle in Beirut, co-founded the intellectual group affiliated to the avant-garde literary journal *Shi'r* (Poetry). He played a key role in establishing modern poetry, which is to say poetry no longer oriented on the traditional rules of mono-rhyme and conventional meters, in Lebanon.

Adonis (b. 1930) made his mark early as an exemplary revolutionary poet; his work prior to 1967 signaled a new experimental poetry and his decidedly secular reconfiguration of the religious in Arab poetry remains unique to the present day. Having migrated to Lebanon from Syria in 1956, Adonis was the focus of intellectual circles in Beirut for a number of years. Explicitly philosophical and often revealing inspiration from the mystic tradition, his poetry is testimony to a universal orientation that transcends contemporary history, also evident in his works of literary criticism and cultural philosophy. Though Adonis is only one of a host of authors who criticize the hold of tradition on Arab society and literature, his verdict is certainly one of the most extreme. In 1974 he wrote a trilogy titled *The Static and the Dynamic*, a critical study of Arabic poetry from its roots to the present day that compares examples from different ages on the basis of creativity versus ossification. He reaches the bleak conclusion that Islam as a socio-political force has inhibited the flourishing of creative thinking and writing within Arab and Muslim society, thus providing – in Akram Khater's view – the most striking example of an intellectual's disillusionment with the cultural and intellectual situation of his time.

One of the keenest experimenters in Syrian prose literature, the short story writer Zakariyya Tamir (b. 1931) is another who has left his homeland. Although he first migrated in 1981 his estrangement from the dominant realism paradigm had already taken place in the 1970s. Written in Damascus, the short stories of this period, which deal with the grotesque situations of life under dictatorship, reveal a new fantastic-absurdist technique of representation unique in Arab literature. Tamir is not unaware of the stifling *longue durée* (long duration) of local experience with absolutist forms of government; to underscore his criticism he resorts to the experience of predecessors who wrote under the threatening umbrella of absolute power, such as the eighth-century writer Ibn al-Muqaffaʾ, whose animal fable on power and overpowering is reflected in some of Tamir's work.

From the June War defeat to civil war: Lebanon

In Beirut, the metropolis of Arab intellectual life, the pan-Arab dream was only one of a number of rival political visions. These diverse political ideals, vying for supremacy and the subject of acrimonious debate until well into the civil war (1975–90), reveal that Lebanese society is anchored in more than one culture. Close affinity to the West, in particular to French culture, and traditional solidarity with the Arab world are pitted against one another, forming a latent source of conflict. As early as 1958, disturbances reminiscent of a civil war broke out over the controversial alternatives of Nasserism or stronger ties to the West; the resultant antagonism would drive a longstanding wedge between particular Christian denominations and Muslims. The events of 1967 heralded a decisive turning point, triggering a dramatic shift in the balance of power: after the occupation of the West Bank, Palestinian resistance was increasingly relocated to Lebanon. For many young Lebanese, the armed liberation movement seemed to be the epitome of a revolutionary movement fighting for emancipation, and it enjoyed enormous support both amongst a rural population already politicized in the 1950s and 1960s and even more among students. A progressive leftist movement transcending denominational lines crystallized; it would later declare its willingness to pursue its aims through armed struggle.

Rising Palestinian militancy, incompatible with the official Lebanese policy of neutrality, and the fact that the supporters of a pan-Arab project began to exploit the militarily defenseless Lebanon as a base, appeared problematic to many Lebanese. The Maronite Christians' party in particular felt provoked by these developments; in response they began preparing for the seemingly inevitable conflict by recruiting their own militias.

At the same time Beirut remained the indisputable cultural metropolis of the Middle East, even after the civil war had commenced. In the words of Samir Khalaf:

> By virtue of its mixed ethnic and religious composition and permissive politi-
> cal atmosphere Beirut had become remarkably innovative and venturesome,
> serving as a safe refuge for dispossessed and marginal groups periodically
> out of favor with the political regimes in the adjacent Arab states. More
> important perhaps it evolved as an intellectual sanctuary, a pace-setter for
> new trends from serious ideological doctrines and political platforms to the
> more frivolous manifestation of fads and fashions. An intellectual sanctuary,
> it fostered, indeed, licensed, experimentation in nearly all domains of public
> and private life.

Already, in the 1950s, intellectual and poetry circles had gathered here from throughout the Arab world, mainly based around the journals *al-Adab* (Literature) and *Shi'r*. The city was a collecting point for avant-garde art, and in turn it swiftly re-circulated the newest trends. Censorship restrictions were minimal. The Palestinians active in the Beirut scene were often also militant pioneers of revolutionary movements. Ghassan Kanafani, for instance, was active as a public affairs commentator whilst simultaneously holding the position of spokesman for the Marxist-oriented PFLP. In the 1960s Kanafani's narrative works had played a key role in helping Palestinian prose literature gain a reputation, while he himself had discovered and brought to the attention of the Arab world the "poets of resistance": the young talented writers living in the Arab enclaves of Israel. Kanafani was assassinated in 1972. Mahmoud Darwish, whose work reflected the eventful years of the 1970s and in particular the situation in the Palestinian refugee camps, was also active in Beirut from the time of his exile in 1971 until the expulsion of the Palestinians in 1982.

The situation deteriorated as the civil war dragged on, before changing drastically and definitively with the Israeli invasion of 1982. After the Arab-international intelligentsia had left the city, Beirut became a mere caricature of itself, reverting to a symbol of the gravest crisis, the bitterest disappointment of Arab cultural hopes. This is not only reflected in Darwish's contemporary poems; it became an irrefutable truth as the voices of many Arab poets and writers, now scattered to the four winds, died away. Beirut was now nothing more than a Babylon, a depraved counter-image to the once celebrated "mistress of the world's cities". The role Beirut played throughout the 1950s, 1960s, and 1970s as an inspiring center for locals and Arab exiles alike appeared in retrospect to be a mere episode, one in which Arab-international intellectuals found and, for a short while, lived out a utopia.

Novels from the civil war

Prior to the civil war poetry had dominated Lebanese literature; indeed, between the 1950s and the late 1970s, Beirut had been home to a number of Arab poets, some of them aligned with the *Shi'r* movement. Outstanding among them is Khalil Hawi (1919–82), who, not unlike Mahmoud Darwish and his role among the Palestinians, was uniquely capable of giving an authentic voice to collective political and personal aspirations. Forcefully cladding his deep frustration with Near Eastern culture and politics in the language of Christian myth, Hawi wrote strikingly poignant narrative poetry, among it unique versifications of Gospel stories, subverting the message of resurrection into testimonies of failed renewal and ongoing decay. Hawi was not forced to endure the Israeli occupation of Beirut – he shot himself in the wake of the Israeli invasion in August 1982.

By that time, the main voice in literature had passed from poetry to the novel. Early Lebanese novels, such as those by Mikhail Naimy (1889–1988) and later Emily Nasrallah (b. 1931), still bore strongly rural-idyllic characteristics. (This was also true of the musical libretti of the celebrated Rahbani brothers, who with Fayrouz as their singer brought local history and myths to the stage.) The first novels set in cities were *I Live* (1958) written by Layla Ba'albaki (b. 1936), and *Death in Beirut* (1972) by Tawfiq Yusuf Awwad (1911–81). The latter exposed the social crisis plaguing Lebanon that culminated in the civil war. But it was the civil war itself that triggered massive ruptures in intellectual and literary traditions amongst those authors who would go on to establish the preeminence of the Lebanese novel in the Arab world.

As divergent as the diverse Christian and Muslim parallel societies are – and their languages, Arabic, French and English, represent a level of diversity unknown elsewhere – their cultural memory concentrates on a common issue: the traumatic experience of the civil war. Authors from the generation that has plotted the social developments leading to the outbreak of violence have attempted to gain a semblance of clarity about their own group's history and trace the reasons triggering the catastrophe through the act of writing. To name only the most prominent: Yusuf Habshi al-Ashqar (1924–92), Elias Khoury (b. 1944), Hoda Barakat (b. 1952), Hassan Daoud (b. 1950), Rashid al-Daif (b. 1945), Sélim Nassib (b. 1946), Rabih Alameddine (b. 1960), Najwa Barakat (b. 1960). In the face of the terror practiced during the war, hushed up by the political establishment, depicting violence is itself already a political statement, which testifies to the authors' willingness to learn as well as their trust in the ability of their readers to do the same. And yet memory goes a step further when, as in the novels of Rashid al-Daif and Sélim Nassib, it undertakes, in an act of self-reflection, to call itself to account and does not shy away from personal confessions of guilt. The juxtaposition of rivaling and alternative recollections of the past is above all a juxtaposition of rival and alternative perspectives and ideas on the future, a parallel most prominently evident in the novels of Elias Khoury. What distinguishes the Lebanese novel from the rest of contemporary Arab literature is not only its introspection and rigorous destruction of political grand narratives but its experimental character, unique in its daringness.

What Edward Said has said about Elias Khoury holds true for an entire generation of Lebanese novelists:

> Khoury ... is an artist giving voice to rooted exiles and trapped refugees, to dissolving boundaries and changing identities, to radical demands and new languages. From this perspective Khoury's work bids Mahfouz an inevitable and yet profoundly respectful farewell.

Postscript: the new politics of memory in the Middle East and the necessity of dismantling the borders between disciplines

Recently, new forms for remembering violence have emerged in the public spheres of various Middle Eastern societies. They are significant expressions of the pressure for political liberalization that has lately begun to manifest itself in the region. Although it is true that this pressure results more immediately from the changing constellations of international politics, the Barcelona Process, and the growth of civil society and independent media inside Arab countries, it is also inseparable from the intellectual movements that preceded and often triggered these developments. The scarcity of studies exploring the lineaments of social and political memory in Arab countries, lamented as an indicator of the lack of intellectual interest in the politics of memory in the Middle East, is deceptive, a misleading impression that arises due to its very limited scope: scholars and theoreticians of social and political phenomena only seldom dare to transgress the borders set by their disciplines and thus simply fail to consider well-documented developments in art and literature – in spite of the striking fact that those public figures who usually play a pivotal role in bringing about change, journalists, are themselves often to be found among the literati. This observation is not limited to literature but applies to theater and the fine arts as well. In Lebanon, Elias Khoury was one of the first to reflect on collective memory on the stage. With his *Memories of Job*, performed at the *Masrah Bayrut* Theater in 1994, he brought to the fore war memories that the official policy of forgetting – endorsed by the amnesty law passed by the Lebanese Parliament in 1991 – had tried to ban. In a video installation from 2005, staged together with Rabih Mroué, he unmasked the production of myth inherent to the contemporary media performances orchestrated to prepare for the broadcast of forthcoming suicide operations. By this time, a new documentation center and forum of debate had been established in Beirut in 2004; called "Umam – Documentation and Research", its explicit aim is "to address the necessity and feasibility of actively revisiting Lebanon's violent past, an undertaking fiercely contested among Lebanese".

As far as the visual arts are concerned, there is hardly more striking proof of the awareness of this ambiguity and the high level of reflection involved in contemporary art practice than the work of the Lebanese artist Walid Raad, who in his art project "The Atlas Group", launched over fifteen years ago, explores the question of the document as such, how it is represented and dealt with in media-based artistic practices; while reflecting on violence and its various physical, psychological, and phenomenal forms. Or take the Lebanese dramatist Lina Saneh's presentation "Appendice", where the artist's persona – out of the desire to be cremated rather than buried after her death – grotesquely plays out the idea of submitting herself to a series of operations in order to have parts of her body removed and sold as art objects, conquering as much of the terrain of her body for her project as she could; a plot whose allegorical undertones are hard to ignore. But even this piece of absurd theater highlighting the role of the media in the interrelation of memory and violence in Lebanon remains strongly self-referential, conscious of the essential role of the artist in the political discourse of memory:

> There is only one thing that I would never cut out, although it is feasible medically speaking: my tongue. But I don't want to. Because without my

tongue I can no longer do theater, I lose my citizenship as well as my war against the enemy.

It is in art and literature, and of course in the scholarly discussion of both, that the meta-discursive dimension of the concept of memory and recollection has most thoroughly been investigated.

While memory studies in Europe have developed interdisciplinary frameworks of analysis, roaming productively between anthropology, political science, psychology, literary and cultural studies as well as the neurosciences and sociology, such a broad scope is still some way from being envisaged in the scholarship on the situation in the Middle East. Yet in view of the often observed fact that speech, psycho-acoustic stage performances and readings are still the most significant and effective means for bracketing Arabic language societies, the various literary voices, including cinematic projections, until now usually excluded from the analysis of the social and political situation, should finally be recognized and given a feasible platform. Works written by and about the intellectual protagonists involved in the strife-ridden struggle for truth and reconciliation should be considered as traces of the debates on memory which have been going on for some time now between intellectuals in the Middle East and Europe.

The authors and works discussed in this volume are not only part of an aesthetic development, they are equally – in view of the still missing consensual historiography in most of the Arab states – highly relevant political witnesses that testify to the immense diversification of historical memory in the Middle East.

WORKS CITED

Salah Abd al-Sabur: *Diwan Abd al-Sabur I, II*, Beirut: Dar al-'Awda 1972–7

Adonis: *al-Thabit wa-l-mutahawwil. Bahth fi l-ittiba' wa-l-ibda' 'ind al-'arab*, 4 vols., Dar al-'Awda 1974–9

Paul Antze, Michael Lambek (eds.): *Tense Past. Cultural Essays in Trauma and Memory*, New York: Routledge 1996

Aleida Assmann: *Erinnerungsräume. Formen und Wandlungen des kulturellen Gedächtnisses*, Munich: Beck 1999

Tawfiq Yusuf Awwad: *Tawahin Bayrut*, Beirut: Dar al-Adab 1972 (English translation: *Death in Beirut*, trans. Leslie McLoughlin, London: Heinemann 1976)

Sadiq Jalal al-Azm: *al-Naqd al-dhati ba'd al-hazima*, Beirut: Dar al-Tali'a 1968

Ariella Azoulay: "Open Doors. Museums of History in Israeli Public Square", in: *Theory and Criticism* 4 (1993), pp. 79–95

Homi K. Bhabha: *The Location of Culture*, London, New York: Routledge 1994

Sidra DeKoven Ezrahi: "Our Homeland, the Text ... Our Text the Homeland. Exile and

Homecoming in the Modern Jewish Imagination", in: *Michigan Quarterly Review* 31 (1992), pp. 463–93

Rachel Feldhay-Brenner: "'Hidden Transcripts' Made Public. Israeli Arabic Fiction and its Reception", in: *Critical Inquiry* 26 (1999), pp. 55–108

Emile Habibi: *al-Waqa'i' al-ghariba fi khtifa' Sa'id Abi l-Nahs al-Mutasha'il*, Haifa: Arabesque 1974 (English translation: *The Secret Life of Saeed, the Ill-fated Pessoptimist*, trans. Salma Khadra Jayyusi and Trevor LeGassick, London: Zed Books 1985)

Maurice Halbwachs: *La topographie légendaire des évangiles en terre sainte*, Paris: Presses Universitaires de France 1941

Jabra Ibrahim Jabra: *al-Bi'r al-ula. Fusul fi sira dhatiyya*, London: Riad El-Rayyes 1987 (English translation: *The First Well. A Bethlehem Boyhood*, trans. Issa J. Boullata, Fayetteville: University of Arkansas Press 1995)

Jabra Ibrahim Jabra: *Shari' al-amirat. Fusul fi sira dhatiyya*, Beirut: al-Mu'assasa al-'Arabiyya li-l-Dirasat wa-l-Nashr 1994

Samir Khalaf: "Culture, Collective Memory and the Restoration of Civility", in: Deirdre Collings (ed.), *Peace for Lebanon? From War to Reconstruction*, London, Boulder: Lynne Rienner Publishers 1994, pp. 273–85

Edwar al-Kharrat: *al-Hassasiyya al-jadida. Maqalat fi l-zahira al-qasasiyya*, Beirut: Dar al-Adab 1993

Daniel Krochmalnik: "9. November 1938. 14. Mai 1948. Zur Entmythologisierung von zwei historischen Ereignissen", in: *Babylon* 5 (1988), pp. 1–24

Amnon Raz-Krakotzkin: "Exile in the Midst of Sovereignty. A Critique of 'Shelilat ha-Galut in Israeli Culture'" [in Hebrew], in: *Theory and Criticism* 4 (1993), pp. 23–55, and *Theory and Criticism* 5 (1996), pp. 113–32

Edward Said: *The Question of Palestine*, New York: Vintage 1992

Badr Shakir al-Sayyab: *Diwan Badr Shakir al-Sayyab I, II*, Beirut: Dar al-'Awda 1971–4

Anton Shammas: *Arabesqot*, Tel Aviv: Am Oved 1986 (English translation: *Arabesques*, trans. Vivian Eden. New York et al.: Harper & Row 1988)

Laurence J. Silberstein: *The Postzionism Debates. Knowledge and Power in Israeli Culture*, New York, London: Routledge 1999

Reuven Snir: "'Hebrew as the Language of Grace'. Arab Palestinian Writers in Hebrew", in: *Prooftexts* 15 (1995), pp. 163–83

Fadwa Tuqan: *Rihla jabaliyya, rihla sa'ba. Sira dhatiyya*, Amman: Dar al-Shuruq 1985 (English translation: *A Mountainous Journey. An Autobiography*, trans. Olive Kenny, poetry translated by Naomi Shihab Nye with the help of the editor, ed. Salma Khadra Jayyusi, London: The Women's Press 1990)

Fadwa Tuqan: *al-Rihla al-as'ab*, Amman: Dar al-Shuruq 1993

Sa'dallah Wannous: *Haflat samar min ajl khamsat huzayran* (1969), Beirut: Dar al-Adab 1977

The Divinity of the Profane
Representations of the Divine
in the Poetry of Adonis

Stefan Weidner

The notion of "modernity" has been applied to a multitude of complex, often very different phenomena over the last two hundred years. It has been used for such divergent purposes that it has probably become more misleading than helpful, and we should be careful not to regard it as a criterion for distinguishing between positive and negative developments. One of the phenomena usually linked with modernity in the cultural sphere is the crisis of religions and growing skepticism towards the theological foundations of religious belief in God. Even if the questioning of traditional religious beliefs has never been as widespread as the social or technological phenomena of modernity, it has nonetheless been one of the most decisive factors of twentieth-century intellectual life, not only in the West but also, albeit to a lesser degree, in the Islamic world. It is in this context that the work of Adonis, a naturalized Lebanese citizen born in the coastal region of northern Syria in 1930 and one of the Arab world's most prominent poets, should be read. No other modern Arab author tackles the crisis of the Divine so directly and forthrightly as Adonis, who seeks to resolve the dilemmas spawned by this crisis through the means of poetry.

Although Adonis's preoccupation with the Divine can be traced back to the early 1950s, it became the main thematic issue addressed by his poetry in his famous collection *The Songs of Mihyar the Damascene*. Expressed fifty-three times according to my count, the word "Allah" and derivations of it, including *rabb* (Lord), is the most used proper noun in the volume.

The importance of the Divine and the superhuman is obvious from the opening pages. The protagonist, introduced in the grammatical third person but not yet named, is presented in the introductory "Psalm" (the title, of course, already hints at the religious dimension of this prose poem) in terms of qualities and characteristics which clearly transcend the human. Not only is he said to encompass opposites – "he is the reality and its contrary, he is the life and its other" – thereby escaping any definition; he has neither an outward bodily appearance – "He has the shape of the wind" – nor an ancestry – "he has no ancestor and his roots are in his footsteps". Furthermore, he has abilities which are marked by power over life and death: "He fills life and no one sees him. He whips it into foam and drowns in it", and: "he scares and vivifies (...) he peels man like an onion".

The character described here shares many of the attributes that are ascribed to God in the Islamic theological tradition. According to this theology, God's main characteristics are his indefinability and his being uncreated, meaning that he has no predecessors. Other features also seem to imply that a God-like character is presented here. For instance, it is said that "he creates his kinds starting from himself", an idea close to the creation of man as depicted in Genesis (1:26–27), although at the same time this seems to contradict the aforementioned traditional Islamic notion of a God who is not supposed to create his own kind precisely because he is uncreated. Moreover, when he is said "to have the shape of the wind", (*rih* (wind) being the last word of the psalm), one is reminded of the conception of God as *pneuma* (soul), or of the "spirit" of God as compared to the "wind" in the Biblical tradition. The etymological link of *rih* and *ruh* (spirit) with the *ruakh* (spirit) of the Hebrew Bible further stresses this idea. In the literary tradition, both Western and Eastern, only gods have been said to have "the shape of the wind".

Quite obviously, however, it is not a God who is presented here. The subject of the poetic speech displays traits that are unquestionably contradictory to the notion of God. Thoroughly inconceivable for a God, he is "dancing for the mud so that it yawns and to the tree so that it falls asleep". More importantly, he shows signs of being "at a loss", as if he were lacking something. It is said that, after having turned "the morrow into game", he runs after it "in despair". His words "are chiseled into the direction of loss" and "perplexity" (a well-known mystical term denoting a degree of the spiritual states of the Sufi) "is his homeland". The protagonist thus appears as a god-like creature, a demigod, or someone who, despite his divine attributes and elusive sense of omnipotence, is not without needs and is certainly familiar with distress. He represents the sphere of the human and the profane as much as he represents the Divine.

The second poem, "He is not a star", brings the reader closer to the protagonist, once again depicted in terms usually associated with the religious sphere. However, his divine character is now explicitly denied: "He is not a star, not the inspiration of a prophet". The distance between the protagonist and the traditional notion of the Divine is further widened and stressed by an imputing simile: "he is coming like a heathen spear, invading the earth of the letters". It is only in the third poem of the volume that the protagonist is finally named, and with the naming given a status: he is called "King Mihyar". The domain of this king is not real, however, but symbolic: he shares his domain with the poet; his castle is the dream; he lives in the kingdom of the wind and rules in the country of secrets. The figure of Mihyar has been compared to the ancient Persian God Mithra. The name Mihyar therefore bears, albeit in a rather remote way, divine connotations.

The whole range of transformations and aspects of the person of Mihyar cannot be explained here. It should however be noted that while he possesses a considerable array of divine traits, he is by no means impervious: the divine is mingled with the human. Indeed, a subsequent poem makes it clear that the "heathen spear" is directed most forcefully against the Divine in the traditional Islamic sense: Mihyar is said to transgress "the frontiers of the Caliphate" and "to reject the Imamat", thus expressing his disregard for the worldly order of Islam.

This "transgression" of the religious order and value system is elaborated and illustrated in several other poems. The titles of poems like "The Holy Barbarian", "The New Noah", or "Shaddad" (the name of a legendary person) indicate a heretical tendency. In "The Holy Barbarian" Mihyar is presented with attributes of sainthood as well as paganism:

> This is Mihyar, your holy barbarian (...)
> He is the suffering creator ...

As a creator he belongs to the sphere of the Divine, but he also suffers and thus belongs to the human.

In the poem "Shaddad" the heresy is more deeply rooted in the Arabic-Islamic tradition. The poem alludes to the myth of "The many columned city of Iram", mentioned in the Qur'an (89:6–7) as having ignored the orders of God. In its very first line the poem tells us that Shaddad, the ruler over Iram, "has come back". An age of rebellion against the orders of God, the reader is led to conclude, has begun anew. According to the poetic persona, the city of Iram, condemned by God in the Qur'an, is "the homeland of those who are desperate and those who refuse". This would seem to be the same refusal associated with the character of Mihyar in the earlier poems, marked by a similar desperation and perplexity. The inhabitants of Iram are blithely careless as to their salvation and ignore the menace of God. Whereas in the Qur'an the Lord unleashed "a scourge of punishment" on the city and its inhabitants, in the poem the city is presented as a home for all those who condone and share the poetic persona's attitude of refusal. The final two verses underline this affiliation, for the poetic persona now switches to the first person plural, "we", merging with those he has previously addressed and designating Iram as "our land and our only heritage". In the final line he goes on to say: "We are its sons who are reprieved until the day of resurrection". The full meaning of this line only becomes clear by tracing its Qur'anic reference. In the Qur'an it is Satan who is said to be among the reprieved: "You [Satan] have respite (...) until the Day of Appointed Time." Employing the first person plural thus creates a parallel to Satan: the poem's final line tells us that we, like Satan, are condemned and will be subjected to the punishment of God on the Day of

Judgment. Only until then are we reprieved. Although this is stated neutrally as a simple fact, when read in conjunction with the preceding poems it becomes clear that the poet regards our state of being in reprieve as the *conditio humana* (human condition) and accepts it as such.

Heresy and the longing for a new worldly or religious order also emerge clearly in the poem "The New Noah". In Islamic tradition Noah is one of the first and most important prophets of the monotheistic God. Here the Islamic Noah is replaced by a new Noah, the narrator. Towards the end of the poem, this new Noah says that he does not listen to the words of God, but "long[s] for another, for a new Lord." Although once again the heretic impact of the poem is quite obvious, it is remarkable that the notion of God is not completely dismissed; rather, there is a longing to replace the traditional God with a new one: the new Noah's most important role is to be one of his prophets. While the meaning of God and Noah as well as the worldview they convey may have changed, what we may call the divine structure remains: there is still a god and there are still prophets – however, they are to symbolize new values.

Another highly interesting poem for our purposes is, at first glance, the homage to one of the most venerated persons of early Islam, "Elegy to 'Umar ibn al-Khattab". At the same time, it is somewhat obscure; it refers to a story told in Abu al-Faraj al-Isfahani's *Book of Songs* that might not be known or recognized by every reader. The story in the *Book of Songs* relates the encounter between Umar and Jabala (the latter is rendered as Jibilla in the poem for reasons of rhyme). Jabala is a Byzantine nobleman and leader who has converted to Islam and performed his visit of duty to the caliph and the holy places in Mecca. During the circumambulation of the Kaaba, a Bedouin inadvertently tears Jabala's robe. Upset, Jabala beats the man. As a result of the assault, Umar allows the Bedouin to ask for satisfaction or to take revenge, justifying this decision to the surprised Jabala by telling him that everybody is equal in Islam. Jabala responds by claiming that under these conditions he would prefer to return to the Christian faith, thereby exacerbating the situation: as an apostate, he is now threatened with death. Umar in fact tolerates Jabala's departure, probably fearing a clash between his adherents and those of Jabala.

The meaning of the poem becomes apparent when read against this backdrop: a "voice" poses the question "when are you beaten, o Jibilla", enabling an interpretation based on the story in the *Book of Songs*. Jabala has not yet been beaten, but he should have been if the promise of Islam to treat every Muslim equally regardless of his origin had been kept. It is this promise which is alluded to in the last two lines:

And we are waiting
for your promise which comes from heaven.

As pronounced by the religion of Islam, the promise is of divine origin but it has remained unfulfilled until now. Justice has not been done. The striking feature of the poem is that this failure is attributed to such a venerated figure as Umar. It was his task to see that the promise was fulfilled, but he preferred a more diplomatic solution. The reader is thus witness to the deconstruction of the myth of the so-called rightly guided caliphs from the Golden Age of Islam, one of the most popular of all Muslim creeds.

The destruction or deconstruction of established religious orders and creeds is not the only way the Divine is treated in *The Songs of Mihyar*. In most cases, the impulse of destruction is matched or accompanied by a creative act or an establishment of positive values. The poem about Umar is thus not only a deconstruction of the myth of early Islam and the rightly guided caliphs, but also an acknowledgement of the value of equality among men regardless of their origin. The dialectic of destruction and creation is also at work in the short poem "Death", which opens with the lines:

> We die, if we do not create gods
> We die if we do not kill gods –

In talking of gods and their creation by men, the poem immediately takes a position beyond the sphere of the Islamic or Christian conception of the Divine. The constant creation and destruction of gods as well as all that they entail, that is, the accompanying worldly and religious order, is presented as the *conditio sine qua non* of life. As obvious as this may be, the last of the poem's three lines is as obscure: an apostrophe (as a means of rhetoric) addresses the "Kingdom of the straying rock", whereby straying forms a significant rhyme with "Gods", a clear echo of Matthew 16:18–19.

The rock is a symbol of stability. Whatever is built on rock will last forever, remain where it is, and stay what it is. The notion of a "straying" rock is thus paradoxical. This poem is the quintessence of how the Divine and God are represented in *The Songs of Mihyar*, encapsulating the worldview of this whole divan. As we will see, it is also a key to understanding the later works of Adonis. The metaphysical security guaranteed by the rock is only that of a fragile equilibrium. It is the equilibrium between creating and killing gods. We still need gods, the poem tells us, and we still need the kingdom, the worldly order created by God. However, as a very condition of our life, this order is no longer built on stable ground. Moreover, the poem seems to imply that the function of the Divine is more important than its particular form, its realization in a specific religion. Although the latter, together with the belief in a particular God, may, indeed must differ and change, there must always be a power comparable to the Divine that "produces" a religion and a "kingdom"; it is this power that is posited as an anthropological necessity. In this way, the poem expresses a Copernican revolution in the field of the Divine: the Divine moves.

Although fully aware of the danger of reading too much into such a short poem, I feel that this interpretation is more than justifiable given that the notions of God or the Divine are by no means dismissed out of hand, but are rather "reworked" or "reconstructed". As we have also seen, the notions of particular gods in the traditional sense or of traditional world orders are dismantled and demystified. This short poem is thus a microcosm of *The Songs of Mihyar* as a whole: gods are destroyed and created.

The Book of Transformations and of Emigration in the Regions of Day and Night, the volume of poetry written after *The Songs of Mihyar*, also betrays an obsession with the Divine. Of particular interest for our theme is the treatment of the Divine in the section titled "The Transformations of the Lover". Here, for the first time in Adonis's poetry, the body shifts to the center of the poet's attention; on the surface at least, the Divine seems to be completely absent. However, a closer analysis of the language and ideas in this poem reveals that the Divine remains important.

To a great extent the thirty-page poem is a collage. As far as I am aware, not all of Adonis's sources have been traced; nonetheless, the most salient have been identified by Arab scholars. The collage technique Adonis uses is rather simple: taking a classical text with a certain religious meaning, he transposes it into a profane context, whereby – this is the decisive transforming moment inherent to the collage approach – he changes precisely those words and expressions which denote the former religious context. The religious is thus erased and replaced by locutions connected to the body or sexuality. The following three examples provide perhaps the clearest testimony of this supplanting of the religious. In the first example, Adonis changes a text by al-Asma'i. Instead of a pilgrimage "to the holy house of God via Syria", Adonis writes of a journey to a woman; the rest of the story is more or less identical. Another striking example is based on a saying by al-Niffari. In *Kitab al-Mukhatabat* 57:9 al-Niffari says: "The Lord stayed me, and said to me: Say to the Sun, O thou that was written by the Pen of the Lord". In Adonis's version, it is not *al-rabb* (the Lord) who says this, but *as-sayyid al-jasad* (Mister Body). Instead of the sun, the beloved is addressed; she is not, like the sun, written by the pen of the Lord, but by the pen of the lover. One need not to be an adherent of the psychoanalytic school of literary analysis to see that here the highly venerated Qur'anic *qalam* (pen) is nothing but another name for the phallus. The heretical impact of this reinterpretation of the Divine is unsurpassable.

The third example of an allusion to a Qur'anic expression is somewhat more subtle and may pass unnoticed. Describing the act of lovemaking, Adonis writes: "I am torn while descending into the depths of the body which are filled with creatures burning, dying down, moaning and wailing." In the Qur'an (11:106) *shahiq* and *zafir* (sighing and groaning) describe the cries of those cast into the fires of Hell. In Adonis's version, these cries become part of the sexual act. Moreover, by incorporating these words into a description of lovemaking Adonis simultaneously revives another meaning of these words: *shahiq* and *zafir* are also the cries of rutting donkeys. As before, we cannot know if Adonis has used this expression consciously. Those Arab readers who know the Qur'an well are most likely to be reminded of how they are employed in the holy text. We may interpret Adonis's provocative appropriation of Qur'anic language thus: that heaven and hell are located in the body, not in a transcendental sphere.

The Divine is thus literally replaced by the profane, the traditional notion of God by an adoration of the body. Simple as it is, this method is even more striking when we realize that the Divine, as a function or system of thought and approach to the world, is largely retained. Although now founded on the body instead of God, it acts as if God were still there. There is still a pilgrimage, we are led to conclude, but it leads to the other gender, to women. There is still a mystical experience, but instead of being concerned with God, it is rooted in sexuality (this shift is the inversion of the Sufi technique, which consists of using the profane terminology of love to describe love of God). There is even a direct and explicit adoration of specific gods. Several times in the poem the poet says "Liber, Libera, Phallus", thus invoking the ancient pagan gods Liber and Libera, who, according to Augustine, were celebrated in processions exposing giant Phalli. Fortunately for the poet, this subtext has largely gone unnoticed.

To summarize, the internal structure of the Divine is kept while its traditional outward shape is replaced by the notion of the body. "The Transformations of the Lover" therefore represents Adonis's first decisive attempt to "create" or determine a new God from the profane and to use the tradition to bestow it with divine traits. Whereas the demigod Mihyar was a rather diffuse, intangible figure, at times interchangeable with the poetic persona or other figures like Odysseus, the body is now presented as the rightful successor to the Divine – and the poet is its herald. From now on, the body remains at the center of the poet's attention and is, in some poems more, in some less, bestowed with divine attributes.

Some poems written during the Lebanese civil war lend a new quality to the relationship between the body and the Divine. To explain this enrichment I would like to briefly analyze two poems written in 1977 and 1982 respectively. From the outset, the text of "Unintended Worship Ritual" is clearly recognizable as a follow-up to "The Transformations of the Lover": "And thus, she was an unintended worship ritual." Instead of God, worship is directed towards a woman. As the poem unfolds, it turns out that it is not a woman who is portrayed, but the city of Damascus, where the poet lives. The city is described in terms of a body and throughout the text the city is rendered in terms largely synonymous with a woman. Several times the poet calls on and evokes his beloved "woman-city". Making love and writing, that is, finding the right words and the language to express his love, are also paralleled:

> Her body being his language by which he spoke
> he listened to her body speak about a travel between ink and paper
> between member and member

Moreover, Damascus here is not only an image of the beloved, but the symbol of the Arab world, the political division of which becomes apparent in the Lebanese civil war. The poet regards it as his task to heal the Arab nation through his poetry, the beloved through his body. This redemptive task of the poet is expressed quite clearly in the last part of the poem:

> your [i.e. Damascus's] name is being doubled now
> and, by the glory of your other name,
> it is now poetry
> that recasts you letter by letter
> in order that you will be in people's reach,
> in order that you will be at hand so long as there is poetry

In short, the task of poetry is to reconcile and to heal the Arab nation of its wounds and defects. In my view, this task is rooted in an almost religious conception of poetry. The model character of the religious in the poet's struggle becomes obvious when he calls his act of love i'jaz (miracle): "I exclude you [the beloved] from how, why, and where, and I practice my inimitable miracle."

The transcendental poetical power of the Qur'an, laid down as a dogma in the term i'jaz, is, by using this term for the sexual act, now projected onto the body, the powers of which are said to be as miraculous as the Qur'anic verses. The body of the poet thus becomes the symbol for the powers of poetry, which now seems to compete even with the Qur'an in its promise to heal and redeem, in short, to exercise its divine powers. As in "The Transformations of the Lover" and *The Songs of Mihyar*, the traditional religious conception of Islam or any other religion is discarded. In a frank admission, the poet says that he is "embraced by heresy". Yet the predominant religious characteristics are maintained and transposed onto the poet, his body and his language. The Divine as a system of thought or the fount of alleged powers remains.

Written in response to the Israeli siege of Beirut in 1982 "The Time" displays a pattern comparable to "Unintended Worship Ritual". The poet overcomes the vicissitudes of the war and the omnipresent destruction by exercising his magic poetical powers. In contrast to his age, marked by destructive forces, the poet embodies the reconciling forces of poetical language, stressed in the last lines of the poem:

> My skin is not a cavern of thoughts, (...)
> my weddings the grafting of two poles; this epoch is mine
> the dead God, the blind machine – (...)
> I am the Alpha of water and the Omega of fire – the mad lover of life

The religious dimension of the last phrase is obvious: by calling himself "the Alpha and the Omega", the poet identifies himself with what was formerly the Divine, the only difference being that here the Divine is not located in the other world; is not transcendental but tellurian, elemental. As in "Unintended Worship Ritual", the definition of the Divine has obviously changed but nonetheless the stance of the Divine is again adopted. The poet has, so to speak, usurped the Divine.

Naturally enough, the credibility of such a stance, as well as its acceptance amongst readers, is a question that needs to be probed. We can enjoy the poem aesthetically – I consider it one of the most perfect of Adonis' later poems – and admire the poet's determination to fight war by means of poetry. The impact of the poem is another matter: to my mind, its textual perfection is tarnished by the pathos-laden, hubristic claim put forward by the poet; moreover, it is unclear as to how poetry could ever manage to overcome war and put an end to its divisiveness – or, as in "Unintended Worship Ritual", reconcile the Arab nation. In assessing these problematic traits, we need to keep the following in mind: while modernity has brought about a crisis in religious beliefs and notions, impressively mirrored in *The Songs of Mihyar*, this crisis is most certainly not limited to a specific religious system but has undermined the Divine itself; more specifically, the pattern or system of thought organizing and guaranteeing the credibility of the Divine. It is this belief system that made dogmas such as the *i'jaz* or phrases like "I am the Alpha and the Omega" (as the word of God in the Apocalypse) true beyond doubt and discussion. Such truths have however been the subject of rigorous scrutiny from the end of the nineteenth century up to the present day. What is more, this questioning has probed religious thought, shaken belief in the Divine as a whole, and not been restricted to any particular dogma or religion.

While leading people to question dogmas and other beliefs, this very same impulse also nourishes our incredulity and skepticism when a figure with a prophetic voice, no matter how exalted an artist or poet they may be, confronts us with an unfounded claim and seeks to garner our belief. The problem resides less in what the poet asks us to accept than in the circumstance that the poet asks us to give up our skepticism, to place our trust in him and follow his path in the attempt to change the world by means of poetry. Only to a public of disbelievers can a poet say that his body performs the *i'jaz* or that he is the Alpha and the Omega of the elements; but, strangely enough, the same public is then asked to accept that a poet reestablishes the Divine. Maybe the poet has reckoned with a different audience, one for which this remains unnoticed or is unproblematic, and not with skeptical Orientalists who do not share his belief in the magical healing powers of poetry.

In any case, the Divine is not only one of the main themes broached by Adonis's poetry, it is its main problem, the unresolved center of the poet's preoccupation and one of his main motivations in writing. The twofold question which haunts this poetry, already detectable in *The Songs of Mihyar*, is how to represent and to found the Divine anew, giving it a new form while ensuring that it does not suffer the same fate as the established religions. For Adonis, poetry is the means of introducing this new type of the Divine and to grant it the necessary credibility.

One of the most gifted poets of the Arab world invests all his powers of expression in the attempt to save the Divine by reconfiguring for it for the modern age and so making it acceptable once more. Although this Divine has lost most of its traditional appearance, its most important functions are retained. We may regard this as an impressive attempt to fuse modernity and tradition. We might read it as a first-hand testament as to how deeply the Divine is still rooted in Middle Eastern society, represented by one of its foremost, most libertine intellectuals. Both, I think, are true. Whether we want to or not, we have to accept that even the most perfect poetry is sometimes subjected to contradictory forces, which multiply its meanings and possible readings. The treatment of the Divine in Adonis's poetry is one of the best examples of this. And last but not least, it is an invitation to debate.

SELECTED WORKS

Aghani Mihyar al-dimashqi (Mihyar of Damascus: His Songs), Beirut: Dar Majallat Shi'r 1961

al-A'mal al-shi'riyya al-kamila (Complete Poetic Works), Beirut: Dar al-'Awda 1985

Kitab al-tahawwulat wa-l-hijra fi aqalim al-nahar wa-l-layl (The Book of Transformations and of Emigration to the Regions of Day and Night), Beirut: al-Maktaba al-'Asriyya 1965

TRANSLATIONS

The Pages of Day and Night, trans. Samuel Hazo, Evanston: The Marlboro Press, 2000

If Only the Sea Could Sleep, trans. Kamal Boullata, Susan Einbinder, Mirène Ghossein, Los Angeles: Green Integer Books 2002

An Introduction to Arab Poetics, London: Saqi 2003

Sufism and Surrealism, London: Saqi 2005

A Time Between Ashes and Roses, trans. Shawkat M. Toorawa, Syracuse, NY: Syracuse University Press 2005

Mihyar of Damascus: His Songs, trans. Adnan Haydar, Michael Beard, Rochester, NY: BOA Editions 2008

FURTHER READING

Adonis. Un poète dans le monde d'aujourd'hui. 1950–2000. Paris: Institut du monde arabe 2000

Stefan Weidner: "A Guardian of Change? The Poetry of Adunis between Hermeticsm and Commitment", in: Stephan Guth, Priska Furrer, Johann Christoph Bürgel (eds.), *Conscious Voices. Concepts of Writing in the Middle East*, Beirut, Stuttgart: Steiner 1999, pp. 277–92

Stefan Weidner: "The Divinity of the Profane", in: Ed de Moor, Gert Borg (eds.), *Representations of the Divine in Arabic Poetry*, Amsterdam: Rodopi 2001, pp. 211–25

OTHER WORKS CITED

Abu al-Faraj al-Isfahani [= al-Isbahani]: *Kitab al-Aghani* [10th century], 24 vols., Cairo: Dar al-Kutub 1927–74

Muhammad ibn 'Abd al-Jabbar al-Niffari: *The Mawaqif and Mukhatabat of Muhammad Ibn 'Abd Al-Jabbar Al-Niffari. With other fragments* [10th century], ed. and trans. Arthur John Arberry, London: Trustees of the "E.J.W. Gibb Memorial" 1935

Days of Amber, City of Saffron
Edwar al-Kharrat Remembers and Writes an Unintended Autobiography

Andreas Pflitsch

In the title story of his book *Bernsteintage* (Days of Amber) Maxim Biller depicts the childhood memories of his protagonist, sounding out in the process the limited possibilities of rendering the work of memory into literature. "His Czech childhood was as firmly enclosed by his memory as a tiny beetle by a block of amber – he was the beetle, but he also observed it from the outside, and that perhaps warped his view." The situation described here – a person remembering, peculiar and almost schizophrenic; the paradox role of someone who is at once subject and object of his own observations – is exacerbated when this person writes. When an author remembers and turns acts of remembrance into a central thematic of a text, the results of these efforts are commonly regarded as an autobiography.

The classical autobiography is defined as the life of a person as told by himself. If it was only that simple: stepping outside of oneself to observe oneself, suspending the rush of time – or more precisely reversing it – to enter the past thinking backwards; while this may not be entirely impossible, it is nonetheless a remarkable undertaking. Drawing attention to the exceptionality of such an everyday experience, Jorge Luis Borges has stated that "viewed philosophically, remembering is no less miraculous than predicting the future." And that is not all. The author of an autobiography has not only to plunge into the past, into the "deep well" that Thomas Mann mentions in the prologue to his *Joseph* tetralogy, moved to ask: "Should one not call it unfathomable?" The autobiographer cannot afford to become lost in these unfathomable depths, but must time and again surface from the well, climb out, and return to the desk, back to the present. In this way the autobiographer commutes between times, and this perpetual back and forth may occasionally turn vertiginous. This too, so we may assume, "perhaps warps their view" now and then.

In any case, the assumption that the autobiographer commits to paper the past exactly as it was can safely be filed away amongst those things that postmodernism, not without a hint of sarcasm, looks down upon as a typical expression of "modern" naivety. The past and its recollection are not the same. To dip into the well again: if the past is the murky water at the bottom of the well, remembering is the often arduous and not always pleasurable act of hauling some of this water out of the depths and bringing it to the top. Inevitably drops are spilt; what arrives at the top probably has something to do with what is down below, but it is by no means identical and most certainly never complete.

Kernels of events, clouds of memories

In *City of Saffron* the Egyptian author Edwar al-Kharrat has written a text that is at once autobiographical and non-autobiographical, illuminating the theme of memory and remembrance in a complexity unrivaled in Arab literature or further afield. *City of Saffron* hovers between genres, neither autobiography nor novel, and yet both. A preliminary remark by the author appears to answer unequivocally the question of its autobiographical character: "These texts are not an autobiography, nor anything like," he begins, before the differences are given more specific contour:

> the flights of fantasy, the artifice herein, bear them far beyond such bounds. They are illusions – incidents and visions – figures; the kernels of events which are but dreams; the clouds of memories which should have taken place, but never did.

In short, al-Kharrat seems to want to disarm the gravest reproach that can be leveled against the classical autobiographer: that nothing written down here is true.

But what does "true" actually mean in this context? In the rivalry between fiction and reality al-Kharrat seems clearly to side with fiction here, with "the flights of fantasy, the artifice herein". Reality may not be his concern, but truth is another matter: it has to be told. With the title of his autobiography *Dichtung und Wahrheit* (Poetry and Truth) Goethe not only specified a mutually exclusive pair but defined them as conditioning concepts. He formulated this stance in a letter in 1830, where he declared the use of "a kind of fiction" within autobiography to be a permissible means for expressing what constitutes the "genuinely fundamental truth" of a life. In this context, fiction is not to be misunderstood as something "contrived"; on the contrary, it is the means for conveying sincerity and truthfulness, the path to be taken for the concentration of the ever-shifting truths of one's own life into text.

Key to understanding the preliminary remark to *City of Saffron* are al-Kharrat's fundamental doubts about representing reality, coupled with his adherence to pursuing the truth. According to Friedrich Schiller, "whoever does not dare to go beyond reality will never capture the truth"; an attitude that can stand in the way of the classical modernist requirements of an autobiography. For a long time now Goethe and Schiller have served as reference points for a myriad of approaches and reproaches, but they will most assuredly never have been suspected of being precursors of postmodernism. The standpoint they propound in this respect – that at times truth lies closer to fiction than reality – is for al-Kharrat merely a first step that is followed by a decisive move, namely the relativization of truth. The work of autobiographical remembrance is particularly apt for illustrating the plural character of truth: what was in the past is never the same as what the author remembers in the present. And for the readers it will be in turn another truth which they believe to have recognized. Al-Kharrat sets awareness of diverging, at times contradictory truths against Goethe's belief in the "genuinely fundamental truth".

Despite his doubts about the existence of a single truth, which brings him close to postmodernist thinking, by adhering to the general claim of "truth" al-Kharrat refuses to countenance the radical disavowal of a concept of truth as postulated by Derrida. Al-Kharrat's work moves between the conflicting poles of doubt and belief in truth, suspended between literary modernism and postmodernism; thus nestling into an interstice position that he, as someone who feels fully at home between genres and cultures, must relish. Viewed from this perspective, *City of Saffron* is a postmodern autobiography that flouts reality and illuminates "truth" in all its diversity, so as once again to give "truth" its rightful place through this act of doubt.

The end of realism

Edwar al-Kharrat is one of the most influential contemporary Arab writers. He has decisively shaped an entire epoch of Arabic literature as the author of novels and short stories; as a literary critic, translator, and editor of anthologies. Twentieth-century Egypt is reflected in his biography. He was born in Alexandria in 1926. After studying law he worked at the National Bank of Egypt. For his active participation in the nationalist movement, he was sentenced to two years of camp detention in May 1948. His first texts were published in Egyptian literary journals in the 1940s. He published his first volume of stories, covering work written since 1943, at his own expense in 1959 after the censors had drastically altered some of the texts. It took another thirteen years before his second volume could be published, and another eight years would pass before his first novel *Rama and the Dragon* could appear in 1980. The gap between publications shortened steadily: today his body of work spans over forty books featuring novels, short stories, poems, and essays.

With his concept of the "new sensibility", al-Kharrat summarized different currents of the turn away from realistic narratives whose initial trigger was the epochal shift following defeat in the June War of 1967. Already in the early 1960s he had discerned the first expressions of this tendency, which in his view is not limited to a specific school but encompasses different manifestations; similar, however, in how they seek to overcome the prevailing realistic style. "Traditional sensibility", according to al-Kharrat, is based on naïve and optimistic notions of perception and cognition, striving to transport and mirror reality. By pursuing such a narrow approach literature betrays its own possibilities. "It would have been far simpler", Peter Handke succinctly objected to mimetic realism in the 1960s, "to take a photo." In al-Kharrat's view, the "new sensibility" questions the classical plot, ruptures the chronological sequence of action, discloses the complexity of language, and gives itself over to the continuous shifting of levels of meaning.

The de-centered subject in *City of Saffron* circumvents auctorial narration; the first and third person narrators alternate, as do passages in the present with those in the past tense. Like flotsam, flakes of remembered life are washed ashore only then to be elusively drawn back by the undulations:

> I can see the boy.
>
> He is small, his legs thin in big white shorts, his shirt open. There is a look in his eyes, which is thoughtful beyond his years. He is standing, at the earliest hour of the morning, on the shore of the empty sea, at el-Mandara.
>
> Before him is a vast, still expanse, a barely rippling radiance, a heavy milky sheen under the light which could almost be a winter light, ending in a transparent froth which sinks with a low continuous hiss into the sand.
>
> After all these long years I can still feel the soft dampness under his bare feet, and the moist air on his face.
>
> And I realize that love, like the pulling of the waves, throws itself incontinently on the shore with arms outstretched, spent, like the onrush of water, from riding on the back of Time; and that it retreats again to the open reaches of the sea, ever to rise and fall, a dream that will ebb and flood and never rest, nor for a moment leave the rippling skyline.
>
> At that hour in the morning there was no one on the wide shore save him.

As external reality is no longer the unchallenged reference point of truthfulness, Kharrat is able to let dreams, myths and visions flow into the texts. He also advocates "writing beyond the genres" (to pick up the title given to a collection of essays of literary criticism published in 1994), which is not least a call for openness towards classical Arab storytelling traditions and Egyptian folk culture. Against literary realism, in particular the broad current of combative committed literature that spawns social realism and claims to provide solutions for social and political problems through literature, al-Kharrat sets the principle of doubt. The literature of the "new sensibility" is an unrelenting questioning that evades giving definitive answers.

The defeat of 1967 and the wave of self-criticism it triggered; the collapse of

Nasserism; and the radical political turnaround to economic openness instigated by Nasser's successor Sadat: taken together, all this amounted to a fundamental convulsion of Egyptian society and a profound loss of authoritative principles. Kharrat described the situation thus: "With this rapid and stormy development, reality itself was even called into question by Arabic literature." His biting and at times polemical rejection of literary realism should be seen against this backdrop of loss. For him, combative-committed literature had nothing more to offer than "declamatory, bombastic slogans", still very much in the grip of the predominant ideological jargon. Kharrat's criticism of realism is always inherently tied to a critique of ideology. Literature is not about asserting set subject matter, but is rather a means of sounding out the realm of possibilities. His texts describe; they do not prescribe. The literary work of memory, as we encounter it in *City of Saffron*, connects the postmodern form of the personal-individual dimension of remembering with the "modern" claim to be sincere. This is a reiteration of Kharrat's position "in between" modernism and postmodernism; an "in between" he is fully aware of, reflects on and readily discusses. Albeit with this he is thoroughly postmodernist.

"Hauling in life"

Remembering through the act of writing is a recollection in the double sense of the word: it is re*collecting* and *re*collecting. Recollections are therefore, as Haruki Murakami's protagonist says in *Kafka on the Beach* (2002), "the only proof that I have lived." The paradoxical situation of the presence of the absent connects the phenomenon of recollecting with Derrida's concept of the "trace", a salient element in postmodern discourse. Recollecting is the trace people leave behind in time.

Time, the past, is the raw material in *City of Saffron*, recollecting the work. The Swiss author Paul Nizon, who in a paradoxical formulation has characterized himself as "a passing-stationary autobiography-fictionizer", hyphenates the word: to re-collect is for him "hauling in 'life' into an enhanced consciousness, an internalized being-aware."

City of Saffron is a text that reflects on its own conditions of production and in turn takes this very reflection as a theme. It is therefore a kind of meta-autobiography that moves far beyond classical memoirs and, as an expression of postmodernist skepticism about what is thoughtlessly taken as "reality", places enormous faith in the power of literature, thus also demanding a great deal from it. Kharrat does not tell stories, he *in-scribes* life. In the process, the plot dissolves into fragments of subjective perception. Instead of proceeding from an objective given reality that the writer transports into literature, in Kharrat's view literature *creates* reality.

Archaeology of recollection

City of Saffron is not the only book by Kharrat that deals with memory and recollection. He once said that he had been writing a single book all his life. Strands from other books are picked up time and again, the reader encountering familiar protagonists in familiar places. For instance, *Girls of Alexandria* (1990) is a continuation of *City of Saffron*. In keeping with the advanced age of the protagonist, the tone here is somewhat more sober, mature and disillusioned: the text no longer revels in the rapture of childlike sensations but instead traces the skeptical observation of an adolescent for whom the disenchantment of the world is well underway. And yet here, too, the narrator is not master of his past; it is the past that overwhelms him: "yesterday inundates".

In *Stones of Bobello* (1992) Kharrat once again varies the theme. The text comprises splinters and frayed threads of the past. More or less eluding rational ordering, for they are neither bound specifically to historical events nor anchored in a definitive time, these fragments are visionary, dreamlike, irreal. More radically than in his previous works, al-Kharrat undertakes here an "archaeology of recollection", as Stefan Weidner put it, using writing as a tool for excavating memory layer by layer; striving for a language of such precision that it bursts the boundaries of syntax, breathless, as though the narrator is at once out of his mind and immersed in himself:

> Be quiet, then, please, I do not want to hear you or even to know who you are – why all this beauty, all this remoteness? – the cruelty of absence is a power-ful charm, attracting the soul of the infatuated man happy to be destroyed of his own free will. The sphere of the universe, your luxuriant hair, your strong eyes, the divinity of your voice has no equal, you say with all your emotion and passion, desire and distress, how can I say that you are not alone, so why am I alone, why, the more devoted to you I become, the more dumb I find myself, and whenever I burst into song, I start to stammer, why am I a pris-oner? No, no, no, I mean that, why then do I just say I have yearned, I have tried to see, to hear, to know, to awake from the pressure of anxiety, I have grown weary of wandering and roaming in more than one tiresome valley, I am in a depression of sand and pebbles.

Powerfully eloquent, evocative, and of an almost baroque sensuality, the intent of all ambitious literature is presented here: to translate life into words. That the outcome of this endeavor ultimately remains only a text is something the author is painfully aware of: "The nets of words are full of holes, they hold nothing. The fish fall back into the sea, dead."

In *City of Saffron* too, the search for lost time ends invariably at the author's desk. The past eludes apprehension: recalling it into the present only succeeds as an approximation that remains shadowy. For this reason, passages where the author reflects on his attempts to remember have a resigned, elegiac tone; doubt about the sense of this strained, brooding, and often gloomy remembering breaks through repeatedly. "And is this a pause in front of scattered ruins, bereft of mercy or tears? What is the use of it? On what is it founded?" These are the types of questions the author/narrator poses himself, only to reply – half defiant, half resigned: "Is there anything we can trust, rather, save the traces of that which has been annihilated?"

It is unsurprising that Arab literary critics often compare Kharrat's work to Marcel Proust's *A la recherche du temps perdu*. In fact, what Hans Robert Jauß has written about Proust's 'poetics of recalled time' also cogently describes Kharrat's works: the text "consummates the enduring that is first formed in the process of remembrance itself." Despite all their differences, both authors share a fascination, bordering on obsession, for the wonder of human memory: man is the animal capable of remembering.

Who could seriously measure these and other texts by Kharrat against the conventional definitions of autobiography, which are at best naïve when compared to the aspirations he pursues? One of the most acknowledged definitions of autobiography (which is indeed a thoroughly magical genre: the closer one looks at it, the more enigmatic it becomes) is given by the French literary theorist Philippe Lejeune. Laconically he states that autobiography is "a retrospective prose narrative by an actual person about their own existence." The belief in the factual reality of autobiography assumes absurd traits when the issue is brought before a court. In August 2003 the Munich District Court stated that autobiographies are to be categorized as nonfiction because "like science and scholarly books" they can claim "to reproduce real events." The court thus concluded it is possible to allege that the author of an autobiography has lied, but not the author of a novel. At this point it must be patently clear that between such legal obstinacy and Kharrat's literary project, these "*études* about the self" as his German translator Hartmut Fähndrich puts it, is a difference of such magnitude that the preliminary remarks to *City of Saffron* gain in plausibility. No, "these texts are not an autobiography", not because they are less true, but because they are truer. For their "flights of fantasy, the artifice herein, bear them far beyond such bounds."

What separates Kharrat's texts from autobiography in the classical sense is, perhaps, what marks the difference between modernism and postmodernism. The individual, the "*self*-conscious" subject, was the focal point of modernity, its foundation and its engine. With the loss of faith in this autonomous, self-determined individual, with the rising suspicion that this concept harbors and forges ideology and the word "I" hides countless elusive identities and realities, it is no longer possible to write ingenuously, as "an actual person", about one's "own existence". The "end of the grand narratives" proclaimed by postmodernism also pertains to the narration of one's own life, in so far as it purports to follow an inner logic and assert continuity, both of which run contrary to the postmodernist focus on overt indeterminateness and all kinds of ambiguities, ruptures, and shifts. Furthermore, Kharrat is by no means interested in the purported completeness of a biography that commences with birth and tells events in sequence. He shares with postmodernism the deep-seated disdain towards any synthesis, and so he dismisses the specific synthesis of traditional autobiography, expressed in the intention to write down one's life in its entirety and as a unity. Instead, he seeks to come nearer to the truths of life through the described fragmentary splinters of remembering, breaching chronological order, and so refusing to indulge synthesis and factitious necessity. The openness emerging here is not to be mistaken for moral relativism. Driven by the "burning need for what I call sincerity", he remarks in *Stones of Bobello*, he is more than capable of indignation:

> My soul was nauseated by this destructive lying; it stank of ruin and desolation.
>
> The murder of thousands, of tens of thousands of children through famine and the ravages of disease in the midst of ruins brought down by rocket strikes from the nightmare intruder, the lies of tyranny, the eloquence of defeat using shameful masks from a pile of clapped out, medieval inspiration, impotent lies sheltering behind worn-out slogans, the lies of the venerable chief of staff, may God protect him, the lies of the shaykh and amir, may God preserve him, lies that light fires, pollute the oceans and rivers, painting earth and heavens black, the lies of rulers and writers, of newspapers, radio and television, lies of enemies and friends alike, lies of love, lies of indifference, lies of the bed, lies from rostrums everywhere ...

No, there can be no question of disinterest, contempt or of groundless querying of truth in the work of Edwar al-Kharrat.

The capital of memory

> All these people made the world a rich place, a place of changing color; a bit frightening, but fascinating...

The wrestling with the past; the work of memory the autobiographer has to undertake; and the observation that the past, when torn out of its protective atmosphere by remembering, comes into contact and interacts with the present, changing its aggregate state: these aspects of individual remembrance are a key but not the sole theme in *City of Saffron*. In many of his works, Kharrat attempts to "decolonize" his home city of Alexandria in and through literature, most predominantly in his creation of a counter image to the portrayal of the city in Lawrence Durrell's famous *Alexandria Quartet*. Alexandria, Durrell wrote, is "the capital of memory." Kharrat criticizes Durrell for having let himself be led astray by Orientalist projections. This perspective results in a distorted portrayal of Alexandria, a literary occupation of his homeland that has outlasted the military one: a hostile takeover of memory. "He was", Kharrat writes about Durrell, "completely alienated from the Alexandria I was born and lived in, during approximately the same time." Kharrat's prime concern, then, is to wrench the history of his city from the clutches of European discourse.

Durrell, Kharrat points out, speaks of "Arabs" and "Copts", of "Turks" and "Armenians"; never of Egyptians. This kind of naming is nothing other than an attempt to divide society, to differentiate the city's population into exclusive groups; whereas he, Kharrat, is concerned with emphasizing common features and saving from oblivion a cultural climate that has evolved over centuries, enriched by diverse ethnic, cultural, religious and language traditions. Kharrat focuses not on the separate, individual elements that the European sees, names, and classifies, but the whole. This whole is at once unity and diversity; it is a *pluralistic* culture that makes up the essential character of Alexandria. This Alexandria is a multicultural Levantine city, not some picturesque ambience conjured by Orientalist sentimentality; a lively, vivid city, not a projection surface for adventurers weary of Europe. Levantine Alexandria, the city of the Greek poet Konstantinos Kavafis, of E.M. Forster; of Greeks, Italians, Maltese, Arabs and Armenians; of Muslims, Copts and Jews, has become for Kharrat a cipher for the whole of Egypt, a pluralistic Egypt that is conscious of the diversity of its traditions and cultures, from which it draws its energy and so creates a counter model to the monoculture of modernity's classical nation state:

> As if he were seeking refuge in an enchanted place, he ran to it (...): The boy was running to Umm Toto's house, Umm Toto "that Greek woman", who lived at the crossroads of shari' el-Ban and al-Nargis. (...) He did not, then, fully understand the import of the word grigiya – Greek woman.
> For him, back then, differences between people were part of the natural course of things.

In this respect too, Kharrat disengages himself from the certainties of a modernity that has petrified into a classical model. The temptation to transfigure Alexandria into a paradise, even into a myth of multicultural harmony, is one to which he occasionally succumbs. But perhaps that is unintentional: he does not shy away from idealizing. The ideals given expression in his texts, which offer a postmodernist interpretation of pre-modern times, may be read as an alternative to the coupling of modern nationalisms and culturalist explanatory models. Alexandria is far more than a mere literary "theme": "not a fictional décor, she is neither the material nor the location of fiction, but the autobiographical fictional act itself."

SELECTED WORKS

Hitan 'aliyya (High Walls), Cairo: n.p. 1959

Sa'at al-kibriya' (Hours of Haughtiness), Beirut: Dar al-Adab 1972

Rama wa-l-tinnin (Rama and the Dragon), Beirut: al-Mu'assasa al-Arabiyya li-l-Dirasat wa-l-Nashr 1980

Turabuha za'faran (City of Saffron), Cairo: al-Mustaqbal al-'Arabi 1985

Ya banat al-Iskandariyya (Girls of Alexandria), Beirut: Dar al-Adab 1990

Hijarat Bubillu (Stones of Bobello), Beirut: Dar al-Adab 1992

al-Kitaba abr al-naw'iyya (Writing Beyond the Genres), Cairo: Dar Sharqiyyat 1994

TRANSLATIONS

City of Saffron, trans. Frances Liardet, London, New York: Quartet 1989

Girls of Alexandria, trans. Frances Liardet, London, New York: Quartet 1993

Rama and the Dragon, trans. Ferial Ghazoul, John Verlenden, Cairo, New York: The American University in Cairo Press 2002

Stones of Bobello, trans. Paul Starkey, London: Saqi 2005

FURTHER READING

Boutros Hallaq: "Autobiography and Polyphony", in: Robin Ostle, Ed de Morr, Stefan Wild (eds.), *Writing the Self. Autobiographical Writing in Modern Arabic Literature*, London: Saqi 1988, pp. 192–206

Marlé Hammond: "Subsuming the Feminine Other: Gender and Narration in Edwar al-Kharrat's *Ya banat Iskandariiya*", in: *Journal of Arabic Literature* 31 (2000), pp. 38–58

Magda al-Nowaihi: "Memory and Imagination in Edwar al-Kharrat's *Turabuha za'faran*", in: *Journal of Arabic Literature* 25 (1994), pp. 34–57

Andreas Pflitsch: *Gegenwelten. Zur Literaturtheorie Idwar al-Harrats*, Wiesbaden: Reichert 2000

Andreas Pflitsch: "Narration against Transitoriness and Temporality. Mythical Time Structure in Idwar al-Kharrat's Works", in: Angelika Neuwirth et al. (eds.), *Myths, Historical Archetypes and Symbolic Figures in Arabic Literature*, Beirut, Stuttgart: Steiner 1999, pp. 363–78

Stefan Weidner: "Archäologie der Kindheit. Edwar al-Charrat erinnert sich", in: Stefan Weidner, *Erlesener Orient. Ein Führer durch die Literaturen der islamischen Welt, Wien*, Edition Selene 2004, pp. 65-67

OTHER WORKS CITED

Maxim Biller: *Bernsteintage*, Cologne: Kiepenheuer & Witsch 2004

Lawrence Durrell: *The Alexandria Quartet* [*Justine, Balthazar, Mountolive, Clea*, 1957-60], London: Faber & Faber 1962

Johann Wolfgang Goethe: *Aus meinem Leben. Dichtung und Wahrheit* [1831], in: *Werke. Hamburger Ausgabe in 14 Bänden*, vol. 9, Munich: Beck 1948

Peter Handke: *Ich bin ein Bewohner des Elfenbeinturms*, Frankfurt/M.: Suhrkamp 1972

Hans Robert Jauß: *Zeit und Erinnerung in Marcel Prousts 'A la recherche du temps perdu'. Ein Beitrag zur Theorie des Romans*, Heidelberg: Winter 1955

Philippe Lejeune: *Le pacte autobiographique*, Paris: Seuil 1975

Thomas Mann: *Joseph und seine Brüder*, Berlin: Fischer 1933

Haruki Murakami: *Umibe no kafuka*, Tokyo: Shinchosha 2002

Paul Nizon: "Ich bin ein vorbeistationierender Autobiographie-Fiktionär", in: Martin Kilchmann (ed.), *Paul Nizon*, Frankfurt/M.: Suhrkamp 1985, pp. 64-87

Marcel Proust: *A la recherche du temps perdu* [1913–27], ed. Jean-Yves Tadié, 4 vols., Paris: Gallimard 1987–89

On the Necessity of Writing the Present
Elias Khoury and the "Birth of the Novel" in Lebanon

Sonja Mejcher-Atassi

"The story is nothing but names", says the narrator in Elias Khoury's novel *The Journey of Little Gandhi* (1989). But as in Khoury's other novels, memories cling to names, and so every new name mentioned leads into a new story, which in turn harbors more names and so branches off into further stories. The novel turns into a game of names that seems to move forward on its own, a narrative flow that starts anew over and over again.

Today, the Lebanese author Elias Khoury is one of the most prominent figures in Lebanon's cultural, intellectual, and literary life. As a novelist, he has gained international recognition. His novels have been translated into several languages and are characterized by a high degree of experimentation and innovativeness that many critics have labeled postmodern. Transgressing literary genres, they reflect the conditions and possibilities of narrative fiction beyond preset models. Their reference points are manifold, ranging from contemporary European and American literature via contemporary literature from Latin America, Africa and India through to classical Arabic literature. The late Palestinian-American intellectual Edward Said described Khoury's novels as "post-Mahfouzian", thus marking a turn away from the Arab novel as it had been influenced over decades by the Egyptian Nobel laureate Naguib Mahfouz (1911–2006). This new tack is primarily the result of a shift in the perception of reality, in Khoury's eyes at once inevitable and necessary in the wake of the Arab defeat in the June War of 1967, and the Lebanese civil war of 1975–1990.

This shift is already discernible in *Little Mountain* (1977), the novel that established Khoury's name as a writer and that Stefan G. Meyer has characterized as "a patchwork novel". *Little Mountain* consists of fragmentary narratives that relate to different spatial and temporal situations and have, at least in part, an autobiographical nature. They recall a Beirut childhood in the Christian neighborhood of Ashrafiyya, also called "the little mountain"; a childhood that is increasingly overshadowed by the events of the civil war. Tensions escalate until roadblocks are set up: then fighting – in which the narrator takes an active part – breaks out between the Palestinian and Christian militias, spreading throughout the streets of Beirut and dominating everyday life.

Black metal devouring me: roadblocks, they say. I see my face tumbling to the ground. Black metal devouring me: my voice slips down alone and stretches to where the corpses of my friends lie buried in mass graves. Black metal devouring me: the raised hands do not wave banners, they clutch death. Metal on the street, terror and empty gas bottles, corpses and smuggled cigarette cartons. The moment of victory has come. The moment of death has come. War has come.

Fully absorbed in the fighting, the narrator himself becomes one of the novel's characters, another of the young fighters who in turn become narrators. Free of any moral positioning or partisanship for one militia group over another, with *Little Mountain* Khoury managed to give a shockingly direct insight into the first years of the civil war. The novel is based on journalistic accounts that Khoury had intended to publish separately. They fitted together to result in a novel that dispenses with the integrative effort to furnish a single coherent picture of reality, allowing instead the diversity of the fragmentary, splintered, and at times contradictory perceptions of this reality to coexist; perceptions that the civil war brought explosively to light.

The interweaving of literature, journalism, and intellectual engagement, already evident in *Little Mountain*, is characteristic of Khoury's work and runs like a thread through his life.

Literature, journalism, and intellectual engagement

Elias Khoury was born in 1948 in Beirut into a Greek Orthodox family and grew up in the mainly Christian neighbourhood of Ashrafiyya. He was a member of the "Orthodox youth movement" founded by the Lebanese bishop and intellectual Georges Khodr, which he left aged sixteen after becoming acquainted with Existentialism. Khoury attended a private school for the Lebanese middle class, which, like most Lebanese schools at the time, followed the French curriculum. After completing his baccalaureate, he studied history and sociology at the Université Libanaise in Beirut, gaining his M.A. with a thesis about the *nahda*, the so-called Arab renaissance of the late nineteenth and early twentieth centuries, and the Muslim intellectual and reformer al-Afghani (1838–1897).

For a time Khoury frequented the "Arab National Club" founded by the Palestinian intellectual George Habash. He sympathized with the ideas of Arab nationalism but was not part of any political group in particular. This changed with the Arab defeat in the June War of 1967. Shocked by the political events, he joined the *fidayyin*, the Palestinian resistance fighters in Jordan. While pursuing his studies in Beirut, he repeatedly took part in military actions in Jordan and southern Lebanon.

After the "Black September" of 1970, which saw the expulsion of the Palestine Liberation Organization (PLO) and its *fidayyin* from Jordan by the Jordanian Army, Khoury left for Paris, where he continued his studies at the École Pratique des Hautes Études, gaining a diploma in sociology with a thesis about the Lebanese civil war of 1860. At the same time he attended seminars in philosophy and literature held by such luminaries as Michel Foucault, Roland Barthes and Maurice Blanchot.

By the time he returned to Beirut in 1973, the political situation in Lebanon had changed dramatically. The PLO now had its headquarters in Beirut and the Palestinian resistance was operating solely from Lebanese territory. The country's internal political crisis erupted into civil war in April 1975: Khoury again joined the *fidayyin*. After being severely wounded and gravitating towards an increasingly critical stance towards the civil war, he withdrew from active participation in 1976. The fighting had gained such momentum that it was now obeying its own logic, decoupled from the ideological goals the parties had formulated at the outset. The Damour massacre in January 1976, where the *fidayyin* killed hundreds of Christian civilians in revenge for the siege of the Palestinian refugee camp Tell al-Zaatar (undertaken by Christian militia with the support of the Syrian Army) and the massacre of its civilian inhabitants, profoundly shocked Khoury. He now openly criticized his own political camp, a criticism clearly expressed in his novel *The White Faces* (1981), where a young woman filmmaker confronts a Palestinian resistance fighter:

- Listen, you don't listen, we have to make our just cause known and reveal the fascist practices, killing, rape, theft, expulsion and destruction of houses. This is the role of the engaged cinema. We have to make it known.
- But we, too … I told her that we, too, had committed crimes, had killed and …
- That's not true, it isn't true.
- I swear it's true, Damour … in Damour we …
- Don't talk about Damour, did you forget al-Maslakh, Karintina, Nabaa, Tal al-Zaatar and …
- Don't talk to me like this. God have mercy on you. I say the truth.
- No, that's not the truth. The truth has to serve the revolution. This kind of talk makes our camp get mixed up.
- The truth has to serve the truth. Listen to me.
- You listen, war is war.
- I know, God knows, these crimes happen in all wars. The most important thing is the political issue. But we, too, have committed crimes.
- No, you just make things worse, how can a fighter like you talk like this?

From 1973 to 1979, Khoury worked at the PLO Research Center in Beirut where, together with the Palestinian poet Mahmoud Darwish, he was in charge of editing the monthly journal *Shu'un filastiniyya* (Palestinian Affairs Review). In 1974, the center published Khoury's first book: a study in literary criticism about the Arab novel after the defeat of 1967. Due to the increased political involvement of the PLO in the center's intellectual work, Khoury and Darwish decided to leave in 1979. Khoury took on the post of editor-in-chief of the culture section at the Lebanese daily *al-Safir*, a position he kept until 1991. Throughout these years, the cultural journal *Mawaqif* (Positions), founded by Adonis and the literary critic Khalida al-Said, was the most important avant-garde platform for intellectuals, writers, and artists across the whole region. Khoury joined its editorial board in 1972. In retrospect, he considers the latter half of the 1970s to be the decisive formative phase in his intellectual life.

Khoury's novels are intricately intertwined with the Lebanese civil war – or the memory of it. If at first he regarded his literary writing as a kind of sideline to his journalistic work, with *Little Mountain* he shifted his priorities. Amidst the chaos of war Khoury's productivity as a writer rose. Whereas in most of his novels the war is dealt with explicitly, *Gates of the City* (1981) offers an allegorical reading of the war. Interspersed with numerous intertextual references to Kahlil Gibran's *The Madman* (1918) and *The City of Brass* from *The Thousand and One Nights*, this novel transforms Beirut into a mythical city whose name is never mentioned. In highly poetic language, unusual for Khoury's fiction (and compared by Stefan G. Meyer to the experimental prose of Gertrude Stein), it describes the apocalyptic demise of a city in which all important topographical landmarks and inner reference points sink into oblivion – an ending that Beirut was facing with the imminent Israeli invasion of 1982.

Since the end of the civil war, Khoury has published many more novels: *The Kingdom of Strangers* (1993), *The Gate of the Sun* (1998), *The Smell of Soap* (2000), *Yalu* (2002), and *As If She Were Sleeping* (2007). He was awarded the Prize of Palestine for *The Gate of the Sun*, which is based on the orally transmitted recollections and stories of Palestinians living in the refugee camps of Lebanon. The voluminous novel, subsequently made into a film by the Egyptian filmmaker Yusri Nasrallah for the TV channel ARTE, and premiered in Cannes in 2004, is an epic account of the *nakba* (disaster), the exodus of the Palestinians caused by the creation of the state of Israel. The novel took years to research as its material is based on countless interviews.

During the first Gulf War, he came into conflict with Syrian interests, which had increasingly influenced the political stance of *al-Safir* since the end of the 1980s. Khoury had openly criticized the participation of Arab countries, in particular that of Syria, in the US-led coalition against Iraq. A year later he became the editor of *Mulhaq*, the cultural supplement of the largest Lebanese newspaper *al-Nahar*, which has since been acclaimed throughout the region for its critical stance.

Besides his journalistic and literary writing, Khoury has taught modern Arabic literature at different universities in Lebanon and the United States. Moreover, he was involved in bringing the Theater of Beirut back to life, acting as its director from 1993 to 1998. He turned it into a veritable cultural center, where apart from plays and film screenings, exhibitions, conferences, and discussion rounds were held.

In the early 1990s Khoury wrote his first play: directed by Roger Assaf, *Job's Memories* premiered on the fiftieth anniversary of Lebanese independence in 1993. The Lebanese Job is cast as a traditional Arab storyteller, a figure usually entrusted with telling heroic legends as a form of entertainment; but this Job has no edifying stories to tell. Instead he relates the fates of three ordinary women whose husbands or children were abducted during the civil war and remain missing, thus addressing a taboo issue in the collective memory of postwar Lebanese society. In 2000 Khoury undertook a similarly subversive confrontation with the memory of the civil war in *Three Posters*, a video performance created in collaboration with the Lebanese actor Rabih Mroué that was shown as part of the annual Aylul Festival, which he organized between 1996 and 2001. *Three Posters* critically tackles the issue of suicide attacks, which were initially carried out by secular, leftist movements resisting the Israeli occupation of southern Lebanon. Taking as its starting point an uncut version of a video in which a suicide bomber declares himself a martyr before carrying out his mission, *Three Posters* opens a discourse about death that calls into question conventional distinctions between reality and fiction, truth and illusion, documentation and manipulation.

The 'birth of the novel' in Lebanon: between memory and amnesia

Memory is a central topic in all of Khoury's novels, as it is in his literary criticism and journalism, as well as his work in theater, film, and video performance. In his work of literary criticism *The Lost Memory* (1982), he explains that the civil war took place not only in reality but also in memory, due to memory itself becoming a point of dispute. Like the buildings and other landmarks in Beirut, memory was also destroyed, until only fragmented memories remained scattered here and there between the rubble, and it seemed as if the people had lost their memory.

An official coming to terms with the civil war, a *travaille de mémoire* (work of memory) has yet to take place in Lebanon, while a broader historical perspective spanning Lebanon's various denominations remains to be accomplished. Even the term "civil war" is disputed; at times reference is made to "the war of the others", "the war in Lebanon", or simply "the events." The unbearable silence has though engendered its own counterpart: in March 2001 a conference titled "Memory for the Future" was held, the first attempt emerging from within civil society to explore the recent past of the civil war critically. Given the lack of any official effort to come to terms with the past, literature assumes an important role in Lebanon. With the civil war the novel has gained unprecedented popularity, while the authors come from different religious, social and cultural backgrounds. For this reason Khoury dates the "birth of the novel" in Lebanon to the outbreak of civil war. Of course novels were written beforehand, but it was not until then that the novel first stepped out of the long shadow cast by poetry. According to Khoury, the "birth of the novel" in Lebanon is not to be understood as the result of national consolidation but rather as a consequence of its destruction. Only the devastation of war enabled society to name directly what was previously shrouded in taboos: the social, political, economic and religious discrepancies within Lebanon.

Like many of the novels written during and since the civil war, Khoury's novels are characterized by a critical coming to terms with Lebanon's recent history. They preserve and transmit what officially still seems to be unspeakable. Khoury is on the lookout for the recollections and stories of ordinary people, of the marginalized and downtrodden; the recollections and stories in which unacknowledged contradictions to official history – written, as is generally known, by the victors – become visible. In this aspect he comes very close to the so-called postcolonial authors, such as the Caribbean writer Edouard Glissant, who emphasize the necessity of claiming a history that remains generally neglected, subjugated to Western historiography. Last but not least is the dispute about who writes history: historians not only define the lineaments of the past but also stamp their authority on the present and shape the future.

Khoury does not restrict the scope of his efforts to filling the "gaps" in historiography. He is not concerned with the past as such but rather with its direct relevance to the present. This is clearly evident in his use of Arabic. Introducing spoken Arabic, the local dialect, into written Standard Arabic – a controversial issue in Arab literature down to the present day – establishes a direct link to the orally transmitted, lived experience of contemporary history. Arabic, Khoury explains, has always consisted of more than one language. Attempts to transform it into a homogenous entity, which have been undertaken repeatedly by nationalist ideologies, would turn it first into an instrument of exclusion and ultimately a dead language.

In his novels Khoury succeeds in retaining the different realities in their plurality whilst simultaneously questioning their fictional nature. As in *The Thousand and One Nights*, his novels become marvelous story machines. The all-knowing narrator merges into countless stories, absorbed by a narrative diversity of voices and languages, much in the vein of the Russian literary theorist Mikhail M. Bakhtin's description of the novel. The stories in Khoury's novels are seemingly self-perpetuating. The end of a novel becomes a "temporary ending". As in *The Thousand and One Nights*, every new name and thus every new character open a new story.

The Journey of Little Gandhi

"The story is nothing but names" says the narrator in *The Journey of Little Gandhi*. The novel's first words, however, point to a more complex situation: "But they're talking." The novel's characters tell their stories in their own peculiar language. The narrator as guarantor of one true version of the story disappears, while the names, voices, languages, and stories multiply, seemingly of their own accord. The novel is prefaced by a quotation from the Arab philosopher and mystic Ibn 'Arabi (1165–1240) which can be understood as the novel's motto: "A face is only one, yet when it's seen in many mirrors, multiplies itself." Whereas Ibn Arabi used this metaphor to express the idea that the prophets and saints mirror God's transcendence, but that ultimately there is only one God, Khoury gives it a different connotation. He transfers it from the religious to the social realm, unmasking the idea of unity as an ideological construct that seeks to negate the existing plurality.

The novel opens with the death of Abd al-Karim Husn, a Beirut shoeshine who was given the nickname "Little Gandhi" by a professor from the American University of Beirut and has been known solely by this name ever since. Each chapter – except for the short first and last chapters – starts with a description of how Alice, a former prostitute, found Little Gandhi dead, shot in the street, and covered him with newspapers, on the morning of the Israeli invasion into West Beirut on 15 September 1982. Each repetition gives the impression that his death is occuring all over again. Any chronological ordering of time is thus dismissed from the outset. Just as the beginning and ending of the narration cannot be determined with any certainty, so the beginning of the civil war cannot be identified, nor is there an end to the conflict in sight.

Alice, a haggard woman in her mid-sixties wearing a long black dress, is seated in the foyer of a rundown hotel in downtown Beirut where she used to ply her trade before the war. Her hands shaking while drinking *araq* (an aniseed flavored liquor), she tells the narrator the story of Little Gandhi. The story goes back to his birth in 1915 in a small village in northern Lebanon, tells of his flight to Tripoli, and from there to Beirut, where he worked as shoeshine in front of the American University of Beirut, until his death on 15 September 1982.

> He was scared. He carried his shoeshine box, hung it around his neck, letting it swing by its old leather strap, and he walked. And they were everywhere. They shouted at him to stop, or they didn't shout, no one knows. But they fired.

Gandhi knew that the bullets which killed him were not only directed at him:

> But he knew why he died, he knew the bullets weren't aimed at him, but
> rather at the heart of a city that destroyed itself (...)

Rather than Gandhi, the city of Beirut during the civil war and the Israeli invasion, with its numerous names, voices, languages, and stories, turns into the novel's protagonist; the true hero, or rather antihero.

The story of Little Gandhi opens the door to a host of other stories, which Alice tells along with her own tales of Beirut's night life: that of the American professor Davies, whose shoes Little Gandhi used to polish; the story of Little Gandhi's son Husn and his girlfriend; or the story of his daughter Souad who suffers from schizophrenia.

"Cities are invisible stories, and stories are invisible cities": this is a dictum Khoury likes to quote. The city lives only through the stories of its inhabitants, who are as numerous and various as their memories. Alice epitomizes the oral memory of the city of Beirut, which, like the city's center, lies in ruins and is about to sink into oblivion. In turn, the narrator resembles the *hakawati* (classical Arab storyteller), the transmitter of collective memory. But while the message passed on by the *hakawati* in his stories remains embedded in the oral tradition, the narrator sets out to put Alice's stories in written form. He thus turns into the novel's fictive author.

When Alice disappears in the course of renewed fighting in February 1984, he begins to look for her. At a cemetery in Ashrafiyya he comes across a damaged gravestone with her portrait as she must have looked like as a young woman:

> I went to Saint Mitr Cemetery. I searched among the scattered graves beneath
> the cypress trees. I read all the names, and on a half-destroyed grave, whose
> white tile had become dust-colored, I saw the image of Alice. I went closer and
> read the name, it was someone else, but the image engraved on the semi-white
> marble resembled Alice as a young woman. That's how I imagined Alice in
> her youth, with a full face, thick lips, a small turned-up nose, big eyes. I went
> closer to Alice, or to whom I thought was Alice, and I read my own name,
> and I read my mother's name, and I read my grandfather's name. They were
> all there, there wasn't a face I saw that I hadn't seen before, it was like a long
> dream from which I couldn't wake up.

The portrait refers not so much to Alice's youthful years but an idealized, nostalgic image of Beirut, of how the city might have looked like before the civil war. It brings back to memory – by contrast – the destruction of Beirut. The name engraved onto the gravestone is not mentioned in the novel. However, the affinity between the names "Alice" and "Elias", in Arabic consisting of the same letters, suggests that the name is that of the real author. Without explicitly mentioning his name, the real author identifies himself with Alice as well as the narrator and fictive author, thus inscribing himself as a dead figure into the novel. Here, the novel's self-referential character, aiming to blur the distinction between fiction and reality, reaches an artful peak.

In *The Journey of Little Gandhi* reality is not presented as a given truth that the narrator is able to transmit or even approximate. Only the protagonists' memories, which break loose from the remembered events and take on an imaginative character, are true. Ultimately, truth and falsehood, reality and dream cannot be separated from one another. The narrator no longer even tries to tell a coherent story; he knows that all stories reveal inconsistencies:

> I recall Alice's words and try to imagine what happened, but I keep finding holes in the story. All stories are full of holes. We no longer know how to tell stories, we don't know anything anymore.

On the day before the Israeli invasion, Beirut is engulfed in whiteness, as if the city in which the civil war seems destined to continue with no end in sight is drowning in silence, as if storytelling itself was coming to an end. Alice is aware of the fact that the ability to forget is a basic trait of humankind and quotes an Arab saying: "man is called man because he forgets"; a wordplay between *insan* (man) and *nisyan* (to forget). The problem is not that we forget. The question raised in *The Journey of Little Gandhi* is what we forget and what we remember, whose stories are being told and written, salvaged from death and transmitted into the future. These are stories of ordinary people, of those on the margins of society, "the stories of those who couldn't run away". None of the characters in *The Journey of Little Gandhi* participate actively in the civil war, but all are exposed to and trapped in it. They, the ordinary people, are the real losers and victims of the civil war.

WORKS

al-Jabal al-saghir (Little Mountain), Beirut: Mu'assasat al-Abhath al-'Arabiyya 1977
Abwab al-madina (Gates of the City), Beirut: Dar Ibn Rushd 1981
al-Wujuh al-bayda' (The White Faces), Beirut: Dar Ibn Rushd 1981
al-Dhakira al-mafquda. Dirasat naqdiyya (The Lost Memory. Critical Studies), Beirut: Mu'assasat al-Abhath al 'Arabiyya 1982
Rihlat Ghandi al-saghir (The Journey of Little Gandhi), Beirut: Dar al-Adab 1989
Mamlakat al-ghuraba' (The Kingdom of Strangers), Beirut: Dar al-Adab 1993
Majma' al-asrar (The Junction of Secrets), Beirut: Dar al-Adab 1994
Bab al-shams (Gate of the Sun), Beirut: Dar al-Adab 1998

Ra'ihat al-sabun (The Smell of Soap), Beirut: Dar al-Adab 2000
Yalu (Yalo), Beirut: Dar al-Adab 2001
Ka'annaha na'ima (As if She Were Asleep), Beirut: Dar al-Adab 2007

TRANSLATIONS

Little Mountain, trans. Maia Tabet, Manchester: Carcanet Press 1989; New York: Picador
2007
Gates of the City, trans. Paula Haydar, Minneapolis, London: University of Minnesota
Press 1993; New York: Picador 2007
The Journey of Little Gandhi, trans. Paula Haydar, Minneapolis, London: University of
Minnesota Press 1994; New York: Picador 2009
The Kingdom of Strangers, trans. Paula Haydar, University of Arkansas Press 1996
Gate of the Sun, trans. Humphrey Davies, New York: Picador 2007
Yalo, trans. Peter Theroux, New York: Archipelago 2008; New York: Picador 2009
White Masks, trans. Maia Tabet, New York: Archipelago 2010

FURTHER READING

Mona Takieddine Amyuni: "The Image of the City. Wounded Beirut," in: Ferial J. Ghazoul,
Barbara Harlow (eds.), *The View from Within: Writers and Critics on Contemporary Arabic
Literature*, Cairo: The American University in Cairo Press 1994, pp. 53–76
Sonja Mejcher: *Geschichten über Geschichten. Erinnerung im Romanwerk von Elias Khoury*,
Wiesbaden: Reichert 2001
Sonja Mejcher: "Interview with Elias Khoury: The necessity to forget and to remember,"
in: *Banipal* 12 (2001), pp. 8-14
Sonja Mejcher-Atassi: "The Martyr and his Image. Elias Khoury's *al-Wujuh al-baida'* (*The
White Faces*)," in: Friederike Pannewick (ed.), *Martyrdom in Literature. Visions of Death
and Meaningful Suffering in Europe and the Middle East from Antiquity to Modernity*,
Wiesbaden: Reichert 2004, pp. 343–55
Friederike Pannewick, Atef Botros: "Elias Khoury," in: *Kritisches Lexikon zur fremdspra-
chigen Gegenwartsliteratur*, Munich: Edition Text + Kritik 2009

OTHER WORKS CITED

Kahlil Gibran: *The Madman. His Parables and Poems*, New York: Knopf 1918

Historical Memory in Times of Decline
Saadallah Wannous and Rereading History

Friederike Pannewick

Saadallah Wannous (1941–97), one of the most important playwrights of the Arab Middle East, belonged to a generation of Arab intellectuals and artists whose political and artistic self-understanding was strongly molded by the Palestine conflict. This tragic conflict reached its dramatic peak with the founding of the state of Israel in 1948 and the Arab defeat in the June War of 1967.

At the end of his life, which was cut short by illness, Wannous gave a bitter appraisal of the situation in an interview with the Syrian stage director Omar Amirlay broadcast by ARTE:

> How is our generation to ever be laid to rest and find peace of mind? It will carry around in its thoughts a dull horror. It will resemble a wound. It will be the horror at the age they have lived through and the bitter, lifelong disillusionment. For Israel will still be there. Even when our generation dies.

By no means was this author always so resigned and disillusioned. After a childhood spent in a village on the Syrian coast near Tartous, Wannous studied journalism in Cairo in the 1950s. At the beginning of the 1960s his theater career commenced, with a few experimental plays influenced by Surrealism and the Absurdist theater. In 1967–68 he studied theater in Paris at the Sorbonne, under the guidance of Jean-Marie Serreau, before becoming editor of the children's journal *Usama*, a position he held between 1969 and 1975. In 1971 he wrote a film scenario that was censored by the Syrian government despite gaining international acclaim at festivals in France and Egypt. He studied French experimental theater in Paris for a second year in 1973. Two years later, he took over the editorship of the cultural section of the Beirut daily *al-Safir*. In 1976 he founded the experimental Qabbani theater in Damascus and in 1977 he launched the theater journal *al-Hayat al-masrahiyya* (Theater Life), where he remained editor-in-chief until 1987.

Politicizing theater

International in his orientation, Wannous was an intellectual who saw himself as part of a worldwide avant-garde movement. The early phase of his writing, from the beginning of the 1960s to the end of the 1970s, was formatively influenced by Erwin Piscator's political theater, but above all by Bertolt Brecht's didactic theater.

His initial works reveal an intensive social engagement, which he characterized in his *Manifesto for a New Arab Theater* (1970) as a "politicizing of theater". In a phase marked by significant social developments triggered by the national defeat at the hands of Israel, Wannous bravely and provocatively formulated the lineaments of a "politicizing" aesthetic which was to make Arab theater into a vehicle of hope, instigating political reforms and speeding the processes of democratization: "We perform theater to develop and change consciousness. We want to deepen the grasp of our collective consciousness for our shared historical consciousness." Wannous's critical rereading of Arab history was thus imbued from the outset with the dynamics of social and political crises and a seemingly inexorable decline.

The first of his plays that was to match his aspirations of political enlightenment was *Gala Evening for the Fifth of June*, where in an ingenious play-within-a-play Wannous staged the traumatic events of recent Arab history. Although written in the immediate aftermath of the defeat of 1967, the play was not permitted to be performed until 1971. The playwright's demand to activate the political consciousness of his fellow citizens was spectacularly successful: around 25,000 people attended the forty-four performances put on in Damascus's Qabbani theater, a sensational response that has yet to be repeated in Syrian theater. From the beginning, though, it was feared that the government would not tolerate a political mobilization of such dimensions.

The culprits are in our midst

Gala Evening for the Fifth of June is a play that seeks to identify those responsible for the momentous defeat suffered in the June War, without sparing the government from criticism. Wannous's strategy is to incite a dialogue between the audience and the actors, continually breaching the "dramatic illusion" by having the actors address the audience directly. Actors covertly placed in the audience take up the dialogue in the hope that others will then become involved. The gala evening announced in the title begins deceptively: a "director" appears on the edge of the stage and apologizes for the delay, explaining that differences have emerged between himself and the "author" of the play. In the auditorium, the "author" stands up to respond, insisting on calling off the performance of a play that has, to his eyes, been distorted, claiming that the political reasons behind the defeat by Israel have been downplayed. Actors disguised as members of the audience get involved in the discussion, trouble is stirred and the auditorium is stormed by "security forces". Calm is finally restored – albeit at the price that the "gala evening for the fifth of June" is cancelled.

With this play, Wannous gets to the very core of the social and political crisis of the time. It becomes clear that the explanations given by government propaganda, which demonized the archfiend Israel and rigorously avoided even the slightest acknowledgement that the causes of the devastating defeat might have lain with the Arab states, were without substance and inevitably led to a political dead-end.

This work laid the foundations for following plays, in each of which Wannous employed the means of epic theater, those devices of estrangement which create a distance between the audience and what takes place on the stage. In this conception, theater serves as a kind of rehearsal room for changing real social relations, one in which people are to be coaxed into thinking for themselves and reflecting critically on dominant ideology.

Over the course of the next ten years Wannous wrote several plays based on this political commitment, which were staged throughout the Arab world. At times he took up stories and themes from the *Thousand and One Nights*; at others he experimented with traditional Arab coffeehouse storytelling or ancient Arabic epics: common to all these dramas was an appeal to approach and appropriate history and the shared Arab cultural heritage *critically*, not to idealize. Wannous became imbued with such a strong sense of the crisis of the age that it encroached upon and damaged his personal life, an effect he emphasized repeatedly in various statements. It was his passionately pursued goal to understand the causes behind the decline through a critical account of history and cultural heritage, and thus eventually to identify a curative solution to the malaise.

Between commitment and despair

Shortly before his death Wannous gave the aforementioned interview with Omar Amiralay, a bitter appraisal which testifies to how politics became entangled with the individual lives of this generation:

> I stride ahead on a winding path, along the borderline between life and death. I believe that Israel has stolen from me, in the true sense of the word, the best years of my life. Israel has robbed the fifty-year-olds – that's how old I am now – of their zest for life. It has destroyed so many opportunities.

This personal dismay and sadness felt by the artist when faced with contemporary political constellations is a characteristic feature of *adab multazim* (*littérature engagée*), to which the majority of Arab writers were committed in the 1950s and 1960s. There was a strong sense of solidarity with the Palestinians and their plight, in particular amongst the Left. Given the oppressive situation in Arab countries, it seemed to these artists that it was simply impossible to present and practice "art for art's sake", detached from everyday politics. The works of this epoch refer directly to contemporary events and show a clearly contoured political commitment; the Palestinian *adab al-muqawama* (literature of resistance) is the most important example of this style.

The 1967 defeat precipitated the first dramatic collapse of the literary movement, hitherto optimistic and firmly believing that the world could be changed. Saadallah Wannous described this traumatic experience gripping an entire generation in an interview in 1997:

> The defeat of '67 ... That was the decisive moment in our collective and individual history. And to be honest: the crisis that broke out made us happy. An idea had become entrenched in our minds: after years and years of mendacious talk we believed that the defeat of 1948 [of the Arab armies and the subsequent founding of the state of Israel, F.P.] had a single cause, namely betrayal and the purchase of inferior weapons. It thus had nothing to do with the superiority of Israeli soldiers. We were even led to believe that they were scared, timid, that they were incapable of confronting their enemies. From then on it seemed that victory over Israel was possible at any time. In 1967 I was not overly optimistic. But I'd never thought that our troops, above all those in Egypt and Syria, were in such a state of inner disarray. We only discovered this during the Six Day War of 1967. (...) Our trauma was enormous. We were wounded, humiliated to the core.

When, ten years later, President Sadat became the first Arab politician to travel to Israel on official business, outlining his plans for peace in a speech to the Israeli parliament, the world came crashing down for Wannous and a whole generation of committed intellectuals in Arab countries. With the unilateral peace offer of 1977 which left unanswered the key issues of the situation of Palestinian refugees and the status of Jerusalem and the occupied territories, a comprehensive and coherent solution to the Near East conflict seemed to recede into the distance. Saadallah Wannous tried to take his own life on the night of this momentous event:

> The news sent me reeling. It was evening ... sunset. To ease the unbearable tension I took a sleeping tablet. Two hours passed. Then I woke up, even more tense and anxious. It was completely dark. I tried to kill myself during the night. It was a time of silence and distress. I read and pondered. I was continually compelled to face up to the painful questions of history.

Wannous did not write a single play for the next twelve years. He finally broke his silence in 1989 with a play that was as celebrated as it was controversial; a play that attempted to relate to the Palestinian conflict from an Israeli viewpoint: *The Rape*.

The enemy mirrored in myself

Analyzing human cruelty and its use of torture and violence, *The Rape* is a drama that itself violated a taboo of Arab society, namely to consider the other side in the conflict and think about Israelis as people, not as a faceless "enemy". In the aforementioned 1997 interview, Wannous explained this approach:

> My play tells of a Jewish man. He denounces the abuse and torture of Pales-
> tinians by the Shin-Beth [secret service]. I was subsequently accused of being
> an Israeli sympathizer. I was seen as paving the way for reconciliation. But
> my goal was to put an end to our feelings of shame. I wanted to destroy the
> notion that Israel is a taboo, a united, homogenous block. An enemy that has
> to be annihilated before it annihilates us. I've called this notion the retreat
> into the eternal animosity.

The play, originally conceived as an adaptation of Antonio Buero Vallejo's drama *La doble historia del Doctor Valmy* (1969), is a harrowing analysis of violence in a state where the rule of law is flouted. Wannous portrays an Israeli security officer who can no longer cope psychologically with torturing Palestinians during interrogations. He becomes impotent and visits a doctor. During the consultation, incidents from interrogations are shown in flashbacks: a Palestinian is beaten and castrated; his wife then raped before his eyes; last he is murdered. Parallel to these scenes, which also present the officer at home, the author unfolds the history of the suffering of the victim's family. The dramatic highpoint of the play is the attempt by the Israeli to break out of the spiral of violence with the help of the doctor. But instead of letting him go, his colleagues, amongst them his stepfather, the chief of the secret service, murder him. His wife is raped by one of them and flees to the United States. The Palestinian wife of the victim assumes her husband's place in the resistance. In the last act, the doctor and the authorial character take the stage to state their positions against the repression and violence being practiced by both sides.

Poetic self-stylization as a victim of history

Although a number of Arab and in particular Palestinian critics condemned this play as being biased towards Israel, it nevertheless proved to be Wannous's greatest success. Initially banned in Syria, it was performed at Arab festivals in a variety of productions and was the subject of critical appraisal in a flood of secondary literature. It is, moreover, the only play to be performed in German translation in various productions in Germany and Austria. Revealingly, many German critics accused the author of presenting a biased, pro-Palestinian view of things.

We thus have a situation where different publics perceive and criticize diametrically opposed tendencies within the play. The fierce reactions allow us to deduce that the author had gotten to the heart of the matter. It was his first direct political response as an artist in a state that strictly censored such open displays of opinion. The staging of the play in Syria in December 1990 was only permitted in the form of "public rehearsals" held in a small room; a proper premiere in a theater was prohibited. In contrast, the text could be purchased in Syrian bookstores without any problem: apparently, the censorship authorities held the written expression of an opinion to be harmless. Due to its public eminence, theater has always attracted the vigilant eyes of rulers.

Despite the ban placed on staging *The Rape*, it was obvious that as the country's most famous playwright Wannous enjoyed an exceptional position. His terminal illness, which was diagnosed shortly after the end of the first Gulf War, lent his words even greater weight. For his own part, Wannous styled himself as a victim of the political history of his age, portraying his illness and imminent death as the result of unsolved political problems:

> I have the impression that our life is an endless series of setbacks. The last setback was especially painful. I believe that it caused the cancer I'm suffering from. By setback I mean the Gulf War. It killed our last hope. It is no coincidence that my first tumor appeared at the time. To be more precise: as the US was bombing Iraq.

In the years between 1991 and his death in May 1997, he wrote, as he put it, against death. His literary techniques and characterization shifted with his perspective: in the final phase of his creative life he addressed specific individual themes, exploring interpersonal problems, furnishing psychological studies and achieving multidimensional characterization. His late dramas reveal narrative finesse with novelistic traits, just as much closet dramas as for theater production.

In an interview with Mari Elias in the mid-1990s, he explained that this turnaround in his work stemmed from the realization that, by the beginning of the 1990s, political involvement in the Arab world was hopeless. Opposition groups were marginalized, established political forces rotten to the core and hopelessly factionalized. Belief in being able to change the world through struggle, heroic acts and martyrdom was suddenly revealed to be an illusion. In these years Wannous bade farewell to the idea that had hitherto guided him: that the problems of the Arab world could be traced back to simple power relations in society.

Literary form and thematic changed accordingly in his work. From the conscious simplification that had aimed to ignite political change and restructure power relations, he now turned to an approach that would generate insights into social problems. More difficult than instigating a change of regime, said Wannous in 1995, is "to stir a society adhering to and petrified in superstition."

This new style of drama led Wannous to a kind of aesthetic liberation and self-discovery, as he stated in an interview with Mari Elias:

> For the first time I've a sense of how writing can be a liberating act. Previously, I had certain ideas: I imposed a kind of self-censorship. An inner censorship which – as I imagined it – consisted in repressing everything that was of secondary importance, and left me to deal exclusively with the purportedly big questions. For the first time, I feel that writing is enjoyable. I was of the view that personal worries or individual problems were bourgeois, were superficial, unimportant affairs which one can put to one side. My whole interest was focused on grappling with and understanding history, and I thought – wrongly – that I had to avoid the traps of petit-bourgeois literature and go beyond all that was individual and personal. For this reason, I never felt as if I were entirely at one with myself in my work as playwright.

Working through history in times of decline

Wannous produced a searching and complex play right at the beginning of this new creative phase. Set against a background of the Mongol invasions at the beginning of the fifteenth century, *Historical Miniatures* (1992) explores the position of the intellectual in a situation of crisis. Taking the example of the historian Ibn Khaldoun (1332–1406), Wannous asks whether scholarship can be objective and pursued detached from political events, or if it is not inevitably the product of its historical setting.

The plot is set in early fifteenth-century Damascus. The Mongol ruler Timur Lenk (Tamerlane) and his army have reached the city gates, news of the horrors committed in the already fallen cities has spread, and panic breaks out. Faced with the superior forces of the enemy, the inhabitants of Damascus split into factions, fluctuating between heroic sacrifice to defend the city, opportunistic eagerness to negotiate, humble submissiveness, and panicky plans to flee. The Sultan's army has arrived to rescue the city, but as soon as the hopelessness of the situation becomes apparent, he withdraws his forces on the pretence of an impending putsch back in Cairo. The people of Damascus are isolated and abandoned. The city's notables agree to enter negotiations with the enemy, hoping to secure advantages for themselves. Sections of the population are enraged by this decision and hole up in the fortress. Neither honorable resistance nor strategic negotiations save the city and its population from torture, murder, plundering and devastation.

Ibn Khaldoun plays a key role in these events: arriving in the city as part of the Sultan's entourage, he stays to chronicle the events. He takes a detached position, defending himself to his pupil (a foil adeptly employed for the play's dramaturgy) with the argument that true scholarship is never permitted to take a stance. This means, however, that the historian must seek the support of those in power if he wishes to work unimpeded. He changes sides deftly, following the fortunes of the powerful, before finally entering a pact with Timur, the conqueror, promising him a written description of northern Africa.

Events are presented in scenes, most of which end with a relatively short bridging passage narrated by the "old chronicler": he prefaces the following scenes as commentator and as a kind of facilitator. For a long time he maintains an extremely neutral position, which, given the reported atrocities of the Mongols, appears cynical. Finally, he gives up this stance and expresses regret that he had to be so cold and clinical. In future he will try to show more compassion, even if he risks comprising his dramatic role.

The "old chronicler" reflects the conflict between scholarly neutrality and the ethical obligation of intellectuals to impart knowledge to society, to warn of dangers, and to instruct; he embodies those intellectuals who withdraw to a position where they simply tally events. Only so can he report the murder, torture and rape without faltering in style or tone.

Civil courage contra the objectivity of scholarship

The conscious detachment and neutrality of Ibn Khaldoun are called into question by his pupil throughout the course of the play. To Shamsaddin, Ibn Khaldoun appears to be an opportunistic researcher who watches violence and injustice with a detached, analytical eye; individual fates fail to move him, everything serves as material for his chronicle. The historian – of whom the Arab world, as "inventor" of modern sociology *avant la lettre*, is very proud – is exposed to a withering judgment by his own pupil in this play. Shamsaddin says of his teacher:

> Ibn Khaldoun hadn't understood a thing, he was too preoccupied with himself and his ambition. The agonies suffered by the people left him unaffected. He didn't hear our sobbing and didn't have the slightest inkling of our situation. All this misfortune was for him merely a tight spot he'd got temporarily caught up in and gotten out of again unscathed. But (...) how did he manage to suppress his tears (...), how could he consider his survival as being safe and sound?

In this play, Wannous draws on a key figure of Arab history and scholarship. Given this figure's enormous significance and fame, the thoroughly negative characterization is startling. It should, however, be kept in mind that in an epoch marked by violent upheavals, intrigues, and countless bloody wars within the

Islamic world, Ibn Khaldoun betrayed his masters and patrons more than once over his lifetime, switching his allegiance whenever he ran into difficulties; in some instances between direct rivals. Alfred Bel described this behavior succinctly in the first edition of the *Encyclopaedia of Islam*: "He possessed the skill, if not the honesty, to always cast his lot with the strongest."

This judgment is shared by Mohammad Talbi in the second edition of the encyclopedia:

> There is certainly no doubt that he behaved in a detached, self-interested, haughty, ambitious and equivocal manner. He himself does not attempt to hide this, and openly describes in his *Ta'rif* his successive changes of allegiance.

Talbi rightly contextualizes this verdict, remarking that in this epoch there was of yet no idea of loyalty towards a country, that solely apostasy was forbidden. Moreover, these facts of Ibn Khaldoun's life are counterbalanced by numerous passages in his autobiography *Ta'rif* (Instruction) in which he bitterly bemoans being dragged into political intrigues and machinations with the result that political reality repeatedly held him back from pursuing his true passions, philosophy and history. To decide whether Ibn Khaldoun was a victim or an opportunist exploiting the bloody history of his epoch for his own ends is not our task here: our interest is to find out what it was about this historical figure that fascinated Wannous so much that he devoted an entire play to him.

Why civilizations perish

The key point of Ibn Khaldoun's historical work was to study the causes of decline, the symptoms and nature of the illnesses that lead to the perishing of civilizations. Talbi traces Ibn Khaldoun's theory of history directly back to his own painful personal experiences; the *Muqaddima* (Introduction):

> ... is very closely linked with the political experience of its author, who had been in fact very vividly aware that he was witnessing a tremendous change in the course of history, which is why he thought it necessary to write a summary of the past of humanity and to draw lessons (...) from it.

Possibly Saadallah Wannous viewed the postcolonial end of the twentieth century in similar terms, or perhaps Ibn Khaldoun's ambivalent character fascinated him because as a critical intellectual in Syria, he himself was repeatedly confronted with the dilemma between active political commitment and individual aesthetic goals. This runs like a connecting thread through almost all of his plays between 1967 and 1997. Whoever wanted to survive politically in Assad's Syria had to devise a well-thought-out plan for dealing with political authority, otherwise persecution, sanctions and exile loomed. How much politics can art actually endure? How much politics does art actually *need*?

In an interview given in 1986, Wannous reflected critically on this dilemma. He characterized himself as the member of a generation of writers "who have made the enormous mistake ... of connecting creative with political work."

The making of a counter-narrative

This radical and unsparing self-criticism is not a rare occurrence at the turn of the twenty-first century. The Syrian-Lebanese poet and literary critic Adonis interprets this intellectual position as stemming from the postcolonial situation. Colonialism has by no means vanished with the withdrawal of the last British and French troops. In a lecture given in March 2007 at a conference in Doha on the theme of "Literature and Exile", Adonis claimed that political authorities in the Arab world are far more aggressive and ruthless than the former colonial masters. This is the reason that many writers searched for new strategies to circumvent or outfox censorship. The new colonist is, so to speak, the local political leader of the Arab world. Most of these politicians, who have ruled violently over the Arabs for decades, are more representative of Western colonialism than their own people.

Muhammad Siddiq explains how authors tried, precisely in the decades after independence, to use literature to develop counter-narratives:

> In the postcolonial era, the state apparatus invariably came under control of a privileged segment of the population: an elite, a party, a family, etc., which sought to collapse the national narrative with its own ideology in order to justify and perpetuate its political domination and culture supremacy. It is precisely at this crucial juncture that each of the national literatures of the contemporary Middle East has made what may yet emerge as its most significant contribution to its respective culture. Over against the essentializing, totalizing, and monolithic thrust of the ideological 'official' narrative, each one of these literatures developed a host of diverse, pluralistic, multivalent, and anti-hegemonic counter-narratives.

It is in this sense that *Historical Miniatures* can be read as a "counter-narrative": as Wannous sees it, the euphoric reception of the glorious Arab heritage which was to serve a reaffirmation of the recaptured national identity – a widespread movement in popular nationalism – cannot go on. "We've become our own worst enemies."

For a "third nahda"

Wannous is by no means the only intellectual to give such a bleak assessment. Sociologists like Tahir Labib, president of the Arab Sociological Society, were no less skeptical about the lack of critical voices in the Arab world and bemoaned "a culture without intellectuals". Tahir Labib sees in Edward Said a model for a new generation of secular Arab intellectuals, in whose development he pins his hopes.

The Lebanese author and journalist Elias Khoury is another who believes that only a blunt and unsparing self-criticism would enable the Arab world to deal adequately with the complex postcolonial situation. In an article, published in 2002 in the leftwing Beirut journal *al-Tariq* (messenger), Khoury backs a "third *nahda*". He too sees in Said a forerunner for a specific type of Arab intellectual, one who willingly assumes a highly visible public profile in intellectual opposition to the ruling powers. Comparable to the position taken by Wannous, Khoury demands that the traditional roles of Arab intellectuality such as king, sheikh, poet, politician, officer, entrepreneur, or journalist be replaced by a new understanding of the role. In the sense of Said's critique, a new oppositional practice and intellectual movement needs to be initiated, one which counters both the repression and the injustices of Arab governments and the xenophobic cultural and religious ideologies circulating in the Arab world. The consequences of "self-colonialism" need to be combated energetically – without turning a blind eye to the neo-imperialist tendencies of today's Western governments.

Historical Miniatures is an unequivocal appeal for such a new model of courageous public engagement by Arab intellectuals. The approach to collective memory elucidated here is not – as in so many works of Arab theater – that of a comparative reflection on the relationship between past and present, whereby whoever reflects on the past from an assured present hauls some aspect of that past into their present, but only because they feel that they are presently on the right path. This mode of reflection serves merely to affirm the present. To adequately characterize Wannous's understanding of history, I would suggest that a more emphatic and critical concept of reflection is needed: reflecting on the past serves to call the present into question; it is to be rethought by reflecting on uncomfortable historical moments.

Saadallah Wannous is not concerned with reaffirming a cultural identity that is already believed to exist; his concern is to instigate a radical change of current political and social reality. Only unsparing critique and courageous engagement can heal the festering wounds of the Arab present – that is the unequivocal credo of this author.

Wannous retained his unstinting commitment to Arab society up until his tragically early death. His final plays testify his pressing wish to give essential humanistic messages to his fellow Arabs on their journey to an open society. These messages have fallen on fertile ground in Syria and Lebanon in recent years. Since 1997 a series of important studies on his dramas of the 1990s have emerged. The award he received from the *Institut International du Théâtre* on World Theater Day in 1996 played an important role. He read an international message, which criticized Syrian society as well as the government in no uncertain terms, at a large event held in Syria's largest festival hall, the *Masrah al-Hamra*. He ended his speech with the words: "We are condemned to hope. What is happening today cannot be the end of the story." In line with this sentiment, his widow, the actress Fayza al-Shawish, organizes a small festival annually to mark the anniversary of his death. In recent years, critics and literary figures such as Faysal Darraj, Mari Elias, Abdelrahman Munif and Mahir al-Sharif have published important works on Saadallah Wannous, ensuring that he is not forgotten.

WORKS

al-A'mal al-kamila (Collected Works), 3 vol., Damascus: Dar al-Ahali 1996

'An al-dhakira wa-l-mawt. Nusus (On Memory and Death. Texts), Damascus, Dar al-Ahali 1997

Institut International du Théâtre (ed.): *World Theater Day, 27th March 1996: International Message, Saadalla Wannous, playwright*, Paris: Maison de l'UNESCO 1996

[with Nadim Mohammed] art. "Syria", in: *The World Encyclopedia of Contemporary Theatre, vol. 4: The Arab World*, ed. Don Rubin, London, New York: Routledge 1999, pp. 234–49

TRANSLATIONS

The King is the King (*al-Malik huwa l-malik*), trans. Ghassan Maleh, Thomas G. Ezzy, in: Salma Khadra Jayyusi, Roger Allen (eds.), *Modern Arabic Drama. An Anthology*. Bloomington: Indiana University Press 1995, pp. 77–120

A journey through the maze of a fleeting death (*Rihla fi majahil mawt 'abir*), trans. Rania Samara, in: *Rive. Revue of Mediterranean Politics and Culture* 5 (1997), pp. 71–2

"A Translation of *Sahrah ma'a Abi Khalil al-Qabbani* by Sa'dallah Wannus", trans. Shawkat M. Toorawa, in: *Arabic and Middle Eastern Literatures* 3 (2000), pp. 19–49

"A Translation of *The Elephant, Oh Lord of the Ages*, by Sa'dallah Wannus" (*al-Fil ya Malik az-zaman*), trans. Peter Clark, in: *Arabic and Middle Eastern Literatures* 4 (2001), pp. 53–68

The Glass Café, trans. Fateh Azzam, Alan Brownjohn, in: Salma Khadra Jayyusi (ed.), *Short Arabic Plays. An Anthology*, Northampton: Interlink 2003, pp. 412–32

The King's Elephant (*al-Fil ya Malik az-zaman*), trans. Ghassan Maleh, Christopher Tingley, in: Salma Khadra Jayyusi (ed.), *Short Arabic Plays. An Anthology*, Northampton: Interlink 2003, pp. 433–45

FURTHER READING

Roger Allen: "Arabic drama in theory and practice. The writings of Sa'dallah Wannus," in: *Journal of Arabic Literature* 15 (1984), pp. 94–113

Omar Amiralay: *There are so Many Things Left I Would Like to Say* [Filmed Interview with Saadallah Wannous], ARTE 1997

Magda Barakat: "Saadallah Wannus: 'Wir sind zur Hoffnung verurteilt'", in: *INAMO* 19 (Summer 1997), pp. 37–8 (incl. interview with Saadallah Wannous by Mari Elias 1995)

Interview with Saadallah Wannous, in: *al-Hurriyya* (Cyprus) 148 (1986), pp. 42f.

Peter Clark: "Remembering Sa'dallah Wannus", in: *Banipal* 1 (1998), pp. 72–3

Rosella Dorigo Ceccato: "Arab Theater and Syrian Folk Culture. Comments on the Relationship between Syrian Dramatic Art and the Present-day Public", in: A. Fodor (ed.), *Proceedings of the 14th Congress of the Union Européenne des Arabisants et Islamisants*, Budapest: Chair for Arabic Studies, Eötvös Loránd Univ. & Sect. of Islamic Studies, Csoma de Körös Soc. 1995, pp. 101–11

Regina Karachouli: "A Heritage Performed on Stage. The Contemporary Arab Theater", in: Günther Barthel, Gerhard Hoffmann (eds.): *Arab Heritage and Tradition – Burden or Challenge?* Special number of *Asien Afrika Lateinamerika*, Berlin 1989, pp. 138–46

Abdelrahman Munif: "A Short but Unforgettable Journey. Saad Allah Wannous' Theater", in: *Rive. Review of Mediterranean Politics and Culture* 5 (1997), pp. 68–70

Sami A. Ofeish: "Gender Challenges to Patriarchy.Wannus' Tuqus al-isharat wa-l-tahawalat", in: Sherifa Zuhur (ed.), *Colors of Enchantment: Theater, Dance, Music, and the Visual Arts of the Middle East*, Cairo, American University in Cairo Press 2001, pp. 142–50

Friederike Pannewick: *Der andere Blick: eine syrische Stimme zur Palästinafrage. Übersetzung und Analyse des Dramas "Die Vergewaltigung" von Sa'dallah Wannus in seinem interkulturellen Kontext*, Berlin: Schwarz 1993

Monica Ruocco, "Islamic Modernism in a Recent Play by Sa'd Allah Wannus", in: U. Vermeulen, J.M.F. Van Reeth (eds.), *Law, Christianity and Modernism in Islamic Society. Proceedings of the Eighteenth Congress of the Union Européenne des Arabisants et Islamisants*, Leuven: Peeters 1998, pp. 279–89

Aleya A. Said: "Wavering Identity. A Pirandellean Reading of Saadalah Wannus's *The King Is the King*", in: *Comparative Drama* 32 (1998), pp. 347–61

OTHER WORKS CITED

Adonis: "Makan akhar fi ma wara' al-watan wa-l-manfa," in: *al-Hayat*, April 8, 2007

Alfred Bel: art. "Ibn Khaldun," in: *Enzyklopädie des Islam*, 1st edition, vol. 2, Leiden: Brill, pp. 419–21

Elias Khoury: "al-Nahda al-thalitha", in: *al-Tariq* 60.1 (Jan./Febr. 2002), pp. 28–39

Muhammad Siddiq: "The Making of a Counter-Narrative. Two Examples from Contemporary Arabic and Hebrew Fiction", in: *Michigan Quarterly Review* 31 (1992), pp. 649–62

Mohammad Talbi: art. "Ibn Khaldun", in: *Encyclopedia of Islam*, 2nd edition, vol. 2, Leiden et al.: Brill, pp. 825–31

Linguistic Temptations and Erotic Unveilings
Rashid al-Daif on Language, Love, War, and Martyrdom

Angelika Neuwirth

Historical memory in Lebanon

There is arguably no other Arab country in which the need for historical memory is so acutely felt than present-day Lebanon. Not least, questions of guilt need to be addressed and resolved. After a brutal civil war lasting fifteen years (1975–90), Lebanon is faced with the daunting task of reevaluating and rewriting its history. Ostensibly, the civil war began as an inevitable, overdue revolutionary movement in a country with antiquated social and political structures. However, over time ethnic sectarian struggle preempted secular and cold war imperatives; military actions fought along clearly recognizable fronts gave way to violent plundering of settlements, massacres of the civilian population in entire districts, and the indiscriminate murder of random individuals. Once unleashed, the violence spread like an epidemic and eventually gripped every segment of the population, with lasting impact on the intellectual movement. As Ken Seigneurie notes:

> In wartime Lebanon the rapid shift from a secular ideological war to an atavist feud between Christians and Muslims dampened the sense of commitment in those who had imagined the cause of martyrdom should, ideally, be for the same cause from one day to the next. In literature, secular chaos punctuated the myth of progress and along with it realist literature predicated on a knowable world. After a half century of serving the Arab cause, realism in the Arabic novel became an overnight anachronism, and from its grip emerged the Lebanese war novel.

After the war, an official amnesty was proclaimed, erasing all war crimes from juridical memory – without these vanishing from the collective memory of the Lebanese. On the contrary: amongst intellectuals the question as to what Lebanese society should remember became one of the most volatile issues. If the country was not to sink into a state of total amnesia, into a dull oblivion, the population had to face up to and tackle what politicians had decided to neglect.

Amongst the multitude of voices commenting on the traumatic events, Rashid al-Daif is one of the few who does not speak from a victim position and steadfastly abides by the overwhelming discovery that guilt for the catastrophic events is to be found in almost all groups in Lebanon. Indeed, he goes further, examining his own past as an individual. He undertakes this search for complicity and guilt in a fictional autobiography which, outwardly at least, has the unmistakable form of a Christian confession. By virtue of this form, with its implied strenuous and far-reaching self-examination, al-Daif's work stands out from the majority of recently published Arab autobiographies.

Social conservatism is primarily blamed for the frequently remarked backwardness of Arab autobiographies in comparison with the self-scrutinizing Western works of this genre. In her monograph on contemporary Palestinian autobiographies, *Unsere Situation schuf unsere Erinnerungen*, Susanne Enderwitz identifies a still existent timidity amongst autobiographers "to come into conflict with their social role." This social role, which is male, is more strictly controlled in the Islamic context than in Christian societies, which are in any case more conversant with verbalizing admissions of guilt due to the established institution of the confessional and its many ramifications. It is therefore to be expected that authors from the Christian tradition would undertake a rigorous examination of historical memory in the manner of a confession. Yet even individualistic self-examinations like those of the Palestinians Jabra Ibrahim Jabra, Edward Said, or Raja Shehadeh, authors with Christian backgrounds, are not confessions despite their introspection, but rather stories of miraculous triumph over painful experiences of loss: stories of survival.

In contrast, self-accusation and taking on the burden of collective disgrace as an individual characterize one of the most prominent Lebanese poets, Khalil Hawi (1925–82). Hawi, who saw political catastrophes crush his dream of a resurgent Arab culture on several occasions, committed suicide on 15 September 1982, the day the Israelis occupied Beirut. One of his most important poems expresses the sense of living an incomplete existence, a decay riddling the body while still alive; the poetic persona is an Arab Lazarus who has risen from the dead only to find himself restored to an incomplete state. Just as this poem takes self-accusation to the extreme, the same is evident, albeit with a different area of impact, in al-Daif's novel of 1995 which is both formally and in its substantive message a confession. Does the author in a subtle way draw on an ecclesial model? If this is the case, then it is not without irony, for his confessor is a "dead writer", the Japanese novelist Yasunari Kawabata (1899–1972), who committed suicide. Al-Daif's book bears the seemingly anachronistic title *Dear Mr. Kawabata*.

The author and his works

Rashid al-Daif was born in 1945 in Ehden, not far from the north Lebanese town of Zghorta. Zghorta is famous and notorious far beyond its immediate surrounds as a bastion of militant Maronite Christians, whose ruthless blood feuds have continued into recent times, provoking controversy. The murder of innocent family members of ostracized persons had also occurred amongst Rashid al-Daif's own family and friends; this cast a shadow over his youth. Formative for the writer, who grew up in a strict conservative family, was the restrictive moral codex of his society, in particular the strict separation of the sexes. But this patriarchal order began to totter in his youth. Compulsory schooling, established under mandate rule, brought the adolescent al-Daif into contact with French teachers, who introduced the young generation to modern ideas. Under this influence they gained a completely new sense of self-esteem, even feeling themselves to be superior to the older generation, whose norm-setting values were perceived "over night" as outdated, no longer holding any weight. Al-Daif was witness to the process that would prove fateful for Lebanon, which is reflected in a number of his novels: the new leftist and cosmopolitan utopias erected insurmountable fronts between the already polarized groupings of the Lebanese population, a situation whose inherent tension would eventually erupt in the civil war.

After graduating from school, al-Daif began studying Arab literature at the Université Libanaise in Beirut in 1965, before moving to Paris to attend the Sorbonne, where he completed doctorates in 1974 and again in 1978. Even more than the academic standards, the intellectual climate in France left an indelible mark on al-Daif. He moved in French communist circles, where he became a political activist and met his French wife. Immediately upon returning to Lebanon in 1974 to become a lecturer at the Université Libanaise, he joined the Progressive Left, a group that hoped a war would revitalize the Lebanese political system and resolve the Palestinian conflict. Although al-Daif never actively engaged in armed combat, he gave committed backing to the revolutionaries with political speeches and the drafting of manifestos. He published his first volumes of poetry in 1979 and 1980.

Things changed dramatically at the peak of the war in 1983 (a year after the devastating Israeli bombing and invasion of Beirut) when al-Daif, like countless other Beirut residents, was driven out of his apartment. The city was now practically ruled by militias who refused to tolerate denominationally mixed districts. Once famous for its cosmopolitan character, the city of Beirut was transformed into a pre-modern oriental town with a ghetto-like partitioning of individual religious groups, a severe setback for those fighting for a secular Lebanon in particular. In the same year, al-Daif was hit by a grenade and nearly died: this brush with death and the experience of being retrieved from its clutches is reflected in several of his novels. In this fateful year he began to write prose.

Between 1983 and 1997 seven novels were published, all of them drawing on experiences of the war, including *Dear Mr. Kawabata*, the work with which he gained his international reputation. He only turned away from the war thematic in his eighth novel, *Learning English* (1998). With his subsequent novels, *To Hell with Meryl Streep* (2000), *Forget the Car!* (2002), *Ma'bad succeeds in Baghdad* (2005) and *O.K. Good-bye* (2008), which focus on gender issues and openly describe sexuality, al-Daif has embarrassed his critics; discussion about the purported pornographic nature of these novels continues unabated. He is currently professor of Arab literature at the Université Libanaise and once again lives in his old apartment, near the Rue Hamra in the center of West Beirut.

Al-Daif on war and love

In 1983 al-Daif's first novel, *The Tyrant*, was published. It is the psychogram of a literature professor named Rashid who continues lecturing during the war. Amidst the ruins and collapse of all social norms, a sexual adventure snaps him out of the lethargy of the day-to-day routine of life in wartime. While the shells rain down, a young woman falls into his arms in the university's dark bunker. He will never see her again. The novel develops in conjunction with its intertexuality: a Camus text quoted right at the novel's opening as a translation task furnishes the pattern for the narrator's attitude and behavior. Like the figure of Dr. Rieux from Camus' *The Plague* (1947), the narrator concentrates exclusively on his private crisis despite the collective catastrophe happening around him. In al-Daif's work, however, the Camusian patterns escalate into an obsession: in his search for the woman the protagonist is prepared to exploit even such destructive acts as the explosion of a car bomb.

The Tyrant is a study of the insoluble relationship between love and death, Eros and Thanatos, exemplified by the narrator's obsessive search for intimate contact with women in moments when death seems imminent. With it, al-Daif joined the increasing number of Lebanese authors attempting to come to terms with the traumatic experience of the war through writing. By the time it was published, Elias Khoury had already written three novels and Hassan Daoud one; writers including Etel Adnan, Hanan al-Shaykh and Vénus Khoury-Ghata had probed the war from a female perspective. Al-Daif's novel stands out from these works by virtue of its pronounced autobiographical character. This is generated not only by the close resemblance between the narrator and the author, but also because the narrator stands at the center of his tale; a stark contrast to the novels of Elias Khoury, for instance, where the plot is told by several different narrative voices and protagonists other than the narrator are the focus of attention.

A very different tack in facing up to the war is evident in *Shadow Creatures* (1986), whose lyrical language emphatically recalls al-Daif's early poetic works. Using the allegorical form, al-Daif reflects on the latent potential for conflict in Lebanese society drawing on a well-known poem by the Lebanese poet and writer

Mikhail Naimy, praising Lebanon as a safe home atop a high mountain, to portray building a house as a dangerous and ominous undertaking. A couple plan to realize their dream of a paradisiacal home. Construction seems to be underway; at other points in the novel, though, it is already completed. In terms of time and location, events are held in a strange limbo. Abysses of hate lurk beneath the tender words, and the love between the two shatters. A child – at times a daughter, at others a son – lives in perpetual angst and is finally fatally bitten by one of the snakes skulking everywhere, the "creatures of the shadows". The woman metamorphoses into a destructive force of nature. Graves begin to open up beneath the house. In 1986, it is blatantly obvious that the "house of Lebanon" is not a viable dwelling but an excavated grave. Language has not kept its promises.

Recourse to surrealist elements is taken a step further in the novel *The Crucial Space between Drowsiness and Sleep* (1987; translated into English as *Passage to Dusk*). The novel opens with the death of the first-person narrator, a scene that is then retold in different versions. The narrator cannot sleep. There is an incessant and menacing knocking on his door. As he finally musters the will to open it, he becomes the voyeur of his own death. In an inner monologue he tries to understand what is happening, struggling to recall what had gone on before. There is the bomb explosion where he loses an arm and is left lying dazed on the street. His blood flows under a manhole, attracting the rats. There is the strange hospital where he fears that he will lose consciousness and reveal his identity, which could well prove disastrous for these are times in which one can lose one's life solely due to religion. Finally he encounters the reader as he attempts – carrying his torn-off arm like a briefcase – to get to his apartment in West Beirut unnoticed. He takes a taxi, reaches his apartment, and lies down. There is a knock on the door. Opening the door, he is gunned down by militiamen, dies, and the novel begins again. Once more the novel reveals autobiographical interests: composed of narrative fragments without fixed temporal organization, its form reflects the narrator's condition, seriously injured both physically and mentally, a state that is a microcosm of the city of Beirut. Written in the middle of the war, the novel drastically satirizes the relationship between the blood-shedding victims and the soil of the fatherland, a topos mythicized frequently at this time.

In the final novel he wrote during the war, *Techniques of Misery* (1989), al-Daif begins a language experiment on which he will continue to expand in later novels: "objectifying prose", a key characteristic of the *nouveau roman*. In its thoroughly neutral depiction of reality the novel follows the lead of Sonallah Ibrahim's *The Committee* (1981), which also describes a siege. Faced with a grim war situation, the protagonist, Hashim, is condemned to spend his life in the dungeon of his apartment with irregular power and water supplies. This place and the routine of day-to-day life in it are meticulously observed, depicted in an endlessly slow tempo. During occasional forays outside the apartment, Hashim is exposed to the rudeness and disparagement of his neighbors. He takes in the humiliation passively, becoming an object, a robot. This novel has been compared with William Kotzwinkle's hippie novel *The Fan Man* (1987): war and drug consumption have in equal measure resulted in the individual's desensitization; they direct attention to circumstances of the simplest, lowest level and lead to the passive acceptance of every experience, even aggressive ones. Through the emotionally disinterested rendering of reality, al-Daif succeeds in mirroring the state of consciousness he wishes to depict in his writing practice. In the process, as he himself put it, "language becomes the genuine subject of the text."

After the war, al-Daif shifted his attention from the devastating psychological effects of violence to the issue of guilt. After his autobiographical novel focusing on guilt, he wrote a novel that, like Elias Khoury's *The Kingdom of the Strangers* (1994), approaches guilt as though it were a phantom, a phenomenon no longer graspable in reality. In *This Side of Innocence* (1997), the theme of guilt tapers into a single question: who could have torn down the poster of a political leader? Here al-Daif plays with a reproach that had crystallized into a topos of literature, an innocent individual accusatively targeted by a repressive state power, as in Orwell's *1984* or Ibrahim's *The Committee*. The plot is vague: the narrator is arrested and the reader encounters him after questioning. The narrator – introduced by name just once in passing as al-Rashid, which means "the reasonable" and is of course also the name of the author – feels guilty even though he has not committed the crime for which he has been arrested. Has he not always harbored the wish to do something similar? And do not wishes of this kind make him suspicious? In the tradition of Joyce and Kafka, the plot unfolds through the "stream of consciousness" of a single person, blurring any clear distinction between real events and the imaginings produced in the narrator's harrowed mind. Is the torture he is subjected to – or the rape of his wife before his eyes – reality or a fantasy spawned by his fear? By raising the question of guilt and innocence the novel furnishes – much like those by Elias Khoury – a collective psychogram. So much collective aggression prevails in the nameless country torn apart by war that no-one can be considered innocent.

Al-Daif has enriched the Arabic war novel through incisive innovations: surrealist elements, elsewhere found only in Francophone literature on the civil war such as that of Ghassan Fawaz, Sélim Nassib, and Vénus Khoury-Ghata; "objectifying prose"; and the exceptional autobiographical coding, which often incorporates the Beirut locality into a larger Lebanese environment.

Tabooed sexuality and the problem of pornography

If al-Daif's early novels are mostly autobiographically tinged accounts of the traumatic experiences of the civil war, his more recent work focuses on the way of life in Maronite north Lebanon, a society dominated by tribal attitudes and practices, and thus on the patriarchal society of the Arab world as a whole. They display plot strands, often bordering on the grotesque, which emerge out of a conflict between the narrator/protagonist and the constraints of the tribal moral codex, in particular the strict segregation of the sexes. As the conflict unfolds, what this codex seeks to conceal, the "illicit", is revealed, the unthinkable expressed; and thus a step is taken in the direction of al-Daif's striven for desacralization of sexuality.

The problem of tabooed sexuality takes center stage in the novel *Learning English*. The innocuous title suggests that the novel's plot is about learning a foreign language; the reader is confronted instead with more of a detective story. Browsing through the police notices in a newspaper, the first-person narrator, university lecturer in Beirut and once more al-Daif's alter ego, reads about the violent death of his father, the victim of a blood revenge killing in his north Lebanese hometown, who has seemingly already been buried. Why have his mother or his father's brothers not told him, the only son?

Old doubts are rekindled as to whether the dead man was indeed his father, doubts not only about the genetic parentage of the dead man but also about the unreserved recognition of this parentage in the extended family. He undertakes agonizingly precise attempts to reconstruct the emotional and sexual past of his mother, who as a young woman gave up plans to emigrate with her lover to America at the very last minute, only to accede to the suit of a man she did not love and who, as it turned out, was disposed to emotional cruelty and physical abuse. The narrator hopes that these attempts at reconstruction can help fathom the secret of his painfully constrictive and disappointing relationships to his closest relatives. Images of the past spring up and some of them conjure his sexual awakening and relationship to a younger friend of his mother, a woman who is privy to his mother's purported secret.

But what is most predominant here is the peculiar acquisition of a language. The narrator reflects on his still imperfect modernity. With subtle irony he presents himself as being suspended between two worlds: a modern life in Beirut determined by individualism and a rural reality governed by atavistic thinking in categories of shame and honor. He feels that he has to learn English, to find a language that is free of this painful ambiguity; a language that does not simultaneously transport along with modern reality its hidden double still complying with the value categories of the traditional society. But prior to the acquisition he scrutinizes the old language by relentlessly uncovering tabooed reality, by expressing the unmentionable. The novel is a fascinating attempt to write the grammar of a mentality, of a Middle Eastern communicative code still dominated by a myriad of subliminally pervasive compulsions, which are almost always tied to sexuality.

It is worth noting that in al-Daif's work tradition does not serve as a hallowed model, even in the form of literary tradition. Any recourse to older literature serves rather the function of a magnifying glass, under which the similarity and yet dissimilarity of lived reality first becomes recognizable in its grotesque character. In almost all of al-Daif's more recent works, readings of earlier texts are mirrored in the drastic magnifying glass of the causes for conflict or the irritating inversion of the plot. Despite their state of minds being considered socially normal, individual persons are revealed as grotesque; such as the narrator in *To Hell with Meryl Streep*, who turns the actual or imputed sexual past of his wife into the subject of obsessive investigations and strives to erase it by whatever means possible. He acts no differently but ultimately more futilely than King Shahryar in *Thousand and One Nights*, whose discovery of his spouse's extramarital pleasures impels him into an obsessive persecution of women. The dubiousness of traditional patriarchal attitudes to sexuality is disclosed by inverting classical Arab or Western European subtexts.

The desacralization of sexuality goes hand in hand with a desacralization of language as such. Al-Daif's new "objectifying prose" is ultimately an act of protest against traditional usages of standard language. This remains a religiously explosive issue in Arabic-speaking regions up to the present day. Arabic is considered by many to be a kind of sacred language demanding special attention and protection. In al-Daif's eyes it is precisely the criteria elevating Arabic to this status that make the language itself problematic; in particular its pronounced tendency to rely on archaic expressions, its evocation of venerable role models through recourse to traditional stylistic patterns, and its seemingly innate aptitude for a euphemistic disguising of reality. Given this extraordinary conservatism, Arabic transports a host of antiquated social and ethical valuations, along with sexual and tribal subtexts, in its lexis and metaphor. The unmasking of such is a tenaciously pursued concern of al-Daif's later novels, in particular *To Hell with Meryl Streep*, *Forget the Car!* and *O.k. and Good-bye*. For him, the burdened language represents the biggest obstacle to liberating and opening Arab society.

But is it only the "enlightening" objective of unmasking existent obsolete attitudes towards sexuality that inspires Daif's recent works? Maher Jarrar has put this question, which more or less imposes itself on readers of Daif's more recent novels, in explicit terms: "Can one differentiate between eroticism and pornography in literature?" For an answer Jarrar extrapolates some important inferences about the form and outcome of sexuality as a literary genre in the postwar setting of Beirut:

The most striking, perhaps, is that al-Daif's strategy must not be seen merely as a radical experimentation with narrative themes and playful prose, inventive and appealing as these may seem. Such virtuosity can be easily seen (...) in al-Daif's inventiveness and skill (at times excessive) in readily manipulating both these literary elements.

The narrative, Jarrar holds:

> ... entails a disguised phobia; both at the level of gender and the reassertion of social and religious affiliation. This indifference to, or phobia of the other is an expression of what Samir Khalaf labels "Geography of Fear" and has become much more pronounced in postwar Lebanon.

He concludes with a skeptical vision:

> The liberty of experimentation in the use of language which mounts up in a satirical parody of many voices and languages, and particularly, his parody of the language of Islamic law and of Arabic love manuals regarding sexual relations and techniques, reveals an anxiety of the symbolic phallus of the other. (...) Eros becomes here a disguised expression of aggression and a prelude to war. This kind of disguised phobic discourse is unprecedented in the Lebanese novel. Are we here confronted with a new type of writing provoked by the degradation of the social and political system which is becoming manifestly sectarian, excluding a major portion of the society and reinforcing lack of democracy and constant violation of civil rights? Whatever the causes, the consequences of such a literary trend might be drastic.

Daif on the Arabic language and on martyrdom

The autobiographical novel *Dear Mr. Kawabata* is not least an engagement with the Middle Eastern concept of martyrdom, unique to modern Arab literature. Although the idea of martyrdom is absent from contemporary Western thinking, the concept of sacrifice is still universally present. It has even been claimed that "the self-consciousness of a society is reflected in its sacrifice metaphoric". This maxim, according to the Catholic theologian Joachim Negel, not only applies to the pre-secular past, but can also hold for post-religious modernity. In applying it however, what emerges is the ambivalence of sacrifice:

> It is one of the peculiarities of our current spiritual situation that the increasing technological-economic networking of the natural life-world and the concomitant withering of forms of life determined by religion generates a thoroughly contradictory situation, oscillating between criticism of sacrifice and

an inflationary metaphoric usage of sacrifice. On the one hand, the category of sacrifice in the sense of Latin *sacrificium* stands (in the modern perception) for a world-negating cult of renunciation, for an obscure mysticism of self-chosen suffering; on the other hand, in the sense of the Latin *victima* the category appears irreplaceable when suffering inflicted by others or brought upon by one's own fault as well as misfortune from external circumstances are brought down to a common denominator.

The inversion of being a victim (*victima*) into an active sacrifice (*sacrificium*) remains an ambiguous step in this perception, suspected to be a dubious act of self-sacrifice. The suspicion of private victimization is only circumvented (...), the sublation of the ambivalence inherent to the term sacrifice only occurs, when the activated self-offering finds acceptance, in the sense of St. Thomas Aquinas' *hostia acceptabilis Deo placens*.

Negel advocates an understanding of sacrifice that necessarily implies transcendence. And it is precisely the question of the sacrificing person's participation or non-participation in the discourse of transcendence which is the crux of the current discussion between Lebanese and Palestinian intellectuals, who present martyrdom as a highly ambivalent phenomenon.

That al-Daif has a fractured relationship to the martyrdom discourse is no surprise given his biography. Born into a Maronite Christian family and educated in secular French tradition, he writes in a world in which ancient prerogatives of Islamic martyrdom have enjoyed a revival since the 1950s. Although the narrator in *Dear Mr. Kawabata* is, like the author, a secular intellectual, he does nonetheless at times adopt and employ ubiquitous images of martyrdom marked by Islamic influences, such the notion of martyrdom as an "act of writing" that necessarily appears in times of crisis or as a physiological consummation of the fighter and is comparable to a full-blossomed flower. At the same time, though, he also calls on the Christian notion of martyrdom as a kind of cultic act that unites the community of the sacrificial actor into a cult community. The narrator only realizes at the end that he has succumbed to an illusion: that martyrdom is nothing more than a construct of language; and more importantly a symptom of the sacralization of Arabic, which fatally hampers any unconditional perception of reality. What lends particular weight to his denunciation of the martyr myth is his sensibility of the origin of the ambivalence in martyrdom, his appreciation that the martyr cult he experienced and practiced is part of the modernity, which legitimized its rise with a verbal deicide, with a loss of transcendence.

In *Dear Mr. Kawabata* the idea of the martyr is embedded in a confession, a Christian intertext that lends the novel a conspicuous ethical dimension repeatedly highlighted by critics such as Ken Seigneurie. By explicitly broaching the issue of guilt for the first time in Lebanese literature, the novel places the debate about the recently concluded civil war on a completely new level. Besides the person confessing, a standard confession requires a confessor to whom a secret or culpable behavior is revealed. The confessing person in the novel is the narrator, who bears the author's name, Rashid, and like the author grew up in the north Lebanese town of Ehden. The Japanese novelist Yasunari Kawabata figures as confessor. The narrator points out the motives for his choice of Kawabata:

> I loved the innocence of the stranger, perhaps I still do. The stranger's lack of preconceptions to me meant neutrality. Perhaps it still does. So here I am, Mr. Kawabata, appointing you as the king, I dreamed of being myself, the arbitrator obeyed because of his sincerity ...

Generally, the urge to confess is precipitated by a limit-experience that triggers sudden insight and self-awareness. For Rashid, the trigger is the shock evoked by a passing doppelganger figure, a man whom he initially takes to be a mirror image of himself. This purported mirror image by no means induces narcissistic self-infatuation; on the contrary, it leads him to the sudden realization of another self hidden away within him, a self that only now, as his doppelganger walks away, breaks loose. This other "dark" self is embodied in his former mentor, his fellow fighter in wartime who has simply dismissed the war as done with and leads a normal civilian life with not the slightest qualm nor any anguished pangs of conscience about his sinister role in the war. This man, whom Rashid encounters unexpectedly on the Rue Hamra, now acts as a trigger to recall and reflect on the repressed past.

The actual guilt to be confessed lies submerged in his recollections of the war, which closely enmesh Rashid with this mentor. As the reader finds out at the end of the novel, the culpable act is a calamitous use of language which drove scores of young people into a violent death intended to be a sacrifice. However, as Rashid recalls it, this culpable agitation during the war is tied to an incident from his youth, an incident that revolves around a particular use of language with a fatal outcome.

Prelude: deicide and the desacralization of language

To make the socialist ideology they will defend for years in the war of their own, Rashid and his contemporaries had first to acquire the "scientifically secured" thinking that, while promising progress, also stood in irreconcilable opposition to the traditional worldview of the milieu of their birth, igniting bitter conflicts.

Rashid grows up in a small, isolated Maronite town as the son of illiterate parents. The father expects nothing good to come from the school education of his children and wants to restrict it to learning to read and write. His fears are not unfounded. His children are going to school in stormy times: geography lessons discuss the earth's spherical form and rotation around the sun, which entirely contradicts the traditional Maronite world image; Soviet cosmonauts turn this revolutionary subject matter into a demonstrable *fait accompli*, with pictures and radio reports reaching as far as Ehden. The boys are swept away by Yuri Gagarin's astronautics, and from their new, scientifically illuminated world they assail the old and jaded world order, ruled over by a God in heaven. Akin to religious warriors, they want to force the older generation to realize the godlessness of the world. Indeed, the suddenly dynamic cosmos is for the older generation a vertiginous world, one in which they literally stagger, no longer able to stand upright. This is demonstrated by Sadiq, an old man who opposes the new view of the world with empirical arguments:

> Our neighbor Sadiq was by far the most argumentative. He used to lie in wait for us, and we could always reckon on meeting him at the same time – once a week, the day of the geography class. In addition, of course, to the chance meetings that happened often, very often. Sadiq would take responsibility for speaking on their behalf. Them. The grown-ups. The older generation, people on whom time had eaten and drunk. This is an expression, Mr. Kawabata, which our teacher used a lot. Fortunately, the geography class was the last period of the day – the day when we had a regular appointment, that is. As soon as the bell went, we were off. Sadiq would stand on one foot and lift up the other one, pretending to be standing on a steep slope. One foot up and one foot down. Then he would stretch his hands out like wings, and say: "So, this is how we stand on the earth, is it! Isn't this how we should stand if the earth were like a ball, as you say it is? Why don't we fall off the earth's surface, then, if the earth is a ball floating in space?"

The dispute reaches its climax as the youths are able to make use of a new weapon: printed words and pictures as testimony. Up until this point the spoken word was the guarantor of authority in rural society, more so when articulated by the elders, who underscored the truth of what they said by leading a life conforming to established norms. The new authority of the printed word, which the analphabetic elders cannot control, disrupts the hitherto irrefutable hierarchical order, including even the boundary between heaven and earth:

> The day after that great day [when Gagarin's spaceship circled the earth] I bought a newspaper for the first time in my life. The first page was indeed about Gagarin's historic voyage into space around the earth. It was full of pictures and news, especially pictures. I read everything written in the newspaper about the event on my way home from the place where newspapers were

sold. I gobbled it up. (...) I looked at the pictures. Pictures from my brother Gagarin. My schoolmate and classmate Gagarin! Dear Mr. Kawabata, how can I describe to you the relationship between Gagarin and myself at that moment? He was part of me. I was him and he was me. (...) Sadiq didn't read and he didn't write. He couldn't distinguish an alif from a telegraph pole. But I showed him the pictures. I said to him: "Look!" (...) He looked at the pictures but gave no indication of having understood anything. I put them under his eyes as he bent over the basket he was making with strips of cane. He thrust them away from in front of his face with his fist ...

The hard evidence of the pictures decides the dispute; for Sadiq and the older generation the traditional edifice of beliefs collapses. Sadiq is not a relative or a loved one, but he is a close friend of Rashid's father, a kindred spirit, or to put it pointedly, an *alter ego* of the father – though with communicative competence. The father is extremely taciturn and in his "omniscience", absolute power and severity he is an unapproachable God, whose countenance the son seeks in vain. The undermining of his beliefs through the new authority of science and its attendant ally, the printed word, is for Sadiq a personal loss; a "robbery of his heaven" in the wake of which only the consciousness of his own mortality remains, followed by no salvation that might redeem the trials and tribulations suffered on earth. For the father, who is as head of the family and guarantor of the clan's honor codex a pillar of the old world order, this new interpretation of the world is nothing less than an act of terrorism.

When the son leaves a newspaper that propagates socialist views and politics at home, the father (unable to read it he relies on others to tell him the contents) remains silent. His son's betrayal of the principles sustaining Maronite society, foremost the politically privileged position of the Christians, is something that he cannot accept: he will never speak to his son again; he has "turned his countenance away" from the son forever. Worse, for the son he is dead. Although he is killed in a vendetta during the son's first year at university, he has long been dead, a God who perished along with his own world order. Patricide and deicide coincide.

Rashid feels burdened by the victims his personal enlightenment has claimed. He can undo neither the patricide nor the deicide that robbed Sadiq of hope. Nonetheless, the dislocation that has taken place in this edifice also has a harrowing effect on him. The first news of the earth's roundness and its rotation around the sun confounded him, propelling him into a state of physical powerlessness. And while the idea of God's expulsion from his heavenly sphere is made somewhat more bearable by reading Brecht's drama *Life of Galileo*, the recollection of Sadiq's lost hopes and the averted countenance of his father resolutely cling to him: the novel ends with a scene from Sadiq's funeral and the countenance of his father, his features concealed as a sign of mourning.

Resacralizing language: communist agitation and the martyr cult

All this is only the prelude to an even graver crime – the role played by Rashid and his intellectual friends in the war. Once again a forceful use of the word is practiced, this time resacralizing language. After the "death of God" a new figure is apotheosized, a virile young God: the hero or martyr. That this new cult follows the disempowerment of the older is more than a mere historical succession. The generational conflict manifesting itself in this constellation is also a conflict between pre-modern mentality and modernity, between maintaining a relationship with transcendence and a rejection of transcendence. This conflict is similarly evident in Palestine, where the *fida'i* martyr cult fashioned in the poetry of Mahmoud Darwish and others supplants the patriarchic model and even counters the disempowered guiding father figure with a mother-son configuration, the mythic female homeland superseding the figure of God the Father. This is certainly no coincidence in Palestine. Although the martyr cult fostered by the secular revolutionaries in Lebanon is a more fleeting phenomenon and most certainly cannot boast a comparably prominent poetic articulation, here too scores of young people are stirred by the magical power of the word to sacrifice themselves for the good of their political cause – or, in the language of the time, to become a "martyr".

As Darwish, resident of the city during this period, has put it, Beirut in these years became:

> ... a factory of posters. Beirut was certainly the first city in the world where posters rivaled with dailies in importance. (...) Faces on the walls – martyrs, freshly emerging from life and the printing presses, a death that is the copy of itself. One martyr takes the place of another on the wall until replaced by yet another or wiped out by the rain.

Countless young people become "martyrs", or "victims" as defined by Jean-Luc Nancy: "Their body has reached the border where it becomes the body of a community, even its spirit, its salient agency, its material symbol, which infuses their bloodstream intimating sense and forges sense as shed blood." This is a sacrifice akin to the model of Christ but without any semblance of a transcendental dimension. The act of sacrifice has turned in on itself, becoming self-reflective.

The images of the dead elevate them into a community of heroes with a glimmer of the divine, a central theme in Elias Khoury's novel *The White Faces*

(1981). Furthermore, no matter how thoroughly secularized the observer may be, the demotic-religious vision of Islam has bestowed upon the martyr a singular status, reinterpreting death suffered in youth as the rite of passage – commensurate with their age – of a wedding with the mythical homeland. They are celebrated, particularly in the Palestinian context, as bridegrooms.

Even if Rashid remains aloof from such an archetypical interpretation of untimely heroic death, he nonetheless accords martyrdom mythical powers: in his eulogy of martyrdom – direct quotations from early speeches given by the author Rashid al-Daif himself – the martyrs undergo a kind of apotheosis, a divinization. They are eulogized in Biblical language, and as is proclaimed of Christ in the Easter liturgy, they are set as the Alpha and Omega, embodiments of the "new alphabet" comparable to the Revelation of St. John the Divine: "I am Alpha and Omega, the beginning and the end, saith the Lord (...)". And like the apostles, they carry the message of freedom "to the ends of the world": "But ye shall receive power, after the Holy Ghost is come upon you: and ye shall be witnesses unto me both in Jerusalem, and in all Judea, and in Samaria, and unto the uttermost part of the earth".

It is Rashid's mentor, known to the reader from the novel's opening, who, although he himself cannot stand the sight of blood, spurs him into eulogizing the martyrs as a means to encourage all the comrades "who are sacrificing themselves":

> Your stomach turned at the sight of blood. Nonetheless you valued my piece highly and congratulated me on it, telling me that we were in need of precisely this sort of literature. This was revolutionary literature that told the truth in an artistic way, revealing and illuminating reality, and producing a deeper knowledge of it. This was literature committed to the interest of the masses, and to the path of history. It raised the morale of our comrades, so that they could confront death proudly. You said it was our duty as intellectuals to raise the morale of our comrades who were sacrificing themselves. This was the least we could do for them.

Martyrdom: death, image, and writing

Martyrdom as an act of writing either invites biting satire, as in Mahmoud Darwish's evocation of the new martyr posters plastered daily on the walls like a newspaper, or it reveals its own monstrous pretensions, as in Elias Khoury's novel *The White Faces*. Here the father of a "martyr" tries to scratch away the letters of his son's name on the poster because real death is oblivious to idealization and the son's demise means the factual end of a genealogy, since this particular branch of the family will now die out. The erasure of the name severs the tie forged in the "image and writing" ensemble that is the hallmark of the poster, and the poster thus loses its mythical powers of persuasion. In both cases, however, this is related only years after the fatal incident had taken place.

Another non-literary testimony of a spontaneous refusal to succumb to the martyr aura, the memoirs of Souha Bechara, a young Lebanese woman involved in the communist resistance, also dates from a later period. In 1988, aged twenty, Souha Bechara took responsibility for carrying out the mission of her political cell: to murder Antoine Lahad, the militia chief of Israeli-occupied southern Lebanon; an operation that meant almost certain death. On the eve of the assassination attempt, she simply cannot come to terms with the self-stylization as a martyr that is expected of her and is unable to complete the "document" testifying to her martyrdom. While willing to write the text of a "martyr testament", she finds it impossible to hand over the conventionally accompanying photograph; here the ensemble comprised of writing and image does not eventuate:

> With Rabih (Bechara's contact man, A.N.) I spent one of my last free nights. He gave me advice and support, and asked me to write a letter explaining my act. I wrote about the civil war, the Israeli invasion, and the death of our heroes. I expressed my admiration for the Palestinian intifada, which had just broken out in the Occupied Territories (...) During my last night at home, I burnt in secret my favorite photos of myself, fearing that they would be used by the Party for propaganda about the "martyrs" of the resistance. (...) This side of things exasperated me, and when Rabih told me the nom de guerre that the Party had chosen for me (...) I rudely cut him short.

The Party had decided that she was to enter the historical annals of the struggle under the name "Flower of the South".

Souha Bechara refuses to allow a myth to be created around her impending act of resistance, as this would deprive her of her secular identity. As mentioned, this act of defiance took place in 1988. In stark contrast, even the leftist revolutionaries rapturously embraced the first years of the war, and they were obviously not disinclined to see their acts of martyrdom as the "writing of history".

Such glorification of martyrdom as an act of writing has a long local tradition. Following an apocryphal word of the Prophet, on Judgment Day the blood of the martyrs and the ink of the scholars will be weighed up. Religious scholars have always been forced to plead that the bloodless writing of their scholarship be recognized as equally salutary as martyrdom, as seen in a text by the eighth-century Shiite Imam Ja'far al-Sadiq: "On the Day of Judgment the ink of the scholars and the blood of the martyrs will be weighed, and the scholars' ink will prove weightier." Radical Muslims of more recent times regard both the "scriptures" in ink and blood as necessary for sustaining the community. Abdallah Azzam, an agitator for the al-Qaida movement, speaks of a "dual writing in black and red", with which the history of the *umma* (religious community) needs to be codified. The eschatological dimension in the apocryphal word of the Prophet is here conspicuous by its absence – transcendence is no longer involved.

The reference to scripture made by the narrator Rashid, informed by Christian images, also transposes the prerogatives of power evident in the Biblical text from eschatology to the here and now. Although secular, the martyrs are sacralized and endowed with almost messianic powers. The same "modern" transposition of divinity, its transcription from the person of God, for whom the martyr sacrifices himself in the original religious context, to the person of the martyr himself is also to be found in the redemptive figure of the *fida'i* as portrayed by Mahmoud Darwish. Likewise marked by Biblical influences, unsurprising given Darwish's acculturation in Israel, this martyr figure, his body bearing bloody wounds, brings about a forging of remembrance, evoking the blood of Christ: he keeps the *al-jurh al-filastini* (mental wound of the collective body) bleeding and thus counters the "Biblical inscription of his land with Hebrew script" with a new "blood-script", one that inscribes the body of the collective while codifying the remembrance of Palestinian victimization and ensuring the continuity of their heroic endurance. To a certain extent, this is a revival of the paradigmatic shift from the Jewish orientation on scripture and writing to the Christian focus on sacrifice that took place in the same land in antiquity, this time in a secular context.

The same figure of the *fida'i* bears even more markedly Christ-like features in the work of the communist novelist Emile Habibi, who was born into a Protestant Palestinian family in Haifa. In *The Pessoptimist* (1974), Habibi reenacts scenes from the Christian Holy Scripture, such as Jesus's miraculous overcoming of the physical limits of time and place, and transforms suffering into triumph. Once again we encounter the same transposition of the transcendental aura to the here and now, only for the narrator to discard it when – like Rashid – he comes to see it merely as a mystifying illusion that is only temporarily uplifting.

Writing and martyrdom are even more tightly interlinked outside literature, for instance in the martyr statements which became so prevalent from 1982 onwards in Lebanon for operations where the chances of survival were slim. The aforementioned activist Souha Bechara only reluctantly and partially went along with this ceremonial practice. The valediction demanded from her was supposed to be read out to the public after her death, printed and if possible even broadcast on television. This latter aspect of a television presence needs to be elucidated briefly. During the civil war, in particular after the Israeli invasion of 1982, Lebanese television was basically reduced to a single channel, Télé Liban. The martyr statements were read out as part of the station's evening news program, and for this reason they left a lasting impression on the collective memory. According to Rabih Mroué, who has integrated martyr statements into his video art:

... back then, the majority of the Lebanese population saw these videos, which is why they are a singular element in the memory of every Lebanese person. The videos were rarely broadcast more than once – and in this, they seemed to resemble the finality of death itself.

The convention of these testaments may stem from the Iranian martyr fighters from the Iran–Iraq war; they were the first to leave behind written statements, in addition to wearing headbands inscribed with the word "martyr" and thus, as it were, themselves embodying the media for the martyrdom manifesto.

The simultaneity of truth and fiction in these martyr statements, whereby the "scribe" (or later the speaker on the video) is transformed into a public symbol of their collective while still alive, is visualized by Elias Khoury and Rabih Mroué in a video performance from 2000. The piece *Three Posters* reenacts the production of such a martyrdom statement video set in 1985. The same text is read out in three slightly different variations by the future martyr, thus posing the question as to the relationship between truth and media representation: when the martyr appears in front of the camera and the "decisive moment of martyrdom" is presented, the viewer still has the preceding presentation of the same scene in mind. Which one is true? And once this doubt is sown, where does truth cease and fiction, the fabrication of truth, begin?

Infused with a sense of pathos reminiscent of religious diction and articulated in a standard Arabic that is itself already ominously sacral, martyr testaments address the collective as recipients and beneficiaries of the sacrifice. In this way they also document how the God figure is supplanted by the "nation", a well-established practice since the rise of nationalist movements throughout the Middle East. All in all, further proof of how the act of sacrifice has become deprived of its transcendental reference point, and a pointed indicator of the ambivalence of martyrdom.

Authorial attempts at erasing the writing

By directing a reflective gaze on himself, Rashid's martyr analysis takes a course different from that of Khoury and Mroué, for it is this inward direction that identifies the ambivalence of martyrdom. He comes to see that his lapse resides in an attitude towards martyrdom that falls back on a religious model, in his verbal transfiguration of the fighter's death, which sends the actually secular agitators into a rapturous state, welding them into a ritual community reminiscent of its religious predecessors. What happens here is to some extent a reprise of the Pentecostal effusions of the illuminating Holy Spirit, an act presumptive of the divine:

Mr. Kawabata, we were drinking together in his house. Tears poured from his eyes and ran down his cheeks, when he read this last sentence: "Our buds envy our flowers." Then he repeated the words, and the eyes of everyone present filled with tears, and we were seized with a violent, pagan joy mingled with a thin mist of sorrow, and a volcanic desire to take our revenge for the comrades who had gone before us to martyrdom.

Words about death move them to tears, not of grief but of triumph. The group manipulates the death of others for the purpose of self-exaltation: the murder set in motion by the eulogy provides the murderer with new vitality. Rashid's own words tap into and unfurl this magical power. He cannot retract them, even when later, in his confession, he recognizes them as a delusion. But at least he can unmask them. He confronts them with a counter text, a litany of the mortifying suffering of the dead, stripped of all pathos, and thus reduces the eulogizing to an absurdity. What the martyrs' self-sacrifice is really about is shown by the inventory of the bestial procedures used to kill the fellow fighters;

> those comrades who had been tortured, those who had been abducted, those whose corpses had not been identified, those who had been murdered, those who had disappeared, and those whose limbs had been amputated as a lesson.

Here the religious text genre of the litany is reclaimed for the process of deconstructing religious pretensions. This dismantling of the myth enshrouding the martyr cult recalls the verses dedicated to a martyr written also in 1982 by Mahmoud Darwish:

> We are so far from him
> We goad him to lunge to his death
> And write polished words of obituary dedicated to him and modern
>   poetry
> And shed the sadness outside in the street café.
> We are so far from him
> At his funeral we ourselves embrace his murderer
> And steal the bandage from his wound
> To polish the medals for persistence and enduring the long wait.

Unlike the voice in the poem, who is resigned to the moral consequences of his action, Rashid believes himself to be personally accountable for the countless and nameless martyrs. He decides to address Kawabata, a dead writer who, like the martyrs, embraced death willingly, albeit soberly, not driven by rapturous words. Rashid confides: "Mr. Kawabata, I lie sleepless in this nightmare: what if the dead were to return – what should I say to them?" It is arguable whether this question has ever been formulated so clearly by any author who was actively embroiled in the war.

Martyrdom revisited
What is the *proton pseudos*: sacralized language or monstrous history?

The question posed by Rashid – "what should I say to them?" – simultaneously raises the linguistic problem key to the novel: one that he, unlike his writer colleagues, combines with the guilt issue in unparalleled clarity. Mahmoud Darwish is another who came to criticize his own work via a studious reflection on the language he had employed and its formative influence on the martyr cult (see chapter on Darwish in this volume for a detailed examination of this).

At this point, a brief look at the Israeli side may prove illuminating. In 1970 the dramatist and satirist Hanoch Levin aroused much attention with his satirical drama *Queen of the Bathtub*. In one frequently quoted poem from the piece, Levin shocks his readers with a new and subversive interpretation of (self-)sacrifice in war. Examining the causal conditionality of violent death in military conflict, he comes to negate any sacrificial dimension claimed to be involved. Whereas for Darwish the sacrificial dimension of martyrdom is traced in terms of language and poetry, Levin holds that not poetry but myth is involved in the sacralization of death in battle. It is Biblical myth, most prominently the martyrdom paradigm of the Aqedah, the binding of Isaac (Genesis 22:1–13), that lives on in Israeli society, converting the "casualty" into *victima*: the father of the young man going to war takes the role of Abraham, prepared to sacrifice his son. The new Abraham, however, will not be relieved of the command to carry out the sacrifice by a divine voice, but must complete the act. This is a transmutation of the Biblical scenario but one that again exemplifies the aforementioned transposition and elimination of the transcendental, which after the Nietzschean "death of God" has become prevalent even across cultural divides.

In Levin's critical view, it is the older generation, sustained by Biblical prerogatives, that is responsible for the death of the younger. Levin deconstructs the reconfiguration of Abraham and Isaac to expose the inopportunity of parental pride for the dead sons. One of the fallen says:

> Dear father, when you stand on my grave
> Old and tired and very lonely,
> And you see how they bury me in the ground,
> Don't be proud,
> But ask me to forgive you, father …

Levin takes up a figure of thought influential in Europe as well – the accusation brought against the father generation by the young war victims, denouncing this generation as "miscast Abraham figures". The British composer Benjamin Britten incorporated into his *War Requiem* dedicated to the victims of the Second World War (1962) a related but more daring rereading of the "Aqedah", a poem written by Wilfred Owen during the Great War:

> Then Abraham bound the youth with belts and straps,
> And built parapets and trenched there,
> And stretched forth the knife to slay his son.
> When lo! an angel called him out of heaven,
> Saying, Lay not thy hand upon the lad,
> Neither do anything to him. Behold,
> A ram, caught in a thicket by its horns;
> Offer the Ram of Pride instead of him.
> But the old man would not so, but slew his son
> And half the seed of Europe, one by one.

The perspective of these verses, which reads European history as a subversive counter-tradition to the norm-setting Biblical text, contrasts with those by Rashid and Darwish, where it is not a father generation that is held responsible but the demagogic words of contemporary intellectuals. History has turned into a monstrous nightmare; they are not concerned with reflecting on it to find the culprits. Since military operations in their case were not set in motion by the state, the tragic outcome could not be blamed on the older generation. The war started as a revolutionary movement, as Ken Seigneurie summarizes:

> The child's commitment to science and the militant's commitment to armed conflict in the name of scientific socialism spring from the same progressive conviction and end in the very same degradation that each had promised to eradicate.

What was needed, therefore, was a more protracted operation: the long overdue de-mythicization of language. Darwish's rethinking of his earlier language enabled him to extricate himself from the role thrust upon him by listeners and readers, of the "Palestinian martyr poet", which by 2002, with the second *intifada* and the emergence of the new martyr, the suicide bomber, had become intolerable.

For the Lebanese al-Daif, however, who feels grave personal culpability, the problem is more deep-seated. The martyr construction is merely the tip of the iceberg. The narrator reflects:

How is it that language writes itself through us? How is it that we are merely its vehicles? We worked for these convictions to the end. To the point of murder. Yes, to the point of murder! Which of us did not kill with his own hand, which of us did not kill with his tongue?

The "canonicity" of Arabic performs the preparatory work for its sacralization; the ambivalent martyr construction is only the culmination. Glorifying the martyrs expresses a flaw, seemingly inherent to Arab culture, which al-Daif perceives as the root of the modern crisis: the ubiquity of religious evocations and, concomitant to this, linguistic control mechanisms over social interaction, which turns Arabic into an ethical, normative medium. One could also say: the pretended immanence of the divine in social reality. With his infiltration into this very language that he tries to reflect anew, al-Daif contradicts and refutes the diagnosis formulated by the historian Dan Diner, who has claimed: "Classical Arabic lacks rootedness in the present. The classical language, *fusha*, (...) arrests time." Yet the intellectual dealings with the Arabic language that al-Daif and many others are involved in reveal that Diner's verdict can at best be taken formally as a premise in the argument about the present situation of the Arabic language, a premise that should be responded to by an antithesis: for it is first and foremost the project of a desacralization of the Arabic language that al-Daif and others are enthusiastically engaged in.

Dear Mr. Kawabata – a *Bildungsroman*?

Samira Aghacy has described *Dear Mr. Kawabata* as an inverted *Bildungsroman*. Unlike the typical heroes of this genre, who move from inwardness and marginality to social activity and commitment, after a promising education and intensive political commitment the novel's protagonist falls into loneliness and disorientation, his dedication to the socialist cause transforming into a nightmare of guilt. This reading of the novel, though suggestive in itself, leaves the question of how to explain the function of the addressee, Kawabata, unanswered. Ken Seigneurie has proposed a convincing solution to this dilemma: it is not solely the narrated material but the act of writing the novel itself that represents the educative process. The narrator schools his thinking and writing on Kawabata's strict expectations and develops from a speaker seduced by the metaphorical and palliative formulations of Arabic into someone sincere and meticulous, acutely aware of language.

Thanks to the triangulation with Kawabata and the reader, Rashid learns a few things about language and commitment that he did not learn by living through the events he recounted. Through Kawabata, the master artist of peerless rectitude, Rashid extends his youthful demystification of faith, clan and sect to the realm of language.

Beyond the catharsis the narrator undergoes, the tripolar relationship between narrator, addressee and reader enables the enlightenment of the reader, who also becomes aware of the pitfalls of his or her language. The novel therefore strives for and attains an ethical goal, one whose political significance cannot be underestimated. At the same time, the novel, which revolves around guilt on the one hand and the problematic of sacralized language on the other, sets the tone for the author's subsequent works, which orchestrate these dual themes anew.

Rashid al-Daif is perhaps the most distinctively "Lebanese" author amongst his writer colleagues. This is evident on the surface from the plots located in easily recognizable Lebanese settings. With his stories of rural life, al-Daif succeeds authors like Kahlil Gibran, Mikhail Naimy and Emily Nasrallah. But as present as Gibran and Naimy may be in his work, al-Daif has inverted their writing practice. Where they lament the disappearance of the idyllic paradise of rural Lebanon is precisely where al-Daif searches for the "gates to hell", the causes for the devastating civil war. He localizes the roots of the malady in the subliminal absurdities, the sacralizing of sexuality and language, which continue to inhibit the quest for happiness. Al-Daif's oeuvre roots out the blockades preventing secularized modernity; be they obsolete ethical principles, the deceptive tricks played by language, or the rapturous experiences evoked by illusions. All these were contributing factors to the developments plunging Lebanon into an infernal state of emergency for years. Rashid al-Daif is their contemporary witness.

WORKS

al-Mustabidd (The Tyrant), Beirut: Dar al-Ab'ad 1983

Fusha mustahdafa bayna l-nu'as wa-l-nawm (Passage to Dusk), Beirut: Dar Mukhtarat 1986

Ahl al-zill (Shadow Creatures), Beirut: Dar Mukhtarat 1987

Taqaniyat al-bu's (Techniques of Misery), Beirut: Dar Mukhtarat 1989

'Azizi l-Sayyid Kawabata (Dear Mr. Kawabata), Beirut: Dar Mukhtarat 1995

Nahiyat al-bara'a (This Side of Innocence), Beirut: Dar Masar 1997

Learning English, Beirut: Dar an-Nahar 1998

Tastafil Meryl Streep (To Hell with Meryl Streep), London: Riad El-Rayyes 2000

Insay al-sayyara (Forget the Car!), London: Riad El-Rayyes 2002

Ma'bad yanjah fi Baghdad (Ma'bad Succeeds in Baghdad), Beirut: Riad El-Rayyes 2005

'Awdat al-almani ila rushdihi (The Return of the German to His Senses), Beirut: Riad El-Rayyes 2006

Uki, ma' al-salama (O.K. Good-bye), Beirut: Riad El-Rayyes 2008

TRANSLATIONS

Dear Mr. Kawabata, trans. Paul Starkey, London: Quartet 1999

This Side of Innocence, trans. Paula Haydar, New York, Northampton: Interlink 2001
Passage to Dusk, trans. Nirvana Tanoukhi, Austin, TX: University of Texas Press 2001
Learning English, trans. Paula Haydar, Adnan Haydar, Northampton: Interlink 2007

FURTHER READING

Samira Aghacy: "Rachid El-Daif's 'An Exposed Space Between Drowsiness and Sleep': abortive representations", in: *Journal of Arabic Literature* 27 (1996), pp. 193–203

Samira Aghacy: "Addictive Interpretation in Rashîd al-Daif's *Learning English*", in: *Edebiyât* 10 (1999), pp. 219–42

Samira Aghacy: "The Use of Autobiography in Rashid al-Daif's 'Dear Mr Kawabata'", in: Robin Ostle, Ed de Roor, Stefan Wild (eds.) *Writing the Self. Autobiographical Writing in Modern Arabic Literature*, London: Saqi 1999, pp. 217–28

Maher Jarrar: "Sexuality, Fantasy and Violence in Lebanon's Postwar Novel", in: Samir Khalaf, John Gagnon (eds.), *Sexuality in the Arab World*, , London, San Francisco, Beirut: Saqi 2006, pp. 278–98

Andreas Pflitsch: "'The Importance of Being Earnest'. Anmerkungen zu einem Buch gewordenen Missverständnis zwischen Joachim Helfer und Rashid al-Daif", in: Georges Tamer (ed.) *Humor in der arabischen Kultur*, Berlin, New York: De Gruyter 2009, pp. 347–66

Ken Seigneurie: "The Importance of Being Kawabata: The Narratee in Today's Literature of Commitment", in: Andreas Pflitsch, Barbara Winckler (eds.), *Poetry's Voice – Society's Norms. Forms of Interaction Between Middle Eastern Writers and their Societies*, Wiesbaden: Reichert 2006, pp. 237–46

Paul Starkey: "Crisis and Memory in Rashid al-Daif's *Dear Mister Kawabata*: An Essay in Narrative Disorder", in: Ken Seigneurie (ed.), *Crisis and Memory. The Representation of Space in Modern Levantine Narrative*, Wiesbaden: Reichert 2003, pp. 115–30

OTHER WORKS CITED

Susanne Enderwitz: *Unsere Situation schuf unsere Erinnerungen. Palästinensische Autobiographien zwischen 1967 und 2000*, Wiesbaden: Reichert 2002

Sonallah Ibrahim: *al-Lajna*, Beirut: Dar al-Kalima 1981 (English translation: *The Committee*, trans. Mary St. Germain and Charlene Constable, Syracuse, NY: Syracuse University Press 2001)

Elias Khoury: *Mamlakat al-ghuraba'*, Beirut: Dar al-Adab, 1993 (English translation: *The Kingdom of Strangers*, trans. Paula Haydar, Fayetteville: University of Arkansas Press 1996)

William Kotzwinkle: *The Fan Man*, New York: Avon 1974

Joachim Negel: *Ambivalentes Opfer. Studien zur Symbolik, Dialektik und Aporetik ines theologischen Fundamentalbegriffs*, Paderborn: Schöningh 2005

Angelika Neuwirth: "Rashid al-Daif" in: *Kritisches Lexikon zur fremdsprachigen Gegenwartsliteratur*, Munich: Edition Text + Kritik, 2004

George Orwell: *Nineteen Eighty-four*, London: Secker & Warburg 1949

Memories for the Future:
Abdelrahman Munif

Susanne Enderwitz

In 1988 the Egyptian Naguib Mahfouz became the first and until now the only Arab writer to be awarded the Nobel Prize for Literature. Rumors had been rife for some time about possible nominations and chances, with many speculating that Abdelrahman Munif would emerge as the winner. They were, of course, to be disappointed. If Munif's name was still generally unknown in the West, for Arabic-speaking readers he was no longer some obscure figure known only to insiders. In any case, Mahfouz and Munif were generally regarded as the two "patriarchs" of twentieth-century Arabic literature, who had elevated the novel to the center stage of Arab literary life. Some commentators were even of the opinion that Munif's oeuvre and its popularity in the Arab world entitled him rather than Mahfouz to take the prize. One argument underlined the case for Munif: compared with the predominantly "Egyptian" Mahfouz, he would have been more of an "all-Arab" prizewinner.

Stations of a life

Born in 1933 in Amman, today the capital of Jordan, Abdelrahman Munif was the eighth child of his Saudi father and his Iraqi mother. At the time Saudi Arabia was a country of abject poverty; the petroleum boom, the beginnings of which Munif was to describe in a novel, was only getting started during this period. As it happened, the year of Munif's birth was also the year in which the Arab-American Oil Company (ARAMCO) was founded, the starting point for a massive restructuring of politics, economics and society.

Traditionally, young men were often forced to go abroad to earn enough to found and maintain a family. Yet this type of exodus was not comparable to the typical migrant fate nowadays. The nation states (Saudi Arabia, Iraq, Syria, Jordan, Lebanon, Kuwait, Oman, the Emirates and Palestine/Israel) were in their nascent phases and the mandate powers Great Britain and France ruled the region, so borders were extremely porous. As in preceding centuries, the cities of Jerusalem, Cairo, Damascus, Beirut and Baghdad were dominant, forming a network about which people and goods moved rather freely. Borders, nationality and passports only gradually became obstacles impeding freedom of movement. In an autobiographical abstract, half of which is a biographical abstract about his father, Munif gives a haunting sketch of his father's wandering in this period of tremendous upheaval between the downfall of the Ottoman Empire and the rise of nation states.

Originating from the Najd, the highland plateau lying in the center of the Arab peninsula, as a young man Munif senior joined a caravan that first took him to Iraq and Syria. No matter how intense his yearning for the Najd was, in later years his wanderlust would keep edging him from place to place. Becoming an established merchant, he travelled incessantly back and forth between Baghdad, Basra, and Damascus. Eventually the family, by this time rather extensive, settled in Amman, where Abdelrahman was born. Initially Amman was to be merely another temporary residence before a definitive return to the Najd, but preparations for the final move proved lengthy and troublesome. During the course of them the father became ill and died, and so the family remained in Amman.

Munif thus spent his childhood and youth in Amman, before this city became capital of the newly founded kingdom of Jordan in 1948. After attending Qu'ran, elementary and high school in Amman, in 1952 Munif decided to study petroleum economics in Baghdad. While Amman at this time could hardly be considered a metropolis, Baghdad was a vibrant cultural center and as Munif was to stress throughout his life, it played a pivotal role in broadening his horizons. Besides pursuing his studies and taking part in cultural life, he was attracted to politics and became involved in organizing the socialist-nationalist Ba'th Party, which after its founding in Syria in the 1940s had also positioned itself as the main opposition to the ruling monarchy in Iraq. His belief in the cause of Arab nationalism moved him to take part in a demonstration against the Baghdad Pact (1955), which, as a US initiative and in collaboration with Britain, foresaw the formation of an "anti-Bolshevist bastion" that would also include Iraq, Turkey, Iran and Pakistan.

Subsequently expelled from Iraq due to his political activities, Munif first went to Cairo to further his studies, before being awarded a scholarship by the Syrian Ba'th Party that enabled him to move to Belgrade in 1958 to complete his doctorate. Although he became estranged from the Ba'th Party over the years, like so many Arab intellectuals of his generation he would remain loyal to another early orientation point; in his case an attachment to Eastern Europe. A cosmopolite, he nonetheless maintained a certain distance from the West and its economic liberalism. Politically he remained an Arab nationalist with socialist leanings, but his basic humanitarianism induced him to search for aesthetic forms of expression.

After obtaining his doctorate in 1961, Munif first worked as an economist specializing in the petroleum business in Syria, Iraq, and the Gulf region, was active as a consultant to the Organization of the Petroleum Exporting Countries (OPEC), and edited a trade journal for the petroleum industry. Ten years later he spent some time in Beirut, where, influenced by his journalistic activities, he increasingly turned his attention to writing. He was stationed in Baghdad from

1975 to 1981, then in Paris from 1981 to 1986, before he and his family finally settled permanently in Damascus. Running like a golden thread through his life, this restless wandering was partly due to external circumstances and partly due to his own inclinations. An unrelenting critic of oligarchic, corrupt and incompetent Arab regimes, he frequently fell foul of the ruling political elites. Several times he was declared, temporarily at least, a *persona non grata*, and a change of residency also entailed a change of nationality. In Saudi Arabia, the authorities rescinded his citizenship rights as early as 1963. Whenever he spoke about his life, however, he tended to focus less on these forced moves, emphasizing instead those journeys he undertook of his own accord. Besides most Arab countries, he also travelled through Europe, the Soviet Union, the US, Canada, and Japan, at times combining his journeys with prolonged stays.

When Munif died of heart failure in Damascus in 2004, he was working on a book about Iraq, the country's plight under the American occupation proving a source of great anguish. His death triggered strong reactions from Arab intellectuals and artists, who underlined his significance as a contemporary writer. This acclaim was not restricted to the Arab world; Munif's work has been translated into ten languages. Nonetheless, he was most famous in the Arab world, where he was awarded numerous literary prizes.

Narrative as awakening

Abdelrahman Munif was a late starter as a writer: he did not make his debut until he was forty, and only made writing his main vocation in 1981. Thereafter, throughout the 1980s, he worked on his magnum opus, the pentalogy *Cities of Salt*, which is about the fate of a desert community during the petroleum boom.

Following the June War of 1967, faced with disquieting developments in the regimes of Syria, Iraq and elsewhere, Munif saw his hopes fading away and he gradually withdrew from active political life. He now turned to writing novels, convinced that this was where his true vocation lay, firmly believing that it would continually lead him to new shores and enable him to contribute to a more humane, freer, and fairer world. Munif's faith in the power of literature was boundless, and he had reason for this unshakable conviction. Censorship was a crucial aspect: literature accrues far greater responsibility in countries where censorship is the norm than in societies enjoying full freedom of the press. Firmly convinced that the aim of literature resides in preparing the way for something new, Munif regarded it as a particularly effective means to initiate change: "While theater and film require capital and facilities which can be easily controlled by the state, the novel leads a life of its own once it has been printed." Like Naguib Mahfouz several years before him, Munif compared the task of contemporary Arabic literature to that of European literature in spreading new ideas in the late nineteenth and early twentieth century.

With this orientation on the classical European novel Munif turned away from the *littérature engagée,* which had dominated Arabic literature in the 1950s and 1960s, promoting the propensity to portray exemplary heroes holding socialist aspirations. The 1970s witnessed a turnaround in orientation, which ended with the emergence of the "new sensibility". The once-dominant realism, activism, and pathos were now supplanted by a focus on the individual in whose "stream of consciousness" reality hallucinations and dreams commingled. Munif did not go as far as to follow the radical subjectivism of this current. This move must have seemed to him like a form of escapism; he was less interested in the inner life of the individual than in the inner life of the society this individual lived in. But he also defended his aesthetic credo of paying careful attention to the divergent facets of everyday life, for which the dogmatic "revolutionaries", seeing in them nothing but worthless details, invariably had nothing but contempt.

Even though critics reproached Munif for having betrayed his political beliefs with and in his writing, he steadfastly adhered to the path he had embarked on. He once remarked that in the novel he had sought and found a means other than politics for communicating possibilities, ideas, and visions. At the same time, he continued, he was well aware that every type of work requires its own tools, and for this reason his novels are not conceived as political manifestos. Nevertheless, Munif remained a political writer throughout his life. This is patently manifest in his wide-ranging essays on political issues, works on contemporary artists, and newspaper and journal articles on the events of everyday political life. He repeatedly declared his solidarity with the Palestinians, and he objected to the process of uniformity gripping world culture; both without ever slipping into the virulent tones of cultural struggle. Although he was anything but a supporter of Saddam Hussein, he condemned US political strategy, which he considered to be a revenant of imperialism. The political writer also came to the fore when he compared the the role of the writer to that of the *fida'i* (freedom fighter), with the book as weapon. Finally, the subject matter also demonstrates Munif to be a political writer, for his novels invariably included a political dimension: individual freedom versus state repression; participation in the political process versus autocratic regimes; and a just distribution of wealth on an international basis versus imperialistic greed.

The June War had painfully revealed to the Arab world that Arab nationalism had not managed to achieve a unity strong enough to prevail against Israel and the West. The years immediately following defeat indicated that the causes of the defeat lay not in the strength of Israel and the West but within the Arab societies, where forces were at work that counteracted modernity and progression towards an enlightened society. This is the thematic Munif addressed in his early works, written throughout the 1970s. Besides a few other books, the following novels were published at roughly two-year intervals: *The Trees and the Assassination of Marzuq* (1973), *East of the Mediterranean* (1975) and *Endings* (1978). With their nightmarish scenarios, Munif's early novels are not entertainment in the generally accepted sense. Like other Arab writers, he found it difficult to bear the burden of responsibility that is accorded to literature *nolens volens* under conditions of political repression; at the same time, though, he was careful to avoid the paternalism of which Arab literature is often accused. The reader should always be mindful of the fictitious nature of the plot, and so develop a sense of the alternatives to existing reality. But even within the framework of the story, Munif refrained from taking his readers by the hand. In their dreadful situations his heroes therefore lead a complex life of their own, albeit without ever emerging victorious.

The title *East of the Mediterranean* is programmatic. East of the Mediterranean is confrontation with a bitter reality when one is an intellectual striving for freedom who must deal with state power. East of the Mediterranean human life is cheap, worth less than a cigarette butt. East of the Mediterranean there is no difference between a life within or outside prison walls. In this situation the prison guards are in no better a position than the prisoners: everyone – the ruling powers, intellectuals, the people – is entrapped in their roles within the same murderous system. No single specific Arab country is a prison in the sense of repression, compulsion, and violence, but rather the whole Arab region represents a system of interacting prisons.

Thanks to his intimate knowledge of a host of Arab countries Munif was able to evoke a tangible scenario in his novels; more precisely, a tangibly menacing scenario which conveyed the impression to his entire Arab readership, irrespective of nationality, that he was addressing them as individuals in their traditional milieus within their own countries. It is one of Munif's artful skills, by means of the setting, the language of the protagonists, and the description of place, to transcend the divide separating the respective national literatures. The fictitious settings usually recall real places, the fictitious countries real states, and yet the plot could be playing out in any Arab city in any Arab country, and the fates portrayed could befall any Arab family. But even more than the configuration of the settings, it is Munif's language which responds and appeals to readers throughout the Arab world. The issue of diglossia, the co-existence of standard language with dialect, has accompanied modern Arab fiction since its beginnings. It was precisely the pioneers of modern literature, writers like Taha Husayn, Tawfik al-Hakim and Naguib Mahfouz, who paraded a marked purism, although this was not a dispensation from deferring to the vernacular (Egyptian in all of these cases) at least in dialogue. Munif solved the problem in his own way: he also employed Standard Arabic for the narrative passages of his works, but in a style instinctively familiar to Arab readers, which he called an "intermediate language", while he fashioned the dialogues to fit the respective dialect and at times even tribal dialects. Munif took the dichotomy between Standard Arabic and dialect extremely seriously. He believed that this dichotomy harbors a grave problem, for the educated and the "people" speak different languages, between which there is no interaction and no translation. In his view this problem could only be solved through a fundamental reform of Arabic, one that would be tantamount to a gradual simplification of the grammar and syntax of Standard Arabic, achieved by a phased approximation of written Arabic to the dialects.

The third of the aforementioned works, *Endings*, represents a significant shift in theme, perspective, and narrative techniques, bringing ecological concerns into play, putting the community at the center of attention, and reverting to the Arab tradition of storytelling. The novel is set in a small desert settlement, its hero an outsider called Assaf who, contrary to his own beliefs but to earn a living, helps city dwellers seeking amusement to hunt birds. After Assaf loses his life during a hunt, the locals and guests gather to hold a mourning ritual, where one by one they recite poetry, reminisce, or tell (animal) stories. The dichotomy between two effectively unconnected parts, the narrative and its stories, is something that Munif would first overcome in his following and most important work.

Despite this rupture in form, with its focus on the desert and the community as well as its recourse to traditional storytelling, *Endings* anticipates *Cities of Salt*. The story begins in the 1930s as Americans searching for oil come into contact with the desert communities of Saudi Arabia for the first time. A leap in time catapults us into the 1950s and a brand new petroleum town, where adventurers from across the globe exploit the inexperience of a young tribe leader to remodel the local tribal values to fit a capitalist system. Rivalries between the tribes break out, and the local ruler emerges victorious. This character is obviously modelled on King Abdul Aziz ibn Saud, the founder of the dynasty that has ruled down to the present day.

Asked why he had titled his novel cycle *Cities of Salt* and not "Cities of Oil" even though he describes the changes and upheavals in Saudi Arabia resulting from the discovery and exploitation of oil, Munif answered:

> Cities of salt means cities that offer no sustainable existence. When the waters come in, the first waves will dissolve the salt and reduce these great glass cities to dust. In antiquity, as you know, many cities simply disappeared. It is possible to foresee the downfall of cities that are inhuman; with no means of livelihood they won't survive. Look at us now and see how the West sees us. The twentieth century is almost over, but when the West looks at us, all they see is oil and petrodollars. Saudi Arabia is still without a constitution; the

people are deprived of elementary rights. Women are treated like third-class citizens. Such a situation produces a desperate citizenry, without a sense of dignity or belongings.

It is above all the first volume of *Cities of Salt* that reverberates in this remark: it portrays the inhabitants of the desert and, in the most pointed contrast within the book, their confrontation with the Americans, who arrive via the sea, consider water to be their element, and tend to vanish again via the sea.

The very first location, where the storyline is laid and which may be read as a prologue for the whole cycle, is Wadi al-Uyun, the "valley of the water springs" in the eastern region of the Arab Peninsula. As remote as it may be, it is still important as a resting place for caravans and thus provides its inhabitants with the means to earn a living: the older people by trading with the travelers, the younger as a steppingstone for migration (as Munif's father once did). One day Americans enter the village, where, invoking the backing of the tribe leader, they begin to study flora and fauna, ask the locals about their customs, and jot down details in their notebooks. They cart in construction machinery, floodlights, and caterpillar trucks, prompting the villagers to wonder and speculate, but only one character foresees the danger: the levelling of the village.

The second location is on the coast, where out of nothing a seaport is to be built overnight and some of the inhabitants from the obliterated village of Wadi al-Uyun find work. The topography of this conglomerate is described vividly and contradicts any notion of an organically evolved town: the Americans settle on one hillside, the local notables on the other; in between lies the original Arab village, and a cheerless housing estate for the workers is being built on the outskirts. This new town serves the author as a means to describe how life unfolds in the new petro-cities, as well as the culture shock people used to life in the desert are exposed to when suddenly confronted with modern technology and laxer morals.

Overwhelmed and left alone with their new fate, they attempt to digest this shock by lending their experiences fantastic, miraculous, or even mythical traits. A group of intermediaries establishes itself between the unsophisticated workers and the Americans and they profit from the situation; however, numerous and sometimes murderous conflicts soon arise between and within the various groups, spawned by cultural misunderstandings and manifest class interests. The tribal leader, out of his depth and increasingly confused, is no longer able to settle disputes. Instead it is the police chief who actually wields power over the locals, and acting in the interests of the oil company he orders the quelling of a riot during an industrial dispute. Although the story has no happy ending, it is not completely hopeless either: a semblance of reconciliation is attained when thirty workers dismissed by the company are reemployed, even though, as another twist, the company refuses to assume responsibility for the victims of the clampdown.

The English translation of the first three volumes meant that *Cities of Salt* was reviewed relatively soon in the US, albeit with mixed success. Francine Prose euphorically compared the novel to a translation of the Victorian novel into Arab calligraphy, even going so far as to see in it a re-narration of *The Thousand and One Nights* by Stendhal. This somewhat exalted effort to incorporate Arab literature into the Western canon led to a diametrically opposite appraisal at the other end of the spectrum. A querulous John Updike remarked that the author had all too obviously failed to appropriate Western narrative strategies, producing a work that was neither fish nor fowl. Updike, patently targeting Munif's dissolution of the chronological plot, the omniscient narrator and realistic depiction, must have been well aware that in the West, too, the postmodern novel displays precisely these characteristics in its adoption of post-colonial narrative styles. It would therefore seem that it was perhaps the portrayal of the Americans which annoyed Updike, a portrayal that reveals elements of an inverted "Orientalism", with the Americans appearing in the eyes of the locals as a curiously interesting, incomprehensible, and profoundly slow-witted exotic species. At the same time, though, Munif captures the seriousness of the looming upheavals, gradually letting his local protagonists recede into the background and become increasingly "absent", as in a colonial novel. The meaning behind the proliferating signs (surveying markers, pipes and machinery) remains obscure, while increasingly frequently their own undertakings come to nothing and the power of effective action is transferred to the foreigners.

Munif enjoys an excellent reputation amongst Arab literary critics and, above all, the Arab reading public. He possesses a detailed a knowledge of the facts, he is aware of cultural differences, he strikes the right tone, he criticizes economic globalization, and he castigates despotic rulers – enough reasons to guarantee him a cult status cutting across the usual boundaries of national literatures. But through these aspects Munif's fame in the public perception feeds mainly on his role as a dissident, as a critic of imperialism, politics, and society. Edward Said, a great admirer of Munif, praised *Cities of Salt* as "the only serious work of fiction that tries to show the effect of oil, Americans, and the local oligarchy on a Gulf country." The Arab regimes shared his view, and Munif's work was censored in Saudi Arabia, the Gulf States and even to some extent in Egypt. But as Munif himself pointed out in an interview, it was the least of his intentions, from *Cities of Salt* onwards, to pursue a simple realism: "The reason for writing this novel was not that it was intended to voice social criticism. In the societies around the gulf there is far more corruption than what's being shown in the book. If anything, the issue of social and political corruption is being treated with kid gloves."

Reflection and identity

The novel is originally a European genre, and that authors from countries of the south often write for the Western book market is evident in the increasing prevalence of English as the original language. Not so Munif, who had the Arab public in mind from the very beginning; besides Western literature, he closely studied Latin American and Japanese literature for stimulating ideas in his search for an original Arab form of expression. Munif was not the only writer to embark on such a search; other Arab writers drew on the Arab "legacy" in the form of literary traditions and employed them to create aesthetic, political, or historical authenticity, to give expression to political and aesthetic resistance, or to substantiate a "counter narrative". The last is the case for Munif's approach; he contrasted the view from outside (foreign observers) or above (the official discourse) with his version from within.

The view from the inside means for Munif dispensing with the omniscient narrator and with him the central plot strand. In his works the action skips from one time level to another, reality merges into fiction (employing elements of magical realism characteristic of Latin American literature), and the "novel" reveals similarities with collections of stories, anecdotes, and even fables from the Arab storytelling tradition. In a similar way, he dispenses with an ever-present hero who holds together the plot as protagonist, central figure, and witness. His protagonists come and go; sometimes their function is passed on to a similar figure, at other times persons simply vanish quietly, leaving behind loose ends in the plot. This generates the impression of an arabesque. For Munif, how a community thinks and acts is more important than individualism, and therefore the interpretative frame of the story gleaned from the indigenous oral tradition is accorded an equally important role as the "objective" account through which the narrator – using both ironic and folkloristic styles – keeps moving the story forward, despite the aforementioned qualifying constraints.

Paradoxically, the recourse to traditional narratives – disrupting the story thread, the multitude of characters, and the paradigms of interpretation – generates effects characteristic of postmodern literature. This insight is not new: it has often been pointed out that the narrative techniques of *The Thousand and One Nights* and other works from the Arab tradition share a structural similarity with postmodernist narrative strategies, most prominently fragmentation and polyphony as well as a resemblance to fables. For his part, Munif, with his extensive knowledge of both traditions, consciously plays with and utilizes this effect, which becomes most clearly manifest in his approach to history. Writing a historically informed story as an "antidote" to official historiography, as a *tertium datur* (third alternative) to the respective views of the West and the Arab rulers, is probably the strongest motive behind *Cities of Salt*. Understood in this light, employing the novel form as a "counter historical writing" no longer needs to serve an overriding purpose, or function as a vehicle for criticizing imperialism, social grievances, and ideology: it represents a commitment in itself and requires no other form. Munif's basic conviction is that historical writing is always contingent (fictive) and inevitably becomes increasingly mendacious the more authoritatively it is espoused. From now on Munif takes to the extreme the insight that truth depends on the observer's viewpoint by substituting the fictions of historical assertions with the fictions of the writer's imagination. Thereby he follows a postulate of European modernism, according to which literary fiction often comes far closer to grasping and conveying the truth than attempts to document historical reality.

Munif generates his postmodernist appeal in the tradition of European modernism by employing a traditional method that dates back to the early period of Arab-Islamic historiography and originally arose from the codification of the Prophetic tradition: the equal status of divergent, in part rivaling versions of one and the same situation, whereby their in- or exclusion depends solely on the credibility of the transmitter. In his novel cycle he employs this method in the exact sense of its original usage, for instance to recount, or let his protagonists recount, the commencement and progress of a battle in different versions. In contrast to the earlier compilers, as a writer Munif is also a creator and so he intervenes with commentaries, queries, and opinions on the credentials of the witnesses and rapporteurs. Bearing witness to the truth as such remains: history may not be permitted to be solely at the command and disposal of a sovereign power; it can only be pieced together like a patchwork quilt. At the same time, history must be compiled like this patchwork quilt if it is to perform its task of forging identity. In the end all these patchwork quilts resemble one another, but no two are exactly alike.

Munif was not fanatical about the past; Bedouin romanticism was as far from his interests as the pureness of the "heritage". His lament that the Arabs were insufficiently concerned with their history, in particular recent history, had nothing to do with nostalgic sentimentality for a lost ideal world. On the contrary: he criticized the prevailing mentality of Arab society, which remained yoked to thinking in terms of clans and continued to be abused by the kleptocracy of the ruling political class. His concerns stemmed more from his insights into the connections between historical knowledge, cultural identity, and personal as well as collective stability. If the present and our visions of the future structure our notions of the past, then conversely the past constitutes the present and future of a community, a people, or a nation.

From its beginnings, Arab-Islamic history has essentially been a history of cities. Consequently, Munif not only lamented the general lack of historical awareness amongst the Arabs, but in particular the lack of modern city biographies. He redressed this with his own (auto)biography in 1994 with *Story of a City: A Childhood in Amman*. Amman as he remembers it is the very antithesis of a "city of salt", an intimate, lively, colorful city, interacting with the surrounding countryside and at the same ready to welcome newcomers.

> Whenever in the forties a tourist came to Amman – which happened frequently – his first impression was that of a continuous carnival of dialects and customs. For instance, there was a turn-off from Mango Street where – at least twice daily, before noon and before sunset – elderly women from Fuhais used to place their water pipes which were over three feet in height ... At the same turn-off there was a tiny English school, which was run by two sisters, Miss Alice and Miss Margot, who both wore state-of-the-art European dresses. Not far away from the school and the water pipes, in both directions, you noticed these high Cherkessian fur caps and you could hear a wide variety of dialects ... But in actual fact the markets, and most of all the vegetable market, were the meeting places. And as the town of Amman and its population were fairly small, most – or nearly all – the people knew each other, or had at least met on numerous occasions.

A lack of democratic participation and a language everyone could comprehend, along with the prevailing historical amnesia: Munif considered these, when taken together, to be the key reasons for the increasing estrangement of the Arabs – and paradigmatically, Saudi Arabians – from their roots, which would in turn crucially curtail their prospects for the future. He often voiced criticism about the spineless – because it lacked identity and thus direction – perverting of the Arab virtues that were rooted in Bedouin society: nepotism instead of family solidarity; a spendthrift spirit instead of generosity; self-seeking instead of pride. He was therefore not that surprised when it emerged that most of the 9/11 assassins were originally from Saudi Arabia. In retrospect, he had already traced the beginnings of their nihilistic fury twenty years earlier, as he described the impoverishment of a Saudi culture overshadowed by the opulent wealth of the ruling dynasty and its entourage.

SELECTED WORKS

al-Ashjar wa-ightiyal Marzuq (The Trees and the Assassination of Marzuq), Beirut: Dar al-'Awda 1973

Sharq al-mutawassit (East of the Mediterranean), Beirut: Dar al-Tali'a 1975

al-Nihayat (Endings), Beirut: Dar al-Adab 1978

Mudun al-milh (Cities of Salt), Beirut: al-Mu'assassa al-'Arabiyya li-l-Dirasat wa-l-Nashr
1984–89

Sirat madina. 'Amman fi l-arba'inat (Story of a City. A Childhood in Amman), Beirut:
al-Mu'assassa al-'Arabiyya li-l-Dirasat wa-l-Nashr 1994

TRANSLATIONS

Cities of Salt, trans. Peter Theroux, New York: Vintage 1987

The Trench, trans. Peter Theroux, New York: Vintage 1993

Variations on Night and Day, trans. Peter Theroux, New York: Vintage 1994

Endings, trans. Roger Allen, London: Quartet 1988

Story of a City. A Childhood in Amman, trans. Samira Kawar, London: Quartet 1996

FURTHER READING

M.M. Badawi: "Two Novelists from Iraq: Jabra and Munif", in: *Journal of Arabic Literature*
23 (1992), 140–54

Issa J. Boullata: "Social Change in Munif's *Cities of Salt*", in: *Edebiyat* 8 (1998), pp.
191–216

Miriam Cooke: "Living in Truth", in: Kamal Abdel-Malek, Wael Hallaq (eds.), *Tradition, Modernity, and Postmodernity in Arabic Literature*, Leiden et al.: Brill 2000, pp.
203–21

Rashid al-Enany: "Cities of Salt. A Literary View of the Theme of Oil and Change in the
Gulf", in: Ian Richard Netton (ed.), *Arabia and the Gulf. From Traditional Society to
Modern States*, London: Croom Helm 1986, pp. 213–22

Interview with Abdelrahman Munif compiled by Samuel Shimon, with comment, review
and analysis from Peter Theroux, Peter Clark & Faisal Darraj, in: *Banipal* 3 (1998), pp.
8–15

Richard van Leeuwen: "Cars in the Desert: Ibrahim al-Kawni, Abd al-Rahman Munif and
André Citroën", in: *Oriente moderno* 16/17 (1997/98), pp. 59–72

Heidi Toëlle: "Individu et pouvoirs dans *Sharq al-mutawassit*", in: *Naqd* 11 (1998), pp.
143–60

OTHER WORKS CITED

Francine Prose: "Sinbad in a White Rolls-Royce," in: *New York Times*, October 27, 1991

Authenticity as Counter-Strategy:
Fighting Sadat's "Open Door" Politics
Gamal al-Ghitani and *The Epistle of Insights into the Destinies*

Stephan Guth

Time and the changes it brings about; the fragility of life and its transitoriness; destiny: these are themes central to the literary production of Gamal al-Ghitani, one of the most prominent and prolific writers of contemporary Egyptian fiction. The author's preoccupation with these fundamental questions of human existence comes as no surprise, however, when one considers his biography. Like so many of his generation who grew up in the heyday of Nasserism, al-Ghitani's life bears the imprint of upheaval and radical change. The formative phases of his life have coincided with decisive moments in Egypt's postwar history.

Early youth

The author, who lives today in the metropolis of Cairo with its fifteen million residents, was born on 9 May 1945, the day after the war ended in Europe, in a period characterized by dramatic changes to Egyptian society. The creation of new and growth of old branches of industry during the war had accelerated labor migration from the countryside to the large cities, the population of Cairo increasing by nearly two-thirds within a few years. Al-Ghitani's family was among the migrants who hoped to benefit from employment opportunities in the booming capital. While Gamal was born far from Cairo and spent his earliest years in a village in Upper Egypt, at the beginning of the 1950s he was sent to the giant metropolis to start school. The family settled in the old city district of al-Gamaliyya.

Schooldays during the Nasser era

It was precisely at this time, in 1952, that Egypt's old regime was overthrown by a coup d'état launched by the Free Officers. Implementing fundamental changes, they abolished the monarchy and the antiquated feudal system, finally stepped out of the shadow cast by the continuing influence of the former colonial master Britain, and sought in a variety of ways to bring genuine independence and autonomy to the country whilst raising the living standards of the masses. Having grown up in near poverty, al-Ghitani belonged to those benefiting from the welfare state propagated by President Nasser, his young life running parallel to the early years of the Egyptian Revolution and the new republican Egypt. A "child of the revolution", he was raised in an atmosphere marked by its noble ideals, élan, enthusiasm for progress and unswerving belief in a better future. Thanks to his parents' self-sacrifice and support, after completing grade school he began vocational training in carpet design and tapestry, graduating with a diploma in 1962; this would have been almost impossible for a boy of his background in pre-republican Egypt.

The system in crisis – new personal horizons

For al-Ghitani's generation, the years of adolescence so important to the formation of personal character – and in which initial attempts at writing might take place – coincided with signs that the edifice of Nasserist ideology and "Arab socialism" was fragmenting. Doubts rose steadily as to the true nature of the system, so much so that for al-Ghitani and many of his contemporaries, puberty soon metamorphosed into a period of revolt against the grand "father figure" Nasser. At the same time as al-Ghitani began to work in his chosen trade (it was 1963: he had just turned eighteen, the Revolution was in its tenth year), his first texts were published. They soon aroused the suspicion of state authorities. It was not long before the young author was arrested along with numerous other critics of the government on the grounds of dissent. Accused of being a member of an illegal Marxist group, he was detained in a camp for six months between October 1966 and March 1967. Following his release, he was for a time secretary of the Arts & Crafts Guild in the old-city quarter of Khan al-Khalili. But his experiences in the detention camp; the Israeli defeat of Arab forces in the June War of 1967; and, in consequence, the final collapse of Nasserism along with all it symbolized; seem to have triggered a decisive shift in young al-Ghitani's life.

Moving away from arts and crafts, he now concentrated exclusively on his writing. It is certainly no coincidence that the first novel he published – *Zayni Barakat* (1974) – focuses on the work of spies and informers in a repressive surveillance state. In 1969, he began to work for the largest Egyptian daily, *al-Akhbar*; he has been employed there, or in publishing houses belonging to the same group, ever since. In 1985 he was appointed editor-in-chief of the feuilleton office, whence he became involved with the *Akhbar al-yawm* publishing house, editing the influential paperback series *Kitab al-yawm*, which occasionally features studies and commentaries on current political and social issues and serves as an important steppingstone in the literary career of young authors. Since 1993 al-Ghitani has been editor of the much respected literary journal *Akhbar al-adab* (Cultural News).

Al-Ghitani and the war

During his first four years at *al-Akhbar* al-Ghitani worked as a war correspondent, covering the so-called war of attrition. In the October War of 1973 as Egyptian forces launched a surprise attack against the Israeli Army, crossed the Suez Canal, and recaptured Israeli-occupied Sinai, which went some way towards making up for the humiliation of the June War, al-Ghitani reported directly from the frontline. His experiences would leave as lasting an impression as the Nasser era, later finding their way into a number of stories. In 1974 he published a non-fiction book, *The Egyptians and the War: from the June Shock to the October Awakening*, followed in 1975 by *The Guardians of the Eastern Gate*, a study of the Iraqi army. Two decades later, he initiated a short-story competition in *Akhbar al-yawm* devoted to the theme of war.

Egypt's Westernization – seeking authenticity in writing

Just as al-Ghitani's first days at school coincided with the Revolution, so was his turn to journalism and writing virtually contemporaneous with another decisive caesura in Egypt's history. In 1970 Anwar al-Sadat, previously vice-president, took office as president of the republic following the death of Nasser. After the 1967 defeat, Nasser had begun to alter his political course, hardly noticed by the majority of Egyptians because the slogans circulating in official discourse generally remained the same. Sadat was bolder. Once he had secured the support of the military in the wake of the successes achieved in the October War of 1973, he changed tack completely and distanced himself openly from the ideals of his predecessor.

Al-Ghitani's decisive breakthrough as a writer, with the novel *Zayni Barakat,* came at around the same time as the first consequences of Sadat's politics of *infitah* (opening) towards the West and foreign investors were being felt. The devastating impact of this primarily economic liberalization, continued in principle after Sadat's assassination in 1981 by his successor Hosni Mubarak, would occupy al-Ghitani and many others in the coming years. He gives his first evaluation of the situation in *al-Ghitani's Topography* (1981), a work whose Arabic title, *Khitat al-Ghitani*, alludes to the *Khitat al-Maqrizi*, a historico-topographical description of Egyptian cities by the medieval scholar Taqi al-Din Ahmad al-Maqrizi (1364–1442). The creative adaptation of historical styles of writing and their narrative integration is typical of al-Ghitani's approach. In his first small collection of stories, *The Papers of a Young Man Who Lived a Thousand Years Ago* (1969), he had employed this historicizing style; it soon became the "signature feature" of his literary work, particularly after the success of *Zayni Barakat*. While in the latter work he borrowed extensively from the chronicler Ibn Iyas (1448–1524), who had described the decline of the Mamluk

Empire in Egypt, for the three volumes of *The Book of Revelations* (1983–87), which continue and deepen his explorations into the Sadat era, he entered into a dialogue with the philosopher and mystic Ibn al-'Arabi (1165–1240). He makes use of a similar style in his *Epistle of Insights into the Destinies* (1989); I shall take this work as a model for examining how his writing technique functions and the purposes it seeks to fulfill.

Al-Ghitani and Cairo

That the author seeks to tap into the literary heritage of classical Arabic writing must partly be due to the fact that he has since childhood been more conversant with older Arab cultural traditions than the large majority of his compatriots. This is founded in his locality: al-Ghitani grew up neither in the new Cairo based on Western models built during the colonial period, nor in the anonymous residential blocks of Nasser's social-welfare state; his milieus were first the countryside and then old Cairo, where the pre-colonial heritage of the Egyptian-Arab tradition is a striking visual presence. Nowhere else in Cairo, or indeed in Egypt, are so many mosques, madrasas, fountains, or mausoleums from this heritage concentrated in one place; nowhere – despite the ravages of time – has the character of a former "Oriental" city of narrow alleys and dead-ends been so well preserved as here, where traditional crafts are still practiced and cultivated. His deep roots in the old city and his love of pre-colonial Arab-Islamic civilization and culture are documented in his non-fiction books, as well as in his novels and short stories. Testimony to this are the volume of essays devoted to the history of Cairo, *The Sights of Cairo Through a Thousand Years* (1983), published to mark the thousandth anniversary of the founding of the old city (today known as "Islamic Cairo") by the Fatimid dynasty, and his *Cairenica* (on the fountains of Cairo), the first volume of which appeared in 1984.

Al-Ghitani and Naguib Mahfouz

Al-Ghitani shares his love of the old city with the outstanding figure of early postwar Egyptian literature, Naguib Mahfouz. Forging a friendship that would last decades, in 1980 al-Ghitani edited and published his conversations with Mahfouz under the title *Naguib Mahfouz Remembers*; more recently, he worked in collaboration with the photographer Britta Le Va to produce *The Cairo of Naguib Mahfouz* (2000). Both writers have a vital interest in politics, a penchant for close observation and the minute description of details, and a sensibility for the alterations in human behavior in times of change. It is with good reason that some critics consider al-Ghitani to be the genuine literary heir of Egypt's Nobel laureate.

The Epistle of Insight into the Destinies – context

The spirit of Mahfouz is also tangible in *The Epistle of Insight into the Destinies* (1989), although in its literary form this work is very different from a Mahfouz novel. Here Gamal al-Ghitani addresses a problematic that had appeared solved under Nasser but which reemerged with Sadat's open-door politics: the increasing dominance of the West and everything Western. First relevant in the colonial period, this issue has once more become pivotal, giving rise to a series of dilemmas: How can Arab culture assert itself against such dominance? How can Arab identity be maintained? Which traits of this culture and identity are capable of countering a modernity which is relentlessly destroying them?

In Egypt (but not only there), these questions, which first became virulent again after the defeat in the June War, were exacerbated through the 1970s and 1980s by the repercussions of Anwar al-Sadat's opening to the West. From the mid-1970s onwards, Sadat reversed the coordinates of his predecessor, performing a *volte-face* that broke with Nasser's fundamental principles. Two changes in tack represent the main thrust of the Sadat era: the accords signed at Camp David with the archenemy Israel; and economic liberalization with all its far-reaching impacts, in particular its radical upheaval of the social order.

Western and Gulf State capital now poured into Egypt, exerting a powerful influence. Pursuing a *laissez faire* policy, the state left economic processes largely uncontrolled, resulting in an expansion of the so-called unproductive branches of the economy. The country was flooded with consumer goods and all manner of articles that were in effect anathema to stable, long-term economic progress. Making a quick profit was what mattered to investors, but a sound economic base was still lacking. Consequently, the 1970s was a decade marked by rapidly rising prices and, above all, radical social change. As the poorer became poorer still and the middle class, which had enjoyed privileges under Nasser, slowly became impoverished, the rich increased their wealth, while wheelers and dealers exploited the numerous "gray zones" in the new economy through semi- or outright illegal business practices, forming a class of *nouveaux riches* parvenus. The fabric of society was in tatters.

Egyptian destinies after "turning to the West"

All this is the theme of al-Ghitani's *Risala*, his "Epistle", in which the author sets himself the task of documenting the "shocking upheavals" of that "distressing time". This is achieved by focusing on several separate episodes, each devoted to a single character and his/her "destiny". These episodes are only loosely interlocked; this has caused some critics to consider the work to be a collection of short stories rather than a novel. Two features unite them into a whole, however: each episode gives a different example of what it means to live under the conditions of a specific time; and they are all variations on the one major theme, the vicissitudes and changes typical of this time.

For this reason, each of the individual stories shows life before the 1970s and then traces the changes in the character's situation and behavior as the decade unfolds. Take the old warden of the mosque-mausoleum of the Mamluk sultan Qalawun, for instance. At the beginning, he is a self-sufficient, honest man, eager to protect "his" mosque from any act of desecration. When we encounter him in the 1970s, he fails to intervene to stop a young tourist couple behaving inappropriately inside the mosque; later he is talked into performing odd jobs for an illegal foreign exchange trader. There is also a young doctor who offers free medical care in a poor quarter: suddenly he starts to buy up property; he then starts erecting luxury high-rise apartment blocks; ultimately he becomes the owner of a chocolate biscuit factory. Lastly, there are two large groups of protagonists: first, the courageous soldiers who risked their lives in numerous wars for their motherland only to be sent into retirement in the 1970s, left to cope on their own in the world that *infitah* (open door) has created. There is also the large group of people driven by the tremendous rise in prices to seek work abroad, in the *ghurba* (outland), who endure terrible danger and fears far away from home, where they had once believed that they would face a brighter and more secure future.

From this brief outline alone it is clear that in terms of subject matter al-Ghitani's primary concern is with the ethical and moral aspects of the "liberalist" turn of the 1970s. An old value system has fallen away, while a new one takes an ironclad grip. How are the events precipitating this profound shift described in the novel?

From the perspective of the sufferers

In the opening chapter the narrator states that he wishes to give a very "neutral" description of the enormous changes that took place in the 1970s. Although this may indeed be the case in the first two chapters, from the third onwards he undoubtedly takes sides. This is particularly evident from the change of narrative perspective: from this point onwards the characters tell their own stories, whether in the form of letters or through free indirect speech, which is to say that the narrator remains present but what he relates are the characters' innermost thoughts and emotions. From this inner perspective, the reader is confronted with a close-up of interminable and unbelievable suffering.

The events plotted by the novel are in themselves touching, if not shocking. There is the story of a young Egyptian, potentially talented enough to become an ambassador, who is forced by unscrupulous hotel managers into becoming the resident gigolo; when he tries to opt out, the racketeers have him thrown into prison. Then there is the family man who is forced to work abroad to fulfill his duty as breadwinner. This gradually leads to an estrangement from his children, climaxing when they no longer even recognize their own father on his return to Egypt for his holidays. In Lebanon, he is almost killed during the civil war; in Libya he becomes entangled in a web of intrigue spun by the secret service; finally, he dies somewhere in Europe from black despair. Another young Egyptian loses his life tragically in *al-ghurba*, leaving behind his parents, who had sacrificed their lives completely to their son and are left to vegetate under the sheer weight of their grief. For no obvious reason, another character is thrown into the torture cells of a state ruled by a brutal dictator, "our most beloved leader" (this may allude to Saddam Hussein's Iraq or Muammar al-Gaddafi's Libya). And those working in the Gulf States are reliant on their local sponsors, entirely at their mercy for better or worse.

All this would be bad enough. But the impact is reinforced by the pathos of the language employed and the construction of the text: the trajectory is that of a continuous escalation, things going from bad to worse, on and on, culminating in the episode telling the story of a man from Aleppo: when his beloved son is sexually abused by a Gulf Arab, the man knifes the lecher in his rage, an act for which he is executed in public.

The causers of suffering

With whom is the reader supposed to take sides? The bogeymen or enemies are easily made out, and they can be roughly classified into four groups. Firstly, there are the profiteers of the "open-door" policy: the powerful entrepreneurs, the foreign exchange speculators, doctors running exploitive private clinics, drug smugglers, the *nouveaux riches* upstarts, and many more. These people care only about money; they are uneducated, immoral if not criminal, and are portrayed as betraying their country. The second group is formed by "Westerners" and the West: sex-obsessed tourists, rapacious American entrepreneurs, coquettish women. Europe appears as an area of homelessness and estrangement emanating coldness, both climatically and on an interpersonal level; a place that is home to alcohol drinkers and the consumerist mentality as well as a stronghold of anti-Arab hostility. The third enemy group is Egypt's political leadership: the president travels to Jerusalem, betraying the Arab cause and dishonoring the Egyptian nation. The state tosses the fighters of yesteryear on the scrapheap, favors or tolerates the profiteers, and is no longer concerned with protecting the interests of the masses. The last enemy group to emerge is the other Arab countries: there the novel's protagonists are confronted with brutal, autocratic dictators and their ubiquitous secret services, or – in the rich Gulf States – with sanctimonious sheikhs, who conduct themselves like slavemasters and exploit their positions as employers and sponsors to abuse the foreigners' wives and children.

The trustees of good tradition

On the other side of the divide are those one can justifiably call the "custodians of heritage" or the "trustees of Good Tradition". The heroes – one might even say the martyrs – come from urban, petit-bourgeois backgrounds or the countryside. They represent four aspects of society. First, they uphold Arab-Islamic cultural heritage: here we find the aforementioned warden and the calligrapher, a character who features in the novel for no other reason than to provide al-Ghitani with an opportunity to praise the beauty of Arabic calligraphy and portray it as the vehicle of an advanced civilization that, having grown organically, is now perishing under Sadat's *infitah*. The protagonists are depicted – and this is the second aspect – as caring a great deal about education, one of the values pivotal in the Nasser era, the years when al-Ghitani attended school. Just as the upholders of heritage are conceived as the antithesis to the decay of cultural identity in an age dominated by consumerism and the "American way of life", these advocates of education are laudable, albeit antiquated exceptions in a climate of unbounded materialism. Then there are those protagonists, in particular the ex-fighters, who symbolize patriotism and pride in one's country, sentiments the government has scandalously cast aside in undertakings such as the Camp David accords. Lastly, al-Ghitani's protagonists also represent a general human heritage, people aware of their familial duties and responsibilities as fathers, mothers, brothers, sisters, who through their behavior set an example for readers, showing us how smoothly and harmoniously society could function if the old social structures were not being slowly but surely eroded by the *infitah*.

Too much pathos?

One could ask if the pathos with which the loss of these values is bemoaned is in fact meant to be taken seriously. In his review of the work for the *Neue Zürcher Zeitung* (2001), Stefan Weidner answered affirmatively. Due to the "excessive frustration" felt about the prevailing conditions of the *infitah* society, an author who is actually progressive has, according to Weidner, become caught up in sentimentality; a stark contrast to earlier novels where the author had succeeded in reclaiming an ironic component from even the most terrible and tragic events: an irony that, by ridiculing the appalling terror, salvaged the victims' dignity (for example the cruel torture scenes in *Zayni Barakat*, or *Incidents in Za'farani Alley*, a novel that addressed the imagined paralysis of the ability to act using the metaphor of a curse of impotence befalling all the men who live in the alley).

Although in some places it almost seems that the text sheds tears, it is questionable to conclude, as Weidner does, that this is simply a surplus of pathos or even snivelling oversensitivity. I suggest that the text is so saturated with pathos that it becomes ridiculous. Moreover, that the narrator's only comment on all these terrible events is "What was God's will happened", and that this becomes an obtrusively repeated motto, should arouse suspicion. It seems to me that a form of irony is indeed at work here – but an irony which by no means exposes the Good Traditions to derision and mockery. Al-Ghitani's attitude in this respect is perhaps best understood on closer examination of his handling of literary heritage in the novel.

Timely tradition

With regard to form, the text is oriented on the classical tradition of Arabic literature. This affinity is evident not only in the language but in an array of other aspects: the quotation from the Qur'an that precedes the text; the adoption by the narrator of the stance of an ancient chronicler striving to give an account of his times for posterity; the title that imitates the rhymed ornamental title of classical Arabic literature; that the work is called a *risala* (epistle) rather than a *riwaya* (novel); and by certain compositional techniques like the insertion of short unconnected episodes into a (albeit strongly reduced) framing narrative, or the numerous intertextual markers referring to works like *The Thousand and One Nights*.

Much of al-Ghitani's text is thus quotation or imitation, full of empathy, of an older writing and narrative tradition. Keeping the past present as a contrastive foil, this "classicism", typical of al-Ghitani's work, performs a twofold task. First, the subject matter of the narrative (the decaying heritage) is countered by his revival and retention of tradition, which, at least textually arrests the decay. In the process, the heritage re-*affirmed* is in principle and at the same time re-*formed*. As the sum of forms of thought that are actually obsolete, this tradition can only prove useful for mastering the problems of the present if, rather than being blindly copied, it is adjusted to the new reality. Two examples illustrate how this happens.

Modern Qur'an

"No soul knows what it will reap tomorrow, and no soul knows in what land it will die" (sura 31:34): this quotation taken from the Qur'an precedes the text as a motto. Three aspects need to be underlined: first, it is a quotation from the holiest text of Islam, that is, it is taken from a religious discourse on reality; second, it deals with the essential insecurity of human existence, arising from worries about assuring a livelihood and the uncertainty as to the place of death; and third, with respect to form, the quotation is comprised of two parallel constructed parts. Placing a Qur'anic quotation at the beginning of a novel generates the impression that it will be a religious tract or something similar. Of course the text then proceeds to disappoint this expectation. At the same time, the novel repeatedly confirms that this verse, revealed fourteen centuries earlier, still rings true today, since earthly existential insecurity is something very real, and thereby elevates Qur'anic heritage to a sustainable model for a discourse on the *infitah* era.

With respect to form, the (post)modern novel also affirms its religious opening; al-Ghitani's *Epistle* not only adopts the pathos of its language but utilizes its formal binary division as the structuring principle throughout. While the first section focuses on the insecurities of human existence, the second revolves around the theme of "death in the outlands". Adopting the exterior form of the Qur'anic motto confirms the enduring validity and adaptability of the model text.

Modern adab

While it seems credible enough when authors of classical *adab* (the amusing and edifying literature of past ages) state that they do not order their anecdotes according to a preset plan, one is more skeptical towards similar pronouncements by Ghitani's narrator. At the outset of the novel, the narrator states that he "does not adhere to a specific method [of presentation and arrangement]", nor does he have a "fixed plan", and he allegedly concludes his "message" (another possible meaning of the word *risala*) because he fears any further stories would only bore the reader. Both statements have a completely different function from those made by *adab* authors: in al-Ghitani's work, the associative narrative mode does not serve as vehicle for entertaining distraction but seeks to convey the confusion and disorientation stemming from the suffering inherent in present circumstances; as for the conclusion, when the narrator follows the description of the torture and execution of the man from Aleppo with an expression of his apprehension that any further stories will bore the reader, it comes across as pure cynicism. In both cases, heritage is adopted as a foil, its structuring principle capable of rendering present events, while its traditional functions are discarded: contemporary *adab* is not a literature of amusement and distraction, but one of political commitment, provoking the reader through its internal tensions.

Making literature authentic

Reviving literary heritage as a source of artistic inspiration is of course not an idea pursued by al-Ghitani alone: it is in broad circulation within contemporary Arab literature. The aesthetic program of *ta'sil* (making authentic) aims at creating a genuinely Arabic literature and discards earlier genres of modern literature, despite the remarkable achievements of its pioneers from Taha Husayn through to Naguib Mahfouz as being ultimately alien forms, imported as part of colonialism and imperialism. It is obvious that the *ta'sil* aesthetics is one part of a broader and multifaceted political ideology which resists heteronomy and infiltration by foreign cultures, demanding a reconnection to the local culture's intrinsic traits, the restoration of cultural continuity that was severed by the rise of foreign dominance, and political self-determination.

When al-Ghitani breaks with the literary practices of his modern predecessors, borrowing instead from classical models to create a form that bears very little resemblance to the conventional genre of the novel, it is no longer a procedure immanent to literature itself but a political statement: wherever local identity is surrendered by opening towards the West, the only option is to counter the concomitant decay of values and social structures by drawing upon and actualizing cultural heritage, a step that also entails its critical reformulation.

Orientation on classical Arabic literature is not, however, a simple affirmation of the old ways. In the discrepancy between (critically revised and reshaped) older forms and contemporary subject matter, there does indeed lie an ironic rupture of any semblance of seamless connection between the two; it is not the form which casts an ironic light on the content, but vice versa. In an era like that of the *infitah*, in which the "good old ways" are being destroyed and seem to have next to no chance of surviving, anyone steadfastly adhering to tradition appears woefully, if not tragically ridiculous, for he/she is fighting a losing battle; a modern Don Quixote. We are thus dealing with a rupture of tragic irony; the irony is not a means for ridiculing the *turath* (upholders of heritage) but demonstrates their tragic situation – and in this way denounces the circumstances responsible for their tragedy. The "classicism" of al-Ghitani's *Risala* configures the almost cynical defiance of an author who, caught in bleak desperation, insists on swimming against the tide. His "classicism" shows an affirmation of identity despite the absence of all hope that it can indeed be preserved.

SELECTED WORKS

Awraq shabb 'asha mundhu alf 'am (The Papers of a Young Man Who Lived a Thousand Years Ago), Cairo 1969

al-Zayni Barakat (Zayni Barakat), Damascus 1974

al-Misriyyun wa-l-harb. Min sadmat yuniyu ila yaqzat uktubar (The Egyptians and the War. From the June Shock to the October Awakening), Cairo 1974

Hurras al-bawwaba al-sharqiyya. al-Jaysh al-'Iraqi min harb "Tishrin al-awwal" ila "Harb al-shimal", Cairo 1975

Waqa'i' harat al-Za'farani (Incidents in Za'farani Alley), Cairo 1976

Hikayat al-gharib (The Stranger's Stories), Cairo 1976

Nagib Mahfuz yatadhakkar (Naguib Mahfouz Remembers), Beirut 1980

Khitat al-Ghitani (al-Ghitani's Topography), Cairo 1981

Malamih al-Qahira fi alf 'am (Views of Cairo over the past 1000 years), Cairo 1983

Kitab al-tajalliyat (The Book of Revelations), 3 vol., Cairo 1983–87
Qahiriyyat (1): Asbilat al-Qahira (Cairenica 1: The Fountains of Cairo), Cairo 1984
Risalat al-basa'ir fi l-masa'ir (The Epistle of Insights into the Destinies), Cairo 1989
Mutun al-ahram (Pyramid Texts), Cairo 1994
The Cairo of Naguib Mahfouz, by Naguib Mahfouz, Britta Le Va and Gamal Al-Ghitani, Cairo 2000

TRANSLATIONS

Incidents in Za'farani Alley, trans. Peter O. Daniel, with an introduction by M. Enani, Cairo: General Egyptian Book Organization 1986
Zayni Barakat, trans. Farouk Abdel Wahab, London, New York: Penguin Books 1990; Cairo: The American University in Cairo Press 2004
Pyramid Texts, trans. Humphrey Davies, Cairo: The American University in Cairo Press 2007

FURTHER READING

Rachid Bencherif Ouedghiri: *L'univers romanesque de Jamâl Al-Gitânî*, Diss. Paris-Sorbonne 1993
Ceza Kassem Draz: "In Quest of New Narrative Forms. Irony in the Works of Four Egyptian Writers. Gamal al-Ghitani, Yahya al-Tahir 'Abdallah, Majid Tubya, Sun'allah Ibrahim (1967–79)", in: *Journal of Arabic Literature* 12 (1981), pp. 137–59
Stephan Guth: *Zeugen einer Endzeit. Fünf Schriftsteller zum Umbruch in der ägyptischen Gesellschaft nach 1970*, Berlin: Schwarz 1992
Richard van Leeuwen: "The Enchantment of Space. Two Novels of Gamal al-Ghitani and Hoda Barakat", in: Boutros Hallaq, Robin Ostle, Stefan Wild (eds.), *La poétique de l'espace dans la littérature arabe moderne*, Paris: Presses Sorbonne Nouvelle 2002
Samia Mehrez: *Egyptian Writers between History and Fiction. Essays on Naguib Mahfouz, Sonallah Ibrahim, and Gamal al-Ghitani*, Cairo: The American University in Cairo Press 1994 (2nd printing 2005)
Nabil Sharaf el-Din: "Gamal el-Ghitani: The Quest for the Authentic and Innovative", in: *Banipal* 13 (2002), pp. 8–11
Rotraud Wielandt: "Mystische Tradition und zeitgenössische Wirklichkeitserfahrung in Gamal al-Gitanis *Kitab at-tagalliyat*", in: *Asiatische Studien/Etudes Asiatiques* 50/2 (1996), pp. 491–523

OTHER WORKS CITED

Alif laila. Book of the Thousand Nights and One Night, commonly known as the "Arabian Nights Entertainments", ed. William H. Macnaghten, Calcutta: Thacker 1839–42
Ibn Iyas: *Bada'i' al-zuhur fi waqa'i' al-duhur* [16th century], 2nd rev. ed., ed. M. Mostafa, Cairo: Bibliotheca Islamica 1960–3 (English translation: *An Account of the Ottoman Conquest of Egypt in the Year A.H. 922 (A.D. 1516)*, trans. W.H. Salmon, London: Royal Asiatic Society 1921)
Ahmad ibn 'Ali al-Maqrizi: *Kitab al-Khitat al-Maqriziyya* [15th century], Shiyyah: Maktabat Ihya' 'Ulum al-Din 1959

"This reality is deplorable"

The Egypt of Sonallah Ibrahim: Between Media Representation and Experienced Everyday Reality

Andrea Haist

On 22 October 2003 Sonallah Ibrahim, one of Egypt's most internationally renowned novelists, was finally due to receive one of the country's most prestigious literary awards, the prize of the High Council for Culture worth some 13,000 Euros. The accolade was long overdue. But state cultural institutions had long avoided honoring an author whose novels, although finding favor amongst readers and critics alike, painted a gloomy picture of the conditions prevailing in Egypt. Moreover, the author had kept his distance from the state and its institutions. Now a jury comprising of ten leading literary critics from the Arab world had decided to honor him for his oeuvre and the achievement it represented – and with this decision brought him a few sleepless nights.

The awards ceremony at the Cairo Opera House ended in scandal. At the end of his speech, the award-winner declared that he could not accept the prize – not in the present political situation and not from this government. It is the fate of Arab writers, he explained, that they cannot ignore what is happening around them: the humiliation of the Arab world from the Persian Gulf to the Mediterranean; Israeli attacks on the West Bank and the systematic displacement of the Palestinians; American hegemony over the region; and the disgraceful acquiescence of Arab governments and regimes to these events. That is by no means all, he went on; the catastrophe reaches even further, into the very fabric of society and the life of its citizens: in Egypt there is no longer any theater, cinema, research, education, industry, agriculture, health system, or justice. Corruption and thievery are endemic, and whoever protests against it is interrogated, beaten, and tortured. This reality is deplorable. A writer who takes his responsibility seriously cannot close his eyes and hope it will all go away, while accepting a prize that lacks credibility because it is awarded by the government. Sonallah Ibrahim then left the stage to sustained applause. Whilst he was surrounded by guests congratulating him for the step he had taken, the Egyptian minister of culture seized the microphone and declared that the speech was in fact an endorsement of the government: if it had not granted him this degree of freedom, then Sonallah Ibrahim could not have been present and able to speak his mind.

As this story demonstrates, Ibrahim is an out-and-out political author. His work is closely tied to political, economic, social, and cultural conditions in Egypt and the Arab world, and to the worries and hardships suffered by people living under such conditions. The thrust of his criticism faces up to uncomfortable truths, and he does not mince his words. His relationship to the apparatus of political power is tense and he has clashed with authority time and time again.

Sonallah Ibrahim was born in 1937 in Cairo. A high-ranking civil servant, his father took a second wife, a nurse – Ibrahim's mother – who was of lower-class background; she was to care for the first wife, who was paralyzed. The boy was thus confronted with the significance of class difference from an early age: his father's family was upper middle-class and they held his mother in contempt due to her poor background. His Marxist convictions, which he has maintained steadfastly up to the present day, stem from these formative experiences of his childhood and youth.

In 1952, shortly after the Free Officers' putsch and the dismantling of the monarchy, Ibrahim began to study law at the University of Cairo. But he was far more attracted to politics and journalism than jurisprudence. Due to his membership in a splinter group of the Communist Party, he was arrested on 1 January 1959 along with some 250 other persons and in 1960 was sentenced by a military tribunal in Alexandria to seven years imprisonment and forced labor. After periods spent in two prisons near Cairo where the prisoners were tortured and abused, he was then sent to a large camp at the al-Kharga oasis in the western desert. Conditions there were no less hard: barefoot and dressed in rags, prisoners were forced to perform strenuous physical labor; they were beaten, and many died under torture. It took a hunger strike in July 1961 to bring about improved conditions, including permission to possess paper and writing implements. With short story and poetry competitions, theater performances, painting courses and the publication of a prison newspaper, the inmates sought to remain intellectually active and stand their ground. Together with friends, Ibrahim followed – in so far as the books and journals smuggled into the prison permitted it – the experimental developments taking place in world literature and began, like many of his fellow prisoners, to write. While still in prison he resolved to become a writer.

As part of a general amnesty Sonallah Ibrahim was released from prison in May 1964. He moved into a furnished room in the Cairo district of Heliopolis, but was still subject to police surveillance and parole restrictions such as a night curfew. During the day he went out and became reacquainted with people and surroundings he had not seen for five years. Each evening he wrote down his impressions in a journal, the material which formed the basis of *Smell of It*, his first novel published in 1966.

Cairo through the eyes of a released political prisoner

From the perspective of an unspecified first-person narrator imprisoned on political grounds, this novel, wherein the author makes use of his daily journal entries, tells of the protagonist's first ten days after release; how he explores reality outside the confines of prison and attempts to pick up the threads of his previous life. He meets up with people who had been close to him in the various phases of his earlier life: the widow of a friend who died in prison, friends and relatives, his parents and grandparents; and visits places he once frequented: a café that was the haunt of his former political comrades-in-arms, the editorial office of a journal he once wrote for, the cinemas in the city center, and finally the house of his childhood.

From the outset the narrator is confronted with a reality that tarnishes the joy of his release: the people he encounters are weary, impoverished and dejected. Relationships, with him and each other, are for the most part infused with egoism, rendering them loveless and fragile, rarely displaying solidarity and affection. The country is clearly in a desolate state – as desolate as the Cairo sewage system, its waters pooling in the streets of the inner city and its stench overwhelming. The hopes for a better, more just and freer future aroused by the 1952 Revolution, Nasserism, and Arab socialism have been dashed; the quintessential insight of the novel.

This return to "ordinary" life is narrated on two levels. In terms of immediate reality, the narrator relates laconically and without comment what he does, sees, and hears in chronological succession. He describes all the banal things that are part of everyday routine: getting up in the morning, going to the toilet, taking a shower, getting dressed, making coffee, eating breakfast and so forth. He expresses his observations in short incisive scenes, and he retells snippets of conversation in which the people he meets tell him about their individual situations or prevailing social conditions. For his own part, however, he says nothing. What he thinks is communicated to the reader on a second level, in passages of a different typescript that are reserved for his inner world; reflections on external events, his daydreams, and memories of childhood, adolescence and the years in prison. Here the descriptive means used to render the reality experienced is very different, with no deference shown to taboos: homosexuality and masturbation are touched on, as are corruption and the forms of violence and contempt with which the state treats its citizens.

It is glaringly obvious that this unadorned picture of reality roused the ire of the censorship authority: the novel was confiscated immediately upon publication and the author called into the Ministry of Information for interrogation. Nevertheless, Ibrahim managed to save a few copies from the clutches of the state and distribute them in secret. The novel was published in a Beirut journal in 1968 and once again in Cairo in 1969, albeit in censored versions. The first uncensored version was the English translation by Denys Johnson-Davies published in 1971. The Arab public was first able to read the uncensored novel in 1986. Such intervention by censorship authorities has had a decisive influence on the author.

After release from prison, Ibrahim first found work as a bookseller and translator, before joining the Egyptian news agency MENA. In 1968 he moved to Beirut, then East Berlin, where he worked for ADN, the GDR state news agency. Granted a scholarship, he began studying cinematography in Moscow in 1971, spending three years there before returning to Egypt. For the next two years he worked for a publishing house, and married in 1976. With the support of his wife, he decided to cease work in publishing and devote all his energies to writing. He earned a basic living through translating books, most of which show a certain affinity to his own work, numerous books for the young, and scripts for film and television.

The construction of the pharaoh

Between 1967 and 1974 Sonallah Ibrahim worked on his second novel, *August Star*, which was published in Damascus in 1974 and two years later in Cairo. The novel is based on material gathered on a journey that the author took with two friends in 1965 to the Aswan High Dam, which he used for a magazine feature story. Like the journey, the novel is set in the year 1965. The first-person narrator, a professional journalist, travels from Cairo to Aswan at the height of summer to observe the construction work on the dam project. Day by day he visits different construction sites and reports meticulously from morning to bedtime on all he does, sees and hears; with whom he talks; and what he finds out. Technological operations and the construction machinery used are described in detail, and the persons involved in the project (Russian and Egyptian workers and engineers, truck drivers, secretaries, functionaries, and military personnel) have their say as well. At times the narrator is accompanied by a friend, a successful Cairo journalist who is covering the construction of the dam. Over the course of his stay he witnesses how those involved in the project and the Egyptian media representatives glorify the building of the dam and registers discrepancies between the image conveyed by the media and the repressive, inhumane reality of the construction site. Later he travels to Abu Simbel, where the rock temple of Ramses II is being dismantled before being reconstructed at another location. This provides an opportunity to draw parallels between the veneration of the pharaoh and the Nasser cult, both of whom erected monuments to themselves by building enormous edifices. The construction of the high dam mirrors post-revolutionary Egyptian society under Nasser with all its contradictions.

Similarly to *The Smell of It*, *August Star* is narrated on two levels. On the level of immediate reality the narrator describes what he does and his sensual impressions without any commentary. These sections are interspersed with typographically highlighted passages featuring recollections of his time in prison, an inner monologue, excerpts from a book about Michelangelo, and an Egyptology essay on Ramses II. These passages place the construction of the dam into a broader autobiographical, philosophical, and historical context.

A satire of the Sadat era

In contrast to previous works, *The Committee*, published in Beirut in 1981, is a sarcastic settling of scores with the Sadat era. Sadat sought to resolve the grave economic crisis gripping Egypt in the late 1960s through a political reorientation. In the early 1970s Egypt turned to the West, in particular the USA, and legislation liberalizing the economy opened the country to Western investors from 1974 onwards. It allowed for joint ventures, the transfer of profits abroad, and the import of foreign goods, which soon flooded the Egyptian market. But only a small elite profited from the opening – primarily leading functionaries and shrewd self-made men. The living standards of large sections of the middle class continually worsened, with rising inflation coupled to stagnating incomes, while the gulf between rich and poor kept widening.

In *The Committee*, a first-person narrator with a leftwing past, who represents Nasser's Egypt as well as the leftist intellectuals of the 1970s, faces questioning by a scurrile committee made up of civilians, high-ranking members of the military, a spinster and a Westerner; to all appearances representatives of the capitalist and pro-Western lobbies. The narrator wishes to begin a new life, and the examination he is put through is supposed to ascertain whether he is suitable for such a change despite the leftist persuasions of his past. For this purpose he has to endure all manner of humiliating procedures and, finally, answer two key questions, which are designed to reveal the depths of his self-denial. The first question is: "What achievement of the twentieth century is so important and global that it will be remembered in the future?" After some thought, the narrator answers "Coca-Cola". Explaining the reason behind his answer, he says that Coca-Cola is a global product which – as the drink of American soldiers – is inextricably linked to the decisive events of the twentieth century: "Coca-Cola took the risk of entering into two world wars – and emerged victorious both times." The Coca-Cola corporation continues to influence American and international politics, in particular in the "Third World". This ironic answer, revealing the link between a large corporation and international politics, fails to please the committee. The second question tests the narrator's historical knowledge of the Cheops pyramid. Alluding to the separate peace concluded between Egypt and Israel in 1979, the narrator replies that the

Egyptians would never have been able to build the pyramid alone, and so one must presume that the Israelis had provided them with the necessary technological support, an answer that satisfies the committee.

Dismissed from the examination, the narrator spends the coming weeks in hope and trepidation. Finally a telegram arrives, requesting that he write a paper on the "greatest contemporary Arab luminary". A difficult task, for the narrator decides to exclude political and government leaders, certain that he would judge them in a manner at odds with the committee's wishes. What is more, none of the defeated Arab military leaders, opportunistic poets and writers, scholars who have migrated abroad, or corruptible judges could be considered luminaries. Leafing through a newspaper, he comes across the colorful figure of the "Doctor", an extremely influential personality in the Arab world, and decides to make him the subject of his paper.

Researching the subject turns out to be difficult, however, as he is hindered by the mysterious fact that records have been removed from the dossiers in the archives of the large dailies, and all articles dealing with the Doctor have been cut out of the newspapers. Finally, he finds leads in a women's magazine and an American magazine. Piecing the information together, he succeeds in reconstructing the Doctor's biography and his rise to multimillionaire status: born into a poor family, but related to one of the post-1952 rulers, he lays the foundations for his future wealth firstly as a film director and later as the president of a construction company. At the beginning of the 1970s, he becomes involved in the arms trade – a lucrative business given the wars and tensions in the Middle East – and after the economy is liberalized he turns to importing airplanes, automobiles, food articles, and other consumer goods. In addition, he possesses a national bottling concession for Coca-Cola.

Just as the narrator has advanced to the stage in his research where he might begin to draw far-reaching conclusions from the gathered material, he is contacted by the examination committee, which strongly suggests that he change his topic. To prevent him from pursuing his research, it even has one of its members shadow the narrator. Watched at every turn, the narrator's life becomes unbearable, and when he discovers that his "minder" carries a revolver, he kills him with a kitchen knife. The wreaths laid in honor of the committee member at the funeral show that those mourning the victim are the political and economic power elites of the Western industrial nations, Israel, and the "Third World".

Unsurprisingly, the narrator is brought before the committee to justify his actions. In a long speech he explains the broader context and connections he was on the verge of identifying. For example, he can explain that the deterioration and shortage of drinking water stems originally from irrigation projects launched by the Coca-Cola corporation in Israel's Negev Desert. The resultant pollution of the drinking water led to a rise in the import of mineral water and soft drink products of the same corporation. These insights displease the committee, and the narrator is convicted.

With nothing more to lose, on the way home he undertakes an act of rebellion against the intolerable state of Egyptian society: of a group witnessing a man harassing a woman, he is the only one to step forward and confront the assailant. Injured during the ensuing tumult, he requires medical treatment, which gives him a welcome opportunity to bluntly tell the doctor that he has helped ruin the state health system by opening a private practice. Back home, he comes to the conclusion that he should have not have testified *before* the committee but *against* it, and that his honorable behavior ultimately means his demise. He then begins to enforce the verdict passed by the committee – and consumes himself.

Even though the narrator consumes himself because the time is not yet ripe to challenge the imperialist-capitalist system openly, *The Committee* is nonetheless an appeal to take a position against the ruling elites, to resist bowing to their tactics of deception, and to cling onto and foster a critical political consciousness; only so is it possible to penetrate the nexuses of power such as the connections between the Doctor, the ruling power elites, and Coca-Cola and, acting on insights of this kind, resist hegemonic impositions, shrugging off the passive tolerance of social injustices.

How to read a newspaper in the Mubarak era

How this could occur in concrete terms is shown in the novel *Zaat*, published in Cairo in 1992. Zaat is the unusual name of novel's heroine, an allusion to the medieval Arab folk epic of the warrior princess Zaat al-Himma ("the lady of noble intentions"), who performed heroic acts in the Arab-Byzantine wars of the eighth and ninth centuries. The word *Zaat* can also mean *self*. The novel is a modern epic in which Zaat, a typical member of the urban middle class, struggles against the adversities of everyday life and performs acts of resistance whenever and wherever possible. For all her efforts, she makes hardly any impression on the worsening living conditions, the decay of public morals, the collapse of state institutions and agencies, and society's drift towards religious fanaticism and obscurantism.

The plot begins in the 1960s, as Zaat, studying media and communications, marries Abd al-Magid, a bank assistant who has discontinued his studies. Together, they establish a household. They have found a cheap apartment in a neighborhood of Heliopolis with new blocks reserved for public service employees. Everything is still going fine at this stage. Abd al-Magid's income is adequate and his future prospects good, while his sense of male self-esteem remains untroubled and the gender hierarchy is still intact: he is in a position to forbid his wife from continuing her studies.

Zaat becomes a housewife and the mother of two daughters, and buries her dream of one day becoming a journalist. But then in the 1970s the cost of living begins to rise, and she has to find work. Through contacts Abd al-Magid finds her a job at a newspaper. There she works in a department responsible for "proof-reading and copy-editing" – a euphemism for censorship – and evaluating the articles published in the paper; this department is in fact redundant, because the Ministry of Information or the President's Office dictates in advance what is permitted to be published. Over time, the department evolves into an important collecting point for news, for its task now is to substitute stories of scandal and white-collar crime with other news. In this way Zaat gains first-hand knowledge of how Egyptian society functions.

At the beginning of the presidency of Hosni Mubarak, who came to power in 1981 following the assassination of Sadat, Zaat is transferred to the archive. This is a punishment for being a Nasser sympathizer and displaying antipathy towards Sadat. There she deals with newspapers and magazines typical of this period; they respond to the malaise in public life by reproducing empty political sermons and slogans. Moreover, she is confronted with apolitical women colleagues, who are predominantly disposed to Islamic ideas and obey Islamic dress codes, and who talk about nothing but the banalities of everyday life as mothers and wives while spurning Zaat due to her obvious leftist leanings.

Zaat and Abd al-Magid are not amongst those able to improve their social and economic position in the 1970s and 1980s. On the contrary, their living conditions worsen. The neat and tidy apartment block becomes rundown, the streets are full of sewage, rubbish lies everywhere, and countless cats patrol the stairwell, causing mischief. Zaat tries vainly to animate the residents into undertaking a joint initiative against the rubbish and plague of cats, only for the particular interests of each resident to prevent a solution. The block continues its inexorable slide into squalor, and the apartment needs urgent repairs. But a new kitchen or bathroom, as advertised on television, are things Zaat and Abd al-Magid simply cannot afford – in contrast to their neighbors, who, as police or army officers or employees in the city administration, are occasionally able to supplement their income with bribes and so renovate their apartments. Because Abd al-Magid is neither willing nor able to finish his studies or emigrate to the rich Gulf States, and because both of them fail in attempts to become self-employed, their only option is to maintain a strict budget and ignore consumer goods. While Abd al-Magid compensates for this restraint by indulging in porno movies and stories about imaginary heroic acts, Zaat wrestles with the routine of day-in, day-out monotony, escaping at night in dreams of heroic men like those portrayed in Egyptian films of the 1950s and 1960s. The birth of a much longed-for son brings about a number of changes. Abd al-Magid alters his lifestyle and becomes pious, while Zaat varies her appearance and dons a veil – all because Abd al-Magid wishes her to. The care and education of her son confront Zaat once again with the grotesque social conditions.

The visit of friends, a married couple who have returned from Europe, opens Zaat's eyes to new political scandal: much of the medication available from Egyptian chemists is unauthorized for sale in Europe because of its damaging effects, and the food sold in Egypt also contains dangerous substances. Moreover, a story is running in the papers about how hormone-treated chicken is having a negative impact on the libido of Egyptian men and enlarging their breasts – symptoms Abd al-Magid has noticed in himself. As a result, meat is struck from their diet, which now becomes very health conscious. A can of olives tagged with a false use-by date finally prompts Zaat to an act of resistance: she decides to make use of her rights and obligations as a citizen to inform the health authorities and the police. But such cases are too numerous for the authorities to take her complaint seriously. The only constructive thing Zaat can do is to report the incident. Supported by her friend Himma, she thus enters the jungle of Egyptian bureaucracy, where submitting a simple statement proves to be a complicated administrative act that takes several days.

Fictionalization of reality

Zaat's story only makes up half of the novel; the other half is comprised of collages of newspaper clippings, most of which are taken from the Egyptian press and presented in alternation with the narrative chapters. They shed light on those national and international developments that have a determining influence on the political, economic, and social conditions prevailing in Egypt at this time, and so impact on Zaat's life. Emerging out of the excerpts is a picture of Egyptian society in the 1980s. The material aims to discredit the ruling political and economic elites; at the same time, the collage method is deployed to counter and expose the ideological character of media coverage.

The alliance with the West, in particular the US, forged under Sadat includes promises of financial and technological aid, which only creates political dependency. Sadat's economic reforms prove to be a "sellout" of state property and result in the destruction of local industry. Leading Egyptian politicians and civil servants are deeply embroiled in the accompanying transfer of Egyptian capital to foreign companies and take advantage of the situation to line their own pockets. National debt rises. The ideological superstructure of society is provided by fundamentalist Islamic theologians, who – nurtured under Sadat as antipodes to communists and adherents of Nasserism – preach the Islamization of society. They go about their business with great fervor, propagating the wearing of the veil while at the same time opening the first fashion boutiques for Muslims. The end of this particular chapter is ironically crowned by a quote from Mubarak: "Extensive development has taken place in all areas of life, thanks to all those who work in all fields of production with a team spirit of solidarity and honesty." The preceding newspaper excerpts contradict this claim emphatically and disclose it to be nothing but idle talk.

In subsequent chapters, we encounter Egyptian-American-Israeli relations; the state of the health system and infrastructure; natural disasters, epidemics, and accidents; rebellions, strikes and their quelling; the Islamization of society, Islamic discourse in the media, and the business practices of Islamic firms and banks; the increasing tension between Muslims and Coptic Christians; and the rise and fall of politicians, captains of industry, theologians, actors and other figures of public life. Even advertisements are included. The collages always contrast headlines and news stories on actual incidents with the statements given by politicians, the explanations churned out by high-ranking functionaries, or the official reports issued by state institutions.

In *The Committee*, the narrator's research is abruptly ended when the collected material leads him to draw explosive conclusions about the connections between politics, capital, and Egypt's decline. In *Zaat*, it is the reader who is now challenged to do what was forbidden the narrator in *The Committee*.

Not only official government statements and announcements are unmasked by the collages – the ideological character of the Islamic discourse is also mercilessly exposed through selected quotations. Among those cited is Shaykh Sharawi, an extraordinarily popular theologian in Egypt – due to his television appearances – whose influence, power and esteem have grown continually since the early 1970s, contributing decisively to the Islamization of Egypt. Sharawi produces ideology in its purest and simplest form, impeding social change – and the state thanks him for it:

> If you see a building, for example, which earns its owner a lot of money, you shouldn't envy the man. Rather you should pray for him because he has earned his money honestly. He hasn't exploited anyone because he has put food in the bellies and clothes on the backs of the poorest workers.

The entwinement between Islamic ideology and tangible business interests is uncovered in numerous newspaper excerpts. For example, the reader is confronted with a scurrilous fusion of Islamic and Western manager rhetoric:

> Sony celebrates its return
> *The fruit of cooperation between the Japanese company Sony, the International*

Islamic Computer Company (Compuland), the International Islamic Bank, and the Benha Electronics Company (public sector).

Professor Mohamed Samir Alish: "Praise be to Allah and thanks be to Allah. This great occasion is the result of years of continued and unstinting effort, of work undertaken quietly and unobtrusively. Today we are able to gather the harvest of all that labor and all that sweat and to see that the dream has finally come true ... Yes, Sony is back in the Egyptian market ... We met with some of the pioneers of Egypt's new economy in the late seventies and resolved to raise the name of Allah and the law of Allah in every field of life ... for the rules of Islam are not mere religious rites to be performed, but a perfect model on which to build our lives ... with the effort and potential of humanity. Here we are today ... witnessing the birth of the International Islamic Company for Computer Technology (Computum), offspring of Compuland, ready to realize its goals and take the world of the future by storm ... the world of information, which until now has been monopolized by a number of nations you could count on one hand".

The chapters featuring newspaper excerpts also contain "photos" and captions. The spaces reserved for these photos remain empty; it is the task of readers to fill them in. Due to their knowledge of reality and its conventional presentation in the media, they are well aware what the image fitting the caption should look like: "President Mubarak shaking hands with Shaykh Sharawi as he awards him the Medal of the Republic" or "Residents of Alexandria wade through sewage inside and outside their homes on the first day of the feast."

These collage chapters are closely interwoven with those of the narrative text. What happens to Zaat and Abd al-Magid in the narrative only becomes fully comprehensible through the collages. To take one example: the reader finds out why the olives Zaat buys are rotten – the Ministry of Health has lifted controls on imported goods. Conversely, the narrative text shows up the ideological character of many a newspaper article, such as when Shaykh Sharawi declares that women are forced to go to work because the masculinity of their husbands is on the wane. From their own experience, however, Egyptian readers know that it is first and foremost the spiraling living costs that are compelling women to find work.

Narrator and reader as accomplices

Following the advice of three lawyers, the publisher prefaced the novel with a declaration:

The events and incidents depicted in some of the chapters of this novel are taken from stories covered by both the state and the opposition Egyptian press. Their reproduction is intended neither to confirm the accuracy of these reports nor damage the reputation of the persons they mention. They are solely to mirror the media climate affecting and influencing the lives of the figures.

This is most certainly only part of the truth. *Zaat* is a text in which the narrator and reader enter into a permanent complicity. Both know full well what is going on in everyday life, what the real circumstances of their lives are like, and that they simply cannot afford to trust all the proclamations and explanations given by the ruling class and disseminated in the media discourse. They utilize the material garnered from the newspapers as a lever of subversion and keep the insights they gain into the machinations of the ruling class for themselves.

It is most certainly no coincidence that the novel was enthusiastically received by Egyptian literary critics. According to an opinion poll, *Zaat* was the best novel of 1992. In the following year, it was supposed to be awarded a state prize as the most important Egyptian novel – but state institutions proved unwilling to endorse the decision. A decade would pass before Sonallah Ibrahim would be nominated for Egypt's most prestigious literary award – and be able to decline the "honor".

WORKS

Tilka l-ra'iha (The Smell of It), Cairo 1966.
Najmat Aghustus (August Star), Damascus 1974
al-Lajna (The Committee), Beirut 1981
Bayrut, Bayrut (Beirut, Beirut), Cairo 1984
Dhat (Zaat), Cairo 1992
Sharaf, Cairo 1997
Warda, Cairo 2000
Amrikanli, Cairo 2003

TRANSLATIONS

The Smell of It and other stories, trans. Denys Johnson-Davies, London: Heinemann 1971
The Committee, trans. Mary St. Germain, Charlene Constable, Syracuse, NY: Syracuse University Press 2001
Zaat, trans. Anthony Calderbank, Cairo, New York: The American University in Cairo Press 2001

FURTHER READING

Ceza Kassem Draz: "Opaque and Transparent Discourse in Sonallah Ibrahim's Works", in: Ferial J. Ghazoul, Barbara Harlow (eds.), *The View from Within. Writers and Critics on Contemporary Arabic Literature*, Cairo: The American University in Cairo Press 1994, pp.134–48

Hartmut Fähndrich: "Trials and The Trial. Sun'allah Ibrahim, Franz Kafka etc.", in: Angelika Neuwirth et al. (eds.), *Myths, Historical Archetypes and Symbolic Figures in Arabic Literature. Towards a New Hermeneutic Approach*, Beirut, Stuttgart: Steiner 1999, pp. 239–45

Stephan Guth: *Zeugen einer Endzeit. Fünf Schriftsteller zum Umbruch in der ägyptischen Gesellschaft nach 1970*, Berlin: Schwarz 1992, pp. 114–49

Samia Mehrez: *Egyptian Writers Between History and Fiction. Essays on Naguib Mahfouz, Sun'allah Ibrahim and Gamal al-Ghitani*, Cairo: The American University in Cairo Press 1994, pp. 119–46

Marina Stagh: *The Limits of Freedom of Speech. Prose Literature and Prose Writers in Egypt under Nasser and Sadat*, Stockholm: Almquist and Wiksell 1993

Ulrike Stehli: "Referenz und Selbstreferenz. Strategien des Erzählens in Sun'allah Ibrahims *Tilka r-ra'iha*", in: Verena Klemm, Beatrice Gründler (eds.), *Understanding Near Eastern Literatures. A Spectrum of Interdisciplinary Approaches*, Wiesbaden: Reichert 2000, pp. 203–14

Hebrew Bible and Arabic Poetry

Reclaiming Palestine as a Homeland Made of Words: Mahmoud Darwish

Angelika Neuwirth

The poet as a liminal figure: in the limbo between individual artist and public symbol

I come from there. I return the sky to its mother when for its mother the sky cries
And I weep for a cloud that returns to know me
I have learned the words of blood-stained courts in order to break the rules.
I have learned and dismantled all speech to construct one single word: "homeland".

Is this voice claiming a transcendent status, coming "from there", aspiring to the role of mediator between heaven and earth, and boasting the achievement of converging fragmented language into a single name; is this voice the poetic persona of a specific poem; or is it the poet's very own prophetic voice? This is a question steeped in history: it begins with the Arab *qasida* poet who, serving as the preserver of collective memory and traditional norms of pre-Islamic society, employed the first person voice in his poems. If the experiences he related were largely stereotypical and the heroic acts he claimed as his own were exemplary renderings of the tribal virtues of his society rather than his own deeds, he was nonetheless held personally responsible for his message, which enabled his listeners to identify with him when he recited his poetry. Throughout subsequent eras, even as scholars of Islamic religious lore assumed their role as guarantors of social norms, Arab poets remained public figures, albeit mostly in the service of courtly patrons.

In cultural memory, however, thanks to such outstanding figures as Abu Nuwas, Abu Tammam and al-Mutanabbi, the poet of classical times is seen as an uncompromising, unbending fighter, championing a purely worldly, individualistic culture of emotion; a realm of freedom wrested from the clutches of the prevailing Islamic norms. In this milieu the heroic stance of the old poet who presented himself as socially active was supplemented by imagination. The poet, deprived of his activist role, resorted to poetic obsession: in the soon predominant *ghazal* genre, the classical poet evoked a passionate love – often, but not necessarily, remaining unfulfilled – to an imagined beloved other. The old poet's role of forging political identity had passed to religious scholarship, his function of extolling princes and patrons serving only to enhance existing power relations. Rather than playing an active political role, the classical poet created a kind of counter-world to outbalance the norm-abiding realm of lived reality.

A substantial political function to affect the collective as such only reemerged in the colonial period, when Arab poets stood for cultural self-assertion against the colonial powers. Mahmoud Darwish (1942–2008) belongs to this newly revived tradition. Although artistically his work is part of a modern poetry that spans regions and cultures, Darwish never entirely disappointed the expectations pinned to a poet in the Middle East: to play a public and therefore political role. He remained committed to both of the functions ascribed to poetry, the personal exploration of the self and the activation of collective memory amidst a political conflict, very much in the vein of his paragons: revolutionary poets like Nazim Hikmet, Louis Aragon, Pablo Neruda and García Lorca, who were concurrently tribunes of their oppressed societies in the struggle for political change.

The lines quoted above, however, make a particularly ambitious claim. The poetic persona presents himself as nothing less than a cosmic agent who reconciles heaven and earth, a kind of Prometheus who shatters the symbols of ruling power structures, while at the same time re-embodying a Biblical figure, namely the first man, Adam, who on divine order gives everything a name. Is this poem a purely poetic and thus justifiably hyperbolic articulation of an artist triumphing over a situation of perversion, or is it a prophetic, covenantal and thus autobiographical statement by "the poet of Palestine"? This is a controversial question among readers of Mahmoud Darwish's work. His poetry has always provoked reinterpretations in which readers and listeners claimed autobiographical validity for the statements expressed by the poetic persona. The poet has become a charismatic figure, his poetry elevated into a "Palestinian canon" by a kind of "canonization from below". Indeed, it is no exaggeration to claim that listeners and readers have construed a prophetic-poetic, "meta-literary" autobiography from Darwish's poems, an autobiography in which they act as his closest allies.

For his own part, Darwish sought continually to repel this popular appropriation, countering the "imposed" autobiography and its mythic dimensions with his own autobiographical works: two memoirs written in different creative phases (*Diary of Daily Sadness*, 1973; *A Memory for Forgetfulness*, 1987), and two more recent divans (*Why Did You Leave the Horse Alone?*, 1995; *The Bed of the Stranger*, 1999). In these two latter works, one intertextual subtext, glimpses of which were already discernible in early poems, comes clearly and explicitly to light: Darwish's reading of the Hebrew Bible.

Against the backdrop of the Palestinian-Israeli conflict, it is to be expected that a non-religious, Arabic reading of the Bible – a body of text that had long been politically instrumentalized by Zionists – might generate a new Arabic counter-tradition, one enabling Palestinians to confront the politicized canon of the "others" with a subversive reading of their own. In his early creative period, Darwish produced such a counter-text, a Palestinian Genesis and Exodus. However, in his later reading of the Bible, his goal is far beyond this: to resolve the antagonism between other and self and localize both in a shared world, albeit one that is in the *ghurba* (outland); the specific *conditio humana* to which the title of the collection *The Bed of the Stranger* (*gharība*) alludes. It is little wonder then that prominent figures of exile from world literature find their way into the context constructed by Darwish in his later poetry, among them the Jewish poet Paul Celan, who with his idiosyncratic reading of the Hebraic Bible appears as Darwish's principal witness for the existential sensibility of exile.

Mahmoud Darwish is – together with Adonis – considered the most prominent Arab poet of his age. Darwish was born in 1942 in Birwa, a Galilean village near Acre that was razed to the ground in 1948; his family, who took refuge in Lebanon only to sneak back a year later, lived as refugees in their own country, farmers who had become day-laborers. Yet Darwish enjoyed a solid education, growing up with both Arabic and Hebrew. He took to writing poetry with overtly political overtones at a very early stage. In his obituary, his friend Elias Khoury tells us:

> ... the 12-year-old poet was called on to recite a verse at school, and wrote a poem about a child who lost his house to strangers who conquered the land. He did not know then that the poem was to be recited in memory of the *Nakba*, which over there they call Independence Day. The next day, he was summoned to the headquarters of the military governor, where they threatened to ban his father from working. 'Then I understood that poetry was more serious than I thought,' he said, 'and I had to choose between resuming this game or giving it up. Thus oppression taught me that poetry could be a weapon.'

Several years later, Darwish joined the editorial staff of the Communist literary journal *al-Jadid* (*The New*), before working for the journal *al-Ittihad* (*The Union*) in Haifa, which was closely affiliated with the Israeli Communist Party. Both press organs supported efforts to establish a transnational culture. Here he worked closely with the novelist, journalist, and politician Emile Habibi.

Written in 1966, his first long poem would mark his emergence as the voice of his society. "A Lover from Palestine" is a work in which "the Palestinian poetic project took the shape of a new language, a means to retrieve the land with words." The poet reflects on the existential experience of a poetic "land appropriation", which he has clad in prose language in his approximately contemporaneous memoir *Diary of Daily Sadness*:

> Suddenly you remember that Palestine is your land. The lost name leads you to lost times, and on the coast of the Mediterranean lies the land like a sleeping woman, who awakes suddenly when you call her by her beautiful name. They have forbidden you to sing the old songs, to recite the poems of your youth and to read the histories of the rebels and poets who have sung of this old Palestine. The old name returns, finally it returns from the void, you open her map as if you opened the buttons of your first love's dress for the first time.

What has been forcibly expunged from the speaker's consciousness returns in a kind of vision, and its erotic radiance restores reality in its full dimension. Darwish was twenty-four at the time.

As he became more prominent, he was subjected to increasingly tighter controls by the Israeli authorities, including several spells in prison, where in fact he wrote "A Lover from Palestine". Shortly after the publication of this poem, the famous Palestinian publicist and prose writer Ghassan Kanafani, working in Beirut, came across the work of Darwish and several other young poets from Israel's Arab enclave. Suitably impressed, he managed to have a number of their poems smuggled to Beirut, presenting them to a broader Arab public as "resistance poetry" – a label that Darwish would later vehemently reject.

Increasing political pressure forced Darwish to leave the country and after a short stay in Cairo he joined the Arab intelligentsia in Beirut in 1971. It was during these years of exile in Beirut that he wrote some of his most impressive poems, creating the *fida'i* (self-sacrificing fighter), or *shahid* (martyr), as an alter ego. When the Israeli Army expelled the Palestinian resistance movement from Lebanon in 1982, Darwish was again forced to leave, moving to Paris. In exile there, he wrote his war memoir *A Memory for Forgetfulness* and embarked on a collection of new poetry, this time distinctively personal in tone. As far as the wider public was concerned, he remained the "voice of Palestine", the congenial translator of the innermost longings of Palestinians, which could only be expressed poetically, in myths and symbols. Although Darwish had begun to "re-write" his past poetically in the 1990s, reappraising it from the perspective of the "estranged" exile, it was nonetheless a surprise for readers when in 2002, six years after returning to the Arab world, he, – "Palestine's poet" for over thirty years, able to attract thousands of listeners to readings and reaching countless readers throughout the Arab world – explicitly cast off this mantle and called into question an essential part of his own mythical production in the volume *State of Siege*.

Palestine: a land inscribed with the Biblical text

An observation by Thorsten Valk about German Romantic poetry seems also to describe a hallmark of modern Arab poetry:

> Since poetry is credited with a world-transforming and time-sublating dimension, reflections about poetry often touch eschatological horizons. The poet [in Novalis' work] bears the traits of the ancient poet Orpheus. Like Orpheus, he appears as a powerful magician who suspends the laws of space and time, connects the remotest realms of reality with one another, and allows all creatures to enter into a comprehensive dialogue. (...) The poet occupies a preeminent position, for he possesses an almost mythical access to the Golden Age. He is capable of tangibly experiencing the unity of the ideal primordial spheres even in the most disparate phenomena of the current world. Endowed with the exclusive gift of the analogical gaze, he can grasp the connective elements in the seemingly unrelated phenomena of the empirical realm. He is able to divine and decipher those enigmatic signs, which are inscribed into everything earthly.

Although it is difficult to identify a universally accepted Golden Age in Arab secular culture, post-colonial poetry of the Near East is nonetheless nostalgic. Poets endeavor to transform reality and recover the vision of a pre-colonial paradisiacal state of their living space beyond its real, politically distorted appearance.

This applies to Palestinian poetry in particular, for its whole self-understanding is predicated by, as Richard van Leeuwen has stressed, the premise that land is the structuring principle to organize individual and collective perceptions of life:

> There are various versions of history inscribed on the land, both by the occupier and by the Palestinians. The relations of power, however, imply that the Israeli version is dominant and that the Palestinian "textual" homeland is threatened by elimination. What remains for the Palestinians is not so much "history", as "memory" consisting of recollections of childhood and of the exodus, emotions symbolizing the attachment to the land and the natural right of the Palestinians to the land.

But these issues remain dispersed, lacking binding power, as long as no aesthetic catalyst is available to re-structure them. This is the function that poetry comes to fulfill.

It must be remembered that for a long time the Palestinian collective did not possess any relevant medium to express their experience of the *Nakba* trauma of 1948; during this period poetry was the only form of public expression left to the traumatized remnants of the population. The poet thus came to be celebrated as the speaker of the collective, a position that made him extremely vulnerable to all kinds of oppression exerted by the authorities and in several cases led to exile and loss of this public role. In spite of exile, Mahmoud Darwish's fame as the voice of Palestine survived such a crisis, thus accumulating even greater symbolic significance. It is no exaggeration to claim that the relevance of his poetry and the impact it has exerted on the memory of the Palestinian catastrophe are no less than that of such internationally cherished manifestations of Jewish memory like commemoration rituals and – more latterly – Holocaust memorials. Darwish's poetry – in his own mind – is a response to a powerful pre-existing writing that is inscribed on the land and serves to ascertain and anchor the legitimacy of the dominance of the "others": the Hebrew Bible.

Zionist inscribing of the land had not come first. A century before, American Protestants had perceived the land as oscillating between sacred ground and Biblical text, or, to quote Hilton Obenzinger, "as a female land inscribed with the male pen of the divine" waiting to be read by the heirs of the Biblical heritage. It is obvious that this vision, which would reemerge in secular form in Zionism, had and has no place for identities, which are not intrinsic to the Bible. Educated in both Arabic and Hebrew, Darwish soon became aware of the inseparable entanglement of text and land in the minds of the dominant Jewish society in his country. In his view, the mission of poetry "is essentially to strive to rewrite or to create its own Book of Genesis, to search for beginnings and to interpret myths of creation. It is through these myths that the poet can return to his origins". The master narrative of the Jewish "natural, historically preordained presence" – and of course its implication of preordained Palestinian absence and exile – had to be de-narrated.

The Palestinian-Israeli struggle is a struggle over a land claimed as the Jewish homeland; a concept that in Zionism is taken to reflect not historical contingency, but an ontological reality, as the reversal of the negative concept of *galut* (exile). This is in contradiction to traditional Jewish thought, where exile was regarded primarily not as territorial, but as spiritual, the Jews being the most obvious witnesses and evidence of a universal state of exile that – when the destruction of the Second Temple left the land devoid of the divine immanence – had affected the world as such. Yet this did not mean the dissolution of the Jews as a people; as the German-Jewish philosopher Franz Rosenzweig held: "unlike other nations, the Jewish nation was able to exist without a common land and a common language because from its very beginning as a people it did not make the peoplehood of Israel dependent on these external factors". *Zikkaron* (memory) thus played a pivotal role in preserving the past and paving the way for *ge'ula* (redemption) by keeping alive the hope for the return of the divine presence.

Zionism, which came to secularize the religious notions of Judaism, replaced the basic binarism of exile/redemption with that of exile/homecoming or homeland.

This binarism is central to Zionism; indeed it is the *shelilat ha-galut* (negation of exile) that provides the conceptual basis for the Zionist territorial claim to the land. Since Zionism – modifying the Christian view of the Jews as being excluded from the "History of Grace" – understood Jewish exile as an absence from history, that is, from historical time, the return to the land was perceived as a return to history. This notion, unique in its ideological dimension, turned the discourse of exile into a primarily Jewish discourse, which for a long time was then considered to be exclusively Jewish.

In modern history it is the plight of the Palestinians that comes closest in its dimensions to the Jewish exile experience, which had long stood as absolutely unique. With the concomitant loss of a political entity, the Palestinian situation evolved into a kind of replica of earlier Jewish exile, entailing a double absence: the absence of the majority from their homeland and the absence of those who had remained from political and cultural participation. It is impossible not to see both "exiles", the Jewish and the Palestinian, as related to and indeed intertwined with each other. The fateful relationship – the ending of one exile producing another, while two mutually exclusive memories coexist – has been poignantly expressed by Darwish, who wondered: "Should the Palestinian have to wait for two thousand years until Jewish memory will permit him to remember?"

Palestinian territorial exile, experienced by those who had to leave the country in 1948 or later in 1967, and the spiritual exile felt by those who had remained, were equally structured by the remembrance of the *status ante* that they yearned to restore. An ideal utopia emerged, one that would be re-established in reality with the anticipated collective *'awda* (return) of the exiles to Palestine. This was the hope cherished by the people. This memory – in striking parallel to the role played by Jewish *zikkaron* – acquired a vast dimension, sometimes to the extent of replacing the real homeland, as is attested in some of Mahmoud Darwish's most popular poems of the 1970s. But Palestinians are not only guided by memory, they also represent memory. To quote Edward Said:

> As a symbol of Arab defeat in 1948 and 1967, the Palestinian represents a form of political memory which is not easy to dismiss. In his wanderings, in his ubiquitous presence, above all in his own self-conscious awareness that he and his writing are the theme of much modern Arab culture, he is a figure of a worrying, a displacing sort of urgency.

Darwish is perfectly aware of the Palestinians' complex relation to memory. As mentioned above and explained by Richard van Leeuwen, in Darwish's view one of the tasks of poetry is to interpret myths of creation, because they are a vehicle for returning to origins. This emphasis on myth is only one aspect of a double strategy. Darwish's response to memory is also historical; as van Leeuwen puts it: "history and myth have become an unavoidable detour to comprehend the present and to mend the gaps created by the violent usurpation of the land and its textual representations."

The poet as the First Man: a tale of Genesis

However exaggerated their desire to be represented by a poet might be, the Palestinian public was not entirely arbitrary when choosing Darwish as their national voice. Darwish's early masterpiece "A Lover from Palestine", a *ghazal* poem dedicated to a Beloved "Palestine", can be understood as a covenant concluded between the poet and his listeners: it initiates the poet's project of de-narrating exile. The poetic persona is a *ghazal* poet, a passionate lover, who opens with a lament about the pain he suffers from the gaze of his Beloved, who is imagined as a kind of goddess, absent, yet present. The original addressee of the mystical *ghazal,* the divine Beloved, is in the postcolonial era re-embodied in the image of the similarly unattainable – whether lost or occupied – homeland. It is thus that the speaker addresses his homeland. But to be able to address her, he has to first restore her to reality. In 1966 the name "Palestine" was still politically taboo, having been officially abolished with the foundation of the state of Israel. It was likewise a tabooed word for the Palestinians of the West Bank after its annexation by the Kingdom of Jordan. Nothing called Palestine existed in political reality.

It is therefore no exaggeration to claim that the poem re-creates Palestine. The poem takes the standard form of a *qasida* with the sequence of three sections, each conveying a different mood: a nostalgic *nasib* lamenting the loss of a Beloved; followed by the *rahil*, a restrained description of a journey that portrays the poet regaining his mental composure; culminating in a pathos-charged *fakhr*, self-praise confirming the heroic virtues of tribal society. In Darwish's poem, the *nasib* laments the absence of the homeland and the resulting muteness of her loved ones:

> Your words were a song
> I sought to sing
> But agony encircled the lips of spring.
> Like swallows, your words took wing.
> Led by love, they deserted the gate of our house
> And its autumnal threshold ...

The poet's *rahil* section, leading to his imagined triumphal union with her, presents a prolonged visual pursuit of the Beloved, taking the poet through various scenes of exile, suffering and misery: to the harbor, locus of involuntary emigration; to abandoned hilltops overgrown with thorn bushes; to the storerooms of poor peasant houses; to cheap nightclubs; to refugee camps where the inhabitants are suffering great hardship.

> I saw you yesterday at the harbor
> a voyager without provisions ...
> I saw you on briar-covered mountains
> a shepherdess without sheep ...
> I saw you in wells of water and in granaries
> broken ...
> I saw you in nightclubs
> waiting on tables ...
> I saw you at the mouth of the cave,
> drying your orphan rags on a rope
> I saw you in stores and streets,
> In stables and sunsets
> I saw you in songs of orphans and wretches.

The long sequence of visions of the Beloved in a state of need and humiliation only reaches a conclusion, and so a turning point, when the Beloved reveals herself in her resplendent beauty. Endowed with an erotic aura – evocative of the poet's prose account of his rediscovery of Palestine at the seaside – she is glimpsed as a sleeping beauty, an aesthetically perfect form:

> I saw you covered all over with salt and sands,
> Your beauty was of earth, of children and jasmine.

With this vision the speaker achieves a new state of mind: he swears an oath of absolute devotion to the homeland. He thus concludes – in the understanding of his listeners – a pact, an autobiographical pact so to speak, with the Palestinian collective, which is of course the hidden addressee behind the salutation. This oath, an overtly meta-textual section placed exactly in the center of the poem, presents the process of poetical creation of the Other as the production of a garment for her, made from parts of the writer's own body, thus constituting a kind of self-sacrifice:

> I swear to you
> I shall weave a veil from my eyelashes embroidered with verses for your eyes
> And a name, when watered with my heart
> Will make the tree spread its branches again
> I shall write a sentence on the veil
> More precious than kisses and the blood of martyrs
> Palestinian she is and will remain.

The speaker in the poem thereby acquires a mythical dimension, namely that of the Biblical Adam. Like Adam, he even cedes a part of his body to make the creation of his female companion possible. The new Eve thus created, Adam's companion, who receives her name through the poet's act of creation, is none other than Palestine. The poem within the poem that echoes the Qur'anic creational imperative "Be – and it is" (Qur'an 2:117 and elsewhere) is a Palestinian transcript of the Genesis story. Because he writes down the covenant, the Adam persona figures as the writer of a new Scripture. A new tale of Genesis, of Palestinian presence, has been written.

But the self-identification of the poet as 'a lover' (*ashiq*) is above all an Arab cultural gesture reaching deep into local poetic tradition: it evokes a love that does not seek fulfillment but demands sacrifice of the lover. Recreating Palestine in poetry, bestowing on her a new identity and giving her a name: this in Darwish's view is an act of devotion that is superior to a real, bloody sacrifice, and no less redemptive than the martyrdom demanded by the Iraqi poet Badr Shakir al-Sayyab, whose "Hymn of the Rain" Darwish is rewriting. Sayyab's "civilization" of violence, turning bloodshed into the symbolic act of a sacrifice, is taken a step further by Darwish: symbolic violence is replaced by a poetic sacrifice. The land perceived as exiled is restored through the power of poetic imagination. Written shortly before the armed struggle started, Darwish's poem still views the sacrifice made to attain union with the Beloved to be a poetical task, the task of the man of the pen. The sword and the pen in Darwish's early poetry are still joined together – a poetical stance that was soon to change.

Exodus: the fighter as the poet's alter ego

Four years after he created "A Lover from Palestine", Darwish left his homeland to join the Arab intellectual elite in Beirut. For a second time he had to distance himself from the way his poetry was being read; this time from its appropriation and incorporation in ideological propaganda, which he had allegedly sanctioned. During his time in Beirut he did indeed extol the resistance fighter as a hero, a figure that since the beginning of armed struggle in the mid-1960s had kindled new hopes that the land could be recuperated. The *fida'i* in Darwish's poetry came to be regarded as a redeemer, a tragic figure who through a highly symbolic act of self-sacrifice leads his people to freedom, without himself participating in it; a hero like the Biblical Moses who led the Israelites in their Exodus to resettle in the Promised Land, himself dying before being able to tread its soil.

The struggle for the land, manifested in the 1960s in the military operations of the *fidayeen*, also took on a textual form as Darwish placed the fighter in the mythical context of his poetry. The poetical achievement of creating a figure called "Palestine" was thus followed by another act of inventing a counter-tradition to sacred history: elevating the fighter to the rank of a redeemer figure. It is thus little surprise that Darwish's poetry celebrating the *fida'i* was again taken as a "canonical expression" of the new collective experience: to take part in a decisive movement promising and delivering liberation, to live the miracle of an Exodus.

Reclaiming the land is not exclusively, however, a matter of poetical words. The poetical tradition of Palestine is closely connected with the deeds of fighters and martyrs who were celebrated as heroes in the 1930s during the British mandate. The figure of the *shahid* (martyr) was the touchstone for the obligation of preserving honor. "My land is my honor, either living in dignity or dying for the sake of it": this was the motto of the poets of the 1930s. The power of the poet, however effective its impact may be, had to be measured against the power of the fighter. The poet's commitment could claim at best to be a metaphoric parallel to the real sacrificial act of the fighter. The poet is only a martyr in terms of intention; in reality he is represented by the fighter, who is his alter ego. In turn, the poet lends the martyr poetical speech, inscribing his deeds into the consciousness of Palestinian society. Darwish himself states in his *Memory of Forgetfulness*:

> The fighters are the genuine founders of poetry and song. After a long period of time the right words will be found to describe their heroism and their amazing lives. How can the new writing crystallize and take form in a battle that has such a rhythm of rockets? And how can traditional verse define the poetry now fermenting in the belly of the volcano?

The fighter is portrayed as a hero who through his self-sacrifice attains sacred, superhuman dimensions; he is the true lover of the homeland, indeed he is her bridegroom, who through his violent death consumes a mythical marriage with her. One of Darwish's most overtly mythopoeic poems is "Weddings", where the moment of the fighter's death in combat is imagined as his wedding night which ends with his death:

> From the war comes a lover to the wedding-day
> Wearing his first suit
> And enters
> The dance floor as a horse
> Of ardor and carnation
> And on the string of women's joyful trilling he meets Fatima
> And to them sing
> All the trees of places of exile
> And soft kerchiefs of mourning ...
> And on the roof of women's joyful trilling come planes
> Planes, planes,

Snatching the lover from the butterfly's embrace
And the kerchiefs of mourning
And the girls sing:
You have married
You have married all the girls
O Muhammad!
You have spent the first night
High on the roof-tiles of Haifa
O Muhammad!
O prince of lovers ...

Acceptance of the idea of the dying fighter's mythic wedding would be unthinkable in isolation from the *ghazal* tradition. In mythic love poetry the lover has to experience, indeed welcome, the death of his ego in order to attain the desired union with the Beloved. In Darwish's poetry, this traditional concept of the "martyr of love" is embedded in a ritual reflecting the most important social rite in the rural milieu. The martyr becomes a bridegroom who guarantees through his marriage the perpetuation of his community.

Redemptive faculties had been ascribed to the martyr during the Palestinian Revolt, by poets like Abdelrahim Mahmud, but the step remained an individual literary device. Darwish involves the martyr in a drama located in the framework of a rite of passage, turning loss into redemption. Unlike the traditional Islamic imagination of the martyr, the postcolonial vision is not concerned with a reward in the Hereafter, his deed being an end in itself. He sacrifices himself, dedicating himself to the Beloved as a *fida'i*. Since there is no military gain either, the achievement of the martyr is primarily symbolic. It is the revival of memory, the crossing of the boundaries between fantasy and heroic activism; it is part of an Exodus into the contested Promised Land.

Darwish's generation of a new canon, the composition of an authoritative text on the redemptive work of the martyr, was greeted with unusual intensity: the public took possession of it in a strikingly ritual fashion. Through a kind of translation of Darwish's poetical speech into rite, the myth of the *fida'i*-redeemer was severed from poetry and given concrete form in daily life. The myth of the freedom fighter as a "dying god", a figure dying a sacrificial death to redeem, or literally "to marry" the mythified Palestine, was performed ritually for every fighter who died in action. Burials took on the traits of wedding ceremonies. The ensuing condolence ceremony, staged by women rather than the male members of the household, betrayed a striking subversion of the customary social order: the patriarchal order – often challenged in times of crisis – was suspended for the duration of the ceremony. The "marriage of the martyr", which upholds the memory of the heroic collective history, was a powerful rite of commemoration.

Darwish's close relationship to the martyr had become increasingly strained during his Beirut exile, as his work was avidly exploited in political propaganda. This is perhaps most evident in his poem "When the martyrs go the sleep" from the 1977 divan *Fewer Roses*. In 1982 he wrote a poem in praise of an individual fighter, inserting into the eulogy highly sarcastic comments on the manipulation of heroic values in society. The poem is an early attempt at dismantling of the myth enshrouding the martyr cult:

> We are so far from him
> We goad him to lunge to his death
> And write polished words of obituary dedicated to him and modern
>   poetry
> And shed the sadness outside in the street café.
> We are so far from him
> At his funeral we ourselves embrace his murderer
> And steal the bandage from his wound
> To polish the medals for persistence and enduring the long wait.

Yet on one occasion it was revived and expressed in a thoroughly positive tenor. Three months after the beginning of the first intifada on 9 December 1987 Darwish published a poem in the Paris-based Arabic-language weekly *al-Yawm al-Sabi'*, titled *Abiruna fi kalamin 'abir* ("Those who pass between fleeting words"). This poem aroused a great deal of attention in Israel and triggered a heated debate among Israeli intellectuals, which, as Issa Boullata has observed, "seemed to have been fostered by right-wing journalists and politicians and joined in by leftists for internal Israeli political reasons." Quickly translated into Hebrew, the poem was published in all major Israeli newspapers, often accompanied by extremely polemical commentary. Darwish was suspected of urging an expulsion of the Jewish population from Israel. The poem was read as documenting the radical revision of the liberal stance he had been known for *vis-à-vis* the Israeli state, though the scholar and translator Mattityahu Peled, a former general, defended it as "a poem of anger" and Uri Avnery, editor of the critical weekly *ha-Olam ha-zeh*, denounced what he termed the arrogance of the Israeli left. The debate culminated in the poem being quoted in the Knesset on 28 April 1988 as "a warning of aggressive Palestinian designs".

The poem was also the subject of lively debate in Western literary and scholarly circles, who – albeit to no avail – tried to rectify the interpretation of the misread text, which *de facto* contrasts the claims to a normal everyday life in the present, as raised by the young Intifada protesters in the West Bank, with those of Jewish settlers in that part of the land, who base their right to it on ancient history and messianic hopes. They are represented as performing an inverted exodus, not passing through the Red Sea or the desert to reach the Promised Land but plaguing an inhabited land with their aggressive presence. It is in this context that the martyrs are mentioned, with the wake celebrated in their honor becoming an integral part of the speakers' lives. The Homeland and the martyrs are imagined as generating each other. A core passage of the poem, quivering with extreme agitation, reads:

> Take your share of our blood and leave!
> We have to watch over the blossom of the martyrs,
> (...)
> Oh you who pass between fleeting words,
> Like bitter dust, pass wherever you wish but do not pass by us,
> like assailing locusts
> (...)
> Take the past if you wish to the market of antiquities,
> And restore the Temple-skeleton if you wish to the hoopoe
> On a porcelain plate.
> (...)
> We have what is lacking in you: a homeland bleeding out a people
> Who bleed out a homeland
> Worthy of oblivion or memory.

Although Darwish banned it from his official divans, it was this poem that remained alive in the Palestinian collective memory and was broadcast on many websites after his untimely death on 9 August 2008.

Multiplying exiles: the poet casts off his mask of Majnun

Darwish can be considered to embody what Foucault once termed a founder of discursivity, a figure who plays a major role in establishing a discourse; in his more recent divans he reflected not only on history as such, but also on the history of the discourse that he himself initiated. Reconsidering his early love poetry on Palestine, he identified his role in "A Lover from Palestine" as a poetic role that he had played in a kind of youthful ecstasy. His divan *The Bed of the Stranger* (1999) contains a particularly revealing poem:

> I found a mask, and it pleased me
> to be my other. I was not
> thirty yet and I thought, the limits
> of being are the words. I was
> sick for Layla like any young man, in whose blood

salt had spread. When she was not
present physically her spiritual image
appeared in everything. She brings me close to
the circuit of the stars. She separates me from my life
on earth. She is not death nor
is she Layla. "I am you,
there is no escape from the blue naught for the last
embrace". The river cured me when I threw myself into it to commit suicide

The poet's estrangement from real life could have lured him into self-annihilation, as it lured Paul Celan, the great poet of exile, who in 1970 committed suicide in the Seine. The Arab poet, however, is returned to life:

Then a man passing by brought me back.
So I asked him: Why do you give me back the air
And extend my death? He said
That you will know me better ... who are you?
I said: I am Qays Layla, who are you?
He said: I am her husband.
So we wandered around in the streets of Granada
Recalling our days on the Gulf without pain,
Recalling our days on the Gulf far away.

He is now prepared to step into the role of a poet who has become an emblem of exile, Louis Aragon's aged poet Medjnoun.

The Marxist Surrealist poet Louis Aragon stages his romance *Le Fou d'Elsa* in Granada at the eve of a new age, in the last decade of the fifteenth century, which witnesses the fall of al-Andalus into Spanish hands. Aragon's Medjnoun is in love with a future "Elsa" who could come true only when freedom and justice would allow love to flourish. He dreams of Elsa, an ideal image not of a homeland but of history, a Layla who does not yet exist; hoping she might come into being in the far future, in a society of freedom, love and justice. Darwish's Majnun merges with that of Aragon, wandering the streets of Granada, the poetical locus of Arab exile. His former rival, his "other", has become his alter ego; together they recall multiple exiles: not only the prototype of the Palestinian exile, the Arab exile from al-Andalus (which is equally the event of a Jewish exilation) but also Badr Shakir al-Sayyab's exile from Iraq, when he cried out standing on the shores of the Gulf.

While remaining Qays Layla, the poet walks no longer in the footsteps of the ancient Arab Majnun alone, but equally in those of modern poets of exile, Western and Eastern alike: Celan, Aragon and Sayyab. As these names presented in his poem betray, his exile is no longer related to territorial exclusion, but is an existential estrangement to the extent that the figure of the poet in the conventional sense is called into question. As Stephan Milich has underlined, the concluding verses of the poem are unique in expressing a complete renunciation of modern self-perception as a subject and in dismissing any essentialist and monolithic understanding of identity, conveying in contrast a self-consciousness that no longer aspires to the status of poethood but only to poetry:

> I am a being that has never been. I am an idea for a poem
> That is without land nor body,
> Without son nor father.
> I am Qays Layla, I
> I am nothing.

The poet's exiles have come full circle: at the beginning of his poetical career, Darwish gave the Palestinians a Genesis story, de-narrating their exile. Later, when celebrating the *fida'i* and the martyr, he created a Palestinian Exodus drama, dramatizing their "return" from exile. From the 1980s he turned his attention to exploring existential exile, *ghurba*, the other (*ghariba*) having become part of his self. In his divan *The Bed of the Stranger* (*ghariba*, the title, is a pun on *ghurba*) numerous heterogeneous experiences of exile emerge and merge together.

The Song of Songs versus ghazal poetry, or, Shulamit versus Layla

Once attained, the poetic recreation of the figure of Palestine is not necessarily questioned by the transformation of the poet's persona, who has ceased to claim the role of her sole partner, nor does the poet explicitly attempt to de-narrate it. Yet, his "ex-centric" self-location is, of course, indicative of the new state of mind attained within the Palestinian intelligentsia.

With the retreat of Layla, the mythic Beloved, the memory of the first real Beloved reemerges. Mahmoud Darwish had named the young Jewish woman with whom he was in love with as a young man residing in Haifa "Rita", or at other times "Shulamit", the "strange woman". Rita first appeared in his early divan *The End of Night*, but, as Elias Khoury observes:

> ... she cast her shadow over all of his poetry, up through his great poem "Mural" in 2000. (...) Darwish devoted a whole collection to love, based on the figure of Rita. *The Bed of the Stranger*, acclaimed as among the most beautiful love poems, is based on his personal experience.

Rita is the heroine of a number of early poems that celebrate love; a love located in sites impossible to inhabit such as an infernal place called Athina or a place simply called Sodom, both pseudonyms of Israel. She reemerges in his war memoir *Memory for Forgetfulness*, where in the apocalyptical situation of the bombardment of Beirut the poet has telephone conversations with her in his daydreams. Elias Khoury insists that:

> ... though she may have been inspired by a relationship that connected Darwish with an Israeli poetess (...) Rita would turn into a symbol, but not of the impossibility of love between enemies, as is commonly assumed. Because Rita became a framework in which The Poet would split the self into two.

This development has a long poetical pre-history. The most elaborate narrative of the love relationship with Rita is told in the divan *Eleven Stars Over the Last Andalusian Scene* (1992), where a long poem titled "Rita's Long Winter" is dedicated to her. Here the scenario is markedly different from that of the early Rita poems. The piece is nothing less than a translation of the Biblical Song of Songs into the reality of a loving Palestinian-Israeli couple: it is no longer the ancient city guards who pose the threat, but a powerful modern ideology adverse to their love. The tension is not between female desire and patriarchal constraints, but between mutual love and political constraints. It is a poem full of motion and vitality, rich in striking bodily metaphors taken from the realm of fauna and flora.

The poem starts with a nocturnal encounter reflecting the nocturnal scene of the beginning of the Song of Songs and, like the literary model, more than once presenting an allusion to sexual arousal: both lovers are reunited in the "room", where a window is opened to invite the moon in, to let imagined palm trees rise up in the room. Through Rita's presence the room becomes spacious, a vast field. Rita's breasts are birds, she is a gazelle. Indeed, what has been remarked about the Song of Songs – that the intricate metaphorical play whereby each of the Beloved's body parts is likened to another object evokes the impression that the lover is attempting to fill the gaps in his knowledge of her body, using as many images as he can to grasp the elusive tenor – could also be transposed to "Rita's Long Winter". Immersed in and part of local nature, the lover is closely related to his Beloved: he feels the needles of the cypress tree under his skin, both feel as if there were bees in their veins, she diffuses the smell of jasmine; when he found himself caught up in the hedge she freed him and cured him, washed him with her tears and spread anemones over him so that he could pass between the swords of her brothers; she outwitted the watchmen of the city.

As in the Song of Songs, there is the experience that on the threshold of fulfillment the Beloved vanishes and the lover is denied the possibility of consummating his desire. The tension between desire and fulfillment continues through the poem. Both texts reveal similarities in structural terms as well: the lovers more than once reverse roles; in several scenes the young woman declares her love to him; she curses or outwits her kinsmen for his sake; and there are frequent amorous dialogues. But unlike the Song of Songs, in Darwish's poem it is not she who is harassed but the lover who is targeted, impeded from entering his familiar space and in the end banished from his happiness.

But as the lover's self-assertions demonstrate, the modern poet is aware of his readers, reminding them that he is rewriting canonical texts, Hebraic as well as Arabic: he has "a part in the Book of Genesis, (...) a part in the Book of Job, (...) a part in the anemones of the *wadis* in the poems of the ancient lovers, a part in the wisdom of the lovers demanding to love the face of the Beloved even when killed by her". The last section is a kind of epilogue disclosing the break-off of the relationship – her military pistol has been laid on the manuscript of his poem and he is forced into exile.

Achieving the ultimate step of transferring Rita from the remote realm of nostalgic memory into the very core of the poet's lyrical persona would not have been possible without a pivotal encounter: that with Paul Celan's work, already alluded to in discussing the "mask" poem. Only seven years later, in a 1999 poem titled "A Cloud from Sodom" that draws on and rewrites a specific verse by Celan, Rita becomes what she will then remain throughout Darwish's later poetic production, to quote his description, "an intensively present absence":

After your night, the last winter night,
The sea road is cleared from the guards.
No shadow follows me since your night dried up
In the sun of my song. Who would tell me now:
"Leave yesterday behind, dream your unconscious!"?
My freedom now sits beside me, with me, on my chair
Like a tame cat regarding me and what you have left from yesterday:
Your lilac shawl, videocassettes
With "dance with the wolves" and a wreath of jasmine on the moss of the
   heart.
What will I do with my freedom after your night,
Your last winter night?
"A cloud moved from Sodom to Babylon",
A hundred years ago, but its poet Paul Celan committed suicide today in a
   river in Paris. You will not take me to the river a second time. No guard
Will ask me: What is your name today? We will no more curse the war. Not
   even
Peace. We will not climb over the wall of the gardens, searching for a night
   between

Two willows und two windows. You will no more ask: When will peace
    open the gates
Of our stronghold for the doves?
After your night, the last winter night,
Soldiers built up their camp at a remote place.
A white moon came down on my balcony,
And I and my freedom – we stare silently at our night.
Who am I? Who am I, after your night,
The last winter night?

The poem presents a new reflection on the story of Rita as told in "Rita's Long Winter": the "plot" is now projected into the present ("videocassettes"). The scenario of the Darwishian Song of Songs – recalled in this poem through the reminiscences of the garden wall, the willows, and the interaction with the watchmen – has been relinquished by the female figure. She is no longer nostalgically evoked but has become this "extensively present absence".

As Stephan Milich has shown, the new poem relocates the Rita story: the end of the relationship between the lovers can no longer simply be balanced by the poet's retreat to his subconscious and thus to poetical creativity. With the poet's entrance into definite exile and the merging of the "strange other", previously represented by the "strange Beloved", with his self, only the lonely "I" of freedom and silence remains. The poet himself now has to pose the question that the guards and soldiers had hitherto posed him:

Who am I, after your night,
The last winter night?

The reminiscence of the infernality of the location, of Sodom – already prefigured in the early Rita poem "A Beautiful Woman From Sodom" – brings the poet back to the past situation of his impending exile when he was about to leave Sodom, the contemporary Israel, for Babylon, the land of exile par excellence. But Sodom is now associated with the experience of another poet of exile, Paul Celan, whose verse *Von Aug' zu Aug' zieht die Wolke / wie Sodom nach Babel* (From eye to eye the cloud passes / as if Sodom passed to Babel) is rephrased by Darwish. The biblical locations of Celan's poem are reinterpreted; words of the other are claimed as words of the self, a strategy that seems to be pursued for poetic and political purposes: in these later reflections on the stages of his poetical creativity, Darwish leaps over the long phase of his mythopoeic creation during his Beirut years, when he was only *manfi* (temporally exiled) and still held hopes of returning. He seems to predate his only later attained consciousness of exile as a definite condition so as to synchronize his discovery of existing in a "land made of words" with that of Celan, who died in 1970. Stephan Milich has drawn attention to the fact that Darwish claims for himself the same stance towards poetry as Celan, who understood poetry as "a point of orientation and who strove to create an exile in language".

Farewell to myth: the deconstruction of the martyr's messianic role

The transition from devotion to the collective ideal of the mythic Palestine to a personal love marks a decisive turn, one that the broader Palestinian public greeted with harsh criticism. It proved even more problematic for Darwish to rethink and ultimately revoke the second act of his invention of sacred history: the *fidā'ī*'s redemptive role as the leader of an exodus. He had tried in the 1980s to distance himself from the figure of the martyr, exchanging the task of being the martyrs' spokesman for the more modest role of their guardian, defending them against their relentless exploitation in political propaganda. Addressing the martyred heroes, seen as sleeping and thus absent from the political scene, he had praised their integrity, their aloofness from the realm of propaganda. His "addresses to the sleeping martyrs" proved of little avail in altering the consciousness of the Palestinian public, which, ever since Darwish's conceptual coupling not only of text and land, but also fighter and poet, had cherished the figure of the martyr as closely related to that of the poet, as an anchor of hope in a situation marked by continuing siege and an increasing desire for redemption.

The poetic creation of the martyr had been a powerful act. The martyr was closely related to traditional Islamic redeemer figures bearing strong mythic characteristics; his *hieros gamos* (sacred marriage) with the mythic earth of Palestine had bestowed on him semi-divine dimensions. Once established through poetic words, "Gods" can only be abolished by those whose words created them. About thirty years after the creation of the martyr, in 2002, Darwish turned the hierarchy upside down by exposing himself to the devastating critique of his poetical creature. He allowed the martyr to correct his poetical perception of martyrdom and to tell him that all his martyr poetry was superfluous, nothing but idle noise. The martyr thus steps out of the creation of the poet, rejecting any part in his poetic imagination. To quote from the final section of Darwish's divan *State of Siege*:

> The martyr besieges me when I live a new day
> He asks me: "Where have you been?
> Return the words you gave me as presents
> To the dictionaries,
> Relieve the sleepers from the buzzing echo."

Step by step, the figure of the martyr as a poetic creation is deconstructed. Thus, the inverted social order – where not men but women determine the social life, staging a wedding in place of a funeral – also needs to be revised:

> The martyr warns me: Do not believe their ululations
> Believe my father when he looks at my picture, crying
> Why did you change turn, my son, walking on ahead of me
> I was to be first.

Martyrdom is no longer a social rite with redemptive power, but an exclusively individual act motivated by personal pride and the defiance of despair:

> To resist means: to be confident of the health,
> Of the heart and of the testicles, to be confident of your incurable malady,
> The malady of hope.

Martyrdom is viewed as an absolutely personal endeavor; it resembles another intimate human experience of transgressing the borders between the self and the other: the transition from real time and real space into the imagined sacred time and space familiar from Islamic ritual prayer. This particular intertextuality is suggested by the concluding verse of the section on the martyr, which echoes the concluding phrase of Islamic ritual prayer, *al-salamu alaykum* (Peace be upon you!). But whereas in prayer those words – uttered at the end of the ceremony and addressed to the real or imagined co-performers of prayer – mark the return of the praying person from imagined sacred time and space into reality, the martyr bids farewell forever: he addresses the "nothing" that he has become and bids farewell to his shadow.

> And in what remains of the dawn – I walk outside myself.
> And in what remains of the night – I hear the echoes of footsteps within
>   me.
> Peace be upon him who shares my alertness at the ecstasy of the light,
> The light of butterflies
> In the night of this tunnel.
> Peace be upon my shadow.

By presenting a wholesale deconstruction of the poetical image of the martyr, Darwish ends his long personal history of being a mythopoeic poet and thus concludes his role as a liminal figure, although never ceasing to reflect on collective, political issues in his poetry. But he did turn from being a kind of "magician poet", immersed vicariously for his community in a mythic time and space, to a more personal and ideologically independent role that comes closer to that of the modern writer. Looking back critically to his role as Majnun, the "Lover of Palestine" and his heroic staging of the fighter as leader of an Exodus, he bids farewell to his own mythic creation. Inspired by the *Song of Songs*, he in his later poems creates a scenario where the self and the other no longer exclude each other but merge to form a composite I-you. It is the "nonpolitical" *Song of Songs* that provides a common poetical space for the exiles among both Palestinians and Jews. Similar to the Islamic mystic who considers existence on earth to be an exile of the soul, and similar to the religious Jew who views the entire world to be in exile, the Palestinian Mahmoud Darwish perceives the world as an exile-home "made of words", *ein aufgeschriebenes Vaterland* (Heinrich Heine), which for an Arab deprived of place must be located in poetry. "In the end, we will ask" – he says in the poem *On the last evening on this earth* (1992) –

Was Andalusia
Here or there? On this earth ... or in poetry?

Postscript

Mahmoud Darwish, one of the most important poets of modern Arabic literature, died on August 8, 2008. He was mourned throughout the entire Arab world as the spokesman of his society – the Palestinian collective – and as the most respected poetic voice in the Arab language community. His death was perceived as a painful loss and lamented in countless speeches, obituaries and worldwide poetry recitals. Whereas such encomia recognized his literary significance for both Arabic and world literature, as well as his political-ideological commitments, they rarely highlighted his particular hermeneutic achievement. It went unsaid that the poet whom the Arab cultural collective had hailed as the "Voice of Palestine" – and who, until the nineties, had not been able to renounce political obligations tied to the Palestinian cause – never lost sight of the 'other' cultural collective: the Israeli, in whose midst he had grown up, and which he continued to address, alongside the Arab, in his poems. This addressing of the other is not always explicit in Darwish's poetry, but hermeneutically conveyed through intertexts from the Jewish literary canon (first and foremost the Hebrew Bible), later through the poetry of Paul Celan, and eventually through the philosophy of Walter Benjamin.

At first sight, Darwish's simultaneous address to two politically and religiously antagonistic audiences – the Arab and the Jewish – is not evident. Though Arab criticism has recognized an Israeli presence in Darwish's poetry, this concession is often tied to the figure of Rita – a figure onto which, in his later poems, Darwish projected his longing for the presence of the "first beloved" who, due to political polarization, had become a symbol of absence. Thus, Elias Khoury writes in his obituary: "We must return to the character of Rita to understand the beginning. Rita first appeared in his early book *The End of Night*, but she cast her shadow over all of his poetry, up through his great poem "Mural" in 2000. Though she may have been inspired by a relationship that connected Darwish with an Israeli poetess whose name he refused to divulge – and I will not divulge it either – Rita would turn into a symbol, but not of the impossibility of love between enemies, as is commonly assumed. Because Rita became a framework in which The Poet would split the self into two." Indeed, a dual perspective permeates Darwish's entire work. It is, however, difficult to grasp for critics unfamiliar with both the Hebrew Bible and the Hebrew and exilic Jewish literature. Likewise, it is hidden from most Israelis, who do not read Arabic. Yet the reception of Darwish's poetry in Israel, which manifested itself earlier primarily through translations in literary periodicals, is presently experiencing a revival. Four volumes of his poetry have been translated into Hebrew by Muhammad Hamza Ghanayim: *The Bed of a Stranger* (2000), *Why Did You Leave the Horse Alone?* (2000), *State of Siege* (2003) and *Mural* (2006). Salman Masalha, another bilingual Arabic-Hebrew writer, has translated his memoir, *Memory for Forgetfulness*, into Hebrew. In March 2000, the liberal minister of education, Yossi Sarid, proposed introducing several poems by Darwish into the high school curriculum. His attempt was defeated by the then Prime Minister Ehud Barak, on the grounds that Israel was "not yet ready". With Darwish's death, however, the debate over his poems's inclusion in the Israeli curriculum seems to have been re-opened.

Although Darwish's poems are undisputed masterpieces (irrespective of their Hebrew and Jewish intertexts), his consideration of the Israeli, or Jewish, audience attests to an intellectual openness in diametric opposition to the antagonism towards the other observed in daily politics. It is challenging to read Darwish's texts as *Vexierbilder*, that is, as texts with two different targets. Such a reading not only permits the discovery of hitherto neglected political-ethical dimensions of his work, but also compels Western readers to re-read familiar texts of "their" tradition that have been merged with Darwish's poetry, and to recognize these texts as palimpsests, or multiple texts, that have gained a new layer of meaning through their inscription in Darwish's poems, becoming – in musical terms – polyphonic.

His poems remain polyphonic, in the sense that they address two audiences, until his very last divan. In one of his last poems, "Do Not Apologize for What You Have Done", Darwish asks who is "I" and who is "you", while refusing to identify with his former self. Referring to a powerful topos of ancient Arabic poetry, he restages the ancient poet's lament over the deserted encampments (*atlal*) that fail to resemble the inhabited encampments of his memory. But whereas the ancient poet stands perplexed in front of the imperishable rocks – on which an unreadable inscription (*wahy*) is engraved – expressing his aporia and asking the unanswerable question, "Where have they gone that were here before (*ubi sunt qui ante nos in mundo fuere*)?" Darwish turns the question around. Rather than inquiring about the blotted-out features of the once-familiar encampment, he asks himself about his own blotted-out identity. He feels an affinity with the wind (whom he addresses in one of his last poems as a relative of fellow-poets). Both his farewell to everything firm and his exclusive maintenance of the aporia that once haunted the ancient poet bring him close, once again, to a biblical voice – that of a Hebrew poet who more than anyone mistrusted securities and placed his trust in the wind, the Ecclesiastes. His initiatory words: "Everything is wind" ("*Ha-kol hevel*"), seem to be echoed in one of Darwish's last poems, which closes: "Then I turned to the wind: Good evening! Good evening!".

SELECTED WORKS

'Ashiq min Filastin (A Lover From Palestine), Haifa: Maktabat al-Nur 1966

Yawmiyyat al-huzn al-'adi (Diary of Daily Sadness), Beirut: Markaz al-Abhath – Munaz-zamat al-Tahrir al-Filastiniyya 1973, reprint: Beirut: Riad El-Rayyes 2008

A'ras (Weddings), Beirut: Dar al-'Awda 1977

Diwan Mahmud Darwish I (Collected Poems of Mahmoud Darwish I), Beirut: Dar al-'Awda 1977

Ahad 'ashar kawkaban 'ala akhir al-mashhad al-andalusi (Eleven Stars over the Last Andalusian Scene), Beirut: Dar al-Jadid 1992; Casablanca: Dar Tubqal 1992

Ward aqall (Fewer Roses), Casablanca: Dar Tubqal 1986

Dhakira li-l-nisyan. al-Zaman: Bayrut, al-makan: yawm min ayyam ab 1982 (Memory for Forgetfulness. August, Beirut 1982), Beirut: al-Mu'assasa al-'Arabiyya li-l-Dirasat wa-l-Nashr 1987

Diwan Mahmud Darwish II (Collected Poems of Mahmoud Darwish II, Beirut: Dar al-'Awda 1994

Limadha tarakta l-hisana wahidan? (Why Did You Leave the Horse Alone?), London: Riad El-Rayyes 1995

Sarir al-ghariba (The Bed of the Stranger), London: Riad El-Rayyes 1999

Halat Hisar (State of Siege), London: Riad El-Rayyes 2002

La ta'tadhir 'amma fa'alta (Do Not Apologize for What You Have Done), London: Riad El-Rayyes 2004

Ka-zahr al-lawz aw ab'ad (Almond Blossoms and Beyond), London: Riad El-Rayyes 2005

Hayrat al-'a'id. Maqalat mukhtara (The Hesitant Homecomer. Selected Essays), London: Riad El-Rayyes 2007

Athar al-farasha. Yawmiyyat (A River Dies of Thirst. A Diary), London: Riad El-Rayyes 2008

TRANSLATIONS

Selected Poems, trans. Ian Wedde, Fawwaz Tuqan, Cheadle Hulme (UK): Carcanet Press 1973

Splinters of Bone, trans. B.M. Bennani, New York: Greenfield Review Press 1974

The Music of Human Flesh. Poems of the Palestinian Struggle, trans. Denys Johnson Davies, London: Heinemann 1980

Sand and other Poems, trans. Rana Qabbani, London: KPI 1986

Memory for Forgetfulness, August, Beirut 1982, trans. Ibrahim Muhawi, Berkeley: University of California Press 1995

The Adam of the Two Edens. Poems, ed. Munir Akash, Daniel Moore, trans. Husain Haddawi, Sinan Antoon, Sargon Boulos, Ferial Ghazoul, Clarissa Burt, Noel Abdulahad, Mona Asali van Engen, Tahiya Khaled Abdulnasser, New York: Syracuse University Press 2000

State of Siege (extracts), trans. Amina Elbendary, in: *Al-Ahram Weekly online*, 581 (11–17 April 2002), http://weekly.ahram.org.eg/2002/581/607.htm

Unfortunately, It Was Paradise. Selected poems, trans. Munir Akash, Carlyn Forche, Sinan Antoon, Amira El-Zein, Berkeley: University of California Press 2003

The Butterfly's Burden, trans. Fady Joudah, Northumberland: Bloodaxe 2007

A River Dies of Thirst. A Diary, trans. Catherine Cobham, London: Saqi 2009

Almond Blossoms and Beyond, trans. Mohammed Shaheen, Northampton: Interlink 2009

FURTHER READING

Sinan Antoon: "Returning to the Wind: On Darwish's La Ta'tadhir 'Amma Fa'alta". In: Hala Khamis, Najat Rahman (eds.): *Mahmoud Darwish. Exile's Poet. Critical Essays*. Northampton: Interlink 2007, 219–38

Issa J. Boullata: "An Arabic Poem in an Israeli Controversy. Mahmoud Darwish's 'Passing words'," in: Asma Afsaruddin, A.H. Mathias Zahniser (eds.): *Humanism, Culture, and Language in the Near East. Studies in Honor of Georg Krotkoff*, Winona Lake: Eisenbrauns 1997, pp. 119–28

Birgit Embaló, Angelika Neuwirth, Friederike Pannewick: *Kulturelle Selbstbehauptung der Palästinenser. Bio-bibliographischer Survey der Modernen Palästinensischen Dichtung*, Beirut, Würzburg: Ergon 2001, pp. 216–46

Hala Khamis, Najat Rahman (eds.): *Mahmoud Darwish. Exile's Poet. Critical Essays*, Northampton: Interlink 2007

Elias Khoury: "The Poet is Dead. Elias Khoury Remembers his Friend Mahmoud Darwish", in: *The Nation*, 29 August 2008

Verena Klemm: "Poems of a Love Impossible to Live. Mahmoud Darwish and Rita", in: Thomas Bauer, Angelika Neuwirth (eds.), *Ghazal as World Literature I: Migrations of a Literary Genre*, Beirut, Würzburg: Ergon 2005, pp. 243–58

Richard van Leeuwen: "Text and Space in Mahmoud Darwish's Prose Works", in: Stephan Guth, Priska Furrer, Johann Christoph Bürgel (eds.), *Conscious Voices. Concepts of Writing in the Middle East*, Beirut, Stuttgart: Steiner 1999, pp. 255–75

Stephan Milich: *"Fremd meinem Namen und fremd meiner Zeit"*. *Identität, Fremdheit und Exil in der Dichtung von Mahmud Darwisch*, Berlin: Schiler 2004

Angelika Neuwirth: "Kulturelle Sprachbarrieren zwischen Nachbarn. Ein neues Gedicht von Mahmud Darwish im Verhör seiner israelischen Leser", in: *Orient* 29 (1988), pp. 440–66

Angelika Neuwirth: "Mahmud Darwish's Re-staging of the Mystic Lover's Relation Toward a Superhuman Beloved", in: Stephan Guth, Priska Furrer, Johann Christoph Bürgel (eds.), *Conscious Voices. Concepts of Writing in the Middle East*, Beirut, Stuttgart: Steiner 1999, pp. 153–71

Stefan Weidner: "Mahmud Darwish", in: *Kritisches Lexikon zur fremdsprachigen Gegenwartsliteratur*, Munich: Edition Text + Kritik 1997

OTHER WORKS CITED

Louis Aragon: *Le Fou d'Elsa*, Paris: Gallimard 1963

Paul Celan: *Mohn und Gedächtnis*, Stuttgart: Deutsche Verlagsanstalt 1952

As'ad Khairallah: *Love, Madness, and Poetry. An Interpretation of the Majnun Legend*, Beirut, Wiesbaden: Steiner 1980

Edward Said: *The Question of Palestine*, New York: Vintage 1979

Thorsten Valk: "Der Dichter als Erlöser. Poetischer Messianismus in einem späten Gedicht des Novalis", in: Olaf Hildebrand (ed.), *Poetologische Lyrik von Klopstock bis Grünbein. Gedichte und Interpretationen*, Cologne et al.: Böhlau 2003, pp. 71–81

Traditions and Counter-Traditions in the Land of the Bible

Emile Habibi's De-Mythologizing of History

Angelika Neuwirth

A modern novel, Hans Wollschläger once remarked, must be able to demonstrate that it was written after James Joyce's *Ulysses*. Emile Habibi's novel *The Secret Life of Saeed, the Ill-fated Pessoptimist* (1974) is one work that can match this demand: its main concerns follow the path carved by Joyce. Although the narrative timeframe is not condensed into a single day but extends across a political epoch, the quarter of a century from 1948 to 1972, like *Ulysses* this novel traces the discrepancy between aspirations and reality, thus disclosing the "surrogate character" of social reality; or more precisely, of the two life-worlds ideologically based respectively on a Jewish messianic "saga", and an Arab heroic ideal. After Salman Rushdie's *The Satanic Verses*, which, as Sadiq al-Azm has pointed out, is underlain by the "great narrative of Islamic culture", namely the canonical vita of the Prophet as a subtext that is then deconstructed, *The Pessoptimist* can be regarded as a further audacious attempt from the Middle East to create a counternarrative, to "foundational texts" setting and sustaining cultural identity.

In his bi-national homeland Israel/Palestine Habibi is faced with not one but two irreconcilably different "foundational texts", called on by both societies to justify their respective claims to the same land. The Jewish claim is based on a secularized Zionist reception of the historical sections of the Hebrew Bible, a reading that has retained its political and theological relevance, accumulated over centuries of allegorical interpretation: the reading of the Bible had already in antiquity crystallized into a grand drama of divine intervention in the historical fate of the people of Israel, recalling the crucial stages from divine election via exodus, the occupation and settlement of the land, to exile and eventually promised salvation. In the Diaspora, this drama was continually re-actualized through synagogal liturgy and theological reflection into a pivotal figure of remembrance for collective memory. The political actualization of this messianological paradigm, inherent to the Zionist ideology of the founders of the state of Israel, enables Jewish society to interpret its own presence in the land as a fulfillment of a historical narrative which begins with being God's elected people, entitled to the promised land, and culminates, after exile, in return and redemption.

The Arab-Palestinian model is entirely different: it is the resolute adherence to a mythicized "prophet-poet-fighter" ideal, a re-actualization of the remembrance of venerable Arab-Islamic figures standing for self-assertion and the gallant defense of collective dignity, whereby the relationship between the land and the Arab population takes on mythical dimensions. Neither society is geared towards rational argument or engagement with its counterpart; they avoid it by interpreting contemporary history in terms of a "return to origins", constructing myths about their own relationship to the land. The paradoxes which emerge for the Palestinian Arabs caught in this field of tension are the real subject matter of Habibi's novel.

Born in 1921 in Shafa Amr near Nazareth, Emile Habibi grew up in modest circumstances in Haifa, by then an emerging city with oil refineries and a busy export harbor that would soon become the cultural center of the Palestine mandate territory. The son of a teacher, he completed part of his school education at Akka, a town steeped in tradition located some thirty kilometers from Haifa and a historical bastion of Islamic-Arab assertion against foreign enemies. Upon leaving school Habibi studied to become a refinery engineer through correspondence courses only to turn to journalism, working for Palestinian radio in Jerusalem. Joining the Communist Party, he gained prominence as the organizer of a political discussion forum for Palestinian intellectuals as early as 1943; in 1944 he co-founded the communist newspaper *al-Ittihad* (The Union), the only press organ that would survive the expulsion of the Arab population from the region in 1948.

During the fighting of 1948 Habibi fled to Lebanon, but he managed to return before the founding of the Israeli state. He worked as a journalist, mainly for *al-Ittihad*, where he advanced to the post of editor in the 1950s; he also acted as editor for two communist-affiliated literary and cultural political monthlies, *al-Jadid* (The New) and *al-Ghad* (The New Tomorrow). These editorial posts not only introduced him to the latest Arab literature written outside the country, otherwise inaccessible for the average Arab reader; they also brought him into close personal contact with Arab literary figures, most of whom also worked in Haifa, like Mahmoud Darwish, Samih al-Qasim and Tawfiq Zayyad, whose poems are referenced frequently in Habibi's work. Furthermore, his editorial work introduced him to important Israeli writers and poets, mostly recent immigrants from Iraq, kindred spirits with the Palestinian communists, whose texts were printed in the Arabic original or in translation from the Hebrew in the state-funded communist journals. After 1967 Habibi appeared in public together with Israeli writers a number of times to defend the rights of Palestinians in the occupied territories.

A member of the central committee and politburo of the Israeli Communist Party, Habibi was a Knesset deputy for three legislative periods, resigning from his seat only in 1972 to devote his energies entirely to his literary work. He spent the following two years working in Prague for the journal *Peace and Socialism* as representative of the Israeli Communist Party. Habibi saw himself as representing

Palestinian society in Israel, which, through the opening of Israel's borders after the 1967 June War, gained the freedom to address the "others" in Israel as well as the Arab world, from which it had been isolated for twenty years. Habibi explored this aspect of postwar development in a cycle of short stories titled *Hexalogy of the Six Days* (1968), which traced the slow return of memory and the faculty of speech to those who had remained in the country. He never lost sight of the ambivalence of this reawakening, which was born of a catastrophe whose repercussions were still unforeseeable at the time. While the short stories were already distinctly self-reflexive, critically interested in probing collective and individual failures, this "work of mourning" forms the very heart of the allegorical drama *Luka', Son of Luka'* (1980) as well as the novels *The Pessoptimist, What a Shame!* (1985) and *Saraya, the Ghul's Daughter* (1991). From 1990 onwards, after resigning from the Communist Party, Habibi ran his own publishing house, Arabesque, until his death in Haifa in 1996.

In his first novel *The Secret Life of Saeed, the Ill-fated Pessoptimist* (1974), which was translated into several languages and for which he was awarded the Israeli State Prize for Literature in 1992, Habibi focuses primarily on recalling the years prior to this opening of borders; the "cryptic", "missed" years during which the first-person narrator, a powerless and inactive man whose naivety borders on scurrility, clings to unrealistic dreams. At the same time, he, the outsider and mere observer, is unable to evade the grotesque traits which accrue to both societies as they superimpose the present with idealized, mythically evoked history.

Contexts and subtexts

This aspect requires a brief look back: with the exodus of Palestinian Arabs in 1948 and the void left in urban centers by the flight of the elites, the groups remaining behind were deprived of the basic intellectual and cultural force necessary to articulate their presence as an identifiable collective. Psychologically uprooted and under threat socially, they also lacked the stability and strength necessary to perceive the "other" objectively, let alone the willingness to enter into open communication. Isolated in this way, they turned to their own traditions for orientation to overcome the myriad difficulties of the catastrophe befalling them.

Initially it was a matter of holding onto the land. This was articulated in poetry, in rural areas the longstanding conventional medium for expressing relevant political and social concerns, mastery of which accorded the poet a kind of spokesman's role. In Palestine this poetry was able to tap into patriotic predecessors from the nationalist movement of the 1930s but the most influential impetus, evident throughout the entire Middle East, was the crucial rediscovery of myth, inspired by the reception of T. S. Eliot's *The Waste Land*. Both the image of self and other are mythicized, as is particularly evident in the early poetry of Mahmoud Darwish. Above all since the June War, Zionist, biblically founded self-awareness confronts a Palestinian self-conception that is embodied in the figure of the heroic fighter or martyr as the liberator of an oppressed society. In the surrounding postcolonial Arab world, where this role is not taken up by armed fighters, it is claimed by poets and the literati; in Palestine, but also in Iraq and the Palestinian diaspora, writers and intellectuals see themselves as fighters, and this role is ascribed almost messianic significance. Poetry, above all that of Darwish, thus forms a continual subtext of *The Pessoptimist*; a seam of meaning that is not always affirmed in the novel but is frequently subject to severe criticism.

A further subtext underlies the novel: Voltaire's picaresque novel *Candide*. As entire passages that quote *Candide* reveal, *The Pessoptimist* borrows from Voltaire's counterpoint between the report given from the perspective of an artless-naïve narrator, a "sheer fool", and the sovereign-satiric commentary given by a reflective critic. The short chapters with their headings in baroque detail; the expressive names; the direct and drastic descriptions of catastrophic events; the simplistic, woodcut-like portrayal of the figures; and the philosophy upon which the work is based: all these aspects are obviously a deliberate paraphrase of *Candide*. For as Voltaire's satire reduces Leibnizian optimism to absurdity – "tout pour le mieux dans le meilleur des mondes" – Habibi's satire makes a mockery of the legacy of Islamic optimism, which assumes that even the direst adversity is a sign of divine intervention and thus assuredly awaits liberation "from beyond". From his Palestinian observation post, Habibi would undoubtedly judge the progress inherent to world history far more pessimistically than Voltaire: instead of the gradual advancement of reason, he observed the endless continuum of repression and new performances of historical tragedies, which, as Marx emphasizes, can only be considered farcical in their repetition. All of his embitterment is reserved for the idea of the repeatability of history in the sense of a return to origins, an idea he detects as predominant amongst both conflict partners.

The baroque syntax employed to expose the grotesque in Habibi's picaresque novel is connected with the strategy to exploit the equivocations of Arabic consciously, as a means of marking and expressing the paradox of the given situation. It is precisely this technique which would spontaneously remind a native language reader of *The Pessoptimist* of genuine Arabic paragons; in particular the *Maqamat* by al-Hariri (1054–1122), which unfold a panorama of settings from the Arab world of the twelfth century, moved along dramatically by the rhetorical brilliance of a vagabond trickster called Abu Zayd al-Saruji who scams his livelihood by disguising his poverty in brilliant imitative performances of literature and philosophy. He too is an antihero, continually forced into playing a double role; at the same time, thanks to his polished command of language and suggestive rendering of ideas into verbal imagery, he manages not only to manipulate his listeners but also to capture the ambiguity and paradox of reality. In the end the trickster's "topsy-turvy world" is exposed and critically rebuked by his follower al-Harith, before being placed right side up once more. The formal structure of *The Pessoptimist* is in places closely modeled on al-Hariri, but even more prominent is the adoption of his playful technique to forge fantastic connections between subjects that, although close to one another etymologically or in pronunciation, are objectively completely unrelated, thus creating a fantastic counter-reality.

Like al-Hariri, Habibi inserts elements of poetry; sometimes to lend the speech a historical dimension, appealing to the shared language of the rich collective cultural heritage; at other times to playfully verify or – even more frequently – expose falsehoods in the facts related. The novel abounds in references to classical texts that are still promulgated as a matrix of collective identity in the school curricula. Peter Heath has characterized this particular employment of historical references as follows:

> Habibi's ironic attitude toward canonical knowledge serves to subvert it. He continually contrasts lofty historical and cultural references from the school canon, which are intended to teach Arab schoolchildren about the greatness and nobility of their past, (with complete disregard for, A.N) the pathetic daily realities (...), in which heroism or idealism are unrealistic expectations. (...) The gap between cultural rhetoric and current fact is too great.

Even more than secular verse, Qur'anic verses possess a "verifying" character. Taken in their respective contexts, it may be assumed that every reader is familiar with them, so that fleeting allusions suffice to call to mind a complete story, the traits of a historical salvation figure, or a theological doctrine. Despite Habibi's non-Muslim education, allusion to Qur'anic verses is one of his preferred techniques; perhaps because they provide him – an author confronting both Jewish and Islamic cultures – with a unique opportunity to refer to both their shared and distinguishing features. Since his main protagonists are decidedly Islamic in character, as is clearly evident in their language, Qur'anic-tinged speech is inevitable. Furthermore, Qur'anic echoes often have a biblical equivalent, to which the Israeli identity is bound as much as the Arab is to a Qur'anic verse. When, for example, the biblical story of Jacob is indirectly referred to in the name given to the Jacob Rothschild foundation Zikhron Ya'qov (literally: "Memory of Jacob"), so must the association – conjured by Saeed with his playful renaming of the settlement in markedly Qur'anic terms, as "A wish Jacob had in mind" (*hajatun fi nafsi Ya'qub*; sura 12:68) – with the Islamic story of Jacob be seen as a satirical attempt to "Arabize" the Jewish settlement by connecting it to a Qur'anic etiology.

These trans-cultural and trans-linguistic associations are only the tip of the iceberg. They form part of a dense web of stratagems introduced to lay bare the political power of each of the two segments of Israeli society, Jewish and Arab. The novel is replete with irony, often expressed through linguistic puns that feed on the apparent similarity between Hebrew and Arabic. Thus the narrator's aunt, mistaking him for a government agent taking the census, exclaims: "I am *mahsiyya*! [I have already been counted in the census!] But she pronounced it *makhsiyya* (castrated) as the soldiers pronounce it..."

This trans-linguistic pun is adduced by Akram Khater as a particularly telling example of Habibi's irony:

> The play on words *mahsiyya* and *makhsiyya* – pronounced as it is differently by the oppressor and the oppressed – hints at the political importance of Palestinians living in Israel when it equates being counted in the census of the state with castration. It is this impotence against a dominant political structure that feeds and nourishes the confusion in the lives of Palestinians living in Israel.

Habibi's political criticism is enshrined in puns like this. Various other devices conveying irony have been highlighted by Ibrahim Taha:

> Hence, language is not only a simple mirror that reflects, but one that charges the reflection with meanings which reside in several layers. It is the intentional, yet unpretentious, depth of these layers (...) that separates Habibi's work from most Palestinian novels.

As Akram Khater points out, in his playful ironic challenge of the hegemony of the Hebrew language Habibi was not only unrivaled in his own time, he also found no emulators. A substantially different approach would be taken only a generation later, when Hebrew had established itself as the second language of Palestinians in Israel.

In his novel *Arabesques* Anton Shammas, the preeminent Palestinian writer of the 1980s and 1990s, uses Hebrew, to quote Khater:

> ... in its most classical fashion to describe the memories and lives of Palestinians living the Jewish state. Thus Hebrew ceases to be exclusively a vessel that contains Jewish memories, for now it must make room – albeit a very small one in the beginning – for the memories of the Arabs of Israel. In this manner, Shammas interjects the reality of Palestinian existence and historical experience into the consciousness of the Jewish Israeli.

Hebrew is no longer the language of the other, but part of the self – again very much in tune with the mutation of the Israeli other into part of the Palestinian self that is reflected in the later poetry of Shammas's older contemporary, Mahmoud Darwish. It is noteworthy, however, that unlike Shammas, whose experiment was doomed to fail, Habibi not only asserted himself as a political figure in Israel but, by writing what has been judged as the most impressive satire in Arabic, also succeeded in attaining his explicitly pronounced goal "to show the absurdity of the ethnic oppression in Israel".

From the life of a Pessoptimist

The reader encounters elements from Habibi's own life in *The Pessoptimist*, in three long letters penned by a first person narrator called "Saeed (literally: "happy"), the Ill-fated Pessoptimist". Nevertheless, the novel is not some encoded autobiography of Habibi's but fiction through and through; at best a "pseudo-autobiography" of the narrator, as Peter Heath claims, or a memoir, as Ibrahim Taha prefers to label it. This is conspicuous from the very outset, with the ironic filtering of the narrative and a large number of intertextual allusions to older Arab and European literature. There is a series of documents, all "verified" in footnotes providing details on persons and dates and which would thus appear to be more the responsibility of an "editor" than a narrator. But even here it is shortsighted to perceive Habibi in the background; the framework – confirmation of the receipt of the letters and investigations into their author – is itself fictional, created by another anonymous first-person narrator, who although reminiscent of Habibi himself, is the ficticious narratee of the novel.

Given this "fiction within the fiction" it is not surprising that, as distinct as the letter-writer and the addressee may seem at first, the two narrative perspectives of the naïve and the sovereign reflective voice often overlap in the figure of Saeed himself. It is precisely this play on the double perspective which gives the letters, in particular those in the first book, their specific appeal: maintained in the narrative strand on the events of 1948, the perspective of the naïve young man, a "weak, passive, dim-witted collaborator" who presents himself as a comical antihero, shifts suddenly to that of the sovereign, seasoned caustic critic, who positions himself and his writing in 1972, the point in time when the report switches to reflection and criticism. This discrepancy, particularly noticeable in the first book in view of the youth of the protagonist, his susceptibility and his dealings with persons with simple, often ridiculous, character traits, diminishes in the second book, covering the post-1948 years, before disappearing completely in the third, set in the years after 1967. Although Saeed still comes across as a foolish and simple person in his dealings with political reality, he is nonetheless now well aware of his paradoxical situation as an Israeli Arab, so that the satirical comments accompanying his report in fact match his own psychological disposition. Moreover, he is confronted with morally superior partners, some of whom are even exemplary in certain aspects. He may thus be looked upon as a "wise fool", a type not unfamiliar in Near Eastern narrative.

A poem is presented as the novel's prefacing motto, an appeal to wait no longer for redemptory messages from otherworldly spheres, but to write one's own messages, to bring about salvation through one's own words. Saeed takes this call literally, writing down his story in three long letters. He claims to be writing from an extra-terrestrial place where he has been transferred by a super-human savior who earlier in his life had initiated him to his role as a writer. He finds himself amidst otherworldly beings, not unfamiliar in the history of Islam as those redemptory figures shrouded in secrecy, the last of whom – in the hope of the folk religion – is the Mahdi, expected at "the end of days", when the social and political order has reached its absolute low and all await the savior. In the novel, however, they feature as extraterrestrial figures without eschatological dimensions, evoking instead models from science fiction and other contemporary surreal literature. Already the introduction of his *fada'iyyun* (extraterrestrial friends) – the word is a pun on the designation of the more familiar representatives of salvation, the *fida'iyyun* (guerrillas) – expresses the narrator's claim to a highly privileged status. His life story, however, ridicules his lofty self-positioning. It is centered on an exilic dream of return. Although the name Layla is never mentioned, Habibi's novel plays on the Majnun Layla story. Saeed has lost the beloved of his youth, Yu'ad ("that which will be returned"), with the eviction of the Arab citizens of his hometown Haifa. He never ceases to yearn for her. But the genre of the picaresque novel does not allow pathos to gain the upper hand; Saeed soon finds consolation with another woman called Baqiya ("she who has remained"). The dream of a return to the beginning (Yu'ad) thus gives way to the acceptance of a life among the remnants (Baqiya) of the people. Though the vision of Yu'ad never fades, Saeed subverts rather than lives the role of Majnun.

The three sections of the novel are named after women, names whose literal meaning refers to a phase in the development of the homeland. The first of these women, Yu'ad, symbolizes the lost homeland, the painfully missed sense of being in the safe hands of one's relatives, friends, and neighbors, most of whom have fled and contact with them been lost. But her name also echoes the beginning of a famous ancient Arabic poem, *Banat Su'ad* ("Su'ad has departed"). In pre-Islamic poetry the topical image of a woman who has left is closely connected to the equally stereotypical motif of an encampment that lies devastated, symbolizing the loss of an emotionally fulfilled past that will not be retrieved. In Habibi's novel, the etymologically charged name Yu'ad stands for the collective vision of regaining an intact homeland, increasingly elevated by the narrator into an ideal, only to be eventually abandoned.

The vision must fade because as the ideal recedes into the distance another no less attractive, but more real figure emerges: the "small homeland", the life-world of those who have remained. For the narrator this figure is embodied in the woman he marries, a young girl who gives herself the name of "al-Tanturiyya" in honor of her lost and devastated home village Tantura, but in the narrative is simply called Baqiya. As his wife she will share his life for almost twenty years. The Baqiya character is linked with a strictly kept secret that makes it possible for her to survive under the pressures exerted by a double loyalty, torn as she is between obedience to the authority of the state and the indomitable wish to maintain her personal dignity, which is severely abused in everyday life. This dignity is like a treasure chest thrown overboard by its owners, nestling on the seabed filled with the weapons of the men and the gold jewelry of the women. To regain this inheritance, of traditional male and female values as well as collective memory, is Baqiya's secret goal; the narrator pledges his support as part of their wedding vows. The realization of this goal is not achieved by her generation, but first comes close to fruition for their son, fittingly named Wala' (fidelity, loyalty), who lends this dignity a new interpretation, one that takes the parents fully by surprise. He has experienced the patient, self-imposed constraint of the older generation as a process of withering away and becoming helplessly muzzled. Seeking to break out of the debilitating impasse (events are dated indirectly to the year before the June War, the beginning of the armed struggle) he engages in an act of resistance which results in his death and that of his mother. The vision of the "small homeland", of a life in the isolated minority, is extinguished.

What remains for the narrator after both visions have been ruined? In the third and final book – titled the "second Yu'ad" – he encounters another embodiment of the homeland amidst the stream of returnees from Lebanon after 1967. She is none other than the daughter of his early love, a member of a young Palestinian generation which has gained new self-confidence in exile. At first the narrator is unable to distinguish her from the "first Yu'ad" he still cherishes and longs for, so he clings to the idea that history is repeatable. But the "second Yu'ad" comes from a thoroughly renewed society, one that has liberated itself from the shackles which have so constricted the Arab minority who remained behind and is capable of engaging in rational discussion with its political opponents.

Influenced by this new way of thinking, Saeed discards all his earlier loyalties. As if sitting atop a hermit pillar, he eventually becomes completely estranged from his life-world: in the allegorical terms of the writer-prophet, he is translated to heaven to join the extraterrestrial beings. It is precisely from this situation of "translation" and its rapture – a madness spawning creativity – that Saeed writes his letters. He is given the role of breaking the silence of his generation, of remembering. An outsider in both societies, he shows them no forbearing respect, always observing life "from below", from the perspective of a childlike-naïve observer. Yet this low status, as Peter Heath observes:

> ... allows him to lay claim to another form of professional identity (...). He is intrinsically a member of that nameless yet ever-present group that the news-papers refer to as "the others," or "the rest," those whose presence is mentioned in news reports although they are never individually identified.

Without letting his observations pass through an inner censor of personal solidarity, Saeed perceives above all else the tragicomic of history. His report offers a chain of demonstrations for his reflections on history, which lead directly back to Marx's *Eighteenth Brumaire*:

> Hegel remarks somewhere that all facts and personages of great importance in world history occur, as it were, twice. He forgot to add: the first time as tragedy, the second as farce.

Does history repeat itself? "Inheriting the land", "gathering the exiles", "making the desert fertile"

Returning from exile in Lebanon, Saeed "entered the state of Israel" to fulfill the last wish of his father: to follow in his footsteps and become an informer for the new state. He enters the country on a donkey, a grotesque Messiah figure. It is 1948. Saeed will become instantly entangled in the "war of independence".

Taken along on an Israeli patrol, he witnesses the specifically Zionist process of gaining independence or, in religious terminology, "inheriting the land". What he observes has little to do with the fulfillment of the Biblical promise of land given to Abraham. It is rather a new staging of a Biblical counter-tradition to inheritance, namely a story of expulsion, the "disinheriting" of "relatives" who have become undesirable. The military governor, who introduces himself to Saeed as "Abu Ishaq" ("father of Isaac") and thus as "Abraham", expels a young woman and her child from the land. Frightening her away at gunpoint, he sends her "to the east", reenacting the story of Abraham's casting out of his own helpless concubine Hagar and her son Ishmael. This act of repudiation does not lead to the striven-for "independence" but to the military governor's irritated observation that the shadows of the expelled are becoming increasingly larger, and will eventually cover the whole country. Viewed critically, this is the essence of the history of the Israeli war of independence.

The language and in particular the conclusion of the scene provide the key to a second reading, one that illuminates the Palestinian story. The Israeli perspective adopted by the narrator, betrayed by Zionist labels such as "war of independence", is in linguistic terms alone an act of self-deconstruction of the text. Arabic texts with this skewed terminology are omnipresent in the propaganda that infiltrates everyday life, in the "hegemonic representation" whose untrustworthiness is clearly evident to its oppressed addressees. In this way the untruth of what is asserted is already part of the text. What remains as the uncompromised message is the subtext of the story, the genesis of resistance prophesied with the event. The village the young woman named as her home was Birwa; the child is thus none other than the future poet Mahmoud Darwish, the voice of Palestinian resistance. The described expulsion, the early experience of dispossession and disenfranchisement, will become the formative moment for his artistic inspiration, as the verse by Darwish quoted at the end of the chapter shows: "We know them, the (inspiring) spirits who turn children into prophets."

Before he can begin serving as an informer like his father, Saeed is briefed by a night in the al-Jazzar mosque in the center of Akka's old quarter, where he is once more witness to a perverted realization of a biblically sanctioned mission. The scene, which like no other demonstrates the lack of communication amongst Palestinians affected by evacuation, is the trigger for his own calling to become a writer, a speaker. On the surface the scene portrays the procedures employed in the expulsion of helpless villagers, involving not only violence on the Zionist side but also collaboration and deceit on the side of educated Palestinians. But on closer inspection, this incident turns out to be the inverted image of a major Zionist claim, that of the "ingathering of the exiles". Peter Heath has pointed to the frequency of Habibi's use of symbol and allegory. He interprets these symbolic representations as:

> ... part of the novel's larger allegorical structure in which every character and event symbolizes aspects of the relationship among and between Palestinians and Israelis. Saeed is the passive survivor, the two Yu'ads different generations of those driven into exile, Baqiya and Wala' two generations of those Israeli Arabs who decide to resist ...

This is certainly true, yet the allegorical structure does not primarily rely on individual figures or issues acquiring symbolic value, but on a cohesive paradigm.

What has hitherto not been given due attention in scholarship is the transnational subtext that underlies the narrative plot. What underpins the entire novel is a tightly knit sequence of counter-representations and subversive deconstructions of major Zionist objectives, passing from the claim of the "ingathering of the exiles" via "making the desert fertile" to the "negation of exile". It is true that this dimension of cultural critique is not as obvious to the non-local reader, who is unaware of the crucial significance of these particular Zionist claims; it may even be hidden to readers unacquainted with the main tenets of Zionist ideology. One of the major objectives of the Zionist settlement was the bringing home of the dispersed members of the Jewish nation, *qibbuts ha-galuyot* (ingathering of the exiles); in the religious context, the work the Messiah will one day achieve and an integral part of Jewish morning prayer. In Zionism, the assumption of responsibility for this objective by politicians is reflected in the name given to the institution that forms a pillar of the state, the *qibbuts* (kibbutz). To disclose the grotesqueness of this claim and its practice, Habibi transposes the idea of the Zionist "gathering" to the Palestinian Arabs involved on the other side, those whose expulsion and dispersion is the price to be paid for the attainment of the Messianic goal.

In the al-Jazzar mosque Saeed meets his old school principal who has been entrusted with the task of organizing the "gathering" of refugees who were detained as they attempted to return to their destroyed villages in the coastal strip and are now interned in the mosque. After the principal has convinced the scared refugees that Saeed is trustworthy, they bombard him with the same question: "We're from the village of so-and-so. Have you met anyone else from so-and-so?" Completely insensitive, Saeed is aware solely of the randomness and comical aspect of the countless names, their questions remaining pointless for him:

> But soon voices erupted again, persisting in drawing out their relationships to their villages, all of which I understood to have been razed by the army: "We are from Ruwais." "We are from al-Hadatha." "We are from el-Damun." "We are from Mazraa." "We are from Shaab." "We are from Miy'ar." "We are from Waarat el-Sarris." "We are from el-Zeeb." "We are from el-Bassa." "We are from el-Kabri." "We are from Iqrit". "We are from Kufr Bir'un." "We are from Dayr el-Qasi." "We are from Saasaa." "We are from el-Ghabisiya." "We are from Suhmata." "We are from el-Safsaf." "We are from Kufr 'Inan." Please do not expect me, my dear sir, after all this time, to remember the names of all the villages laid waste to which these figures made claim that evening in the courtyard of the Jazzar Mosque.

While this is certainly a new "gathering of the exiles", which the principal then indeed calls a *jam' shaml*, the equivalent Arab phrase (bringing together the dispersed), it is in reality an utter travesty of the Messianic *qibbuts ha-galuyot*, serving the purpose of smoothing the deportation of the refugees across the border that will take place at daybreak.

Language is presented here as caught in a dead end. The scene demonstrates the grievance raised by Darwish in an early poem: that in the situation of collective catastrophe individual loss is not named, and as such the loss simply vanishes, is "forgotten in the crowd of names." The countless names of lost villages are nothing more than fragments of a memory yet to be restored. The evocation of names is for both Darwish and Habibi not a viable way to "gather the exiled" in memory.

This gathering, as the act constituting remembrance, must be preceded by a reflection on the role of language, which in this context seems not merely to be pointless but indeed a medium of deception. By modeling the scene on the classical *maqama*, Habibi marks it as a cynical farce for his readers, who are able to grasp the intertextual foil. Like the trickster in the *maqama*, the principal dupes the refugees with euphemisms like "bringing together" and "return" so as to make them submissive. Only the rebuke of the deceiver by his pupil, which in the *maqama* is an essential part of events, in the novel text fails to materialize: Saeed's reflection gestates slowly. Without the protests of their educated co-patriots – this is Habibi's message – the helpless refugees are betrayed by their own political leaders.

Other Zionist prerogatives are exposed as propaganda, in reality achieved through Palestinian involvement. Thus, in the Zionist perspective the actual confirmation of the successful regaining of the land is *hafrakhat ha-shemama* (making the desert fertile), very much an end-of-days vision, although again one that the Zionist settlers take into their own hands and seek to realize through their own *avoda ivrit* (Hebrew labor); a project that is known in religious terms as the *ge'ulat ha-arets* (redemption of the land). The biblical basis for the repossession of the land, texts about the promises of inheriting the land, are inscribed on boards set in many places throughout the land. In reality of course the land is not uninhabited, and the Zionist project relies heavily on the Arabs who have remained behind:

> How was this tiny place (Tantura, A.N.) along with its sister village, Fraydis – 'Paradise', that is – able to withstand the catastrophes of war and dispossession … ? Fraydis … survived to fulfill "a wish that Jacob had in mind", James (Jacob) de Rothschild who had nearby established the colony of Zikhron Ya'qub, in memory of Jacob, at the close of the nineteenth century. Its settlers who all come from Europe, began procuring fine wines. … Yes, it's a fact that the people of Fraydis, the Fraydisis, or "Paradisers", were saved from the storms of war by the grape juice in Ya'qub's jars. It's true to say that the huge profits that the settlers of Zikhron Ya'qub won from the toil of the Fraydisis' arms and legs strengthened their back when their Zionist brethren attacked them, the advocates of the purely "Hebrew work" – a principle as pure as the wine in those jars.

Those who have remained become, as it were, one with the fruits of the land; they are physically absorbed by the land: "And who would be unfair as to blame the people of Fraydis for staying, the residue of the winepress?" Habibi counters the Zionist claim of "purity" with its opposite, the tangled roots of the traditional rural population in the land.

By the 1970s speaking about the land was no longer a simple, unmediated act; literary discourse had already set the coordinates for perceiving the land allegorically. Darwish's poetry celebrates Palestine in the image of a desirable young woman whose honor can only be preserved by the self-sacrifice of the fighter or the absolute devotion of his alter ego, the poet. Habibi counters this with a strikingly unemotional image of the land and its people. He reveals the grotesqueness of allegorical interpretations of the land in the mirror of the analogous practice of the adversaries, in whose language the land is also subjected to erotic mythicizing. The aggressive, indeed obsessive aspects of claiming exclusive responsibility for "making the desert fertile", of claiming to be the sole "redeemers of the land", are given distinctive expression in a lecture by his "employer" that Saeed is forced to listen to during his transportation to prison. Here the land is portrayed as a female in need of protection and whose dignity, the "covering of her shame", is first achieved by her liberators, her "redeemers":

> "Verdant fields! Green on your right and on your left; green everywhere! We have given life to what was dead. This is why we have named the borders of former Israel the Green Belt. For beyond them lie barren mountains and desert reaches, a wilderness calling out to us, 'Come ye hither, tractors of civilization!' If you had been with me, boy, when we crossed the Latrun road on our way to Jerusalem, you would really have seen the Green Belt: the greenery of our pine-clad hills, trees everywhere hugging one another, branch intertwined with branch, while lovers embraced beneath them. Then you would have seen, facing these green robed hills, your barren mountains devoid of any cover that could hide their naked rocks. There they remained, weeping for a quarter of a century, shedding all their earth. Let us wipe their tears dry ..." "Was this why you demolished the Latrun villages, 'Imwas, Yalu and Bait Nuba, and drove their inhabitants away, master? "But we gave the monastery to the monks, for a tourist attraction and we left the graveyards to those buried there, out of our faith in God. These great expanses, however, are ours, our inheritance from the war. Let bygones be bygones ..."

Diminishment as survival strategy

Viewed from this angle, the Israeli counterparts lose much of their superior status: from the military governor, Saeed's superior, the "big man of small stature", through to his most senior "employer", they all seem in some way "small". Perhaps the sharpest criticism leveled against the arrogant pretense of authority, which is perceived by Saeed to be utterly excessive, is also tied to a diminished figure. This criticism is, however, concealed, encoded in a name. It targets the practice of legitimizing claims to the land by referring to a permit granted by God, laid out in the Bible as a kind of land register. This practice, the narrator feels, means not only that one has deduced religiously founded rights for one's own group; it also creates a peculiar image of God, assigning God a very human, massively diminished role which for outsiders recalls that of a real estate agent. The "all-powerful" figure hovering in the background for most of the novel, whom Saeed is told to "serve" by his dying father, is called Adon (master) Safsarsheck, a Hebrew designation complemented by a Slavic ending which in fact roughly means "small broker". The mere mention of this name is enough for Saeed to obtain protection; he occasionally resorts to "this refuge", and is told during their one meeting to "serve us like your father did". His curse will haunt Saeed and his offspring "from generation to generation" should he ever refuse to perform his duty.

With the state ruled by the small God, Adon Safsarsheck, something like a new religion has been founded, intolerant of apostasy. It is striking that the state claiming divine prerogatives has also become a problem for others in the Middle East, despite being of the Jewish faith. For instance the Israeli author Sami Mikhael, born in Iraq, has expressed his criticism:

> I never feared a great, true, wise, and all-powerful God with the power to make decisions and ensure that they are carried out. But I'm scared of a small, miserable, deaf-mute, helpless God who needs creatures born of women to carry out his work and articulate his wishes. I can oppose this God, for he fakes and rewrites my past.

Implementing the three grand Zionist prerogatives has thus had a Palestinian flipside. Outside the myth, "the land" only has reality together with its Arab inhabitants, whose bodies form, as it were, the surface terrain upon which Zionist history is played out.

The fida'i put to the test

People diminished in stature, a massively miniaturized God – how does one survive in the "small homeland"? Several models of self-assertion are presented in the novel. One is the intensive work put in by the people of Fraydis, disarming the adversary by their absorption into the land itself as the "residue in the winepress". Then, there is self-enclosure in a village on the edge of reality, like the people in the legendary Sulaka, where Saeed journeys with the "second Yu'ad"; a village where one can go into hiding by observing the rules regulating language, which even succeed in covering up family relationships. Lastly, there is the option of sheer persistence in the steadfast hope of regaining the dignity that although buried one still knows is there, as evidenced by Saeed and Baqiya. None of these self-diminishments are able to create an outlet; indeed, they make the lack of space to maneuver seem even more constricting.

One of the key chapters of the novel is devoted to the attempt undertaken by Wala' to break out of this suffocating confinement. Overcautiously named Wala' by his parents – "a name that turns out to be two edged, since the state cannot determine to whom Wala' should give his loyalty" – this young man proves to be the faithful warrant of his parents' hidden pledge: after a failed act of resistance he confronts them, before disappearing into the vast sea, repeating the warning with which they had poisoned his childhood and adolescence: "Careful what you say!" Following an unsuccessful guerilla action he has holed up in the basement of a devastated house in his mother's deserted home village; she stands before him with the task of persuading him to capitulate. But with the litany-like repetition of the old warning he evokes the suffocating atmosphere of home, the self-imposed speechlessness, which drove him to rebel. His resistance is only realizable by paying the ultimate price – his own life. Baqiya calls out to him, "Out into the open air, my son! That cellar is too small, too shut in. You'll suffocate down there!" To which Wala' replies:

> Suffocate? It was to breathe free that I came to this cellar, to breathe in free-
> dom just once. In my cradle you stifled my crying. As I grew and tried to learn
> how to talk from what you said, I heard only whispers. As I went to school
> you warned me, "Careful what you say!" When I told you my teacher was my
> friend, you whispered, "He may be spying on you". When I heard what had
> happened to Tantura and cursed them, you murmured, "Careful what you
> say!" When they cursed my, you repeated, "Careful what you say!" When I
> met with my schoolmates to announce a strike, they told me, "Careful what
> you say!" One morning you told me, Mother, "You talk in your sleep, careful
> what you say in your sleep!" I used to sing in the bath, but father would shout
> at me, "Change that tune! The walls have ears. Careful what you say!" ... I was
> suffocating. This may be a poky little cellar, Mother, but there's more room
> here than you have ever had! Shut in it may be, but it's also a way out!

It was Wala', the son, who hauled the chest from the seabed and recast the regained treasure into a new understanding of dignity as a total commitment to the national cause, a willingness to break through the language barriers erected out of overriding caution. While this change in tack enabled him to leap from confinement into the wider world, it has failed to provide him with a future.

The suicidal aspect revealed here in an act of untimely and isolated resistance; the negation of future and the rational explanation of active resistance as stemming from social and psychological distress: all this represents a rebuke of any mythicizing interpretation. Wala''s way out of the impasse does not lead to a renewal of the vision of the homeland in acts of remembrance, but drags the remaining homeland into the abyss.

The figure of Wala' is juxtaposed with another freedom fighter, a young man who – borrowing from a Darwish poem written in roughly the same period – is portrayed in a strikingly emotional tone. While serving another stint in prison, the narrator gets to know the youthful Saeed, a figure who leaves a deep impression on him:

> The hand to my left was shaking mine and pressing it reassuringly ... I turned my head to the left and saw a very long form lying there on a straw mattress like my own. He was naked, and at first sight his body seemed to have been painted with a deep red pigment. Had it not been for his eyes smiling silently to me in encouragement, and for his hand pressing mine and telling me to be brave, I would have thought the body lying to my left was a corpse. ... He forced himself to stand up. And I saw him bend his head down so that it would not hit the ceiling, or perhaps he was bending his tall figure down to look at me. ... He healed my wounds by talking about his own. He kept widening that single tiny window in the wall until it became a broad horizon that I had never seen before. Its netted bars became bridges to the moon, and between his bed and mine were hanging gardens.

Capable of transforming suffering into triumph and so of converting signs of suffering into symbols of sovereignty in emulation of the Sufis' mystical transcending of the woes of earthly existence, the young Saeed character appears to be inspired by the well-known poem *Radd al-fi'l* ("The Reaction"):

> When they barred all the windows in the prison cell
> Sunlight appeared, emanating from plenty of torches.
> When they drew on the wall the image of my executioner
> The shadow of ears of wheat appeared to extinguish it.
> The victors shall see nothing other than the shining of my forehead
> They shall hear nothing other than the rattling of my chains
> Once I burn on the cross of my adoration
> I have become a saint – in the guise of a fighter.

It is this type of activist who helps the protagonist Saeed toward a new level of self-knowledge and sense of self-dignity. There can be no doubts about the significance of the active resistance exiled Palestinians dared to undertake for Palestinians in Israel to regain self-respect. The concept of armed conflict to recover the land, though, is not only presented in a positive light; it is subjected to rigorous critique at a later point in the novel. It is not the old Saeed, continually looking for redemptive figures, who is given the right to judge the would-be liberators, but the self-confident, optimistic young Yu'ad, the revitalized embodiment of the homeland. In the eyes of this "modern" character, who is no longer dependent on the old ideals, it is precisely the "messianic" element, the freedom fighter's ignorance of real historical circumstances, which disqualifies him: "If they'd really learnt anything, then they wouldn't talk about a return to the beginning." The "second Yu'ad" is the spitting image of the first but not identical to her; her self-confidence reveals the changes wrought in a generation for whom exile has become normal and her demeanor serves to disclose the misperceptions that can be generated by idealized memory.

A shared Arab ideal in a distorting mirror: the poet/prophet

The freedom fighters that for a while impress Saeed, who is forever searching for a savior, as the epitome of hope are toppled from the pedestal in the end. But it is the representatives of literary culture that are much more studiously targeted, for they are or should be "the genuinely legitimate partners", the "selfless lovers of the homeland". One strand of the plot threaded throughout the novel – albeit not always in the foreground – follows Saeed's development into a writer in the sense of becoming a spokesman for his society. At the outset of the novel, he, like the spokesman of the society par excellence, the prophet Muhammad, experiences a calling. This occurs in the wake of the incident at the al-Jazzar mosque, when he is hailed and advised by the otherworldly beings. Like the Prophet, he is in contact with supernatural powers for the entire duration of the narrative. After his calling – like the Prophet, but also like kindred writers in colonial and postcolonial society – he suffers from a sense of isolation so severe that it borders on madness. Finally – again like the Prophet – in consolation and as initiation into the society of the elected he experiences a "heavenly journey" on the back of a wondrous mount, after which he is able to pursue his calling in the true sense of the word: he becomes a writer.

But how are these experiences concretely portrayed? In the novel's depictions, continually refracted by irony, a retarding element is inherent to the calling, namely Saeed's sluggish appreciation of what is going on around him. After his fortunate "entry into the country" despite adverse circumstances, and on the night of his meeting the speechless "ghosts" in the al-Jazzar mosque, Saeed has a supernatural encounter with an otherworldly redeemer figure, identifiable in the Islamic context as a *mahdi*, who calls him to take up a role the import of which initially eludes him. In decisive features the scene evokes the Prophet Muhammad's own calling: in both, the novitiate is hailed several times and he answers with "here I am"; the otherworldly hailer comes closer, the novitiate tries to escape, before finally following the call:

Suddenly, though not really unexpectedly, I heard a voice calling to me, "Saeed! Saeed!"; I felt like a man peeping through a keyhole at a virgin in her chamber. I was embarrassed and wanted to retreat, but the voice urged me forward. I said, "Here I am". I saw the figure of a man emerging from the rocks of the lighthouse as the light shone toward me and then disappearing as it receded. He was wrapped in a blue cloak flecked with white foam, like the lighthouse itself. As he approached I walked toward him, we met in the middle of the open space between one end of the sea wall to the right and the other end to the left, in the Fakhura quarter.

But Saeed, here assigned the mission to preserve the dignity of his homeland, attempts instead to use the encounter as a means to win over his counterpart as a guardian:

> He stared hard at me ... Then he said, "That is the way you always are. When you can no longer endure your misery, yet you cannot bear to pay the high price you know is needed to change it, you come to me for help. But I see what other people do and the price they pay, allowing no one to squeeze them into one of these tunnels, and then I become furious with you. What is it you lack? Is any one of you lacking a life he can offer, or lacking a death to make him fear for his life?" I felt stunned, absolutely breathless, as I listened. The tunnel swam before my eyes. Then I remembered the promised dawn in my beloved city of Haifa. My sense of foreboding grew stronger. I explained to him, "Tomorrow, reverend, I shall return to my city of Haifa and live there. So please give me advice." He grew calmer and replied, "My advice will not help you. However, I will tell you a story I heard, set in Persia, about an axe without a handle that was thrown among some trees. The trees said to each other, 'This has not been thrown here for any good reason.' But one perfectly ordinary tree observed, 'Provided none of you supply a stick for its arse, you have nothing to fear from it.' You'd better go now; this story's not fit to repeat." "May I see you again, reverend?" "Whenever you want. Just come down to these tunnels." "At what time, reverend?" "When you feel completely drained of strength." "When?" But he had disappeared.

For a long time Saeed evades his mission, keeping it a "secret". But although his calling will only be concretely realized in his taking up writing at the end of his development, it occupies his mind already at an earlier stage, when, after realizing that the vision of the "small homeland" has been lost as a result of the June War, he sees his personal situation as a haunting nightmare. He finds himself condemned to a "martyr's stake" of helplessness, totally isolated and alienated from himself. He suffers psychological torments typical of a figure who, by virtue of his orientation on an unattainable ideal, feels and presents himself to be "extolled on the cross":

the poet committed to the political cause. Stripped of pathos, as the ironic novel prescribes, the cross evoked by poets has turned into a banal stake. Although through acts of self-diminution Saeed continues to try and come back down to earth, he only finds himself exposed to even greater shocks. In prison he meets his alter ego, the young Saeed, whose invigorating presence brings about a catharsis but cannot show him a way out of his plight. Only the encounter with the young Yu'ad drives home how untimely he is and how obsolete are the ideological options that his stance offers.

In this situation bordering on madness, when on the humiliating stake of total isolation and abject despair he suffers a martyrdom of crucifixion inverted into absolute meaningless, he is seized by the supernatural force, the *mahdi*, reviving his earlier calling. The *mahdi* transports him out of his unbearable position, carrying him like the fabled mount of the Prophet on its back, and in heaven – so we must conclude from the beginning of the novel, which depicts his joyous induction amongst the otherworldly elected – initiates him to the role of the writer. As related at the outset of the second letter, he thus becomes a *natiq* (speaker), a figure familiar not only from the traditional Shiite road to salvation, where he acts as the herald of an imminent liberation from humiliation, but also from a modern interpretation, where the *natiq* is embodied in the *littérateur*, the genuinely legitimate representative of society in modernity. Is the calling, the probation proved in suffering and the exaltation of the Prophet, being restaged here?

It is more like an arduous path, a path that narrowly passes by clinical madness; in any case it is not a path that would qualify for the highly charged role of the prophet-poet-fighter, the liberator and the creator of identity who is so prominent in committed modern Arab literature. Moreover, the revitalized homeland no longer has a need for such an ideal figure: the new Yu'ad is unable to perceive any trace of a miracle-verifying prophetic status in Saeed's "journey to the heavens"; on the contrary, she takes his disappearance to be a sign of hope. Rising up from his martyr's stake with the help of the *mahdi*, the last thing Saeed is able to recognize of his receding surroundings is Yu'ad, who, pointing up at him, prophesies: "When this cloud passes the sun will shine once more!"

This release from his social role also represents a freeing of the writer: he has stepped out of the mythical triad configuration – real homeland, the intellectual as its liberator, and the ideal homeland – in which he, the gallant deliverer, was bound more to the ideal image of the homeland than its reality. Only now can he follow his mission to recall what has been lost, without mythically "bringing it back". His discourse is now "remembrance which tolerates occasional forgetting", very much in tune with the stance reached more than a decade later by Mahmoud Darwish, who chose this very motto for the title of his Beirut war memoir, published 1986: *A Memory for Forgetfulness*. It is a discourse shared too by contemporary Palestinian filmmakers such as Michel Khleifi. It refers to the living physique of the land and expresses its real emotional value, without allowing itself to be misled by the limits imposed by existing political misappropriation.

When his "employer" informs him about a change in the ownership of a strip of land, documented by a new Hebrew name, Saeed points out the reality of the homeland that transcends all naming, citing a line from Romeo and Juliet:

> What's in a name? That which we call a rose
> By any other name would smell as sweet.

The right to possess the homeland may be controversial, the hope to regain it futile, but what remains nevertheless is what unifies all exiles: the longing for the homeland. Habibi shares this conviction with post-Zionist Israeli thinkers who have developed a concept of *galut* (exiled existence) as an "imperfect presence" the only viable, livable alternative. This "exile presence" would permit a remembrance of both the denied Jewish past and the denied Palestinian past. This is a prospect Habibi fully endorses when, at the beginning of his second novel, *What a Shame!* (1985), he asks: "Is my trust to be shaken in our freedom to long for this land in this land – for Haifa in Haifa?"

Habibi's work, one of the most powerful effects of which is the continuous subversion and problematizing of the collective obsession with remembering and forgetting that is inscribed in the hegemonic Israeli narrative, thus dramatizes the concept of a life led in "exile inside the homeland". This perception deliberately projects the situation of Jewish exiles in pre-Holocaust Europe onto the contemporary Israel/Palestine constellation. Not only articulated in his fictional work but also in his political writings, the full significance of this idea has only been realized with the emergence of post-Zionist thinking, which has deconstructed the negative notion of *galut*.

Habibi's perception of the Palestinian situation in Israel has found its fitting sequel in the vision of the one most innovative post-Zionist thinkers, Amnon Raz-Krakotzkin, whose critique of Zionist discourse focuses on the fundamental concept of *shelilat ha-galut* (negation of exile). He calls for a thorough revision of the denigrated concept of *galut*, which in his theory constitutes a key notion for describing the reality of the Jewish situation even after the recovery of the land. A revised concept of *galut* would enable "a Jewish identity based on the recognition of the potential embodied in the bi-nationality of the land." The consequences are far-reaching, for this in turn would set the parameters of a political discourse whose starting point would be the recognition of the Palestinian collective as a group with a historical consciousness. There is hope that an intensified reception of postmodern thinking will eventually trigger not only a deeper insight into these still hidden dimensions of Palestinian and Israeli memory, but also help them to achieve greater public recognition.

WORKS

Sudasiyyat al-ayyam al-sitta (Hexalogy of the Six Days), Haifa: Matba'at al-Ittihad al-Ta'awuniyya 1968

al-Waqa'i' al-ghariba fi khitifa' Sa'id Abi l-Nahs al-Mutasha'il (The Secret Life of Saeed, the Ill-fated Pessoptimist), Haifa: Arabesque 1974

Luka' ibn Luka' (Luka', Son of Luka'), Nazareth: 30 Adhar 1980

Ikhtayya (What a Shame!), Nikosia: Bisan Press 1985

Saraya bint al-ghul (Saraya, the Ghul's Daughter), Haifa: Arabesque 1991

TRANSLATIONS

The Secret Life of Saeed, the Ill-fated Pessoptimist, trans. Salma Khadra Jayyusi, Trevor LeGassick, London: Zed Books 1985

FURTHER READING

Sobhi Boustani: "Terre natale et paysages urbains dans le roman palestinien. Essai sur les œuvres de Ghassan Kanafani et Emile Habibi", in: Ken Seigneurie (ed.), *Crisis and Memory. The Representation of Space in Modern Levantine Narrative*, Wiesbaden: Reichert 2003, pp. 145–76

Peter Heath: "Creativity in the Novels of Emile Habibi, with special reference to *Saeed the Pessoptimist*", in: Kamal Abdel-Malek, Wael Hallaq (eds.), *Tradition, Modernity, and Postmodernity in Arabic Literature*, Leiden et al.: Brill 2000, pp. 158–72

Akram F. Khater: "Emile Habibi: The Mirror of Irony in Palestinian Literature", in: *Journal of Arabic Literature* 24 (1993), pp. 75–94

Angelika Neuwirth: "Israelisch-palästinensische Paradoxien. Emil Habibis Roman *Der Peptimist* als Versuch einer Entmythisierung von Geschichte", in: *Quaderni di Studi Arabi* 12 (1994), pp. 95–128

Saleh Srouji: *Emil Habibi, ein arabischer Literat aus Israel. Die Suche des Palästinensers nach dem Selbst unter verschärften Bedingungen*, Augsburg: Wißner 1993

Ibrahim Taha: "The Author as a Serious Comedian. The Pessoptimist by Emile Habibi", in: Ibrahim Taha, *The Palestinian Novel. A Communication Study*, London: Curzon 2002, pp. 55–96

OTHER WORKS CITED

Sadik Jalal al-Azm: "The Importance of Being Earnest about Salman Rushdie", in: *Die Welt des Islams* 31 (1991), pp. 1–49

Mahmoud Darwish: *Dhakira li-l-nisyan. al-Zaman: Bayrut, al-makan: yawm min ayyam ab 1982*, Beirut: al-Mu'assasa al-'Arabiyya li-l-Dirasat wa-l-Nashr 1987 (English translation: *Memory for Forgetfulness. August, Beirut, 1982*, trans. Ibrahim Muhawi, Berkeley: University of California Press 1995)

Karl Marx: *Der achtzehnte Brumaire des Louis Bonaparte* [1852], ed. Hauke Brunkhorst, Frankfurt/M: Suhrkamp 2007

Sami Michael: "On Being an Iraqi-Jewish Writer in Israel," in: *Prooftexts* 4 (1984), pp. 23–33

Amnon Raz-Krakotzkin: "Exile in the Midst of Sovereignty. A Critique of 'Shelilat ha-Galut in Israeli Culture'" [in Hebrew], in: *Theory and Criticism* 4 (1993), pp. 23–55, and *Theory and Criticism* 5 (1996), pp. 113–32

The Poet of the Arabic Short Story: Zakariyya Tamir

Ulrike Stehli-Werbeck

> On the first day hunger was created. On the second day music was created. On the third day books and cats were created. On the fourth day cigarettes were created. On the fifth day cafés were created. On the sixth day wrath was created. On the seventh day sparrows with their nests hidden in the trees were created. On the eighth day examining magistrates were created, who immediately swarmed over the cities, accompanied by policemen, prisons, and handcuffs.
>
> *Zakariyya Tamir, "He Who Burnt the Ships"*

The most important feature of Zakariyya Tamir's short stories is the tension between a world characterized by despotism, deprivation, and absurdity and a dense, seemingly simple, poetic language. Regarded as one of the most important authors not only of Syrian storytelling but of the Arab short story in general, Tamir has devoted his entire literary life solely to this genre. "Until now the short story has been for me the knife with which I can peel a fruit and kill an enemy", he once said in an interview. Between the 1960s and the present day, he has published ten short story collections, and on each occasion their style has exerted its own intrinsic fascination. Tamir has greatly influenced younger short story writers, especially in Syria, Egypt and Iraq.

The author and his country

Zakariyya Tamir was born in 1931 in a modest quarter of the old town in Damascus, at a time when Syria was still under French mandate. Due to his family's circumstances, he was forced to leave school at the age of thirteen, working as a smith and in other skilled trades from 1944 until 1960. Encouraged by his contact with intellectuals, he continued his education at night school and on his own initiative embarked on an intensive study of Arab and world literature.

These years of his autodidactic apprenticeship coincided with the postcolonial phase of optimism and hope after attaining independence in 1946. In Syria this phase was characterized by political instability and numerous military coups on the one hand and the idea of Arab unity on the other, which led to a temporary union between Syria and Egypt from 1958 to 1961. During this period, in 1957 Tamir began to write. His very first collection of short stories, *The Neighing of the White*

Steed, caused a sensation upon publication in 1960 and he immediately established himself as a new, independent voice in the field of the Arab short story. From this year onwards, he devoted himself completely to writing, both as an author and as a journalist in various media and institutions. Inevitably, he became entangled in the conflict that faces every intellectual in a non-democratic or totalitarian state: out of the material necessity to earn a living and – at least temporarily – the hope of instigating change from within, he assumed responsibilities in the state's cultural apparatus, even though he took a critical stance on the repressive actions of each respective regime. From 1960 to 1963 he thus worked for the Publications and Translations Department in the Syrian Ministry of Culture.

In 1963 his second collection, *Spring in the Ashes*, was published as part of the ministry's program. In the same year the Ba'th Party, which had taken up the cause of "[Arab] unity, freedom, socialism", launched a military coup and seized power in Syria. The parliamentary system was replaced by a "people's republic" based on the Eastern European model, in fact a disguised military dictatorship, and a socialist economic system was installed, accompanied by agrarian reforms and the nationalization of enterprises. During these years Tamir was editor-in-chief of the weekly magazine *al-Mawqif al-'Arabi* (The Arabic Point of View), worked for a short period as scenarist for Saudi-Arabian Television in Jeddah, and was eventually appointed to the censorship board in the Syrian Ministry of Information. The shock of military and political defeat which the Arabs suffered at the hands of Israel in the June War 1967 also hurled Syria into a deep crisis, demanding fundamental analysis and self-criticism. In Tamir's case, this critical reflection was expressed in the short story collection *The Thunder* (1970). Between 1967 and 1970 he worked in Syrian state television as director of the drama department.

Although the rule of President Hafez al-Asad (1970–2000) was marked by limited liberalization and a modest economic upswing, repression by the police and secret service apparatuses continued unabated. Co-founder of the Syrian Writers' Union in 1969, Tamir was its vice-president and editor-in-chief of its magazine *al-Mawqif al-Adabi* (The Literary Point of View) between 1973 and 1975. He published his third (the aforementioned *The Thunder*) and fourth (*Damascus in Flames*, 1973) short story collections as part of the Union's literary program. The fifth collection, *Tigers on the Tenth Day* (1978), was once again published in Beirut, which unlike Syria was a paradise of freedom of expression during the Lebanese Civil War. In spite of his grave reservations about the political line taken by the regime, from 1978 to 1980 Tamir acted as editor-in-chief of *al-Ma'rifa* (Knowledge), a culture and philosophy journal published by the Syrian Ministry of Culture. A committed supporter of children's literature throughout his life, he has written numerous children's stories, while from 1970 to 1971 he was involved in the publication of *Rafi'*, a weekly magazine for children, and from 1975 to 1977 he was editor-in-chief of the youth magazine *Usama*.

1979 and 1980 were marked by a series of assassinations of high-ranking members of the Ba'th Party. With the Muslim Brotherhood accused of staging a coordinated campaign, state repression was intensified. Like numerous others from the intellectual elite during these years, Tamir left Syria in 1981 and moved to London. Since the 1990s he has lived in Oxford, where he works as a freelance writer and journalist for diverse Arab newspapers and magazines and occasionally as contributing editor of Arabic cultural journals published in Britain.

The 1990s witnessed a second fruitful phase of creativity. In just eleven years he published – still written in Arabic – five short story collections: *Noah's Summons* (1994), *We Shall Laugh* (1998), *Sour Grapes* (2000), *Breaking Knees* (2002), and *The Hedgehog* (2005). For his literary work he was awarded the prestigious Sultan Uways Prize of Culture from Abu Dhabi in 2001, the Syrian Medal of Merit, First Class, in 2002 and the Blue Metropolis Montreal Internation Literary Award as well as the first Prize of the Arabic Short Story in 2009.

Visionary and apocalyptic counter-worlds

When Zakariyya Tamir began writing in 1957, heated and controversial debates about the political commitment (be it nationalist or socialist) of the writer in society were taking place in the Arab world. From the First World War onwards, the literary aesthetic concept of realism had been predominant in the short story field, only to evolve in the 1950s into an Arab "socialist" realism. At the same time though, harbingers of a change in paradigm were already being heralded in the works of the Egyptian writers Edwar al-Kharrat and Yusuf al-Sharuni. In Syria, where authors committed to literary realism like Abd al-Salam al-Ujayli, Said Hawraniyya, Hanna Mina and Ulfat al-Idlibi dominated the narrative genres, Tamir broke the realist mould in a single move.

A world whose causal connections have ceased to be comprehensible to the individual and seem more than ever resilient to change, whose values one no longer shares and to which one feels defenselessly exposed – such a world can no longer be represented by the devices of literary realism. Even if Tamir's stories open in what is generally considered to be "realistic" mode, in town quarters, lanes, or cafés typical of ordinary everyday life, the realistic depiction is soon ruptured by fantastic, grotesque or absurd events and notions. The laws of logic, the limits of space and time, conventional distinctions between dreams, fantasy and reality, as well as life and death, are suspended. By employing stream of consciousness, generating alienation effects, using bold imagery bordering on Surrealism, and positioning these often abruptly at key junctures in the text, Tamir opens up visionary, partly apocalyptic counter-worlds.

Tamir taps into and exploits new areas for the stream of consciousness technique in both its forms as interior monologue or free indirect speech: wishes, dreams and visions are constructed in meticulous detail and expressed in graphic descriptions, while often simultaneously presented as fragile or illusionary.

Elaborate in their composition, Tamir's stories are characterized by a complex network of (inter)textual connections and references as well as a subtle, at times iconoclastic use of metaphor, symbol, and allegory. Typical compositional techniques, in both content and structure, are montage and shocking contrasts: realistically narrated passages are confronted with starkly marked metaphorical ones; the same holds good for different time layers, perspectives, and text types. Tamir's language is concise and impressive. He operates with stylistic devices more readily associated with verse, positioning key words as leitmotifs, using a seemingly inexhaustible reservoir of figures of speech, and generating various rhythms. For this reason, his works often convey the impression of being *prose poems*. The literary critic Sabry Hafez has rightly called him "the poet of the Arabic short story *par excellence.*"

Tamir's imagery encompasses all senses. Light, colors, sounds, and smells are depicted frequently and in all their diversity. The symbolism of colors is accorded a particular role: colors are often repeated as a leitmotif. While black and yellow mostly have negative, pessimistic or ominous connotations, green and blue as colors of nature generally signal intactness, innocence, youth, and hope. Red stands for passion, for it is the color of a bright red mouth but also of blood, while gold signals permanence but also hardness.

> At that silence and fright overcame the members of the delegation, and life appeared to them at this moment as something beautiful. For is not the sky deep blue? And are not red roses lovelier than the love songs sung by a yearning lover's voice? Does not a child's first cry sprout green grass in the blood? And is not the woman's quivering mouth a moon, which slaughters the nights with a knife of silver?
> *Zakariyya Tamir, "The Beards"*

Fearlessly, Tamir dares to broach the three great taboo topics of Arab societies: politics, religion, and sexuality. His works focus on existential mood and the human condition in a world characterized by despotism, deprivation, and alienation. The characters of his stories are confronted with and subjected to a diverse array of oppressive practices and attitudes stemming from various sources: the state with its judges, executioners, policemen, and jailers, the privileged, but also the social pressures exerted by patriarchal traditions, and rigid moral and honor codes. As an antihero, the individual is left largely defenseless, forced to submit to threatening superior powers; imprisonment, interrogation, execution, killings, and mutilation occur repeatedly. Clashes between the individual and repressive authorities are representative of Syrian reality, about which the author has said the following:

> Violence in my stories is not an imported product or a psychological complex or some kind of agitation or device to raise tension, it is only an expression of our daily life. We live in a violent, murderous world, which bestows on us nothing but prisons, failure, and ashes and crowns us with defeats. Arabs see themselves daily confronted with brutal massacres; therefore it is not possible to write about the lovely jasmine while napalm burns its fire into the human flesh.

Bearing certain autobiographical traits, Tamir's first collection took the perspective of the working and oppressed classes: material deprivation, hunger and joylessness on the one hand; modest pleasures and the dream of a better life on the other. Unable to realize their dreams, the poor resort to acts of violence as a means of expressing their rebellion, acts that are performed in a ritualistic way and with cold brutality.

Later, his focus moved increasingly towards political matters, especially after the 1967 defeat: the passivity, cowardice, and corruption rampant in the Arab world are now rebuked. Moreover, the author is uncompromising in his criticism of the sexual morals and honor codes which assign responsibility and blame to women alone, requiring murder upon the slightest suspicion of violated honor as a means of restoring the prevailing patriarchal order. The practiced form of organized religion is also denounced as a means of securing and maintaining power. Tamir castigates every kind of hypocrisy, in particular those concealed under a facade of respectability, no matter if motivated by religion or tradition. He is masterful in characterizing his characters with concise, pointed attributes as well as by their way of speaking and thinking, thus exposing their shortcomings and revealing their hopes to be illusions.

Displaying a tendency towards caricature and anecdotal ellipsis, his more recent short stories (also to be categorized as *short short stories*) are variations on general human weaknesses such as malevolence, envy, conceitedness, and arrogance. Sexuality and morality remain an inexhaustible topic – even if they are now given an obscene slant.

The inhuman, depressing reality depicted in Tamir's stories is counterbalanced on the one hand by irony, at times witty but more often than not biting. On the other hand, this reality is further relativized by glimmers of hope: even if they cannot be asserted and established in society, there is awareness that justice and decency do exist; then there are the moments of innocence, happiness, and childhood memories which occasionally illuminate daily routine; finally, nature – mostly – preserves its original unspoiled state. *The Hedgehog* (2005), a small cycle of narratives, gently leads back to childhood: twenty-two episodes from the point of view of a six-year-old boy give impressions of his sense of security and his fantasy, but also his disillusionment when coping with the world of grownups.

(Hi)stories – the cultural memory

Ever since he started writing, Zakariyya Tamir has incorporated historical, mythical, and literary figures and materials gleaned from the Arabic and Islamic tradition, a narrative strategy that a number of other Arab authors have employed in a variety of ways since the 1970s on a larger scale.

Tamir drew on myths and archetypes already in the title stories of his first two collections. *The Neighing of the White Horse* refers to a symbol of freedom widespread in the Arab world. The title *Spring in the Ashes*, which combines the myth of phoenix with Near Eastern fertility myths, links into notions of the resurrection of a god and the return of fertility after a period of drought, which, especially in Arab poetry of the 1950s, expressed the hope for a better future. The author also returns to the biblical myth of Adam and Eve. All of these examples are archetypes of creation and survival.

Other stories feature characters, well known in the Arab world, associated with specific events, behavior, or characteristics, which however, although they do not always concur with historical tradition. While quantitatively historical figures are easily the most frequent, literary characters also appear, such as Scheherazade and Shahryar, the famous couple from the frame story of *The Thousand and One Nights*, Sinbad the Sailor, and Juha the jester. Tamir also employs this strategy in his children's stories, such as *Badiʿ al-Zaman* (a proper name meaning "unique of his time"), a story set "in olden times" in Baghdad, and *The Steed of the Green Land* (1980).

Tamir's stories are not concerned with historicity or the fictional reconstruction of historical figures, as is the case to a certain extent in novels by the Egyptian writer Gamal al-Ghitani and the Moroccan Bin Salim Himmish. They are rather satires targeting fault and injustice in contemporary (not only Arab) societies. Tamir frequently places the characters in a literary present, wherein contemporary conditions are denounced by the resultant confrontation between divergent standards and value systems. If the stories are set in a mythical past, a reference to the present is achieved by alienation effects.

Individual stories call to mind the memory of Napoleon Bonaparte's expedition to the Near East, the time of French colonialism or the occupation of Palestine. Others tackle the traumatic defeat of 1967 when the Arab armies were overpowered by the pre-emptive strike of the Israeli army. Moreover, certain Syrian special units were not sent into action on purpose, for example during the conquest of Qunaytra, the capital of Golan. One of Tamir's masterpieces is to be read against this background: "The Beards" (1970) is supposedly set around 1400, when the Mongol Timur Lenk (known as Tamerlane in Europe) conquered Damascus, but anachronistic references are made to the present, such as by the mention of petrol. The men of the town want to relinquish it and all its women without a fight. Timur Lenk presents them with a choice: either to have their beards shaved or to be killed. When they decide to save their beards, the town is ignominiously destroyed. This attitude is exaggerated in caricature form through a parodistic variation of Descartes' maxim *Cogito ergo sum* (I think, therefore I am), now rendered as: "war needs only he who does not exist (...), we, however – God be praised – have beards, therefore we are." Presented here is a population that is paralyzed by its religious and patriarchal traditions and unable to cope with a changed reality and a concrete military and political threat; this was exactly what the Arab states had to reproach themselves for in 1967. By addressing an imaginary public at the beginning and end, allowing the story to be told by a fictional storyteller, Tamir places it in the context of the Arabic oral tradition of storytelling.

The story "He Who Burnt the Ships", from the same collection (1970), revolves around the Arab commander and conqueror Tariq Ibn Ziyad. As an Arab legend would have it, the Muslim conquest of Andalusia in 711 was successful because the commander had the ships burnt after landing, thereby preventing his army from retreat and leading it towards victory. Here this famous hero is transferred to a fictitious present, accused by the subaltern henchmen of a despotic regime who did *not* fight in the June War, of having wasted state funds and collaborated with the enemy. Thus the law is employed to get rid of potential critics, whose scent is picked up even in the myths of the past. This story is a collage of five different passages varying in length and subject matter, which are not all directly connected with one another. The parts are also stylistically different in terms of language: while the first and fourth focus exclusively on the plot involving Tariq Ibn Ziyad, the second additionally presents the creation story quoted at the beginning of this essay, the third is a parody of a political speech in the pathos-charged style of Syrian and Arab politicians, and the fifth and final part is an official letter. As early as 1970, Tamir was playing with various types of text and styles of language, an approach now considered characteristic of postmodernist writing.

A further thematic revolves around the role of the intellectual. In "'Abdallah Ibn al-Muqaffa' the Third" (1994), the eighth-century scholar is accused of having incited the people to think through his writings. The irony resides in the Caliph's claim that he follows the prophet Muhammad's admonition to search for knowledge always and everywhere, while in fact he prevents any free intellectual development.

He employs the scholar as his secretary, subjecting him to his control, whereupon Ibn al-Muqaffaʿ finds himself confronted with seven more Ibn al-Muqaffaʿs, all forced into line: the exaggerated representation of a dilemma that Tamir may well have also experienced.

"The Accused" (1970) is also about the "offence" of critical thinking and owning books. Here the Persian poet and freethinker Omar al-Khayyam, famous not least for his wine poems, is dragged from his grave and prosecuted in court on the basis of national protectionist laws. Convicted of exhorting the people to enjoy and consume wine and to import foreign goods, he is banned by the court from writing. In the author's words, this is "a satire of the enthusiastic, empty slogans in many countries of the Third World."

In other short stories Tamir utilizes intertextuality by transposing figures of the Arab literary heritage to a new context. Sinbad the Sailor, of *The Thousand and One Nights*, endures another shipwreck. Arriving on an island, he comes across a community of donkeys, which redounds to an example for mankind. And the Arabic Eulenspiegel figure, Juha, has his appearance in satirical, at times very brief and pithy anecdotes. "Tales of Juha the Damascene" (1994) exemplifies a tendency in Zakariyya Tamir's recent work: satire and parody are given even greater emphasis, along with the tightening of the narrative economy and pithiness of representation, while the author continues to hone in on human shortcomings and the absurdity of prevailing conditions.

The intertextual strategy of quoting literally from an older text to concretize references and allusions is employed in the story "Kafur al-Ikhshidi's Prophecy"(1994): to introduce himself to the Egyptian ruler Kafur, the famous poet al-Mutanabbi (915–965) quotes a section from one of his own poems that he once used with great aplomb when taking a stand against his former patron Sayf al-Dawla. In contrast to this spirited defense, al-Mutanabbi, subjected to torture, now writes for Kafur anything the ruler commands: first a panegyric poem, then an invective.

Tamir also makes numerous references to typical genres within the Arabic storytelling tradition: foremost to the fairytale, by employing specific introductory and ending formulas and calling on countless magical elements, but also to the fable and to the popular epic. A hero stemming from this genre, Antara Ibn Shaddad, becomes the alter ego of a modern antihero, who cannot get over the loss of his curved dagger, the symbol of his manliness.

Without elevating this to the status of a program, Tamir's short stories are deeply rooted in cultural memory, foremost that of Arab-Islamic society; at the same time, he also explores the possibilities afforded by other Oriental cultures and the European-Western tradition. This phenomenon is illustrated by the title of the short story collection *Noah's Summons* (1994) – a collection which contains a particularly great number of stories of this tendency – which refers to the oldest example of a warning and admonishing voice equally in Judaism, Christendom and Islam. Another example is the version of the creation story quoted above. In contrast to those authors who demand a genuinely Arabic literature drawing inspiration solely from its own literary and cultural heritage, Tamir does not hesitate to use elements from the European-Western tradition, such as the rationalist Descartes' maxim, as a foil or to weave references to European writers and composers into his texts; in this way he draws on the creative reservoirs of the literary and cultural heritage of the entire world.

Parodistic playing with elements of tradition, enhanced intertextual references to older texts, the combination of different types of texts and discourses, the meta-fictional reflection on the act of narration, diffusing clarity in favor of ambiguity, and thus questioning the single, dominant and generally accepted discourse by presenting different versions of the same story: all these are aspects of postmodernist narration.

A successful example for the manifold possibilities engendered by intertextual references is the short story "Shahryar and Scheherazade" (1994). It consists of two parts, both parodies of the frame of *The Thousand and One Nights*. As is well-known, the vizier's wise daughter Scheherazade marries King Shahryar, who has vowed revenge against all women in response to the betrayal of his first wife. She tells him stories every night until he is finally healed of his fury. The first part of Tamir's short story, titled "The Forgery", offers the same story with changed roles that twist and estrange the familiar: when on the thousand and first night Queen Scheherazade demands of her husband Shahryar that he entertains her with exciting stories as he has done every other night, he refuses, arguing that after a thousand nights of toil he now deserves a rest. Confronted with this defiance, she has him beheaded like her former husbands and orders "reliable men of letters" to rewrite *The Thousand and One Nights* in the following days. Thematically this part is about despotism and the faking of (hi)stories. The transmitted discourse is called into question, a current topic, not only in societies that are characterized by political propaganda and indoctrination.

The second part, "The Last Night", relocates the action onto another layer of society and into the present: the shoemaker's daughter Scheherazade proposes to her newly-wed husband, the shoe polisher Shahryar, to tell him stories on their wedding night, as in future the tradition will say it happened. But Shahryar prefers to watch television: a game of football, a soap-opera and the film *Superman*; he even threatens to kill Scheherazade if she does not keep quiet. "And hence Scheherazade was scared and fell silent – as every Arab man and every Arab woman." Here two reasons are given for the decline of the culture of storytelling: firstly, the supplanting of the word by the modern visual media of film and television; and secondly, the suppression of freedom of speech, which impacts on both sexes.

Both texts are about the end of storytelling. While Scheherazade in *The Thousand and One Nights* saved her life by narrating, in Tamir's story the refusal to narrate leads to death, while forbidding narration ends in silence. After the "last night" nobody will tell stories any more. The message presented in the content is supported by the form: although there is a division into nights, the story is ultimately and foremost concerned with the end; we are given only the finale, the thousand and first and "last" night. And in contrast to the voluminous, intricately woven form of the original text, here we have only the juxtaposition of two disparate stories, the smallest variant possible of a cycle of narration, reduced to its absolute minimum, before Scheherazade falls silent.

By inverting the "pre-text" in terms of both content and form Tamir combines in a parodistic way the affirmation of heritage – in this case of the highly-developed, centuries-old Arab tradition of storytelling – with criticism of the cultural development and political conditions of the present day. Fortunately, Tamir's entire oeuvre belies this swansong on the art of storytelling.

SELECTED WORKS

Sahil al-jawad al-abyad (The Neighing of the White Steed), Beirut: Dar Majallat Shi'r 1960

Rabi' fi l-ramad (Spring in the Ashes), Damascus: Wizarat al-Thaqafa 1963

al-Ra'd (The Thunder), Damascus: Ittihad al-Kuttab al-'Arab 1970

Dimashq al-hara'iq (Damascus in Flames), Damascus: Ittihad al-Kuttab al-'Arab 1973

Badi' al-Zaman (proper name), Beirut: Dar al-Fata al-'Arabi 1975

al-Numur fi l-yawm al-'ashir (Tigers on the Tenth Day), Beirut: Dar al-Adab 1978

Jawad al-ard al-khadra' (The Steed of the Green Land), Beirut: Dar al-Fata al-'Arabi 1980

Nida' Nuh (Noah's Summons), London: Riad El Rayyes 1994

Sa-nadhak (We Shall Laugh), Beirut: Riad El Rayyes 1998

al-Hisrim (Sour Grapes), Beirut: Riad El Rayyes 2000

Taksir rukab (Breaking Knees), Beirut: Riad El Rayyes 2002

al-Qunfudh (The Hedgehog), Beirut: Riad El Rayyes 2005

TRANSLATIONS

Tigers on the Tenth Day & and Other Stories, trans. Denys Johnson-Davies, London: Quartet 1985

Breaking Knees. Modern Arabic Stories from Syria, trans. Ibrahim Muhawi, Reading: Garnet 2008

The Hedgehog. A Modern Arabic Novella and Short Stories, trans. Brian O' Rourke, Denys Johnson-Davies, Cairo: The American University Press in Cairo 2009

FURTHER READING

Peter Bachmann: "Hundert Jahre arabische Kurzgeschichte: Bemerkungen zu den neuesten Werken des Syrers Zakariya Tamir", in: Gernot Wießner (ed.), *Erkenntnisse und Meinungen I*, Wiesbaden: Harrassowitz 1973, pp. 46–82

Eros Baldissera: "Syrian Narrative and the Topic of Sex: Šakib al-Ğabiri and Muhammad al-Naǧǧar via Zakariyya Tamir", in: *Quaderni di Studi Arabi* 10 (1992/93), pp. 99–108

Peter Dové: *Erzählte Tradition. Historische und literarische Figuren im Werk Zakariya Tamirs. Eine narratologische Analyse*, Wiesbaden: Reichert 2006

Mahmud Kayyal: "Damascene Sharazad: The Image of Women in Zakariyya Tamir's Short Stories", in: *Hawwa* 4,1 (2006), pp. 93–113

Husam al-Khateeb: "A Modern Syrian Short Story: 'Wajh al-qamar'", in: *Journal of Arabic Literature* 3 (1972), pp. 96–105

Baian Rayhanova: "Mythological and Folkloric Motifs in Syrian Prose: the Short Stories of Zakariyya Tamir", in: *Journal of Arabic and Islamic Studies* 5 (2003/04), pp. 1–12

Ulrike Stehli-Werbeck, Hartmut Fähndrich: "Nachwort", in: Sakarija Tamer: *Die Hinrichtung des Todes. Unbekannte Geschichten von bekannten Figuren*, trans. Hartmut Fähndrich, Ulrike Stehli-Werbeck, Basel: Lenos 2004, pp. 129–37

Ulrike Stehli-Werbeck: "Transformations of the Thousand and One Nights: Zakariya Tamir's *Šahriyar wa-Šahrazad* and Muhammad Ğibril's *Zahrat as-Sabah*", in: Luc Deheuvels, Barbara Michalak-Pikulska, Paul Starkey (eds.), *Intertextuality in Modern Arabic Literature since 1967*, Durham: Durham University Press 2006, pp. 103–16

Emma Westney: "Individuation and Literature: Zakariyya Tamir and his Café Man", in: Robin Ostle (ed.), *Marginal Voices in Literature and Society. Individual and Society in the Mediterranean Muslim World*, Straßburg et al.: European Science Foundation 2001, pp. 189–99

Part Two

Polygamy of Place

Introduction

Andreas Pflitsch

Time and place are becoming increasingly independent of each other. We live in a global village, networked with one another, always reachable; and, if they are deemed newsworthy, informed immediately about even the most innocuous incidents in the remotest places. Depending on the perspective, this condition, generally labeled globalization, is either a constituent feature, the continuation or the supplanting of postmodernism. At present it would seem that the processes of cultural globalization are forking in two directions: either it amounts to nothing more than another manifestation of predominantly Western popular culture, interested almost exclusively in fast-paced consumerism and marketability, in which deep-rooted traditions are pulped into insipid uniformity, spelling the end of their rich diversity of form and variation; or, in contrast, cultural globalization processes replicate the "purified" homogenous cultures of nation states. Numerous examples and indicators point in both directions.

There is, on the one hand, the McDonaldization of society: the standardization of everyday culture, where consumer products are readily available across the globe, fostering uniform eating, drinking, viewing, and listening habits; under whose oppressive omnipotence local cultures are in danger of atrophying and eventually dying. There is also the diametrically opposed tendency: an enrichment of everyday culture by virtue of borrowing elements and tapping into influences from across the globe. To take the deceptively simple example of food: globalization means not just that burgers and coke are consumed everywhere, but also that one may choose from Chinese, French, Greek, Italian, or Turkish cuisine, alongside which local cooking has become exotic in some places. Globalization proves to be an extremely paradoxical phenomenon, for it provokes its own opposite, namely localization. The global and the local relate to one another dialectically; the world is universe and "pluriverse" in one. As the globalization theorist Ulrich Beck has remarked, "we all live glocally."

For the German philosopher Rüdiger Safranski, this reveals the "fundamental anthropological condition that mobility and cosmopolitanism need to be counterbalanced by a strong sense of place": an observation that leads him to advocate "a positive interpretation of home" that goes beyond its coupling with rigid nationalist or other ideological constructs. Home and the local do not form an anachronistic counterweight to globalization but represent a corrective, one without which globalization is simply inoperable and intolerable. In his essay *Wieviel Globalisierung verträgt der Mensch*, Safranski postulates the following formula: "The more intense the emotional connection to place, the greater the capacity and willingness for cosmopolitanism."

Similar mechanisms and phenomena involving this curious enmeshment of the global with the local are also evident in literature. Trends towards a standardized literary aesthetic are observable worldwide, and these go hand in hand with rediscovered traditions. Modern Arabic literature has a long history of using traditional narrative forms, genres, or stylistic elements; aspects of this history are touched upon in the essays in the preceding section devoted to remembrance. Resorting to local traditions in times of confusing global complexity – no longer so "new" as Jürgen Habermas claimed back in 1985 – is not the only point of intersection between the two thematic blocks "remembrance" and "polygamy of place": independent of the traditions, the acute crises in the Arab world are what connect these two themes. The enforced polygamy of place that is foisted upon displaced persons and expellees, depriving them of a sense of orientation in space and so triggering a concomitant loss of identity, is a theme addressed by Christian Szyska and Christian Junge, who explore the works of Anton Shammas and Sélim Nassib respectively: the former a Palestinian author living in the United States who writes in Arabic, Hebrew, and English; the latter a Jewish-Lebanese Francophone author and publicist resident in Paris.

Writing in the "global village"

Arabic literature has long ceased depicting and discussing only Arab society. Crossing conventional boundaries has become common practice. Hybrid identities come about in the "global village", with migration and telecommunications, tourism and the internet radically altering the relationship between time and space. Categories like "belonging" or "home" are being scrutinized, and thus the signs employed to mark the boundless complexity of identity are altered.

"To be married to more than one place", writes the creator of the term "polygamy of place", Ulrich Beck, "is the gateway for globalization to enter one's own life." A place-polygamous existence, a globalized biography, often leads to a "zapping across continents, eras and cultures", according to Regina Keil-Sagawe's essay on the Algerian author Habib Tengour in this volume.

The literary canon also shifts under the influence of these processes; new benchmarks emerge. Elements of a popular culture now spanning the world, Hollywood movies, and the emergent global everyday culture are finding their way into Arabic literature, whereas superficial ornamental representations of Arab culture have long had a place in the global canon. Pessimists envision that the process will end with rehashed and easily digestible snacks, deprived of their potential complexity and so stripped of any disturbing and stimulating impulse, while optimists rave about diversity, exchange, and bridges of understanding. For the moment, it seems that the scales could tip either way.

What is certain is that classical points of orientation for forming collective identities are on the decline and losing their importance. The European paradigm of the nation state, dominant throughout the nineteenth and twentieth centuries, is now being questioned and is losing its status as sole benchmark for collective identity. Under closer inspection, national identity is fading, revealing itself to be no more than another fiction, hardly any different from folklore.

Native country, native language

While the ideal of a nation is based on congruency between the native population, territory, and language, the reality is often decidedly different. Mass migration is once again prevalent; authors live and work in one country while writing in the language of another about the history of a third. A good example of this is the American novelist Jeffrey Eugenides, author of the novel *Middlesex*: "Descended from Asia Minor Greeks, born in America, I live in Europe now. Specifically, in the Schöneberg district of Berlin", states the narrator of the novel. "You used to be able to tell a person's nationality by their face", he continues. "Immigration ended that. Next you discerned nationality via the footwear. Globalization ended that. (...) Only Nikes, on Basque, on Dutch, on Siberian feet."

Nationalities are recognized more easily today by language than footwear. Language often proves to be a firmer, more durable tie than place but even this does not always hold for a lifetime. Nations have native languages; whoever migrates is place polygamous and thus perforce polyglot, forced to deal with an adopted language. The Turkish author Emine Sevgi Özdamar made her writing debut in German in 1990 with a collection of short stories titled *Mutterzunge* (Mothertongue). "In my language tongue means: language." Özdamar speaks in tongues and realizes that "the tongue is boneless and whereto one rolls it, it rolls there."

Born in 1960 in Tokyo and resident of Hamburg and Berlin since 1982, Yoko Tawada switches between Japanese and German when writing. Taking the title of one of her books *Überseezungen*, literally, we may say that she speaks in "overseas tongues": she translates because she has crossed over from overseas.

> A week later a woman asked me: Do you have a velo [bike]? I was shocked, because "velo" sounds remarkably like the Japanese word for "tongue". Do you have a tongue? That's an important question. Do you have the tongue one needs to belong here?

"What's interesting lies in-between", says Yoko Tawada. When "either / or" contends with "both one and the other", when it is yet to be decided if opposites are to exclude or cancel out one another, when everything hangs in the balance – this is when something new can arise. The author is exasperated by the endlessly posed question: "what language do you dream in?" Unable to answer, the enquirer usually goes on to inform her that one dreams in the language of the country where the soul resides. "To which I answer cheerfully: 'I've lots of souls and lots of tongues.'"

Canons

Models of place polygamy are multifaceted. They must not always go hand in hand with a change of language and do not even presuppose a conclusive physical change of place. Wei Hui is a Chinese citizen who lives in China and writes in Chinese. Her fast-paced novel *Shanghai Baobei* (1999) – described in the novel as "true and chaotic stories about the postcolonial flower garden called Shanghai" – is set in the artists' milieu of the Chinese harbor city which although currently booming still clings to the myth of its past. Icons of popular culture and authors mark out the framework with the novel's very first sentence:

> My name is Nikki but my friends all call me Coco after Coco Chanel, a French lady who lived to be almost ninety. She's my idol, after Henry Miller.

Nikki's furniture is from IKEA; her boyfriend's car is a VW. She reads ELLE, watches movies like *Natural Born Killers*, and listens to Portishead, Marilyn Manson and Alanis Morissette. She works in an Adidas store during the day and plays in a rock band in the evenings, before watching the late-night news bulletin, where she sees horrific images from the war in Kosovo. Is this a Westernized or a globalized life? To put it differently: is the lifestyle depicted here a freely chosen adaptation or a kind of friendly takeover by the West?

Ordinary eccentrics

Today cross-over seems to be the norm: "British" authors like Amitav Ghosh, Arundhati Roy, Jhumpa Lahiri, Salman Rushdie and Hanif Kureishi, or "German" writers such as Feridun Zaimoglu, Renan Demirkan, Selim Özdogan and Aysel Özakin are prominent figures on the literary stage. Kureishi's novel *The Buddha of Suburbia* (1989) begins with a confession: "My name is Karim Amir, and I am Englishman born and bred, almost." In Zaimoglu's powerfully eloquent novel *Liebesmale, scharlachrot* (2000), the first-person narrator is moved to say: "What a strange Turk I am."

Of course, writers going into exile and adopting the language of the host country is nothing new. Great names like Samuel Beckett, James Joyce, Milan Kundera and Vladimir Nabokov recall that this process can have a variety of causes and circumstances. And works by authors who in exile continue to write in their native tongue are hardly comprehensible without considering the alienation inherent to exile. Here one need only recall Heinrich Heine or Thomas Mann. No matter if chosen or enforced, if accompanied by a change of language or not, authors in exile tend to abandon old certainties and pose new questions. For this reason, exile literature was always particularly innovative. The Tuareg author Ibrahim al-Koni, presented in this volume by Hartmut Fähndrich, is convinced of the value of living in alien surrounds "because under the conditions of exile one ceases to live in space" and is thus no longer caught "in an environment that robs a person of their inner self." Al-Koni realizes that losing one's sense of self is not necessarily a flaw, "for whoever wishes to find their soul must first lose it". The days seem long past in which the Syrian poet Adel Karasholi, living in Germany, spoke of being torn between languages and cultures, emphasizing the suffering this turmoil caused him.

In recent years, Turkish authors, or those with a Turkish background, as well as writers from Eastern European and the Balkans have entered the stage of German-language literature. The real existing crossover and mixing of languages, national affiliation, and place of residence, in short a bursting out of the corset of nationalism, has created multifaceted overlapping spaces. Whereas such spaces were perceived and accepted somewhat ashamedly as a necessary evil in modernism, if not outright suppressed, postmodern authors are extremely adept at highlighting the charm and value of their position "betwixt and between". Authors no longer feel torn between cultures, between languages, and between countries; instead, they grasp this "neither-nor" situation as an advantage. While "guest-worker" literature in Germany and *beur* (migrant) literature in France pursued a predominantly defensive approach, expressing self-assertion in a foreign country, young authors are now performing the balancing act between cultures with assurance and self-confidence. They are simply place polygamous, without the faintest hint of guilt either way. They are not starting from a position behind the blocks and having to play catch up, but actually have a head start. This new-found confidence stems not least from the observation that genuinely important literary texts are often written from a peripheral position. Jamal Tuschick, editor of an anthology of "recent German literature" titled *Morgen Land* (2000) featuring authors of non-German background, has remarked that "German literature is being intensively pollinated from the ethnic margins of society." Authors have nestled into the interstices and margins and their insights are uncomfortable for the so-called majority society seeking to assuage its discontents with the fiction of a "guiding German culture".

In the meantime, Arabic literature is being written in German – or should that be: German literature is being written by Arabs? Solely a question of perspective, this alternative adds nothing insightful to what is happening. Born in southern Iraq, Hussain Al-Mozany has lived, after a spell in Beirut, in Germany since 1980. After publishing short stories and a novel in Arabic, in 1999 his first novel written in German, *Der Marschländer*, was released. In his second "German" novel, *Mansur oder Der Duft des Abendlandes* (2002), he tells the absurd-comic story of the Iraqi Mansur, who has taken legal action against the Federal Republic of Germany on the grounds that he is the descendant of a certain Peter the Solitary. As the story goes, Peter journeyed to Iraq at the time of the "good friendship" between the Abbasid caliph Harun al-Rashid and Charlemagne from Aachen and left behind the fruit of an amorous adventure he shared with a woman called Aischa. Mansur therefore heads off to the "old homeland" of Germany, where he experiences a couple of adventures of his own, narrated in the tradition of the picaresque novel. At first, sitting next to a couple of Turks in a packed bus, he wonders about the similarity between German and his native Arabic, while he fails to recognize that the author "Fulfschtanscht fun Tschuta," who he surmises must be a Bulgarian or perhaps a Frenchman, is in fact the icon of German highbrow culture, Johann Wolfgang von Goethe. Al-Mozany spares nothing or no-one: neither the *jus sanguinis* (right of blood) basis of the right to German citizenship, nor language and culture as criterion and pride of the German nation.

As an idea, nationalism is deep-seated – even if the high degree of ideology that was necessary for its popular assertion has long been recognized, even if we are now well aware "that ethnicity exists first of all in the imagination of man" and cannot be proven empirically, as the historian Patrick J. Geary has shown lucidly, even if it has long been established that the national languages were much more the result of homogenization typical of nineteenth-century Europe than any kind of natural tradition. Thus, even if today the "nation" has to be considered a constructed and more or less arbitrary entity, this does not diminish its prevalence or significance. Ever since Woodrow Wilson formulated the principle of national self-determination in 1918, the nation was definitively established as the organizing norm for the body politic. The most important European multinational states, the Habsburg monarchy, Tsarist Russia, and the Ottoman Empire, were all dismantled in the wake of the First World War.

The nation as an "imagined community", to evoke Benedict Anderson's succinct formulation, went and goes hand in hand with erecting the "alien" and the "other" as a counter-image and means of demarcation. As the dark underbelly of the search for any national or collective identity, an excluded and excluding counterpart is inevitable. A shift in the coordinating points of the term "imagined communities" has become discernible in recent years: the "nation" fades into the background as "culture" comes to the fore. Nonetheless, the reflex to demarcate remains.

The cosmopolite in interstitial spaces

Not only those authors who actually move between various physical locations are place polygamous, but so too those who live intellectually in several different worlds. The Arab poet Adonis is a prime example, his work rooted in both the Arab-Islamic and the Western-European traditions. Drawn for descriptive purposes, this distinction is in fact indiscernible in his work, for it is less an addition of two elements than their blending, as when two different colors mixed together create a third – and defy renewed separation by stirring in the opposite direction. Adonis' literature is cosmopolitan without ever succumbing to the danger of shallowness lurking in any attempt to harmonize divergent sources.

Place polygamy in both its spatial-geographical and cultural-intellectual forms draws its particular stimulus from what Homi K. Bhabha has characterized as interstices. This spatial conception refers to domains defying exclusive ascription to hegemonic structures; their openness and quality of "not belonging", generated by overlapping and displacement, enhance the potential of difference. Here a no-man's land emerges between the established coordinates of dominant discourse, a space conducive to creating or recreating ideas, where a sense of lostness is at home and home has been lost. "Everything that I have done lives from spaces in between", writes Peter Handke, who has repeatedly characterized himself as a "place-bound writer": "my starting point is never that of a story or an event, an incident, but always a place." As Regina Keil-Sagawe points out in her essay on Habib Tengour, a distinction needs to be drawn between chosen and enforced alienation nevertheless: "mirror- and counter-worlds are worlds of 'estranged nearness' – artificially created distance sharpens the gaze. Exilic worlds, on the other hand, are worlds of 'alienated nearness' – a daily lived distance dims the gaze."

Multinational states: the "myth of the Levant"

In his essays on Ukraine, Yuri Andrukhovych sings the praises of the old Danube Monarchy. Here Austria-Hungary is not – and this is decisive – idealized from a centralist position, motivated by a restorative impulse concerned with reestablishing a vanished empire. Andrukhovych adopts the perspective of the periphery. His "apologia for blessed Austria" has absolutely nothing in common with nationalism; on the contrary, it focuses on the transnational character of the monarchy, specifically the fact "that the Ukrainian element was able to survive thanks to precisely the endless linguistic and ethnic diversity of this world." The classical nation states of the age granted cultural and linguistic minorities precious little room to develop. Against this background, one can only be filled with appreciation and gratitude for the Danube Monarchy: "I think that for this reason alone, the 'old Prohazka,' Kaiser Franz Joseph I, earned a Nobel Prize for the Cultural Conversation of a Species if there was such a prize at all and it could be awarded posthumously."

With the caveat that comparisons are inevitably somewhat askew, here seems to be the ideal place to turn our attention to another large multinational state, a direct neighbor of the Danube Monarchy: the Ottoman Empire. Between the early sixteenth century and its demise at the end of the First World War, the Ottoman Empire spanned today's Arab countries. In recent years, Arab intellectuals have begun to reappraise Ottoman history and their approach is cognate to Yuri Andrukhovych's Austria-Hungary apologia. Whereas previously the "Ottoman yoke" dominated, a simplistic and demonized version of four centuries of continuous decline traditionally propagated in historical works legitimizing the "new" Arab nation states, focus has now shifted to the transnational and multicultural "Levant" as the paradigm of a regional culture. A realignment of perspective, a simple shift in key, and it suddenly becomes possible to write historical studies bearing titles – referring to Lebanon under Ottoman rule – like *The Long Peace*. Historical novels evoke the "myth of the Levant", the ideal or utopia of an open, tolerant, multicultural Middle East prior to the demarcating of borders – first and foremost securing the interests of the European powers – at the beginning of the twentieth century.

The biography of the painter and writer Etel Adnan represents this Levant. Born in Beirut in 1925 to a Greek mother and Syrian father – her parents had met in Izmir – she grew up in the cosmopolitan climate of Beirut. She attended a French school where speaking Arabic was punished. In 1949 she left Beirut to study in Paris, moved in 1955 to the United States, and today commutes between Beirut, Paris, and Sausalito in California. As Sonja Mejcher-Atassi shows in her essay, Adnan has developed her own unique approach to Arabic as a language and script. Writing in English and French, she has learnt "to paint in Arabic". Another example of a "Levantine" biography is that of Andrée Chedid, born in Cairo in 1920 to Lebanese parents. After attending school in France, she returned to Egypt to study. At first she published poems written in English before switching to French. Today her work is part of the French literary canon taught in French schools.

The co-existence of religions, peoples, and languages in the eastern Mediterranean region lends itself, indeed imposes itself as a model of globalization *avant la lettre*, whereas such potentiality is completely missing in successfully homogenized nation states like – albeit very belatedly – Germany. Remnants of cultural diversity, to stay with the German example for the moment, like the Danes in Schleswig or the Sorbs in Lusatia, are perceived, if at all, as attractive curiosities and cultivated within an enclosure marked out by special bureaucratic rules. In contrast, Arab authors, with Lebanese and Palestinians leading the way, have the opportunity of linking into the myth of the Levant. In his *Balthasar's Odyssey*, the Lebanese author Amin Maalouf (b. 1949) provides a panoramic representation of a complex Mediterranean cultural region, shaped by Jewish, Christian, and Islamic influences, and travelled by traders and scholars from north and south, Orient and Occident alike. The paradigm of a multinational state turns out to be a viable option in times when, according to conventional categories of ethnicity, nationality, and race, almost a billion people belong to "minorities", reducing the concept of "minority" itself to an absurdity.

For Maalouf, the *Ports of Call* (the title of one of his novels) in the Levant are synonymous with the openness of the pre- and postmodern transnational state, much like Alexandria for the Egyptian Edwar al-Kharrat and İzmir for Jeffrey Eugenides, who calls it "the most cosmopolitan city of the Middle East" and describes it as a city which "was actually not exactly a place, which did not belong to any one country because it harbored all countries."

Wei Hui is another who bridges pre-modern and modern cosmopolitanism with postmodern globality by breathing new life into the myth of Shanghai. As in her novel, a new tone is resonating in the works of younger Arab authors born in the 1960s and 1970s. Whereas preceding generations revealed an aching lack of self-confidence typical of a backward "Third World" vis-à-vis the overwhelming superiority of the West, they are enunciating a new-found sense of assuredness, crystallizing out of the realization that the Western emperor is often enough caught out with nothing on.

No other writer shows this with more wit than the Lebanese author Hani Hammoud. In his satirical novel *L'Occidentaliste* (1997), he reverses the clichés of Orientalism and fixes the ethnological gaze on the Americans. An American rival in love, backed by rough and ready reinforcements, waylays the Lebanese protagonist, who is then subjected to a barrage of verbal abuse that, however, does not faze him due to the geographical ignorance put on show:

> If I still had even the slightest doubts about their intentions, he dispelled them by hurling a "fuck Iran" in my direction, obviously the fruit of geo-political deliberations which couldn't have taken that long. The mob instantly repeated this war cry, complemented by a couple of shouts of "fuck Khomeini" for the more educated. I'd have liked to answer through my indifference, not to mention my quite exceptional tolerance towards the sexual propositions they wanted to solicit to the heirs of the Persian throne and its subjects.

In Hammoud's novel the Americans are the truly exotic figures. Unlike the greater majority of their writer colleagues of older generations, authors such as Hani Hammoud, Rabih Alameddine, and Tony Hanania are neither awestruck nor plagued by inferiority complexes when facing self-confident, if not narcissistic, Americans and Europeans.

At times, place polygamy leads to temporal asymmetries: at a gala marking American Independence Day held at the university, the "Occidentalist" is asked by the mother of a fellow student sitting next to him if the Fourth of July is also celebrated in Lebanon, to which he answers: "Yes, madam. But we celebrate on the fifth, because of the time difference."

WORKS CITED

Engin Deniz Akarli: *The Long Peace. Ottoman Lebanon, 1861–1920*, London, New York: Tauris 1993

Benedict Anderson: *Imagined Communities. Reflections on the Origin and Spread of Nationalism*, London, New York: Verso 1983

Yuri Andrukhovych (= Juri Andruchowytsch): *Das letzte Territorium*, Frankfurt/M.: Suhrkamp 2003

Ulrich Beck: *Was ist Globalisierung? Irrtümer des Globalismus – Antworten auf Globalisierung*, Frankfurt/M.: Suhrkamp 1998

Homi K. Bhabha: *The Location of Culture*, London, New York: Routledge 1994

Jeffrey Eugenides: *Middlesex*, New York: Farrar, Straus & Giroux 2002

Patrick J. Geary: *Europäische Völker im frühen Mittelalter. Zur Legende vom Werden der Nationen*, Frankfurt/M.: Fischer 2002

Hani Hammoud: *L'Occidentaliste*, Beirut: Editions Dar an-Nahar 1997

Peter Handke: *Aber ich lebe nur von den Zwischenräumen*, Zurich: Ammann 1987

Hanif Kureishi: *The Buddha of Suburbia*, London: Faber & Faber 1990

Amin Maalouf: *Le périple de Baldassare*, Paris: Grasset & Fasquelle 2000 (English translation: *Balthasar's Odyssey*, trans. Barbara Bray, London: Harvill 2002)

Amin Maalouf: *Les échelles du Levant*, Paris: Grasset & Fasquelle 1996 (English translation: *Ports of Call*, trans. Alberto Manguel, London: Harvill 1998)

Hussain Al-Mozany: *Mansur oder Der Duft des Abendlandes*, Leipzig: Reclam 2002

Emine Sevgi Özdamar: *Mutterzunge*, Berlin: Rotbuch 1990

Rüdiger Safranski: *Wieviel Globalisierung verträgt der Mensch?*, Munich, Vienna: Hanser 2003

Yoko Tawada: *Überseezungen*, Tübingen: Konkursbuch 2002

Jamal Tuschik (ed.): *MorgenLand. Neueste deutsche Literatur*, Frankfurt/M.: Fischer 2000

Wei Hui [= Zhou Weihui]: *Shanghai Baobei*, Shenyang: Chunfeng wenyi chubanshe 1999

Feridun Zaimoglu: *Liebesmale, scharlachrot*, Hamburg: Rotbuch 2000

"From the Orient to the Occident it is just a reflection"
The Mirror-Worlds of Habib Tengour

Regina Keil-Sagawe

The wave
a hollow mirror
confuses the crew
Nobody wants to set over
Who could anyway?
This offshore island
glimmers strangely

Habib Tengour, The Far Island

Jazirat al-maghrib (island of the West, or island of the setting sun) is the sonorous name thought up by seventh-century geographers in distant Baghdad for the newly conquered Western province at the extreme edge of the Arab empire. In later German texts it was arrogantly referred to as the "Barbary Coast". The Ancients even fancied that this was where the world ended ... where the Pillars of Hercules rose into the sky and Atlas carried the burden of the heavens on his shoulders, where the shadow world of Hades began and where the Hesperides, Islands of the Blessed, lay.

Al-Jaza'ir (The Islands) is still the name of Algeria. Authors have played with this: *Coeur Insulaire* ("Island heart", 2000) is the name of a volume of poems by Mohammed Dib, the *grand seigneur* of Algerian literature who died in 2003. Even today, the "West" is preserved in country names such as: *al-maghrib al-adna, al-ausat, al-aqsa*: (the "near", the "middle" and the "far" West) – for Tunisia, Algeria and Morocco. (In contrast, the countries of the Near East are known as the *mashriq,* the countries of the "rising sun"). These names derive from the same word root as that of the Portuguese Algarve region, *gh-r-b* (leave, emigrate, move to foreign parts; to go West, become Westernized). Related to this are *gharib* (foreign, foreigner, strange, odd) and *ghurba* (the outland, exile).

This has far-reaching consequences, as Mohammed Dib describes in his essay *L'arbre à dires* ("The Tree of Sayings", 1998):

> Even if exile were to lead us into the east, for us, etymologically speaking, it would still lie in the West. In the language and thus mental substrate of an Arab-speaking Muslim, there is no other exile than the western one.

Under the dictates of this root, anyone who lives in the Maghreb lives in dangerous proximity to "exile". This is very close to Heidegger's vision of modern man's existential predicament and his concept of *Geworfensein* (being thrown into the world). Habib Tengour, "one of the Maghreb's most forceful and visionary francophone poetic voices of the post-colonial era" (Pierre Joris), who was born in 1947 in a port town of western Algeria and migrated to Paris as a child, puts it this way:

> The Maghrebian is always elsewhere. And that is where he fulfils himself. Jugurtha lacked money to buy Rome. / Tariq gave his name to a Spanish mountain. / Ibn Khaldûn found himself obliged to hand over his steed to Tamerlane. / Abd el Krim corresponded with the Third International ...

Tengour formulated this statement in 1981, in his *Manifesto of Maghrebian Surrealism*, which was written in the spirit of Arthur Rimbaud and André Breton's famous *Surrealist Manifesto*. The muted cynicism underlying this poetic worldview has recently received further macabre confirmation in the exodus of Algerian and other young people who, fleeing the lack of prospects in their home countries, have drifted to France, Spain, Canada, Australia or even as far as Afghanistan.

Transit station Peshawar

> How he had dreamed of this resting station during the tribulations of the journey! The city did not correspond in the least to the magic world of the *Thousand and One Nights*. From the sound of the name he had imagined an enchanted atmosphere. What a disappointment! A squalid settlement. The run-down Orient as portrayed in documentaries!

Mourad, the main character of Tengour's novel *Le Poisson de Moïse*, ("Moses's Fish", 2001) is a young scientist living in Paris and enjoying professional success. World-weariness drives him to Afghanistan on a quest to find the meaning of life; the "old dream of Medina", of an "original Muslim community in all its fraternal coherence!" He soon gives up, disappointed and irritated by the numerous rival factions entangled in bloody feuds. In perplexed meditation, he withdraws to the seclusion of "The Cave"; the mystical eighteenth sura that deals with the enigmatic will of God, which can manifest itself in incomprehensible violence and yet aims for and tends towards what is right. This sura runs through the novel as a leitmotif, with Moses and his companion, al-Khidr, the sage sent by God, arguing about Good and Evil:

He asks himself if the initiation of Moses, which is the point of the parable, doesn't perhaps have something to do with the course of his own life ... Of course he has his doubts that someday Al-Khidr could cross his path. The times have changed. The characters in tatters who people the streets these days are only poor devils, abandoned by the whole world, devoid of any illumination.

"Homecoming from Afghanistan" was the original title of Tengour's film script for a feature movie on the lives of adventurous Algerian volunteers in Islamist Afghan camps. The film never materialized, but the scenario became a novel that was published simultaneously in Paris and Algiers in December 2001 – only a few weeks after the 9/11 terrorist attacks on New York and Washington. It is a mixture of road movie and *Bildungsroman*, reflecting on the wanderings of three young Algerians between Paris and Peshawar as well as on the correct use of Islam.

Tengour recognized the extraordinarily controversial nature of the theme early on:

It started in the summer of 1993: for the Algerians the "Afghanis" were people who fought in the underground and founded the GIA, the Armed Islamic Groups. Many of those had indeed returned from Afghanistan. What mattered to me was to show a modern hero, someone who until then had not played a role in the cinema or in literature, but who would become the typical hero figure in the contemporary Muslim world: the figure of the "Afghani," of the "terrorist," the fundamentalist Islamic resistance fighter ...

Anything but coherent, Tengour stages this figure in a variety of ways using Mourad, Hasni and Kadirou, the dissimilar trio of friends from Oran who meet again during the battle for Kabul. The motives leading them to Afghanistan could not be more different. Kadirou is an unemployed second-hand clothes dealer, driven by boredom and a lust for adventure. Hasni is a car mechanic and suburban preacher driven by fanaticism. As for Mourad, he is a physicist, driven by idealism and his inferiority complex as an Arab. When Tengour started working on the scenario, in 1994, he was accused of a lack of realism. In retrospect, he comments:

Two years ago it was simply unthinkable that a figure such as my hero could even exist, i.e., someone who has a doctorate in physics, lives in the West, has a French girlfriend, and comes from a respectable family. I was told it was impossible that someone like that would go and fight in Afghanistan. But I had done my homework thoroughly, and it was clear to me even then that it was quite possible for someone who had studied in the US or in Britain to somehow end up as an Islamic fundamentalist.

"... end up." Indeed, the modern heroes Tengour portrays are unviable; they are antiheroes, like their models in real life, and their models in literature: "Julien Sorel, for example, or Lucien Leuwen: the heroes, the fighters in Algeria are exactly like them. Too young to have fought in the revolution, they are people who were born too late in a fast-changing world that doesn't live up to their ideal"; a world in which they will ultimately founder and come to a bad end.

Like Stendhal in *Le Rouge et le Noir*, Tengour intertwines the individual and psychological with historical and temporal perspectives. The novel falls into two clearly separated parts. Part One, "The Road to Kandahar", is a fast-paced action thriller, with backdrops of multicolored bazaars and high mountain peaks. Part Two, "Stopover in Paris", breaks this pace: Mourad is hanging around in Paris, desperately searching for Hasni and his share of the stolen million dollars but even more desperately searching for himself as he drifts through the spectrum of the Algerian immigrant world, on the tracks of a wounded Algerian exile identity vegetating in bars and dives, shops and old people's homes.

West-East mirrorings

From "road movie" to "street ethnology": a rupture intended by Tengour, this stopover in Paris gives insights into the ethnographic work of the author. It echoes literary forbears in the Orient and the Occident, such as Aragon's *Paysan de Paris*, a classic Surrealist novel; or Niffari's concept of the *mawaqif*, a key Sufist idea, which refers to a concentrated "pause" between two phases of roaming that broadens the view and creates historical connections. In his 1998 study, *Fugues de Barbarie*, the Tunisian scholar Hédi Abdeljaouad coined the term *soufialisme* (Sufialism), meaning a merging of the essential aspects of Surrealism and Sufism, when characterizing Tengour's literary technique as a prime example of modern Maghrebian writing.

What excites Tengour about Surrealism are the surprising parallels between the central concepts of that movement and the Sufi mysticism he has been familiar with since boyhood: *amour fou* (crazy love), "objective chance", "automatic writing" and hermetic speech. "The longer I immersed myself in Surrealism, the more reconnected I felt to my childhood in Mostaganem."

Under the influence of the Surrealists and their image of the Orient, which is based on that of the Symbolists and the Romantics, Tengour's own, "naïve" image of the Orient shifted considerably:

It is the Romantics who were the first to rediscover the *Thousand and One Nights*. Baudelaire sings a song in praise of hashish and wine ... With these authors I have discovered an image of the Orient which radically differs from mine. It is a doubly or triply filtered gaze. I work on authors who work on the Orient, and through them I work on the Orient and the Occident ...

This leads Mourad to ask himself for an embarrassed second if it was not in fact the "French Romantics" who "through strange mirror-effects had awoken his Arab soul in him, this elusive matter for which he has searched so laboriously in Islamism." Indeed, he even suspects them "of being more Arab than the ideologists of the Arab Renaissance."

Some literary reflections touch upon a controversial subject: the genesis and solidification of images of self and other in their complex interplay. Tengour, who presents heroes tormented by self-doubt and shows ambivalent and contradictory characters, takes the risk of disrupting the prevalent Western discourse, which having passed through Orientalist phantasms and colonial clichés now seems afflicted with Bin-Laden syndrome. He does not, like Montesquieu exclaim *Comment peut-on être Persan?* (How can one be a Persian?) Instead, he tries to explain, in the vein of Enlightenment: *Comment devient-on Afghan?* (How does one become an Afghani?) He insists that for him it is neither a matter of "action" nor a matter of writing about Algeria, as the media would then expect scenes of violence and massacres, which are purely superficial phenomena. It is much more important for him to "trace the deeper underlying structures of Arab-Islamic culture this opens up. All of this with the backdrop of myths, historical events and collective phantasms, in order to understand how they affect the world of today in those countries." In the novel this all culminates in Mourad's desperate outcry, revolting against the Orient-Occident stereotypes. Futile, of course:

> There's no Orient or Occident, that's all literary bull, there's only a North and a South, locked in lethal combat. That's the truth. And it's brutal. Especially if you are on the wrong side. The strong have no memory, they have only remembrances and commemoration days, which they celebrate at great financial cost. The weak are ruined by their memory. It is like an evil curse that can't be shaken off. (...) Then religion works like a balm (...) I thought I had split because I was fed up with Europe and setting out in search for an authentic identity. Today I'm not so sure anymore. Afghanistan or Peru, these places are interchangeable; you always carry your old ego and the memory of your kin with you! There's no escape ...

Fictions of the distant – stations on the way to a nomad poetics

Afghanistan or Peru – indeed, the places are interchangeable, for the appeal of the far-away places is omnipresent in the texts of this author, whom fate exiled early to France and who even today lives and writes between the two shores of the Mediterranean, between Paris and Constantine, seemingly always on the move.

He is a nomad of the word, a writer considered – thus Jacqueline Arnaud, holder of the first French chair in Maghrebian literature – as "the very first author of the second generation of Algerian immigrants." In her 1995 study, *Les fous cartographes*, Geneviève Mouillaud-Fraisse asserts that Tengour's books are different from nearly everything one has read before. His writing technique is an accurate illustration of the main features of a "nomad poetics", as defined by Pierre Joris, the Luxembourg poet and scholar from America, in his manifesto *The Millenium will be nomadic or it will not be. Notes Towards a Nomadic Poetics* – translated, significantly enough, into French by Habib Tengour:

> A nomadic poetics is always on the move, always changing, morphing, moving through languages, cultures, terrains, times without stopping.

Indeed, a foray through Tengour's literary oeuvre – presently consisting of seven volumes of prose and thirteen of poetry, besides a mass of short texts, uncollected poems and narrations, published in France, Algeria, Italy, the US, Britain, Belgium, Germany and Switzerland – almost constantly highlights Tengour's writing "position" or rather, as it is anything other than static or fixed, his "between-ness". This is the state Joris defines as "the fundamental nomadic state"; as a ceaseless forward movement, an absence of stasis, a continuous becoming, a "line of flight" away from a final state of being, which would be akin to death.

Three such lines of flight can be traced in Habib Tengour's work. They are lines that keep intersecting, coming together only to separate once again; structuring a poetic universe, carrying readers and characters away into imaginary worlds; strange, estranged and alienated worlds where one thing is mirrored above all: the process of writing as an unending search for an Algerian identity.

Imagined distance ... desire- and dream-worlds

> To Valparaíso! To the other end of the world!
> A burning desire he could name any time.
> *Habib Tengour,* Gens de Mosta

This unending search goes hand in hand with a flight from reality. Place-names become the ciphers of a yearning set aflame by the stories told by sailors in a harbor bar. Country-names take on an erotic overtone, as in *L'épreuve de l'arc* ("The Trial of the Bow", 1990):

Sweden! Denmark! Norway! Finland! (...) The magnetic North (...) It was said that up there the girls, and what girls! were sugar dolls, easily approachable, completely taken with the dark, curly heads, melting like cream pies, blonde, svelte and adorable, slender honey candies...

And fantasies of desire fuse with shimmering mythological projections, where fear and fascination keep equal balance: "Was Paris the abyss into which we fell upon awakening? The ogress from our mothers' fairy tales? Circe who changed us into whatever she wanted? Maybe Calypso, able to fetter us imperceptibly?"

"Imagined distance" one could call such fantasies of desire: strategies of evasion through which Tengour's characters escape the frustrations of everyday life; they fantasize themselves out of their drab, gray present, the time of a daydream, a conversation in a bar, a passing remark ... They do not, however, withstand confrontation with real life, as Mourad shows.

Feigned distance ... mirror- and counter-worlds

I am a foreigner among all these Greeks.
Habib Tengour, Tapapakitaques

Against this stands the "feigned distance", a quintessential structuring dimension of Tengour's texts. It is a simulated, (pre-)mirrored, mirror-image distance, indeed; for between the lines that superficially set the event in distant regions and times, the Algerian present flashes again and again, along with occasional snippets from Tengour's own biography.

Tengour loves to deceive, to tease and to confuse. A recurring theme in all his texts is the question of Algeria's cultural identity at the confluence of East and West. All his work can be read as a chronicle of postcolonial Algeria. Admittedly it reads as an estranged chronicle, one in which borrowings from Arab literature blend with the tradition of Maghreb narratives and influences drawn from European Classicism and Modernism. It reads as a blend of documentation and fiction, too, that wittily recycles dark chapters of history while resorting at times to grim, surreal humor: 1983 and the rise of fundamentalism in the mirror of the medieval movement of the Assassins; 1985 and the failed Algerian socialist experiment in the light of the Russian October Revolution; 1990 and the attitude towards life amongst the youth of Algiers in the 1980s, with echoes from the Odyssey and Arab picaresque literature.

The ever-present recourse to the Odysseus myth, with its motif of exile, yearning and return, is most significant. Odysseus almost becomes the author's *alter ego*, as the opening sentence of his literary debut shows: "My name is Odysseus, I am twenty-two and I am studying sociology because I flunked law." *Tapapakitaques* is a burlesque chronicle of the Parisian student milieu in the 1960s, which also catches the political and emotional mood at the time of Boumedienne's 1965 coup in sentimental, subversive text fragments ("Cogito argo boum"). This text is a surreal predecessor of *beur* (migrant) literature; the main protagonist a "displaced" Romantic with nothing but love, revolution and poetry – the Surrealists' credo – in his head. Being abroad is a source of pain for him: "I wandered all over like a fool lost in a hothouse in the suburbs of Paris. I drank milk to become white and strong ... the Champ-Elysées made me throw up my merguez." He wants to return to his island, that Ithaca-Algeria where the first blemishes of socialism have started to show, although he guesses how all this would end one day: "they hung him, the ethnologist-spy. In those days we were a bit wild."

In 1972, after graduating in sociology, Tengour, who had followed his parents, committed activists for Algerian independence, to Paris in 1958, returned to Algeria. He was appointed director of the newly founded Institute for Social Sciences at the University in Constantine, which was to become the stronghold of fundamentalism. Twenty years later, in September 1992, Tengour's colleague Abderrahmane Benlazhar would be murdered there by Islamic extremists, the first victim of the terrorist onslaught that was to decimate the Algerian intelligentsia.

Tengour's obituary for his friend, *La mort de Abderrahman* ("The Death of Abderrahman"), first published in the newspaper *Alger Républicain*, is considered to be the very first, and very discreet literary example of a lamentation for the dead – "you, who are dead / yesterday still / you were leaning against the dream" – that would later on, during the 1990s, take on much shriller forms (so-called "literature of urgency"), whereas Tengour continues referring to and rewriting mythological models, be it the Qur'an, as in the above example of the *al-Rahman* ("The Compassionate") sura, or the Odyssey, as in the poem cycle "In the Country of the Dead":

> is there need for one more massacre
> and even more tears and the mute ash of the poem
> to show us the way beneath the earth.

The recourse to myth is not only motivated by aesthetics. It also serves as a way to bypass censorship, as well as having therapeutic and cognitive functions, as Tengour insisted in 1980 when writing about the Greek poet Georges Seferis: "Myth attenuates the shock, sublimates the pain, frees the gaze" ... also the gaze upon corruption and mismanagement, on growing intolerance and bigotry.

Tengour's experiences in the Algeria of the 1970s, his frustrations and premonitions, are woven into two subtle and enigmatic prose texts that rework the past and present history of the country in poetic fragments:

> He planned to write the history of the Tartars, a giant anecdote, but he was refused access to any official documentation. Dream would have to make up for the lack of archives.

Thus Tengour in the first text, *Sultan Galièv ou la rupture des stocks* ("Sultan Galiev or the Shortfall of Supplies", 1981) a text so controversial that at first it circulated only secretly, *samizdat*-fashion, in Algeria. Conceived, in fact, "only" as a pastiche of socialism in Algerian garb with the Russian Revolution as a background, it anticipates the later worldwide decline of socialism and points to the potential for unrest in the South of the former Soviet Union:

> Those were the days when in Algeria we lived under a Marxist system, and I, I described the collapse of the Soviet empire. My friends said, how can you write something like that, have you suddenly become an anti-communist, or why do you do this? To which I answered, no, that has simply come to an end ... I have always had a sort of time-delay in regard to these events.

Tengour's approach to fundamentalism is similar: even before the Islamic Revolution in Iran in 1979 he picked up the themes of religious totalitarianism and the responsibility of the intellectual in relation to war, corruption and ideological sclerosis. In the *Le Vieux de la Montagne* ("The Old Man of the Mountain", 1983), Tengour offers a poetic variation on Hassan i-Sabbah, the famous "old man of the mountain" prototype: the fanatic Shiite sect leader who, in his mountain retreat Alamut in the Persian Khorassan, trained his followers during their hashish highs to become terrorist "assassins" and eliminate his political rivals. That was in the eleventh and twelfth centuries. Right up to the present day the French and English word "assassin" recalls them, and Tengour's surreal version of war and peace in the distant Orient seems more real than ever:

> Hassan wanted power. Absolute power ... His assassins terrorized the empire, without winning the people to their cause, for their doctrine was complicated and demanded absolute obedience. Submission.

As if in a laboratory, Tengour sets up three emblematic historical figures and lets them collide: Hassan i-Sabbah, the fanatic warrior; the Persian Grand Vizier Nizam al-Mulik, the incarnation of the ruthless, pragmatic politician with an insatiable thirst for power; and Omar Khayyam, the astronomer-poet from Nishapur, to whom the world owes melancholy epigrams, the *Ruba'iyyat* and the solution of third-degree algebraic equations. In Tengour's text, however, the latter wastes his life locked in his observatory, held back by a fear of getting his hands dirty. A fatal blood-brother alliance unites the three unequal friends, each one of them searching for the only one, bliss-bringing Truth. The experiment fails tragically: when posited and pursued in absolute terms, neither religion, politics, nor science are viable ways towards "truth".

Tengour's text is a poetic plea for pluralism and tolerance against the backdrop of the decadent decay of the once glorious Abbasid Empire (720–1258), which created a unique cultural synthesis in the ninth and tenth centuries together with Arab, Persian, Indian and Greek substrates. In those days Paris was a village; Baghdad a city of millions, the center of the civilized world, radiating through Spain to the rest of Europe. Then came a time when "the gates of *ijtihad*" (the individual exertion towards the interpretation of religion) "were shut", when the courage to make use of one's intelligence vanished. Schools of thought and law were established, blocking the emergence of new ideas. The Empire was beset by obscurantism, stagnation, fatalism and resignation, before it was conquered in 1055 by Turkish Seljuks and finally swept away by the Mongol invasions. The fall of Baghdad in 1258 disrupted the whole Arab world and is portrayed even centuries later by Arab chroniclers in purely apocalyptic terms. Tengour, similarly:

> Elsewhere too the Mongols terrorized the nations. Their advance brought the Day of Judgment ever closer. At the head of the host rode Azrael, on a black she-donkey, whose shadow had the width of ten ploughshares ... They were numberless and awe-inspiring. / Fear gave birth to the new faith. / The Mongols were the whips of our erring souls, apprehensive turbulence. (...) The only means to conquer our infantile fears would have been free and honest information. / But who wants to know about freedom. / In the Alamut-bar, under the protection of a muted neon-idyll and the usual jokes, the regulars emptied glass after glass to the health of the Mongols.

Of course, Tengour has Algeria in mind, but he will not be instrumentalized: "I never wanted to be a critical writer, someone who is applauded in Europe. I am interested in bearing witness in ambiguity, for things are never one-sided. What interests me is to see how things could work." And his literature "works" – herein lies its attraction and provocation – only in so far as the reader accepts zapping across the continents, eras and cultures on Tengour's somewhat vertiginous tracks.

For Tengour is a passionate moviegoer, and this shapes his narrative technique. The very first sentence of *The Old Man of the Mountain* blends Persia and Paris in a cinematographic manner: "The first street off the Ourcq Canal led to Alamut, a neighborhood under demolition." From locations in the Oriental Middle Ages – Alamut, Nishapur, Qom and Baghdad – readers and characters are catapulted without warning sometimes into the immigrant milieu in Paris, sometimes into present-day Algeria. Politically charged poetic kaleidoscopes are formed continuously: "A birdman was named Great Cultural Councilor for having trained parrots to teach the renovated classical language to the young cadres of the Nation."

Sultan Galiev works in the same way: the two figures onto which the narrator projects himself, the political one, Sultan Galiev, a follower of Lenin and figurehead of the liberation movements of the so-called Third World (Stalin stopped his attempt to create an autonomous, Islamic Tataro-Bashkirian republic in 1923), and the poetic one, the reprobate poet Sergei Yesenin, meet up in a fictive universe that resists any attempt to pin it down:

> I became Sultan Galiev, I separated myself from him, a Tatar gone astray, I drifted through Baku, Constantine, Kasan, Mosta or Moscow, I spied on life and in the lining of my leather jacket tanned by fantasy, I keep a confession ready to draw its last breath.

Ingeniously blended collages, worlds intermingled in one sentence, and blurring contours paradoxically widen the horizon and sharpen the gaze, subtly criticizing the present and revealing the cyclical nature of history: while historical novels like *Samarkand* (1990) by Amin Maalouf or *Alamut* (1938) by Vladimir Bartol describe medieval Persia in an epic vein, Tengour draws audaciously from what Hilde Domin has called "the reserve of the unsaid", in absolute accordance with Novalis's statement that "poetry is the truly absolute Real. (...) The more poetic it is, the truer it is." Indeed, history's coordinate system draws past his texts, in the course of time revealing ever newer ways of reading, suggesting parallels between the Mongol and other desert storms, between *Pax Mongolica* and the New World Order.

Experienced distance … exilic worlds, everyday worlds

> the long crossing from deserts to cities
> these buried peoples with strange languages
> ...
> there are only scattered signs
> truth surprises you
> at a metro gate
> *Habib Tengour*, Empedocles's Sandal

Mirror- and counter-worlds are worlds of "estranged nearness" – artificially created distance sharpens the gaze. Exilic worlds, on the other hand, are worlds of "alienated nearness" – a daily lived distance dims the gaze. In the exilic variant, the motif of distance has received its most painful, but also most intense and richest arrangement in Tengour's work.

For Tengour, the experience of exile is first of all an experience of and in language: "to confront the crew with my indigenous French", he notes in *L'Ancêtre cinéphile*, ("The Movie-Crazed Ancestor", 1989), impressions of his first crossing of the Mediterranean, from Oran to Marseille in 1958. He will carefully tend this "indigenous French". His style is thus characterized by a highly refined reflection on language, a conscious delimitation within the spectrum of French language literature, and a continuous search for an adequate mode of expression or, as Rimbaud puts it, a search for "the words of the tribe" that give justice to his cultural identity in an intertextual dialogue spanning the world. His technique of literary recycling is applied not only at the level of content but also at the formal level. Once again this is in tune with Joris's nomad poetics and its idea that language should follow the subject's wanderings and, in Celan's terms, be literally "underway".

"Dwellings of maya asma om awf or khawla"

To mention only a few examples: Tengour sets his long poem *"La sandale d'Empédocle"* ("Empedocle's Sandal", 1993) in the tradition of pre-Islamic poetry: the *mu'allaqat*; he opens both sections of his novel *Moses's Fish* with ironic allusions to the classic Bedouin camp topos with which every old Arab text was supposed to start – here the fundamentalists' camp near Peshawar, there the bazaar tent in front of the Paris Institute of the Arab World; he writes a complete novel, *L'épreuve de l'arc* ("The Trial of the Bow", 1990), in the style of Arab picaresque literature, and a complete volume of short stories echoing James Joyce: *Gens de Mosta* ("People from Mosta", 1997).

These "Algerian Dubliners", as Tengour calls them, were created on neutral ground, while he was writer-in-residence at the Münsterland artist's colony of Schöppingen; a new experience for Tengour. Relativizing France as the ever-present reference point for Algerians, he writes: "When in Germany, France practically no longer exists. That's a good experience for an Algerian." These fifteen short stories offer nostalgic snapshots of Tengour's birthplace, the city of Mostaganem, and amusing side-glances at provincial Germany, but above all they save Algerian immigrant experiences in Paris during the 1940s, 1950s and 1960s from oblivion. In the story "Paris-October", Tengour may have been the first writer to evoke in a subdued tone that disastrous day of October 17, 1961, when the Seine ran red with the blood of the Algerians who had been demonstrating in the streets of Paris:

Among my generation there are not many Algerians who can write, and among the previous one even fewer; if we do not leave some traces, then those who will come after us will simply not know what our life was like. What I am doing is memory-work.

"Exile is my trade"

This memory-work questions the ethnologist no less than the poet. In some thirty publications so far, Tengour tracks collective Algerian memory: through identity-creating myths and saints' legends as well as Raï music; through the oral tradition of ancient tales just as much as through the memory that constitutes itself anew in Paris exile and that, again and again, pushes him to write. In his long poem "*Traverser*" ("Crossing", 2002), he says:

> exile is an imitation leather armchair
> a word that has never seen the light of day
> ritual mutilations
> the ingrained difference
> an obstruction
> a telepathic idea
> a painless index card
> and then
> all that you never thought of in your distraction
> (busy building a house over there)
> falls on your head
> a flood

Since 1992 he has practiced oral history as a field ethnologist, collecting the life stories of Algerian immigrants, mainly elderly men. *Ce Tatar-là 2* ("This Particular Tartar 2", 1999) arose as the poetic protocol of that research: the portrait of a "particular Tatar" who becomes the phantom image of the self-alienated migrant, who spends his life waiting, "at the edge of a dirt road" near the Paris suburb Kremlin-Bicêtre, knowing well that "the steppe no longer feeds the Tatars", even "mugwort and wild mint dried up long ago"; a solitary, suspicious, diffident Tatar, who is to be questioned "in the context of a study about traveling people" but "is suspicious of the sociologist", as he confuses him "with the social welfare office" and anyway believes that "a sociological survey will only erase their traces" ... Tengour seems to agree with him indirectly.

"The trace of the poem in fragments shows the way"

Thus the figure of the (im)migrant, doubly familiar to Tengour through his own experience and his research, finally becomes the cipher of a modern (and not only Maghrebian) sense of life, as well as the cipher of his writing. His literary project, the exploration of virtual Maghrebian worlds of writing and living, is by definition open towards the future: this is precisely what constitutes its extraordinary modernity, even post-modernity; and its implicit controversial political charge, as it does protect against hasty imputations, ex- and inclusions. Tengour designs shimmering visions between Orient and Occident, between yesterday and tomorrow: visions of possible Maghrebian identities from a postmodern patchwork optic that can neither be pre-scribed nor fixed in writing, but only kept after in the process of writing; that have to be invented more than discovered in a dialogue with world literature. Take Odysseus, for instance, for whom the return to Ithaca at the end of Tengour's novel *The Trial of the Bow*, turns out to be a flop. "What kind of pleasure is there," he asks himself, "in regaining one's ancestral rights" – on this "island of need," "this island "without anchorage"...?

Anchorage is proposed by poetry alone: *Island Poetry*, as Tengour already subtitles his first volume, *Tapapakitaques*, in 1976. And Pierre Joris speaks of the *poem-oasis*, a *poasis*, as a stance of movement along nomadic lines of flight. The poem itself is to be understood as an oasis that invites for a stay, before the nomad moves on again, along his "line of flight" ...

Indeed it is restlessness, it is exile and erring, nostalgia and yearning, that is at the very heart of Tengour's texts, as a common *condition humaine* and the specific *condition arabe*, and even more so in his poetry than in his prose; a poetry that seems to oscillate between Novalis and Rimbaud, Tarafa, Hölderlin and Diderot at the meeting-point of the archaic and the avant-garde. In this context, the fragmentary character of Tengour's writing is perfectly appropriate: the fragment was appreciated by the pre-Socratics as well as the Romantics, and it corresponds to the "molecular structure" of ancient Arabic poetry as well as to the oral tradition of Maghrebian narration, refusing the confidence trick of the linear and logical sequence of events in a world whose meaning stopped revealing itself long ago: "the bird that takes its flight at midnight is blind."

To splintered meanings and identities corresponds a splintered language. But from the ruins flash finely honed language shards:

"the instant contains its light – cursive resonance (...) the voyage completes itself."

(Text and citations translated from German and French by Pierre Joris)

The author is especially grateful to Cécile Oumhani for her helpful comments on an earlier version of this text.

SELECTED WORKS

Tapapakitaques – La poésie-île. Chronique 196 567 897 012 (Island Poetry), Paris: Oswald 1976

Sultan Galièv ou La Rupture des Stocks. Cahiers, 1972/1977 (Sultan Galiev or the Shortfall of Supplies), Paris: Sindbad 1985 (Oran 1981)

Le Vieux de la Montagne. Relation, 1977/1981 (The Old Man and the Mountain), Paris: Sindbad 1983 (new edition: *Le Vieux de la Montagne suivi par Nuit avec Hassan* (The Old Man and the Mountain, followed by One Night with Hassan), Paris: Editions de la Différence 2008)

L'épreuve de l'Arc. Séances 1982/1989 (The Trial of the Bow), Paris: Sindbad 1990

Gens de Mosta. Moments, 1990/1994 (People from Mosta), Arles: Actes Sud/Sindbad 1997

Ce Tatar-là 2 (This Particular Tartar 2), Launay Rollet : Dana 1999

Le Poisson de Moïse. Fiction 1994/2001 (Moses's Fish), Paris: Paris-Méditerranée/ Algiers: EDIF 2001

Epreuve 2 (Ordeal 2), Rennes: Dana 2002

Traverser (Crossing), La Rochelle : Rumeur des Ages 2002

Gravité de l'Ange (The Angel's Gravity), Paris : Editions de la Différence 2004

Retraite – Halwa (Retreat), Manosque: Le Bec en l'Air 2004 (with photos by Olivier de Sépibus and an Arabic translation by Saïd Djabelkheir and Esma Hind Tengour)

L'Arc et la cicatrice (The Bow and the Scar), Paris : Editions de la Différence 2006

La Sandale d'Empédocle / Il sandalo di Empedocle (Bilingual edition, translated into Italian and with a foreword by Egi Volterrani), Genova: San Marco dei Giustiniani 2006

Le Maître de l'Heure (The Master of the Hour), Paris : Editions de la Différence 2008

Beau Fraisier, Paris: Editions de l'Amandier 2009 (with illustrations from Pascale Bougeault)

Seelenperlmutt – La nacre à l'âme (Soul Nacre: Bilingual edition, translated into German and with an afterword by Regina Keil-Sagawe), Berlin: Schiler 2009

L'Ancêtre Cinéphile (The Movie Crazed Ancestor), Paris: Editions de la Différence 2010

Dans le soulèvement. Jalons (Collection d'essais), Paris: Editions de la Différence 2010

SELECTED TRANSLATIONS

Empedocles's Sandal, trans. Pierre Joris, Sausalito: Duration Press 1999

"The Old Man of the Mountain", trans. Pierre Joris, in: Pierre Joris (ed.), *4 x 1: Rainer Maria Rilke, Tristan Tzara, Jean-Pierre Duprey, Habib Tengour*, Inconundrum Press 2002, pp. 179–201

"In the Country of the Dead", trans. Marilyn Hacker, in: Khaled Mattawa, Marilyn Hacker (eds.), *New Arab Poetry* (*rattapallax* 7, 2002), pp. 34–8

"L'Ile au loin/The Far Island", trans. Donald Winkler, in: *La Traductière* 21: "Miroirs et frontières/Reflections and Borders", June 2003, pp. 66–9

"Café Marine", trans. Pierre Joris, in: Brian Henry, Andrew Zawacki (ed.): *Verse magazine* 23, 1-3 (2009), pp 357–61.

"The Manifesto of Maghrebian Surrealism", trans. Pierre Joris, in: *Celaan Review*, vol. 7, number 3, Fall 2009, pp. 189–94.

"Ordeal 2", trans. Pierre Joris, in: *Cerise Press. A Journal of Literature, Art and Culture*, vol. 2, issue 1, Spring/Summer 2010 (www.cerisepress.com).

"This particular Tartar 2", trans. Marilyn Hacker, in: *Virginia Quarterly Review*, Winter 2010 (also online: www.vqronline.org/).

FURTHER READING

Hédi Abdeljaoud: *Fugues de Barbarie. Les Ecrivains maghrébins et le surréalisme*, New York, Tunis: Les Mains Secrètes 1998

Pierre Joris: *Towards a Nomadic Poetics, a Manifesto-Essay*, Hereford, UK, Spanner Editions 1999

Pierre Joris (ed.): *Exile is my Trade: A Habib Tengour Reader*, Boston: Black Widow Press 2010 (forthcoming)

Regina Keil-Sagawe: "'L'Exil est mon métier ...' Le Poète-Ethnologue Habib Tengour", in: *Letterature di Frontiera/Littératures Frontalières* 25 (XIII/1, 2003), "Littérature maghrébine: Interactions culturelles et méditerranée", Vol II: "Ecritures algériennes", pp. 159–77

Regina Keil-Sagawe: "Der Dichter als Fährtenleser und Fahrtenschreiber. Transkulturelles Gedächtnis und Nomadenpoetik bei Habib Tengour", in: Habib Tengour: *Seelenperlmutt – La nacre à l'âme*, Berlin: Schiler 2009, pp. 115–26.

Geneviève Mouillaud-Fraisse: *Les fous cartographes*, Paris: Harmattan 1995

Giovanni Miraglia: "Habib Tengour o del nomadismo della scrittura", in: Habib Tengour, *Traversata decisiva*, Caltarivone : Altavoz 2006, pp. 7–15 (Foreword to *Traverser* trans. Manuela Cardiel; bilingual edition)

Mourad Yelles (ed.) : *Habib Tengour ou l'ancre et la vague: Traverses et détours du texte maghrébin*, Paris: Karthala 2003

Mourad Yelles (ed.): *Habib Tengour. L'arc et la lyre. Dialogues (1988–2004)*, Algiers : Casbah Editions 2006

OTHER WORKS CITED

Louis Aragon: *Le paysan de Paris*, Paris: Gallimard 1926

Vladimir Bartol: *Alamut*, Ljubljana: Ptica 1938

Mohammed Dib: *L'arbre à dires*, Paris: Albin Michel 1998

Mohammed Dib: *Le coeur insulaire*, Paris: La Différence 2000

Hilde Domin: *Das Gedicht als Augenblick von Freiheit*, München: Piper 1988

Omar Khayyam: *The Quatrains of Omar Khayyam. The Persian Text with English Verse Translation by E.H. Whitfield*, London: Octagon Press 1980

Amin Maalouf: *Samarcande*, Paris: Lattès 1988 (English translation: *Samarkand*, trans. Russell Harris, London: Quartet 1992)

"I dream in no man's land": Anton Shammas

Christian Szyska

> The blackbird does not dream.
> The blackbird knows.
> Wherefrom it knows
> it does not tell us.
>
> I do not know.
> A language beyond this,
> and a language beyond this.
> And I dream in no man's land.

Anton Shammas' collection of poems *Shetah hefqer* (*No Man's Land*) concludes with these lines, which leave the poetic persona in a state of abeyance between places and languages. "Beyond this", in the interstices of the political, linguistic, and cultural traces of power, is where the work and thought of one of the most demanding authors, essayists, translators, and intellectuals from the Middle East meander. His thought seeks out and traces the unsaid and the unsayable, strives to give them a language, helps them to emerge out of the background noise of power claims, and by interweaving them with what is already marked and labeled he lends them contour and existence. In a climate of enmity and vulnerability, of pride and nationalistic torpidity in the Middle East, this was and is no easy task, in particular when the aim is to make the individual voice audible again against this background.

This is mirrored in the life and work of Anton Shammas, born in 1950 in Fassouta, a Christian village in Galilee, Israel. He is a member of the first generation of Arabs who passed through the Israeli school system. His talent for languages was obvious early on; naturally this includes a command of Hebrew. At times one has the impression that he thinks he has to apologize for this gift. In Jerusalem he studied English, Arab literature, and art history, wrote articles for Arab and Hebrew journals, and translated literature such as the novella *Star Eternal* by K. Zetnik, a Holocaust survivor, from Hebrew into Arabic. In the other direction, from Arabic into Hebrew, he translated the works of famous Palestinian poets and authors like Mahmoud Darwish and Emile Habibi. He has also brought plays by Dario Fo and Samuel Beckett into both languages. Beckett's *Waiting for Godot*, a play written in three languages, was performed impressively at the Haifa City Theater in the 1980s, and Shammas provided the translation. In this production, the figures of

Estragon and Vladimir are Arab day laborers who try to eke out a living in Israel. The dialogue between them is in local Arab dialect, while Pozzo speaks Hebrew, only lapsing into Arabic when delivering a tirade. Vladimir and Estragon answer in their accented "guest worker Hebrew". Only Lucky's monologues are delivered in standard Arabic. In a way Shammas's rendering relocates the play from the level of absurd theater to that of absurd realism.

Explorations into language and metaphor

Playing with and between languages as well as with the meaning of language and its relationship to culture and power – all this is already manifest in Shammas's first collections of poems. 1974 saw the publication of both a collection of poems in Arabic, *Imprisoned in My Own Awakening and Sleep* (*Imprisoned*), and one in Hebrew, *Hardcover*. Both encompass several cycles, circling in with a language rich in metaphor on themes like loneliness, homelessness, unfulfilled love, the ebbing of desire, and death. A good example can be found in the cycle "After that how can the poem be on the way" from *Imprisoned*.

> Just as desire grows,
> Between the upsurges of the body, so creeps
> Sadness between my fingers at night's end.
> I bury my face in your neck and weep for
> All the pelicans which have flown to the
> Western isles to die.
> Along the coast I hurry after them, reach them,
> After they have buried their bills in the sand
> As a sign of defeat
> And their whiteness on the rocks has faded.

Although the images here clearly resonate with the tenor of politically committed Palestinian poetry, they are nonetheless unburdened of the usual pathos and point more to an individual search than a collective identity and tie to the land. One looks in vain for words like "Palestine" or "Arabs" in Shammas's poetry; in fact he caricatures some of the slogans proclaimed by Palestinian "blood-and-soil" poetry by polishing them into flat phrases. For this reason there is all the more emphasis on a deeply felt sense of homelessness and the wish to establish contact with the past and so learn about one's forebears:

> I unfold the map of the world
> And on it look for a village
> Which I have lost.

I search in the pockets of a grandfather, who I never knew,
For the vestiges of a story and the smells of the unusual,
Clinging like a butterfly to his neck.

Many of the poems reveal a poet searching for his own poetic diction, who, having found this diction, wishes to condense and reinforce it through metaphors. There is a clearly recognizable tendency in early texts to try out everything in the reservoir of myths from Arab, Christian, Jewish, and European cultures.

Don't look at me (but the lover looks)!
And see, he is a white bull of salt
Whose shirt (and I saw the sleeper
Draw out the city's virgins to the mountain
Looks around to weep the lost innocence of Europe) is torn on the back.

In these lines the poetic persona's thoughts at once pervade and compress Greek, Jewish-Christian, and Muslim material. When upon glimpsing the alluring Europa the bull turns into a pillar of salt like Lot's wife, its torn shirt is evidence of how it has resisted succumbing to her charms, exactly like the Qur'anic Joseph who resisted the seductive advances of the Pharaoh's wife. In his Hebrew poetry Shammas wrestles on more than one occasion with the Song of Songs. In "Love Poem" the poetic persona ponders over his inability to put his feelings into words. He then muses:

I await your voice from afar. Dreams
Perch on the edge of the bed
Like in a waiting room. The air blows in
Under the closed door: they lift their feet.
They await sleep. I wait in vain. In this
Position sleep fails to recognize me. The weatherman
Sits alone in his tower and awaits rain. Now, perhaps,
He thinks of me. I think
Of the line 'My friend is myrrh between my breasts.' I think
Of the zipper in your flesh, which
Runs down the length of your body.
Like a sleeping bag.

The concretion of language often even exceeds the interweaving of ideas, with fragments of thoughts pressing to the surface in an associative simultaneity until the words finally tumble into one another, as happens in *Imprisoned*:

The wrinkles – in face – and the body

I know them now
By memory,
An old cathe
Dral.

The poet pursues this technique to a point where a kind of concrete poetry emerges, which emphasizes (written) form and sound. Shammas undertakes similar language and sound experiments in Hebrew. In the poem "Collage" we read:

In my unfathomable dream
Full of *eyelids* and steps.

Birdsinflighttheirpupils
EX PLO DED like the shards of the sky
Last autumn.

Jerusalem as goal and dream, as well as the suffering on the way and life, there are thematic focal points of both volumes. In both the Hebrew "Five Gates to Jerusalem" and the Arabic cycle "Suddenly on the Road of the Prophets", the image arises of an ambivalent relationship to a city that is defined by affection, desire, and rejection. In both languages the poetic persona feels threatened by the squishing sound of a citrus juicer as he roams the deserted streets at night, trying to destroy the magic of the city and its myths.

Another element reaching far beyond these early poems is how memories force themselves upon the poetic persona; memories of a past that, defying their repression, repeatedly raise their voice and intrude on consciousness with images and splinters of thoughts: at times in the character of a small child, then with the image of the house of childhood, the mother, the father, or the drawer in which the feelings of childhood have survived.

I have a drawer where lullabies
Lie. It is closed. I stand in front of it and
Grow, in the hope, one day
To find the key which my mother
Has hung on the hook of her death.

Just as this thought connects access to memory with growing up and death, so in Shammas's best-known work, the autobiographical novel *Arabesques*, death unravels the knots of memory.

Inhabitant of the self

In 1979 Anton Shammas published his third and, thus far, last volume of poetry, *No Man's Land*, which, like *Hardcover*, was composed in Hebrew. While many of the themes prominent in the first two volumes are broached once again, the author has enriched and streamlined his poetic language. The early experiences are now rendered in a metaphoric and complex style that is nonetheless lucid. These experiences are even more personal and the love poems are confined to "you" and "I". The memories springing up continue to create disharmony, though. Nonetheless, we encounter at the beginning of the volume a poetic persona who has found his place:

> I apologize.
> Allow me to begin in the first-person singular:
> I apologize.
> I did not know that I would need so long
> To get here.
> The end of memory, sunk to the bottom of the lake
> Enters the unconscious. Relatively calmly,
> To be sure.
> The voice cloaks itself with velvety bloom
> Like the antlers of the unhappy stag. Up to the time when the
> Great rutting comes. And including.
> I am an inhabitant of my self. A dependable citizen
> Of my loved ones. My loved ones who were there.
> I touched them with the palms of my hands.
> The voice cloaks itself with velvety bloom, but not my hand.
> My Isaac resolved a long time ago: not the voice alone,
> And not the hands alone. But now is not the time.
> Nevertheless, finally I arrived, see, I am here. I would be glad
> If my childhood, jammed into the elevator of memory,
> Wasn't pressing the emergency button.

Arrival is not completely successful, a tension between now and memory remains. Some of the lyrical tableaus from *No Man's Land* are devoted to this inexhaustible memory, as in "A Photo", which we also encounter later in *Arabesques*.

> Three young women are in my photo album.
> Beautiful, it seems they knew that they are beautiful,
> In Sidon, Lebanon, 1938.
> Behind them steps and a brittle railing.
> At their feet a flower tub was placed.

As if the sensitive photographer had so
Arranged this for reasons of composition.
In the right corner one sees a bright circle
In the middle of the floor, which over the years
Carried the weight of this flower tub with wonderful grace.
Now it lies in front of the camera,
Exposed to shame in its nakedness.
It seems that no one took the effort,
After the click,
To move the tub back to its place.
And perhaps this floor bears
In its middle, the mark of shame
To the present day.
And I would not have evoked this modest recollection
Of this tub on paper
If it had not frequently appeared
In my dreams.
The young woman dressed in black in the center,
She would in future, after a long time, become my mother.

Whereas in Palestinian poetry scenes like these are often symbolized as a grating wound, this snapshot positions them as accidentals. As in "I apologize", the essential lies in the people, not in place.

The extent to which the hope of Zion in the verse *ba-shana ha-ba'a b'irushalayim* ("Next year in Jerusalem"), that Jews recite or sing as part of the Passover feast actually expresses the wish to arrive in a real earthly Jerusalem need not concern us here. Modern Israeli Jerusalem appears to be a place of disillusionment, isolation, and disappointment.

In my ninth year in Jerusalem,
I no longer dream. Unfortunately. For some time.
Only a few friends still ask what I am doing.
And I contemplate with a fixed gaze my hands:
Arm myself for the great death.
And maybe I'll manage that as long as time permits.
Every morning I contemplate the soles of my feet –
The hoped-for roots have yet to sprout,
Although the rustle of falling leaves has long dried my skin.
"I'd like an extension" –
I carve in the trunk the remnants of my speech –
In Braille, just like the wood carver wishes.
In my ninth year in Jerusalem

Each morning I count anew
The fingers of my hand.
In clear light I look at the intruding yesterday
That threatens me.
I am weary of letting
The desired voice being heard.
And meanwhile I arm myself
For the great death.

Arabesques: shimmering facets of existence

Deaths form the beginning of the novel *Arabesques*, which Anton Shammas published in 1986 and that made him a well-known literary figure both in Israel and internationally. Whereas in the poem, the key to the drawer holding memories hangs on the "hook of mother's death", in this semiautobiographical novel it is the death of the grandmother that resources and swells the narrative flow. The chapters headed "The Tale" gather the various stories of the narrating figure Uncle Yusef. These are less interconnected through a continuous plot line than an account of the wanderings of the Shammas family, which lead from Syria via Lebanon and Palestine to Argentina; wartime events through to the founding of the state of Israel; and numerous anecdotes, legends, and fates connected to the various people and places. Shimmering through the abundance of stories, which otherwise defy any summarizing overview, are the inscriptions etched into the geography of these places, which Zionism, with its myth of a "land without people", sought to deprive of any history. They emerge here as in the memory of the child, who, trapped in an elevator for so long, finally presses the emergency button.

The death of the father, another of the scenes positioned at the novel's outset, enables the author-narrator to order and unfold his stories. This occurs in chapters headed "The Teller". The author-narrator's personal odyssey takes him from Israel and France to the United States, where he takes part in an international writers' workshop in Iowa City. This wandering provides him with an opportunity to ponder over his frustrated love, a triangular relationship which one may read as an allegory of his relationship to Israeli culture and the Hebrew language. During the international writers' workshop a microcosm of literature emerges, in which authors of varying cultures and nationalities meet and interact. This situation and the conflicts and stories it spawns call into question the very meaning of identity based on culture, language, and nationality, illuminating the suffering which coerced identity can bring about.

Arabesques: an intertextual adventure

The wanderings of the narrator are therefore also a kind of odyssey through cultures and their literatures. The reader thus experiences *Arabesques* as an intertextual adventure. As in many of Anton Shammas's preceding poems, the traces of numerous important texts of world literature are discernible in the novel. Modern Hebrew literature, to which *Arabesques* is inextricably bound, naturally enough assumes a key role. Embarking on this path of literatures, the author-narrator is able to extricate himself through writing from nationalist, linguistic, and intellectual dead-ends.

As a Christian Arab, Shammas struck a number of sensitive points in Hebrew literature. He used an autobiographical text to counter the nationalist Israeli narrative in which, as the Israeli literary critic Yaron Ezrahi has put it, the individual frequently withdraws behind the collective. With this counterpoint, *Arabesques* triggered heated debate amongst Israeli critics. Besides the question of the work's literary merits, the problem of language dominated discussion. By writing a novel in Hebrew that was acclaimed for its literary and language qualities, Shammas, a non-Jew, questioned the Jewish-Israeli identity, connected as it is with the use and command of Hebrew. Amos Oz for instance characterized the presence of this novel as "a triumph (…) not necessarily for Israeli society, but definitely for the Hebrew language"; it seems attractive to a non-Jewish author as a literary language – a notion that the Israeli literary critic Hanan Hever sees as actually expressing distance and caution rather than acceptance.

The crossroads to the self

In order to elucidate the question of language and identity somewhat and illustrate the novel's intertextual depth, it seems appropriate here to present a section of the novel in detail rather than provide an abstract analysis. The chapter set in Paris, "The Teller: Père Lachaise", is one of the novel's pivotal points wherein the paths of several figures intersect. Paris is a stopover point for the autobiographical narrator on his way from Israel to North America. Comprised of shifting perspectives, those narrating include the "narrator in the third person", that is, the author-narrator of the novel, his Lebanese cousin Nadia, Yehoshua Bar-On, an Israeli writer, and Amira, a French woman writer of Alexandrian-Jewish descent; they all recount the time they spent in Paris. With the exception of Nadia, all the characters will meet again at the aforementioned international writers' workshop held in Iowa City. The chapter is prefaced with a poem by Yehuda Amichai:

A shop window is decorated with
dresses of beautiful women, in blue and white.

And everything in three languages:
Hebrew, Arabic, and Death.

This description effectively outlines the characters' network of relationships, determined by different languages, cultures, and nationalities, grouped around a heterotopic space, the famous Paris cemetery Père Lachaise, where a host of important artists and literary figures have found their last resting place. The third person narrator – the text suggests that it is Anton Shammas himself – traces the events and circumstances of his journey from Jerusalem to Iowa City. Traveling recalls moments of transition for him. The text ushers in this state of being in-between when in Paris the narrator begins to write about, amongst other things, a lost love. In an allusion to the opening of Lawrence Durrell's *The Alexandria Quartet*, this occurs "far away from everything".

The Israeli writer Yehoshua Bar-On grabbed the attention of Israeli critics, and he was frequently seen as a parodic allusion to the writer Abraham B. Yehoshua. His acronym gave the character in the novel his name. Critics agreed that within the hegemonic intellectual discourse in Israel, Yehoshua forms a kind of antipode to Shammas's views on language, literature, and identity. The figure of Bar-On waits in Paris for the narrator to call him, the two having arranged to meet while still in Israel. Bar-On's motivation for the meeting stems from his plan to write a novel wherein the hero is to be an Israeli Arab. While this project recognizes the existence of the "other" in his own country, or more specifically its literature, this "other" is to gain contour and become manifest only within the limits marked out by the writer's own culture. Bar-On thus sits in a Parisian café and ponders the "Arab" he plans to create. But his Arab shall be quite distinctive from all those hitherto represented in Hebrew literature. He thinks about some of the Arab heroes Hebrew literature has produced and decides that under no circumstances may his proposed character be someone in love with a Jewish-Israeli girl, a clear reference to the main protagonist in Abraham B. Yehoshua's *The Lover*.

The language of power

Although Bar-On endows his Arab with an excellent command of Hebrew, this shall remain confined within the "limits of what is permissible". It would certainly not be befitting for him to know the Kaddish, the Jewish prayer of mourning. The Hebrew line of the prayer "He who make peace in his heights", taken from the Book of Job, is deemed as something within his range, but the older Aramaic "speedily and soon" is to remain barred to him, for it underlines the wish that the "House of Israel" gain in power. The phrase "speedily and soon" flows into Yehoshua Bar-On's monologue.

The Arab's linguistic limitation touches on the close connection between New Hebrew and Israeli-Jewish identity. New Hebrew was invented and established as a national language by a cultural elite during the Haskalah, the Jewish Enlightenment, and grew later under the influence of Zionism; it is one of the key national symbols of independence. This was a conscious strategy designed to draw a clear distinction from the vernacular generally used by Jews in Europe, Yiddish, on the one hand, and those championing assimilation on the other, in particular in Western Europe and Germany. Evading the identity posited between language and nation would constitute a threat. It seems that Bar-On realizes this as well: he thinks about how his Arab would mock and rant about his habit of taking a "nap", for which Bar-On himself uses the Yiddish word. Hence, Yiddish must also remain a taboo for the Arab. If he were to have a command of Yiddish he could evade the control of the author.

The languages of love and home

Juxtaposed to Bar-On and his thoughts about his Arab is the figure of the French author Amira, a Jewish woman born in Alexandria. Her portrayal clearly recalls features of Durrell's Justine from *The Alexandria Quartet*. A dream ushers us into her past. The language of the dream is Arabic, and Amira suddenly finds herself at the Jewish cemetery in Alexandria, where she stands together with her deceased father at his grave. The gravestone is inscribed in Hebrew. A person photographs them as they stand there, while the surreal aspect of this dream image escalates when the camera metamorphoses into a lizard, which then slips into the eye of the formerly blind caretaker 'Amm Sayid, another of Durrell's characters. With a dose of irony, Amichai's lines quoted above are referenced as it transpires that Hebrew has remained the language of the gravestone. Trying to explain this to her Greek lover, Amira says:

> "You know, I'm half Arab," Amira says, "because the creative side of my mind comes from Alexandria. I love you in a Jewish way, but I write about it Arab style. I used to write to my father in Arabic, and he would answer me in French. But you could sense the smell of the beach at Alexandria behind his words. Also the smells of my mother's kitchen. I didn't understand every-thing he wrote, but the dried up stream of his Hebrew somehow flowed into my Arabic. Do you know that the Hebrew letters that were fastened to his tombstone were stolen? An Arab stonecutter came and carved them into the stone. I was surprised to see Hebrew letters on it, because he lived his life in Arabic. So why should his death be in Hebrew? Come to think of it, maybe that's why Hebrew is the language of death for me."

The lover's reply ("That, as you know, the camera can't catch") is an admission of his one-dimensional perception, while Amira's description attests to the superiority of the narrative mediation of the self. Her languages are not tied to nations. "Jewish love" is given in an Arab style, and the feelings of home are not coupled to a national language or a single place, but rather to intimate personal memories like her mother's cooking. In this way "Jewish love" is liberated from Hebrew and can be expressed in other languages, while conversely the Hebrew tradition of her father lives on in her idioms. Amira thus circumvents Bar-On's monolithic notions, which interconnect language, homeland, and religion into a nationalist identity. Hebrew in the sense posited by Bar-On appears to her as the language on the tombstone of her father, finally chiseled at great effort after the initial letters were stolen; as the language of death. At the same time, it seems to her problematic that a hybrid self can occasion wounding projections.

Like the narrator, Amira and Yehoshua Bar-On take part in the international writers' workshop in Iowa City. There they are all lodged in a student dormitory called Mayflower – a reference to the famous ship of the Pilgrims. The figure of the narrator gains contour against the backdrop of the multicultural atmosphere of the workshop. On the plane from Chicago Bar-On waxes lyrical about his great plan to write a novel about an "educated" Arab, to which the narrator dryly replies that he would consider himself an "intellectual" and not an "educated Arab". With this he defies a discursive practice which establishes and perpetuates ethnic difference and excludes the individual. Over the course of the workshop Bar-On remains imprisoned within the Israeli-nationalist discourse and turns into a sour carper; finally, aggravated by his obvious isolation, he becomes aggressive. The one exception is Paco, with whom he becomes friends, a Palestinian author with nationalistic views structured similarly to his own. Bar-On eventually takes him as the model for his novel.

The narrator gravitates towards Amira, and the two soon start an affair, eyed with jealous suspicion by Bar-On, which deepens the ties between the two figures, whose respective hybridity reveals striking similarities. She is a Jewish Arab who has forsaken Hebrew in favor of Arabic and French, Hebrew now re-channeled and living on in her Arabic; the narrator has passed through a development in the other direction and, when one considers Anton Shammas's description of his own situation, we may say that Arabic lives on in his Hebrew. Amira can live out her hybridity undisturbed because she is not exposed to the demands raised by Israeli society. On account of this cross-over, it is hardly surprising that the text attributes the authorship of this chapter to both of them: "And between the glasses and sighs we sat and scribbled the first draft of 'Père Lachaise' together."

This remark naturally raises the question about the chapter's autobiographical aspect. In *Arabesques* Anton Shammas has created a text that runs counter to chronological and spatial logic. By means of this text, the author is ultimately able to determine the discourses he had been exposed to in his past. This explains the subdivision of the text into two levels: narration and narrator. On the first level the story narrates and guides the subject, while on the second level the subject guides the story. Now that the subject has gained mastery over the story it can become immersed in the universes of the narrated worlds and orchestrate the intertextual connections.

"Père Lachaise" stands at the beginning of this second phase of writing in which the subject becomes autonomous. The narrator is obviously capable of this with only the help of Amira, who must also come to terms with similarly confusing identities but whose experience of such dilemmas is, at this point in time, clearly greater. With another reference to Durrell's *The Alexandria Quartet*, Amira feels that it is distance that makes it possible to write about home.

The narrator's odyssey turned out to be prescient. Anton Shammas is now an American citizen. He has published neither a novel nor any poetry since. Alongside teaching Middle Eastern literature at the University of Michigan, he continues to translate Arabic works of literature into Hebrew. He has also emerged as an important essayist, discussing and querying both Israeli and Palestinian nationalism. In the process he has pinpointed that the happiness of the individual, a right anchored in the American constitution, has no importance for either Israeli or Palestinian texts delineating the goals of the state.

WORKS

Asir yaqzati wa-nawmi (Imprisoned in My Own Awakening and Sleep), Jerusalem: Isdar Majallat al-Sharq 1974

Krikha qasha (Hardcover), n.p.: Sifriyat Poalim, Hotsa'at ha-Qibbuts ha-Artsi, ha-Shomer ha-Tsa'ir 1974

Shetah hefqer (No Man's Land), Tel Aviv: ha-Qibbuts ha-Me'uhad 1979

Arabesqot (Arabesques), Tel Aviv: Am Oved 1986

TRANSLATIONS

Arabesques, trans. Vivian Eden, New York et al.: Harper & Row 1988

FURTHER READING

Rachel Feldhay Brenner: *Inextricably Bonded. Israeli Arab and Jewish Writers Re-Visioning Culture*, Madinson: The University of Wisconsin Press 2003

Hanan Hever: "Hebrew in an Israeli Arab Hand. Six Miniatures on Anton Shammas's Arabesques", in: *Cultural Critique* 7 (1987), pp. 47–76

Christian Szyska: "Geographies of the Self. Text and Space in Anton Shammas's Arabesques", in: Roxane Haag-Higuchi, Christian Szyska (eds.), *Erzählter Raum in Literaturen der*

Islamischen Welt / Narrated Space in the Literature of the Islamic World, Wiesbaden: Harrassowitz 2001, pp. 217–32

OTHER WORKS CITED

Yehuda Amichai: *The Selected Poetry of Yehuda Amichai*, trans. Chana Bloch and Stephen Mitchell, Berkeley: University of California Press 1996

Samuel Beckett: *Waiting for Godot. A Tragicomedy in Two Acts*, New York: Grove Press 1954

Lawrence Durrell: *The Alexandria Quartet* [*Justine, Balthazar, Mountolive, Clea*, 1957–60], London: Faber & Faber 1962

Ka-tzetnik 135633 [Yahiel De-Nur]: *Kokhav ha-efer*, Tel Aviv: Menorah, 1967 (English translation: *Star Eternal*, trans. Nina DeNur, New York: Arbor House 1971)

Abraham B. Yehoshua: *Me'ahev, Jerusalem: Shoken 1977* (English translation: *The Lover*, trans. Philip Simpson, Garden City, NY: Doubleday 1978)

Exile at Home

Samir Naqqash – Prophecy as Poetics

Osman Hajjar

With his autobiographical story *Prophecies of a Madman in a Cursed City* (1995),
Samir Naqqash (1938–2004) presents a blistering manifesto against the advocates
of postmodernism – a polemical thrust pursuing a particular tactic, namely to
deconstruct itself in the vein of postmodernism and then forge its own poetics
anew and individually.

Captivatingly, the Jewish-Arab author calls on biblical stories as an argument
against postmodernism (in the sense of being a contingent period of history),
stories which already in themselves harbor an overcoming of modernity by the
dissolution of history. Viewed in this light, this process of overcoming loses itself
in the vastness of historical space and contradicts the idea of merely becoming
blurred here and there. Naqqash thus reveals the often bemoaned loss of ideological
centeredness to be a thoroughly routine, age-old phenomenon and reclaims the
account of how the people of Israel turned to the divinity Baal-Peor (Hosea 9:10)
as testimony to an early pluralization of the Absolute, disclosed and witnessed in
"Prophecies" proclaimed by the narrator. He is a contemporary prophet of both
the one as well as the other God:

> There I see myself like countless times before prostrating myself in front of
> my other ruler, the dwarf giant. And the echo of my recitation, impotent and
> defeated, reverberates mechanically: "Here I am." And his voice silenced me,
> the way the Lord's voice had silenced me ...

Israel and Judea; two kingdoms, two Gods: the splitting of belief as a disintegration
of ideology. As further evidence for the origin of globalization in the Old Testament,
the author also refers to Babel – where the Prophet, heeding God's command,
is to reconstruct the Tower – whose multicultural disaster now articulates itself
"postmodern" in a Pisa-like lopsidedness. Naqqash seems to be a wolf in Joseph's
bloody shirt: he dons the postmodern aesthetical guise in order to expose the
postmodernist's lack of historical groundwork. A comparable "short-circuiting"
of history is to be found in the story *This Logic*, also published in 1995. In his
reflections the protagonist mixes religion and Darwinism into a kind of "fizzy soft
drink", the surprising result of which is a tasteless poly-monad:

The order of Creation, as it is mentioned in the "heavenly" books, is almost identical with the principle of development and evolution and what biologists and natural scientists have found out. The only difference is that the Holy Books have reduced millions of years to six contemptible days and that they proclaim that the LORD had created man in his image. Using the logical equation and the conclusions drawn from it as an aid, we can say:

If my grandfather was an ape and the Lord created me in his image, my LORD is thus an ape. And when the grandfather of my grandfather was a sea cucumber, and my LORD created me in his image, my LORD is thus a sea cucumber. And so if the grandfather of my grandfather's grandfather was a protozoon, and my LORD created me in his image, my LORD is thus a protozoon. Therefore, if my great-great-great-great grandfather was a protozoon, and the source of the protozoon is nothingness and my LORD created me in his image, this means that my LORD is nothingness. My LORD – a nothing. Me – a nothing. Everything – a nothing. Everything is nothing except this logic!

The sacredness of God is corrupted here, crumbled into a glib nihilism. Nonetheless, something remains: the authorial logic – logos, word, fable – through which religion is ceremoniously restored, even if now it is nothing but an empty husk which, following the dictate of language, makes the author into a submissive creator of his own world.

The naked word also assumes a prominent place in *Prophecies*. The story opens with a devout call to God: "Here I am." The man remarking his presence for God is a prophet in a city that may with Heisenbergian probability be identified as modern Tel Aviv. Although this prophet is of a traditional mould, scrupulous in his morality, his principal God, Baal-Peor, obviously moves with the times and shows regional preferences. The fissured duality is mirrored in the contrast between language and culture: Arabic words on Israeli territory. This is clearly marked out in the meekly stammered announcement of the prophet's presence. As the text emphasizes, it is the pronouncement spoken by the narrator, which in its Arabic original (as word) refers to the Islamic credo: there is no god but God ... This declaration of faith marks the very contradiction between God's singularity and God's binarity, and the seemingly irreconcilability between Israeli identity and the Arab language.

While the first contradiction is put into practice in Naqqash's idiosyncratic poetics, the latter has mercilessly consigned the reception of his literary work to a vacuum. The readership void that envelops the genius of Naqqash is articulated after his death in a house full of unsellable books that the author bequeathed to his wife. They are unsellable because most Israelis cannot read Arabic, while Arabs will hardly engage with the work of an Israeli writer; the more so because his pacifist story *The Mistake* (1971) was thoroughly misunderstood by Palestinians. In Naqqash's work the word is thus (bi-)politicized to a high degree, even if in the *Prophecies*, as this essay hopes to show, we are dealing with a subjective voice plying literary theory. For this reason it is necessary to highlight Naqqash's personal history in the context of the collective tragedy of Iraqi Jewry.

When Samir Naqqash recalled his youth in interviews, these years glimmered nostalgically for the most part, evoking the subdued atmosphere of a three-storied palatial home in Baghdad – a cosmopolitan salon to which anyone who knew how to contribute to cultivated conversation was granted access. No importance was attached to religious or ethnic affiliations. Although smoky swathes of intellectuality unfurled throughout the rooms, dimming the sunlight which might have created a more light-hearted childhood, Samir was able to foster the strong passion for metaphysical trains of thought which would later run through his work systematically. His (anti-)political literary program corresponds essentially to the mentality of Baghdad Jews, with which Naqqash became familiar in these formative years, an attitude that aimed not at being political but at thinking and acting metropolitically. In this vein the Jewish community in Baghdad – despite a pogrom in 1941 that resulted in 150 deaths – pursued a philosophy of normality, which enabled them to develop into an educational elite within society. The establishment of Jewish Alliance Schools oriented on the West sustained this development, and Naqqash was amongst those pupils who profited from a progressive thinking that did not shy away from self-denial (for example, Hebrew was soon declared to be of little use and removed from the curriculum). Rightly considering themselves to be an integral part of Arab society, the Baghdad Jews accordingly viewed the Zionism forming at this point in time critically. They were not willing to leave Iraq and "return" to a homeland that was alive only in the Torah. After all, they saw themselves as the descendants of the Babylon exiles and thus as inheritors of the most important tradition of Jewish learning, which in the spring awakening of Modernity seemed to be on the verge of a renaissance.

A series of attacks on Jewish organizations finally induced Iraqi Jews to immigrate to Israel. Before an Israeli commission of inquiry, the majority of migrants blamed Zionist activities for these attacks. By no means did they consider themselves to be refugees, but rather as pawn sacrifices in a "Zionist gambit". It cost the Naqqash family a great deal to overcome their qualms and leave the place of their ancestral roots, waiting to the very last minute before the right to leave granted to Jewish Iraqis expired and finally deciding to take this step in March 1951. This move entailed the loss of their Iraqi citizenship; as new arrivals in Israel they felt robbed not only of their nationality but moreover of their human dignity: if credence is to be given to the accounts of Arab Jews, they were greeted to the Holy Land as if they were a locust plague that had to be combated with a douse of pesticide.

The family was housed in a reception camp in an area where there was incessant rain. Their makeshift accommodation was inadequate to provide shelter from the deluge, and Samir's father gradually lost the will to live. He died of a blood clot in the brain just two years later. In 1954, aged sixteen, Naqqash tried to flee to Lebanon with his cousin. According to Naqqash, they were tracked down by an Israeli agent and held captive for six months in Beirut. He was then transferred to an Israeli prison, where he spent a further six months and claimed to have been tortured. In 1958 he travelled to Turkey, where he unsuccessfully sought to save the family possessions that had left behind in Iraq. He then moved on to Tehran, then Bombay, before managing to return to Iraq where he worked for the American embassy for two years. Upon receiving news of his mother's worsening health he felt obligated to return to Israel.

It is thus no exaggeration to claim that Samir Naqqash was a citizen of the world, whereby he probably felt more like a moving target than a cultural globetrotter who pitched his tent wherever he felt inclined. Consequently, Naqqash's homelessness was anything but an expression of freedom; rather a traumatic intermediate state that the author defended by clinging almost neurotically to Arabic despite his command of several languages. With a seemingly tragicomic, forlorn air he petrified like a pillar of salt in his search for a different time, and his children, all of whom grew up learning to speak Hebrew, probably have no real inkling that their father was one of the most important figures in contemporary Arab literature.

Given a life spent in quarantine, it is only natural that Naqqash's maxim is: man is condemned to suffer. It forms the leitmotif of his stories and finds expression in the descriptions of individual misfortune, which is unrelenting and thus strips life of all meaning. Perhaps as a way of enduring the misery of such pointless suffering, Naqqash unfolds his Kafkaesque nightmares with the nonchalance of a butterfly, creating strange characters which he then endows in his second creative phase with various colloquial tones of the (Jewish) Baghdad dialect he had heard in his younger years.

These masterworks of linguistic *veduta* painting are all the more poignant in that they evoke a time and space that had ceased to exist as "home", while in actual fact the author and his family sacrificed the purchase of a home to finance the printing of his first collection of stories in 1971, which was then anything but a success. In this failure, with its very real consequences, Naqqash's memories of Baghdad merge with his present existence to repeat the mutation of person into "pest". The author inscribes this mutation in his stories, whilst allowing it to step out of them and materialize through the books that litter the cramped dwelling.

In view of such painful experiences, it would be sarcastic to describe the geographical polyvalency in Naqqash's work as "place polygamy". The world he describes, inwardly consuming itself, is a far cry from a lascivious harem palace where charming intrigues are spun. In *The Fourth Disaster* the narrator muses: "The world is a *She*, and she is of enchanting countenance, squirming inwardly into a blazing hell."

If the visages of metropolises across the world all display the same glittering facades, the wonderful blue sky they mirror is an illusion. The reality is the ethically hollow world of glass and steel constructions, behind which, according to Naqqash, naked immorality reigns and a depraved, deservedly doomed society reproduces itself sterilely. A more adequate term for such a morally charged notion of globalization is undoubtedly "place sodomy". In *Prophecies*, the reader is confronted with a particularly picturesque version of the Naqqashian Sodom and Gomorra. The interpenetration of the dead craving for life provokes nothing but disgust in the prophetic narrator. Here, Naqqash describes the world as the incarnation of lechery, much like a Hieronymus Bosch tableau:

> I see a wasteland, my Lord, filled with bodies, and I see the bodies; they are the bodies of men and women. And they are naked as you created them, shamelessly exposed. And behold, the naked bodies are rising to their feet. The men, my Lord, are seeking the women, and the women, my Lord, are seeking the men. I see them all craving flesh and in this frenzied, delirious craving, the male is drawn to the female and the female drawn to the male. Some kind of unstoppable match is taking place in which the players make no distinctions between one another nor is anything loathsome to them. A father refrains not from coupling with his daughter nor does a sister recoil from mating with her brother. Each cleaves to the other. Then the wilderness returns heaped with naked, enmeshed bodies.

The earth turns into a genetic mass that produces its own ignominy. Suffering bodies merge together to form the geography of a spiritual emptiness. This vacuum arises not only out of the meaninglessness of sexual excess and frenzy but also out of a ravenous lust for gold, which, like a curse, rains down from the sky, everyone grabbing for it like predators ... a vile scramble that – now through a zoom focus – shows a sanctimonious daughter, casting off civilized behavior, who strangles her begetter to get at the seed of the gold. Seized by gold fever, the sinner murders her father and her copulation partner; decency is not merely transgressed but done away with entirely: genealogy is brought into a state of disorder, history sprouts ingrown spirals, thrusting into its own flesh. This becomes even clearer as events, transported by various biblical narratives, gorge their way through to the present, dissolving any orientation of time and place. Thus, the Exodus becomes a flight to Babylon, to Tel Abib, the place in southern Iraq where Ezekiel settled – which in turn may be identified with the Israeli city bearing its name, Tel Aviv, in which the author concretely positions his modern prophet.

My Lord, this gold of yours is turning into a calf at the blink of an eye. They're all around the calf, making noise, rejoicing, dancing and carousing.

And the Lord whose spirit had descended upon me said: "Do you know, Son of Adam, who these people are? (...) These are the dry bones that I showed your friend the seer in Tel Abib and I restored them to life."

I couldn't control myself and I cut the Lord short as I beseeched and requested: "By your mercy, my Lord, restore them to what they were before, the dust of bones. They deny you, acting licentiously and indulging in the vilest of sins and, as if this were not enough, THEY WORSHIP THE IDOL OF THE CALF."

The resurrected dead not only want to indulge in sacrilegious sex but idolize the golden calf, thus going against the order of the universe at precisely the moment that the stone tablets provide Moses with knowledge of the divine laws. Akin to tearing down the canopy over the world, this act is repeated endlessly; for once humanity embarks on this path outside divine law, history loses its innocence: it will now bring forth the guilt of its iniquitous deflowering time and time again. With history in disarray, the people are once again on a journey of exodus, searching for the Holy Land, seeking asylum in Iraq, dancing around the golden calf in Israeli Tel Aviv – worshipping capital, which has conjured their city out of money and shares like a mirage shimmers in the desert. The despair of his people that overcame Moses is palpably present here, reincarnated in the narrator as a modern prophet. The sinfulness of man outgrows divine authority. On the beaches of hedonism, where people turn themselves into "gold" like Midas to enhance the value of their bodies as artificial sex objects, the ascetic voice of a prophet is completely out of place. The people make fun of him, palter with him, and take him to the cleaners:

I said to my friends: "Tonight I'm melancholy and spent."
As one of my friends said: "Your mood doesn't matter to us – it's your money that matters."
Infirmity took the upper hand and sadness reigned over me. I mumbled: "I don't have a cent on me tonight."
Like a chorus who knew the words by heart they said: "We'll lend you the sum."
I asked my friends: "And would you lend it to me at the going rate?"
Ridiculing me, they laughed till they were about to drop ...

As the offspring of a decidedly wealthy Jewish family, Samir Naqqash, who surrounds his childhood with the aura of a paradise, is not interested in formulating a Marxist critique of society, let alone reasserting a centuries-old prejudice against Jews in general. In the context of *Prophecies* this passage is to be read as an allusion to the economic order of late capitalism, where the money flow is no longer regulated and steered by ideological considerations, but where capital itself, just like the idolized calf, has become a god that rules absolutely and is celebrated in the guise of postmodern art production. As the author emphasizes, it is not the class enemies who exploit the narrator but his friends, whose actions, as we will see, are nothing compared with what his wife Gomer gets up to. Here the fight for justice is an impossible undertaking, for the belief in justice itself has lost all legitimacy. Whoever acts like a prophet in this climate is indeed "insane".

The loss of faith in justice was taken up as early as 1978 in the story *The Symbol*. Set in the time of the Farhud, the Baghdad pogrom of 1941, a carrier called Kamil Dahham, who the Left adopt as a "man of the people" and make the figurehead of their class struggle, testifies to his belief in equality by pointing out that he killed twenty-six Jews, forty-three Muslims, and five Christians during the pogrom. The concepts of justice and equality become interchangeable terms in an abuse of enlightened discourse, and are played out one against the other. Equality now means injustice for all. Kamil gains an intellectual freedom, which inspires him to implement a fratricidal sense of equality, unapologetically placing the idea of justice on the guillotine.

Naqqash articulates an even more significant loss of faith in the story *Tantal* (1978). Here the hubristic self-assuredness of a discipline that believes itself capable of explaining the world tips into existential insecurity. Although the narrator initially describes his characters' ghostly visions aloofly, labeling the djinn Tantal as a figment of their imaginations, by the end of the story – when the characters themselves begin to query their superstitions – he is convinced that there are no rational explanations for the haunting events. With these points of view running contrary to each other, the polymorph djinn now appears not only in Iraq, where belief in spirits is normal and part of everyday life, but also turns up in modern Israel. This occurrence entices one to follow a specific train of thought: 1. If the djinn is not a phenomenon particular to Iraq, then it must be identifiable on the basis of its perceivable form. 2. But as we know, it is principally without perceivable form, so that it can only be identified on the basis of its local particularity. Ergo: Tantal can only be sighted in Israel when Israel is Iraq. Logic of this kind deprives localities of their identity, resulting in the loss of coordinates, and so collapsing the contours of each and every map.

Like the geography in *Tantal*, the prophetic architecture in *Prophecies* is to be understood as a set of *Einstürzende Neubauten* (collapsing new buildings). God, the "dwarf giant Lord", commands the narrator to build a tower that will rival the one in Pisa in its lopsidedness and the one in Babel in its hubris. The result is not only a postmodern skyscraper but also an anthropological symbol: as the Pisa campanile it is the place of Galileo's free fall experiments, a sublime example of man's aspirations to bring the world under control by grasping the laws of physics, but in its leaning testimony to the failure of Renaissance construction engineering; as the Babylonian tower it is even more dazzling and enigmatic than "Pisa". Although the construction of the Tower of Babel could not be completed for organizational reasons, it is nonetheless the first of the two Babylonian wonders of the world. While it is driven by the ambition to reach heaven, the second wonder, the Hanging Gardens, represents an imperfect paradise, a compromise. The Tower may thus be regarded as a symbol of Jewish-Babylonian learning that guides humanity on the path to bliss, whereby the tragic end of the project in turn recalls the linguistic and cultural alienation awaiting the New Babylonian Jews in the Holy Land.

In *Prophecies* the new Tower is not only a sign of religious ambition and theological confusion; it is a lighthouse that shall act as a beacon for the swarms of the tourists, the ephemeral wandering migrants of capitalism:

> That is the folly, and this is the crime. How could we contend with the Tower of Pisa if the building were straight? And do you think it could become a new wonder that would attract millions of people to it if its crookedness does not outdo the crookedness of the Tower of Pisa?

If God commands the prophet to drill a Babylonian skyscraper like *Burj Dubai* into heaven, it should – in the postmodern fashion – rise up crookedly, recalling the *Burj al-Arab*: an arch for the superrich; a sail bulging with the wind as modern pirates conquer the world, swept along by capital markets. Muslim readers will also recognize the prophet Abraham, who was entrusted, together with his son Ishmael, with the task of erecting the Kaaba, a perfectly rectangular stone cube, without any windows or other architectural extravagances. The crookedness of Naqqash's tower does not reside primarily in its perfect giant hunch, but in the fact that on its grounds, directly beneath Mount Sinai, the Tigris and Arno flow together. It represents a wasteland, which with a pinch of perspicacity may be identified as the architectural desert of modern high-rise Tel Aviv but is no different from any other metropolis.

This city, which is by no means unequivocally located in Israel or anywhere else, is the city *par excellence*, the realized utopia, a perverted paradise, a lively Moloch that sprawls across the borders, a monster, a virus, or a natural disaster:

> When I had gone well astray from this city's curse, I could see its malediction like an octopus, spreading its branching tentacles out to other cities and infecting them with the curse. This is the plague. A scourge. Spreading like quivering triviality.

Triviality, valorized in the postmodern age, inheres nothing positive here, but then populism is not in Naqqash's poetical program: what does the voice of the people yield when, as in the case of the carrier Kamil Dahhak, it turns into a malicious satire of humanism?

Although Naqqash contributed like no other to the meticulous conservation of the Jewish Baghdad dialect, this undertaking is not to be confused with a Romantic interest in folk culture, for this dialect is not that of a *homo simplex* but the language of the cultured educational elite. To give this language a literary form posthumously is to restore a universal space, to fight for the freedom of thought that the author sought vainly in the real linguistic landscape into which he was catapulted. The desolate stretch where the spirit of the Lord first descends to the Naqqash prophet and calls him "Son of Man" is indeed a wasteland of intellectual homelessness. In it the senses are blunted and faith deteriorates to a simple-minded opportunism:

> Obliviously, I found myself wretchedly castigated, the roaring of harsh winds deafening me. Grains of desert sand filled my mouth and blinded my eyes. Like the Lord in the eye of the raging storm. He had been looking on at my thoughts, and trailing after my abundant heart. The strength of the storm made me realize how angry the Lord was. But for a split second, so rare and wonderful, I overcame my weakness, I routed my defeat. For this awesome moment it became clear to me that I was at the height of my insanity and that I had never used reason to think for I was drawn to my surging heart and my own desolation without recourse to the citizens of the cursed city. And as for the Lord – (...) What crime did I commit for him to decree what he had decreed to no man before me? And for the first time, I said: 'No!' As loud as I could I said: "No" ... The call thundered throughout the wilderness and got stronger as it reverberated, ringing "No" a thousand times ... a million times "No" ...

At the peak of madness, atop the new Tower of Pisa-Babel, human reason is suspended. The prophet resists the pull of poststructuralist thinking. He shouts his protest into the void, into a labyrinthine space that absorbs the individual "no" and reflects the bewildered expression of a fragmentary mind. The more the prophet struggles against this intellectual wasteland, the more ruthlessly it takes possession of him, makes him *nolens volens* into the prophet of what he denounces and thus into an architect of postmodernism.

It is God's will not only that an architecture of madness be erected, but also that his prophet marry Gomer, just as he once commanded Hosea: "Go, take unto a wife of whoredoms and children of whoredoms: for the land hath committed great whoredom, departing from the Lord. So he went and took Gomer ..."

The reader gets the creeping suspicion that the autobiographical moment of the story has little to do with Naqqash's wife, referring in fact to his "muse", who sucks him dry:

> So it is I feel nothing but the obedience permeating my being. But I found consolation in Gomer not finding any more blood in my veins to suck from now on.
>
> The minute I get home, she'll tell me: "Bare your chest ..."

Gomer is a vampire, a whip-swinging dominatrix who is also profoundly tacky. In her thirst for blood she commands her husband to steal. He is torn between his submissiveness towards the voice that has forced this rip-off upon him and the sensibility of his conscience, which emphatically rejects the rip-off. Finally, the afflicted personality of the artistically inclined prophet splits: bifurcating into a form of postcolonial schizophrenia; oscillating between immersion in reproducible consumerism, the new import historicism, and the claim of indigenous Arabness. While postmodernist versions of self-discovery joyously dispense with the luxury of steadfast identity, Naqqash's prophet is anything but a survival artist able to sell his personality breakdown and loss to his Arab reading audience. He is an art thief without any prophetic aura about him, except for when he confronts the authority of the state. After the narrator has plundered the blood bank to satisfy Gomer, the police turn up at his door. They search his nightmares, informed by his wife, the pitiless vampire, who – as the narrator now realizes – rummages in the depths of his psyche, revealing how porous the boundaries between dreams and reality, between literature and life have become.

If Gomer is the curse of consumerism, the second curse is the old man who degrades him to his personal slave. Within the city, he makes the narrator carry him around on his shoulders, grinding him down with the weight of civilization. In contrast, his own oriental face is like the palm hollowed by worms that the city's residents avoid. Unable to ignore his responsibility to other humans, the prophet carries the old man to his primitive robbers' cave and thereby becomes a victim of his own good upbringing: in the old man's cave he is not only clamped between the thighs of this merciless dictator but caught in the clutches of the story of Sinbad, who on his fifth voyage is enslaved by the Old Man of the Sea:

> ... a spring of running water, by which well sat an old man of venerable aspect, girt about with a waist-cloth made of the fibre of palm-fronds. Quoth I to myself, "Haply this Shaykh is one of those who were wrecked in the ship and hath made his way to this island." So I drew near to him and saluted him, and he returned my salam by signs, but spoke not; and I said to him, "O nuncle mine, what causeth thee to sit here?" He shook his head and moaned and signed to me with his hands as who should say, "Take me on thy shoulders

and carry me to the other side of the well-channel." And quoth I in my mind, "I will deal kindly with him and do what he desireth; it may be I shall win me a reward in Heaven for he may be a paralytic." So I took him on my back and carrying him to the place whereat he pointed, said to him, "Dismount at thy leisure." But he would not get off my back and wound his legs about my neck. I looked at them and seeing that they were like a buffalo's hide for blackness and roughness, was affrighted and would have cast him off ...

The moment the narrator realizes that he has been cast into a Sinbad story, he is able to get rid of the old man, for he recalls the trick played in the literary model: he tricks the old geezer, whose thighs are fastened around his neck, into getting drunk. When the old man is overcome by drowsiness the narrator can now dislodge him from his shoulders, and at this point the old man vanishes from the story.

Both the Old Testament and the *Thousand and One Nights* are treasure troves for the storyteller and can be looted at will. This entwining of Sinbad with Hosea is somewhat too shrill for my taste, but the saving grace for the perturbed reader is provided by a glance at Naqqash's biographical map. With Sinbad, who like Naqqash comes from Baghdad, the author plunges into the idyll of his youth, but immediately sets sail with the old geezer on his shoulders and crosses as the fabulous adventurer with a piratesque (sic!) attitude the seas of world literature.

Through this incursion in the pre-modern oriental corpus, the narrative spirals of which steer European authors into new orbits with cyclical regularity, Naqqash cuts up Biblical geography and rearranges the pieces into a fantastic collage, in which the real-imaginary becomes the literary home of his hero. Naqqash theoretically anticipates this process in his 1980 story *The Day In Which The World Was Conceived And Miscarried*. There we can read:

> He hadn't changed. But the world had changed. The face of all kinds of things had turned inside out. If truths appear as myths, myths for their part perish in truths. The story of the Iranian Princess Dawud al-A'jami, woven completely out of love, becomes pale, is pressed between the lines of the yellowed pages of *Thousand and One Nights*.

If the inscription of the *Thousand and One Nights* is conceived as the recollection of a poetically painted future, the interlacing with Ezekiel (4:12–15) in *Prophecies* leads rather to a drastic "can't be bothered" poetic: it's all bullshit. The Lord commands Naqqash's prophet to eat his own feces until his divine wrath has subsided. Despite his submissiveness, the Tel Aviv prophet argues that his colleague Ezekiel was not forced to make his bread out of human feces, this ignominy toned down to using dung. Given that the Lord in the *Prophecies* is an art connoisseur and has a skyscraper built with all manner of architectural pizzazz as the House of God, it is not too farfetched to compare eating excrement with the breach of the great postmodernist taboo, namely the recycling of historical forms without consideration of good taste. The association between a re-eaten lunch and a postmodernist architectural program is first shown when his doctor sends the prophet to a psychiatric ward because of his coprophagy. He succeeds in escaping; on the run in the desert he has his prophetic vision, where the crookedly built Tower awaits him.

In this wasteland God's spirit descends upon the prophet and their spirits begin to squabble. Incensed, God screams at him to flee and get out of his sight. As Naqqash's postmodern God is omnipresent, there is no place of asylum and so fleeing is endless. *Prophecies* thus ends like a stage farce: the prophet flees, pursued by his wife Gomer, his children, the old geezer, the giant dwarf Lord, and the psychiatrist. The stage remains behind, empty, and the story peters out in a nowhere.

Asked about a possible location of his literature in an interview, Naqqash gave a revealing answer. The author did not believe that Jews should write about Jewish problems and Palestinians about Palestinian problems. He demanded universality from writing, not to mention individuality. Accordingly, he drew his literary map from a global perspective, shouldering the grand myths of human tragedy as an individual. In this way they regained their natural disorder. For Naqqash, chaos is the basis of his thinking; existence itself is principally without structure:

> We can't even control our own thoughts, we don't even know what we're going to think next. The past, the future, it's all mixed up, that's the reality ...

In *Prophecies* Naqqash formulates a poetic that faces up to the graveness of chaos, takes it seriously and declares war on a postmodernist aesthetic inimical to meaning, precisely by denying the candor of its flippancy and by taking its allegedly playful revelry in meaninglessness seriously. He anticipated this subversion of contemporary agnosticism with his story *Tantal*. Although in an enlightened world djinns only haunt us as ridiculous figures in books and films (although they are referred to as serious phenomena in the sphere of "backward Iraq"), *Tantal* can resurface as superstition in modern Israel due to his polymorphous form, whereby he takes possession of enlightened people in a perturbing manner.

When in *Prophecies* Ezekiel and Hosea encounter Sinbad, the holiness of the biblical saying is perverted in a Babylonian babble of voices to something comic and, as in *Tantal*, recaptures its meaningfulness through this; for Naqqash's prophet is a real prophet, whose helplessness in this "cursed" world simultaneously represents his most profound truth. Naqqash claimed its discovery already in 1971 in *The Death of Saint Nicholas*:

> That man experiences the truth in this world which God has cursed, is a thou-
> sand times better than that he stays in paradise, blinded by neglect, wrapped
> entirely in a burial shroud of darkness.

If here the falsehood can only be redeemed through metaphysics, Naqqash's philosophy in *Prophecies* is uncompromising: the prophet flees from the word of the Lord and finds his new faith in an affluent society of excess that denies the truth. Here the lie itself becomes an eternal truth which has existed since the beginning of human history. That falsehood is elevated to truth by no means weakens it, for when God is present in *Prophecies* – even if as a specter that hunts people through the desert of being – falsehood does not lose its deceptive quality.

With the falsehood preserved, suffering and the topos of the wandering Jew also remain. If postmodernism turns this into a myth of the Jewish as the "Other", Naqqash's prophet is not the "Other" simply because he is not a "Jew". He is rather a universal wanderer; his sufferings are limitless and deeply anchored in being. This is expressed above all in a feeling of homelessness. In *Me and Them and The Disassociation* from 1978, Naqqash writes:

> We lived and live in Iraq. We are Iraqis. Here is our land. However, over there
> is also our land.

This uncertainty about here and there is not just a poetical pose, but the painfully felt reality of the author. Shortly before his death, he lamented that he did not exist in Israel, either as writer or as a human being, that he had not had a feeling of belonging somewhere since his roots were ripped out of Iraqi soil. In such a global homelessness, the relationship of human to place resides only in it being wrested from us.

> It is a fact that I was a "person" in my homeland and in this cursed country
> I've now become a "madman". Meanwhile, the seriousness of events in recent
> times (namely the transcending in all conceivable excesses beneath the WALL)
> forced me to quickly go to my doctor without the slightest hope of recovery.
> (...) Recovery would presuppose that I would create myself anew! The visible
> traces on my body forced me to assume that I'm mad and the ill-logic of what
> has happened as being primarily responsible for everything.

Naqqash's prophet cannot be created anew because he does not possess a "new" truth. He is not Europe, which believes it can rise out of the ashes era by era, which mutates from the Middle Ages to Humanism, from modernity to postmodernity (which has admittedly figured out that there is something foul about this belief). His body is the Iraqi "Ezekiel", Sinbad, Naqqash; a Jewish-Arab history is inscribed on his body which cannot be washed off. For this reason, Gomer has to engrave the new map in his skin with lashes of the whip – the map of Israel, whose invented language seeks to abrogate historical geography, just like postmodernism. If the author Naqqash steadfastly defied Hebrew, his prophet obeys and submits to Gomer. But finally his body rebels and where the whip leaves its cuts, it ignites and inflames the pain. This reemerges as human, fragile truth, as the literary expression of a double alienation from the world of which he writes and from the body infected by this world, body and world no longer inseparable. Accordingly, Naqqash's work is he himself – his lifeless body a final legacy of Jewish-Babylonian world literature, the body of a martyr, who tries to save what he believes in through his own death.

WORKS

al-Khata' (The Mistake), Jerusalem 1971

Ana wa-ha'ula' wa-l-fisam (Me and Them and the Disassociation), Tel Aviv 1978

Hikayat kull zaman wa-makan (The Story of Any Time and Place), Tel Aviv 1978

Yawm habilat wa-ajhadat al-dunya (The Day in Which the World Was Conceived and Miscarried), Jerusalem 1980

al-Junuh wa-l-insiyab (Caught on a Reef), Shefar'am 1980

Fi ghiyabihi (In His Absence), Shefar'am 1981

'Indama tasqut adla' al-muthallathat (When the Sides of Triangles Fall), Shefar'am 1984

Nuzula wa-khayt al-shaytan (Courtyard Dwellers and Cobwebs), Jerusalem 1986

al-Rijs (The Abomination), Jerusalem, 1987

al-Maqrurun (The Chilly People), Shefar'am 1990

'Awrat al-mala'ika (The Angels' Genitalia), Collogne 1991

Nubu'at rajul majnun fi madina mal'una (Prophecies of a Madman in a Cursed City), Jerusalem 1995

TRANSLATIONS

"Prophecies of a Madman in a Cursed City", trans. Ammiel Alcalay, M. Joseph Halabi, Ali Jimale Ahmed, in: Ammiel Alcalay (ed.), *Keys to the Garden. New Israeli Writing*, San Francisco: City Lights Books 1996, pp. 111–24

"The Angels' Genitalia", trans. Ammiel Alcalay, M. Joseph Halabi, Ali Jimale Ahmed, in: Ammiel Alcalay (ed.), *Keys to the Garden. New Israeli Writing*, San Francisco: City Lights Books 1996, pp. 124–32

"Selections from Samir Naqqash, Tenens and Cobwebs (*Nzulah u-Khait el-Shitan*)", trans. Sadok H. Masliyah, in: *Edebiyat* 13 (2002), pp. 49–67

FURTHER READING

Ammiel Alcalay: "Signs in the Great Disorder. An Interview with Samir Naqqash by Ammiel Alcalay", in Ammiel Alcalay (ed.), *Keys to the Garden. New Israeli Writing*, San Francisco: City Lights Books 1996, pp. 100–32

Markus Lemke: *Im Labyrinth des verlorenen Paradieses. Samir Naqqash – ein jüdisch-arabischer Schriftsteller aus dem Irak und die Immigration nach Israel im Spiegel ausgewählter Werke*, MA-thesis, Bochum-University 1996

Angelika Neuwirth: "'Zieh fort aus der Heimat, dem Land deiner Väter ... '. Arabische Kurzprosa irakisch-jüdischer Autoren in Israel", in: Shalom Darwish, Samir Naqqash: *Zieh fort aus der Heimat, dem Land deiner Väter. Arabische Kurzprosa irakisch-jüdischer Autoren in Israel*, eds. Angelika Neuwirth, Nesrine Jamoud, Berlin: Schiler 2007, pp. 107–22

Alexandra Nocke: "Rewriting Israeliness. Arabs Writing in Hebrew and Jews Writing in Arabic", in: Andreas Pflitsch, Barbara Winckler (eds.), *Poetry's Voice – Society's Norms. Forms of Interaction between Middle Eastern Writers and their Societies*, Wiesbaden: Reichert 2006, pp. 173–88

Reuven Snir: "'Arabs of the Mosaic Faith'. Jewish Writers in Modern Iraq and the Clash of Narratives after their Immigration to Israel", in: Andreas Pflitsch, Barbara Winckler (eds.), *Poetry's Voice – Society's Norms. Forms of Interaction between Middle Eastern Writers and their Societies*, Wiesbaden: Reichert 2006, pp. 147–72

Reuven Snir: "'Religion is for God, the Fatherland is for Everyone', Arab-Jewish Writers in Modern Iraq and the Clash of Narratives after their Immigration to Israel", in: *The Journal of the American Oriental Society* 126 (2006), pp. 217–38

Reading the Ruins

Repressed Memory and Multiple Identity in the Work of Sélim Nassib

Christian Junge

The civil war and the process of coming to terms with its repercussions is the main anguished theme of modern Lebanese literature. Confronted with the inconceivability of a fratricidal war, a generation of young writers is searching for new forms of expression capable of grasping this past. In sharp contrast to the usual slogans tagging the conflict as having been a "war of the others" or a "war for others", this generation is seeking to enter into a dialogue with the dichotomous self. The Lebanese-Jewish francophone author Sélim Nassib, born in 1946 in Beirut, experienced the civil war directly while working as a journalist for the French newspaper *Libération*. As a writer, he approaches it from the retrospective.

In the very first days after the war has ended, the nameless protagonist of his novel *Fou de Beyrouth* (1992) relapses successively into the mechanisms which had determined life and behavior in the war years. Totally cut off from the outside world, as if under laboratory conditions, the "insanity" of war becomes manifest once more in this character, the insanity that turns a normal person into a cold-blooded murderer.

The setting of the novel is the "Green Line", the strip of land that once formed the line of demarcation running through the destroyed old quarter of Beirut. Overgrown with weeds, after the war this area quickly becomes a huge construction site for prestigious projects designed to erase the scars of war as quickly as possible. A brochure entitled "Information on the Reconstruction of the City Center" states the rationale behind this building frenzy: "The historic and geographic core of the town, once a place of bustling commercial activity, is in a coma-like state and cloaked in sadness. Today Beirut and the whole of Lebanon awaits its reconstruction with impatience and generosity."

The eccentric protagonist of *Fou de Beyrouth* reveals the mood of a new beginning and the spirit of burgeoning postwar optimism as a naïve belief in peace and opportunism. In a race against the ever-advancing clearing operations, he tries to save the evidence of war, namely the ruins. Instead of disposing of the war rubble, he demands a coming to terms with the horrific past – the ruins are to be a memento.

Vomiting against forgetting

> I believe it is the taste in my mouth that wakes me up. Bitter, nauseous. It was still dark. Nina was not there, I was alone in bed. I switched on the radio and listened. I let the news enter me, piece by piece, like poison. (...) The war is over, the war is over, this thought alone puts me in a state of shock.

In 1990 fifteen years of civil war in Lebanon officially end with the founding of the Second Republic. But the protagonist cannot rejoice. He wanders aimlessly through Beirut's destroyed streets and tries to find an explanation for the war in the ruins.

> The ruins are left all to themselves. Everybody is at home here. Here, the war started, it swallowed public space, before it went elsewhere and didn't think about it anymore. Of course I know that everything is destroyed, but it is not the destruction that astonishes me, on the contrary. It is the vegetation. It has taken possession of the naked body, covered it, and is trying to digest it in front of my eyes, like a pleasant, carnivorous forest.

Under the veil of nature, the city afflicted by war becomes a kind of innocent rainforest. But the nameless figure is not seduced by this "bucolic unreality", neither does he find here a *locus amoenus*. Instead, he becomes a witness of how nature overgrows the city ruins and the human corpses, devouring and decomposing them, and thus downplaying the war as something easily digestible. His body reacts violently against these mighty assimilation processes of nature: it reverses the digestive process. "A small desire to throw up, like a very refined pleasure." For the protagonist, the war is not easily disposable:

> They will say we have never stopped being brothers, a state of mental derange-
> ment, the page has to be turned, forgotten, start all over from scratch. They
> are crazy. Iron and lead have left their graffiti on the walls, on every shadow of
> a window, they have written history. It is worthless, but that's the way it is.

Following the traces of the ruins leads him to the center of Beirut, and he dares to advance into the prohibited zone, where no one has set foot for years. This area, once the epicenter of the fighting, has become a symbol of the tabooed war. His intrusion is the first breaking of this taboo and gives him access to the "war archive" made up of ruins, the repressed architectural memory. "It is the center of town that consoles me, that comforts my soul. Because it doesn't lie. I look at it and recognize myself."

A war-time Crusoe

A sudden deluge of rain soaks the streets, turning the ground into a mass of mud and causing it to slide, along with the intruder, into a hollow beneath the ruins. He falls into a deep subterranean cathedral, from which there is no escape. "And yet, suddenly, in this rat hole, for the first time I feel protected in an unexplainable way. I am happy." His prison gives him shelter from peace.

> The city has woken up. The whole weekend it has dozed, but now it no longer closes its eyes to the news. It will take revenge. The strain built up over all these years, the explosions, the nights spent in shelters, it will want everything it missed back in one go. The blood will go to its head. I would rather not be there.

The narrator stumbles into a parallel world *en miniature*. He thus shares the fate of the shipwrecked Robinson Crusoe. Far away from civilization, the Englishman managed to establish his old way of life by tilling the land, finding a servant, and keeping a logbook. The protagonist of *Fou de Beyrouth* also remains within his accustomed way of life, namely that of war. Cut off from the clearing work of peacetime, he becomes entangled in the mechanisms and automatic reflexes of civil-war life.

This war-time variation of a Crusoe-like figure begins with the protagonist's fall into the abyss:

> I roll head forward, whatever I eat I spit back out, on my lips I notice the taste of blood, I leave my body to itself like a sack filled with sand, my head hits an object that makes a dull sound, I'm not here anymore.

The metaphysical changes can be read from the estranged perception of his body: it becomes a sack full of sand. The human body is here mere matter without a soul, no longer subject to ethical norms because it no longer acts according to a will but purely instinctively: "Eat, sleep, keep the organism running." Once under the dictate of this materialistic logic, the cruelties of war cease to be an ethical dilemma and become solely an organic problem: "It wasn't a fight anymore, but a disease, a weird virus, a protracted, cancer-causing process."

After all attempts to escape end in failure, the search for something edible begins. By coincidence he stumbles across a cellar filled with plenty of provisions; with his physical needs covered, the struggle to survive ceases for the time being. At this point, just like Robison Crusoe, the wish to return home stirs in the eccentric. As the nameless Crusoe-like figure breaks through the wall of the cellar, crosses the minefield of the "prohibited zone", and reenters postwar Beirut, his way is blocked by a gang of children. Instinctively he beats a retreat to his "rat hole." "My border is a real one. It's over, I've arrived and there is nothing they can do. I'm on my territory, I'm at home."

Once an unloved prison, his home now turns into a military castle. More and more the character sees himself as the owner rather than a tenant of the theater of war, so that every change is considered a "dispossession" or even "profanation" of his territory. The distinction between the possessed object and the possessor subject wanes successively. The symbiosis culminates in a physical and mental assimilation.

> The traits of the ruins have entered me, they have become a part of my substance. The smallest change is visible immediately, my body reacts instantly, all by itself, just as it would if invaded by a foreign substance.

This dominant sense of ownership of his territorial ground evokes in him an excessive willingness to inflict violence:

> In order to protect my four walls I'll break skulls with my rifle butt, I'll slit open bellies, I'll cut throats, I'll park cars loaded with explosives on crowded streets. All this out of love.

With a critique that reveals Marxist overtones, the moral decay that turns civilians into murderers and fighters into militiamen, a betrayal of ideals and values for material reasons, is described.

At the end of this "ownership spiral", the character no longer controls his possession, but is swallowed by it: the theater of war absorbs him into "its flesh" and turns him into a ruin, a human wreck. When a major thoroughfare is built in the city center as part of reconstruction, he shares the same fate as the ruins: a construction worker hauls him onto his shoulder and carries him away "as if I was only a common bag of bones", while the rubble piles up in the bay of Beirut like a peninsula of debris.

On the remote island Robinson Crusoe successfully overcomes what we may call, borrowing from Heidegger, the threat of his existential *Geworfenheit* ("thrownness"). While in the beginning the island's natural riches provide him with all he needs to survive, later he can even lead a comfortable life by (re-) inventing civilization. The triumph of civilization over barbarism is so compelling and indeed inevitable that even Friday renounces his cannibalistic cravings. In Nassib's Crusoe, set in a war situation, civilization cannot yield the same power. Finding the provisions does not lead the protagonist to live a homely life, but rather, embedded in the logic of war, he is forced to continue the struggle for sheer survival. Here war triumphs over civilization and indulges in anthropophagic atrocity: *this* Robinson becomes a cannibal.

By all the rules of war

> I didn't go crazy. What I thought before, I still think now. My mind is in a healthy state. Even if it has never been so clear. It is so simple: an incident has tilted me into the logic of war, I simply accept it, it could have been madness to act differently.

Similar to civilization, war also has its own rules and logic. With journalistic clarity and conciseness, Nassib describes the mechanism suspending peaceful civilization. In doing so, the author reveals his adeptness as an experienced war correspondent, masterfully arranging and commenting on the protagonist's recollections:

> Over the years I have observed the mechanisms in the mirror, the catenation of cause and effect, the war that loops into itself. I was fascinated by this kind of insanity, which turns normal persons into murderers.

Once sensitized for the signs of war, it becomes impossible to miss them. Everywhere in Beirut he runs into anthropomorphic ruins, which, as architectural heaps of corpses, tell the story of the buildings and their inhabitants.

> Never have I seen a body tortured to this degree, attacked down to the substance, and still erect despite everything. The whole façade is like a flat face, yellowish-rusty, hollowed out by the numerous wide open mouths, grimaces of shock, black mouths that let out ceaselessly inaudible screams.

In the midst of the horror he runs into a group of kids playing soccer:

> They are born into the war, they know nothing else. (...) Their world is strictly binary: they/we, who resemble us like brothers. Nobody sees them, nobody bothers them. They're wearing uniforms and cover their heads under hoods. They're faceless, simply the tools of an interchangeable death.

Marked by the experiences of gang warfare, the protagonist flees the group instinctively, which only gives them a reason to follow him, for they are conditioned to react to the reflex of taking flight like a predator. What follows is a repeat of the war:

> It's done. In a few seconds I understood that the situation has to turn out for the worse, that it was the only way. I wounded one of these little scumbags

severely, perhaps I even killed him – I'm positive I killed him – what's happened, happened. They have their martyr, they have to avenge him, that is the supreme law, that's the core. And I certainly won't accept that I obey this law, which I reject, without defending myself. So that's it then, I'll defend myself, nothing more, nothing less.

For his own protection, he splits his territory into a "subterranean kingdom" and observation building. Later, when the construction workers invade his area, he dodges them by moving to the old flea market, where he sets up a fallback camp for himself in a former brothel. To defend this area he develops a tight military surveillance system:

No one could claim that I underestimate the enemy, no one can say that. It's weird, even my sleep has changed. I'm now capable of waking up exactly every two hours, patrol the area quickly, lie back down and fall asleep again right away, as if nothing had happened.

In the process, he reduces his life to the demands of war and turns himself into a military body par excellence. Dispossessed of his civilian shell by seeing his own obituary posted on the walls, he has become a martyr against his will. This portrait of him on the walls, a minimal ritual for the "killed soldier", has consequently put him in the service of one of the warring groups: "Now I only have to step on to a mine for everything to be put back in order and for everyone to be happy."

In this bitterly fought trench warfare, his desire to provoke the enemy through swift raids increases. "It's dumb, I know that it doesn't make any sense. It is symbolic; I accept it that it is symbolic. The desire is too strong, like the urge to strike back with your fist." This is why he throws a stone at a truck being used in construction work – but his throw falls short of the target and the rock hits a mine. "I have miraculously brought about a full-scale assault. Everybody ready for full combat!" The minor provocation results unexpectedly in a devastating attack which only serves to escalate the spiral of violence.

Although peace is emerging as a tangible reality, the war is paradoxically not over. When a café is opened in the ruins, it seems as if an idyllic place of peace has been created, only for the illusion to be severely shaken shortly afterwards by the arrival of a group of men bearing weapons ostentatiously. The protagonist can make them out easily as former militiamen, "well shaved assassins" who became bodyguards after the war. Although they have changed their profession, they didn't change their manners, behaving as self-confidently as ever before, so that the other customers leave the place with "eyes turned down and backbones bent". For them, peace doesn't possesses the power of a caesura or a new beginning but proves to be just another phase of an ongoing war, because former murderers still live at ease in the postwar period. The protagonist prefers not to be part of *this* society but rather to be the odd one out.

The lovers

During the war the protagonist had met the twenty-eight-year-old Nina, who lost her husband in a shelling attack, which she herself only escaped by a miracle. "She had concluded from this that another life had been given to her, a second life, Baksheesh." She formed a new opinion of the war through this experience, paying no attention to the political situation in the newspapers and on television, and not bothering to scamper for the bunker when danger arises. Instead she led a life that totally ignored the war: she left the light on at night and did not avoid standing at open windows. "Nina talks about everything, except about the war, she never talks about that." Without a single word, they became lovers. "My life has become impermeable, it runs in fixed tracks, out of reach. It's becoming clear to me now that my world was perfect."

One day Nina simply disappeared, an event that the protagonist pushed aside during the days of war. As peacetime dawns, he is unable to share the general mood of optimism because he is waiting for her to return. Unable to face up to this new reality without her, he flees to the empty center of the city, where, as in the war days, he can manage to ignore her absence. Here all his contradictions come to the fore: while on the one hand, he wants to keep alive signs of the past, on the other he tries to repress them. Only as the ruins are being transported away does he dare to read them: Nina is dead. One night during the war he had switched on the lights, drawing the attention of several militiamen, who then broke into his apartment and killed Nina. He hid in a wardrobe, from where he, as tragic hero, had experienced and survived the murder of Nina, for which he was responsible. After this he had fallen into a deep sleep of oblivion, forgetting the incident until he awoke as peace dawned. Here one can see the irony of fate at work: for him, Nina has died when peace is declared.

Mad about Beirut: a madman from Beirut

The tragic hero of *Fou de Beyrouth* is named Fou by the outside world: an eccentric madman, a crackpot, or a lunatic. But he is not insane, only lovesick. He is consumed by his longing for Nina. Behind this stands the old Arab legend of the unfortunate love between Qays and Layla, who are forbidden from marrying because of tribal conventions. As Layla then reluctantly marries another man, Qays goes mad, in Arabic: *majnun*. Lovesick, he retreats to the desert and becomes the poet of his unhappy love. Obsessed by Layla, he turns into *majnun Layla*.

At first glance, the constellation of the couple Layla-Majnun seems to have nothing to do with the love between Nina and the eccentric madman, for the two lovers from Beirut seem to have lived their love, albeit for a limited time. During the war they enjoyed peace, a relationship that ignored the compulsions of war. But it is precisely because of this lack of concern that the madman was responsible for Nina's death. Afterwards he flees the war and is only confronted with her death when peace invades his ivory tower and calls him to account:

> Even our beautiful souls should be part of the fuel. The fire has spread. Nobody was innocent, no one, not even us, I've needed a long time to admit it. I was reprieved for ten years, that's clear to me now. Ten years with Nina, just for the two of us alone, out of time. But even so, I didn't escape. My encounter with myself took place here, now, in the belly of this city, this cave of the living dead.

In peacetime he cannot relive the relationship with Nina, because Nina is dead. Inevitably, he falls back on his wartime relationship: he represses her disappearance up until the point where he – now insane – withdraws to the ruins. There he shares Majnun's fate: he consciously surrenders to an unhappy love.

Unlike the Arab legend, where the fulfillment of love is prevented by tribal conventions, in *Fou de Beyrouth* it is the war that intrudes. This twist to the traditional Majnun-Layla story is prefigured in the poem "Le Fou d'Elsa" (1963) by Louis Aragon. This love story is set in Andalusia at the time of the *Reconquista* (Reconquest), when the Catholic monarchs recaptured the Iberian Peninsula from the Moors. With any chance of realizing his love thwarted under Arab rule, Majnun sets his hopes in a change of power. These hopes are dashed, however, and while living as a recluse in a grotto near Granada he gazes into the future, only to see that even the twentieth century will not be ready to accept that "the time of the couple" has come. The impact of the Second World War is simply too great:

> To be happy eyes needed not be shut,
> Nothing heard
> But nowadays, since there are so many unloved ones
> That to live means burning and wind tastes like ashes
> Our blood is rushing
> All happiness, oh my happiness, one could have had it
> By not knowing
> But not to know, can one really pay the price
> The world is here; we are part of the suffering
> Whether one wants to or complains

There is no happy love, you know this
It can be sung.

In an interview with Francis Crémieux in 1964, Louis Aragon explicitly makes
the connection between *Le Fou d'Elsa* and everyday reality:

And what astonishes the distanced observer [Majnun] here again is the
impossibility of happiness amidst the general unhappiness. For if there is no
happy love in the time of Elsa, then, I repeat, because one has to be egoistic to
be happy amidst the misery of others. As an example I think about the huge
furor that the fact of a war in Algeria could have on contemporary youth.

In *Fou de Beyrouth* the protagonist is both a madman from Beirut and mad about
Beirut. As the former he is a lover from Beirut who loses his beloved through the
war. Despite his perfectly cloistered bliss of love, he has not remained innocent
in terms of the war, and thus in relation to Nina's death. "LOVE OH / TO SAY
THAT YOU ARE HAPPY / WHAT PECULIAR EGOISM" is the message the
Fou of Granada eventually scribbles on the wall of his grotto. Under the aegis of
peace, the "time of the couple" could now have arrived for the lovers from Beirut,
allowing them to live out their love without egoism. But Nina is dead – and in
any case the postwar period is anything but innocent and pristine. The "time of
the couple" is yet to come.

Consequently, we encounter here a madman possessed with a radical will to
remember, a willingness to face up to guilt without evading accountability. This
paradox became politically possible in the 1990s when a general amnesty was
declared, only a few assassinations excepted. In 1955 Heinrich Böll commented
on the German memoir literature of the postwar years, cuttingly calling such a
form of self-amnesty "human equanimity", "the tired shoulder shrug of Pontius
Pilate, who washes his hands in innocence." The will to remember of the *Fou de
Beyrouth* is accusatory, at the same time renouncing the usual slogans laying the
blame elsewhere, the "war of the others" or the "war for the others". Instead, the
madman examines his contradictory self for an explanation and finds that both
victim and perpetrator reside in his innermost self. In his refusal to resolve this
contradiction in innocence, one can locate a thematic affinity to another postwar
literature, that of Germany. In Wolfgang Borchert's play *The Man Outside* the
conscience of an entire people, both perpetrators and victims, ticks on:

And then comes the one-legged man-tick-tock-tick-tock (...) and walks
through the life of his murderer-tick-tock-tick-tock! And I am the murderer.
I? I, the murdered, I whom that they have murdered, I am the murderer?
Who protects us from becoming murderers? We are murdered each day,

and each day we commit murder! And the murderer Beckmann can stand it no longer, murdering and being murdered. And he screams in the face of the world: I die!

Nassib's nameless protagonist shares a similar fate. His experience as a Crusoe-like figure of war has made him a victim and perpetrator at once. Similar to Borchert's Beckmann character, no one wants to hear or see him. The city center of Beirut thus becomes his voice, the suffering of the war finding an architectural analogy: the ruins. The relationship he enters and fosters with them is incredibly intimate and close. He becomes obsessed with Beirut, indeed possessed by the city, and so crazy about it, a *Majnun-Bayrut*.

> They want to flatten it [the center], they want to erase it, that's what they want! One is better off dying. I alone know the secret hidden under these lifeless rocks. It is not meaningless that the war has destroyed specifically this place. It didn't create anything but this piece of art, this monument that is dedicated to its own stupidity.

In this extraordinary twist to the Majnun-Layla legend, the lovesick man becomes not a poet but the protector of the inadvertent poetry of war. The ruins, this artwork of war, are not distractive entertainment but seek confrontation. An unsightly stigma, they are steamrollered by the grinding wheels of peacetime, a Beirut being built with "impatience and generosity" and stripped of memory. The protagonist turns against this architectural imagination of a future without a past, the more so as it would not be able to give him back his Nina or the Beirut that existed before the war. Instead of "disposing of the war" he demands "confronting and coming to terms with it":

> They have lost their minds, they believe that the ruins won't take revenge. They don't realize that something has happened here, one even doesn't know what. If they bury them [the ruins] like that, it will reappear somewhere else.

Layla and Majnun of the Orient

In his work *Oum*, published in 1994 and translated into English in 2006 under the title *I Loved You for Your Voice*, Nassib once again takes up the *Majnun-Layla* legend. By means of the fictive memoirs of the poet Ahmad Rami, he allows the reader to take part in the public and private life of Umm Kulthum, the most famous singer in the Arab world. For nearly her entire life Rami, the impeded lover and preferred poet, has escorted the diva through all her ups and downs. Ostensibly, then, we have an entertaining novel about the biggest star of Arab music; beneath this glittering surface, the novel is also a thoughtful biography of an artist who sacrificed love for her unrivalled fame.

As with Layla and Majnun, unhappy love is the fulcrum of the novel. In the case of Ahmad Rami and Umm Kalthum it fails not because of the strict dictates of tradition but rather due to the singer's insatiable thirst for success; she, having grown up in poor circumstances, wishes to marry into the upper echelons of society. She thus voluntarily renounces her love of Rami – as well as other suitors – in her unbridled desire to become a singer, a singer possessed by love, a *majnuna*. It is this image of an unhappy lover that advances her career and enables a broad audience to identify with her "fate".

> Every single one of us has an unsatisfied desire. My poetry brought this feeling that something is missing; in her mouth it turned into something that the whole country spared. Her voice lulled the anger and the pain, the yearning for a world to come that didn't want to come.

Whenever she lends her voice to rulers, such as the Egyptian President Nasser, the "twosome" love is elevated, sometimes directly, sometimes allegorically, into patriotism. In the Arab legend, Majnun is a poet who creates an ideal image of Layla as a compensatory substitute for the beloved he has lost in real life. When the real Layla visits him in the desert, he is unable to recognize her. He has drifted too far from reality. Against this background, *Oum* gains political brisance, because it dares to broach the topic of how "escapist idealism and fear of realization" are seemingly inherent to nationalist dreams.

In Nassib's novel, the Umm Kulthum character lends itself not only to being interpreted as *majnuna*, but also as a Layla for her countless listeners and admirers. As such, the "Star of the Orient" offers a tempting projection space, not only through her art, but also as an unreachable diva. Commenting on this, Nassib writes: "Arabs define themselves through Umm Kulthum. I give them a glance in the mirror, one that also shows ugly spots. It would not be amiss for them to think about idolization and about themselves a bit."

Borderlines

While *Fou de Beyrouth* and, to a lesser degree, *I Loved You for Your Voice* deal with strategies of memory repression, displacement and escapism, the other weighty theme addressed by Sélim Nassib is identity. In the novel *The Palestinian Lover* (2004), Nassib narrates the doomed love story between the Palestinian aristocrat Albert Pharaon and the young Jewish Zionist Golda Meir, who later became Prime Minister of Israel.

An impossible story? *Almost* impossible, obliged to unfold in the tiny space of this *almost*, where things that should not happen do happen, the narrow patch of earth where forbidden flowers grow, instinctive impulses, life itself.

This novel explores the "narrow patch" where one can step outside the well-defined lines of identity and cross the border of societal norms. This is prefigured in earlier works, for example the novel *Clandestin* (1998), in which Nassib highlights the "multiple identity" of a Jewish Lebanese boy whose first language is French; hardly a surprising constellation for an author of the Jewish faith who grew up in Lebanon, regards French as his native tongue, and speaks fluent Arabic. Nor can it be surprising that inclusive identities are replaced by patchwork identities in his work. Life is no longer played out within the confines of firmly established borders, but rather along them, a phenomenon Homi K. Bhabha characterizes as "border life" in *The Location of Culture*:

> These "in-between" spaces provide the terrain for elaborating strategies of selfhood – singular or communal – that initiate new signs of identity, and innovative sites of collaboration, and contestation, in the act of defining the idea of society itself.

The novel *Clandestin* shows how one can help shape his or her own identity. Following the model of inner-city adventure novel, a boy named Jussuf finds a way out of the narrow confines of a local small street and enters the turbulent life of the large city of Beirut. Confronted with a multitude of different ways of life, the greatest adventure awaits him there: the search for his own identity.

Tom Sawyer learns Arabic

> My father is Iraqi and my mother is from Syria. I was born in Paris. We live next to the lighthouse, on the other side of town. I'm visiting a friend. His name is Fuad. Fuad Hussein. My religion? Muslim, that is too risky. Let's say Christian. I should know more about Christianity than them.

Jussuf, the main character of the novel, attends a Jewish school in Beirut. He speaks French as his native tongue and is bored to death with the lack of anything exciting to do in his street. "I could have been a witness to violence and hate, of obscene gestures. But this street is so calm (...). Only normal people pass here. (...) Where is it, *the other street?*" He yearns for great adventure, like Tom Sawyer. To get away from his sheltered life at home, both use, among other things, what Mikhail M. Bakhtin called the "carnivalesque" power of language. While Tom

Sawyer discovers the inimitable slang of Huckleberry Finn, Jussuf has to switch into another language.

> Arabic is reserved for the communication with grocers or maids, but it is also the language of all the dirty things. Fucking, cock, whore, pimp, masturbate, and to play for a sucker, all these words don't exist in French. The French language is as well raised as I am, in a small velvet costume with straps and satin shirts, an innocent little boy of his mummy, obedient, almost gay.

Seemingly impotent, French loses its appeal when up against vulgar Arabic. When Jussuf meets Fuad, the only Muslim in his school, he finds his ideal counterpart. Through him he discovers the other language. One day they skip the elaborate funeral service held for an important rabbi and visit Fuad's family in the Muslim part of town.

> The sidewalks are just like the ones in my quarter, grey with small checkers that make you dizzy. The buildings are the same (...). The same dust, the same red sand between the cobblestones. I have never been here, I'm sure of that. And that is the exciting thing. Everything is familiar and unknown; one could say it is a projection of my quarter just much bigger. A grown-up town compared to my childlike town. It's like walking around in a dream, where I recognize everything without recognizing it. *The other street*, maybe it is here.

But he is soon confronted with his otherness: "The pedestrians look at me curiously. Maybe I'm too young to walk around by myself, or could it be my clothes, my air. I definitely have to be like everyone else, but what is everyone like?" Here the naïve astuteness of a Tom Sawyer is already evident. On a par with his thirteen years, he poses seemingly simple questions which though undermine standard answers. By asking "but what is everyone like?" he doubts the conception of the homogeneous mass for the first time and goes on to "deconstruct" the notion. His questions about identity have a maieutic effect: like the Socratic art of dialogue, they induce new answers. Through this mode of questioning, Jussuf finds out that he is not Syrian, even though his mother was born in Aleppo, and that, even though his father was born in Baghdad, he is not an Iraqi, because neither have Syrian or Iraqi papers. Then again, they are not Iranian, although they hold Iranian passports. Their Arabian accent is Jewish, and is very similar to that spoken by Syrians, but stands out from the Lebanese Muslim and the Lebanese Christian.

In the end, religion, origins and family turn out to be less relevant to his identity than his accent. Obsessed with the idea of wiping out the Jewish accent in his Arabic, he takes lessons from Fuad. He no longer wants to be noticed in the "other street", and he soon achieves his goal, which affords him unlimited access to the other world. By learning the accent perfectly, Jussuf the imitator has reached his goal: he has become a counterfeiter of identity.

The self-defined "rite de passage"

To escape the father's high gambling debts, the family decides to flee secretly to Israel on Jussuf's bar mitzvah, the Jewish celebration of initiation that witnesses a young man becoming a full member of the community. Jussuf had hoped to attract the attention of all the girls and women present, in the expectation that he would be able to lose his virginity. Now that his bar mitzvah has been cancelled, he decides to take matters into his own hands. On the last night, a few hours before the planned flight, he and his friend Fuad go to a brothel. Instead of waiting for official initiation into the Jewish community, he has celebrated his own *rite de passage*, with and in front of Fuad. The religious ceremony is turned into a profane celebration, which though is no less the forging of a communal bond. "Fuad and I are brothers forever."

Jussuf returns home late, just as the night is coming to an end. From afar he sees his parents waiting for him, only for the Syrian police to turn up and arrest them. In this moment Jussuf decides to follow them and jumps on the truck loaded with the furniture.

> I cannot start to escape. (...) If one day I leave this place, then it will be my own wish. Until then I'll stay in the Orient. My proper place is here, hidden.

Clandestin most certainly contains autobiographical traces of its Jewish Lebanese francophone author. Nevertheless, the interest in the self, whether autobiographical or fictional, is not to be equated with narcissistic navel-gazing. Far removed from any monologue, Lebanese literature discovers in the self a cultural polyphony characteristic of Lebanon. As the son of Syrian-Iraqi parents, the Jewish Tom Sawyer learns to overcome the narrow, constrictive borders: the borders of accent, language, and religion. The protagonist counteracts this polyphony with a multilingualism that sees his multifaceted identity not as a handicap, but as a chance he has to seize.

WORKS

Selim Nassib, Caroline Tisdall: *Beirut: Frontline Story*, Trenton: Africa World Press 1983

L'homme assis (The Sitting Man), Paris: Editions Balland 1991

Fou de Beyrouth (Mad about Beirut), Paris: Editions Balland 1992

Oum (I Loved You for Your Voice), Paris: Editions Balland 1994
Clandestin (Clandestine), Paris: Editions Balland 1998
Un amant en Palestine (The Palestinian Lover), Paris: Editions Robert Laffont 2004

TRANSLATIONS

I Loved You for Your Voice, trans. Alison Anderson, New York: Europa Editions 2006
The Palestinian Lover, trans. Alison Anderson, New York: Europa Editions 2007

FURTHER READING

Angelika Neuwirth: "Sélim Nassib. Der Besessene von Beirut", in: Angelika Neuwirth, Andreas Pflitsch, *Agonie und Aufbruch. Neue libanesische Prosa*, Beirut: Dergham 2000, pp. 145–47
Barbara Winckler: "Utopische Kriegslandschaften. Sélim Nassib, Huda Barakat und die Debatte um den Wiederaufbau des Beiruter Stadtzentrums", in: Andreas Pflitsch, Barbara Winckler (eds.), *Poetry's Voice – Society's Norms. Forms of Interaction between Middle Eastern Writers and their Societies*, Wiesbaden: Reichert 2006, pp. 259–80

OTHER WORKS CITED

Louis Aragon: *Entretiens avec Francis Crémieux*, Paris: Gallimard 1964
Louis Aragon: *Le Fou d'Elsa*, Paris: Gallimard 1963
Homi K. Bhabha: *The Location of Culture*, London, New York: Routledge 1994
Heinrich Böll: "Die Stimme Wolfgang Borcherts", in: Heinrich Böll, *Werke. Kölner Ausgabe*, vol. 9 (1954–56), ed. J. H. Reid, Cologne: Kiepenheuer & Witsch 2006, pp. 276–80
Wolfgang Borchert: "Draußen vor der Tür. Ein Stück, das kein Theater spielen will und kein Publikum sehen will", in: Wolfgang Borchert, *Das Gesamtwerk*, ed. Michael Töteberg, Reinbek: Rowohlt 2007, pp. 115–92

British-Lebanese Identity Fallacies
Tony Hanania and a Malady Called Homesickness

Andreas Pflitsch

Homesick, the title of Tony Hanania's first novel, not only indicates a yearning for home, an aching desire to return, and so presupposes "having a home"; but it can also be read as indicating a suffering *because* of this home, suffering from one's own origins. A third possible reading is that the homeland itself is ill. It is this third meaning suggesting a privation, a morbid affliction of the homeland as well as a suffering felt at this state, which Hanania's novel takes as its central theme.

Ostensibly, the novel tells of the inner workings of a "closed society": torn away from the idyll of his childhood in Lebanon (the novel opens with the words "Leaving town"), the narrator Toby Shadrach is sent to an English boarding school; a situation that he by no means grasps as advancement or improvement. The very first hours in this new environment are enough for him to suspect that difficult times are ahead:

> Later that night I had been awakened by the sounds of a struggle. Some of the lights had been switched on again. Three of the older boys were on the floor wrestling for what appeared to be one of the drawers with wooden knobs. This confirmed my worst suspicions. I had been abandoned in a wild and savage place.

Initial encounters with the "indigenous" pan out accordingly. Upon learning that he is from the Middle East, his roommates are initially confused: "Does that mean you're a foreigner?", asks one. Then "some bright spark" observes that Jews come from the Middle East, triggering all kinds of politically dubious remarks. As it finally emerges that he is an Arab they assail him with seemingly obvious questions: "Does your father ride a *camel*? How many wives does he have? Is he the colour of crap? Does he live in a tent? Do you wipe your bottom with your hand?" The adolescent boy retorts with a precocious, if reflex-like counter question: didn't they know "that we went to Church and had baths when you were still throwing each other into bogs?" Such ignorance is not limited to the pupils, however; the teachers are not immune, and this is exposed most blatantly by the geography master of all people, whose face lights up as Toby says where he comes from, and begins to rave about the "swelling sublimities of the Opera." The teacher has obviously confused

Beirut with Bayreuth. Only later will Toby learn to turn the expectations of his classmates and teachers to his own advantage.

Transistor radios in boarding school and the car dealer Abu Shawki

The frequently brutal rituals of boarding-school life, in particular the power struggles raging among the pupils, which blur the boundary between childlike play and crushing earnestness, echo what is happening in Toby's homeland, where the civil war is raging. The military vocabulary, one of demarcations, territories, power struggles, taking sides, and alliances, which Hanania employs to describe English boarding-school life, resonates with the situation in Lebanon. The author inscribes one into the other, confounding and blending the two worlds and the modes used to speak about them. The chapters are titled "blood feud", "my enemy's enemy", "despite the curfew", and "continued attacks by unknown assailants". There is continual talk of "defense lines", "batteries of water-bombs", "hostage taking", and being "lightly armed with sock-balls". The brawling in the boarding school and the anarchy in Beirut mirror each other: charismatic pupils who rally their (school) comrades around them and enlist their services reveal a disturbing similarity to the no less charismatic feudal lords and militia leaders in Lebanon. Children become monsters, warlords become childish – and both are anything but harmless.

Much of the behavior in the English boarding school is a cipher for specific historical incidents from the Lebanese Civil War.

> In the first weeks Ferrers, supported by a band of senior Hounds and Curlews, had waged a vigorous campaign against transistor radios, mounting sound patrols across the dormitories and gardens, probing the bog-houses and music cubicles for headphone solitaires. But this purge had proved a victim of its own success. Such quantities of equipment were confiscated in those first weeks that the trading values of all batteries and every species of tyranny soared to levels that ensured that extortion and racketeering among the sound patrollers rapidly became endemic. It was even mooted that Standish had provoked Ferrers into orchestrating the war against the tyrannies with only this end in mind. Whatever the truth of this, by the end of the first month of the campaign the black trade in Sony and Philips and Panasonics and Ever-Readies of all specifications had reached such a feverish pitch that one set might be confiscated from a junior in the morning and change hands half-a-dozen times on the floor of the washroom before being ransomed back that night to the same junior for over six times its original trading price. In short, while the sound patrols were kept up there was a tyranny bonanza the likes of which may never be seen again.

Hanania is alluding here to the lively trade in stolen cars which flourished during the civil war. In *Beirut Fragments*, a memoir of the war years published in 1990, Jean Said Makdisi relates that it was the significant rise in car theft that first alarmed the Beirut population, which until then had not taken the fighting particularly seriously. Makdisi's journalistic autobiographical notes tell of a new line of business that emerged at the outset of the war, the reselling of cars to the actual owners:

> Soon no one could leave a car on the streets without running the risk of losing it. With insurance no longer available and the police increasingly powerless, a brisk business grew up of reselling cars to their rightful owners. You would go to the center of the trade in Baalbek, far away from the reach of what little government authority was left. There you would be greeted by the redoubtable Abu Shawki, who would accord friendly hospitality, offering cigarettes, coffee, or a cold drink. You would then be escorted around the great parking lot to pick out your own car, showing papers to prove ownership, and then pay whatever fee Abu Shawki saw fit to charge. A friend of ours paid 10,000 pounds for his 50,000 pound car and drove it home, deeming himself lucky to have found it at all.

Abu Shawki and his car racket are one of a myriad of incidents that became legendary during the course of the war and have over time gestated into a myth of everyday life in war-racked society. Makdisi, who witnessed the war in Lebanon first hand, gives a comparatively sober account. "Non-local" authors like Hanania or Rabih Alameddine, a Lebanese painter and writer living in California, observe events from a distance. In these cases there is a conscious propensity to exaggerate. Alameddine also seized on this topos in his 1998 novel *Koolaids: The Art of War*. In comparison with Makdisi's report of what is anyway a rather absurd story, Alameddine's version magnifies it into a horrific grotesque:

> *December 24th, 1987*
>
> Dear Diary,
> What a day. We had to drive all the way to Ba'albak to buy our car back. It was our second trip. The first time, they told us, our car had not arrived yet. They did have it, they assured us. It just hadn't arrived at the depot yet. Apparently it takes about five days for a stolen car to get up there. They had the gall to tell us they are trying to get more efficient. Soon it would take only three days for them to steal the car, drive it up to Ba'albak, for it to be ready to be sold back to its owner. What is this world coming to?

Place-polygamous authors like Alameddine and Hanania, looking in from a distance, may well have an unfocused view of some things; for that however, they often have a sharper sense for others. In particular, the unintentional comedy of situations that seem tragic when seen from close quarters rarely escapes their attention.

Identity mania: Eve and the tomato

The Lebanese situation and its mirroring in British boarding-school life are not the only themes addressed in *Homesick*. Hanania's novel broaches the central theme of modern Arabic literature, of intellectual and cultural engagement with the West, and inverts it. Far from being subjected to the almost stifling earnestness, sentimentality and palpable pressure of justification evident in earlier Arab works on this theme, in the figure of Toby Shadrach we encounter a boy oozing in self-confidence who is adept at turning prejudices to his advantage. He manages to see the idiocy nestling in clichés and succeeds in converting any situation into one where he enjoys predominance, which he then exploits. A good example is when he dodges having to eat the despised stewed tomatoes at boarding school. Toby claims to be a member of a special group in the Eastern Church that believes that Eve tempted Adam with a tomato and has therefore forbidden its consumption. The teachers and school board show utmost sympathy for Toby's "religious tomato ban" and with a hint of political correctness go so far as to prohibit the other pupils from even mentioning tomatoes in Toby's presence.

Here identity does not spring, as is so often the case, from an anxiety-ridden reflex to draw distinctions. The mechanism behind cultural demarcations of this kind, the drawing of exclusivist borders, is ironized and subversively undermined. Hanania is on the trail of the mechanisms of identity formation. Problems are found not only in the views others have of one, clichés, and prejudices, but also in that one's own feelings of belonging prove to be contingent on the mirror held up by others:

> When there was a slide lecture on mining, for instance, and Barnsley found himself brocked from all sides as a *scully northener*, though his family had lived in Norfolk for generations, he would rally to the miners' cause with a degree of heartfelt conviction and eloquence which would have put many union men to shame.

The literary configuration of this mechanism, by virtue of which the prejudices of others decisively influence perspective of one's own identity, can be read as a variation of the theme addressed by Max Frisch in his play *Andorra*, first performed in 1961.

A kind of symbiotic relationship develops between Toby Shadrach, the

"Oriental", and the slightly elder Ferrers, who displays an interest in the Middle East bordering on obsession and puts Toby on the spot with his questions. As Ferrers wants to find out "all about camels and sheikhs and dancing-girls", Toby is forced to admit that his experience in this field is limited, for "apart from the two-cylinder models in Regents' Park" his "experience of camels was confined to the moth-eaten creature which squatted among the souvenir stalls in Baalbeck with a disdainful expression." Arab terrorism fascinates Ferrers the most. Toby gladly satisfies his seemingly insatiable thirst for new and increasingly adventuresome stories about George Habash and Ahmad Jibril. Flattered by the interest shown in his homeland, he begins, once the stories he's heard run out, to invent new ones.

The abuse of the longing for identity, whether through a wrathful insistence on the identity asserted or the imputation of an identity by others, is regarded by many zeitgeist diagnosticians as one of the gravest dangers of the present age. In his book *Identitätspolitik* the political scientist Thomas Meyer has coined the concept of "identity mania" to designate this phenomenon, a malady he defines as the "fundamentalist form of the construction of cultural identity". This malady does not only afflict non-European or Muslim societies but is just as prevalent in the West, where in harmless cases the symptoms are ethnic-nationalist political parties or talk of a "national guiding culture"; in less harmful cases, the ever-increasing erosion of civil liberties and human rights as part of the so-called war on international terrorism. The aim is always homogenization and hierarchical classification. Identity strives towards purity. Whatever meddles with symmetry needs to be abolished; culture and identity are to be had only in the singular. The explosive potential lying in the debate about identity and culture, seemingly academic, is no longer of an intellectual nature, but has become very real. "Viewed in its entirety, the politicization of cultural difference". writes Meyer, "is therefore a suicidal undertaking for everyone".

This warning of the excesses of identity mania has nothing to do with denying cultural differences or neglecting the human need to belong to a group or identity. Meyer's critique targets the *how* and not the *if,* because: "the search for identity only becomes identity mania where it is able to enter a field of action as nothing but itself, without distance to its own roles, without empathy for the diverse roles and identities of others, without the will and capacity to endure ambivalences." What Meyer expresses here in the jargon of political science and sociology has been put into far simpler words by the Lebanese author Rashid al-Daif. The narrator of his novel *Dear Mr Kawabata* (1995) succinctly encapsulates the distinction between a healthy, self-assured sense of identity and the pathological mania fixated on erecting rigid cultural barriers: "I the Maronite, who loves goat's milk, loves it just because I do and not in defiance of someone else."

The Levantine advantage

Foresters are not the only ones who realize that monocultures are especially susceptible to diseases and infestation by pests. Authors like Tony Hanania, who due to his biography alone is adept at moving between cultures, know this as well. Hanania was born in 1964 in Beirut and grew up in Lebanon. In the 1970s he attended boarding school at Winchester in England before studying art history at the Warburg Institute in London. He has worked for Sotheby's in Madrid as well as the Tate Gallery in London, where he lives today.

As an author with a broad experience of the world, Hanania is not only a practitioner in transgressing borders, he also enjoys the advantage of having witnessed firsthand the multicultural coexistence afforded by the Levantine tradition. His novel *Eros Island* is a Levantine family saga that relates the odyssey of a family which fled to Lebanon in 1948 after the founding of the state of Israel. The story spans the family's fate from the 1930s in Palestine to the 1980s and 1990s in Lebanon, the United States, England and Spain. Radical social transformation and ultimately far-reaching changes affecting the material culture of everyday life characterize the 1930s in Palestine. Canned meat and Nestlé milk chocolate testify to these changes. Some rise from poverty to affluence, like Anton, a forefather of the narrator, who is able to fulfill a dream:

> With his new salary he buys a Model T Ford from the new showroom on the Jaffa Road. Every evening under the tasselled lamp he reads the User's Manual. He intones the lines like scripture. "A few drops of oil may be added to the petrol to improve the running of the engine."

With exquisite virtuosity, Hanania plays the full register of world and everyday culture in *Eros Island*, depicting a frame of reference, already existent at that time, that is today ascribed to the phenomenon of globalization. Agfa, Carl Zeiss Jena, and Leica surface as "exotic hieroglyphics" – once more Hanania undertakes a shift in perspective, a reversal of views – in the streets of Palestine. Traversing different historical eras and spaces, the reader encounters Barthes, Trakl, Heine, Schiller and Goethe; Ford, Plymouth, Thomas Cook and Barclays Bank; Bach, Beethoven, Mozart, Vivaldi and Schumann's songs; Ilie Nastase; and the Wimbledon semi-final between Boris Becker and Michael Stich; in short: insignia of Western high, everyday, and popular culture. The reader also becomes acquainted with Umm Kulthum, a mufti, and with *jibneh* and other Arabic words, which Hanania neither explains nor translates and so stand for something strange and alien, although their meaning is in fact very familiar, in this instance "cheese".

It all fits together in Hanania's weaving of the text; nothing is so manifoldly baffling than reality itself. It is a well-known and familiar world that Hanania describes, blended and intertwined with the exotically unfamiliar; with Jerusalem and Beirut, cities that the European imagination conceives as sacred and filled with war, terror, and violence – all of which are "borderline experiences". These cities, so charged and overloaded with images, have rarely been so stripped of mystique whilst rendered so captivating as they are in the work of Tony Hanania. He pulls away the veil of exoticization without any pathos, so that one looks on astonished and almost startled at just how normal things there are: "It is raining in Jerusalem."

When a chapter opens in such a lapidary fashion, so harmlessly and undramatically, freed from the ballast of myths and history, one begins to sense that syncretism, the mixing of cultures, is the rule and not the exception. That it has been repackaged and resold under the buzzword of globalization over the last few years may be due to the fact that this "normal state" threatened to fall into oblivion under the burden of massive homogenization that inherently accompanied the flourishing of modernity. The paradigm of the Levantine expresses a counter model. The scenario of imminent danger so virulent today across the globe, the fear of "others", appears to be a collective hysteria when juxtaposed with the unobtrusive, calm approach to dealing with differences that potentially shimmers through in this utopia. The clash of civilizations is unlikely, but it would be altogether harmless if the colliding cultures had "soft" edges and fluid boundaries.

The calm self-assuredness we encounter in the texts of Tony Hanania and other Lebanese diaspora authors of the younger generation like Rabih Alameddine, Elias Abou Haidar and Hani Hammoud has introduced an entirely new tone into Arabic literature. The pathos of cultural emancipation characteristic of post-colonialism, itself long become classical, is as alien to them as the fundamentalist return to the purported roots of a "Golden Age" or the slavish imitation of admired Western role models. Nothing is sacred to them; myths are there to be unmasked. As members of a generation whose parents more often than not raised the West onto a pedestal in limitless admiration, it has become their task to shatter the mystique. They were quick to notice that everyone in the West also puts on their pants one leg at a time. In a single sentence Hanania turns the creation of proud legends enshrouding the British Empire into ridicule:

> We had been told that the town itself had once been the capital of all Christian England, the seat of legendary warrior kings, but all I had seen was a muggy high street and some boys outside the Wimpy with long hair and silly lapels, smoking in the drizzle.

Nostography

Despite the irony and notwithstanding the underlying utopian-optimistic sentiment, in *Eros Island* Hanania also tells a tragic story: that of the Palestinians in the twentieth century. Although this story reaches back to a time before the narrator was born, it still determines his life. Whereas his father, an academic in the US, could never feel at home in his homelessness, for the narrator, a member of the "third generation" in exile, London and later New York have become natural homes. Homesickness has lost its direction. Passé it is not. "I had become a stranger", says the narrator in *Eros Island* with an unmistakable melancholic tinge, "by staying where I was".

As noted above, the title of Hanania's debut, *Homesick*, can be understood in a double or even a triple sense. In *False Papers: Essays on Exile and Memory* (2000) André Aciman, a Jew from Alexandria, living and teaching in the USA and so another place polygamist, undertakes an etymological plotting of nostalgia, a genealogy of return. Starting from the Greek word *nostos* (return home), he writes:

> Nostalgia is the ache to return, to come home; nostophobia, the fear of returning; nostomania, the obsession with going back; nostography, writing about the return.

Nostalgia as the longing to return entails erasing itself through its fulfillment. Home is at its most alluring when one is not there and can pine for it from afar. The Czech writer and politician Jiří Gruša spoke on the "value of homelessness" in a review of Milan Kundera's novel *Ignorance*. Gruša's review ends with praise for how Kundera, who has lived for over thirty years in exile in France and meanwhile writes in French, "has achieved something rare: namely a return without having to." He gave the review the following title: "Strange return: how the greatest Czech writer has turned feeling strange into his home." Tony Hanania has described many a strange return, an odd staying put in foreign lands and departing to what is familiar. Mirrorings of the home country and the foreign land, of comings and goings are to be found in his texts. He recalls places and travels in times. And is sometimes homesick.

WORKS

Homesick, London: Bloomsbury 1997
Unreal City, London: Bloomsbury 1999
Eros Island, London: Bloomsbury 2000

FURTHER READING

Syrine C. Hout: "Of Fathers and the Fatherland in the Post-1995 Lebanese Exilic Novel", in: *World Literature Today* 75,2 (2001), pp. 285–93

Andreas Pflitsch: "Tony Hanania. Heimweh. Unwirkliche Stadt. Eros Island," in: Angelika Neuwirth, Andreas Pflitsch, *Agonie und Aufbruch. Neue libanesische Prosa*, Beirut: Dergham 2000, pp. 102–09

OTHER WORKS CITED

André Aciman: *False Papers. Essays on Exile and Memory*, New York: Farrar, Straus & Giroux 2000

Rabih Alameddine: *Koolaids. The Art of War*, New York: Picador 1998

Rashid al-Daif: '*Azizi l-Sayyid Kawabata*, Beirut: Dar Mukhtarat 1995 (English translation: *Dear Mr Kawabata*, trans. Paul Starkey, London: Quartet 1999)

Max Frisch: *Andorra* [1957], Frankfurt/M: Suhrkamp 1961

Thomas Meyer: *Identitätspolitik. Vom Missbrauch kultureller Unterschiede*, Frankfurt/M.: Suhrkamp 2002

Jean Said Makdisi: *Beirut Fragments. A War Memoir*, New York: Persea 1990

The Forbidden Paradise
How Etel Adnan Learnt to Paint in Arabic

Sonja Mejcher-Atassi

The writer Etel Adnan has gained international renown for her acclaimed novel *Sitt Marie Rose*, which was published in Paris in 1977 and subsequently translated into several languages. *Sitt Marie Rose* is one of the first novels to deal with the Lebanese civil war that articulates a position opposed to the conflict. The text, which has been taught at many universities in the US as an exemplary work of gender and postcolonial literature, is based on a true story: the abduction, imprisonment and killing of Marie Rose Boulos by Christian militiamen. Boulos, a Christian Lebanese of Syrian origin, had become involved in the plight of Palestinian refugees.

Adnan has published more than a dozen books, most of which are collections of poetry. She has also written essays, short stories, plays, scenarios for documentaries, and, together with the British composer Gavin Bryars, contributed to Robert Wilson's opera *Civil Wars* (1984). Moreover, she is a visual artist. Her art has been shown in solo and group exhibitions in museums and galleries in the US, Europe, the Middle East, Russia, and Japan. Although mainly an abstract painter, she has also experimented with different media. She has produced numerous *livres d'artistes* (artists' books), most of which focus on modern Arabic literature. By turning Arabic script – in the form of her own handwriting – into an integral component of her abstract painting, she has reclaimed artistically the Arabic language, and with it part of her identity, which had remained inaccessible to her as a writer.

Adnan writes in French and English. She speaks Arabic (the Lebanese dialect) but does not have sufficient command of the language to compose literary texts. Whereas most anthologies and encyclopedias of Arabic literature exclude Adnan on the grounds that she does not write in Arabic, she considers her literary works to be part of Arabic literature. To underline her claim, she points out that she draws on a tradition of cultural mobility in the Middle East. Famous writers such as Ibn Sina (d. 1037), Jalal al-Din Rumi (d. 1273), and Kahlil Gibran (1883–1931) have written in more than one language. In Adnan's view, literary writing is not solely based on national language but is informed by other elements such as poetic sensibility, historical memory and political experience.

Adnan is often considered to be a francophone writer, a term she rejects, because, as she explains, this term stems from France's colonial past and is applied as a tag for authors from so-called Third World countries only, whereas writers from other European countries who choose to write in French are recognized as French authors. More recently, Adnan has also been labeled an Arab-American author. This description should be seen in the context of the emerging body of Arab-American literature within multiethnic literature in the US. This characterization is only partially apt for Adnan and her work, however, since it neglects her rich cultural background, which also includes Greek, Turkish (Ottoman), and French influences.

A life in geographical and cultural "in-between spaces"

Adnan was born in 1925 in Beirut. Her mother was a Greek Orthodox Christian from Smyrna, today's Izmir; her father a Sunni Muslim from Damascus. He met his wife while serving as an officer in the Ottoman Army. After the breakup of the Ottoman Empire, Adnan's parents settled in Beirut. The Levantine coastal city was even then marked by a cosmopolitan character which attracted diverse religious and ethnic groups from the whole region. After the Sykes-Picot Agreement of 1916, which divided the Arab provinces of the Ottoman Empire among the entente powers, Lebanon became a French mandate. In 1920 the French High Commissioner in Beirut proclaimed the founding of Greater Lebanon. Following internal political unrest and heated disputes with the French, Lebanon was finally granted independence in 1943. In line with the unwritten "national pact", a democracy was established in which political power and positions were divided proportionally among the seventeen religious communities officially recognized by the French in 1936, among them various Christian and Muslim communities as well as Druze and Jews.

Adnan grew up amidst a multitude of languages, cultures, and religions. At home, she spoke Turkish and Greek, at school, French. Arabic remained a "forbidden paradise", she explains; speaking Arabic in school was not only punished, it was "equated with the notion of sin." The children were educated after the French model; French was considered superior to Arabic. Adnan's father tried to teach her Arabic at home. His efforts were rather old fashioned. He made her copy an Arabic grammar, which she faithfully reproduced word for word without really understanding the meaning. Nonetheless, it is these Arabic lessons that come to mind today when she works on her *livres d'artistes*. Her frequent visits with her father to see his family in Damascus, however, established a profound familiarity with Arabic-Islamic culture. "I got used to standing between situations, to being a bit marginal and still a native", she recalls.

The difficult economic situation during the Second World War had an impact on Adnan's family and forced her to leave school prematurely. Working for the French Information Bureau, she managed to make a living and finish her baccalaureate at the same time. Afterwards, she studied French literature at the newly founded École Supérieure des Lettres de Beyrouth. In 1949 she accepted a scholarship to study philosophy at the Sorbonne in Paris. The effects of the Second World War and the German occupation could still be felt in the French capital. In 1955 she left for the US to pursue her graduate studies at the University of California in Berkeley; she spent a year at Harvard University, but then decided not to complete her PhD. She found a job teaching humanities and philosophy of art at Dominican College in San Rafael, California, and stayed in the US. The cultural revolution of the 1960s set the context in which she found the freedom to pursue and develop her literary and artistic interests.

In 1972 Adnan returned to Beirut to work as a journalist for the cultural section of the French-language Lebanese daily *L'Orient-Le Jour*. Here she met her partner Simone Fattal who, like Adnan, had studied French literature at the École Supérieure des Lettres de Beyrouth and philosophy at the Sorbonne in Paris, before returning to Beirut at the end of the 1960s to devote herself to painting and sculpture. Beirut in the early 1970s was known for its cosmopolitan character, attracting intellectuals, writers, and artists from across the region. However, the Israeli-Palestinian conflict and the growing Lebanese crisis produced a highly volatile political atmosphere that eventually erupted into a full-blown civil war in 1975. In 1977, Adnan left Beirut once again. She has since divided her time between California (Sausalito), Paris and Beirut, devoting herself entirely to literature and art.

Adnan has lived all her life in "in-between spaces", a term used by Homi K. Bhabha in *The Location of Culture* (1994) to designate the spaces between cultures. In response to the question whether she feels exiled, she says: "Yes, I do. But it goes back so far, it lasted so long, that it became my own nature."

Exile and diaspora represent a place of transformation and difference, where cultural identities are continually redefined. Identity has never been a homogenous entity in Adnan's life. She has been committed to maintaining her Arab identity as one among other identities. Not only has she returned regularly to the Middle East, she has followed cultural life and political events with great interest and participated even from exile in many debates – as an intellectual, a writer, and an artist. Living between three countries, the notion of "home" has acquired a transnational and transcultural meaning for Adnan, one that lies beyond any geographical borders. Without diminishing the severity of the loss that every exile entails – be it voluntary or involuntary – Adnan's exile can at the same time be considered an asset. Continually crossing national as well as cultural borders, she has liberated herself from various conventions. Her literary and artistic practices are marked by a highly avant-garde character. They have anticipated developments that have generally come to be described as postmodern and postcolonial. This may explain her popularity and influence among younger generations of writers and artists in particular.

Literary and artistic transgressions

Adnan wrote her early poetry in French. One of her first poems, "The Book of the Sea", confronted her with serious linguistic problems when she undertook a translation into Arabic. The poem examines the relationship between the sea and the sun as a kind of cosmic love affair. Whereas the sea in French is a feminine noun and the sun masculine, thus corresponding to Adnan's depiction of the two as a woman and a warrior, in Arabic it is in fact the other way round. But expressing herself in French has not only caused her linguistic problems. With the Algerian War of Independence (1956–1962) it became a political problem. Like many North African authors, she was repulsed by the idea of writing in the language of the French colonial power. For some time she stopped writing altogether. It is most certainly no coincidence that she turned to visual art, more precisely abstract painting, in which she believed to have discovered a new language that disregards national and cultural borders. Only in the course of the American peace movement triggered by the Vietnam War in the late 1960s and early 1970s did she go back to writing poetry, this time in English. She published numerous poems against the war, for example in Walter Lowenfels' famous anthology *Where is Vietnam? American Poets Respond. An Anthology of Contemporary Poems* (1967). Since then Adnan has written in both French and English, at times translating her own work from one language into the other.

It was with the publication of her long prose poem "Five Senses for One Death" (1971) that Adnan first came to be considered a feminist writer. The poem may be one of the first poems in modern Arabic literature written by a woman poet and addressed to a woman. Her next book of poetry *Jébu suivi de L'Express Beyrouth --> Enfer* (*Jebu followed by Beirut Express --> Hell*, 1973) deals with the Israeli-Palestinian conflict and the growing political crisis in Lebanon, which she foresees turning into a veritable earthquake. In 1977 she published her only novel, the aforementioned *Sitt Marie Rose*. Her following book, *L'Apocalypse Arabe* (*The Arab Apocalypse*, 1980), is again concerned with the political crisis in Lebanon. However, her poetry collections *From A to Z* (1982) and *The Indian Never Had a Horse* (1985) are set in American contexts, the nuclear accident of Three Mile Island and the genocide of the Native Americans respectively. It is clear from these publications that Adnan is not only committed to one region of the world, but addresses crucial issues wherever she is currently at home.

Her poetic essay *Journey to Mount Tamalpais* (1986) brings together philosophical reflections about the relationships between art and nature, featuring diary entries and a selection of Adnan's aquarelles and drawings of Mount Tamalpais in California. This work delineates a notion of home beyond national and cultural borders. Comparable to the significance of Mount Saint-Victoire in Paul Cézanne's life and work, to which Adnan refers explicitly in her essay, in her eyes Mount Tamalpais has ceased to be a mere geographical reference point: it has become spiritual.

> Year after year (...), Tamalpais appeared as a constant point of reference, the way a desert traveller will see an oasis, not only for water, but as the very idea of home. In such cases geographical spots become spiritual concepts.

Wandering between worlds, exile, fragmented identity, and marginality – key terms of postcolonial and postmodern literary theories – are at the center of Adnan's recent texts. In *The Spring Flowers Own & The Manifestations of the Voyage* (1990), the linden tree figures as a symbol of exile, a loss she associates with the cities of Damascus and Beirut, powerfully evoked in the poem "A Return to Earth, a Linden Tree". In *Paris, When It's Naked* (1993), she describes the French capital as "the heart of a lingering colonial power", torn between feelings of repulsion and fascination. In *Of Cities & Women (Letters to Fawwaz)* (1993), she gives testimony of her nomadic lifestyle. The book consists of letters Adnan wrote from different cities while attending book fairs, conferences, or exhibitions: Barcelona, Aix-en-Provence, Skopelos, Murcia, Amsterdam, Berlin, Rome and finally Beirut, where she is overwhelmed by a profound feeling of homecoming. Adnan describes these cities through the streets and alleys she walks in, the houses and museums she enters, and the artists who lived in them, like Paul Cézanne, Pablo Picasso and Antoni Tàpies, but foremost through the women she encounters. In the long prose poem *There: In the Light and the Darkness of the Self and the Other* (1997), she discusses questions of identity and difference. Transgressing borders (external ones, like the borders between nation states, as well as internal ones, like the borders between the self and other), Adnan centers her poetic reflections on the question: "Do I have to have a nationality in order to be human?"

Adnan's literary practices are manifold and cannot easily be subsumed into literary genres. In her view, all literary writing is part of one and the same creative process in which poetry and prose often merge. No matter if written in French or English, translated into Arabic, Italian, German, Dutch, Greek or Urdu, Adnan's literary practices defy the narrowing confines of national literatures. They are part of postmodern and postcolonial tendencies, as described in Western literary theory, as well as of Middle Eastern traditions of cultural mobility, and they are capable of interweaving both aspects in highly innovative ways. They can best be described in terms of an *écriture métissée* or a transnational literature – as elucidated by critics such as Homi K. Bhabha, Gloria Anzaldúa, Françoise Lionnet, Edouard Glissant and Abdelkebir Khatibi – which in transgressing national borders breaks open literary conventions.

The Arab Apocalypse

The Arab Apocalypse is a good example of transnational literature. The typographical arrangement of the text, published in a large and unusual format, is of central importance. It includes blank spaces, words written in capital letters and small, sketch-like images. Placed in the context of European avant-garde literature, *The Arab Apocalypse* brings to mind texts by Stéphane Mallarmé, Ezra Pound and the Dadaist poets, which broke with conventional ways of writing and reading. In the context of modern Arabic literature, however, *The Arab Apocalypse* is rather exceptional; it represents a highly innovative approach.

The typographical arrangement of the text brings to the fore the crisis of language experienced by many authors during the Lebanese civil war, a crisis that can best be expressed in French as *le mal de la page blanche* (the blank page malady). Speechlessness, the shortcomings of trying to grapple with the horror of the civil war verbally: in this work, Adnan seeks to bridge this void visually.

The Arab Apocalypse consists of fifty-nine numbered poems that mirror the fifty-nine days of the siege of Tell al-Zaatar – a Palestinian refugee camp in Beirut whose inhabitants were massacred by Christian militiamen in March 1976. As in Mallarmé's famous poem *Un coup de dés* ("A Throw of the Dice", 1897), the blank spaces in *The Arab Apocalypse* provide places for the reader to halt and create connections in their own mind that narrative continuity would foreclose. Words written in capital letters are reminiscent of telegrams. Used in telegrams to indicate the end of a sentence, the word STOP in *The Arab Apocalypse* is placed within lines of words which are not organized according to syntax. At times, it takes on an imperative meaning – for instance in poem XXXVIII, demanding the end of the sorrow inflicted by the civil war:

> A clear morning of cold rocks lost on an oceanic trail ...
> A lighthouse calls the tide of Palestinians branded with red
> Their guts protrude as umbilical cords
> Savage is the enemy who settles in their eyes STOP O sorrow!

The small, sketch-like images can be compared to the Chinese characters inserted into Pound's *Cantos* (1925–69). As ideograms, the visual images do not represent anything in relation to the written text – for example, visual as opposed to verbal

– but rather emphasize the visual aspect of writing. They are an integral part of the narrative, as becomes clear with the very first lines of poem I:

The images come to replace the adjectives, the color attributes of the sun, and then the noun, the sun itself. The sun in *The Arab Apocalypse* is a divine, powerful, and omnipresent entity. Reminiscent of Adnan's early poems *Le livre de la mer*, it enters into a cosmic love affair with the sea.

A yellow sun a sun ——➤ toward the sea a sun reckless and in love with the sea

The sun dominates the sea as colonial powers dominate the people they subordinate, be they Hopi Indians or Palestinians, both mentioned frequently in the text. But the sun is not only described as a dominant colonial power. It is also referred to as a violent potential in any human being, a potential dramatically manifest in the civil war, as a dead or a dying sun. *The Arab Apocalypse* cannot be reduced to a critique of the colonial past that continues to have an impact in the Middle East today. The oppression described is a double one: originated by colonial and neocolonial powers and passed on to dictatorial regimes and, in the case of Lebanon, militias. It amounts to destruction, violence, suffering and death, without any prospect of change. The outcome is apocalyptic. The only remaining hope is the extinction of the sun, when oppression is finally overcome. The last line of the poem reads: "In the night in the night we shall find knowledge love and peace".

The Arab Apocalypse was written in the highly charged political situation of the Lebanese civil war. However, it has not lost its actuality – especially when read against the background of the current crisis in Iraq. As the Lebanese literary critic Yumna al-'Id writes, the literary texts written during the Lebanese civil war carry within them traces of violence and destruction; nevertheless, their authors have managed to create the beautiful so that we can read its negation, the non-beautiful. What can be read in *The Arab Apocalypse* is anything but beautiful. It is a vision of the Arab Middle East destroyed by colonial and neocolonial powers, repressive regimes, and militias. Nevertheless, it is a beautiful text, owing much of its beauty to the playfulness of its typographical arrangement, which enables a reading that surpasses verbal and visual boundaries.

Adnan's "livres d'artistes"

As a writer and visual artist, Adnan does not limit herself to breaking conventions within the fields of literature and art. She also questions the boundaries between different art forms. This is particularly evident in her *livres d'artistes*. They dismantle the whole notion of a separation between verbal and visual art forms in favor of a "purity" of media, a theory postulated by Clement Greenberg that gained credence in modernist discourses on art. In this sense, Adnan's *livres d'artistes* can be described as "verbo-visual hybrids", a term frequently used to describe postmodern art.

Adnan produced her first *livre d'artiste* in the early 1960s. Inspired by a friend, she started to draw on Japanese folding paper, which at first she used like ordinary sketchbooks. But the new format preoccupied her; it soon reminded her of literature, especially modern Arabic poetry. She started incorporating Arabic script into her drawings. Later on, shattered by the Arab defeat in the June War of 1967, she saw this use of Arabic as a compelling means to reassure herself of her Arab identity. She has since produced more than two hundred *livres d'artistes*, each one a unicum. Although they include works devoted to French and English literature, these do not have the same significance for Adnan as the large majority, which are on Arabic literature. The latter include texts written by famous contemporary authors such as Badr Shakir al-Sayyab, Yusuf al-Khal, Adonis, Mahmoud Darwish and Elias Khoury. In some *livres d'artistes* she has also employed her own poetry translated into Arabic. As she explains, the at times vague knowledge of a text fascinated her. It rendered the text more mysterious.

When closed, the format of the *livre d'artiste* is comparable to a pocketbook; once unfolded, it turns into a concertina, a long, horizontal scroll measuring almost two meters. Like her oil on canvas paintings, her *livres d'artistes* feature abstract drawings: colorful brush strokes interspersed with geometric signs, little squares, triangles, or circles. The Arabic script is clearly legible. However, it reminds one of a child's handwriting, as can be seen in her *livre d'artiste* on Elias Khoury's novel *The Journey of Little Gandhi* (1989). Writing in Arabic turns into drawing and brings back memories of how she used to learn Arabic with her father as a child, copying Arabic sentences for hours on end without really trying to understand their meaning.

Working on her *livres d'artistes* has led Adnan to a new understanding of translation. Translation not only takes place from one verbal language into another but also from verbal into visual language, from one art form into another. Transgressing verbal and visual boundaries, Adnan's *livres d'artistes* transform a literary text into a visual text; rather than representing a finalized translation, it unfurls across meter-long scrolls of paper like an ongoing translation.

Adnan's *livres d'artistes* are of a very personal nature. In most cases, she has given them to the authors of the texts she chose to work on. Some, however, have become part of important public collections such as the British Museum or the Institut du Monde Arabe in Paris. They are viewed in the context of a contemporary art movement in the Middle East that is characterized by the use of Arabic script and known as *al-hurufiyya al-arabiyya* (Arabic letters). While this movement draws inspiration from the tradition of Arabic calligraphy, an essential component of Islamic art, its orientation is nevertheless decidedly contemporary.

Comparable to her literary practices, Adnan's *livres d'artistes* bring together different cultural traditions – the European tradition of the *livre d'artiste* with the Japanese tradition of folding paper and the Arabic-Islamic tradition of calligraphy – and thus break with artistic conventions. "Painting in Arabic", as Adnan puts it, has enabled her to appropriate the "forbidden paradise" of her childhood. Whereas she has rarely been recognized as an Arab or Lebanese author because she does not write in Arabic, with her *livres d'artistes* she has literally re-inscribed her way into the Arab Middle East. They embody a sense of a homecoming for Adnan who has lived all her life in "in-between spaces". "These works," she concludes, "represent to me a coming to terms which I would never have expected until it happened, with the many threads that make up the tapestry of my life. I integrated myself in the cultural destiny of the Arabs by very indirect ways, and I hope that the search is not over."

WORKS

Moonshots, Beirut: Reveil 1966

Five Senses for One Death, New York: The Smiths 1971

Sitt Marie Rose, Paris: des femmes 1977

L'Apocalypse Arabe, Paris: Papyrus 1980

From A to Z, Sausalito: The Post-Apollo Press 1982

Pablo Neruda Is a Banana Tree, Lisbon: De Almeida 1982

The Indian Never Had a Horse & Other Poems, Sausalito: The Post-Apollo Press 1985

Journey to Mount Tamalpais, Sausalito: The Post-Apollo Press 1986

The Spring Flowers Own & The Manifestations of the Voyage, Sausalito: The Post-Apollo Press 1990

Paris, When It's Naked, Sausalito: The Post-Apollo Press 1993

Of Cities and Women (Letters to Fawwaz), Sausalito: The Post-Apollo Press 1993

There. In the Light and the Darkness of the Self and of the Other, Sausalito: The Post-Apollo Press 1997

In the Heart of the Heart of Another Country, San Francisco: City Lights Books 2005

Seasons, Sausalito: The Post-Apollo Press 2008

TRANSLATIONS

Sitt Marie Rose, trans. Georgina Kleege, Sausalito: The Post-Apollo Press 1982

The Arab Apocalypse, trans. Etel Adnan, Sausalito: The Post-Apollo Press 2007 (first edition 1989)

FURTHER READING

Etel Adnan: "Growing up to Be a Woman Writer in Lebanon", (1986) in: Margot Badran, Miriam Cooke (eds.), *Opening the Gates. A Century of Arab Feminist Writing*, London: Virago 1990

Mona Amyuni: "'The Secret of Being a Woman'. On Etel Adnan's Quest", in: *Al Jadid* vol. 4 (1998) no. 25, pp. 30–1

Mona Takeddine Amyuni: "Etel Adnan & Hoda Barakat. De-Centered Perspectives –Subversive Voices", in: Andreas Pflitsch, Barbara Winckler (eds.), *Poetry's Voice – Society's Norms. Forms of Interaction between Middle Eastern Writers and their Societies*, Wiesbaden: Reichert 2006, pp. 211–21

Thomas Foster: "Circles of Oppression, Circles of Repression. Etel Adnan's *Sitt Marie Rose*", in: *PMLA* 110 (1995) no. 1, pp. 59–74

Lisa Suhair Majaj, Amal Amireh (eds.): *Etel Adnan. Critical Essays on the Arab-American Writer and Artist*. Jefferson: McFarland & Company 2002

Lisa Suhair Majaj: "Voice, Representation, and Resistance. Etel Adnan's *Sitt Marie Rose*", in: Lisa Suhair Majaj, Paula W. Sunderman, Therese Saliba (eds.), *Intersections. Gender, Nation, and Community in Arab Women's Novels*, New York: Syracuse, 2002, pp. 200–30

Sonja Mejcher-Atassi: "Re-inscribing Oneself into the Middle East. Etel Adnan and her livres d'artistes in the Context of *al-hurufiyya al-'arabiyya*", in: *Beiruter Blätter* 10/11 (2004), pp. 90–95

Sonja Mejcher-Atassi: "Breaking the Silence. Etel Adnan's *Sitt Marie Rose* and *The Arab Apocalypse*", in: Andreas Pflitsch, Barbara Winckler (eds.), *Poetry's Voice, Society's Norms. Forms of Interaction between Middle Eastern Writers and their Societies*, Wiesbaden: Reichert 2006, pp. 201–10

OTHER WORKS CITED

Homi K. Bhabha: *The Location of Culture*, London, New York: Routledge 1994

Elias Khoury: *Rihlat Ghandi al-saghir*, Beirut: Dar al-Adab 1989 (English translation: *The Journey of Little Gandhi*, trans. Paula Haydar, Minneapolis, London: University of Minnesota Press 1994)

Walter Lowenfels (ed.): *Where is Vietnam? American Poets Respond*, Garden City, NY: Anchor Books 1967

"So we are called Lebanese"
Rabih Alameddine on the Unbearable Lightness of Being Nowhere at Home

Andreas Pflitsch

Survival of the fittest

Identity and a sense of belonging are proving less and less self-evident. "In America, I fit, but I do not belong. In Lebanon, I belong but I do not fit." This is the succinct and laconic tone of one of the vast array of narrators in Rabih Alameddine's debut novel *Koolaids. The Art of War* when putting his in-between position in a nutshell. Conventionally regarded and accepted as a given, the sense of belonging attached to the idea of one's homeland or native country is increasingly turning into a problem which needs to be confronted and reflected upon; indeed, it can escalate into the dominant fixed point of an *ex-centric* diaspora identity. In his novels and stories Alameddine shows what opening this Pandora's Box means.

The author himself was born in 1959 to Lebanese Druze parents in Jordan, grew up in Kuwait, Lebanon and England, and lives today as a painter and writer in San Francisco and Beirut. Published in 1998, his novel *Koolaids* is a multi-perspectival collage without a plot; a text that in its condensed, almost aphoristic pointedness interlinks fiction and documentation. "Death comes in many shapes and sizes, but it always comes", is the opening sentence, which then runs like a refrain throughout the novel. The AIDS epidemic in America and the civil war in Lebanon merge, as *Publisher's Weekly* put it, into a "graphic portrait of two cultures torn from the inside." Perhaps the most apt characterization of the novel, which despite its tragic, bleak subject matter sparkles with wit, is to be found in the text itself: "I wanted to write an endless book of time", states one of the several self-referential passages of the book, where the author becomes the narrator and the narrator the author – and where a placement in the literary tradition is offered as a suggestion while simultaneously rupturing the historical lineage, thus leaving it in abeyance:

> It would have no beginning and no end. It would not flow in order. The tenses would make no sense. A book whose first page is almost identical to the last, and all the pages in between are jumbled with an interminable story. A book that would make both Kant and Jung proud. – I was not able to do it. I would have been copying the master. Borges did it before me.

From Jorge Luis Borges (1899–1986) this narrator has also learnt to call into question what is generally considered to be historical truth: "Cervantes told me history is the mother of truth. Borges told me historical truth is not what took place; it is what we think took place." Mistrusting history and historical writing is unsurprising for Lebanon in particular, where up to the present day a "national history" accepted by all of the country's confessional and ethnic communities has yet to gain a foothold. It is precisely for this reason that the narrator can claim: "Rewriting history is a passion for most Lebanese."

Accordingly, the narrator propounds a number of theses in cavalier fashion which, as proof of a motley cocktail of ideological delusion, cliché-laden prejudice, and bitter truth, underline the view that reality sometimes offers fictions more fantastic than anything the imagination could come up with:

> So Billy Shakespeare was queer.
> Ronnie was the greatest president in history, right up there on Mount Rushmore.
> AIDS is mankind's greatest plague.
> Israel only kills terrorists.
> America never bombed Lebanon.
> Jesus was straight. Judas and he were just friends.
> Roseanne's parents molested her as an infant.
> Menachim Begin and Yasser Arafat deserved their Nobels.
> And Gaetan Dugas started the AIDS epidemic.

Alameddine's novel, wrote Amy Tan in a review,

> is the companion guide to The Tibetan Book of the Dead, The Diary of Anne Frank, and the history of the world. It is hysterical in both senses, hilarious and loudly disturbing. (Where else does Krishnamurti meet Eleanor Roosevelt and Tom Cruise?). Like Zen koans, Koolaids issues pronouncements while pointing out the absurdities of any kind of truth. It contemplates the meaning of death while redefining the meaninglessness of life. It looks at the great cycle of history, destiny, and literature and puts them on spin and recycle. This is an absolutely brilliant book – daring in its somersault of literary feasts and allusions, an antidote for anyone who suffers from the blahs or an excess of self-satisfaction.

The gates usually keeping normality and madness, reason and the phantasmal neatly apart are sprung wide open. Reason is only useful, so we read, "to mummify reality in moments of calm or analyze its future storms, never to resolve a crisis of the moment." In contrast, delusional madness, ostensibly ignoring factual evidence, is more attuned to reality in its confusing plurality than any form of realism: "I wonder if being sane means disregarding the chaos that is life, pretending only an infinitesimal segment of it is reality."

In *Koolaids* the catastrophic challenges presented by the spread of the AIDS virus and the civil war that raged in Lebanon for fifteen years, so different and yet similar in their deadly menace, are repeatedly paralleled; for instance, when one of the protagonists crosses out the telephone numbers of friends in his address book who have died of AIDS. This reminds his mother of what she once did. She writes in her diary: "In the eighties, I would go through my phone book every year. So many friends died, so many simply moved away, emigrated. The war took a terrible toll." In another diary entry we read:

> *March 20th, 1976*
> Dear Diary,
> This day is without a doubt the worst day of my life. The shelling was
> getting closer to our apartment.

Just a few pages on we read how she is affected, twelve and a half years later, by the news of her son's fatal illness, a delayed echo of the "worst day" of her life:

> *September 5th, 1988*
> Dear Diary,
> Today is without doubt the worst day of my life. Samir told me he has the
> AIDS virus.

There is a third parallel passage:

> *July 4th, 1967*
> Dear Diary,
> This is without a doubt the worst day of my life. It looks like we have to go
> back to Beirut. My husband can't take it here in Washington anymore.

The date of the diary entry represents the overlapping of American and Lebanese situations and events which runs throughout the novel: July 4th is Independence Day in the United States, while 1967 marks the catastrophic defeat suffered by the Arab states at the hands of Israel.

When the "good old days" are talked about, the reader is never quite sure whether Lebanon prior to the outbreak of war is meant, or life prior to the AIDS is being recalled. "The good old days": that was the time of promiscuity, when men enjoyed life to the full in the gay subculture without having to fear fatal consequences; a carefree hedonistic time about which the narrator only knows through hearsay, for he suffers under the merciless dictate of having been born too late: "I did not really know the good old days. People started dying when I came out." "The good old days" were also those when one could move around freely in Beirut, without having to risk life and limb: "No Israeli planes, no Syrian tanks, no shelling waking you up at night." Our narrator, though, is always too late: "I did not really know the good old days. I was too young when the war started." War and AIDS, those two catastrophes, merge in the figure of US President Ronald Reagan, joined together by his blanket ignorance of both: "Lebanon, like AIDS, was hardly ever mentioned by our president."

Home sweet home? A self-accusation

The definitions of Lebanon and the Lebanese that the narrator in Alameddine's novel tries to give are extremely laconic and thus, despite the grand words of pathos, restrained and comparatively emotionless:

> Lebanon is a piece of land (not a piece of heaven at all – you only have to be in Beirut in the summer) but it's *our* land, *our home* (even if we are not actually living there). It's our Sweet Home and we *love* it. So we are called Lebanese.

But "being Lebanese" in a foreign country is not as uncomplicated as the narrator asserts here, particularly when this foreign country is gradually becoming more familiar and proving more normal than "home", which seems ever more alien and distant. Inner conflicts can mushroom into a veritable schizophrenia, which brings forth aggression and remains dissatisfied and unsatisfied in both directions. One character claims that the "happiest day in my life" was when he received American citizenship and could finally rip up his Lebanese passport: "That was great. Then I got to hate Americans. And I really do." To finally belong officially to the second homeland does not prove to be fulfilling, because "America is the birthplace of *Wheel of Fortune* and I will never forgive it for that." Identity can turn out to be a prison, a heavy burden, and the effort to cast it off can become the task of a lifetime, an obsession pursued passionately and full of suffering. National clichés and cultural stereotypes beset and besiege Alameddine's narrator until he begins to lash out verbally and breathlessly stutters:

> Something English. That's what I want. I am too tired of America and the Americans. Still they are better than the French. I hate the French, probably more than I hate Americans. Such arrogant bastards. (...) But they are better than the Lebanese. The Lebanese are just arrogant. I fucking hate the Lebanese. I hate them. They are so fucked up. They think they are so great, and for what reason? Has there been a single artist of note? A scientist, an athlete? They

are so proud of Gibran. Probably the most overrated writer in history. I don't think any Lebanese has ever read him.

This swipe against all and sundry shows that our hero has difficulties embracing not only his new American identity but also his Lebanese roots, which he despairingly and vainly tries to shed. Running away proves to be pointless, impossible, and at times even counterproductive, when his attempt to extricate himself from this grip at all costs turns out to pull the chains even tighter:

> I tried hard to rid myself of anything Lebanese. I hate everything Lebanese. But I never could. It seeps through my entire being. The harder I tried, the more it showed up in the unlikeliest of places. But I never gave up. I do not want to be considered a Lebanese. But that is not up to me (...) Nothing in my life is up to me.

Homeland as utopia

A year after his debut, Alameddine published a collection of stories under the title *The Perv* (1999), while his second novel *I, the Divine. A Novel in First Chapters* followed in 2002. The "novel" does indeed comprise of forty-three "first" chapters. Sarah Nour el-Din, the Lebanese-American protagonist, tries to write her memoirs. She was named after the actress Sarah Bernhardt, also known as "the divine Sarah", who her grandfather adored so gushingly that he regarded having once met her personally as the most important event in his life. Again and again Sarah Nour el-Din begins the first chapter of her memoirs. She tries out different stylistic levels; changes the tone of voice; employs the first person, then the third person; experiments with dialogues, then with detailed descriptions of landscapes or impressions of cities; even using different languages: two "first" chapters are written in French. Some chapters are just a few lines in length while others stretch over ten, twenty, or more pages. The author also employs "fictionalized" paratexts like title pages and dedications.

In the forty-third "first" chapter, the last in Alameddine's book, Sarah sits in front of the television, eating ice cream, and remarks: "I was having trouble writing my memoir, not being able to figure out how to attack it. I had tried different methods, but the memoir parried back expertly." In this self-referential passage, typical of Alameddine, the narrator contradicts herself, being right and wrong at the same time: she has failed to write down the story of her life but taken together, the failed attempts to write her memoir yield nothing other than her memoirs.

What at first glance looks like little more than a nice and witty idea, a "structural gimmick" as *Publisher's Weekly* put it, in fact turns out to be an intricate and

effective plot device that enables the author to depict Sarah's life in all its diversity
and turmoil, with its conflicts and ruptures, and to write a biography in fragments,
which, although running contrary to the conventional chronological trajectory,
is consequential and consistent in a way that traditionally related life stories
can hardly achieve. For Amy Tan, the novel's structure and composition reveal
a "literary genius" and are "perfect to the notion of someone reinventing and
revising herself." While learning to see herself in a new light, reinventing herself
and repeatedly attempting to write down what she sees and believes she knows,
Sarah, like most of the male protagonists in *Koolaids*, thinks continually about
identity, belonging somewhere and home. "Whenever she is in Beirut", we are told,
"home is New York. Whenever she is in New York, home is Beirut. Home is never
where she is, but where she is not." Home and a sense of belonging somewhere
prove paradoxically to imply not the place where one is, but the place one yearns
for. Sarah is therefore defining "home" as a *non-place*, as a *utopia*, which first gains
specific value and meaning through being imagined. As imagination and a blank
space, such a "home" is more concrete than reality ever could be.

Similar thoughts overcome André Aciman while following the footsteps of
Marcel Proust and exploring one of the key settings of his *In Search of Lost Time*.
He wanders around Illier-Combray:

> How could Marcel have ever loved such a place? Or had he never loved it?
> Had he loved only the act of returning to it on paper, because that was how
> he lived his life – first by wanting to live it, and later by remembering having
> wanted to, and ultimately by writing about the two? The part in between –
> the actual living – was what had been lost.

True life takes place in literature; reality regains itself in art.

Sarah Nour el-Din's foremost concern is with her arrival in New York, where
she becomes familiar with loneliness as the other side of the glittering coin of
freedom, described in a "first" chapter titled "Here and There":

> She feels alone, experiences the solitude of a strange city where no one looks
> you straight in the eye. She does not feel part of this cool world, free for the first
> time. But at what price? How can she tell the difference between freedom and
> unburdening? Is freedom anything more than ignoring responsibilities, than
> denying duty? (...) In New York, she can disappear. What is the purpose of a city
> if not to grant the greatest of all gifts, anonymity? Beirut offered no refuge from
> unwavering gazes, no respite from pernicious tongues. But her heart remains
> there. To survive here, she must hack off a part of herself, chop, chop, chop.

Home *and* homelessness are always ambivalent in Alameddine's work. Any loss entails a gain, while an enchantment inheres to each farewell, along with a dread. Sarah suffers a lot because of her situation:

> I have been blessed with many curses in my life, not the least of which was being born half Lebanese and half American. Throughout my life, these contradictory parts battled endlessly, clashed, never coming to a satisfactory conclusion. I shuffled ad nauseam between the need to assert my individuality and the need to belong to my clan, being terrified of loneliness and terrorized of losing myself in relationships. I was the black sheep of my family, yet an essential part of it.

This desperate, strained will to settle into American life, already encountered in *Koolaids*, takes hold of Sarah and finds expression in her split feelings about *the* icon of Arab pop music, the Egyptian singer Umm Kulthum:

> I hated Umm Kulthum. I wanted to identify with only my American half. I wanted to be special. I could not envision how to be Lebanese and keep any sense of individuality. Lebanese culture was all consuming. Only recently have I begun to realize that like my city, my American patina covers an Arab soul. These days I avoid Umm Kulthum, but not because I hate her. I avoid her because every time I hear that Egyptian bitch, I cry hysterically.

But where his protagonists are forced to mull on the instability of an identity between cultures – a lack of home, belonging or normality – the author himself sees advantages in this kind of clash between cultures, which is capable of sparking creative energy. Not belonging and assuming the position of an outsider is for him a pivotal condition for every form of art.

Transcendental homelessness

In his *Theory of the Novel*, published in 1920, Georg Lukács affirmed the claim made by the German Romantics, who had drawn "a close connection" between the concepts of the novel and the Romantic, for, as he formulated it, "the novel form is, like no other, an expression of transcendental homelessness." Here Lukács takes up the prototypical Romantic position of Novalis, for whom astonishment was not the incitement to philosophy but the anxiety felt when confronted with the strange: "Philosophy is really homesickness," quotes Lukács, "it is the urge to be at home everywhere."

Besides this general disposition, which points out that the feeling of being caught in a stymie demands an attempt to deal with it in art and thought, for authors like Alameddine, who live and write between cultures, more tangible questions emerge on the very constitution of culture. Biographies not tied to one place; literary works that do not originate from one (linguistic) community alone are characterized by processes of transition, overlapping and fluctuation: these essential qualities mean that they fall through the gaps of conventionally employed concepts that still divide the history of literature into national categories and thus necessarily overlook the peculiarities of such transnational literature. Only the attempt to reverse the perspective and grasp the normal and normalized as the exception, and conversely deal with deviation as the rule, can enable us to take cultural hybridity and syncretic creativity seriously, understanding them in terms of their own premises. As it turns out, the outsider position occupied by authors like Alameddine should be seen as an advantage, not as a deficit or disadvantage.

What Lebanon?

Since its beginnings, attempts to define and characterize modern Lebanese literature as a national literature have demanded caveats due to its multilingualism, the role played by migrant literature in North and South America, and the lack of agreement on who and what even constitutes the Lebanese nation. The Lebanese diaspora greatly outnumbers the Lebanese living in Lebanon itself. Up until the present day, the greater part of Lebanese literature has been written and published beyond the linguistic and geographical boundaries of the nation. Authors like Elias Abou-Haidar, Dominique Eddé, Hani Hammoud, Tony Hanania, Sélim Nassib and Elie-Pierre Sabbag live in Morocco, England and France, and write in English or French. This phenomenon is not limited to literature written in French and English; authors like Hanan al-Shaykh and Hoda Barakat write in Arabic while living in London and Paris respectively. Switching languages is not infrequent. After producing three novels in Arabic, Najwa Barakat wrote one in French, while the painter and author Etel Adnan, who divides her time between the US, Paris and Beirut, writes in both English and French.

The concept of home is a pivotal theme of this literature, as is indicated in the titles alone; for instance Nada Awar Jarrar's *Somewhere, Home* (2003) or Tony Hanania's *Homesick* (1997). Home, for the protagonist in Nada Awar Jarrar's novel, is somewhere where no road continues on, and hence signifies arrival, but this also inevitably indicates stasis and end. There, where no road continues on, one makes oneself at home and adjusts. Return seems impossible; one does not wade in the same river twice; and those who, feeling estranged from the second homeland, wish to return to the first unexpectedly find themselves foreigners in a land that to them had always been known as "home".

"Home" is passed from generation to generation and does not remain unscathed in this process, as the Brazilian author Milton Hatoum, son of Lebanese migrants, forcefully testifies in his novels. When Yacub, one of the heroes referred to in the title of Hatoum's second novel *Dois irmãos* (*Two Brothers*), is asked by Talib during a family dinner if he misses Lebanon, he turns pale, pauses, and replies: "What Lebanon?" Talib's answer highlights the subjective foundation upon which identity is experienced: "As far as I know, there's only one Lebanon", he replies defiantly to the question he obviously feels to be a provocation, before continuing, "or rather there are many, and one of them lies here inside." He then points to his heart.

Literature, mobile

To describe literature of the type presented here, which for all its differences revolves around a similar theme, the concepts available to analyze cultural identity need a critical overhaul and distinctions drawn between multi-, inter- and transcultural approaches. As Ottmar Ette, an expert in Romance literatures, writes, "*multi*cultural coexistence and *inter*cultural mingling has been joined by – and I mean in this in a positive sense – a *trans*cultural tangle in which different cultures reciprocally permeate and change one another." Whereas the first two concepts of this triad mark an exception, continuing to take rigid cultural unities defined nationally – or at times religiously – as their contrastive rule, the concept of transcultural identity assumes fluent borders, with overlapping and continuous fluctuation.

The evidence – not least in the literature of authors like Alameddine – suggests that the burden of proof as to what is the rule and what the exception has long been overturned: the ideal of a collective cultural identity, distinctly separate from and coexisting alongside others, which continues to be asserted by the prevailing conceptions, simply does not exist. Instead, there is only what we might term "individual mixing ratios". Today, it can no longer be the task of analysis to separate the individual components of this mixture by identifying the relative share of patterns and themes influenced by one culture, as if listing the ingredients of a recipe. Identity is more than the sum of its parts. To defend its unique complexity against simplistic discourses is becoming an increasingly important task of literature. With his novels and stories Rabih Alameddine has stepped into the breach.

WORKS

Koolaids. The Art of War, New York: Picador 1998
The Perv. Stories, New York: Picador 1999
I, The Divine. A Novel in First Chapters, New York: W.W. Norton 2001

The Hakawati, New York: Alfred A. Knopf 2008

FURTHER READING

Kieron Devlin: "A Conversation with Rabih Alameddine", in: *Mississippi Review*, http://www.mississippireview.com/2002/leilani-devlin-alameddine.html

Syrine C. Hout: "Of Fathers and the Fatherland in the Post-1995 Lebanese Exilic Novel", in: *World Literature Today* 75,2 (2001), pp. 285–93

Andreas Pflitsch: "'Peter Gabriel left Genesis in the summer of 1975'. Rabih Alameddine über unterschiedliche Unterschiede", in: *Figurationen. Gender, Literatur, Kultur* 6, 1 (2005), pp. 13–22

OTHER WORKS CITED

André Aciman: *False Papers. Essays on Exile and Memory*, New York: Farrar, Straus & Giroux 2000

Nada Awar Jarrar: *Somewhere, Home*, London: Heinemann 2003

Ottmar Ette: *Literatur in Bewegung. Raum und Dynamik grenzüberschreitenden Schreibens in Europa und Amerika*, Weilerswist: Velbrück Wissenschaft 2001

Tony Hanania: *Homesick*, London: Bloomsbury 1997

Milton Hatoum: *Dois irmãos*, São Paulo: Companhia das Letras 2000

Georg Lukács: *Die Theorie des Romans*, Berlin: Cassirer 1920

The Desert as Homeland and Metaphor
Reflections on the Novels of the
Tuareg Writer Ibrahim al-Koni

Hartmut Fähndrich

The desert is life, life is a desert. Or to put it differently: "the desert is God's home", or "the desert is a paradise of nothingness" and "we go into the desert in order to quench our thirst for freedom."

One could easily continue to present aphorisms coined by Ibrahim al-Koni about the desert, about the space that is the concrete and symbolic background of his writing. In al-Koni's desert everything is symbolic, impregnated by myth. Every plant and every animal, every grain of sand and every rock points beyond itself. Even stones are not without significance as this would mean they would be without myth, nor the shifting sand dunes, nor the vastness and the emptiness. For not even for the briefest of moments does he allow his readers to forget that sand and stone, mountain and plain, gazelle and moufflon, acacia tree and retem bush, wind and sun, well and wadi; that all this is certainly the reality of the desert but that at the same time, they invite us to ponder the universe and human existence.

In line with publishing habits, the first two novels by Ibrahim al-Koni translated into German were given the subheading "Novel from Libya". The author intervened, asking for a modification. His argument was that political Libya, the modern nation-state, is not the essential origin of his literary work. The desert is his decisive influence. And so the following novels are characterized as "Novel from the Sahara".

Virtually all of al-Koni's novels and short stories published so far are set in this desert, the Sahara, which encompasses some 3,320,000 square miles and is the largest desert on earth. His essays and collections of aphorisms are also primarily rooted in this landscape, drawing their objects and themes, their wisdom and ideas from there. "Heaven is the desert up there. The desert is heaven down here," claims one of his aphorisms. Or to quote another: "The desert is the home of the soul and exile for the body." This vast desert stretches out in front of every human being, "bleak as transience". And like the silence reigning over it, the bleakness of the desert is of legendary origin. In his novel *The Magus* the author puts it as follows:

> There is the stillness of the desert – the language of complete isolation, the
> sanctuary of infinity, the ballad of melancholic eternity. In the heights of the

Hamada desert, this stillness rumbles with an astonishing clamor, like the howl of whistling winds. Some days it plays songs, like melodies plucked on the amzad. In the deep sandy reaches, the stillness beats its drums at night, while the old men crane their necks to listen, hearing the conversations of distant ancestors and their advice to vanished generations.

Legend has it that the Creator emptied the world, clearing it of all life so that people would be alone. Thus, he made the great Sahara. He created man and the stillness of the desert was pleasing to Him, so He blessed it and set in its heart the oasis of Waw and then, when he had done so, breathed a sigh of relief. This divine sigh can still be heard in the silence of the wastes, and the sands that pulse like songs in the empty space are His divine breaths. Listening to the stillness became a form of worship, yet only old people, only those who have tasted this stillness, can fathom the secrets of its language. (trans. Elliott Colla)

The Sahara, Ibrahim al-Koni's literary space

Ibrahim al-Koni's real desert is situated in the southwestern region of what today is Libya, where this states borders on Algeria and Niger. But political borders of this kind do not play a role in his work. His world consists of the regions prior to the imposition of national borders: Asjirr, Tadrart, Hammada; or, somewhat further away, Tassili, Ahaggar, Air, Adrar ... This is a world without borders and therefore limitless, the world where the Tuareg are at home. The Tuareg are a Berber people numbering between one and one and a half million, who populate the western Central Sahara and the Sahel belt running along its southern tip; from Touat to Lake Chad, from Timbuktu to Ghadames. Divided by national borders, today the Tuareg people live in different countries, the majority – about half a million respectively – in Mali and Niger.

Ibrahim al-Koni was born in 1948 in Ghadames Oasis at the edge of the Red Hammâda. Wandering with animals and life in a tent are the memories of his childhood, the region there in the southwest corner of Libya its space. He first learnt Arabic, the language in which he expresses himself artistically, at the age of eleven; his stylistic command of this language has gained widespread praise from Arab literary critics.

At the age of twenty, al-Koni left his homeland and went to Russia, at that time the Soviet Union, to study literature at the famous Maxim Gorky Institute in Moscow. This explains the obvious influence on his writing of Russian literature, especially Dostoyevsky. After completing his studies al-Koni worked for two decades at the Libyan Cultural Institute in both Moscow and Warsaw until in 1993 he moved to Switzerland, not as a refugee but as a voluntary expatriate, who has described the advantage of living abroad in exile, no matter what the circumstances, as follows:

> From the ancients stems the advice that whosoever wants to succeed in philosophy has to leave his homeland and live somewhere else. The exile, so the argument runs, ignites the flame of homesickness and, thus, stimulates philosophical thought. No doubt, this can also be applied to literary creativity. For the feeling of loss and being lost is stimulating and creative as someone in any kind of exile stops living in a particular space. He does no longer live in a specific environment that would deprive a person of himself, that drives him to dissipate himself and to fill himself with trivialities. The exile turns inward, occupies himself with his soul and gives testimony of the great changes inside himself. Thus, his homeland assumes a different value and the world receives another face. The distance between the exile and his topic shrinks and he discovers that the external distance has not estranged him from his homeland but has, in fact, brought him closer to it. And what he deemed exile and loss has, in reality, turned out to be nothing but a journey to his inner self unknown to him before this change. Finally, he will understand the necessity of being without a determined path as he learns that losing himself is nothing to be ashamed of for anybody searching for his soul must have lost it first. The experience of being alienated is a completely spiritual one, and any true homeland is rooted in the soul.

The heritage of the Tuareg

In spite of his distance from his origins, the life of the Tuareg has remained the major topic of al-Koni's works. Living abroad has only provided him with the opportunity to acquire and then develop the literary techniques he needed to depict this world adequately. He has called it his self-imposed task to represent the thoughts and feelings of the Tuareg and preserve this for posterity, to hand down their myths and their tales; and he is acutely aware that it is high time to document what once was, for the traditional nomadic way of life of the Tuareg is doomed to disappear. For this reason he regards his work as something quite unique. Asked in which tradition he sees himself, al-Koni once answered:

> I do not really know the meaning of tradition for an author who set out to create one. We are talking here about a world in which there is no novelistic tradition whatsoever. Not only in Libya but in North Africa in general, which, by nature and culture, is a prolongation of the Sahara. Leaving aside oral culture, I dare take the adventure to lay the foundation of a culture of the "novel of the desert" that is not only new for the world but also for Arabic literature. Europeans often think Arabs would write desert-literature simply

because they live at the edge of the desert. In fact, Arab culture has all through history never created anything like a "literature of the desert novel". With the exception of Abdelrahman Munif's pentalogy *Cities of Salt* the desert has remained to date an untouched area. I know quite well the dangers for someone willing to take such a burden upon his shoulders. But now, the desert has begun to talk, after a silence that started with creation when the desert became the desert. But then, I do not want to diminish the merits of oral literature for the myths of the Tuareg.

In his works al-Koni thus describes the life of the Tuareg, or should we say their heritage? For as he has said elsewhere, by the time his literary work becomes known through translation the living culture and way of life of the Tuareg will have vanished. This is why he calls his efforts to present their life, thoughts and feelings, and to preserve it for posterity a "mission", his legacy.

But not only geographical space is boundless in his work. Dividing lines of any kind are absent. The distinction between reality and unreality lapses, so too that between the visible and the invisible – even the distinction between humans and animals is partly blurred. This is particularly true for the two animals most frequently found in Ibrahim al-Koni's work: the gazelle and the moufflon, two animals that once populated the vast realms of the desert but whose numbers in the wild have declined greatly, a process drastically depicted in the novel *Nazif al-hajar* (*The Bleeding of the Stone*, 1990).

The gazelle and the moufflon are animals that had a special relationship to humans. In the desert setting, both are symbols of a particular way of life. The gazelle is the animal of the plain, shy and slender; in its often tear-filled eyes there is a deeply sad look that fascinates humans and reminds them of the never-ending pain of life. In contrast, the moufflon is the animal of the mountain range, its body broad-shouldered at the front and tapering at the rear, with powerful, curved horns; according to mythology an animal occasionally inhabited by persons who have gone missing, visible only in the animal's gaze, which tells of their fate. The moufflon, it is said, has saved the life of many a human, and so entered a protective pact with mankind –woe betide anybody who dares to break the pact and attacks the moufflon.

Then there is a third animal, the snake; in Jewish, Christian, and Muslim traditions the primordial enemy of man, always ready to lead him into temptation, to deceive, and even to kill; the snake, which is only harmless once its head has been severed from its body. And of course there is the camel, able to become man's best friend, as depicted in the novel *al-Tibr* (*Gold Dust*, 1990). A deep conviction as to the unity of the universe underpins Ibrahim al-Koni's oeuvre, and any violation of this unity is presented as a grave crime.

The author considers all this to be part of the legacy of the Tuareg, who are presented in all his novels as symbolic of humanity or man. Taking their life as an example, he explores the basic questions of earthly existence: love; death and immortality; order and tradition; commitment and freedom; movement and stasis. For this purpose al-Koni calls on metaphor, which he has characterized as a "miracle":

> It is with the Metaphor that the real history of creative writing began. It is with the Metaphor that the transformation of the world into a symbol began. With the Metaphor began the activity of solemn veiling, of making of human existence metaphorical material expelled from its visible homeland. And with the Metaphor can be achieved the actualization and the grasping of the world outside existence.
>
> This quite miraculous procedure is, in Ortega y Gasset's words, like an instrument forgotten by the creator inside his creature at the moment of creation, the way a surgeon might forget one of his utensils inside his patient. The Metaphor was given the quality of suggestion, comparable to what Muslim Sufis see in the 'sign' (âya), it took, indeed, the role of the magicians' stone of wisdom, as it is capable of changing things not only in their external appearance but in their essence.
>
> It is the aim of the metaphor in art to grasp the world in its real, its religious being.

The desert as human destiny

In mystical traditions the desert is often used as a metaphor for the world, while crossing it is seen as a symbol of man's path through life. Life is movement, wandering. In contrast, staying somewhere or settling down is the beginning of the end. Nomadic existence is the epitome of human existence. Any kind of stasis or sedentary life is tantamount to stagnation, because it intimates a loss of longing. However, as al-Koni formulates it in his magnum opus *The Magus*, longing is

> the most essential fate of the desert dweller. It is his double sense of belonging that made it so. Ever since the day his divine spirit separated him from his mother earth by breathing life into his clay mass, he had been made to suffer a double exile. On the one hand, he had been expelled from Paradise, and separated from God. On the other, he had alighted on earth, though never become one with the desert – never grasped its expanse, its barrenness, its freedom. He had come to be, a handful of clay, before reaching the other, greater and more merciful source – the desert. The creature remained suspended between Heaven and Earth: his body seeking to return to its point

of origin – the desert; his soul longing, pining, to free itself from its earthly cage and fly toward its heavenly source.

From here arises the plight of the desert dweller – the tension between the heavenly and earthly aspects of his being. Whenever he makes camp for a few days in the desert, he hears the obscure call to pack up his tent, to take up his load, and set off on a journey – the long journey to himself, to his divine source, to God. Whenever travel drags on, and his soul flies to the wind, his body then protests and his heart begins to bleed with longing for his homeland – for his mother, for Earth. Then the call of the world goes up, and his mother insists on taking her share of her lost son. A desert dweller's entire life is a struggle between Heaven and Earth, father and mother, each claiming the larger share of the son they share in common. His mother says she gave him a body, consciousness, and that without her, Adam never would have existed. The father reasons that the other part, the inner, spiritual part, is what gives the lump of clay its worth, and what injected life into his speck, and that without that, man would have remained a useless slab of clay. This double sense of belonging was not of man's making, yet from it sprang forth his entire struggle and thus misery. The two forces pull on him and split him in two. He suffers, but has neither the right to protest, nor the right to curse the cruelty of his destiny.

(trans. Elliot Colla)

The tribe that stays for too long in one place and thus indulges in comfort, the vice of sedentary life, will inevitably perish. This is in essence the story told in the novel *The Magus*, set in the shadow of the Idenân mountain range not far from the town of Ghat, where the djinns dwell.

There the age-old struggle unfolds once more: the struggle between the nomadic and the sedentary; between roaming herdsmen and farmers; between Romulus and Remus; between Cain and Abel; between being on the move, which means living, and resting, which means gathering rust. Neither of the two groups emerges victorious. The struggle is attritional and the groups wear each other down. The only victors are the djinns, the spirits mentioned in the Qur'an made of smokeless flames, who appear to humans in alternating guises. The Idenân mountain range has provided them with shelter and in return they protect the summit from the south wind, without which the same fate would befall the Idenân as its companions further south, where the rocky peaks have been eroded away by wind and sand.

"Before him stretched the desert, vast and bleak as transience." This is the last sentence of the novel. At the same time, these words point to the beginning of a new life and the resumption of the wandering that is life across the emptiness that is the world.

The history of a desert town

In such a gaping emptiness there is, of course, no town. There are not even solid dwellings, since a life on the move has no need of permanent shelters, and a protective roof would only induce man to deviate from his determined "straight path". Each and every place made of mud and stone becomes the object of dreams and desires on the one hand, and vituperation and fears on the other. In any case, such constructions would be places for a life completely different from the life of desert nomads – for Ibrahim al-Koni the true life.

But *The Magus* is first and foremost a novel about a town! At the end of the novel there is no longer any town. What still exists are some remnants, a few ruins of the town that once stood there and has disappeared. Under these circumstances two survivors return to their true life, to their destiny: the crossing of the desert. They are an old man and a young woman, an almost mythical couple reminiscent of Biblical characters such as Abraham and Hagar.

The Magus opens in an age when a town is yet to be founded in the part of the desert where most of the events in the novel take place; it ends, as mentioned, at a point in time when there is no longer any town. In between there are eight hundred pages which tell the story of a town, or rather the biography of a town. The town is called Wâw, a name used by Ibrahim al-Koni in several of his works, and indeed in the title of *The Smaller Waw* (1997). There, as in *The Magus*, Wâw is given a real existence in the middle of the desert. Mostly however, it does not possess an existence, for Wâw is a space between imagination and reality, between heaven and earth, between this world and longing. The discussion about the actual existence and the character of this town as well as the human search for it is one of the central themes that Ibrahim al-Koni broaches in his work, not only in *The Magus*.

The original Wâw is called the "Large Wâw". It is, of course, Paradise, which through the sin committed by the first humans and their subsequent expulsion has become paradise lost. It is at this point that al-Koni's characters, the desert dwellers, begin to long for and wonder about Wâw and the possibilities of regaining this paradise. So the dream of Wâw begins, and along with it the fantasies about what it is like.

Wâw is lost and it is precisely for this reason that it has metamorphosed into a dream in the human imagination, an object of hope and desire. It has become a place of refuge, a place of salvation, the home of bliss and the goal of longing. Many a person doomed to death in the endless desert has had this experience. Just before dying of thirst, long after having given up hope, there appeared before them Wâw, opening its doors and saving them from imminent perdition. But like Paradise, Wâw is invisible, unreachable; any attempt to find it, construct it or recreate it in this world is nothing other than hubris. It is exactly this attempt that is the central topic in *The Magus*: the development and history of a fixed settlement, a town; its founding, rise and flourishing; its attraction for and influence over the people living in its vicinity in the desert, no matter whether they wish to live in this town or refuse even to come near it.

At the beginning of the novel a group of people arrives from Timbuktu. They wish to settle in the area near a well where a tribe is camping. The tribal leader permits the newcomers to use the well's water. But their intentions are anything but innocent with regard to the tribe, which under its own laws may not stay at the same place for more than forty days. The newcomers are not content simply to build a few houses and use the water allotted to them. Their true intention is to seize control of the well and enclose it within the walls of their new, inexorably growing town. They do not shy away from using gold and thus provoke the ire of the djinns, who regard all the gold of this world to be theirs. Finally, the newcomers harbor a secret and bear a curse. They are fleeing from destiny, the god of the wind, who is demanding their princess as a sacrifice.

The friction between ways of life

The intentions and activities of the newly arrived town founders collide with the life led by the tribe on various levels in *The Magus*: they expose the tribe to physical danger by seizing the well; they expose them to economic danger by trading with gold; and through their obsession with gold, they expose them to metaphysical danger by provoking the curse of a wrathful god who had followed them.

This contrast to the tribe's values and way of life becomes most obvious in a discussion between the tribal leader and the sultan of the new town. It is certainly no coincidence that this discussion about the pros and cons of desert and town life – as metaphors for forms of human existence – is located in the middle of the novel. It is its centerpiece.

In part heated, the debate focuses first on the characteristics of sedentary and nomadic life. The sultan considers urban life to be the culmination of human existence, guaranteeing as it does tranquility and providing livelihoods, while the tribal leader describes it as the end of true human existence, for it turns men lazy and indolent, depriving them of their vitality and longing for distant horizons. Second, the debaters deal with the values of the new and the old. The sultan calls the basic tenets quoted by the tribal leader from the Book of the Ancients insipid stories, while the tribal leader considers the sultan's way of thinking, which might be called pragmatic, godless. They next talk about the possibility of free will and the necessity that every individual should have the right to exert it. This conviction of the tribal leader is challenged by the sultan, who is of the opinion that man in general has no notion of what is best for him and must therefore be led to his happiness, "even if in chains seventy yards long." Sedentary and nomadic life are not simply two different ways of existence but also two contradictory ways of thinking.

Power triumphs in the end. The tribal leader gives in and chooses exile in the stark desert, from which he returns only after the town has been destroyed and his tribe, who had been unable to resist the lure of comfortable sedentary life, have perished. The tribe had betrayed nomadic life – true life in Ibrahim al-Koni's logic. In the end both the tribal leader and the sultan are losers. But the sultan has not only lost his town, which was destroyed in a final battle; he also loses his life, which of course robs him of the possibility to continue his civilizing project. On the other hand, the tribal leader has lost "only" his tribe, their demise sealed in the same battle; but he has remained alive and embarks from the site of his defeat for new horizons where he will continue his project.

In the world of Ibrahim al-Koni's novels town life is the obverse of true life. It is non-life because it is an obstacle on the path to realizing genuine life; it prevents man from following his real destiny of wandering from cradle to coffin.

Al-Koni's literary world is the real desert. He makes it into an abstract world, through which he reveals his philosophy of life: because our life is transitory, our fate resembles that of the tribal leader who leaves behind the scene of the desolated town – "Before him stretched the desert, vast and bleak as transience."

But this desert, the symbol of life's path, is richly endowed with "signs" and frequently points beyond earthly life; not only because it is on the distant horizon that desert and sky merge or because at night heaven and desert lie in a warm embrace, separated only by the first streak of morning light. It is also because the desert is not always the same desert. The author uses almost a dozen different Arabic words for desert, most of them associated with vastness and emptiness, others differentiating between mountain and plain, sand and stone. This is not least because the sand in the desert is always shifting, sustained by the wind. Dunes wander, blocking paths or routes, filling or liberating wells. Nothing is stable in the desert.

In conclusion

A journey with Ibrahim al-Koni through "his" desert, the region of his childhood and youth, is a journey into the past; his personal past and that of his people. Members of his family still live there between Ghat and Ghadames. An old man accompanying us once wandered here with his father. The author himself remembers the 1950s and a life lived in a tent and with animals.

But a journey like this is also one into mythology. Suddenly he makes the driver of the Landrover stop. He has caught sight of a small plant, symbiotic with truffles, the sort of champignon that in springtime grows under the surface of the earth, much like a little potato, breaking open the crust of the earth with its own strength. Behind this, Ibrahim al-Koni explains, one has to see the "sign". Using this word, his discourse becomes very Islamic, because in Islam man is asked to see God's signs everywhere. The little knob of the truffle lifts and breaks open the arid soil of the desert under which it lives like other plants and plantlets, having survived long periods of drought as a seed before, moistened by a few raindrops, beginning to stir with new life. This too is a sign, for as Ibrahim al-Koni puts it in an aphorism: "Only water connects heaven and earth, falling down and then soaring again."

But little rain has fallen over the last few years. The wadi at the northeastern edge of the Red Hammâda, once a childhood paradise for Ibrahim al-Koni and his brothers; with rainfall in autumn and winter and lush vegetation in spring, providing enough food for many animals, both wild and domesticated: this wadi shows traces of thirst. Dry bushes and an empty well; not a man or animal in sight. Only stones; and they are entitled to be proud or even haughty, as they are, in al-Koni's words, "the beloved and the lover of eternity." Supported by the wind, they also sing eternity's song and serve as its notebook, into which the history of past generations is inscribed. But men neither hear nor understand it. Ibrahim al-Koni's literary work tries to help them overcome this deficiency.

SELECTED WORKS

al-Salat kharij nitaq al-awqat al-khamsa (The Prayer Outside Praying Times), Tripolis: Dar al-Fikr al-'Arabi 1974

Jur'a min dam (A Gulp of Blood), Tripolis: Dar al-Jamahiriyya 1983

al-Tibr (Golddust), Limasol: Dar al-Tanwir 1990

Nazif al-hajar (The Bleeding of the Stone), London: Riad El-Rayyes 1990

al-Majus (The Magus), Limasol: Dar al-Tanwir 1990–91

Waw al-sughra' (The Little Waw), Beirut: al-Mu'assasa al-'Arabiyya li-l-Dirasat wa-l-Nashr 1997

'Ushb al-layl (Herb of the Night), Beirut: al-Mu'assasa al-'Arabiyya li-l-Dirasat wa-l-Nashr 1997

Anubis (Anubis), Beirut: al-Mu'assasa al-'Arabiyya li-l-Dirasat wa-l-Nashr 2002

al-Bath 'an al-makan al-da'i (The Seven Veils of Seth), Beirut: al-Mu'assasa al-'Arabiyya li-l-Dirasat wa-l-Nashr 2003

TRANSLATIONS

The Bleeding of the Stone, trans. May Jayyusi, Christopher Tingley, Brooklyn, NY: Interlink 2001

Anubis. A Desert Novel, trans. William M. Hutchins, Cairo: The American University in Cairo Press 2005

Golddust, trans. Elliott Colla, Cairo: The American University in Cairo Press 2008

The Seven Veils of Seth, trans. William M. Hutchins, Cairo: The American University in Cairo Press 2008

FURTHER READING

Roger Allen: *The Arabic Novel. An Historical and Critical Introduction*, Syracuse: Syracuse University Press 1995, pp. 244–58

Pierre Bataillon: *Le Désert et la vie bédouine dans la littérature arabe contemporaine. Un romancier libyen: Ibrahim al-Koni*, Maîtrise, INALCO, Paris 1996

Hartmut Fähndrich: "Ibrahim al-Koni. Le désert e(s)t la vie", in: *Feuxcroisés* (Lausanne/ Geneva) 4 (2000), pp. 155–64

Jean Fontaine: "Un roman-fleuve libyen: al-Magûs d'Ibrahim al-Kûni", in: *IBLA* 59/177 (1996), pp. 87–115

Richard van Leeuwen: "Cars in the Desert: Ibrahim al-Kawni, Abd al-Rahman Munif and André Citroën", in: *Oriente Moderno* 16 (77), n.s. (1997), pp. 59–72

Ewa Machut-Mendecke: "Magic and realism in the desert (The prose of Ibrahim al-Kawnî)", in: *Studia Arabistyczne i Islamistyczne* 2 (1995), pp. 53–60

Ewa Machut-Mendecke: "The visionary Art of Ibrahim al-Kawni", in: *Research in African Literatures* 28 (1997), 141–49

A Surrealist Trip to Paradise and Back
The Iraqi Author Abdalqadir al-Janabi

Sibylla Krainick

Although a resident of Paris since 1972, the Iraqi poet and commentator Abdalqadir al-Janabi is still largely unknown in the West. In his extensive literary oeuvre, al-Janabi willingly presents himself as the heir of Surrealism in the Arab world and as an iconoclastic agitator against Arab-Islamic culture. Both in its creative fusion of art and literature and even more in its provocative character, his prose stands out from the contemporary Arabic literary landscape. Breaking literary categories, his poetry introduces the reader to a venturous avant-garde poet, who distinguishes himself by his thematic individuality, as well as by his idiosyncratic language. This author's intellectual development bears witness to a syncretic adoption of Western ideas, first and foremost of Surrealism.

Al-Janabi was born in Baghdad in 1944 into a lower middle-class family. He came into contact with Western culture at an early stage. Cinema played a vital role for al-Janabi during the bloody political upheavals of 1963, enabling him to maintain his intellectual individuality amidst the oppressive atmosphere created by the state's increasingly ominous efforts to control institutional and civilian life. His political and literary development is rooted in the Baghdad intellectual scene of the 1960s. He read numerous Western writers, amongst them Herbert Marcuse, Norman Mailer, and Jack Kerouac. The literary periodicals *Shi'r* and *Hiwar* introduced him to the French Surrealists and Arab avant-garde poets such as Adonis and Unsi al-Hajj, while he became acquainted with the idea of literary commitment through the writings of the Egyptian reformist intellectual Salama Musa. As an "innate" sympathizer of the Iraqi Communist Party, due to his mother's political orientation, al-Janabi became an active propagandist for a Trotskyist splinter group and eventually came under the influence of the Iraqi "1960s generation", who sought to realize far-reaching innovations in literature and art. Thus, like many others of his generation, commitment to poetic innovation and openness to Western culture were the initial focus of his literary career.

After the disastrous defeat of Arab forces at the hands of Israel in 1967 and under the total control exerted by the military in the wake of the 1968 *coup d'état*, the situation became precarious for Iraqi intellectuals. In 1970 al-Janabi emigrated to London, where he took part in numerous demonstrations and an occupation of the Jordanian embassy. He also discovered pop music and drugs, which led him to call himself the "first Iraqi hippie." He eagerly soaked up all the impressions of the Western metropolis, which he considers the origin of his "true education". Above all, London appeared to him as a "grand library," so he seized the opportunity for intensive reading.

Two years later he was forced to leave Britain – the reasons for his expulsion remain obscure. He went to Paris, where he met other Arab exiles. Cutting ties with the Trotskyists, he switched his allegiance to soviet council communism. Even after breaking formally with a small workers' council group, he continued to share their radicalism, categorically condemning any party organization. Intrigued by the Surrealists, he sought to gain deeper insights into the movement and so established contact with the Situationist International, a movement which would strongly influence his further intellectual development.

Karl Kraus, Theodor Adorno, Paul Celan, the Surrealists – what is striking about these diverse sources of "education" is that they are exclusively Western. It is André Breton who assumes the mantle of supreme authority in al-Janabi's intellectual pantheon. Al-Janabi follows his idol in claiming an exclusive understanding of Surrealism and he has attempted to establish himself as the pivot of a "Surrealist group." This ideational and practical identification with the Surrealist "father figure" borders on apotheosis and is at times unintentionally comical. This glorification reaches its climax in al-Janabi's autobiography *Tarbiyat Abdalqadir al-Janabi* (*Abdalqadir al-Janabi's Education*, 1995), which ends with his having a vision of Breton: he has attained the *point suprême* with his alter ego and his intellectual formation is completed.

Imitation, adaptation, interpretation: al-Janabi and Surrealism

In a strict sense, there is no such thing as a genuine "Surrealist movement" in the Arab world. Surrealism was one of numerous important Western influences on modernist Arabic literature. The Egyptian authors' and artists' group *Art et Liberté* (Art and Freedom), founded by Georges Henein (1914–1973) and Ramsis Yunan (1913–1966), maintained close ties to the French Surrealists. From the late 1930s up to the 1950s the group published journals and organized exhibitions. Their members followed the Trotskyist principle of an independent revolutionary art and advocated a predominantly "social Surrealism". The group did not regard Surrealism as an aesthetic end in itself, but foremost as a mode of political and social protest against the prevailing conditions in Arab society. Surrealism was also a source of inspiration to the Lebanese and Iraqi modernist poets of the 1960s, in particular the movement around the literary avant-garde periodical *Shi'r*.

As the self-appointed "heir of Surrealism" in the Arab world, al-Janabi deemed it his mission to accomplish the task that, as he saw it, *Art et Liberté* had failed to complete: to translate Surrealism into the Arab present. In 1979 he described his relationship to Surrealism as a "political choice," as his "means to develop a manner of political thinking which protests against the possibilities available in the Arab world."

From the outset his oeuvre shows obvious signs of Surrealist ideas and methods, and his early literary and artistic work is partly an imitation, right down to the smallest detail. The vehement damnation of the "war of the regimes" was the basis of the French Surrealist group, along with the "pacifist fight" on a literary level. Al-Janabi also advocates anti-nationalism – for a long time he felt neither an Iraqi nor an Arab identity. He categorically rejects the nation state as well as all institutional organizations; in his eyes they are incompatible with writing as a creative activity: "When I write I do not belong to anything, but tear up my identity card. Frontiers and history do not matter to me."

Further Surrealist leitmotifs are hostility towards religion and the rejection of religiously based civil morality. Adapting his fundamentally anti-religious position to fit the Arab-Islamic world, al-Janabi relishes quoting the "spiritual fathers" of the Surrealists, de Sade, Rimbaud, and Lautréamont, in his fight against Islam. He also cultivates the Surrealist tradition of excessive polemics, both in writing and in action. This inclination came to the fore early on and he gained a reputation for his polemical confrontation, expressed mostly in terms of personal insults. His favorite target is the poet Adonis, whom he once accused in a pamphlet of collaborating with the Syrian regime. However, in al-Janabi's view this poet's most inexcusable misdemeanor was his "perverted" understanding of Surrealism.

Al-Janabi's consequential pursuit and realization of a universal conception of art is another Surrealist borrowing. In his autobiography he emphasizes the uniqueness of the Iraqi movement for cultural modernization in the 1960s, which confirms him in his general rejection of any borders separating art and literature. He himself realizes this unity through his provocative and mostly obscene collages, which in their combination of elements without any directly apparent semantic coherence follow the Surrealist theory of images.

> Criticizing everyday life, criticizing cultural sublimation of individual drives, criticizing morals, insulting all integrisms, revolting against all prevailing values and stupidity, instigating the liberation of sexuality and of the body by realizing love and delivering power to the imagination.

Abdalqadir al-Janabi considers these Surrealist tasks "more relevant than ever before in the Arab world". His oeuvre reveals a development from simply adopting and imitating Surrealist ideas and methods, through adapting them to Arab culture, to finally interpreting them in his own way.

Al-Janabi's Critique of the Arab Situation

Politics: Oriental despotism

Essentially, al-Janabi's entire work represents a criticism of the contemporary Arab situation, condemning all its various manifestations. He proceeds from a position associated with a non-institutionalized Arab Left, whose theoreticians analyze in a mostly radical manner those elements which in their view hinder the progress of Arab society. The origin of their critique lies in the June War of 1967.

Al-Janabi's political criticism is anything but elaborate or refined and is mostly limited to slogans. It is leveled mainly at Arab revolutionaries and their "unholy alliance" with despotic regimes. He regards revolutionary organizations to be just as repressive as the regimes they fight.

With his "anti-nationalist" attitude towards the Arab-Israeli conflict, al-Janabi has clearly distanced himself from the one-sided approach to this subject taken by the majority of the Arabs: "Zionism is primarily an Arab unionist or isolationist regime. But the Arab presidents and kings know very well what it is about: annihilating Israel implicates the definitive annihilation of their own rotten regimes." His commitment to dialogue with Israel has found a vehicle in his literary collaboration with Israeli writers. The culmination point of this political provocation thus far was his participation in the International Poets Festival in Jerusalem in 1997. But he does not view the Israel issue solely as a territorial conflict but rather as an essential problem, which ultimately finds its expression on a cultural level in the taboo placed on "Jewish literature" by Arab literary circles. In this respect, his intensive interest in Celan's poetry has an undeniably political aspect, so too his demand "to accept the outstretched hand of the Israeli intellectuals."

Religion: the source of all evil

In his usual self-dramatizing manner, al-Janabi dates his intransigent anti-religious attitude to his birth. With ironic, enigmatic playfulness, he describes the devastating impact of his very first breath on the representatives of faith:

> They say on the day of my birth three mosques were closed, and the follow-ing day the neighbors found a cleric hanged in his room. Nobody knew the reason, but at that time a newspaper reported that this cleric had left behind a sheet of paper reading "A light ordered me to do this."

Al-Janabi's fiercest affronts are aimed at the representatives of religion: "It is impossible to kill a God unless you kill his shadow on earth." His position is radical and unforgiving:

Who alone befuddles society's leadership? The clerics. Who defiles the dignity of our women and children every day? (...) Who are the most dangerous enemies of any government? (...) Who provokes civil wars and perpetuates them? (...) Who dispossesses us even of our last vital spark? (...) Who exploits our good will and our naiveté? (...) Who works mercilessly on the final extermination of humankind? (...) If we are still hesitating to eradicate this stinking vermin from the face of the earth, we deserve everything that befalls us.

As religion has continued to gain ground in numerous Arab countries since the Islamic Revolution in Iran, al-Janabi has shifted from a general, Marxist-inspired critique of religion to a specifically anti-Islamic assault. Yet this, too, is limited to slogan-like statements, in truth directed more at Arab society shaped by Islam than at Islam itself. One feature common to all his texts and caricatures on this issue is the blatant, mostly obscene provocation.

Arab society: an ahistorical complex

"Arab reality does not even deserve that one revolt against it", or "The crisis of the Arabs lies in the fact that they do not have a crisis." Such sweeping claims, devoid of any semblance of differentiation, are the *modus operandi* of al-Janabi's attacks on Arab society. Influenced by Marxism, his conception of history regards society more as an idea than a real phenomenon: "The principal characteristic of Arab society is that it is, from a historical point of view, an ahistorical society."

One problem inherent to this theme attracts the author's particular interest – the Arab woman as the culmination of sexual repression. "There is no free society without a woman liberated from the chains of the Arab man." Here, too, he takes up his preferred device, provocation: "Run, sex, the Arabs are chasing you." He diagnoses Arab society as suffering from sexual inhibitions, which he regards as responsible for its alleged stagnation.

Given that al-Janabi wishes to follow the Surrealist concept of *amour fou* and the woman as poetic inspiration, it is even more astonishing that he exploits extremely sexualized female characters, while an aggressive, misogynic attitude emanates from his collages, culminating in this slogan: "Rape is another way to discover the undiscoverable body." Unsurprisingly, this standpoint, underpinning his initiatives to "liberate the Arab woman," has found little support amongst female audiences.

Culture: a mirror of society

Arab culture's alleged lack of a "liberating" reference is a *leitmotif* of al-Janabi's criticism: "A healthy civilization, i.e. a civilization healed from its complex of the past's glory, must create its contemporary instance in order to destroy it." At the same time, he condemns all twentieth-century Arab literature as "inane". This leaves him no choice but to resort to Arabic translations of Western literature. Here, however, lurks a major problem: the falsifying translation, the "Arabization" that he considers a fundamental factor contributing to Arab society's cultural "backwardness". The Situationist *détournement* seems to offer a way out of this dilemma. In *La société du spectacle*, Guy Debord writes: "The *détournement* is the antonym of citation, of theoretical authority, always falsified by the fact alone of having become citation. (...) The *détournement* is the fluid language of anti-ideology." But al-Janabi reduces this concept to a mere device by divorcing it from the theoretical context of a global critique of language and then making abundant playful use of it, for instance through *détournements* of Qur'anic verses and Arabic idiomatic expressions in his poetry. Most importantly, the *détournement* serves him as a means to identify a "genuine revolutionary" text: such a text defies *détournement*.

Al-Janabi's declared intention to write exclusively in French in the future, as in his anthology *Reflets dans le miroir des sables* (2003), is consistent with the context of his critique. In abandoning his mother tongue as a literary medium, the author dissociates himself completely from his Arab-Islamic culture and identity. This is nothing more than the logical conclusion of a process initiated by his first contact with Western culture.

The consequence: (inner) exile

For al-Janabi, the sole consequence of this perceived Arab cultural malaise is a life distant – at least geographically – from "Oriental despotism". The idea of the writer's "inner" migration in search of poetical individuality and the Arab intellectual's inner migration within his homeland run like threads throughout his oeuvre. However, he has never touched on his own life in a foreign culture and society in his literary work. He claims not to be a political refugee, nor his longtime residence in Europe to be a forced exile: rather, he emphasizes that he left Iraq of his own accord, and neither personal threats nor political reprisals played a role in his decision. As he sees it, for the Arab intellectual the real place of exile is not in the Western host country but in the Arab world itself, due to its political and religious situation, which has compelled many intellectuals into deciding between the humiliation of remaining silent in their home country or migration to the West: "He is in exile who lives in Egypt or in any Arab country, deprived of his freedom and of the freedom to create without purpose, the essential of any genuine freedom."

The West: the fallen ideal

An experience of Western culture is something that al-Janabi shares with various Arab intellectuals who have absorbed Western cultural currents with keen interest and used them to inject their own culture with fresh impetus. For his part, though, he cannot or will not take the step from imitation to cultural integration. In his initially uncritical idealization, a utopian West epitomizes an inverted mirror image of the Arab world. His first encounter with Western films and literature gave him a limited, if not idealized image. What is striking is that his conception of the West is monolithic, devoid of any political, geographical, or cultural differentiation. In his glorification of the West as a stronghold of culture and civilization, al-Janabi appears to overlook the fact that he himself reveals the very inferiority complex for which he reproaches the Arabs.

The Gulf War of 1991 – a conflict al-Janabi initially saw as a chance to usher in a new political and social beginning – destroyed this ideal. In its wake, the West is now showing its ugly face:

> This culture among whose highest values are enlightenment, freedom rights, and human rights, both imagination as well as rational thinking (...), the West we so admired and revered, has been superseded by another. By a West acting violently and militaristically, regarding us with contempt.

He thus now calls for a

> ... distinction between the West of the media, of the arms industry, with its customers from all countries, and the real West, the West for everyone. (...) The victory of the former over the Orient is a victory over our only chance (not over the West as a geographic place, but as the center of all revolts of the human spirit for freedom, poetry, and human rights).

From Surrealism to Realism: al-Janabi's vision

In accordance with his respective political position, al-Janabi's vision was at first extremely ideologized, bearing witness to his revolutionary (Marxist, Trotzkyist, Surrealist or Situationist) attitude, but soon its alliance with poetry became vital: "It is revolution alone that creates poetry. We master the poetic act, for it is the illustrative voice of the coming revolution."

Nonetheless, the call for revolution has never challenged the status of individuality. The possibility of individual creative freedom always remained the highest goal, allowing the author to maintain his vision even after having abandoned his political commitment in the narrower sense. In spite of his universal and abstract conception of "revolution", he has never lost his interest in modern Arab society, which he regards as the real problem. Yet since he has dissociated himself from the 1960s-based idea of revolution, the author has also refrained from expressing his view on this matter.

All in all, al-Janabi's vision for the Arab World is the opposite of its present conditions: a utopia, embodied by his former ideal of the West. After the disillusion the poetic revolution takes the place of the political revolution. Abolishing integrism still remains his goal, but now he demands for this purpose "an acceleration of economic and social development". Nor has he lost his interest in politics. Being a severe provocation to the Arab public, his journey to Israel had an unequivocal political message.

Al-Janabi is well aware of the utopian nature of his vision as part of the extremely leftist mindset he has always been close to. Thus, he feels a "cosmic despair" that eliminates any eschatological expectation. However, it does not impede poetic activity, untinged by any drive for results. The poet's political commitment still plays a central role, but now it does so on a universal level. Whenever threatened by despair and resignation, al-Janabi takes refuge in poetry as a symbolic-abstract universal remedy:

> When the crepuscular regression comes, there is nothing left for me but to walk along the banks of poetry, like along the bay of a life where I embrace a universe lacking neither the splendors of isolation nor the depths of rupture.

Anarchy, desire, paradises: al-Janabi's journals

The journal *The Libertine Desire* (1973–75) was "devoted to the essence of language in order to protect writing, as the pen does not enjoy any esteem." It was "the dawn of the Arabic language, aware of a dark night lying ahead of it, the Arab darkness." Published in collaboration with a small group of Arab avant-garde writers and artists, *The Libertine Desire* was intended as a counterpart to André Breton's *La Révolution surréaliste* – and as an attempt to provide Arab readers with a "pedagogical" introduction to Surrealism. The modern meaning of the adjective *ibahi* (pornographic) also fits al-Janabi's provocative intent perfectly. The first issue of the journal explains the intellectual context of its founding in unmistakably Marxist tones:

> The total bankruptcy of everyday thinking and practice in established Arab society (...) encourages us to publish such a journal (...). After a long period of material, cultural, and intellectual misery and the violent, bloody repression of creative freedom, opposition, and scientific thinking ... we think that this is enough ... (...) Hence, we announce a vendetta against everything established

in the Arab homeland. We are aiming not only a theoretical revolutionary critique at the Arab situation; if necessary, we will be gladly adding (...) a sadistic practice against anyone who impedes this campaign, the basis of which is clarity, a dialectical vision of reality, and revolutionary critique.

The Arabic-French series *The Libertine Desire, new series* (1980–81) heralds a new phase, in which political-militant motivation gives way to a predominantly literary-aesthetic orientation:

The objective of the new series is not an attempt to agitate, to instigate a revolution or to multiply the entities of rebellion in the Arab scene. (...) We rather wish for a critical laboratory for the experience of creative intuition.

The four issues of the journal *The Base* (1983–84) mark both a return to the beginning and a transition to something new. Intended as a "mouthpiece of free humans against the oppressor and the oppressed", *The Base* represents a commitment to the "Arab cause". Surrealism features somewhat reticently, in the form of typical themes, puns, and provocations – for instance, instructions on how to commit suicide with an enclosed razorblade. The vast number of texts criticizing religion and Islam is striking, while a political discourse in the narrow sense is missing.

The ten voluminous issues of *Paradises* (1990–95) represent a contrast to their predecessors, conceptually as well as in form and content, giving a considerably more professional impression. Their literary-aesthetic orientation is distinctly programmatic and it would seem that political and socio-critical commitment has become altogether secondary. Al-Janabi's subsequent journal *Arapoetica* (2000–2003) is of an exclusively literary nature, introducing contemporary Arab poets to a Western audience.

Poetry and the individual: al-Janabi's poetic conception

"Poetry is the only thing that Arabic poetry lacks." Criticizing the Arab poet was al-Janabi's poetic leitmotif from the outset: "As for me, everything moronic, ugly, ignoble, and of bad repute is concentrated in one word: Arab poet." Himself a "true poet", al-Janabi stands in irreconcilable opposition to this figure. A true poet is characterized by a tolerance of the "other." In this way he embodies "critique in itself: the thread in the fabric of any poetic unfolding, which wants language to be a free sphere within the space of sense." This leads to the problem of the relationship between poetry and political action and thence to the poet's "commitment."

Initially, al-Janabi regarded poetry simply as a medium of revolution, in line with the Surrealist concept of "militant" poetry: "To the extent to which it is immoral, revolution is the sole Surrealist and irrational act capable of achieving the essence of the game: the poetry-individual." He believed that the unity of poetry with the individual was not only of theoretical significance but was part of life in itself. However, after al-Janabi's encounter with *Art et Liberté* poetry lost its revolutionary function, becoming an independent aesthetic imperative: "I want writing to free itself from reality." This by no means a break with his "revolutionary" past. Although his formerly militant and political notion of revolution now has a predominant nature of cultural criticism, rebellion and protest remain closely linked to poetry. While it was once the revolution's task to overcome the discrepancy between the poet and social reality, it now rests with poetry to establish the line of demarcation between the poet and the society he rejects. However, the poet's distance from political and social conflicts does not entail turning away from universal problems:

> I have never stopped believing that writing is a struggle, and struggle is an ecstatic matter. Any ecstatic activity is in the first instance an exposure of the social lie.

Two factors contributed to his poetological reorientation: his reading of Paul Celan and the 1991 Gulf War. Through Celan, he became "aware that the modern poem does not fondle feelings anymore, but hurts them. It undresses humans, confronts them with themselves, and unsettles them." Through his aspiration for a poetic identification with Celan, al-Janabi bears witness to the fundamental influence which this literary encounter had on his own poetic conception. The "lyrical optimism" of avant-garde poetry was no longer feasible. The tremor of the Gulf War is apparent in his turn away from a rather obscure poetry towards a more direct poetic expression, determined by the urgency of protest.

By its title alone, the anthology *Là où il n'existerait plus de dialogue authentique, il n'y aurait plus de poème* (1990) calls attention to al-Janabi's new position: poetry as dialogue. In the same vein, after visiting Israel he admonished that "the poets have but their visions as a weapon, common visions, in spite of different languages." Having started with a militant Dadaist-Surrealist phase, al-Janabi's poetic conception reverts to a "political" function, now as a dialogue for peace: "Perhaps the whole peace project is just the result of a telepathic dialogue between an Arab and an Israeli poet."

Al-Janabi's poetical development

In terms of form and content, al-Janabi's poetical development was initially determined by Surrealism. Since his political view of poetry has turned to an aestheticizing vision, his poetic œuvre is of greater thematic and stylistic clarity, even though it will never completely abjure Surrealism. But even in his Surrealist phase, his poetical work sometimes left the obscurity of *écriture automatique*. Using a more transparent imagery, it becomes accessible, gradually assuming a stronger individual character. The poetic encounter with Celan evoked in him the tendency to intellectualize his poetry through religious and philosophical allusions.

Al-Janabi owes his integration into the Arabic literary scene to his anthology *The Joy of the Oriental Foreignness* (1988), a kind of retrospective catalogue of his poetical work since 1974 that provided the literary *enfant terrible* with a wider audience and a certain prestige. The subsequent anthology *Life After Z* (1995) represents the pinnacle of his poetry at the time: not only has the provocative tone disappeared for the most part; the anthology also reveals the author's great interest in linguistic perfection.

The poetic experience of life: from individual to community

Life After Z is determined by two thematic poles: "ideational poems" in a rather theorizing style, and "poems of experience", which are mostly autobiographical. The elaborate ideational poems are diametrically opposed to the unconscious spontaneity of *écriture automatique*. They reveal a rich diversity of themes, where any event may bring about existential reflection, such as in "Ibn al-Muqaffa's Misdeed":

> An ego, undisturbed by any other
> An ego, whose excavations in the alcoves of the past are not a business
>   venture
> An ego, whose present is midday, a non-reflecting mirror
> An ego, a fact, not a creation, fabricated [or: written] by the scholastics,
> So as to be interpreted by the groups of infidels
> An ego, the custodian of the science of fire
> An ego, circling in the highest spheres of expression
> Emerging from the mercury of dreams
> As a flower of self-obliteration

Al-Janabi's poems of experience take up those events in life that shape individual and collective experience. The poem "Every Sea has a Boat which fills it" is a funereal oration to a whole generation's poetic project:

> We were a scream
> Exploding between the brain's lines
> In the face of these Bedouin poets
> Who, as soon as the water came in, took refuge on terra firma
> We were this and not that

To annul any belief
Poetry's ephemeral sketch
We were the moment of movements
Dream's expelled revolutions
In the project of *écriture automatique*

Other poems of experience represent an immediate written response to current events. Along with the collective catastrophe of the Gulf War, al-Janabi raises the issue of his personal catastrophe in "Mary in the Sphere of Eternity". In his attempt to give expression to sorrow and shock, he writes in a simple, spontaneous style that contrasts starkly with the intellectualized and discursive tone of his ideational poems:

> Today my brother Salah called, telling me that my mother died twenty-five days ago, i.e. 600 hours ago. So the hour which bears the number 600 was one of this morning's hours when I was lying in bed, having breakfast with my wife, and watching TV as usual. (...) She exhaled her breath, in agony without medication, she was rolling on the bed of a land beneath which rivers with acrid waters are flowing.

The Gulf War

The Gulf War of 1991 assumes a special place in al-Janabi's poetry. For all his personal concern, in his poetry he assigns this war a rather symbolic meaning. The poem "January 17, 1991" ends with the balance sheet-like statement: "the Tower of Babel, suddenly captured by the imams of the North". After this first poetic reaction under the impression of current events, a series of poems obviously influenced by Celan appears in *Life After Z*. These poems seem more reflective in tenor; the war in Iraq is raised to the universal level of human catastrophe:

To the horizon
The tunnels opened up
Like flowers
Like flowers
To the horizon
Shreds [of human bodies]
Higher than the sky
The horizon, outstretched on its belly like a meadow
Where the eye ploughs the visible
And the clouds are the sky's scrambled eggs
An invisible earth covers – (...)
Every soul is an image
Every image is a breath

Woman

Despite his autobiography's rich embellishment with more or less detailed depictions of his amorous adventures, women rarely appear in al-Janabi's poems.

> Love, fate has dispossessed me of it
> It has restricted it to a movement
> Between the phrase and the body
> It has robbed me of love

Such grief and resignation as are found in the poem "Your Sex is the Obsession of My Madness" are diametrically opposed to the complacent tone of his autobiography and to the aggressive, misogynic attitude of *The Libertine Desire*. "Blond Haze" seems to confirm al-Janabi's depiction of his relationships in his autobiography as being mostly focused on the physical aspect of love:

> I ran the dagger over the forest's lip before she said a word
> I pressed, there the blood spouted, blended with the cry's milk
> there a bird with tousled hair emerged from the navel

Viewed as "erotic poetry" in a Surrealist sense, this poem may be read as a poetic rebellion against social and cultural norms.

Language and religion

Language and religion are closely linked in Arab culture, and al-Janabi's poetry is no exception: initially, as if echoing his critical and intellectual texts, it turns away from this entwinement of Islam and Arabic. The poem "Between Alive and Dead" exudes a black despair of having to write in a "dying language":

> My mother tongue
> Has closed its door
> There it is, humming on the bed
> Needless to get up
> The heat of sleep
> Bars it from the expression
> Of salutation
> From buying things for its funeral
> Go
> It is in the other room
> Wake it up
> The funeral will soon take place

In later works, the motif of language vanishes as the anti-religious topos accrues a more elaborate character. "Superstition" contrasts strongly with this sad and resigned tone. Here the poet holds the Arabic language itself responsible for its fate.

> They said the language of *dad*
> Has told man
> To spread destruction
> To strike the earth with lightning
> In order to make the rain come down
> The wasteland is becoming stained with ink

The parody of the Qur'anic text is blatantly obvious through the construction, rhythm, and rhyme. Compared with the respective Qur'anic passage, it is striking that Arabic usurps God's position but is not a creative power; it devastates the world. The ancient Arabic connotation of rain is also perverted: instead of providing fertile green, religious obscurantism pours down over the Arabs.

"Muhammad's Image", a prime example of al-Janabi's anti-religious poems, consists for the most part of allusions and puns based upon texts from the Qur'an and from prophetic tradition.

> It was night. I found my image, stamped in the forefathers' books. A voice resounded in my room. It said "look", there I saw: a small opening, out of which the atmosphere of distant generations was pouring. An opening … it may fill up, then, with my image.
> I shook the vesture off my father's dust, I began to snare the tribes,
> Oedipus between the paths, I cast two birds at a single stone.
> …
> So, my image existed.
> Lo, there it turned into the others' night, a malformed nation

The scene alludes to the Prophet Muhammad's encounter with the archangel Gabriel, who delivers the revelation to him. The Qur'anic "read/recite" is replaced by "look," while the "opening", the void now filled by the usurping prophet, recalls the first Qur'anic sura, *al-Fatiha*. The following paragraph, an almost humorous résumé of Muhammad's prophethood, lies on quite a different linguistic and referential level. The first image, a *détournement*, shows Muhammad exempting himself from Arab traditions. "To snare the tribes" does not cast too favorable a light on his uniting the Arabs under Islam, and the reference to Oedipus alludes to the large difference in age between the prophet and his wife Khadija. The last image – "I cast two birds at a single stone" – is a *détournement* of an idiomatic Arabic expression:

in the poet's eyes, Muhammad adopted any means necessary for his purpose. The consequences of the prophet's egoism are disastrous: the Islamic nation, created to worship *his* (!) image, is a *khadij* (malformed) community amidst religious obscurantism; the barbed pun on the name Khadija is more than obvious.

The poem "Ink" shows the prophet Muhammad in deep solitude just before his death. The revelation now seems strange to him and he comes to recognize it as a fatal illusion. His followers administer their religion; nobody needs the prophet any longer. Even God has forsaken him and no longer speaks to him. Muhammad is no more than an old man whose lifework has spun out of his control. His agony appears as an "anti-revelation", a short clear-sighted moment in which he tries to retrieve his project from those who have institutionalized it. His prophethood is represented as a selfish choice and an unforgivable mistake. In these two poems, al-Janabi allows himself as a (poetic) creator not only to speak in the prophet's name, but even to take God's place within his own universe:

God is a table
and I am His carpenter.

The echo: al-Janabi's resonance

For all his homage to individualism, al-Janabi no longer seems content with the literary offside, but eager to replace his questionable (and not overwhelming) reputation as an *enfant terrible* with the prestige of a respectable poet and critic – even if it is only in the eyes of the Western audience. The French and German versions of his autobiography, his anthologies of Arabic poetry in French translation (such as *Le Poème arabe moderne*, 1999), his contributions to cultural journals like *Banipal* or *Qantara*, and his commitment to literary reconciliation with Israel are all successful measures that help him to gain publicity. Although contradictory to his self-perception as a revolutionary poet, a tendency towards "consolidation" and an abating of his radical impetus are striking.

Al-Janabi is known in the Arab world more as a commentator, agitator, and outsider than as a poet. His distance from the Arab world does not make his position any easier; the reception of his work certainly suffers because instead of providing constructive critique, the sole solution he presents to save an Arab society he sees as being appallingly desolate is his dual panacea of Surrealism and Western culture. His excessive provocation also aroused most Arab readers' irritation and disapproval. A further problem resides in his mostly uncritical idealization of the West and the categorical damnation of Arab culture: the Arab audience can only interpret this as a complete loss of identity and so dismiss it.

Al-Janabi's turning to the Western audience goes hand in hand with his decreasing interest in the Arab press. His journey to Israel attracted little interest in the Arab world, but it enjoyed at least a faint echo in the French media, which invariably present him in a positive light. Besides his wide-ranging Western cultural orientation, the author's break with the Arab-Islamic tradition is regarded with favor: here, he avails himself unhesitatingly of all prejudices and clichés.

Not the last word: conclusion

Seeing al-Janabi as an individual case within a cultural vacuum would distort the picture; as original as the author and his oeuvre may be, they must nevertheless be classed as part of Iraqi exile culture.

It is the question of identity in particular that represents the central problem in al-Janabi's work, which can as a whole be seen as an attempt at "cultural translation". His ambition to transfer Surrealism – a European movement, created by a small group within unique historical, social, and cultural conditions – to Arab culture is predestined to fail. Thus, the author's prophecy from the 1970s that Arab society will be "shaken from the ground up by the most tremendous scandal" has not come to pass. With his construct of a "history of Surrealism in the Arab world", however, al-Janabi deserves credit for having created a historical continuity from the Egyptian Surrealists of *Art et Liberté* to the modernist movements in Arabic poetry of the 1960s.

Al-Janabi's importance is not confined to his literary work, to his enrichment of Arabic literature with an idiosyncratic interpretation of Surrealism, or his role as an *agent provocateur* for Arab-Islamic culture and society. It lies rather in how a charismatic initiator is capable of gathering the most diverse characters around him, inspiring creative literary and artistic projects apart from the established cultural scene. However one may judge the content and expression of his ideas, this *enfant terrible* seems to have no equal within the contemporary Arab literary scene.

SELECTED WORKS

Marah al-ghurba al-sharqiyya (The Joy of the Oriental Foreignness/Emigration) London: Riad El-Rayyes 1988

Hayat ma ba'd al-ya' (Life After Z), Paris: Manshurat Faradis 1995

Tarbiyat Abdalqadir al-Janabi (Abdalqadir al-Janabi's Education), Beirut: Dar al-Jadid 1995

[Abdul Kader El Janabi] *Ce qui fut et jamais plus ne sera. poèmes*, Paris: Paris-Méditerranée 2002

[Abdul Kader El Janabi] *Reflets dans le miroir des sables*, Bordeaux: L'Escampette 2003

FURTHER READING

Özkan Ezli: "Literarische Geschwindigkeiten. Ein Vergleich autobiographischer Texte der irakischen Autoren 'Abd al-Qādir al-Djanābi und 'Aliya Mamduh", in: *Figurationen. Gender – Literatur – Kultur* 6,1 (2005), pp. 53–65

Sibylla Krainick: *Arabischer Surrealismus im Exil: Der irakische Dichter und Publizist 'Abd al-Qadir al-Ganabi*, Wiesbaden: Reichert 2001

OTHER WORKS CITED

Guy Debord: *La société du spectacle*, Paris: Buchet-Chastel 1967

Part Three

Gender Transgressions

Introduction

Barbara Winckler

Shahrazad and veils everywhere

The presence of Arabic literature on the Western book market has increased significantly in recent years. Yet for some time, we have been witness to a phenomenon that may at first seem surprising: In publications providing the general public with a glimpse into Arabic literature, women authors have enjoyed far greater representation than their male colleagues. What would initially seem to be a positive trend from a feminist perspective turns out to be a handicap upon closer inspection. The strong female presence is to be explained in the first instance through a voyeuristic interest in the "oppression of women in Islam" and clichéd notions about their plight: a controversial, if not surreptitiously exciting, topic, which obviously appeals to buyers. Accordingly, this literature is not seen as art but reviewed and received as a form of female self-assertion or a faithful depiction of social reality. In publications whose titles play with catchphrases like "Shahrazad" or "veil", their covers adorned with women wearing headscarves or yashmaks, Arab women writers are asked about their own personal experiences of the "restrictions placed on the life of an Arab woman" and how they managed to emancipate themselves from these shackles through writing. How astonished we would be if German, French or Anglo-American woman writers were presented in this fashion, the aesthetic aspects of their work completely ignored.

The following essays show that the issues addressed by authors from the Arab world, both men and women, are very different. Without wishing to negate the differences that obviously exist, in particular those of daily life, we have to concede that Arab intellectuals are not so far removed from us as we imagine – or rather, we from them. This is predominantly because they are intimately acquainted with the Western world and its philosophy and literature, while the reverse is seldom the case. The "periphery" knows more than the "center" because it knows itself *and* the center. The essays collected here show just how worthwhile it is to read this literature as literature, as expressions of aesthetic approaches, as renderings of specific worldviews, as statements of political and social commitment by authors and intellectuals. We need to recognize that Arabic writing is a part of world literature and that its works delve into the circumstances of their authors' life-worlds, without reducing their complexity to a mere "illustration" of it. This section is devoted to how gender codes are played with in literature, how they are approached and negotiated by both male and female authors.

Post-feminism and gender studies

Distinct from biological "sex", "gender" is culturally connoted and characterizes the historically shifting interpretations of masculinity and femininity. Gender is not connected causally with biologically-defined sex but is rather to be understood as a cultural reading of the body, one which through gender identity and roles assign the individual a specific place in the social order. At once a semiotic and socio-cultural category, gender therefore represents the meaning(s) that a culture confers upon the distinction between men and women. These meanings may overlap or interfere with other foundational generations of meaning, they may also stabilize them, but above all they serve to establish and naturalize hierarchies. Literary criticism oriented on gender analyzes how gender operates as the determining principle, how it is reproduced, and on occasion how it is deconstructed in the composition of literary texts, in questions of authorship and in literary reception.

Based on this cultural understanding of gender, the concept of post-feminism emerged and evolved parallel to that of postmodernism; like the latter it is characterized by the concepts of heterogeneity and de-centering. The turn away from the "classical" feminism of the so-called second feminist movement of the 1960s stems from the context of the 1980s, when awareness of and ideas about class, sexual, racist, and ethnic affiliations underwent far-reaching changes and feminist politics began to take a critical stance towards "meta-narratives". The notion of "the woman" as a universal subject of feminism was identified and duly criticized as essentialist. In particular, the insight that gender difference is constituted through language, society, and culture unmasked the prevailing categories and hierarchies of gender as nothing other than discourses of domination. One key consequence of this shift is that "man the enemy" is no longer at the center of feminist theory. The prime concern is no longer to fight "men" as repressors and representatives of the patriarchal order. Like femininity, masculinity is also a construct that places specific demands on an individual and is the result of social processes of arrangement and negotiation.

This paradigmatic shift from women's studies to gender studies is reflected in literature. The texts of "classical" feminist literature were primarily an expression of how women, acutely conscious of their position and gaining in self-confidence, actively challenged patriarchal restrictions and demanded the unhindered development of the female subject. Striking examples in Arabic literature are texts of the 1950s and 1960s by authors such as Nawal al-Sa'adawi from Egypt, Layla Ba'albaki and Emily Nasrallah from Lebanon or the early novels of Assia Djebar from Algeria. Layla Ba'albaki's novel *I Live* (1958), which may be considered a prototype of this literature, depicts the protagonist's rebellion against the constraints imposed by family and society. In contrast to most of the other authors, who grew up and lived in urban environments, in her novels Emily Nasrallah portrays village life and how women "flee" to the city, motivated by the hope to lead a less constricted life. In numerous works Nawal al-Sa'adawi, a physician, writer and feminist activist, gives an insight into the situation of women caught on the bottom rung of the social ladder.

Gender crossings, gender transgressions

To transgress means to cross a boundary or limit; moreover, to violate rules that are considered to be authoritative in a specific historical situation. The concept of "transgression" first gained currency in Anglo-American circles, most predominantly as part of the New Historicism and Cultural Materialism. In German, for instance, the understanding of "transgression" is generally limited to the sense of violation, specifically acts that violate norms and thus embody deviant behavior, the realm of nonconformists or outsiders. This is in contrast to the broader contouring of the concept in English, where the sense of crossing resonates. Ambivalence and creative potential are thus included, in particular when gender relations are involved.

But not every crossing is a transgression. The crossing of borders is only transgressive in the narrower sense when it becomes a topic in the public sphere, when a scandal marks the aberrance. Transgressions entail a more or less subversive socio-cultural transformation of values. In the symbolic representation and discursive elaboration of violations, real or imagined, society reaches a consensus on what lies within and outside acceptable limits. This is how social norms are called into question, endorsed, adjusted and repudiated.

Transgressions are thus not simply limited to questioning dominant values and norms; their inherent potential for protest may give rise to new values and norms. In other words, transgressing norms may become the founding act of new conventions; what was once considered a transgression may later become an established norm. Our contemporary postmodern situation, in which ambiguity and rapid change have supplanted clearly defined rules and continuity, besets many people with a sense of insecurity. They feel forced into determining their own limits, either creating their own classification systems or selecting from the plethora of norm-setting instances those which in their view should be binding.

As women are always considered the "other", the "exception" in patriarchal structured societies, with men taken to be "normal", the categories of "femininity" and "masculinity" are particularly apposite indicators of social classification models. When men and women transgress the limits imposed on them by their gender roles, their actions frequently call into question the self-understanding of a whole society. In principle there are two types of transgressors or nonconformists who cross the line and become outsiders: There are those who consciously and deliberately transgress; and those for whom their outsider status appears to be "fate". The latter are marginalized because of their gender, origins, or physical or psychological disposition: Their sheer existence marks an inherent crossing of a threshold.

The social impact of transgressions or even inversions – as exemplified by Mikhail Bakhtin in his conception of the carnivalesque, or in trangressions and inversions of gender roles when members of one gender wear clothing usually associated with the other – is thoroughly ambivalent: They may have a subversive effect and galvanize resistance; or they may stabilize the dominant order by functioning as a mere outlet for conflicts. Once "steam" has been let off, things are once again turned the "right way up".

Staging gender

The idea that gender is staged, of its performative character, became popular with Judith Butler's *Gender Trouble* (1990). The American philosopher drew attention to the fact that most societies are organized on the basis that bi-genderism is natural. This assumes that the two genders are characterized by different attitudes, behavioral patterns and attributes. Hence, behavior is routinely perceived as that typical of a man or a woman, and – by referring to gender prototypes – interpreted and evaluated as to whether or not it is congruous with the representation of the respective gender.

Butler explains a performative theory whereby gender is not something one *has* but something that one *does*: "doing gender" is the key formula. Comparable to Pascal's deliberations on religiosity (that it crystallizes cumulatively through the practice of prayer and is not simply given by faith), Butler begins from the premise that it is the practice of being a man or a woman which produces male or female identity. Femininity and masculinity are thus effects generated by ritualized actions and modes of speech, reinforced by clothing and gestural conventions. As Butler underlines, however, this does not mean that the individual is free to pick out and slip on gender identities as if they were costumes from a theater wardrobe. The performative act is not to be understood as that of a "role" or "costuming" but as an effect of socially anchored gender discourses, an effect expressed in a non-concludable and non-intentional repetition and restaging of norms: This is how identity is constituted. This process of "doing gender" is to be viewed as an unavoidable everyday occurrence. Gender is thus acquired in the context of a routinized, permanently repeated practice.

A further key anti-essentialist concept within gender studies is that of the masquerade, the parody. It refers to the level of representation, to the cultural act of producing and embodying gender, distinguishing it as a discursive product that can be subverted ironically. One form of the masquerade is travesty or cross-dressing, taking on the (dis)guise of the other gender. The figure of the "woman in men's clothing" is a common literary motif that has also been used in popular feature films such as *Yentl* (1983) and *Shakespeare in Love* (1998). Whether the game with gender identities proves subversive or affirmative is not a foregone conclusion – this can only be determined from the respective social context.

Border crossings: androgyny

A number of protagonists in contemporary Arabic literature cross borders. Either they profit by their conscious alternation between different worlds, exploiting it as a means of extending their range of opportunities, the reach of their living environment and the scope of their experiences; or they suffer, having failed to find a place in any of these worlds, not feeling a part of any group and unable to establish a "clear-cut" identity.

One special form of gender crossing is the motif of androgyny, which appears in literature and philosophy from Plato's circular creatures to the present day in a variety of forms that are assigned a variety of meanings. In the androgyne, femininity and masculinity are imagined as being unified in one person. Studies devoted to androgynous figures in literature often focus on the sociological aspects, such as the literary rendering of efforts at liberation. The androgyne is an extremely ambivalent figure: Negatively, it is seen as deficient, without a distinctive and definitive identity, and socially marginalized; interpreted positively, it stands for perfection, self-sufficiency and autarchy, and – in its characterization as an "intermediate being" – is regarded as an ideal mediatory instance.

Reflecting on androgyny almost inevitably leads to the concept of the "liminal". The cultural anthropologist Victor Turner, who intensively studied rituals, in particular rites of passage like those performed in initiation or marriage ceremonies, singled out the middle phase as the most interesting: After cleaving from the original state and prior to reintegration into the community with a newly acquired status, the person is in a liminal state, a threshold position. This state is characterized by playing with the known, estranging it and arranging chosen elements into new combinations. It is thus a creative phase, one in which something new can develop. By virtue of its threshold character, the androgyne is the liminal figure par excellence.

Elements of androgyny are present in contemporary Arabic literature in a diverse array of contexts, performing a wide variety of functions. The idea of gender transgression in the form of an androgyne or hermaphrodite is of key relevance in two novels by the Lebanese author Hoda Barakat. In *Disciples of Passion* (1993) it is the desire of a man to merge with the woman he loves into a single being, to "absorb her completely", even if it means killing her; in contrast, the protagonist in *The Stone of Laughter* (1990) is an example of an "outsider fate", stranded in a no-man's-land between the masculine and feminine spheres: Incapable of exploiting the creative potential of his liminal position, he ultimately assumes a stereotypical male role. A case of involuntary cross-dressing is the crux of two novels by the Moroccan Tahar Ben Jelloun, *The Sand Child* (1985) and *The Sacred Night* (1987). Following one of Roland Spiller's interpretations in this volume, a woman brought up to be a man stands for the colonized land: "In the historical master plot, her search for identity thus represents decolonization."

A further form of androgyny, this time external to the text, is the "androgyny of writing": Some women authors, like Hoda Barakat, choose mostly males as their central characters, while men authors like Tahar Ben Jelloun create female protagonists. The motivation behind this can vary greatly. Ben Jelloun believes that women, as the crystallization point of social conflict, are of crucial significance for the description and analysis of the antagonisms flaming such conflict. In contrast, for Hoda Barakat a male protagonist is more interesting because he offers greater plot scope than a female figure. Moreover, Barakat describes her own writing practice as an attempt to go beyond being man or woman, thereby stepping out of all limitations and restrictions.

Gender relations as the expression of other hierarchical relations

When questions of sex and gender are mentioned and discussed it is not always what is primarily at issue. Because the distinction between male and female represents *the* key dualism, to a certain extent it stands for all those other binary pairings – like nature/ culture, inferiority/ superiority or emotionality/ rationality – where the opposing elements are connoted as "female" or "male". Gender relations often stand for other hierarchical relations in society. Sexuality is accorded a key role here. Sexual relationships, in particular those which are violent, often mirror other – violent – social relations.

Rachid Boudjedra, all of whose work is characterized by transgressions, focuses on women and their social situation, employing an offensive depiction of sexuality and physicality. It is Doris Ruhe's thesis that Boudjedra's texts only seek to change gender hierarchy on the surface. Under this mantel are conflicts which concern homo-social relations and the reconciliation of the interests of different social groups, potentially so explosive that they can only be approached in an encoded formulation. In her essay, Monika Moster-Eichberger plots the relationship between sexuality and war in the novels of Vénus Khoury-Ghata. Sex is described with the vocabulary of war, war with a sexual vocabulary. On another level the violence dominating family life is set parallel to that of war: In this way the family functions "as the microcosm of a society at war." Without the war context, but nonetheless bristling with violence and brutality, sexuality and family relationships are depicted as transgressions of various types in the work of Mohamed Choukri. "Besides the obvious transgression of moral ideas about (homo)sexuality and the sacred institution of the family," writes Özkan Ezli, "Choukri also transgresses any coherent form of identity formation, in particular that of sexual identity."

"Gendered spaces"

Transgressions and crossovers also occur in "gendered spaces", real or imagined spaces connoted with gender in which literary characters move, from which they strive to escape, or between which they switch back and forth. Such spaces are central to Alia Mamdouh's novel *Naphtalene* (1986). As Verena Klemm remarks, female spaces possess a double connotation: On the one hand they are shaped and characterized by suffering and male violence – symbolic or real –, mere "interstices" bordered by male spheres of power. On the other hand they are the spheres where the female personality unfolds and the body is explored, places of sensuality, sexuality and subversion.

Tahar Ben Jelloun's novels feature utopian and heterotopian spaces. One example is the *hammam* (public baths), which each gender experiences differently. As Roland Spiller shows, for the women it represents a closed space where they can realize a utopia and speak openly about taboo topics like sexuality. In contrast, in the male baths "a mute, utterly prosaic atmosphere prevails, which conveys an impression of toilsome work".

Autobiographies of collective femininity

Another kind of transgression is perhaps a particular form of the search for identity that is considered to be both a female and a postcolonial phenomenon: the "collective autobiography". As a focus on the individual amounts to challenging the ideal of the collective, writing an autobiography represents a transgression in itself. The collective autobiography is transgressive in a broader sense, because it crosses the borders drawn between the individual and the community in order to bring them together. Alia Mamdouh connects personal recollections with the experiences of other women. As she once put it, "the personal pronoun 'I' is not an autobiographical confession for me. It is a convergence of the self with the other."

The result, as Verena Klemm demonstrates, is a "poly-biography", which "leads the isolated, exiled individual back into a symbolic form of community." Assia Djebar pursues a similar goal in her autobiographical novel *Fantasia* (1985). Through an extremely complex narrative strategy, the author entwines autobiographical material with a diverse array of voices from the history of her country. In the attempt to overcome her personal dislocation – the result of her schooling in the colonial system – she creates a female genealogy.

WORKS CITED

Layla Ba'albaki: *Ana ahya*, Beirut: Dar Majallat Shiʿr 1958

Hoda Barakat: *Hajar al-dahik*, London: Riad El-Rayyes 1990 (English translation: *The Stone of Laughter*, trans. Sophie Bennett, Reading: Garnet 1994)

Hoda Barakat: *Ahl al-hawa*, Beirut: Dar an-Nahar 1993 (English translation: *Disciples of Passion*, trans. Marilyn Booth, Cairo, New York: The American University in Cairo Press 2001)

Tahar Ben Jelloun: *L'enfant de sable*, Paris: Seuil 1985 (English translation: *The Sand Child*, trans. Alan Sheridon, San Diego: Harcourt 1987)

Tahar Ben Jelloun: *La nuit sacrée*, Paris: Seuil 1987 (English translation: *The Sacred Night*, trans. Alan Sheridon, London: Quartet 1989)

Judith Butler: *Gender Trouble. Feminism and the Subversion of Identity*, New York: Routledge 1990

Assia Djebar: *L'Amour, la fantasia*, Paris: Lattès 1985 (English translation: *Fantasia. An Algerian Cavalcade*, trans. Dorothy S. Blair, London: Quartet 1989)

Alia Mamdouh: *Habbat al-naftalin*, Cairo: al-Hay'a al-Misriyya li-l-Kitab 1986 (English translation: *Naphtalene. A Novel of Baghdad*, trans. Peter Theroux, New York: Feminist Press at CUNY 2005)

Changing the Sexes between Utopia and Heterotopia

Tahar Ben Jelloun's *The Sand Child* and *The Sacred Night*

Roland Spiller

A son of Scheherazade

Can you defend a good cause in a bad manner? In other words: can male authors support the female cause effectively and wholeheartedly? Even if they are of Arabic origin? Tahar Ben Jelloun, born in 1944 in Fez, Morocco, is one of the most influential authors of the French-speaking literature of the Maghreb. Living mostly in Paris, he vehemently advocates the emancipation of women. All his prose work, starting with *Harrouda* (1973), is a clear testimony of his endeavors.

The main character, a legendary female figure of North African mythology, appears in the novel as a social outcast. She is the object of desire for adolescent boys in Fez. What is more, she embodies the desire for freedom. The narrator's mother is the second outstanding female figure. She is illiterate; precisely because of this, she represents the very source of writing itself. The mother-son relationship performs a number of fundamental functions for Ben Jelloun: she reminds him that spoken Arabic dialect is the source of the written language; she is also decisive for his literary self positioning (he articulates himself in *L'écrivain public* (1983) to be a "public writer", that is an author who is writing for his mostly illiterate countrymen and women). Rendered as a literary figure, she represents women seizing the opportunity to have a say in society, even if this would hardly have been possible in reality at the time that the book was published; finally, she embodies the distinctive relationship to the mother that is characteristic of Mediterranean culture.

The mother's fictional *prise de parole* touches the gender-specific dimensions of literary texts. In literature, the distinction between biological sex and culturally constructed gender, searchingly analyzed by Judith Butler, seems initially not to play a role. Literary characters are always artifacts constructed through specific narrative and discursive techniques. As they first spring to life, however, when the projections of the author and the reader overlap, they also fulfill functions that go beyond constructs. The sexes are a nodal point in the relational networks of literature. This becomes manifest in the thematic of the body in particular. The body and sex of protagonists and narrators immanent to the text correspond by virtue of their construction to the concept of gender. Sex as gender. Biology as an aesthetic construct? The distinction cannot be sublated so neatly and easily, because the question then arises: if sex becomes gender, what happens to gender?

Characters created by literary means frequently reflect the cultural conditions that determine gender roles. In postcolonial literature, the dichotomy between sex and gender explored by Butler becomes a central theme. The novels of Ben Jelloun anticipate, sometimes in staggeringly prescient ways, the discussion sparked by Butler's work, which characterized theoretical developments in the 1990s. If this dual model of a distinction between sex and gender is to be retained, then with regards to literature one must speak of a secondary gender level; one that reflects the primary historical and cultural mechanisms of construction. Moreover, consideration needs to be given to how the literary character, as an anthropomorphic illusion, fulfils elementary functions anchored in the reader's own real life, such as the wish for identification.

Ben Jelloun enhances the gender-specific potential of the acts of writing and reading in every conceivable direction. His characters develop their own sexuality and sexual identity by reading and writing about others, while they in turn are being read and written about by others. The *lecture dans le corps* (act of reading inside or of the body) developed in *Harrouda* leads inside the body, but it also "touches" the body of the reader. The sensual and political potential of this mechanism of transference is passed on to readers, embracing them in their life-world. The fascination of this spark, the seemingly immediate emotional embrace of life by the narrated story, is closely connected with the gender problematic.

The passage from the real woman mutely bearing her fate to the speaking women and then further to the author as her advocate is repeated in manifold textual ruptures in the novels *L'enfant de sable* (*The Sand Child*, 1989) and *Le nuit sacrée* (*The Sacred Night*, 2000). Women narrators also feature in the preceding and subsequent novels: *Le prière de l'absent* (*State of Absence*, 1983) and *Les yeux baissés* (*With Downcast Eyes*, 1993). The narrating woman refers to the influential and prominent figure of Scheherazade. The principle of securing survival through storytelling is called on by numerous Arab as well as Francophone and other writers, such as Assia Djebar and the Chilean Isabel Allende. The reference to *The Thousand and One Nights* illustrates through the example of the fairytale that literary genres contain their own discursive patterns of gender-specific dimensions. Like Djebar, Ben Jelloun redefines the boundaries of the sex and gender patterns inherent to the novel. In particular, the connection between literature and life, set and performed by Scheherazade herself, is renegotiated in experimental, fictionalized autobiographies. In the hybrid interpretative patterns of the novel genre, Ben Jelloun multiplies the meanings of ascribed gender and identity.

At the same time, Ben Jelloun's commitment to the female cause has provoked controversy: a man amongst the daughters of Scheherazade? Arab gender studies in French? To examine if doubts of this kind have any credence, it seems necessary to combine a close reading of these texts with a superordinate perspective.

Close readings have shown that auto-exotic and Orientalizing elements, indicative of a patriarchal perspective, are indeed evident in Tahar Ben Jelloun's works. These readings can be corroborated in terms of the overall context of the narrative logic. The often complex arrangement of the narrative demands that any potentially patriarchal subject matter be minutely examined as to its function in the entire structure. It is a signature feature of Ben Jelloun's work that he transfers the text-specific reflection on the gender problematic onto the various communication levels of the text. Characters, narrator and implied readers switch roles in breathtaking pirouettes. This sets their gender-defined roles in motion. The dynamic generated encroaches upon the relationship between narrator figures and reader/listeners, both internal and external to the text. A close analysis of the narrative situation in the communication system of literature, indispensable for Ben Jelloun's fiction, may furnish the basis for depicting gender relations.

From a socio-historical viewpoint, a wish to improve the living conditions of women is part of the discourse of decolonization. It is questionable whether a society can be decolonized if relations between the sexes are not also expurgated of the structures of conquest and violence. In Ben Jelloun's novels, the oppression of women is inseparable from the repressive and alienating forces that characterize subjectivization in Moroccan society. Three interlinked factors are the main causes: the persistence of the colonial system, Islamic institutions and state repression. Women acquire an outstanding position when criticizing these three instances: they symbolize the struggle for liberation, because their example most clearly expresses the alienation running through Moroccan society.

The imaginary and the constructing of gender between utopia and heterotopia

How are the "semantics" of the sexes in Ben Jelloun's writing to be determined more accurately? In general, one could argue that transgressing fixed identities plays a key role here. This transgression is manifest in the motif of metamorphosis, a process through which both male and female figures pass. Borrowing from the model of literary space articulated by the Russian cultural semiotician Yuri Lotman, the sex changes that take place in *The Sand Child* and *The Sacred Night* represent what may be called a signifying transgression of borders. As a sign of decolonization, the woman who was brought up as a man stands for Morocco colonized by France and the entire Maghreb. In the historical master plot, her search for identity thus represents decolonization. Vital to the movement from a closed, repressive system of alienation to one that is open and self-determined is a process of linguistic and cultural hybridization. Because the liberation is played out in French, dichotomies like colonizer *versus* colonized, oppressor *versus* oppressed, and man *versus* woman are ruptured.

Ben Jelloun's early poetry is marked by his pangs of bad conscience at seeking freedom in the language of the oppressor. In the context of the Arab world, where the language of the Qur'an enjoys extraordinary prestige, this (self-)accusation carries even greater weight. Out of the resultant guilt, Ben Jelloun develops the idea of the writer as a thief of language, comparable – albeit without the guilt – to Jean Genet, to whom he was extremely close, and Roland Barthes. Like that of the more commonly employed metaphoric of the mistress, the metaphor of the thief serves the self-projection in the intercultural field: "I take the Moroccan universe and transport it into the French language, which is extremely subtle and I love greatly: I have stolen into it like a thief."

One of the most important tasks for a society that has just gained independence after phases of state violence and repression by colonial powers is to forge a new identity. How can such a society navigate a way between coming to terms with its past and the political pragmatism needed to look towards the future, and thus assume responsibility for the past *and* the future? The thoroughgoing Arabization demanded by nationalists has proven to be unrealistic. The modernization of Moroccan society is easier to achieve through cooperation with France and its cultural legacy than without. Such a differentiated view of the options enables the vicious circle of perpetrator-victim relations to be breached.

In order to transfer the macro-structural tension between the utopian horizon of liberation and the possibility of its genuine realization onto the textual level, I would like to draw on Michel Foucault's concept of heterotopia. Foucault attributes the category of space to the twentieth century. He elaborates the definition of heterotopia by contrasting it to utopia, which he understands as an irreal space that shall perfect or reverse existing society. Ben Jelloun's novels present utopian spaces which, for instance at the end of *The Sacred Night*, can even be achieved. Nonetheless, the arrival in *u-topia* is paradox. For this reason, the status of the reality of these placeless places needs to be determined more precisely. Ben Jelloun invokes the literary traditions of fairytales and fantasy to furnish models of this reality. It is out of this intercultural mixture of genres that he generates the dynamic to fabulate. The fictionalized figure of Jorge Luis Borges in *The Sand Child* personifies this dynamic. The title refers to Borges' *Libro de la arena* (*The Book of Sand*). The Argentinean author is one of the few writers Ben Jelloun professes to have modeled his work on – we shall return to this relationship later.

Foucault's concept of heterotopia is particularly suited to analyzing French literature of the Maghreb. Put simply, heterotopia denotes the utopias already realized in society which thus function as counter models. Heterotopias

> are something like counter-sites, a kind of effectively enacted utopia in which the real sites, all the other real sites that can be found within the culture, are simultaneously represented, contested, and inverted. Places of this kind are outside of all places, even though it may be possible to indicate their location in reality. Because these places are *absolutely different* from all the sites that they reflect and speak about, I shall call them, by way of contrast to utopias, *heterotopias*.

From the examples given by Foucault, the cemetery, the library, the prison and the brothel, as well as diverse crisis and deviate heterotopias, are particularly relevant for Ben Jelloun. The *hammam* (public bathhouse) is crucial. Ben Jelloun stages it as a threshold site: it is the space where the decisive event of the sex change takes place. In *The Sand Child*, a visit to the female bathhouse in the chapter "The Friday Gate" marks the transition from the imposed male role to the search for a female identity.

Even more prevalent than crisis heterotopias are those of deviation, defined by their differing from established norms of behavior: convalescent homes, psychiatric hospitals, prisons and nursing homes. Ben Jelloun's oeuvre is based primarily on his protagonists' oscillation between the imagined spaces of utopia and the real heterotopias of crisis and deviation. The crossing of boundaries this involves goes hand in hand with questioning and negotiating existing gender roles.

Before looking at the concrete representation of such places, I should point out that literature itself originates from the tension between utopia and heterotopia. As a form expressing the Imaginary, literature fulfils a mediating function between the real conditions of a society and its wishes and dreams. Drawing on the Greek philosopher, sociologist, psychoanalyst and economist Cornélius Castoriadis, one can consider the Imaginary to be an epistemological and ontological principle of creation; this principle thus determines not only the artistic but also the economic system as a concretization of the Imaginary. Seemingly "naturally" given categories like sex or nature are therefore to be grasped as cultural constructs of the Imaginary.

Ben Jelloun's aesthetic testifies to the primordial force exerted by the Imaginary. A wild imagination is at work in all of the novels presented here. The forces of the irrational, dreams, fantasies and wishful thinking driven by desire lend the subconscious a defining status – one could characterize this aesthetic as a "poetics of the night". The desire for liberation thus springs not just from more or less consciously experienced social conditions, but from an inner drive which escapes the conscious control of reason. Conscious and subconscious experience overlap.

Ben Jelloun positions and stages this overlapping at the existing borders drawn between the sexes. The fact that this border zone is also profoundly intercultural lends the gender and cultural conflicts an irreducible complexity.

The Sand Child and *The Sacred Night*. The hammam and the library as heterotopias

The movement of the subject outlined above is already observable in *The Sand Child* and *The Sacred Night*, before the immigration texts where cultural conflict is set in France. In terms of content, the transgressive crossing of borders is tied to the motifs of the *blessure* (injury), *itinéraire* (itinerary, translated from the Arab *rihla*), or *errance* (aberration or erring path). All of Ben Jelloun's novels vary this basic constellation. The two aforementioned novels in fact vary the very same story. They tell the story of Zahra, a Moroccan woman bearing the wounds of a violation suffered in childhood, and her journey to herself. Her father feels ashamed because his wife has already bore him seven daughters. He therefore brings up his eighth daughter as a son called Ahmed. Only after the death of her father can she begin her journey to discover her female self. The healing of the "wounded inner child", as the family psychologist John Bradshaw would put it, proceeds mainly as *itinéraire* and *errance*. To some extent, we also find traces of pilgrimage and epiphany as teleological master patterns. Developing out of these are forms of a travesty of the sexes, de-sacralized and in part grotesque. This development, presented on a content level, finds expression in the form as well. The narrative situation shifts continually. Inspired by traditional Moroccan storytellers, who recite their tales in the *halqa* (public squares), a storytelling competition begins: no less than four narrators relate starkly diverging versions of Zahra's story in *The Sand Child*. Fatouma, a woman, takes the floor. She provides the insider perspective by slipping into Zahra's story:

> My story is old ..., older than Islam ... My word has no great weight .... I'm only a woman, I have no tears left. I was taught at an early age that a weeping woman is a lost woman ... I decided never to be a weeping woman. I've lived in the illusion of another body, with the clothes and feelings of another person. I deceived the whole world, until I finally noticed that I was deceiving myself.

Two aspects are crucial here. Firstly, there is the principle of nesting: all the narrators use the diary of the figure whose story they are telling. In this way the aforementioned secondary modeling of gender is reflected. Secondly, there is the relationship the narrators have to the story they tell. They are all in danger of being devoured, like the first narrator, by their own sentences.

The semantic coordinates of this *errance* are the Foucaultian utopian and heterotopian spaces. Ciphers of interculturality, by no means do they lead straight to freedom. The stages of female self-discovery are portrayed by all the narrators as a passage through harrowing violence: rapes, betrayal, forced labor in a traveling circus, prison; culminating in a descent to the netherworld, which in *The Sacred Night* climaxes in an inhumane excision before the magical denouement in utopia, that might as well be read as death.

The Sand Child is the prototype for *The Sacred Night*. The image of a child made of sand evoked by the title refers to both Ahmed/Zahra and the narrative style. The double existence of a woman brought up as man expresses the thematic complex of gender differences, androgyny, and emancipation. There occur occasional phases of stability: "I was no longer a being of sand and dust with an uncertain identity that crumbled upon meeting even the slightest resistance."

Zahra's identity, built on sand and so susceptible to crumbling, concerns not only what the story tells but how the story is told, the narration of this crumbling. The multiple rupture of narrative perspective and the nesting of competing storytellers show that narration itself – not only in the sense of the aforementioned *prise de parole* but as an inspired creative speech act – is at issue here: the development of the woman proceeds from her being the narrated object through to being the narrating subject. This development has no ending, however. The danger of being devoured by one's own sentences is great. It would seem obvious to regard this as parable for the situation of a Maghrebian writer who is unable to establish his identity in the language of the colonizers. And in Arabic? Hardly, for the ambiguity of non-arrival is a core element of Ben Jelloun's storytelling.

Finally, it is a phantasm nurtured by many writers to be devoured by their own creation. It is in this context that Borges appears as a "blind troubadour" in the chain of narrators. The particularly complex nesting structure of *The Sand Child* is based on the Borges story *Las ruinas circulares* (*The Circular Ruins*). There a magician dreams up a person only to discover at the end that he himself is the dream of another magician, who in turn is ... and so on. Ben Jelloun also interlocks the internal fictional levels of reality, in line with the principle of a dream in a dream or a book in a book. Distinguishing clearly between dream and reality is therefore not his greatest concern; his interest centers on the space in between that separates and connects these realms. How great is the space between them? Of what quality is the relationship between them? These are the crucial questions.

Ben Jelloun anchors narration in the Moroccan tradition of public storytelling on the one hand, while on the other configuring this performance with the meta-fictional strategies of postmodernism, permanently calling into question the existence of an original, the "true story". Meaning arises out of the insight into how a meaning grounded in an origin inevitably evades fixation. At the same time though, the plot seems to baulk at the prospect of this structurally evident insight. The search for a narrator who finally brings the story under control ends, after diverse failed attempts, in a diary that contains the "true story" of the woman raised as a man. Its pages, though, were expunged by the light cast by a full moon. What remains is the act of narrating, the construction of fictions as the work of the Imaginary, never completely controllable and always unfinished. The reader eager to know the denouement is ironically invited to write their own: "I put before you the book, the inkwell, and the quill." Doubtlessly an open text, but Ben Jelloun goes even further. Activating the Imaginary changes the relationship between fact and fiction. This approach shakes the elementary components of semantics – protagonists, times and spaces. Analogous to the fixation of sexual identity, the relationship between fact and fiction, between dream and reality is shaken. Dream and fiction are often more real than reality itself. For the narrating characters this represents the ultimate threat, for the stories seize hold of their storytellers, swallowing them whole; they inscribe themselves in their bodies. As the stories are about the sexes and so about violence and alienation, they have *incorporated* this violence; thus embodied, it is readable from their bodies, particularly in their faces. Literature inhabits the body. The womb becomes the location of truth. Body and womb are not passive storage places where collective violence is inscribed – they produce ever new stories. Borges abstracts this insight, he *disembodies* it. Ben Jelloun leads it back to the flesh. His exploration of the body through writing, a characteristic typical of so-called women's literature, also explores the narrative mediating of this exploration.

How does this writing "grounded" in the body work? This is best explained by considering heterotopian spaces. Representative of such spaces is the aforementioned female bathhouse. Foucault sees the *hammam* as an example of a heterotopia that presupposes a system of openings and closures that both isolates and makes it penetrable. In this scene Ben Jelloun combines the depiction of the imagination process with the closed world of women, who live out their need for purification, communication and openness during their weekly visit to the *hammam*. In the enclosed space of the steam bath they effectively enact a utopia. It is a place "outside of all places", even though its location in reality can be clearly identified. Only here can the women speak openly about taboo topics like sexuality. The radical otherness of this place is lent particular significance through the mirroring and rupturing of the narrative strands characteristic of Ben Jelloun's work, because it reflects the process of imagination triggered by words: "The ceiling was like picture or gleamed like a stone tablet." In the process the young woman brought up as a man comes to the conclusion: "And for all of these women life is so limited (...):

kitchen, housekeeping, waiting, and once a week relaxing in the *hammam*. Secretly I was glad not to be part of this confined world."

The subsequent visit to the male bathhouse is like entering a different world: a muted, prosaic atmosphere reigns, conveying the impression of work. Taken together, both scenes demonstrate a double mimicry. Zahra has to leave the female bathhouse because she is no longer allowed in as a pubescent boy. She explores the intimate spheres of the sexes under reversed guises.

With *The Sacred Night*, Ben Jelloun presents a version of Zahra's story tending towards closure. Readers thanked him. The novel was awarded the *Prix Goncourt* in 1987. The first aspect that needs to be pointed out is the Qur'anic context of the title. The Arabic expression *lailat al-qadr* can be translated variously, for instance as the "Night of Glory" (sura 97) but with overtones of meeting one's destiny. The night deciding Zahra's fate is that of the twenty-sixth and twenty-seventh day of Ramadan, a highpoint of the Islamic year. The month of fasting recalls the revelatory experience of the prophet Muhammad. The Qur'anic pre-text is one of Islam's founding myths. Suras 96 and 53 describe the revelation of God's word to Muhammad. Muslims believe that a prayer recited on this night is worth a thousand said on other days. Ben Jelloun employs the associations tied to this – truth, legitimacy of speech and origin – but transforms the religious dimension of revelation into a spiritual one with an accent on family psychology: the father himself sets his daughter free.

Less radically than in *Harrouda* and *The Sand Child*, here Ben Jelloun is once again combining Arab and European genres of biographical writing. The initiation into the realm of the in-between ensues from the work performed by the Imaginary. Arising from the unconscious and nourished by dreams, the force of the imagination propels the endless process of storytelling in the intercultural field. Once again the author presents and positions his trademark feature in this field of tension: threatened with extinction, the voices of oral telling enter the universe of the cosmopolitan library. Continuing the tradition of the Borges figure in *The Sand Child*, the blind consul dreams of a "feminized" library of world literature. In his vision strikingly beautiful women recite literary masterpieces. A good dozen of them, "dressed as Scheherazade", read from *The Thousand and One Nights*. A young girl balancing on a trapeze reads from James Joyce's *Ulysses*.

This heterotopian space of literature embodied by women is located beneath a gigantic word depot, to where people come to pick up the words and phrases they'll need in the coming week: a spatialized dictionary. With the dictionary above and the literature represented by women below, the entire construction continues the utopian-Arcadian tradition. Superstructure and substructure both illustrate Borges' famous statement: "I've always imagined paradise as a kind of library." The dreaming consul, an extremely nervous person (and writer), finds supreme peace there: "I felt myself to be at peace with myself and others." According to Foucault, the heterotopia that is the library is characterized by its temporal dimension. Ben Jelloun configures this heterochrony interculturally by citing titles from different epochs and, moreover, different cultures, foremost the Arab and European traditions. The literary effectiveness of this scene first comes into its own through the transfer between different levels of narrative and reality. More importantly, it is a dream. The consul tells Zahra his dream in a romantic-amorous dialogue scene, which in turn is itself part of the superordinate narrative situation of the *halqa* on the Djemaa el Fna, the legendary square of the storytellers in Marrakech. The framework story is thus anchored firmly in reality on the one hand, while being destabilized by strong signs of ambiguity on the other.

Love bestows light and clarity to this text standing under the auspices of night. The protagonist finds stability in love: "There was no confusion anymore. I was at peace with myself and this is something that had perhaps never happened to me before." While this time love, a thoroughly sensual experience, ends in (re)union with the blind man, who has mutated into a spiritual master, overall the erring between sexual and cultural identities remains dominant. The novel does not end in Moroccan reality, but in a utopian nowhere, the mythic land to the south, that might also represent death. There are no really viable spaces of liberation for the woman in Morocco. In this hymn to the night, Ben Jelloun kindles the poetical potential of the imagination. His concern for the social cause of emancipation is embedded in an aesthetic governed by the imagination. Insight arises out of the paradoxical tension between a sensual experience of the world and its ascetic denial or suppression, for instance the conscious refusal to use the sense of sight in prison. In particular, dreaming, leading as it does to the unconscious, forms the basis for the image of humanity portrayed in the diptych of novel presented here.

Sibling constellations, psychoanalysis and *The Thousand and One Nights*

Can psychoanalysis be transferred to *The Thousand and One Nights*? Ben Jelloun has done so. Ever since studying social psychiatry in Paris he has been familiar with Freud's theories. He grants the unconscious great importance in his narrative universe. One example of this is the incestuous relationship between the consul and his sister Assise. The scene takes place in the *hammam*. Zahra watches the man soon to become her lover in the arms of his sister. This ugly and massive figure, almost grotesque, is readily identifiable as a pre-figuration of Zina, the main female character of *La nuit de l'erreur*. The man sucks his sister's breasts. Zahra is shocked: "How's it possible! Such a refined, intelligent man in the arms of this woman shrunk to a child!"

Indeed, the text can be read as a "family saga". Family ties are formative for all the main characters. Along with the child-parent relationship, sibling constellations play a crucial role. Zahra's father suffers from his relationship from his brothers. Their envy and greed are one reason behind his changing the sex of his eighth daughter. Zahra's development is hampered by her difficult relationships with her sisters. The conflict-ridden relationship to one uncle escalates; she shoots him and is sent to prison.

Her marriage to Fatima is another example. This physically maimed, moribund woman provides enough thought-provoking material for an independent analysis, not only because she is the only one to see through Zahra's male disguise but also because her body expresses the violent suppression of female identity. A chastity belt bars her sex, analogous to Zahra binding her breasts tightly to her chest and masking herself as a man. Fatima's violated psyche is signified by a monstrous physical deformation, one even more hideous than that of Assise. With almost clairvoyant clear-sightedness, she thus calls herself Zahra's "sister". The consul is also entangled in a fateful sibling constellation, encapsulated in the image of the man regressing to suckling his sister's breast.

Julia Kristeva's psychoanalytical approach may serve to explain this image. Moments of a sense of being cared for and the fulfillment of desire correspond to a return to the motherly realm of licentious being, which Kristeva calls the *chora*. The man experiences the pre-Oedipal phase of uncensored lust with his grotesque sister. However, a permanent return to the motherly order is not possible: the extreme experience of loss is what connects the siblings. This weakens the vertical axis of parental ties. At the same time, the sibling bond is not stable enough for genuine solidarity to emerge. It remains a fateful communion, revealing partly tragic, partly grotesque and even comic characteristics at times. The "siblings" Fatima and Zahra, two women disguised as brother and sister, are the tragic version, the consul and Assise the grotesque-comical. This does not deprive the search to heal the violated inner child of its earnestness: on the contrary. As the creative work of the Imaginary, literature furnishes the possibility of representing the violated child playfully in the form of fictions and trying out new directions. Freud and Scheherazade take the child by the hand.

SELECTED WORKS

Cicatrices du soleil (Cicatrices of the Sun), Paris: Maspero 1972

Harrouda (Harrouda), Paris: Denoël 1973

Les amandiers sont morts de leurs blessures (The Almond Trees Died from Their Injuries),
   Paris: Maspero 1976

La réclusion solitaire (Solitaire), Paris: Denoël 1976

La plus haute des solitudes (The Ultimate of All Solitudes), Paris: Seuil 1977

Moha le fou, Moha le sage (Moha the Fool, Moha the Wise), Paris: Seuil 1978

La prière de l'absent (The Prayer of the Absent), Paris: Seuil 1981

L'écrivain public (The Public Scribe), Paris: Seuil 1983

L'enfant de sable (The Sand Child), Paris: Seuil 1985

La nuit sacrée (The Sacred Night) Paris: Seuil 1987

Jour de silence à Tanger (Silent Day in Tangier), Paris: Seuil 1990

Les yeux baissés (With Downcast Eyes), Paris: Seuil 1991

L'ange aveugle (State of Absence), Paris: Seuil 1992

L'homme rompu (Corruption), Paris: Seuil 1994

Le premier amour est toujours le dernier (The First Love is Always the Last One), Paris: Seuil 1995

La nuit de l'érreur (The Night of Error), Paris: Seuil 1997

Le racisme expliqué à ma fille (Racism Explained to My Daughter), Paris: Seuil 1998

L'auberge des pauvres (The Harbourage of the Poor), Paris: Seuil 1999

Labyrinthe des sentiments (Labyrinth of Emotions), Paris: Stock 1999

Cette aveuglante absence de lumière (This Blinding Absence of Light), Paris: Seuil 2001

Le dernier ami (The Last Friend), Paris: Seuil 2004

Partir (Leaving Tangier), Paris: Gallimard 2006

Sur ma mère (About My Mother), Paris: Gallimard 2008

TRANSLATIONS

The Sand Child, trans. Alan Sheridan, San Diego: Harcourt 1987

Solitaire, trans. Nick Hindley, London: Quartet 1988

The Sacred Night, trans. Alan Sheridan, San Diego: Harcourt Brace Jovanovich & London: Quartet 1989

Silent Day in Tangier, trans. David Lobdell, San Diego: Harcourt Brace Jovanovich & London: Quartet 1991

With Downcast Eyes, trans. Joachim Neugroschel, Boston: Little Brown 1993

State of Absence, trans. James Kirkup, London: Quartet 1994

Corruption, trans. Carol Volk, New York: New Press 1995

Racism Explained to My Daughter, trans Carol Volk, New York: W.W. Norton 1999

This Blinding Absence of Light, trans. Linda Coverdale, New York: New Press 2002

The Last Friend, trans. Kevin Michel Capé, Hazel Rowley, New York: New Press 2006

Leaving Tangier, trans. Linda Coverdale, New York: New Press 2009

FURTHER READING

Hanita Brand: "'Fragmentary, But Not Without Meaning'. Androgynous Constructs and Their Enhanced Signification", in: *Edebiyât* 11 (2000), pp. 57–83

Roland Spiller: *Tahar Ben Jelloun: Schreiben zwischen den Kulturen*, Darmstadt: Wissenschaftliche Buchgesellschaft 2000

Roland Spiller: "L'intertextualité circulaire ou le désir dans la bibliothèque: Ben Jelloun lit

Borges, lecteur de Cervantes", in: Charles Bonn, Arnold Rothe (eds.), *Contexte mondial de la littérature maghrébine*, Würzburg: Königshausen & Neumann 1995, pp. 171–80

Roland Spiller: "Tahar Ben Jelloun", in: *Kritisches Lexikon zur fremdsprachigen Gegenwartsliteratur*, Munich: Edition Text + Kritik 1998

Sabine Tamm: "Réalisation de 'La liberté dans l'écriture': Le portrait de Borges dans 'L'enfant de sable'", in: Charles Bonn, Arnold Rothe (eds.), *Contexte mondial de la littérature maghrébine*, Würzburg: Königshausen & Neumann 1995, pp. 161–71

OTHER WORKS CITED

Jorge Luis Borges: *El libro de arena*, Buenos Aires: Emecé 1975

Jorge Luis Borges: "Las ruinas circulares", in: *Ficciones 1935–1944*, Buenos Aires: Sur 1944

Michel Foucault: "Des éspaces autres" [1967/1984], in: Michel Foucault: *Dits et écrits, 1954–1988*, ed. Daniel Defert, vol. 4 (1980–88), Paris: Gallimard 1994, pp. 752–62

James Joyce: *Ulysses*, Paris: Shakespeare and Company 1922

Androgyny as Metaphor
Hoda Barakat and *The Stone of Laughter*

Barbara Winckler

"I'm the man of my book and its woman all at once", says Hoda Barakat, one of Lebanon's most prominent and inventive novelists. Although since 1989 she has lived in Paris, where she has produced most of her work, Hoda Barakat does not write about life in exile, about France or Europe. All of her novels are set in Lebanon during the years of the civil war (1975–90). In her work the war functions as a kind of "blind spot", one that, although not the focus of attention, nevertheless determines events. Gender transgressions, often occurring subliminally, are important in her works, particularly in her debut novel *The Stone of Laughter* (1990), which focuses on the protagonist's character development in a society racked by civil war. Androgyny and homosexuality, distinguishing characteristics of this person, can be read as metaphors for ambiguity, uncertainty, and marginalization.

Barakat does not belong to the generation of young Lebanese authors who has known nothing but life in a war-torn society. Born in 1952 in Beirut, she is a member of a generation that experienced the outbreak of the civil war as adolescents. Unlike the older generation, represented for instance by Elias Khoury, which had a political "orientation", or was politically organized prior to the war and actively involved in the social issues and conflicts that triggered it, some even taking part in the fighting, the consciousness of Barakat's generation first evolved under the conditions of war and hence was decisively shaped by it.

Barakat studied French literature at the Lebanese University in Beirut. After completing her studies in 1974 she taught at a school in southern Lebanon for a year. Her first stay in Paris was intended as preparation for a dissertation, but she abandoned it after just a few months, when the civil war broke out, and returned to Lebanon in 1976. During the war she lived mainly in Beirut, working variously as a teacher, journalist, and translator as well as being a staff member at the Center for Lebanese Studies from 1985 to 1987. The circumstances of her exile seem somewhat absurd. After almost fifteen years of living through a war, with no end to hostilities in sight, holding out any further appeared to her to be senseless and unbearable. She fled to Paris with her two small children in the autumn of 1989; a few months later the war finally came to an end. Today Hoda Barakat works in Paris as a journalist for *Radio Orient*, an Arabic-language station broadcasting its programs in Paris and throughout the Middle East.

War as "alibi"

The civil war is omnipresent in contemporary Lebanese literature. This is of course unsurprising, given that it dragged on for fifteen years and had a massive impact on the population. The people suffered enormously under recurring shortages of basic necessities, the mounting scale of material destruction and the perpetual threat to life and limb, but in particular they suffered psychological trauma. The unity of the nation was shattered and countless splinter groups were formed, whose "opponents" and "coalition partners" rotated at ever-diminishing intervals. If the fronts of the conflict were initially clearly recognizable, as it unfolded the war seemed increasingly irrational and unfathomable. No end was in sight, or, rather, time and again it seemed as if the fighting had ended, only for it to flare up again shortly afterwards.

In this way, war mutated from being an exceptional state into an integral part of everyday life and normality; an entire generation grew up whose sole lived reality was a war situation. This was further exacerbated by the way in which clashes in a civil war are fought out "right on the doorstep" and literally into the buildings, while the "enemy" is not some stranger but "one of us".

Ken Seigneurie, a literary scholar teaching in Beirut, underlines the importance of literature to working through war experiences: Stories are seen as crucial to gaining understanding of and coming to terms with the experiences and traumas of this war. This is true for stories told in everyday life, but in particular for those related in literature. By responding to the implicit questions of who, where, when, how and why, stories transform random happenings and incidents into graspable and so potentially meaningful occurrences. "Without stories, an event – the war in this case – remains vague and ultimately a meaningless affair that may in turn re-emerge." Many intellectuals lament that after the war people preferred "to look to the future", to get on with the work of reconstruction and let bygones be bygones. Discussions and arguments about guilt and responsibility are dodged in social and political discourse. The process of accounting for and coming to terms with what occurred is undertaken to a significant degree by literature. Authors like Elias Khoury, Rashid al-Daif, Etel Adnan and Vénus Khoury-Ghata confront the collective amnesia in their work.

Commenting on her own writing, Hoda Barakat has said that she did not freely choose to write about the war. Her generation is so profoundly shaped by it and its consciousness indelibly stamped by the war experience that writing "outside" the war is simply inconceivable. "The war will be with me forever. I will carry with me what I went through wherever I may go." The civil war is therefore present in all her novels; it does, however, gravitate more and more into the background. Are her works therefore to be characterized as "war novels"? Or are they texts whose plots are played out against the backdrop of a civil war, but in which other themes are pivotal? This question as to the appropriateness of classifying a work as "(civil) war literature" is particularly relevant to Barakat's work. She herself does not regard her work as war literature, and especially not in the sense of a "propagandistic literature". Her work does not defend one standpoint against another. She is concerned neither with depicting the occurrences of war nor with analyzing the "logic of war" or political events, "to comprehend the incomprehensible". "In my novels", explains the author in an interview, "I do not trace events. I speak about tiny fragments, about the distant echo of what occurs. I begin where the event ends, because literature has nothing to do with newspaper reports."

In her literary work Hoda Barakat is interested less in what is conditioned by social forces than in the psychological constitution of man and the human condition. The individual, with his/her inner conflicts and obsessions, is the pivot around which her texts revolve.

> My writing expresses what I have learnt about human nature under the conditions of war. In my novels depicting the war is not the actual goal but a kind of alibi. The war functions as one of many possible extreme situations, one in which what lies under the flimsy veneer of value judgments and morality becomes visible.

Take violence, in her eyes a key element of human life, not only under the conditions of war. "We're all immensely violent, even and especially women. I'm not one of those authors who believe in the goodness of human nature."

With the war behind and its shadow in view

Since the publication of her first novel in 1990 which – after her debut in 1985 with a volume of short stories, *Women Visitors* – marks the genuine beginning of her literary production, Hoda Barakat has published three further, likewise extremely complex novels. The language, densely woven and frequently of a brutal beauty, gets under the reader's skin. She connects narrative with the metaphoric, and time and again interweaves into the plot general reflections on mankind that lead the story onto byways. Behind each "clause curve", a new universe opens up. Through her empathy with the protagonists, to whom we become increasingly attached as the story unfolds, the texts deeply engage the reader, only to leave him irritated and without precise answers in the end. As soon as we think we have found a key to understanding the text, it slips away again to confront us with new twists, creating a new set of conundrums. Barakat has developed a unique narrative position: The novels turn their back on the war while keeping the shadow it casts firmly in view.

Three years after *The Stone of Laughter*, Barakat published her second novel. *Disciples of Passion* (1993) attempts to fathom the relationship between love, madness, and death against the backdrop of the civil war. The novel examines a man's obsession with a woman, which is marked by the desire to merge with the beloved into a hermaphroditic creature, as well as the panic-stricken angst of loss. The narration of events by the narrator-protagonist suggests that this – and not the man's war experiences, which include abduction and torture – is the cause of his "madness". It is perhaps ultimately nothing more than an inability to come to terms with the world in which he lives. Now a patient in a psychiatric clinic, he looks back at the past only for the boundaries between reality and imagination to blur. In the end he himself doubts that what he has reported really happened: that he killed the woman "to assimilate her soul".

Barakat's third novel, published in 1998, adopts a new, at times almost legendary tone. Described by Angelika Neuwirth as a "postmodern refracted Levantine saga", *The Tiller of Waters* oscillates between myth and reality. It is the story of Niqula, the son of a mercer, and his relationship with the young Kurdish maid Shamsa. The story of his life and his experiences before and in the first years of the civil war are interwoven with the history of the fabrics and their various characteristics, which he relates to Shamsa. In the process the fabric history turns out to be the history of mankind, of peoples and kings. The dramaturgical arch from simple to precious fabrics – cotton, linen, velvet to silk – is closely tied to the development of the individual from child to adult, which in its final stage – that of silk – can culminate in madness. After militiamen seize his apartment, Niqula builds a new "home" in his extensively gutted shop, amidst the devastated souks of Beirut's city center. In the heart of the fiercely contested city he lives in a kind of utopia – a "non-place" –, in fully deserted surroundings, where wolf-like dogs roam the streets, one of which he takes for a companion. Even after the fighting comes to an end, the "biotope" of this doppelganger of Sélim Nassib's *Fou de Beyrouth* initially remains untouched, until finally, long after the end of the war, the outside world eventually penetrates into his "utopia".

In her fourth novel *My Master and My Lover* (2004) Barakat again works with a male narrator and main protagonist. Wadiʿ tells of his childhood and youth, of his father, who works as a cook for the rich – in the eyes of his son all too submissively –, of a close friendship that ends tragically, of how he somewhat unwillingly became a successful drug and arms dealer, and of the flame of his youth, Samia, with whom he finally flees to Cyprus as the situation in Beirut becomes too risky. When he vanishes at the end, Samia takes over the narrative.

The androgyny of writing

A striking feature of Hoda Barakat's work is that – in contrast to the majority of works penned by women – the main protagonists of all her novels are male. In the first instance this needs to be seen as a strategy safeguarding against an autobiographical reading. Women authors are often "automatically'" identified with their protagonists and their texts banished to the niche of "women's literature". That she is asked about the absence of the "women's rights question" in her work is something that annoys her:

> The "women problematic" is in the first instance a social question. I'm more interested in what lies underneath this, the hidden regions of humans – a woman has regions of strength, a man some of vulnerability. It would be stupid to think that each gender should only speak about itself.

Ultimately, the choice of male protagonists is a way of expanding the scope of her novels:

> A male character opens up for me as a female author another, more complex field. On the one hand men in our society have more opportunities than women, while on the other they have to – and this applies especially in a war situation – face up to more challenges.

Particularly in Arabic literature, the suffering and resistance of women and the oppressed have been portrayed repeatedly. "It is essentially more complex and interesting," comments the author, "to attempt to understand the oppressors and the mechanism of oppression than the victim."

Not least, she writes from the perspective and with the voice of a man so as to experience more about him. For writing is not merely the act of conveying what she already knows, but a process of gaining insight. "When I write about a man and in his name, I do this of course with my instruments and my consciousness as a woman." Barakat thus performs an androgyny of writing: "When I write about men and women I try to be man and woman – and to go beyond both. After all, writing means stepping outside all boundaries."

As she transgresses the boundary between the genders in the act of writing, so too she breaches the confessional divides that play such a key role in Lebanon and along which the conflict lines of the civil war were frequently drawn. The protagonists of her novels belong to different sects; exactly which ones they are affiliated to is mostly extrapolated only indirectly, by those privy to the significance of certain details, for instance how they brew their tea. This also prevents the author from being identified with her characters – an approach diametrically opposite to that of Rashid al-Daif, who deliberately seeks to engage his own community.

The alchemy of war

The Stone of Laughter, awarded the renowned prize of the literary journal *al-Naqid* for best debut novel the year it was published, is set in Beirut during the final years of the civil war. Khalil, the (anti)hero of the novel, a young man with androgynous traits and homosexual inclinations who is in harmony with neither himself nor his body, attempts amidst the turmoil of war to define his relationships to society and himself. Living reclusively in his room, he preoccupies himself with reading, cooking, and cleaning – particularly after bombardments – and does his utmost to keep out of what's going on "outside". He has very few contacts but occasionally he meets up with a group of leftwing intellectuals, one of whom is a friend from university, Nayif, who works for the newspaper of a leftist "organization" and indulges in belligerent revolutionary speeches, although he lives a very bourgeois life. Khalil constantly spurns Nayif's repeated exhortation to get involved in the newspaper.

The novel accompanies Khalil through his everyday life; through his eyes we see Lebanese society and what it is like to live in a divided city. Neighbors of the "other faith" leave their apartments and move to the (predominantly Christian) eastern part of the city – including his best friend Naji, with whom he is secretly in love and who is shot dead by a sniper a little later. Khalil takes care of the unoccupied apartment belonging to Naji and his mother; later he lets the family of his uncle, refugees from southern Lebanon, stay there. He falls in love with his much younger cousin Yusuf, who joins a militia. When Yusuf is killed, Khalil, plagued by stomach pains, shuts himself off from society completely.

Khalil's personality eventually changes dramatically. His nagging sense of being at odds with himself and the world has mutated into a stomach ulcer. Having narrowly escaped death during surgery to remove the ulcer, for the first time he realizes the value of life. He decides to "love himself" from now on and be solely concerned with his own well-being, even if this means disregarding ethical principles. He rents out Naji's apartment and sells everything of worth he finds there. He becomes attached to the newspaper circle and socializes with individuals there who are embroiled in the war, but continues to reject any involvement with the paper. Something is still missing in his realization, though, and this is first revealed to him when he sees the "truth" of the war with his own eyes: The drugs and arms trade is flourishing, even amongst the fiercest of enemies, and people from his "own side" beat him up "by mistake". Only now does he realize that actively taking part as a member of one side is the only way to survive, that he has no choice: "Loving oneself" means hating others. He gets involved in the arms trade and rapes a young woman from the neighborhood.

The novel eschews the obvious signs of war: the street battles, exploding car bombs and snipers; or people in fear of their life huddled in shelters, their conversation revolving around the inexplicable reality of war, who weep for their dead and worry about their "loved ones". Neither the problematic of the country being split along religious or ideological divides nor the question of emigration is directly addressed. The novel tells the story of Khalil, his inner life, his dreams and obsessions, into which the outside world appears to penetrate only at the edges. Nevertheless, the novel includes all these aspects of a war reality. They are shown in small, often absurd details, which reveal a great deal more than heroic deeds and gestures, so that they often seem more grotesque than threatening.

"Alone in a narrow passing place" – in the cleavage of gender

The Stone of Laughter can be read as a negative *Bildungsroman* set in a war context. The protagonist develops from an antihero to a man who finds a "positive" attitude to life and performs a role accepted in society. This development, which appears here as negative, is formulated – like the conflict of the protagonist by and large – in terms of gender and sexual orientation. The ambiguity of his gender identity, assigned a key role in this novel, goes far beyond the mere ascription of a gender role in its implications. Khalil's androgynous traits and homosexual inclinations need to be approached metaphorically.

"Khalil's legs were not long enough." The novel's opening sentence characterizes Khalil as an antihero. This is more than a physical description; his legs stand *pars pro toto* for Khalil's "deficient" physical and psychological constitution. The opening chapter of the novel, comprising of only two sentences, anticipates in a seemingly ordinary scene Khalil's characterization, his relationship to Naji and his environment in general:

> Khalil's legs were not long enough.
> While Naji tossed his head, scattering the raindrops, Khalil panted behind him, on the step before last, stamping his feet to get rid of the mud on his shoes before he caught up and went into the flat with him ...

Khalil's deficient manliness is first conveyed through his physical attributes. His body, "unfinished", yet to fully mature, resembling that of an adolescent, implies that he is not a "real man". The first sign of a "psychological" deficit, of the protagonist's androgynous traits, is his reaction to the street battles:

> Whenever a battle draws to an end, Khalil feels the need for order and

cleanliness and the feeling grows, spreads until it becomes almost an obsession. (...) The line of the striped blanket on the bed is exactly parallel to the ground. On the table with the gas stove is a newspaper, still folded, and the whiteness of its pages, like the gleam of the dishes and little cups on the clean polished edges hidden away in the corner, suggest that a woman, a housewife – or a snow-white old maid – has lived for some time, quietly, in this little house.

How he cleans up and cooks, bakes bread or knits is described in meticulous detail: Khalil's way of life stands in sharp contrast to the usual male gender role. By withdrawing to his room and devoting his attention to housework while a war rages on, he is assuming a distinctly female-connoted role. Instead of actively taking part in the war, as becomes a man, he sets his cleaning and tidying up against the fighting. In these moments, he succeeds in shielding himself off from the demands imposed by the outside world; he is content and has a sense of self-harmony.

With its detailed, in places paralyzing descriptions, which in extensive digressions pull the narrative through languid loops, the text itself obstinately sets itself against the dominance of the war and its tumultuous hectic – just as the protagonist does. Khalil's dissociation from the fighting and the war, however, is not an act of commitment or active resistance but rather, as the author herself once put it, "a kind of physiological reaction." This primarily physical reaction to the war is expressed particularly poignantly in a scene where Khalil cuts his hand on a shattered windowpane and becomes nauseous just by looking at the small wound. As is so often the case, here Barakat counters the reader's expectations by choosing an example that does not directly stem from the war context. Confronting Khalil with the agonizing suffering of the wounded or the dead to demonstrate his "unmanly" reaction would have been too obvious.

Society at war furnishes two models for masculinity, neither of which are an option for Khalil. He cannot identify with the younger males who have become men at a single stroke and are now fully concerned with the practical demands of day-to-day life in a war situation, nor can he feel any affiliation to men of his own age who, involved in politics and working in the press, espouse their theories about the "the big questions of life". He is suited to neither the role of a militiaman nor of a cadre.

But the doors of both kinds of manhood were closed to Khalil and so he remained, alone in his narrow passing place, in a stagnant, feminine state of submission to a purely vegetable life, just within reach of two very attractive versions of masculinity, that force which makes the volcano of life explode.

Khalil finds himself in a no-man's-land between the male and female spheres. On the one hand he cannot and will not be part of the male sphere, associated with "outside", with violence and ideologies. And yet the female world, in which he strives to live by withdrawing to his room, concentrating on housework, and trying to remain aloof from the war and its logic, is denied him. He does not possess the "wisdom of women" – particularly in the face of death – and he cannot become part of the consoling community of women he so achingly longs for.

> Women, thought Khalil, moaning in envy alone in his room ... all the wisdom is given to women. Wisdom of life and death and wisdom of what is farthest from it ... (...)
>
> They tame death, instinctively. (...) They feed it, they give it coffee to drink and they walk by its side until it becomes like one of the family and they do not hesitate to tell it their little problems as if it were a friendly neighbor picking over lentils with you on the big brass tray.

In marked contrast to these imaginings of femininity are the images of women Khalil identifies with in the context of the two "love stories" he experiences, which follow the same pattern. Khalil adores Naji and lives in constant fear of being rejected by him. Full of self-disgust he feels like a "castoff wife" whenever he waits longingly for Naji to visit. Consumed by worry about Naji's safety when he dares to cross the demarcation line after his family has moved to the city's eastern sector, Khalil is torn "like the son of the two mothers in the story of King Solomon." He even goes so far as to identify with the "true" mother from the Old Testament parable, who out of love and genuine care relinquishes the child, as Khalil does Naji's visit.

Unlike Naji, the much younger Yusuf looks up to Khalil as an older brother, but he is just as little inclined to reciprocate his love. When Yusuf joins a militia to provide for his family, Khalil – who also profits from this – sees himself in the position of the wife who stays at home while "his husband" Yusuf provides for their livelihood. Creating another intertextual connection, he refers – once again identifying with a female figure – to the Qur'anic story of Joseph to illustrate his unrequited love:

> I cling to Youssef, like Potiphar's wife, Zuleikha, clung to him. (...) I am a wife of the wrong sex as if, in my stupidity, I wait for Youssef to come one day to ask for my hand. To knock at the door in his most splendid raiment and ask me ... while I blush, shyly, hesitating a little before nodding my head in agreement ...

In both cases Khalil remains trapped in a passive attitude, more a plaything than the master of the situation. Both Naji and Yusuf are for the main part present in Khalil's thoughts, and he feels that they show him too little respect and appreciation. Both die violently in unclear circumstances, prompting doubt about their character. Was Naji perhaps a double agent after all, as a friend had once intimated? Did Yusuf only keep watch to protect the neighborhood, or was he a brutal fighter? These questions gnaw away at Khalil, sowing doubt as to just how intimately he knew his two beloved friends, and as a consequence he is not only robbed of their companionship in the present but also of their shared past. Grief and doubt consume him inwardly – not only in the figurative sense: He develops a stomach ulcer.

Homosexuality and androgyny as metaphors

Is Khalil a homosexual? Is *The Stone of Laughter* "a welcome contribution to contemporary gay fiction", as claimed by *The Bookseller*? Such an understanding overlooks the intentional trajectory of the novel. Khalil's homosexuality is portrayed as thoroughly contradictory. Although he twice falls in love with other men, the newspaper photos of fallen combatants stripped to the waist arouse him, and after Naji's death he is beset by homoerotic dreams, at no point does the text state a definite sexual orientation. Khalil never lives out a relationship; everything is played out in his mind: a state of being in love, an infatuation that he confesses to no one. On another occasion Khalil is physically attracted to his female neighbor; she however has something masculine about her, "something that resembles him". He spurns the advances of men and women alike. His homosexual inclination – and furthermore his choice of the "objects" of his love, who do not reciprocate his feelings – appears more akin to a fleeing from relationships, an intensification of his marginal position.

Stefan Meyer has pointed out the significance of the homosexuality theme for the "'feminization' of the novel form" in the West. "Western modernism is unthinkable without the contribution of homoerotic texts which continuously undermine a patriarchal legacy in the form as well as the themes, the underlying values, and concerns." In modern Arabic literature, Meyer continues, this thematic complex is addressed mostly by women writers.

The Stone of Laughter is not concerned with broaching the issue of homosexuality as a social taboo – a taboo that has only rarely been addressed in Arabic literature. Barakat's concern is not the emancipation of homosexuals. A scandal like the one ignited by the depiction of homoerotic relationships between women in Hanan al-Shaykh's novel *Women of Sand and Myrrh* published two years before this one failed to materialize. This is most probably due to the fact that the novel does not describe any homoerotic scenes and homosexuality is accorded a very different function.

Khalil's gender ambiguity is extremely complex and admits a host of divergent interpretations. In the first instance it is an expression of general destabilization. Khalil's position between the sexes is the expression of his oscillation, his uncertainty, and his doubts. In contrast to the other characters, who always seem to know what is right and "true", Khalil doubts everything. He is never sure about how he should act and who he should believe, in particular as to the deaths of his friends.

The androgyne has been a recurrent motif in literature since Plato's circular creatures of a "double nature". An androgynous figure is always ambivalent: On the one hand, it is viewed as deficient because it has no clearly defined identity and is excluded from mainstream society; on the other hand, the androgyne is a symbol of perfection, of self-reliance, and autarchy. As an "intermediate being", it also appears predestined to play the role of mediator. Alternatively, the adoption of expressly feminine elements in a male figure can be seen as a way of approximating the ideal of androgyny – or even that of the hermaphrodite – and thus depict a character capable of transgressing conventional divides and belonging to two spheres in an enriching way. As already indicated, this is the basic idea behind Hoda Barakat's second novel, *Disciples of Passion*. For the protagonist, obsessed with the fear of losing the woman he loves, this idea means the realization of his cherished dream of autonomy: to merge with the other to avert the danger of loss and be one with himself and the other. In *The Stone of Laughter* this attempt is doomed to failure: Khalil is unable to grasp his borderline situation as something positive, and in the end he fully embraces the male role. The hybrid gender identity, which in the Lebanese context may be taken as alluding to national and religious identity, serves as a means to subvert rigid social roles as well as social norms and conventions.

Finally, the strong presence of feminine elements in a male figure also serves to dissociate Khalil from the image of the male as a killer predestined to be killed himself. Here the gender designations stand for the "masculine" and "feminine" principle in every person:

> Khalil knew that a fear of blood to the point of faintness, having short legs, a slight build, straight chestnut hair and large eyes, all these do not make a man a hermaphrodite, or effeminate, or make him any less masculine, or ... queer ... he knew that there were certainly more female hormones in him than there should naturally be, for they protected him from committing the crime of the act, so it was only a passing crisis, it would come to an end ...

"He has become a man who laughs" – the transformation

Khalil's process of transformation follows the pattern of a *rite de passage* that usually accompanies a critical transition: Separation from social context is followed by the liminal phase, characterized by ambiguous status and isolation from external influences, before there is a reincorporation into the social and cultural framework, connected to acquiring a new status. Khalil is a marginal or "liminal" figure from the outset, one whose character and social position are not unambiguous. His transformation only sets in during his stay in hospital, a place secluded from the outside world, finally allowing him to assume a socially recognized position as a result. The process that is set in motion here results from Khalil's close shave with death, which remarkably has little to do with the direct impact of the war. Moreover, the hospital is not represented as a place of suffering and death but as a paradise where everything is geared to benefiting its patients.

Not until the fifth and final section of the novel, spanning a mere four pages, does the reader realize the full extent of Khalil's transformation: On a cold and rainy night he supervises the unloading of arms and munitions and then rapes his neighbor. With a metafictional device the narrative voice intervenes – for the first time in such a direct form – and reveals itself to be female:

> I went up to the rear window ... Khalil had a moustache and a pair of sunglasses.
> Where are you going, I asked, and he did not hear me.
> It's me, I told him, and he did not turn around.
> The car moved off and, from the back window, Khalil seemed broad-shouldered in his brown leather jacket ...
> The car moved off and began to draw away. Khalil was leaving the street as if he were rising upwards.
> You've changed so much since I described you in the first pages. You've come to know more than I do. Alchemy. The stone of laughter.
> Khalil is gone, he has become a man who laughs. And I remain a woman who writes.
> Khalil: my darling hero.
> My darling hero ...

The novel ends with this parting between the narrator and her transformed hero. Kitted out with the clichéd accessories – sun glasses, moustache, and leather jacket – Khalil is seeking to compensate for this "deficiencies" and become a "real man". "He has become a man who laughs." With *dhakar* Hoda Barakat employs a term that is similar to "male" in English, and so underlines the stereotypical character of his new identity. Khalil adopts the "male" role and all that it connotes: power, oppression, and use of force. By discarding the "female" elements of his personality, he becomes – seen positively – "fully" male, able finally to take his place in society. On the other hand, he turns his back on the possibilities afforded by his androgynous personality to unify both poles.

The androgynous Khalil stays out of the war, while the "male" Khalil, succumbing to the attraction of a war reality, turns corrupt and violent. Here one could hastily conclude that the author wishes to exploit a common cliché: Men are for war, women against it. Khalil observes women, full of envy at how nature has given them "true wisdom", how they stand by one another, and do nothing to enflame the raging war; it would however be amiss to interpret this as an authorial statement. The text makes it clear that these (peaceable) images of women in fact spring from Khalil's imagination of what the female world, which he longs to join, is like. The female figures in the novel are, barring a few exceptions, generally portrayed in a bad light: There is Claude, the moody and arrogant wife of Nayif who wants to leave the country as quickly as possible; or the women who flirt with the men working at the newspaper to assume an air of importance; or the "young bride" who even flaunts her feminine charms in the shelter during the shelling, as well as the wife of the paper's editor-in-chief who plays the devoted, supportive spouse while directing subtle barbs against him and who is in truth interested only in sharing his prestige. In terms of their behavior these women are just like the men. Instead of spurning the war, their only difference to the men is in that they have less room to maneuver, less options to act. Without grand declarations Hoda Barakat implicitly undermines the automatic association of "man = fascination with war *versus* woman = hostility to war". A femininity that is not only a characteristic of women is posited as a positive counterpart to a perverted masculinity. Her novel thus differs fundamentally from classical feminist novels. The "modern" struggle for female self-assertion is supplanted here by a postmodern subversion of how society constructs gender.

The author does not declare that Khalil has changed, or explain how it took place, tracing instead his thoughts and inner conflicts, only revealing the transformed "hero" in the very last scene. Having followed Khalil's life, suffering, and thoughts "first hand", the reader is now suddenly confronted with a *fait accompli* as Khalil is presented as a completely "changed" character. This is the shock effect generated by the novel's end: After the reader has been privy to the most intimate feelings and innermost thoughts of the protagonist throughout the novel, a "closed" figure now stands before him, its inner life inaccessible, its transformation inexplicable.

The narrator is just as alienated as the reader. It is as if she herself is merely an observer who together with the reader suddenly experiences what has happened, and is no longer the narrator who created the protagonist and determined what happens to him. She has merely accompanied her hero, without knowing in advance the path he would eventually take or exerting any influence on his development. The novel thus ends with the protagonist, whom the narrator has hitherto followed from a position in the background, deciding to follow a path along which she can no longer follow him. She regrets this, experiences this as a loss, the loss of her "darling hero". And yet this sad regret does not harbor any condemnation. She does not reproach him, but accepts his decision and lets him go. The metafictional twist serves neither to undermine the meaningfulness and credibility of the preceding story, nor to enhance the text's authenticity. Instead, the twist contributes – through the narrator's sadness – to generating a stronger emotional impact, bewildering the reader when the threads of the story slip out of the narrator's own hands and she has no sway over its progress. Asked why the antiwar figure could not be kept until the finale, the author answered that it had been simply impossible to stay out of the war. The only options were to be victim or perpetrator. Khalil could not maintain his ambiguity because humans – and in particular men – can only be "one hundred per cent" in war and must utterly conform to one of the communities within society. Homosexuality and androgyny, or the ambiguity for which they act as metaphors in this novel, are only acceptable in a stable society.

WORKS

Za'irat (Women Visitors), Beirut: al-Matbu'at al-Sharqiyya 1985

Hajar al-dahik (The Stone of Laughter), London: Riad El-Rayyes 1990; Beirut: Dar an-Nahar 2005

Ahl al-hawa (Disciples of Passion), Beirut: Dar an-Nahar 1993

Harith al-miyah (The Tiller of Waters), Beirut: Dar an-Nahar 1998

Rasa'il al-ghariba (Letters of the Stranger), Beirut: Dar an-Nahar 2004

Sayyidi wa-habibi (My Master and My Lover), Beirut: Dar an-Nahar 2004

Viva la Diva. Masrahiyya bi-l-'ammiyya al-lubnaniyya (Viva la Diva. A Play in the Lebanese Colloquial), Beirut: Dar an-Nahar 2009

TRANSLATIONS

The Stone of Laughter, trans. Sophie Bennett, Reading: Garnet 1994; New York: Interlink 1995

The Tiller of Waters, trans. Marilyn Booth, Cairo, New York: The American University in Cairo Press 2001

Disciples of Passion, trans. Marilyn Booth, Syracuse, NY: Syracuse University Press 2005

FURTHER READING

Samira Aghacy: "Hoda Barakat's *The Stone of Laughter*: Androgyny or Polarization?", in: *Journal of Arabic Literature* 29 (1998), pp. 185–201

Hoda Barakat: "I write against my hand", in: Fadia Faqir (ed.), *In the House of Silence. Autobiographical Essays by Arab Women Writers*, Reading: Garnet 1998, pp. 41–7

Mona Takeddine Amyuni: "Etel Adnan & Hoda Barakat. De-Centered Perspectives – Subversive Voices", in: Andreas Pflitsch, Barbara Winckler (eds.), *Poetry's Voice – Society's Norms. Forms of Interaction between Middle Eastern Writers and their Societies*, Wiesbaden: Reichert 2006, pp. 211–21

Sobhi Boustani: "Réalisme et fantastique dans le roman Hârith al-miyâh de Hodâ Barakât",
in: *Middle Eastern Literatures* 6 (2003), pp. 225–35

Mona Fayad: "Strategic Androgyny: Passing as Masculine in Barakat's *Stone of Laughter*",
in: Lisa Suhair Majaj, Paula W. Sunderman, Therese Saliba (eds.), *Intersections. Gender,
Nation, and Community in Arab Women's Novels*, Syracuse, NY: Syracuse University
Press 2003, pp. 162–79

Michelle Hartman: "Intertextuality and Gender Identity in Huda Barakat's 'Ahl al-Hawa'"
in: Robin Ostle (ed.), *Marginal Voices in Literature and Society. Individual and Society
in the Mediterranean Muslim World*, Strasbourg et al.: European Science Foundation
2001, pp. 171–88

Michelle Hartman: "A Wife of the Wrong Sex: A Re-vision of Joseph", in: Michelle Hartman, *Jesus, Joseph and Job. Reading Rescriptions of Religious Figures in Lebanese Women's
Fiction*, Wiesbaden: Reichert 2002, pp. 123–48

Nisrine Jaafar: "'Unmaking' the Erotic in Hoda Barakat's *Hajar al-dahik*", in: *Al-Abhath*
52–3 (2004–05), pp. 89–98

Richard van Leeuwen: "The Enchantment of Space: Two Novels of Gamal al-Ghitani
and Hoda Barakat", in: Boutros Hallaq, Robin Ostle, Stefan Wild (eds.), *La poétique de
l'espace dans la littérature arabe moderne*, Paris: Presses Sorbonne Nouvelle 2002

Stefan G. Meyer: *The Experimental Arabic Novel. Postcolonial Literary Modernism in the
Levant*, New York: State University of New York Press 2001, pp. 153–59, 231–34

Angelika Neuwirth: "Huda Barakat. Der die Wogen durchpflügt", in: Angelika Neuwirth,
Andreas Pflitsch, *Agonie und Aufbruch. Neue libanesische Prosa*, Beirut: Dergham 2000,
p. 49

Ken Seigneurie: "Anointing with Rubble. Ruins in the Lebanese War Novel", in: *Comparative Studies of South Asia, Africa and the Middle East* 28,1 (2008), pp. 50–60

Ken Seigneurie: "Ongoing War and Arab Humanism", in: Laura Doyle, Laura A. Wienkiel
(eds.), *Geomodernisms: Race, Modernism, Modernity*, Bloomington, IN: Indiana University Press 2005, pp. 96–113

Barbara Winckler: "Utopische Kriegslandschaften. Sélim Nassib, Huda Barakat und die
Debatte um den Wiederaufbau des Beiruter Stadtzentrums", in: Andreas Pflitsch, Barbara
Winckler (eds.), *Poetry's Voice – Society's Norms. Forms of Interaction between Middle
Eastern Writers and their Societies*, Wiesbaden: Reichert 2006, pp. 259–80

Barbara Winckler: *Grenzgänge. Androgynie – Wahnsinn – Utopie im Romanwerk von
Huda Barakat*, Wiesbaden: Reichert (forthcoming)

OTHER WORKS CITED

Sélim Nassib: *Fou de Beyrouth*, Paris: Editions Balland 1992

Ken Seigneurie: "The Storying of Space in Hassan Daoud's Binayat Mathilde", unpublished
paper, The 2nd Annual Conference on Contemporary Arabic Literature: "The War
Novel", 3–4 May 2000, Lebanese American University (LAU), Beirut

Hanan al-Shaykh: *Misk al-ghazal*, Beirut: Dar al-Adab 1988 (English translation: *Women
of Sand and Myrrh*, trans. Catherine Cobham, London: Quartet 1989)

Transgression as Program

On the Novels of Rachid Boudjedra

Doris Ruhe

Rachid Boudjedra's career as a writer began when his first book was awarded a prize whose name in retrospect seems prescient for what was to follow: the *Prix des enfants terribles*, initiated by Jean Cocteau, which recognizes literary works that depart from generally accepted norms and confront society with its very own taboos. Understood in this sense, transgression is a program inherent to Boudjedra's work that is put into practice on diverse levels.

Like Kateb Yacine and Assia Djebar, Boudjedra's early years were decisively influenced by two factors stemming from an act of fatherly authority. While for Kateb and Djebar attending a French school meant separation from their families and the milieu of their native language but not from their country, this phase took a different course for Boudjedra. Born in 1941 in Aïn Beïda in eastern Algeria, in line with his father's wish the author was given an education that would introduce him to the best of both worlds, the Orient and the Occident. Such an education was not possible in French-colonized Algeria of the 1950s, where Arabic remained excluded from school curriculums. For this reason, the ten-year-old Rachid had to cross borders in a tangible sense: those marking family life and his country. Boudjedra attended the elite Lycée Saddiki in Tunis as a boarder, where he came into contact with the essentials not only of Arab but also ancient Greek, Latin and French cultures. He spent a year in Spain in the 1950s, before returning to Algeria after the country gained independence, where he began to study philosophy, which he then concluded in Paris with a degree from the Sorbonne.

A plurality of cultures and languages were thus the resources Boudjedra could draw on from the outset of his literary work. They enabled him to switch to writing in Arabic in 1981 after having published six novels in French. With this step – extremely significant for an author who uses language as a means not only of communication but also of artistic expression – Boudjedra followed the Arabization policy of the Algerian government; he claims it was out of personal conviction and the need to immerse himself once more in his native language. As it became clear in the mid-1990s that fundamentalists were seeking to exploit Arabic as a political weapon, he returned to writing in French.

It would seem that Boudjedra experiences the diversity and heterogeneity of the worlds in which he moves (not always of his own accord and often determined by external circumstances) not as uprooting and dislocation but as an opening and broadening of his horizons, which on the literary level in particular are boundless. He is probably the most modern Algerian author of his generation, perhaps also the most ambitious; he is the author who has pressed ahead most resolutely in the endeavor to renew the novel, explore new narrative strategies, and attain formal perfection. As decisive influences he has named not only the classic novelists of Modernism like Flaubert, Proust, Joyce and Faulkner, but also Günter Grass and above all Claude Simon. In Simon's work he sees the realization of the "Mediterranean" novel he envisions – a novel that is anchored in the climate and social reality of the Mediterranean region with its respective specific local conditions, while simultaneously making the formal devices of Postmodernism productive for Maghreb literature.

Schooled in the *nouveau roman*, Boudjedra has developed a style that critics such as Jean-François Revel have described as "verbally excessive", often making the text virtually impenetrable for the reader. Words cascade page after page with hardly any punctuation to provide orientation, demanding from the reader enormous effort and perseverance. This stylistic trait is particularly evident in his early work. In his novel *The Funeral* (2003), more formally structured than its immediate predecessors and thus somewhat more accessible, the author tells the reader with a wink that he is going to hold back from using punctuation as an aid to reading and comprehending the text. One of the protagonists, a school pupil, admits: "I don't like commas or full stops. I've never liked them. Neither in arithmetic, in dictation, or in essay writing."

On the formal level, the author is concerned with appropriating what has gained currency under the term "world literature" in the postcolonial context. On the level of content though, he locates his texts very precisely in his own Maghreb culture. Tapping into what Jean Ricardou has characterized as the reservoir – the sum of determinants forming an author's personal profile, in which historical, social, ideological and emotional elements converge – Boudjedra creates a narrative cosmos that, similar to Faulkner's sagas of extended families, allows the social figurations and problems behind the individual fate to shimmer through. Even if in the process the authorial gaze is fixed pointedly on the sexual morals and thus the situation of women in Algerian society, it should be asked whether even more contentious and explosive issues, perhaps evading formulation, are not also addressed and other struggles fought out in the medium of this thematic. The way in which the author uses his exploration of the rigid ordering of gender relations to broach vital societal issues at both collective and individual levels can be clearly shown in four novels, ranging from his early literary work through to the present.

The revolt against the tabooed gaze

The typical architecture of the Arabian house, with its high walls and organization around the inner courtyard, unobservable to prying eyes from the outside, may be read as a metaphor for the sheltered spaces that enclose the family in a sphere of intimacy and whose innermost sanctum protects the female body from the outside gaze. This taboo on the gaze, turning curiosity into an illicit act, is purposefully breached by Boudjedra time and again. Speaking figuratively, he demolishes the obstructing walls with his targeted critique of Algerian society, furnishing us with an insight into what traditionally remains concealed.

Gender studies have sharpened awareness that all cultures describe the female body in accordance with social norms, which subjugate the right to gaze, or its restriction, to sets of fixed rules. Is it even possible to break free of these shackles that simultaneously express power relations and codify the traditional asymmetry between male and female in the gender hierarchy? This is the question raised by the repeated breaking of taboos, which take center stage in Boudjedra's novels.

The Repudiation, his debut novel (1969), sets all the signs of a provocation of dominant conventions on the very first page. The text opens with a description of intercourse between the narrator Rachid and his French lover Céline, closing in on the female genital, which is represented as being at once an object of desire and repellant and disgusting. What is generally strictly withdrawn from sight exerts the most powerful stimulation on visual curiosity, but also arouses the greatest trepidation. Starkly exposing the difference to the female other, this focus triggers extremely conflicting feelings. They range from the desire to submit to the woman – thus reacting within the economy of the socially sanctioned attitude – through to disgust at the "terrifying swelling". Even if intended as a rebellion against duplicitous morality, exposing a woman to view in this way is nonetheless a demonstration of power, with which the female body is made malleable to the demands of the male.

Although desired as a sexual object and welcomed as a means of bolstering the male ego – "as lust subsided she used the short time between fulfillment and bitterness to thank me, to idolize me ... " – the woman remains alien. The unhindered gaze directed at her body fails to bring about the hoped-for release from the repressive tradition; on the contrary, it only serves to sharpen awareness of the difference between the sexes and triggers an anxiety slumbering in the depths of childhood memory. The narrator speaks of his nightmares, in which images of his mother's menstrual blood, accidentally glimpsed, return as terrifying streams. This motif surfaces in countless variations in almost all of Boudjedra's works, as if obeying a compulsion. In *The Repudiation*, this passage follows as a digression to the narrator's often repeated admission of his desire to lock up the woman and claim her as his possession, as is customarily practiced. The link between exercising power and coping with anxiety is clearly drawn. However, the narrator at once repels and reverses his temptation: thinking about the physiological nature shared by all women, he equates his lover with the women of his own culture and thus posits her as someone who is to be pitied: "for she too was a victim, just like all the other women in the country where she had come to live." Hence, the victimization of the woman is regretted against the background of implied collective power structures on the one hand, while on the other it conforms to the phantasmagorical desires of the narrator, desires that his culture run unimpeded through in the trails grooved by the imprints of collective experiences and attitudes.

It is not without a certain ironic logic that the woman whose depiction in *The Repudiation* breaches the taboo, marking the author's beginning as a novelist, is a "foreigner", a Frenchwoman. She remains shadowy; in terms of narrative, she is the catalyst for the male subject to find and refine his voice, which is the only voice articulated in the novel. The strangeness existing between men and women, generated and upheld in this society by the separation of the sexes, is transposed here onto the level of national and ethnic difference and in its impact is a factor facilitating the transgression. The break with the prevailing norms of his own society – a kind of initiation – would only seem to have been possible with a partner who is not marked by the same restrictive cultural imprint; it is precisely for this reason, however, that she does not provide the desired liberating effect. Breaking the taboo with a woman from another culture is no way to extinguish it, even less to change the entrenched hierarchy of sexual relations.

This failure has its correlate in a significant structural feature of Boudjedra's texts. In frequent repetitions, specific traumatic experiences are presented in variations and new settings, in particular the event that we may call the primal scene of his writing: the despotic father repudiates the mother of the narrator, accusing her of adultery, but in reality he only wants to legitimate turning his attention to his new, fifteen-year-old wife. Viewing the figures of the mother and young stepmother as the narrative focus of *The Repudiation* would entail accepting what appears to be obvious, that the intention is to give the repressed women a voice and so liberate them from their status as mere objects. In fact, they are the mediums of the dispute between father and son, between a powerful generation of "elders" defending their "rights" and a rebellious "younger" generation. The evocation of the suffering inflicted on the mother, about which the son feels just as aggrieved, serves as a means of denouncing the father. When, as the novel unfolds, the narrator seduces his young stepmother – or willingly yields to her advances – this is at once an act of revenge and an appropriation of an object of sexual desire: an object to which, by virtue of its youthful zest and freshness, the father is not entitled; it should belong to a member of the young generation. There could be no clearer indication that the female body is the site where the male generational conflict is played out.

The revolt against a sexual morality that, as the plot shows, is based on hypocrisy, violence and exclusion, is thus only a secondary goal. Primarily, the revolt is geared towards assigning blame to the fathers' generation, which has let down the sons but still retains power. As is shown by the father, still overpowering in spite of everything, and the continuing effect of the taboo enshrouding women, the symbolic order responds to attack not by accommodating the desired changes, but by excluding the transgressor.

Solidarity amongst siblings

A dozen years later, with *The Fraying* (1981), Boudjedra published a novel which, for the first time in his work, explores the possibility of integrating diverging social forces. The basis for this development is an alteration of the power relations within the narrative cosmos, an alteration through which a specific social dynamic becomes transparent, even if its impact is anticipated rather than concretely realized. Now old and feeble, the father figure of *The Fraying* has lost his power over the younger generation. In this situation, solidarity between the siblings is forged; its gradual flourishing supports the formation of their individual identities and indicates tendencies towards a harmonization of social relations. It even seems possible that, across the generations, there might be a regeneration of those forces which the older generation had regarded as its enemies.

The text unfolds as a dialogue between the twenty-five-year-old Selma and the sixty-year-old Tahar al Ghomri. He is a former Communist Party member: after Algerian independence, he managed to survive liquidation by the new rulers by luck and now lives a miserable existence in a corrugated-iron shack on the edge of the city. This dialogical structure alone, wherein the main male character is joined by a female narrative voice of comparable authority, reveals that a decisive shift has taken place. Selma is perhaps the most likeable female figure Boudjedra had hitherto created, definitely the most optimistic. Her features make it obvious that she represents the new, independent Algeria: born in 1954, Selma belongs to, as Tahar reminds her, the "generation of the tremors"; a reference to the two earthshaking events that rocked the country in this year: the devastating earthquake of Orléansville and, crucially, the start of the war of liberation. Selma is a child of Algerian independence, burdened neither by the repressive mechanisms of the colonial period, nor by the restrictive regulations enforced through a revitalized tradition. She and the young women of her generation are stylized into torchbearers of hope who are to lead a "puritanical and intellectually backward society" into a better future. All the qualities relevant to an open and tolerant society are projected onto Selma: she is at home in the world of knowledge and has found an intellectual niche – she is the director of the Central Library in Algiers. Of just as weighty symbolic importance as the year of her birth is her profession as librarian: she maintains the country's cultural memory. Her friendship with the old communist Tahar al Ghomri, who becomes her "intellectual father", represents the postulate that the country needs to face up to its history and abandon longstanding hostilities. At the same time, she stands for the demands of those marginalized by official discourse to be embraced as part of the symbolic order. The basis for this integration could be the old man's diary, which Selma inherits after his death, a gift that obliges her to uphold his legacy.

The "new" woman envisioned in this novel refuses to be restrained by conventions. She has no time for female coquetry but cultivates an array of traits traditionally regarded as male prerogatives: she is a chain smoker, swears like a trooper, and her seemingly inexhaustible reservoirs of energy keep an entire institution going. This tendency to lend her traits usually ascribable to a virile masculinity is counter balanced by descriptions of a tantalizingly attractive woman: "magnificent breasts" in tight-fitting pullovers, casually bared legs, "voluptuous lips" which she continually moistens with a lick of her "thrillingly red tongue". Whenever these alluring charms animate men to approach her, they are sharply rebutted by Selma. The contraceptive pills she always has at the ready in her handbag stand not only for the sexual freedom the "new woman" claims for herself, but moreover for a rejection of motherhood and thus for a refusal by the young generation of women to fulfill the reproductive function, the sole positive social value assigned to women in the traditional community.

Any woman who challenges the male dominion over progeny in this way generates castration fear amongst men, who now lose their brash self-assurance in the presence of such a woman. At first Boudjedra weaves this problem into a joke about the insubordinate hens which refuse to breed, standing up to the dominant rooster in the chicken yard. Male anxieties about losing power become more clearly configured in connection with the characterization of the relationship between Selma and her father. He hates his daughter, because he relates her birth – and that of the modern woman in Algeria – to the extinguishing of his capacity to beget further children: "He began to hate her and considered her to be the reason for his sterility and the main obstacle to the proliferation of his race."

It is thus the old generation, characterized as no longer of sound mind, which resists this new role of the women. More precisely, they are the most obvious opponents; as the plot unfolds, although never explicitly addressed, it emerges that the sons' relationship to femininity is just as problematic.

Brothers and sisters enjoy, however, a new sense of solidarity. If Selma's sense of self-esteem has survived the deprecatory remarks of her father unscathed, this is only because as a younger sister she can count on the support of her older brother. It is he who faces up to the father whenever her self-confidence needs to be bolstered, and in this he is also a role model for the younger brother.

The positive view of the relationship between the siblings (and thereby of the young generation) that characterizes this novel is paralleled by a greater flexibility in gender roles. Ambivalence in relation to traditional role models now seems at least possible for women and it is no longer the motive for their exclusion. Selma is assigned all too obviously virile traits despite the highly charged portrayal of her womanly physique, traits which prove very useful in her professional life.

Things are very different when men like Selma's elder brother, who is almost incestuously attached to her, and the younger Latif, whose name refers to his character (kind), do not fit traditional clichés. The two brothers are sensitive, fragile, caring and often need a shoulder to lean on – all characteristics that, when shown by men, exact mockery and contempt from society. When Latif, like his older brother, "outs" himself as gay, this only corresponds to the prejudices firmly anchored in society, which are thus confirmed in a roundabout way. Whereas the older brother, who remains nameless, dies because he believes that he has to conceal his "otherness" and can see no place for himself in society, Selma "saves" her younger brother from his forced social isolation by persuading him to admit his sexual preference, fully embracing him and his personal truth. The harmony depicted here is accentuated by reference to Latif's lover. Married because it is what his parents wish, he even gifts them a grandchild. Privy to his relationship with Latif, his wife countenances it without letting it diminish her love for him.

There can be no doubt that with this utopia of a society tolerant of transgressions Boudjedra is seeking to dismantle prejudices and overcome exclusion. But just how much the text remains cleaved to the rigid economy of opposites is revealed in the way that the view of gender roles steadfastly transports old fears and clichés: the active, intelligent, working woman refuses motherhood and indulges, when she is not masturbating, in a promiscuous sexual life; the "soft" man that forgoes virile attitudes is inevitably homosexual, thus likewise a danger to the community's survival.

The ardent wish for a society tolerant of openness and difference on both the political and individual levels has given birth in this novel to a utopian figure, Selma, who, despite the continuing restricted gaze, is intended to send signals of reconciliation and optimism. However, the constellation between the characters and the plot highlight deep-seated social uncertainties about the new order. Selma, the embodiment of the progressive young state, refuses the reproductive role. The child born in this novel owes its genesis solely to the wish of the old generation to reproduce – a motif that sheds an ambivalent light on the hopeful prospects.

Portrait of the artist as a young woman

Lailiyyat imra'a ariq (*Nights of a Sleepless Woman*) is the original title of a novel published in Arabic in 1985; two years later, the work was published in French translation as *La pluie* (*The Rain*). Over six nights, a female first-person narrator writes down fragments of her remembered past, what she experiences in daily life, and reflections. This text is often read as the counterpart to *The Obstinate Snail*, published ten years before, the inner monologue of a neurotic civil servant divided into six sections, each devoted to a single day. Director of the municipal agency responsible for eliminating rats, he seeks to master his mental chaos through an elaborate control system before finally, after he has killed a snail that followed him persistently (which he probably sees as being a kind of *alter ego*), admitting himself to prison.

Metaphorically, the opposition between day and night connotes that between male and female. This counterpoint seems to demonstrate a kind of systematic compulsion within the author's work. To put on the mask of a female protagonist means breaking another taboo; in terms of hierarchical categories he abdicates the dominant position and moves "down" to that of the dominated and disregarded. The benefit generated by this move lies in its transgressive potential: traditionally indiscernible, a female figure can now be presented from an inner perspective. She breaks the imposed silence and thus violates *a fortiori* prevailing conventions.

The nameless protagonist of *The Rain*, who works in a hospital as a doctor, has a male double, the author, who steers her according to his desires and fears. He refrains from giving her the freedom and self-confidence he afforded Selma. This young woman is a person shaken by neuroses, who has suffered from "the misfortune of womanhood" ever since experiencing the shock of her first menstruation; she tries to deaden her body by depriving herself of food and sleep, and her first sexual contact with a man, "enmeshed" in "his old fantasies and old arrogance", is so repellent and humiliating that it ends in disaster: "in the end I vomited in the washbasin."

All the factors that burden the male protagonist of *The Repudiation* are projected here onto the woman: the disastrous familial situation with a weak, humiliated mother and a constantly absent father, who nonetheless retains firm control over the family members; the insecurity triggered by the death of the older brother, who committed suicide presumably because of his homosexuality; and the seething hatred the numerous siblings feel for one another. Characteristic motifs like the shock caused by the sight of menstrual blood are transferred to the woman: caught completely unprepared, the young protagonist takes her first period to be a sign of imminent death. In her distress she turns to her brother, but he cynically rejects her plea for help. Her initiation into life as an adult woman turns into a "primordial deficiency", a reason for her to retreat fully into her shell.

A diary becomes the sole possibility she has to avert the ever-present threat of suicide in this isolation. She writes against death, and this writing is initially characterized by her internalized compulsions and prohibitions: "But there are things I can't mention. Self-censorship." Gradually however, "the ecstasy of writing" brings about reconciliation with her inner self as she becomes aware "that bliss resides in scribbling smooth blank paper." In writing the protagonist recognizes "the ability of a person to realize a plan."

With the difference between the name on the title page and the first person of the fiction having already sharpened awareness of the ambivalences of this novel's female figure, passages like the ones quoted above emphatically suggest a double reading of the text: the authorial, self-referential level continually intersects with that of the plot. Behind the young woman, who is a specialist in diseases of the reproductive organs, looms the author, who examines the maladies plaguing society with her. It is all a matter of diagnosing pathological developments; this demands a painstakingly observant gaze, even if the symptoms are repulsive and trigger nauseous disgust. This gaze is needed to speak the truth and overcome self-censorship. The figure of the woman doctor, who sometimes formulates her diagnoses harshly and cynically, merges with that of the author, who delivers with these passages a meta-textual justification for the shocking openness he is so often reproached for. Both figures ultimately want to heal but both encounter the inertia of their compatriots, a mentality that is absolutely resistant to change.

The futility of writing as a means of bringing about the author's wish to change social consciousness is just one of the interpretative levels to emerge through the inner perspective of the female character in *The Rain*. A second unfolds in the reflections on the act of writing as a therapeutic power and source of pleasure. For the protagonist, keeping a diary becomes an antidote to self-loss, which is an ever-present threat: "I lose my balance. My center point. My inner self goes all limp. Anxiety spirals." It is only by writing that she can brace herself against the constraints of self-censorship: "I'd like to keep writing my diary. Be frank and sincere. Until the very end. Not censor myself. (...) Put two or three thoughts in order which I haven't been able to write in my diary. Due to a lack of pluck, courage, and honesty." By writing she overcomes the "prohibition on women to probe their body" and can finally abandon herself to the pleasures of masturbation without being plagued by guilt. Having broken through the constraints to find the truth of writing, she can now experience the truth of her body, and the text suggests that this enables her to name the origin of her neurosis and so overcome it. Writing is a sign of this breakthrough as well: "Having written this diary to the end I could reread my words at leisure. Calmly. With all the time in the world."

As mentioned, seen from the hierarchy of values adhered to by a traditionally organized society, the male author has lowered himself by slipping on the mask of a woman. This act of displacement may well be seen as a gesture of humility in *The Rain*, for on the level of plot this kind of identification directs the gaze to "the curse of being an Arab woman", a formulation Boudjedra has repeated in his most recent novel, *The Funeral*. As far as the meta-textual strategy is concerned, the author's implied admission of his failure to influence his society is also a gesture of humility, one that is coupled here with the avowal of writing as a form of self-therapy, whereby the futility coalesces with the transgressive image of masturbation. For the female protagonist, an embodiment of the new model of professional young women, as well as for the authorial figure discernible behind her like an emerging shadow, the motif of self-gratification in melancholic resignation portends the impossibility of reaching others and the petering out of communication between the various social forces.

Reconciliation through harmonizing alignment?

Rachid Boudjedra's novel *The Funeral*, written after a prolonged period of violence which rocked Algeria in the 1990s, contrasts starkly to the resigned conclusion drawn long before the outbreak of the embryonic civil war. As traumatic experiences are evoked, the hope of liberation from obsessions and burdensome memories also flickers in Boudjedra's texts. As we have already pointed out, this hope is usually pinned to female protagonists. Selma in *The Fraying* and the doctor in *The Rain* incarnate the ideal of a polity striving for enlightenment, openness and tolerance. However, these texts also reveal the deep divisions in the country. The refusal to face up to history, the clinging to authoritarian structures and jaded traditions with the fateful consequences that arise from this paralysis, and not least the gulf between the sexes are comparable to the cancerous tumors the doctor in *The Rain* identifies in her patients, who represent Algerian society. Elaborating on this metaphor, one could say that in the years which followed this novel, the diagnosed diseases have spread and taken grip of enfeebled bodies: their frightful disfiguration is there for all to see. In *The Funeral*, the horrific events of these years are depicted in often shocking explicitness; nonetheless, the conclusion of this novel presents a turning point in the true sense of the word.

Here, too, the relationship between men and women furnishes the paradigm facilitating discussion on the political and social situation. The plot advances year by year from 1995 to the turn of the millennium, covering the period from the worst phase of terrorism until the highly controversial national reconciliation proclaimed by President Bouteflika.

The novel's heroes are Sarah and Salim (it is no coincidence that their names begin with the same letter), members of an anti-terror brigade who are presented as lovers from the outset. Sarah is the dominant voice in the narrative structure, the character with the say in many respects. Salim's voice intervenes through long letters, a narrative device which at once admits and overcomes the blocking of dialogue between the sexes as being typical of the male inability to communicate: "I'm not used to talking, so I'm sending you this letter, to say to you in writing what I cannot express directly in words."

Salim's letters revolve around his childhood: as it turns out, his recollections bear an astounding similarity to Sarah's; indeed, they seem practically identical. Both suffered under the absence of their father, the submissiveness of their mother and conflict with their siblings. The experiences shaping their lives are so similar that Sarah is moved to say: "We were almost twins."

The annulment of polarities indicated here can be designated as a main feature of the text, which also pleads, on a crucially trickier level, (that of the political groups embroiled in fighting), for the overcoming of antagonisms. While the atrocities committed by the terrorists are described with almost unbearable meticulousness, the distinctions between victims and perpetrators, innocent and guilty, persecuted and persecutors nonetheless become indistinct as the plot unfolds: everyone seems to be both at once. By giving Sarah the same name as an eleven-year-old girl who is gruesomely tortured, mutilated, raped and finally killed, the author forges identification between his heroine and the victim. As for the male protagonists, the connection with Salim is accordingly less obvious, but nonetheless recognizable: Salim's name contains that of two characters who are decisive for the plot, Ali (S-ali-m). Both Alis are victims of terrorist attacks; one killed, the other horrifically maimed.

Both protagonists also have affinities to the perpetrator side. Sarah feels an impulse to torture when interrogating detainees and must fight the temptation to resemble the persecutors: "Most of all I didn't want to imitate them, become like them, lose my humanity." In turn, statements about the terrorists do not deny that they have some positive motives, for example when it is portrayed that in their "ridiculous belief" they hope to purify their victims through the inflicted torments, so that "they leave this perfidious world, enter paradise, and dine at the table of the Prophet every evening."

Salim, whose activities in the fight against terrorism are not reported on in any relevant detail, finally becomes utterly ambivalent when the author gives him a twin brother, who is characterized as Salim's dark shadow. Originating from the same ovum, the brother is the enemy under the same roof: he contested Salim's preeminent position as eldest son, was favored by the mother and always hated by Salim, who faced up to him with "a murderous fury." It is easy to see in this couple the enemy groups whose mutual hatred plunged the country into bloody chaos. Portrayed by Boudjedra as clever, educated in philosophy and self-possessed, Salim represents the state, his brother its enemies, although the author is careful to avoid directly identifying this figure with the terrorists, preferring instead to depict him as a weakling and trickster. As the novel would have it, Salim realizes that he and his brother are fatefully linked as the positive and negative of the same development, a narrative strategy conceived to smooth over differences between the twins and blur contrasts. In the past locked in a state of war, Salim, a soldier fighting terrorism, now discovers a quasi-identity with his shadow, the lawbreaker who "is at once his front and back, his recto and verso." This alignment, not unproblematic, blurs the difference between victim and perpetrator in a way similar to what actually happened on the political level, where (former) terrorists were able to return to normal civilian life without their involvement in criminal acts being investigated.

When the novel concludes with a classical happy ending – Salim proposes to Sarah and wishes for twins – the desire for harmony between the sexes expressed here is at best of secondary importance. The prime concern is to resolve conflicts between men and political groups – a postulate consistent with the policy of national reconciliation propagated by President Bouteflika, which eschews probing into issues of guilt and responsibility. The auxiliary function given to the female for propagating this strategy could not find a more blatant expression than the final infinitive construct which connects the two clauses of Salim's proposal: "Will you marry me and give me twins so to reconcile me with my existence as a twin and this strange brother of mine?" In spite of all the desires to establish a different hierarchy between the sexes, ultimately the woman remains merely a means of realizing male goals.

SELECTED WORKS

La répudation (The Repudiation), Paris: Denoël 1969

L'insolation (Sunstroke), Paris: Denoël 1972

Journal palestinien (Palestinian Journal), Paris: Hachette 1972

Topographie idéale pour une aggression caractérisée (Ideal Topography for a Specific Aggression), Paris: Denoël 1975

L'escargot entêté (The Stubborn Snail), Paris: Denoël 1977

Les 1001 années de la nostalgie (1001 Years of Nostalgia), Paris: Denoël 1979

Le vainqueur de coupe (The Prizewinner), Paris: Denoël 1981

al-Tafakkuk (The Fraying), Beirut: Dar Ibn Rushd 1981

La macération (The Maceration), Paris: Denoël 1984

Layliyyat imra'a ariq (Rain. Diary of an Insomniac), Algier: ENAL 1985

La prise de Gibraltar (The Taking of Gibraltar), Paris: Denoël 1987

Le désordre des choses (The Disorder of Things), Paris: Denoël 1991
Fils de la haine (The Son of Hatred), Paris: Denoël 1992
Timimoun (Timimoun), Paris: Denoël 1994
Les Funérailles (The Funeral*)*, Paris: Grasset 2003

TRANSLATIONS

The Repudiation, trans. Golda Lambrova, Colorado Springs: Three Continent Press 1995
Rain. Diary of an Insomniac, trans. Angela M. Brewer, New York: Les Mains Secrètes 2002

FURTHER READING

Farida Abu-Haidar: "The Bipolarity of Rachid Boudjedra", in: *Journal of Arabic Literature* 20 (1989), pp. 40–56
Debbie Cox: "Autobiography and Intertextuality: Rashid Bujadra", in: Robin Ostle, Ed de Moor, Stefan Wild (eds.), *Writing the Self. Autobiographical Writing in Modern Arabic Literature*, London: Saqi 1998, pp. 229–40
Armel Crouzières-Ingenthron: *Le double pluriel dans les romans de Rachid Boudjedra*, Paris: L'Harmattan 2001
Hafid Gafaïti: *Boudjedra ou la passion de la modernité*, Paris: Denoël 1987
Hafid Gafaïti: "Rachid Boudjedra: The Bard of Modernity", in: *Research in African Literatures* 23 (1992), pp. 89–102
Hafid Gafaïti (ed.): *Rachid Boudjedra. Une poétique de la subversion*, Paris: L'Harmattan 2000
Alfred Hornung, Ernstpeter Ruhe (eds.): *Autobiographie & avant-garde. Alain Robbe-Grillet, Serge Doubovsky, Rachid Boudjedra, Maxine Hong Kingston, Raymond Federman, Ronald Sukenick*, Tübingen: Narr 1990

An Egyptian Don Quixote?
Salah Abd al-Sabur's Rethinking of the Majnun-Layla Paradigm

Angelika Neuwirth

The poet and playwright Salah Abd al-Sabur (1931–81) is one of the most prominent cultural figures of modern Egypt. Hailing from Zagazig, a provincial town in the Nile Delta, he moved to Cairo in 1947 to study Arab language and literature. His enthusiasm for the Arab Romantic literature of the turn of the century, in particular the prose of Kahlil Gibran, had been aroused during his high-school years, and it was through Gibran that he became familiar with the work of Nietzsche, whose *Thus Spoke Zarathustra* was published in Arabic translation in 1938. In Cairo, Abd al-Sabur soon banded together with a number of fellow students, some of whom would go on to become literati and critics, to form an Egyptian literary society, a discussion circle through which he discovered the works of Rilke, Yeats, Auden and most importantly, T. S. Eliot.

As it was for so many of his colleagues in the Arab world, Eliot's influence was crucial to Abd al-Sabur, imparting a new notion of poetic language and so pointing him in the direction of *al-shi'r al-hurr* (free verse), which the Iraqi avant-garde had recently initiated. "Free verse" – in contrast to the hitherto authoritative *qasida* form that originated from pre-Islamic times – signifies a form of Arab poetry "freed" from the fetters of a single meter, strictly adhered to, and a continuously held mono-rhyme; whereby the verses are still based on fixed metrical feet, but there are no set rules regarding the number of feet. Along with the rigid traditional form, the barriers restricting diction and morphology, which had for so long interposed themselves like a light filter between the poet and his changed reality, also fell away.

These epochal changes did not mean that the old poets were no longer of interest to Abd al-Sabur: he worked through a broad spectrum of old Arabic and classical poetry methodically, reading them from a newly acquired distance and applying modern lines of questioning.

Abd al-Sabur's beginnings as publicist and literary critic, as well as his earliest poems, which are distinctly realist, date to his student days. After teaching for seven years, he started working as a literary editor for various renowned journals and newspapers in 1958. In 1967, after he had made his mark with his philosophically inspired poems and essays, most notably receiving the Egyptian State Prize for

Literature for his first drama *The Tragedy of al-Hallaj* (1964), he was appointed publications director in the Ministry of Culture. Almost ten years later, when he was at the peak of his literary fame, with five volumes of poetry, five verse plays, and numerous essays and collections of critical pieces to his credit, President Sadat sent him to Delhi as a cultural attaché. Returning to Cairo in 1979, he took the influential position of director of the State Book Organization and was awarded the status of State Secretary, a position that he held until he died, aged just fifty, on 14 September 1981. His friends link his premature death to a conflict he could never master: his contradictory roles as politically prominent state official and committed writer concerned with enunciating his unique vision.

Abd al-Sabur and his drama *Layla and the Majnun*

The relationship between a literary work and the ideological conviction of its author may be subtly understated or cryptically concealed; it will, however, particularly in modern Arab literature, hardly ever be missing. Tracing this relationship in the works of authors who combine literary creativity with social-critical engagement can be extremely fruitful. Salah Abd al-Sabur is a consummate embodiment of this type of author. Parallel to his development into one of the most sophisticated, demanding poets and dramatists of his generation, he acquired through his essays and countless critical prose writings a reputation as a spearhead for a new, liberal society; a society in which the individual is politically enlightened and responsible, but also enters into a more natural, unbiased and uninhibited relationship with his or her real environment in all its diversity. Ultimately, in such a society the liberation of women from the spell cast by age-old prejudices should enable both sexes to attain deeper self-awareness.

Abd al-Sabur's small body of dramatic work, comprising only five plays, stems from the last fifteen years of his creative life. As in his late role-poems, here the author shows a clear tendency to endow his characters with symbolism that leads beyond the narrow framework of what is immediately represented, thus rendering transparent the psychological conditionality of both individual and collective forms of behavior, which he considers analogous. His last three dramas are parables; the earliest, *The Tragedy of al-Hallaj*, attempts to disclose the archetypical structures underlying the self-sacrifice of the well-known Islamic mystic, very much in the vein of T. S. Eliot's modernist "mystery play" *Murder in the Cathedral*.

The penultimate drama, *Layla and the Majnun* (1970), which places contemporary figures from Cairo literary circles on the stage, assumes an exceptional position. The interval between the action of the plot and the drama's composition is little more than twenty years; the characters, confronted by everyday constraints familiar to the audience, discuss modern problems, not least the gender discrimination that still agonizes Near Eastern societies. Should the play therefore be understood as "realistic drama"? This reading enforces a preemptive narrowing of the scope of interpretation: if the play is isolated from the illuminating context of the author's contemporaneously written parables, references geared towards the symbolic layer of meaning common to all these dramas are suppressed; insight into the deeper dimensions of the text is blocked from the outset. Moreover, the problem arises as to how to justify the verse play form employed by Abd al-Sabur both here and in the other works, for this form entails a semiotization in itself, pointing to a poetical intent that goes beyond what is directly acted out on the stage. To quote Roland Barthes on the comparable poetic form of the French classical drama: "The alexandrine, for instance, has value both as meaning of a discourse and as signifier of a new whole, which is its poetic signification."

Abd al-Sabur never commented explicitly on this aspect of *Layla and the Majnun*, in contrast to his discussion of his other plays. Through various epic devices, he clearly marked the symbolism of individual scenes. Above all, the connection of the main character with the Majnun of legend signals the multi-layered nature of the play. Indeed, in this and other works his main characters form a coherent allegorical paradigm that is always present as a subtext and becomes manifest on stage at the end of the drama. The play has not generally been granted the recognition it deserves; this extends to its reception abroad, where only one translation into a Western European language (German in 1991) has been undertaken.

Given that it was written in 1969–70 it seems obvious to read *Layla and the Majnun* as Abd al-Sabur's response to the Arab defeat in the June War, a context already extrapolated by the critic Nagi Naguib. The thesis that the work is another revision of ideological positions from the 1960s is readily substantiated by the metaphors and language associated with individual characters. But Abd al-Sabur's critique goes beyond ideology. In *Layla and the Majnun*, he undertakes a critical illumination of a phenomenon that, although not unique to the Arab culture of his time, was particularly prevalent therein: committed intellectuals taking refuge in ideals drawn from the past, dimming their perceptions of actual reality and blocking the very inner renewal they strove to instigate. This perspective shifts the focus fundamentally: instead of infusing his characters' ripostes with a polemical discourse, Abd al-Sabur (who always insisted stridently on the clear separation of his essayistic and artistic works) is concerned with translating abstract psychological contexts into ideas and images. In turn, the various combinations of these stereotyped ideas and images, such as the "Majnun Layla paradigm", are revealed to exert a strong influence on an intellectual type then prevalent in Arab societies, enmeshing their thinking – should the discrete proportionality of these paradigms be disturbed by the vicissitudes of real life – into practically irresolvable conflicts. Following this hypothesis, *Layla and the Majnun* could lay claim to a special position within Abd al-Sabur's dramatic work, going further than his other renderings of the dilemmas facing intellectuals insofar as it exposes the danger inherent to this particular intellectual orientation.

What are the lineaments of this critique? It homes in on those who are particularly susceptible to overlaying reality with ideality: committed poets and the literati. The legend of the poet *par excellence*, Majnun, is set as a foil to elucidate *their* specific problematic and disclose its archetypical pattern,. However, this Arab "legend" is by no means fixed; it is not even available in a "classical" version. As Stefan Leder has shown, even in its oldest complete version by Ibn Qutayba (st. 889) the narrative clearly betrays a specific authorial intention, to furnish a refined psychological interpretation of the phenomenon of poetic inspiration, which has subsequently inspired countless new renderings. It is this potential interpretative richness, pursued by writers of various historical periods, which enables Abd al-Sabur to make use of the legend in his very idiosyncratic way. Although he uses them to orient the plot of his own drama, the age-old narrative and its single episodes are of less interest to him than the etiology of poetic inspiration and this permanent rebellion against the sense of existence that pervades society; revealed by a legendary figure who writes verse out of a state of emotional turmoil, caused by the loss of the beloved "thou", and renounces the real world completely.

Depending on the interpretative tradition, it is possible to emphasize different facets of the story: either focus is placed on the untimely end of the lovers, in particular Majnun, who is ultimately consumed by his suffering; or greater consideration is given to the new intimacy between the lovers, which results from their very separation; an intimacy that, willingly embraced by Majnun, is the source not only of poetical creativity but also everlasting devotion to the beloved. Abd al-Sabur works with both these interpretations, brought forth by two distinct traditions, bringing them together for the first time in a new rendering and, moreover, placing them in a dialectical relationship. Simplifying the issue, one could characterize them as the basic fable and the Sufi-amplified fable.

The basic fable employed as the foil for the plot is essentially the same as the story as told by Ibn Qutayba, minus the introductory and concluding frames; although its direct source is Ahmad Shawqi's romantic drama *Majnun Layla* (1934). In this fable, tribal conventions prevent the young poet Qays ibn al-Mulawwah from marrying his passionate love Layla, who contrary to her own feelings then marries another man. The pain of parting is so intense that Qays loses his mind; after a brief encounter with Layla, he severs all human ties and retreats into the desert, where, now a *majnun* (madman), he continues to write poetry dedicated to the lost beloved until, withered by his consuming pain, he follows Layla, who has already perished under the weight of her suffering, into death. In this version, his madness is the expression of a wound that has cut him to the quick; the pain of parting cleaves him apart, resulting in his ruin and ultimately his death.

Far more important to the play is the Sufi-amplified fable that is reflected in the early development of the protagonist Sa'id, presented to the audience in a flashback. The major difference from the basic fable resides in a new assessment of Majnun's madness. For the Majnun figure marked by Sufi influences, *junun* (madness) is not a defect or a lack of reason, but rather an expression of supreme emotion. Indeed, it is an obsession which at once ensures poetical inspiration (*shi'r*) and enables pure devotion to an ideal (*'ishq*) while willingly renouncing real-life personification of the beloved "thou". The *Liebestod* (love-death) is thus not annihilation but the genuine fulfillment of this absolute bond. The Sufi-amplified fable, which – contrary to the "basic version" – shifts the external, private fate of the main character into the background, represents an exemplary model for the particular relationship modern intellectuals have had with society since the 1960s, as evinced by other contemporary recourses to the Majnun-Layla thematic.

Exile

This relationship may be understood as exilic. Majnun has been labeled an "emblem of exile". As As'ad Khairallah has shown, the Majnun figure does not represent a real, historical individual so much as an archetype. Indeed, he has no life history in literary tradition. He should not, however, be understood as a static image emerging from the collective unconscious in the sense established by C.G. Jung; he is employed in modern literature to express a particular condition of modern life or to reveal a historical crisis. It could be subsumed under the category of "historical archetypes" as formulated by Harold Fisch. As such, it has by now become a key pattern for exilic condition all over the Arab world; used by some authors to vindicate their exilic situation, by others to de-construct ideological, essentialist notions of exile, and by others again to reflect on history as a state of exile. An important signpost for this course was Mahmoud Darwish's poem "A Lover from Palestine" (1966); (for a detailed analysis, see the essay on Darwish in this volume).

Layla and the Majnun was written less than four years later, shortly after the devastating June War. A reckoning with the "defeated generation" of Egyptian intellectuals, it brings to the stage a group of revolutionary journalists in Cairo 1952. They are easily recognized as pre-figurations of Abd al-Sabur's own intellectual generation. Although the reader is struck by the harsh judgment leveled against the idealistic intellectual, "the problematic of the poet torn between action and dream, and of the intellectual's uneasy relations with the authorities, is not simply theoretical". The critic Nagi Naguib highlights the tension between language, poetic persona and society that paralyzed Egyptian intellectuals between the 1950s and 1980s. He labels them a "floating intelligentsia", that is to say an intelligentsia in inner exile, obsessed with the love for a utopian ideal of their homeland but unable to achieve it. Abd al-Sabur's Majnun typifies this exiled group, representing the pathetic situation of a defeated generation, which having renounced normal life gives itself up to the lofty ideal of the homeland, dislocates itself from reality and is condemned to suffering in its futile attempts to redeem the homeland. Although the author presents what appears to be a specifically Egyptian problematic, his critical objective to de-mythicize the intellectual's or the poet's self-image as an exilic figure suffering for his homeland is re-encountered in several later texts: for instance in the novels of Emile Habibi, Anton Shammas and Sélim Nasib, to name only the most prominent authors.

The title of the drama

An allusion encrypted into the title evokes the specific affinity between the modern intellectual and the Sufi-amplified fable of *Majnun Layla*. Compared with the customary configurations of *Majnun Layla* or – as in Persian – *Majnun o Layli*, the title *Layla wa-l-Majnun* features two striking aspects. Firstly, there is the rearrangement of the names, which points clearly to the Sufi reception of the legend, most prominent in Persian epic, where the title sometimes appeared as *Layli o-Majnun*. Yet, as As'ad Khairallah points out

> in spite of the appearance of Layla as the point of reference (...), the one char-
> acter which exists more or less fully is Majnun, while Layla is a transparent
> kind of symbol for God's beauty, having little meaning in herself (...) Being
> put on such a high pedestal, she seems abstracted from real life.

This observation leads us directly to the second aspect: by manipulating the original name Majnun, which now becomes an appellative noun by virtue of the definite article, Abd al-Sabur's title excludes exactly this kind of understanding. The immediately obvious, literal interpretation of *al-Majnun* as "the madman", taken up by critics such as Sami Khashaba, Nagi Naguib, and M.M. Badawi, is not supported by the play's actual content: a pathological state of madness is ascribable to Sa'id only at the very end, if at all. It therefore seems more plausible to assume that the article serves to emphasize that the character is a replica, conforming to the Majnun type frequently drawn on by modern writers. In this sense, the title would then stand for *Layla wa-l-Majnun al-asri*, which could be rendered in exaggerated form as "Layla and the (modern) Majnun epigone", or, more soberly, by relinquishing the name correlate, as "Layla and the man possessed by an ideal."

An interpretation of Majnun as an instantly comprehensible reference to a specifically male form of self-understanding, characterizing a contemporary literary archetype in the Arab world, is certainly something Abd al-Sabur could expect from his native tongue readership and audience: there is a close connection between the experiences of committed poets and writers in modern Arab society and a matrix of manifest images and conceptions which refer implicitly or explicitly to Majnun. This need not follow the path into pathological madness itself, where Salah Jahin (d. 1986) sends his intellectual protagonist in the drama *Inqilab*; a play whose main female character is also called Layla. Nor must it explicitly assume the name Majnun, as in the case of Abdellatif Laâbi, whose memoirs bear the title *Le fou d'espoir* (in Arabic, *Majnun al-amal*), or that of Shakir al-Nabulsi, whose Darwish biography is titled *Majnun al-turab*. It suffices to recall the basis of the self-understanding oriented on Majnun: the experience of the world as a desolate "wasteland", dominated by the suffering of existential loss and an insatiable thirst for a reunion with the beloved "thou"; the plight that modern writers so emphatically believe themselves to share with Majnun. Three dispositions above all – passion, obsession with an ideal, and poetic calling – forge this empathy between the modern writer and Majnun into an organic whole: his creativity stems from his self-imposed, fully embraced emotional imbalance. Abd al-Sabur expressed his own disposition in the following terms:

> My poetry – in general – is testimony of a veneration of these ideals [*hurriyya* (freedom), *sidq* (truthfulness) and *adala* (justice)] and protest against their derision. These values are my heart, my wound, and the knife, all at once.

In this declaration, where he ranks himself amongst the "*majanin*," the "Majnuns", Abd al-Sabur could just as easily have used a more abstract conceptual inventory and spoken of his poetical calling, his obsession, and his passion.

The characters and external framework of the plot

The characters are a group of young journalists who are working for an opposition periodical in Cairo on the eve of the 1952 Revolution. While unified in their desire to initiate political change, they cannot agree on the course of action to take. The impatient Hassan agitates for a sudden violent overthrow, while Ziyad is content to play the role of the ironic observer. Only the poet amongst them, the main character Sa'id, believes unconditionally in the power of the word and sees it as the vehicle for realizing the ideals of freedom and justice. It is obvious that each of the three male characters represents a type embodying specific conceptions, whereby Hassan by virtue of his basic destructive attitude and Ziyad in his egocentric smugness are disqualified from gaining the audience's empathy from the very outset, unlike the figure of Sa'id. He confronts us with a problematic already evident in Abd al-Sabur's earliest drama *Ma'sat al-Hallaj*; as Nagi Naguib has put it, the intellectual "imprisoned in words suffering from a consuming yearning to make an impact." The positions of the three female characters, other than Layla minor parts, remain vague.

The *spiritus rector* of the group is the editor-in-chief, *al-ustadh* (the maestro), who is given to a vehement rhetoric drawing on the imagery of the Tammuz poets and seeks to cast the spell of grand political and social ideals over his younger colleagues by evoking poetically embellished visions of the future. Freedom and justice are to be their guiding stars:

> their rays pour so brightly in our eyes
> that they make us as obsessed
> as passionate lovers.

For this character, the persona of Majnun is elevated to a goal of cultural refinement and education. Peculiar to him is an elegiac tone that resonates from the outset, a premonition of the inevitable failure of the shared struggle; moreover –in keeping with the stage set of the scenes in which he features, dominated by a Daumierian image of Don Quixote – he characterizes his younger fellow campaigners as "knights of sad countenance".

The *ustadh* persuades the group to stage Ahmad Shawqi's verse drama *Majnun Layla* for a variety of reasons: to prevent pessimistic doubts from paralyzing the group after one of its members, Husam, is placed in political detention; to help ease the tensions between the group members and deepen their relationships; above all, to generate with this experiment an important emotional prerequisite for the Majnun disposition, namely erotic tension. Sa'id and Layla quickly identify with their roles as the main characters, Qays and Layla. Starkly contrasting the present as a state of exile with an early childhood envisioned as a paradisiacal landscape, the Shawqi verses recited during rehearsals strike a highly charged cord in Sa'id. Layla's speech addressing him, taken from Shawqi's fourth act, is directed in the original text at Qays already scarred by loss, whose suffering she is seeking to alleviate. The verses faithfully match Sa'id's inner disposition; they reach him as the expression of the deeply felt bond Layla has with him, a willingness to leave behind a milieu perceived as hostile and "alien" and to embark on the search for the pristine world of childhood.

> Layla:
> Is it really you my sweetheart by my side,
> It's not a dream from which we shall soon awake?

> Are we now cast far from the places of our childhood, in Amir's Land
> Strangers in the Land of the Thaqif?

Sa'id's part, taken from the same context, has him join in enthusiastically:

> Come with me Layla, to the shaded land of solitude,
> To the distant wildness where no foot has yet tread.

But as the model of the legend dictates, the love between Sa'id and Layla encounters difficulties, albeit here they are of an inward nature. Layla grasps the transformation triggered by her experience of love as a process of liberation that is natural and miraculous at once:

> Two months of rehearsals,
> the quake in your voice when you call me
> to follow you and leave behind my past
> like a pearl in its black shell
> to step into the sun, into the light

In contrast, Sa'id remains entangled in nagging doubts:

> Two months of doubt have fully worn me out ...

Continually looking back at the past, he is plagued by the idea that Layla has been sullied by an earlier relationship with Husam, a doubt he can only stifle temporarily and with enormous effort. When Layla confides her wish to marry soon and so enable the physical consummation of their love, the relationship breaks down. The offer of her love causes him severe torment, moving him to scrap thoughts of their future together. Recognizing the futility of her courtship, she ends their relationship.

The idealizing image of the beloved as a distorting mirror of reality

The key to understanding this behavior is provided by Sa'id's recollections, which he relates to Layla, presented to the audience as a "play within a play". It traces his bleak youth at home with his sexually abused mother, a widow, who is forced into marrying a brutal man of no social standing to provide for her son. Observing its obscenity, sexuality becomes something repulsive for Sa'id; his disgust has remained with him, manifest in his outward attitude. The seared impressions go even deeper: flashbacks bring to light a matrix of images which betray vestiges of the classical Majnun figure. His mother's lament at the premature loss of her first husband evokes the image of the wasteland:

> Uprooted is our shady tree
> and our herb-adorned gate is destroyed

The young Sa'id's often repeated cry of "hunger!" is unmistakably a variation of the thirst motif, evoking Majnun's suffering in the desert. Above all, the experience of the imminent loss of the key female attachment figure, the mother, who is forced into a debasing sexual relationship to survive, is crucial; it ushers in the development that will bring Sa'id ever closer to the classical Majnun marked by Sufi influences. He now elevates an ideal image of a woman to the object of his veneration, one he is to selflessly serve, while renouncing any contact or relationship with the real figure, which even entails a moral degrading of the woman herself. This ideal image is complex: it is an idea of the city, of home, of *Misr* (Egypt), of *al-madina* (the city), "the polis", represented in the image of a woman. Like the mother, this city is also defiled and sullied in reality; in its idealized vision, it is placed in the context of chivalrous love, elevated to a noble woman held captive. Her ill fate must be averted, in other words, it is the obligation of her chivalrous champions to restore freedom and justice, a task entrusted here to poets and writers. As an engaged poet, Sa'id is a lover of this Madina, an interpretation of his role that is by no means unusual in his cultural context. For our Majnun, this transposing of ideal love from the personal into the political ensues from the personal experience of loss marking his youth, inseparable from political events. The death of his father, guarantor of family integrity, coincides with the violent quelling of a student demonstration in support of greater civil liberties in Cairo, so that mother and Madina are branded simultaneously into his memory as robbed and defiled. This analogous structure of personal and political loss, illustrated by epic devices, is also constitutive for the complex ideal figure of the beloved, the mythically evoked personification of Madina in which the mother is also merged.

The veneration of such a sublime ideal figure allows little room for loving a real person; above all, it casts dark shadows back on reality, where the individual woman – and the real Madina corresponding to her on the collective level – appears to be promiscuous, incapable of distinguishing between pure and egoistical love, and eager to yield to any random partner or ruler.

Layla's desire to consummate their love physically seems to verify this notion of the real woman: it not only thrusts him down into the seamy and profane realms of life, but once again sets him up for a painful confrontation with the figure who in his mind has negatively occupied the role of the man in sexual relations – the intruder into the world of his childhood:

Everything is dismal and futile. No matter which door I open – it is he who
I always face!

Here the mythical veneration of the beloved, as an omnipresent image, changes into
a negative: she is supplanted by the paralyzing awareness of an equally omnipresent
sinister rival. Overwhelmed by this personification of his past suffering, Sa'id
himself expresses his renouncement of love, along with it a personal future:

Oh, sex again!
This curse follows us everywhere,
the travesty of true love!
... An impure fire
that only begets impurity!

This represents a change of paradigm: from the poet-rebel, commensurate to the
Sufi-influenced Qays, he has regressed to the enfeebled, mad Qays, vanquished by
his pain. Layla is the first to recognize this transformation:

Sa'id ... My Love!
What a pity!
You're a devastated wreck
You're only good for hanging around within
the walls of your black ruins.
What a pity!
I fell in love with death!
I fell in love with death!

In the classical model, after the lovers separate Layla enters a relationship with
another man while Qays retreats to the desert. Accordingly, we encounter Sa'id in
the next scene, the peripety of the drama, in an utterly sterile wasteland, namely
a bordello, where love is contorted into obscenity and poetry into pornography.
Here the prostitutes hold sway, evoking the image of the dishonored Madina; also
present is a blind singer who performs an ambiguous *Mawwal*, reciting a stanza
composed in Egyptian dialect; an accolade for Misr, portrayed as a beauty available
to all suitors, a crier soliciting them every evening – a travesty of the image of the
ideal Madina that Sa'id had cherished:

By God, should it be granted me
to dwell in you, oh Cairo,
I'll make you into a garden for me and build a castle above it,
and send a messenger to call out each night:
Cairo is this, a paradise for who dwells in her

and tastes her sweetness
she is made of halva!
oh night ... oh heart!

But Sa'id, too, recites poetry in this desert: stanzas in which he, himself once combative, now invokes the coming of a chivalrous figure with eschatological traits:

Oh Lord, who will come after me,
have you arranged your troops to send to us? ...
have you saddled your steed? ...
is your sword drawn and your visor lowered? ...

An unflinching resolve to settle accounts with his own passive generation and an irate, vulgar mocking of professional poets and writers are clear indications of a transformation in Sa'id's own self-understanding: he has lost confidence in his power and in the power of the word, and now awaits an act of salvation from another figure, a Mahdi. The final stanza of this poem betrays the burning impatience with which the salvation of the Madina is awaited:

Oh Lord, is your speech ready
And your words set?
- No, eternal and inexhaustible are my words! –
- Oh Lord, our patience has ebbed,
The night expands. –
- I descend only in deepest night!
In deepest loneliness,
In deepest despair,
In the rigor of death! –
- Oh Lord, you must reach us before the coming horrors,
Or you will reach us never!

This finds a cynical echo in the reprise of the ambiguous stanza devoted to Cairo already recited by the blind singer; Cairo as an object of pure pleasure, a "frivolous woman". The chivalrous figure of the liberator has receded into the distance, as far away as ever before; the imprisoned woman has surrendered to her illegitimate rulers.

Meanwhile, the catastrophe takes its course and engulfs Sa'id and his friends. Husam, induced to become an informer while in prison, has denounced the group to the secret police. Hassan hatches a plan to take revenge, only for it to go awry, and the apartment block where Husam lives becomes the setting for the discovery of the defilement of Layla. Although this discovery is calamitous for Sa'id, its impact is now of a different vein, for it comes after the change in paradigm, after he has included Layla amongst his spiritual, untouchable ideals:

> She is my life like my life for tomorrow,
> for freedom and for justice,
> for the dream,
> a dream that I'll never possess but always desire

The discovery triggers his memory, invoking his earlier experiences of the scorn for female dignity. The new encounter between Sa'id and Layla corresponds to that in Shawqi's drama where Qays and Layla meet up again in the land of the Thaqif, where according to the legend she had ended up as result of her marriage. By once again reciting Shawqi's verses – pertinent to the situation and known to the audience – and viewing one another in the mirror of the poetry, outside the reality corrupting them, they manage to revive their bond in the roles of the classical couple. One Shawqi verse in particular, recited by Layla, is instrumental for this coming together. In the classical original context Layla accuses Qays of having precipitated the separation and so sealed their fates through the imprudent spreading of his verses. Sa'id reinterprets this accusation, grasping it as an expression of the fate foisted on them by outside forces, personified by the traitor/intruder. Layla responds:

> So you know now, Qays, that the arrow is only one,
> and we both the targets of passion?

Both adversaries – the individual egoistic lover who defiles the mother and the beloved, and the political usurper, the illegitimate ruler who brings the homeland under his tyranny – merge for Sa'id, who loves all these female figures, into a *single* omnipresent figure.

From now on, the real Layla will increasingly become one with her allegorical counterpart, with Madina. The imagery associated with them becomes superimposed, overlapping explicitly in his ripostes. While he manages to repel the traitor and defiler violently, when Husam once again tries to take possession of Layla, he can do nothing to avert another political catastrophe occurring simultaneously; a desecration of the homeland, which seals his impotence in front of the beloved: a newsvendor exclaims that Cairo is in flames.

In the closing scene Sa'id is in prison, his mind in turmoil, evading, if not incapable of, human communication, even with his one-time mentor, the *ustadh* – he embodies the traits of the mad Qays. As Qays once drew figures in the sand, Sa'id is now fully preoccupied with a geometric form, a construct that brutally reveals how senseless his martyrdom has become. Prior to being overcome by the traumas of his past, he had readily professed his willingness to bear the cross he had chosen:

> Layla! I hang from my wrists on two ropes,
> a cross to me and resurrection!
> freedom and love

Now that the ropes have snapped, he recognizes that his sense of mission, rendered meaningless, is nothing but the perverted form of the cross, a trivial mechanism that degrades him to a puppet:

> Find a toy for me,
> one like I saw as a child.
> A man in a clown's costume,
> speared and hung,
> on a wire trapeze.
> You press, he swings up,
> you press again, he falls down,
> of course, normally he falls down.
> But he never plummets or jumps out
> of the wire frame.

In this situation he meets Layla once again, this time in a new light. She remains silent, distanced from events, standing there as a mere apparition, and her mute presence evokes in the audience the symbolic figure of Madina. Although at first still caught in his distorting clichéd image of her, Sa'id addresses his parting words to her, words which finally do her justice. Only now, in this final setting, is the circle closed – for the audience as well – in which Sa'id's "great love" becomes one with his "little love".

Critique of the contemporary Majnun type

This configuration of the finale disengages the drama from the legend: it is not Layla and Qays who die in this version from the sorrow of separation, but Sa'id alone who perishes from the torments of his anguish – Layla survives.

Placing the two main characters on different levels, this conclusion provides an explanation of the precedence given to Layla in the title: Layla, the real homeland understood as a female figure, is confronted with an intellectual type already marked by an experience of loss, with a man obsessed with and possessed by an ideal, a Majnun. What befalls her, the real society, with this partner; their relationship failing or suffering because of the positions he advocates and defends: elaborating this dynamic is what the title programmatically announces. This much is clear: the relationship between the modern Majnun and the Madina, conceived here as society, cannot be sincere as long as his shy restraint, his insistence on traditional norms of behavior, his "overanxious concern with purity", and his refusal to open up to the other, the new, admit only a selective perception of his environment, in particular the psychological and emotional state of his beloved. In short: as long as he evades reality.

One critic has claimed that Sa'id's end is an honorable, moral suicide, a capitulation understandable given the overwhelming injustices. This is a misjudgment of Abd al-Sabur's critical intent. Sa'id is not the victim of external forces and circumstances, but rather the victim of his own backward-looking perspective, his fatal *idée fixe* of an intruder personified in ever anew guises: causer of the deep wound he suffered so long ago, of his impotence, of his loss; the defiler of his mother, his beloved, and his homeland – an idea that for the audience at least is dispelled by the renewed appearance of an integer Layla/Madina. Looking back from the vantage point of this scene, it seems appropriate to consider that Sa'id has fallen victim to a syndrome: his consciousness is stamped by the undercurrents of the early loss of a sense of security, trigged by the death of his father; or put in more general terms the legitimate family head; an experience of loss that, with a glance at Abd al-Sabur's other verse dramas, may well be connected to the "death of God". Upon this foundation, all later experiences of loss constitute a repetition of what has been already suffered. That he connects his realization of the profound caesura in the past – of the loss of security in his own cultural environment – with the intrusion of alien, illegitimate powers usurping rightful authority is therefore understandable. Tragically, the connection takes the form of a compulsive entrapment in visions of the past; this leads him to perceive openness towards life outside him, any contact with the new, as dangerous for maintaining his sense of self, even as contaminating. He thus withdraws into an attitude that – as Abd al-Sabur has elaborated in detail in his prose works – cannot match the demand pivotal to an energetic and productive relationship between intellectuals and society – truthfulness.

The literary type on which Abd al-Sabur pins his hopes is thus not a completely new figure who casts aside the old behavioral pattern of the self-sacrificing lover so deeply rooted in Arab-Islamic culture – the vanguard poet fighting for the liberation of the beloved. The demand is more modest and for that, all the more far-reaching: a Majnun who is truthful and sincere towards himself and his society, who no longer allows the horrific images of the past to prevent him from accepting them in their present manifestation, and who – to quote Sa'id's parting words to Layla:

... recognizes that you are Layla,
and calls you by your name.

The "allegorical paradigm"

In conclusion, a few words about the symbolic dimension, the undercurrent sub-textual matrix that has "transported" these lines of thought. The equation forged between Layla as the beloved Qays has known intimately since childhood, and Layla as the allegory of the homeland, which the local intellectuals claim as an intimate partner, becomes obvious when Sa'id himself identifies the beloved with Madina. Layla-Madina, that is, the homeland, in reality and in the vision of its intellectuals, is readily recognizable as the key figure of the paradigmatic configuration. Besides Layla there is Majnun, the pivotal figure of this configuration; her singer, her poet. He alone – out of his intimate knowledge of her essence – is her truthful lover and thus her legitimate partner. Transposed to Madina, this means that as the repository of the culture of the expressive word and defender of political-social ideals, he is the authoritative speaker of his society. This role already ensues from society's natural need for his words, through which it first becomes aware of its identity; but his presence becomes all the more important when the prevailing situation is felt to be catastrophic, when Madina is held "captive". By seeking to "liberate" Madina through his words, he takes on the traits of a chivalrous fighter; Qays metamorphoses into the poet-fighter Antara. The Sufi interpretation of the fable permits this close relationship between purely verbal and heroic self-sacrifice. In contrast to the "basic" Qays figure, the combative Qays' words do not bring about the loss of the Beloved, but in fact restore her by lending her identity, making her own essence recognizable for her, and providing her with a new awareness – precisely as the Qays of our play at times manages for the real Layla.

As the main male figure of the allegorical paradigm then, the chivalrous, warrior-like poet stands next to the female counterpart, envisaged as a noble captive in the hands of illegitimate rulers; this is precisely in keeping with the configurations played out on the stage in Abd al-Sabur's two purely allegorical dramas, *The Princess Waits* and *When the King Has Died*. The task facing the poet-warrior in both these dramas, in which the paradigm is directly discernible in the fabric of the plot's events, arises out of a catastrophic situation of loss. In one case, the legitimate ruler is killed (the father of the princess in *The Princess Waits*, comparable to the motif of Sa'id's prematurely deceased father embedded in a flashback and the lingering illness of Layla's father), while in the other he has proven to be impotent (the husband of the queen in *When the King Has Died*); the princess has fallen into the hands of Samandal, the defiling usurper who has killed the king, while the queen is threatened by the court officials who know of the king's death. The third figure is thus always that of the usurper, who after the murder/death/illness of the legitimate ruler/family head, that is, the fourth figure, seeks to take his place. In *Layla and the Majnun* the "intruder" occupies the place of Sa'id's father; in the black comedy *The Night Traveller*, where the figure of Madina is replaced by the chorus and the poet figure reduced completely to the victim role, the usurper – a ticket inspector – is in fact the main character; moreover, it is this character who explicitly names the loss responsible for the prevailing consciousness and sense of loss: "God is dead."

In our play these four symbolic figures are active on different levels: firstly and most obviously as characters on the stage and secondly as personified ideas, pervasive influences on the minds of Sa'id and his friends. The third level is that of the paradigm, which forms the foundation upon which Abd al-Sabur erects his vision of the future relationship between engaged intellectuals and their society. Having lost the legitimate ruler-figure of the past, an intellectual type will emerge as speaker for the Madina in the future, a type who is unquestionably modeled on the "Majnun"; related to our protagonist in his complex mentality but an idealist, or even more emphatically, a figure obsessed with and possessed by an ideal, who is dauntless in facing up to reality. It is patently obvious that this type, again, originates from a vision of the past, bearing traits abundantly evident in Islamic history: those of the age-old rebel-poet, the chivalrous lover, and finally the warrior prepared for martyrdom in defense of the faith, the *fida'i*. If the new Majnun is to do justice to this conception, then like the *fida'i* he will not seek self-fulfillment in the tangible attaining of his goal but rather in the striving for the goal itself, in the consciously accepted suffering entailed in redressing the imbalance, in an inextinguishable longing for the ideal, an abiding vision of utopia. The poetic watchword of this spokesman type, which Abd al-Sabur borrows from Shawqi's drama, is a pure "profession of faith" to this utopia:

> I beg you, Layla, there is no homeland to him who loves
> than that where he is with his dearest united.
> Let every land that is close to you, be my abode,
> and every place where you are dwelling, be mine.

Is not this vision of a society represented by a poetic spokesman a distant echo of the old Islamic longing for the restoration of a legitimacy which was once assuredly given in a remote past? Jacques Berque may well have such an interpretation in mind when he discerns in Abd al-Sabur's dramatic work a tendency towards "historicizing immanentism" and comments: "After myths were destroyed, myths are being created anew."

Viewed in this light, Abd al-Sabur's *Layla and the Majnun* goes far beyond the historically limited scope of ideological critique of the catastrophe of 1967. What the author shows on the stage with a vividness and clarity he would never achieve in later works is at once an analytical operation and appeal: the careful, sensitive, and yet critical disclosure of the diverse psychological strata which form the basis of the painful identity crisis plaguing his contemporary Arab intellectuals, and at the same time an encouragement to reflect on this complex situation anew.

SELECTED WORKS

Layla wa-l-Majnun (Layla and the Majnun), in: *Diwan 'Abd al-Sabur II*, Beirut: Dar al-'Awda 1983, pp. 703–874

al-Amira tantazir (The Princess Waits), in: *Diwan 'Abd al-Sabur II*, Beirut: Dar al-'Awda 1983, pp. 351–444

Musafir Layl (Night Traveller), in: *Diwan 'Abd al-Sabur II*, Beirut: Dar al-'Awda 1983, pp. 613–81

Ma'sat al-Hallaj (Murder in Baghdad), in: *Diwan 'Abd al-Sabur II*, Beirut: Dar al-'Awda 1983, pp. 445–601

Ba'd an yamut al-malik (When the King Has Died), in: *Diwan 'Abd al-Sabur II*, Beirut: Dar al-'Awda 1983, pp. 227–443

TRANSLATIONS

The Princess Waits, trans. Shafik Megally et al, Cairo: The American University in Cairo Press 1975

Murder in Baghdad, trans. Semaan Khalil, Leiden: Brill 1972

Night Traveller. A Black Comedy, trans. M. M. Enani, Cairo: General Egyptian Book Organization 1980

FURTHER READING

M.M. Badawi: *Modern Arabic Drama in Egypt*, Cambridge: Cambridge University Press 1987, pp. 220–28

As'ad Khairallah: "The Individual and Society: Salah 'Abdassabur's Layla wal-Majnun," in: Johann Christoph Bürgel, Stephan Guth (eds.): *Gesellschaftlicher Umbruch und Historie im zeitgenössischen Drama der islamischen Welt*, Beirut, Stuttgart: Steiner 1995, pp. 161–78

Nagi Naguib: "Materialien", in: Salah Abd al-Sabur: *Der Nachtreisende. Eine schwarze Komödie*, Berlin: Edition Orient 1982, pp. 115–37

Angelika Neuwirth: "Identität und Verwirklichungsängste. Zu einer modernen Bearbeitung des Majnun-Layla-Stoffes bei Salah 'Abdassabur", in: Johann Christoph Bürgel, Stephan Guth (eds.): *Gesellschaftlicher Umbruch und Historie im zeitgenössischen Drama der islamischen Welt*, Beirut, Stuttgart: Steiner 1995, pp. 205–34

Angelika Neuwirth: "Emblems of Exile. Layla und Majnun in Egypt, Palestine, Israel and Lebanon", in: *Mélanges de l'Université Saint-Joseph* 58 (2005), pp. 163–87

OTHER WORKS CITED

Jacques Berque: *Languages arabes du présent*, Paris: Gallimard 1974

T.S. Eliot: *Murder in the Cathedral*, London: Faber & Faber 1947

Abdellatif Laâbi: *Le fou d'espoir ou Le chemin des ordalies* [1982], Casablanca: Eddif; Paris: Autres Temps 2000

Shakir al-Nabulsi: *Majnun al-turab. Dirasa fi shi'r wa-fikr Mahmud Darwish*, Beirut: al-Mu'assasa al-'Arabiyya li-l-Dirasa wa-l-Nashr 1987

Friedrich Nietzsche: *Thus Spoke Zarathustra*, [1887] New York: Penguin Books 1978

Ahmad Shawqi: *Majnun Layla*, Cairo: Matba'at Misr 1916 (English translation: *Majnun Layla. A Poetical Drama in Five Acts*, trans. Arthur John Arberry, Cairo 1933)

On Writing in the "Language of the Enemy"

Assia Djebar and the Buried Voices of Algerian History

Barbara Winckler

For some time now Assia Djebar, the *grande dame* of Algerian literature, indeed of the Francophone literature of the Maghreb, has generated great interest amongst a broad public beyond the Francophone world; this acclaim long preceded her election to the *Académie française* in 2005. This admission to the forty "immortals" or life-long members of France's most prestigious cultural institution represents the summit of an array of accolades that Djebar has gained in the course of her literary life, another of them being the prestigious Peace Prize of the German Book Traders' Association in 2000. In its awards statement the sponsoring organization honored her as an author "who has given the Maghreb a forceful voice in contemporary European literature. In her work she has set an example of hope for Algeria's democratic renewal, for peace in her home country, and for understanding between cultures. Committed to the diverse roots of her culture, Assia Djebar has contributed decisively to spreading a new self-confidence amongst women in the Arab world." This appreciation touches on some of the diverse elements in the work of Assia Djebar, who, variously active as a historian, writer and filmmaker, can look back on an œuvre that is as extensive as it is important and in which these three aspects of her creativity are continuously interlinked. Djebar would justifiably find a place in any of this volume's thematic blocks: The life and work of this author are profoundly "place polygamous", they are deeply infused with history and broach issues of memory – and, as fits this section, their perspective is distinctly gender specific.

A life between the fronts

Assia Djebar is the pseudonym the author assumed upon the publication of her first novel in 1957 because at that time it was still a scandal for an Algerian woman to enter the public stage as a writer. This step into the public sphere was ultimately the consequence of an earlier decision made by her father that would influence her whole life and work: the decision to send her to a French school. She shares this experience with many "colonized" authors. Djebar's Algerian colleague Kateb Yacine has compared the same decision made by his father with "being thrown into the lions' den." For a girl, though, it had much more ambivalent consequences.

Born in 1936 in Cherchell on the Algerian coast as Fatima-Zohra Imalayène, in 1955 Assia Djebar became the first Algerian woman to be permitted to study at the Ecole Normale Supérieure in Sèvres. In 1956 as the Algerian students went on strike in support of the Algerian liberation struggle, Djebar, having only recently turned twenty, wrote her first novel, *The Mischief/Nadia*, in just a few weeks – and was thereupon exmatriculated. Her second novel, *The Impatient*, followed a year later. Both deal with the conflicts endured by young women in Algerian society as they search for their identity. Due to this "unpolitical" thematic, the texts were criticized as being out of touch with the concerns of a country caught in a struggle for independence, their author reproached for showing a perceived lack of loyalty to her country.

An unsettled life followed, working in university positions and as a journalist. She married in 1958 and followed her husband, who was forced underground, to Tunis, at that time a center of Algerian resistance. There, she studied and worked at the university as well as for the press section of the *Front de Libération Nationale* (FLN), the Algerian liberation movement, until the following year, when she was appointed to a position as historian at the University of Rabat in Morocco. In 1962 – the year Algeria gained independence – she returned to her home country, where she began to teach history at the University of Algiers and work for Algerian journals and radio. From 1965 she lived and worked for almost ten years in Paris, where along with her journalistic work she turned her attention to theater. On returning to Algiers, she taught theater studies at the city's university. In two further novels she deals with the experiences of the war of independence and exile, reflecting a stronger political interest and commitment. From 1980 onwards she has lived mostly in Paris, commuting as much as possible between Paris and Algiers, and teaching in the US and Europe. Since 2002 she has held the position of Silver Chair Professor of French and Francophone Studies at New York University.

Her literary work, at present encompassing more than a dozen novels, two volumes of short stories, a number of dramas, poems, and numerous essays, is closely tied to her life and the situation of her country.

Observing history with the eyes of the present

Assia Djebar approaches the history and present of her country from many different perspectives. She has thus directed her critical eye not only at the brutalities and injustices of colonial history, but also on the patriarchal structures of society and the corrupt behavior of the political class in independent Algeria. One outstanding feature of this perspectivism is how history and the present illuminate one another. As a historian, she confronts the rise of Islamic fundamentalism in her country – in particular the attacks upon women who refuse to keep out of public life as the fundamentalists believe "true Islam" dictates – by researching early Islamic sources for evidence of the (often very active) role played by women. She fills the gaps and ruptures in the tradition with literary imagination; this is the fabric of the novel *Far from Medina* (1991), a reconstruction of the life led by women in early Islam. Furthermore, the increasing Islamic violence in the Algeria of the 1990s is addressed in texts like *Algerian White* (1996), an appreciation of and dialogue with the dead that counters murder with memory, and *The Tongue's Blood Does not Run Dry* (1997).

With *Strasbourg Nights* (1997), Djebar sets a story in Europe for the first time. One constant remains: The Alsace, a pawn in the power struggle between Germany and France, is a location where borders are continually transgressed and several cultures coexist, not always peacefully. In an extremely elaborate construction, a constellation involving two couples embodies two historical conflicts: The love between a thirty-year-old Algerian woman and a Frenchman, twenty years her elder, is overshadowed by the memory of the Algerian war of independence, while the relationship between an Algerian Jewish woman and a German brings the Holocaust into focus.

A female memoria

One ever-present thread in Assia Djebar's work is the female perspective. In her works she establishes a female *memoria*, reconstructing stories about women that had been cast aside and forgotten or even repressed and consciously faded out, and so effaced from history. Whether she employs oral history to bring to light the recollections of Algerian women as in *Fantasia. An Algerian Cavalcade* and *So Vast the Prison* or, as already mentioned, elaborates the stories of peripheral female figures gleaned from early Islamic sources in *Far from Medina*, she always lends a voice to those who are usually not heard. To put it differently: She translates the memory of women, passed on orally, into the medium of writing, conventionally the domain of men. "Writing does not silence the voice, but awakens it, above all to resurrect so many vanished sisters."

Language as a crystallization point of the colonial conflict

The thematic complex of language plays a key role in the work of Assia Djebar, encompassing a series of contradictions: In spoken or written form language is paired to its opposite silence; however, the "indigenous" native tongue is also opposed to the language of the colonizers. Language is the crystallization point for conflicts arising from the colonial situation.

Language is always a political issue in the Maghreb, the subject of reflection and discussion. The choice of language is closely tied to the question of identity and often implies taking a cultural position and, along with it, a political one. For Algerian authors, the question of which language to write in is particularly prickly, if not explosive. The reason for this lies in the long and far-reaching colonization of the country, which even today continues to have a formative influence on its relations with France as well as on the linguistic situation and the education system. Unlike Morocco and Tunisia, Algeria was attached to the "motherland" and its education system was French throughout the colonial era. The few Algerians who had access to schools prior to independence were therefore educated exclusively in French. While most authors from this generation speak their native tongue, they do not feel that their command meets the rigors necessary for literary expression. Algerians who have received a bilingual education by studying in other Arab countries, such as Rachid Boudjedra in Tunis, are the exception. Djebar once formulated her hope that this deficit be overcome,

> to put an end to the inner turmoil caused by a bilingualism which seems
> to limp with both legs. To one day stop speaking your native language like
> a child learning to walk, and the language of one's education like a masked
> foreigner.

But beyond the sense of a personal shortcoming, the choice of language also has a political dimension: Francophone authors are often seen as denying their own cultural identity, accused of being "westernized" and thus disloyal to their own country; they are perceived as having taken the side of the former colonial masters.

Algerian women writers find themselves entangled in a double conflict in relation to language and identity. On the one hand, this conflict is gender specific, on the other culture specific. It is embedded in the cleft between French and their native language, which are connoted with different historical roles, with different perceptions of women, with different spaces and social groups, as well as different forms of expression (oral and written). In *Fantasia*, her first autobiographical novel, Djebar attempts to clarify this conflict-ridden situation by analyzing her own relationship to language.

An autobiography under the sign of collective memory

After 1969 Assia Djebar did not publish a single literary work for ten years. During this period she devoted her attention to other lines of work, which would eventually lead to the text that will be discussed in detail here. She undertook historical research into the biographies of families and women and focused on the medium of film.

The significance of film resides for Djebar in how it offers an opportunity for re-appropriating the gaze long monopolized by patriarchy and clarifying her relationship to language. She realized that the reason behind her inability to write in Arabic lay not only in the lack of linguistic competence stemming from her French education but also in the diglossia of Arabic, the discrepancy between everyday colloquial and formal written language. Filming therefore does not mean for her an abandoning of the word in favor of the image but, as she puts it, an engagement with the "image-sound".

After extended stays with her mother's Berber tribe, Djebar created her first film, *The Nouba of the Women of Mont Chenoua*, in 1978. Based on conversations with the countrywomen of her home region, it looks at the world in which they live and their recollections, in particular those concerning the final years of French colonial rule. The film was subsequently awarded the critics' prize at the Venice Biennale. Her second film, *The Zerda or the Chants of Forgetting* (1982), is a montage of French documentary film material from the colonial period. Originally shot from the hegemonic perspective, it creates a new, Algerian perspective through the way the material of an alien gaze is montaged and underlain with a fictive Algerian voice.

This historical and cinematographic work found expression in an autobiographical tetralogy, the first part of which, *Fantasia*, was published in 1985. Two further volumes, *A Sister to Scheherazade* and *So Vast the Prison*, followed in 1987 and 1995. Here, Assia Djebar develops a unique form of autobiographical writing by intertwining autobiography with the history of Algeria, individual with collective memory. Over the course of her literary work, Assia Djebar has continuously approached autobiographical writing, always hovering on the threshold to the fictional. In her work the individual story is unfailingly part of collective history. Her personal conflict stands as exemplary for that of the whole country.

A concert of voices, an entwinement of bodies

In *Fantasia*, probably her most complex work, Djebar calls on and orchestrates an immense number of very different voices. The text reads like the synthesis of all her work hitherto. An intricately constructed narrative structure interlaces three levels, with varying types of text employed for each. The autobiographical narrative, made up of fragments from childhood and adolescence, is set in the 1940s through to the 1960s. In the first two parts, titled "The Capture of the City or Love-letters" and "The Cries of the Fantasia", chapters concerned with this autobiographical narrative alternate with accounts of the fighting and atrocities which took place during the French conquest of Algeria between 1830 and 1852. For these accounts, the author draws on written source materials – colonial, military and administrative reports, diaries and letters, mostly penned by Frenchmen – at once quoting and elaborating on them. In the novel's extensive third section, titled "Voices from the Past", the autobiographical chapters are once again interlaced with historical material, this time oral accounts of the Algerian war of independence (1954–62). In each of these historical chapters – always bearing the same title of "Voice" – an Algerian woman tells of her suffering and active engagement in the war. In this case, however, the two levels are not only juxtaposed but are brought together in a fourth type of text – "Embraces" – where the female narrator seeks out the women and a dialogue ensues. A fifth type emerges in the form of poetical meditations, which are typographically distinguishable from the rest and, situated on a meta-level, reflect on the previous texts and encounters.

As Mildred Mortimer has noted, by juxtaposing French, male, and written sources with Algerian, female, and oral accounts, Assia Djebar is here connecting *kalam* (Arabic "speech") with *écriture* (French "writing") as well as *herstory* – relating the personal recollections of women – with *history* in the form of paper records.

On the necessity of historical rootedness

What purpose does this complicated construct serve? Why are seemingly disparate texts juxtaposed in this way? The significance of the historiographic level becomes evident when consideration is given to the course taken by the autobiographical narrative. Due to her path through life, atypical for an Algerian woman, the author/narrator finds herself in an ambivalent situation: On the one hand she has achieved considerable freedom, while on the other she feels excluded from her community of origin, in particular from the circle of women. The necessity of the two documentary levels arises from this dilemma. The starting point of the conflict, which crystallizes around language, is the father's decision to send the girl to school. The novel opens with a key scene:

> A little Arab girl going to school for the first time, one autumn morning, walk-
> ing hand in hand with her father. A tall erect figure in a fez and a European
> suit, carrying a bag of school books. He is a teacher at the French primary
> school. A little Arab girl in a village in the Algerian Sahel.

By attending the French school, the little girl is stepping out of the norms of her society, daring – unknowingly – to breach long-entrenched borders; a transgression that will determine her subsequent path through life and the conflicts she will go through. Leaving home is tied to learning to write. Writing in turn triggers the first impulse towards self-emancipation, towards asserting her own will against limits imposed by outside forces as well as internalized norms. For the narrator, writing is in the first instance a means to finding her identity and self-affirmation. The "love" letters she writes are less an exchange with someone else than her rebellion against her father's will and, in place of a diary, "simply a way of saying I exist."

Writing is a daring and risky move for a woman to make, for it is akin to an unveiling, making her vulnerable, and exposing her to the scorn of society: Her dignity would otherwise be protected by the veil.

> Its script is a public unveiling in front of sniggering onlookers ... A queen walks down the street, white, anonymous, draped, but when the shroud of rough wool is torn away and drops suddenly at her feet, which a moment ago were hidden, she becomes a beggar again, squatting in the dust, to be spat at, the target of cruel comments.

But it is not only writing – a domain ruled by men – that is problematic for women. Merely raising one's voice brings disgrace. Speaking out is not something women do. Even amongst the women themselves, a hierarchy of age determines who is allowed to speak and who must remain silent. Communication between women is limited to truisms and commonplace phrases, a codex preventing exposure and individualization. It is a taboo to speak openly and thus step out of the collective. Should a woman feel the need to speak about herself, she must "veil" her feelings in idioms:

> The 'I' of the first person is never used; (...) by means of understatement, proverbs, even riddles or traditional fables, handed down from generation to generation, the women dramatize their fate, or exorcize it, but never expose it directly.

Against this backdrop, how is it even possible to write autobiographically? This represents a further act of transgression. To write her autobiography means to consider her own life in terms of individual experience, although the prevailing norm dictates a suppression of individuality and a complete merging into the female collective. By refusing to adhere to this norm, the narrator risks losing her place in the community.

At first the girl embraces the changes French brings in its wake as something positive. The French language, associated with a different, modern social and feminine model, has an emancipating effect. In the relationship between her parents she had already noticed a development brought about by the French language that she sees as positive but her milieu finds appalling. Algerian women never explicitly name their husbands in conversation, referring to them indirectly as "he". After beginning to learn French her mother dares – albeit initially with some trepidation – to say "my husband" when speaking to French women. Later she extends this use to conversations with same-aged relatives in Arabic:

> Nevertheless, I can sense how much it cost her modesty to refer to my father directly in this way. It was as if a flood-gate had opened within her, perhaps in her relationship with her husband. Years later (...) my mother would refer to him quite naturally by his first name, even with a touch of superiority. What a daring innovation! Yes, quite unhesitatingly – I was going to say, unequivocally – in any case, without any of the usual euphemisms and verbal circumlocutions. (...) My mother, with lowered eyes, would calmly pronounce his name 'Tahar' (...), and even when a suspicion of a smile flickered across the other women's faces or they looked half ill at ease, half indulgent, I thought that a rare distinction lit up my mother's face.

With this development the relationship between the parents also changes. They now form a couple, almost like a French husband and wife, even if initially only in the limited public sphere of women. Some time later the father goes even further: He dares to address a postcard to his wife.

> The radical change in customs was apparent for all to see: my father had quite brazenly written his wife's name, in his own handwriting, on a postcard which was going to travel from one town to another, which was going to be exposed to so many masculine eyes, including eventually our village postman – a Muslim postman to boot – and, what is more, he had dared to refer to her in the Western manner as 'Madame So-and-So...' (...).

While the other women are appalled at this "disgrace", the mother feels flattered – although suddenly embarrassed in front of the others. That her parents now call each other by their names "was tantamount to declaring openly their love for each other." The girl has "some intuition of the possible happiness, the mystery in the union of a man and a woman, a first intimation of the possible happiness and secret (...) connecting husband and wife."

It is against this background that the narrator grows up. The process of her emancipation from the constricting conventions runs, as it did for her mother, parallel to the process of learning French and is conditioned by it. Even her body changes under the influence of French, it becomes "westernized" and learns to move freely. "When I write and read in the foreign language, my body travels far in subversive space, in spite of the neighbours and suspicious matrons; it would not need much for it to take wing and fly away!" Gradually her body and voice depart from those of the other women. Her throat can no longer properly articulate the traditional whooping of joy exclaimed by women. Her body becomes detached from the feeling of security afforded by the closed circle of women and gains a greater sense of joy from PE classes in the sun-drenched stadium of the boarding school where she is sent after completing primary school.

> At all the regular family gatherings, I had lost the knack of sitting cross-legged: this posture no longer indicated that I was one of all the women and shared their warmth – at the most it simply meant squatting uncomfortably. (...) My adolescent body imperceptibly breaks away from this bunch of female forms ...

French not only changes the narrator – it appears to exert a magical effect on her surrounds as well:

> (...) so, as soon as I learned the foreign script, my body began to move as if by instinct. As if the French language suddenly had eyes, and lent them me to see into liberty; as if the French language blinded the peeping-toms of my clan and, at this price, I could move freely (...).

Through this development, she becomes caught between two worlds. Outwardly she lives like a young French schoolgirl, while inwardly she feels the very same constraints and taboos as a veiled, entrapped Algerian. At boarding school she participates in sporting activities like the others, but is scared her father could catch a glimpse of her "exposed" and is assailed by the "'sense of shame' of an Arab woman." She can only live out the changes by keeping silent about them. She is not (yet) strong enough to openly act and advocate her position, which would mean exposing herself to words – from others but also her own. She cannot confide in her French classmates. Unfamiliar with this other world, they would not be able to understand her problems. As a result, the girl increasingly detaches herself physically and intellectually from her original surroundings, without ever really gaining the freedoms of French society or becoming a part of it. She is "neither completely outside nor still really in the harem." She is aware that French furnishes her with a perspective on new worlds but she shuts out any reciprocal look back at her. When a male addresses a compliment to her she is shocked; she had assumed that her body was invisible to others and thus protected from forbidden approaches.

> I discovered that I too was veiled, not so much disguised as anonymous. Although I had a body just like that of a Western girl, I had thought it to be invisible, in spite of evidence to the contrary; I suffered because this illusion did not turn out to be shared.

On the one hand an instrument of emancipation for her body and spirit, the French language also erects a blockade to expressing feelings or even love:

> (...) from the time of my adolescence I experienced a kind of aphasia in mat-
> ters of love: the written word, the words I had learned, retreated before me
> as soon as the slightest heart-felt emotion sought for expression.

At first she explains this foreign-language "aphasia of love" as a result of history, taking place at a time when love between European men and Arab women was impossible: She carries within the collective memory of her forbears. Moreover, the French she has learnt at school bears no relationship to her life and world. She has learnt the names of animals and plants that do not exist in her country. The situations and familial relations depicted in French schoolbooks are for her devoid of reality. Torn between the world of school, to which she has no emotional tie, and the world of home, which her education has no place for and indeed does not recognize, she begins to feel insecure as to where precisely she belongs. In all intellectual areas the French language provides the narrator with a rich set of tools, but on the emotional level it remains sealed to her: "the French language could offer me all its inexhaustible treasures, but not a single one of its terms of endearment would be destined for my use..."

The alternation between languages allows for play between intimacy and distance. If "a man whose mother tongue was the same as mine" – whose identity is defined, strangely, on the basis of language and not place of origin – makes an approach in French, then the words transform into a veil. Here though cultures and gender roles are reversed:

> It was he, in the last resort, who put on a veil, to venture to approach. If the
> whim took me to react to the man's advances, I did not need to put on some
> show of graciousness. All I had to do was to revert to the mother tongue:
> by returning to the sounds of childhood to express some detail, (...) I finally
> recover my power of speech, use the same understatements, interlace the
> allusiveness of tone and accent, letting inflexions, whispers, sounds and pro-
> nunciation be a promise of embraces ... At last, voice answers to voice and
> body can approach body.

Language and the sounds of childhood are a direct gateway to the heart. In this way intimacy can arise, an intimacy of voices and bodies. In contrast to French, which may liberate the body but blocks emotion, her mother tongue, although veiling and confining the (female) body, opens the way to the heart.

Overcoming the divide – a female genealogy

The two languages the young girl learns simultaneously, French at primary school and Arabic at Qur'anic school, drive a wedge between two worlds: outside and inside, connected either with freedom to move or entrapment. At first the narrator does not realize that the two are incompatible. Moreover, these two very different places of learning have quite different significance for her: Her success at the French school has a national component, whereby she values it as the achievement of an Algerian over the French; in contrast, she can revel in her personal success at the Qur'anic school without worrying about conflict because it is something her mother wholeheartedly acclaims and is therefore paradisiacal.

> At every prize-giving ceremony at the French school, every prize I obtained strengthened my solidarity with my own family; but I felt there was more glory in this ostentatious clamor. The Quranic school (…) became, thanks to the joy my mother demonstrated in this way, an island of bliss – Paradise regained.

Attending a French school is initially a source of pride. Suddenly though she is overcome by scruples about the privilege granted to her. Is it not tantamount to an act of betrayal to enter the world of the colonial masters, the "enemy," and benefit from what it offers? Is it not her duty to stay at home with the other women? At once she feels the French language to be a "tunic of Nessus", a "gift of love" from her father, an opportunity that he has given in the best possible intentions, only for this gift to fissure her inwardly with insurmountable conflicts.

She feels like one of the young Algerian girls married off at an early age, only she has been sent off to the enemy camp. The French in her is a "stepmother tongue" and so she embarks on the search for her mother tongue "that left me standing and disappeared." Her inner world has become a battlefield, with both languages engaged in a struggle that resembles the conquering of Algeria.

> After more than a century of French occupation – which ended not long ago in such butchery – a similar no-man's land still exists between the French and the indigenous languages, between two national memories: the French tongue, with its body and voice, has established a proud *presidio* within me, while the mother-tongue, all oral tradition, all rags and tatters, resists and attacks between two breathing spaces.

Despite the seemingly overwhelming imbalance, the outcome of the struggle is still open. She is torn between and by the antagonistic forces; she carries both sides within, and is unable to choose one over the other. Neither as a child nor an adult does she have the option of turning exclusively to one language and identity while definitively shedding the other. How could she regain the roots and sense of security afforded by the female community of her childhood without giving up the freedom and self-determination of a "modern woman"? She now attempts to combine on a literary level that which proves to be utterly incompatible in lived reality. And so she turns to autobiography as a means of solving the dilemma, only to be confronted again by the problem of language: While her command of her mother tongue is inadequate for literary expression, writing in the "language of the enemy" leaves her all too painfully exposed.

> To attempt an autobiography using French words alone is to lend oneself to the vivisector's scalpel, revealing what lies beneath the skin. The flesh flakes off and with it, seemingly, the last shreds of the unwritten language of my childhood. Wounds are reopened, veins weep, one's own blood flows and that of others, which has never dried.

After failing to find a solution in the present, a look into history proves to be the step towards reconciling her split identity. She discovers that before her, other Maghrebians wrote in the language of the occupying power, albeit seemingly without the inner conflict:

> After five centuries of Roman occupation, an Algerian named Augustine undertakes to write his own biography in Latin. (...) And his writing presses into service, in all innocence, the same language as Caesar or Sulla – writers and generals of the successful "African Campaign". The same language has passed from the conquerors to the assimilated people; has grown more flexible after the corpses of the past have been enshrouded in words ... (...) After the Bishop of Hippo Regio, a thousand years elapse. The Maghrib sees a procession of new invasions, new occupations... Repeated raids by the Banu Hilal tribesmen finally bleed the country white. Soon after this fatal turning point, the historian Ibn Khaldoun, the innovatory author of *The History of the Berbers*, as great a figure as Augustine, rounds off a life of adventure and meditation by composing his autobiography in Arabic. (...) As with Augustine, it matters little to him that he writes in a language introduced into the land of his fathers by conquest and accompanied by bloodshed! A language imposed by rape as much as by love ...

In placing herself in the tradition of these authors, she links into local history. Hitherto uprooted, she now re-anchors herself in the soil of her country. While researching its history she gains a surprising insight:

I am forced to acknowledge a curious fact: the date of my birth is *eighteen hundred and forty-two*, the year when General Saint-Arnaud arrives to burn down the zaouia of the Beni Menacer, the tribe from which I am descended, and he goes into raptures over the orchards, the olive groves, "the finest in the whole of Algeria", as he writes in a letter to his brother – orchards which have now disappeared. It is Saint-Arnaud's fire that lights my way out of the harem one hundred years later: because its glow still surrounds me I find the strength to speak. Before I catch the sound of my own voice I can hear the death-rattles, the moans of those immured in the Dahra mountains and the prisoners on the Island of Sainte Marguerite; they provide my orchestral accompaniment. They summon me, encouraging my faltering steps, so that at the given signal my solitary song takes off.

The narrator's development is the result of French occupation. Her path through life was made possible by the suffering and death of her forbears. Nevertheless she – who had felt a traitor – will not be condemned by them; on the contrary, they stand by her. At the end another voice speaks to her: Pauline, a French revolutionary who came to Algeria in 1852 – not as an occupier but banished into exile. In sensitive and insightful letters she tells of life in Algeria, enabling reconciliation with the French world. "Affectionate words from a woman, pregnant with the future: they give off light before my eyes and finally set me free."

Except for Pauline, the voices from the distant past were all male, the sources French. Searching for the voices of Algerian women, the narrator encounters only their silence; they are absent from all historical writing. This has continued into recent times. The voices of women have remained unrecognized; their contribution to the war of independence is passed over. The narrator thus begins to collect the war recollections of Algerian women, excavating the buried voice of history. At the same time, she taps into the Algerian side of her personality anew, reestablishes the ties to the community of women in her home village she had believed to be severed forever, and in this way creates a female genealogy. Both sides, coming closer to each other once again, benefit from the narrator's development. It is precisely (French) education, the opting out of the enclosed female world – in other words, the gulf separating her from the women of her family and society – that enables her to overcome the divide through writing.

SELECTED WORKS

La Soif (The Mischief/Nadia), Paris: Julliard 1957
Les Impatients (The Impatients), Paris: Julliard 1958
Les Enfants du nouveau monde (Children of the New World), Paris: Julliard 1962

Les Alouettes naïves (The Naïve Larks), Paris: Julliard 1967

Femmes d'Alger dans leur appartement (Women of Algiers in their Apartment), Paris: Edition des femmes 1980; Albin Michel 2002

L'Amour, la fantasia (Fantasia. An Algerian Cavalcade), Paris: Lattès 1985; Albin Michel
1995

Ombre sultane (A Sister to Scheherazade), Paris: Lattès 1987

Loin de Médine. Filles d'Ismaël (Far from Medina), Paris: Albin Michel 1991

Vaste est la prison (So Vast the Prison), Paris: Albin Michel 1995

Le Blanc de l'Algérie (Algerian White), Paris: Albin Michel 1995

Oran, langue morte (The Tongue's Blood Does not Run Dry), Arles: Actes Sud 1997

Les Nuits de Strasbourg (Strasbourg Nights), Arles: Actes Sud 1997

La Femme sans sépulture (The Woman without a Sepulchre), Paris: Albin Michel 2002

La Disparition de la langue française (The Disappearance of the French Language), Paris:
Albin Michel 2003

Nulle part dans la maison de mon père (Nowhere in the house of my father), Paris: Fayard
2007

TRANSLATIONS

The Mischief, trans. Frances Frenaye, London: Elek Books 1958; New York: Simon &
Schuster 1958

Nadia, trans. Frances Frenaye, New York: Avon 1958

Fantasia. An Algerian Cavalcade, trans. Dorothy S. Blair, London: Quartet 1989; Portsmouth, NH: Heinemann 1993

A Sister to Scheherazade, trans. Dorothy S. Blair, London: Quartet 1989; Portsmouth,
NH: Heinemann 1993

Women of Algiers in their Apartment, trans. Marjolijn De Jager, Charlottesville, London:
University Press of Virginia 1992

Far from Medina, trans. Dorothy S. Blair, London: Quartet 1994

So Vast the Prison, trans. Betsy Wing, New York: Seven Stories Press 1999

Algerian White, trans. David Kelley, Marjolijn De Jager, New York: Seven Stories Press
2000; London: Turnaround 2001

Children of the New World. A Novel of the Algerian War, trans. Marjolijn De Jager, New
York: The Feminist Press at the City University of New York 2005

The Tongue's Blood Does not Run Dry, trans. Tegan Raleigh, New York: Seven Stories
Press 2006

Strasbourg Nights, trans. Betsy Wing, Evanston, Ill.: Northwestern University Press
2008

FURTHER READING

Victoria Best: "Between the Harem and the Battlefield. Domestic Space in the Work of
Assia Djebar", in: *Signs* 27,3 (2002), pp. 873–79

Mireille Calle-Gruber: *Assia Djebar ou la résistance de l'écriture. Regards d'un écrivain
d'Algérie*, Paris: Maisonneuve & Larose 2001

Assia Djebar: "Neustadt Prize Acceptance Speech", in: *World Literature Today* 70,4 (1996), p. 783

Assia Djebar. Friedenspreis des Deutschen Buchhandels 2000. Ansprachen aus Anlass der Verleihung, Frankfurt/M: Verlag der Buchhändler-Vereinigung 2000

Elizabeth Fallaize: "In Search of a Liturgy: Assia Djebar's *Le Blanc de l'Algérie* (1995)", in: *French Studies* 59,1 (2005), pp. 55–62

Andrea Flores: "Affect and Ruin in Assia Djebar's 'La Soif'", in: *Alif. Journal of Comparative Poetics* 20 (2000), pp. 234–56

Soheila Ghaussy: "A Stepmother Tongue. 'Feminine Writing' in Assia Djebar's *Fantasia. An Algerian Cavalcade*", in: *World Literature Today* 68 (1994), pp. 457–62

Jane Hiddleston: "Feminism and the Question of 'Woman' in Assia Djebar's *Vaste est la prison*", in: *Research in African Literatures* 35, 4 (2004), pp. 91–104

Florence Martin: "The Poetics of Memory in Assia Djebar's *La Femme sans sépulture*: A Study in Paradoxes", in: Alec G. Hargreaves (ed.), *Memory, Empire, and Postcolonialism. Legacies of French Colonialism*, Lanham, MD: Lexington 2005, pp. 160–73

Mildred Mortimer: "Assia Djebar's Algerian Quartet: A Study in Fragmented Autobiography", in: *Research in African Literatures* 28 (1997), pp. 102–17

Doris Ruhe: "Which Society's Norms? Francophone Writers in Algeria Facing the Postcolonial Dilemma", in: Andreas Pflitsch, Barbara Winckler (eds.), *Poetry's Voice – Society's Norms. Forms of Interaction between Middle Eastern Writers and their Societies*, Wiesbaden: Reichert 2006, pp. 135–46

Zahia Smail Salhi: "Between the Languages of Silence and the Woman's Word. Gender and Language in the Work of Assia Djebar", in: *International Journal of the Sociology of Language* 19 (2008), pp. 79–101

World Literature Today 70,4 (1996) [Special Issue on Assia Djebar]

Clarisse Zimra: "Hearing Voices, or, Who You Calling Postcolonial? The Evolution of Djebar's Poetic", in: *Research in African Literatures* 35,4 (2004), pp. 149–59

I Write, Therefore I Am

Metafiction as Self-Assertion in Mustafa Dhikri's
Much Ado About a Gothic Labyrinth

Christian Junge

> Life is an activity and passion in search of a narrative.
> *Paul Ricœur*

The "Generation of the 90s"

No fatherland, no brokenness, no glorious defeats. Just writing with all its formal playing. And if there have to be fatherlands, brokenness and defeats then there are fatherlands of the body, brokenness of the soul and defeats of desire. It is a writing ... that belongs to the individual; it turns away from the collective and with it, politics, history, and society.

Mustafa Dhikri

The Egyptian author and screenwriter Mustafa Dhikri is a distinctive representative of the so-called "Generation of the 90s" in Egypt. This generation of young writers published their first works during the 1990s, mostly through the small publishing houses *Sharqiyyat* and *Mirit*. They can be considered as the second generation of the *hassasiyya jadida* (New Sensibility), a term coined by the Egyptian writer and critic Edwar al-Kharrat. In the aftermath of the political and ideological disillusionment of the 1960s, Arabic literature underwent a "crisis of representation"; writers turned away from realism and romanticism and their established aesthetic and poetic norms. The "New Sensibility" thus resulted in a literature "breaking the preordained order of narration (...) plunging into the interiority of the character (...) or incorporating or re-incorporating dreams, legends, and implicit poetry", as Kharrat has put it.

The literature of the 1990s allows for greater artistic freedom and radicalizes the renouncement of the collective. In consequence, it deals intensively with the self – and the text. While some critics disregard it as narcissistic, one has to see this preoccupation in a broader context. Sabry Hafez has said that the "Generation of the 90s" experiences continuous political, social and even urban marginalization and helplessness, which influence both the content and form of the new novel. One could even say that as a consequence of Cairo's ever increasing population density and the lack of green space, the self and the text are the last "rooms of one's own" in which writing can take place. But instead of retreating into solitude and silence, the literature of the 1990s tells of the struggle of the decentered, marginalized self for self-assertion. Unlike in the "literature of the *infitah*" (open door), this struggle often loses its concrete historical and social dimensions, turning instead towards an "absolute present", a more existential conflict taking place in the here and now. Thus, this literature moves away from politics, history and society to become "a chaos of art without opinion or illusions", as the Egyptian writer and critic May Telmissany has put it.

Like the "New Sensibility", the "Generation of the 90s" should not be considered as a homogenous school or movement. It includes various tendencies and such diverse writers as Miral al-Tahawi, Somaya Ramadan, May Telmissany, Ibrahim Farghali, Adil Ismat, Muntassir al-Qaffash, Nora Amin and Husni Hassan – to name a few. Among them, Mustafa Dhikri may be called the *enfant terrible* for his taboo-breaking work, his radical combinations of high- and lowbrow literature and of high standard Arabic and vernacular Egyptian and for his experimental kind of *Gedankenprosa*, or contemplative prose.

Born in 1966, Mustafa Dhikri studied philosophy and received a degree from the Cairo Film and Television Academy in 1992. As a screenwriter he wrote the two feature films *'Afarit al-asfalt* (*Devils of the Road*, 1996) and *Gannat ash-shayatin* (*Paradise of the Devils*, 1999), both of which are celebrated for their innovative ways in which they deal with violence and death – ways that go far beyond mainstream cinema. Dhikri has published two collections of short stories, five novels and a diary; his novel *Lamsa min 'alam gharib* (*Touch From a Strange World*, 2000) was awarded a State Encouragement Prize in 2004.

Hura' mataha qutiyya (*Much Ado About a Gothic Labyrinth*, literal translation: *Idle Talk of a Gothic Labyrinth*) was published in 1997 and contains two *riwayatan* (novels). The first novel, *Ma ya'rifuhu Amin* (*What Amin Knows*), recounts one day in the life of Amin, who is a helpless intellectual from Helwan (a suburb of Cairo). In the second novel, *Much Ado About a Gothic Labyrinth*, the marginalized protagonist, who also lives in Helwan, tells of his painful encounter with an attractive nurse in the hospital. Here, the self-conscious narrator intertwines digressions, anecdotes, day-dreams, reflections and stories, so that the text becomes a confusing labyrinth of plot and time. *Much Ado About a Gothic Labyrinth* may therefore serve as a good example of the "chaos of art" that the literature of the 1990s represents, as well as a telling narrative of the self.

By way of departure into Dhikri's text, this essay will first explore the link between a literature that reflects upon itself as literature, namely metafiction, and the self that writes about itself.

Metafiction and Writing the Self

I write, I erase. I write. What if someone reads these leaves of paper before they're ... complete? Writing is never complete ... Not being is more merciful surely. For being demands that we never end ... never. Being demands that we erase and return to writing and life once again, a writing and life that might be.

Somaya Ramadan

A major feature of the writers of the 1990s is a preoccupation with the self. Indeed, Mustafa Dhikri has stated that they all write autobiographies but differ in their approaches. Certainly, one will rarely find traditional confessions; instead their works tend more towards fictionalised autobiographies and/or autobiographical novels in the vein of Edwar al-Kharrat's influential *Turabuha za'faran* (*City of Saffron*, 1985). In regard to this novel, Stephan Guth has remarked that "writing autobiography means producing a fictional account." This postmodern conviction is related to the notion of the "narrative self" that Wolfgang Kraus describes as follows in his study on transitory identity:

> Language doesn't carry the inner life outside, but produces it. Since we are all involved in social structures, there is no thinking about and feeling ourselves possible outside of language (...) By narration, the self organizes his multifaceted experience in contexts referring to each other. The narrative structures are no creation made by the self, but anchored in and influenced by the social context, so that their genesis and transformation take place in a complex context of constructing social reality.

As a consequence, the narrative self challenges the idea of a stable and prior identity by highlighting the various processes of its own construction through narration, or, so to say, through fiction. This conviction has an important impact on metafiction, the literary strategy of self-reference that Linda Hutcheon defines as "fiction about fiction – that is, fiction that provides within itself a commentary on its own status as fiction and as language, and also on its own processes of production and reception." Because the self is constructed by narration, preoccupation with the text equals a preoccupation with the textually constructed self – and with the narrative norms of society. When the self is the text and the text is the self, then metafiction becomes more than fiction about fiction: it becomes fiction about the fiction(s) of the self, a tendency that one could call "autobiographic metafiction". Unlike traditional autobiography, autobiographic metafiction does not necessarily deal with the historical author outside the text. Instead, it deals mainly with the fictional author within the text and is therefore a kind of meta-autobiography.

This autobiographic tendency can be found in varying intensity in the novels of the 1990s, ranging from Miral al-Tahawi's *al-Khiba'* (*The Tent*, 1996) to May Telmissany's *Dunyazad* (1997); and even more so in Nora Amin's *Qamis wardi farigh* (*An Empty Pink Shirt*, 1997), where the female protagonist writes about the writing of her love story and so produces a multi-layered palimpsest of the narrative self.

Autobiographic metafiction is not a mere narrative narcissism, as one might think. In his study of *The Postcolonial Arabic Novel*, al-Musawi has highlighted the "critical endeavor" of the metafictional discourse in Arabic literature, which leads towards cultural contestation and self-definition. Autobiographic metafiction narrates the various struggles of the self in and with narration. In the case of the Egyptian literature of the 1990s, it deals less with societal narration and its norms, instead bringing to the fore the narrative ambitions of the self that is not struggling for a national or cultural assertion, but seeking its own very individual self-assertion. In the end, despite their uneasiness with the collective, these novels nevertheless provide an account of the narrative rules and constraints of society – even if they do so *ex negativo*.

The cinematic humiliation: what Amin knows

Therefore, marginalization appears to be one of the major and lasting concerns in that kind of modern prose that especially the new generation of authors writes.

Sabry Hafez

Despite their differences, the two novels of *Much Ado About a Gothic Labyrinth* both feature an intellectual protagonist who suffers marginalization and humiliation. Since each deals with these misfortunes differently, the two novels can be interpreted as two versions of a single antihero's story. In this regard, the generic term *riwayatan* may equally signify *Doppelroman*, or double novel, that is a single novel using strategies of double or multiple narrations; here, the two narrators' points of view on intellectuals living in Helwan, the suburb of Cairo. In the second part of the novel, the reader plunges deeply into the interior life of the first person narrator, whereas in the first part of the novel (which Dhikri initially wrote as a screenplay) the reader observes Amin through the dispassionate lens of a third-person narrator. Against this background, the first part deals with self-assertion in the outside world, the second with self-assertion in the inner world.

Amin wants to watch *The Misfits*. But driven by compulsion, he involuntarily leaves his home and castle and finds himself on the street. There he falls victim to his social tormentors, who make fun of him, mock him and even beat him up.

Feeling that there is nowhere safe to watch the movie, he flees from Helwan to the center of Cairo, where he rents a room in a hotel. Even there, he can't escape humiliation. When he falls asleep in the hotel lobby, two children put his finger in cold water, so that he wets himself, to their great delight.

Despite all his efforts, Amin cannot assert himself. As an intellectual, he has no niche in society, whether in unsophisticated Helwan or in highbrow Cairo. He is as much of a misfit as the protagonists of the movie, except that whereas Gay Langland (played by Clark Gable, the "King of Hollywood") is a "clear symbol of masculinity", Amin is a real misfit, a loser. In its cinematic rewriting of *The Misfits*, the novel rejects the common transfigurations of the outsider's role as cowboy, Steppenwolf or Zarathustra. Instead, it recounts the marginalization of the intellectual who cannot even find himself an ivory tower. Amongst the manifold dimensions of marginalization, Dhikri also highlights the results of the exploding population of Cairo: an urban marginalization, where spatial restrictions enhance the feeling of mental or intellectual restrictions.

In the "literature of the *infitah*", the antihero often undergoes a process of disillusionment, a good example of which can be found in Sonallah Ibrahim's novel *al-Lajna* (*The Committee*, 1981). During the course of events the highly committed hero turns into a frustrated antihero, who withdraws into his own world and finally consumes himself. In contrast, in the metafictional autobiographies of the 1990s, disillusionment is not the final result but rather the starting point. Amin's neurotic compulsions, which may be interpreted as the psychological effects of previous humiliations, initiate a merciless odyssey that never ends.

The artist's novel: art or life

> I say to you that I'm often dead tired of portraying human life without taking part in it (...) Is the artist a man at all? One must ask the woman! It seems to me that we, the artists, share the same fate as those modified papal singers (...) We sing quite touchingly, but ...
>
> *Thomas Mann*

In the second part of the novel, the reader's view shifts from the outside world to the inner world of a first-person narrator, an author who lives in Helwan. While witnessing a street-fight, he is accidentally injured and taken to the hospital, where he encounters the frivolous and mocking nurse, Ragawat; an encounter that awakens his sexual desires and opens up old sores. Brought up in the unsophisticated social sphere of Helwan, he has been an outsider from his early childhood. While the others prove to be highly talented when it comes to "life", which signifies women, sex, violence and suburban eloquence, the protagonist suffers the fate of literature:

> Cursed should be literature and all who practice it. Is it always my fate to know everything later – a cold, neutral knowledge only suitable to be written down and to be documented? Or are writing down, documenting and the ideas of writing things that, by nature, only occur afterwards?

Feeling estranged from life, he worries that his profession handicaps him by preventing him from taking part in the world. This fear leads to humiliation when Ragawat rejects him sexually; he believes that her reason is that he is a writer and so cannot assert himself as a man. The binary opposition between life and art is a classic topos of the artist's novel, as is well expressed in Thomas Mann's novella *Tonio Kröger* (1903). In *Much Ado About a Gothic Labyrinth*, this dichotomy is clearly embodied in the figure of a poet, who, in his old age, is finally successful with both poetry and women, but he is no longer able to have sexual intercourse, so that he has to satisfy his women by alternate means. Instead of using his penis, the poet uses his hand – to write. Writing is considered as a kind of Freudian ersatz, a pale imitation of the authentic life that the story's author can never achieve. The only possible way towards life, or towards participation in life, is to write it.

Unsurprisingly, in many autobiographic metafictions of the 1990s, the "self-conscious narrator" is not a lay narrator writing for the first time, but an experienced professional author. As a consequence, these texts offer heterogeneous and multi-layered concepts of writing.

In *Much Ado About a Gothic Labyrinth* the narrator creates a polyphony by intermingling two distinct writing concepts with one another. On the one hand, he "documents" incidents such as the humiliating encounter with the nurse, the eloquent vernacular *bon mots* of the others and his own inability to be as quick-witted as they are. This kind of "mimetic representation" reinforces the narrator's marginalization and underscores his inability to assert himself. On the other hand, he presents himself as a "tricky author", who does not consider writing to be a substitute for life, but celebrates it as a stage for himself. Here, he appears as a witty trickster, reminiscent to a certain degree of the eloquent and artful protagonist of the classical Arabic *maqama* genre. This kind of "poietic representation" offers the narrator the narrative freedom to assert himself:

> Now you will say, dear reader, that I'm a tricky author and that I pursue a labyrinthine and digressive way. And I say: Yes! I'm crazy about labyrinths and corridors that lead to nowhere.

These two modes of writing do not remain separate and distinct, but are intertwined throughout the novel, shaping its narrative maze.

The narrating self and the narrated self

Here we find the mysterious double play of both the selves, the superior narrating one and the stunned experiencing one; therefore also the natural intellectualism.

Leo Spitzer

In his famous study on Proust, Leo Spitzer distinguishes between the *erzählendes Ich* (narrating self) and the *erlebendes Ich* (experiencing self, or narrated self). The first person narrator (autodiegetic narrator) can emphasize the temporal and/ or spatial difference between himself as narrator and himself as protagonist, or even highlight the transitory aspects of his identity. In *Much Ado About a Gothic Labyrinth*, the first person narrator subverts the marginalized role he plays as protagonist with the picaresque role he plays as narrator.

During a nocturnal fight, the protagonist and the very sportive Nunna start in pursuit of a friend. But when the protagonist catches Wafdiya's mocking and scornful glance, he gives up the pursuit, feeling stigmatized as an author who can't stand his ground. The narrator recounts this scene twice. The first time, he depicts it very concisely in a neutral tone; the second time he changes his tune, subtly making fun of his "rival" Nunna. Using an "as-if" construction, he compares him to a runner on a treadmill who doesn't get anywhere, no matter how fast he runs. This causes "the author's moving away from the narrated subject, a distance between the narrating self and the experiencing self", as Spitzer puts it in regard to Proust. In the case of *Much Ado About a Gothic Labyrinth*, the narrator creates an ironic distance to Nunna, offering the humiliated protagonist a hidden counter-narrative to his experience of social defeat. Ultimately, this irony cannot change the course of events, but it helps him to a subtle self-assertion.

The frequent use of "as-if" comparisons in the novel keeps the mysterious double play of the selves going. Unlike in many traditional autobiographies, the narrating self is not superior because of its wisdom, knowledge and life experience. It is superior because writing offers the narrator an extended freedom to act. To write means to re-read, rewrite the story and to provide supplementary narratives. The narrator suggests to the reader elsewhere that a certain detail is "brought into the story by force", so that he can use it for his own purposes. The focus is no longer the story, but the way in which the story can be written. Or, as Jean Ricardou has put it in reference to *nouveau roman*, literature is not the writing of an adventure, but the adventure of writing. As a consequence, the story consists only of "minimal narratives", leaving room for the sparkling intellectualism of the narrating self. This *Gedankenprosa* is implicitly metafictional insofar as it shows the narrator using and abusing the protagonist's story for his own purposes.

Between fusha and 'ammiyya: the narrator's carnival

Carnival brings together, unifies, weds, and combines the sacred with the profane, the lofty with the low, the great with the insignificant, the wise with the stupid.

Mikhail M. Bakhtin

The mysterious double play between the narrating and the narrated selves must also be interpreted against the background of such dichotomies inherent in the novel as *'ammiyya* (Egyptian vernacular) and *fusha* (high standard Arabic), periphery and center, lowbrow and highbrow, provocation and taboo, frivolous and frigid sexuality ... Although the protagonist suffers marginalization in the periphery, he does not disregard his surroundings in a Freudian sublimation. Instead, he admires in others the vernacular eloquence and quick-wittedness that he can never achieve – or if he does, one of the others "steals" it from the tip of his tongue. The only thing he can do, as he complains, is to "document" their witticisms. But this documentation can easily shift toward self-presentation, as the beginning of the novel illustrates:

> About the corpulent and stout nurse Ragawat, Nunna used to say in his vulgar and direct tone: "Perfect is just her bone frame." Her stout figure can be related – though only from afar and with some good will and clemency – to the old Arabic standard of beauty, when they used to say: "That is a beautiful woman with shapely limbs. She feeds the nursling and warms the darling."

With this commentary, the narrator introduces himself as someone who is at least as eloquent as Nunna. At the same time, he offers the highbrow reader an *intraduction* that combines a *traduction* (translation) of the periphery with an *introduction* to the center: he translates the Egyptian vernacular to high standard Arabic and prose rhyme (*saj'*). But with the notion that only goodwill and clemency will justify his commentary and translation, he treats his speech ironically. As a result, he implicitly brings to the fore the artfulness of a rather far-fetched self-presentation. He also claims a *mésalliance* that unifies what doesn't fit together, like the classical Arabic rhetoric and the vulgar Egyptian vernacular – or the sexuality of the periphery and the one of the center, as the following "carnivalization" demonstrates.

The narrator derives the high standard word *thuwwa* (road-sign) from the vernacular word *suwwa* (mons veneris), since *thuwwa* is explained in the dictionaries as "what is raised above the earth and visible" and shares a similar shape with the *suwwa*. By this ironic philological *ishtiqaq* (derivation), which is based on the vernacular homophony of the letters *tha'* and *sin*, the narrator offers a vernacular reading of high standard Arabic. In what follows, he uses the words *thuwwa* and *suwwa* interchangeably. This carnivalization of pure language and culture offers the narrating self a space "in-between" the center and the periphery, the *fusha* and the *'ammiyya* and so on. Foregrounding the far-fetched pretexts for his misalliances, he appears as a self-conscious narrator, seeking to convince his audience indirectly that he is an eloquent and masterful trickster.

The imaginary labyrinth: an example of the riwaya qasira

> The composition of vast books is a laborious and impoverishing extravagance
> ... A better course of procedure is to pretend that these books already exist,
> and then to offer a résumé, a commentary ... More reasonable, more inept,
> more indolent, I have preferred to write notes upon imaginary works.
>
> *Jorge Luis Borges*

From implicit metafiction, Dhikri's novel shifts to explicit metafiction, where the narrator addresses himself directly to the reader in order to convince him of his wit:

> Now I will tell you a story devoted to labyrinths that I wrote a long time
> ago. I've always been of the opinion that it is skilled and proficient to kill
> two birds with one stone. So what do you think about killing all birds with
> one stone?

By virtue of this rhetorical question, the narrator performs a kind of modern *fakhr* (boasting), celebrating his skill and proficiency as author. The birds that he claims to kill, are, as he elaborates, threefold: the story devoted to labyrinths, the novel he is writing about the events in the hospital and finally the reader. For him, killing the three birds with one stone means creating a genre suitable for his purposes. Therefore, he combines the *riwaya* (novel) with the *qissa qasira* (short story) into a kind of *riwaya qasira* (short novel); a term not mentioned in the novel itself, but employed by several authors of the "Generation of the 90s" and also mentioned by Dhikri in an interview. This term is reminiscent of al-Kharrat's *qissa qasida*, a poetic prose that combines the *qissa qasira* (short story) with the *qasida* (poem) to create a new hybrid genre. Dhikri's text also denies the traditional rules of genres, "so that [these rules] will not help you to know if what I am telling you is a novel or a story." For the narrator, the *écriture transgénérique* (writing beyond the genres) serves as a picaresque genre allowing him to "kill two birds with one stone and little effort and to become narrator and novelist with a single blow".

In the story of the labyrinths, the narrator makes use of this waning of generic borders to challenge the borders between reality and fiction. He constructs a labyrinth in order to confuse the Argentine author Jorge Luis Borges, the labyrinth's doyen. While he describes the labyrinth to him over the phone, he gets the impression that Borges uses his words against him: "Does he make fun of me and weave threads of a labyrinth out of my mouth, without my recognizing it? For his own labyrinth, not for mine." In consequence, it is not Borges who is confused but the narrator, who lost this *munazara* (dispute). At the end, he notices that his readers and critics are confused by the order of the literary labyrinths and cannot distinguish clearly between them. Taking advantage of this confusion, he suggests to the reader that he first constructed Borges' labyrinth and is now inventing his own. With this tricky maneuver, he rearranges the labyrinth and its counter-labyrinth in his own favor, demonstrating how brilliantly he can manipulate the story.

Just as Borges deals with "imaginary books", the narrator prefers "imaginary labyrinths" to constructing complete labyrinths. Once again, it is not the labyrinths but the re-reading and rewriting of the labyrinths that is the focus: "But I admire the possibility of seizing a literal expression as if it were a concrete thing that could be stolen unexpectedly in order to serve a purpose that nobody yet knows." Such is the narrator's artfulness.

The *riwaya qasira* appears frequently in the autobiographic metafiction of the 1990s, such as in Telmissany's *Dunyazad* or Somaya Ramadan's *Leaves of Narcissus* (2001, *Awraq al-Narjis*). As *Much Ado About a Gothic Labyrinth* exemplifies, this genre challenges the clear-cut boundaries between the embedded stories and their contexts; between the imaginary books and their notes; between the "story about a labyrinth" and the genesis of this "story about a labyrinth". Confusing, or even erasing, the distinctions between the meta-, intra- and extradiegetic levels of narration, these short novels – despite their brevity – can be considered an extension of the fictional battlefield.

Rewriting the Arabian Nights: never ending details

In *Bouvard et Pécuchet*, I read this sentence, which gives me pleasure: "Cloths, sheets, napkins were hanging vertically, attached by wooden clothespins to taut lines." Here I enjoy an excess of precision, a kind of maniacal exactitude of language, a descriptive madness ... The exactitude in question is not the result of taking greater pains, it is not a rhetorical increment in value, as though things were increasingly well described – but of a change of codes:

the (remote) model of description is no longer oratorical discourse (nothing at all is being "painted"), but a kind of lexicographical artefact.

Roland Barthes

Metafiction in *Much Ado About a Gothic Labyrinth* elaborates as much on the state of the text as on the state of the self. While the narrator describes his "poetics of detail", he asks himself whether a normal person in Helwan – Hajj Abdallah, for example – would understand his elaborations or if he would in fact be considered abnormal or even "sexually deviant". First, he tries to explain his passion, desperately but quite unsuccessfully, before he suddenly recognizes that to "stop talking would be my death or sexual violation by the six sons of the Hajj." This reminds him of Scheherazade in the Arabian Nights, who saves her life by telling stories. As a consequence, he pursues his speech not in order to convince the Hajj, but merely for the sake of talking:

> I said to myself: (...) Let it be a vociferous speech (*hadith*), without drawing a breath. Let it be a crazy, incorrect speech combining *fusha* and *'ammiyya*. Let it be a speech unguided, merging in my mind and in the mind of both reader and critic. Let it be a rousing speech whose only goal is to increase the number of pages, so that the author – that is me – is convinced that he is able to narrate, to narrate truth and untruth. So be it then the story (*hadith*) of Harun al-Rashid and the story of the enchanted bag.

Metafiction explains not only how the text is made, but why the text is made in this manner. The continuous narration serves the author as a means of self-assertion. It is no longer important *what* he narrates, but *that* he narrates.

This paradigmatic change of representation is well expressed by Dhikri's rewriting of the story of "Ali, the Persian" from the *Arabian Nights*. This story deals with two persons who claim ownership of the same bag. To find out who is the legitimate owner, the judge orders each of them to describe the contents of "their" bag. Both exaggerate to such a degree that the bag could not possibly hold everything that they have described; therefore, neither could be the true owner. When the bag is finally opened, it contains only "bread, a lemon, cheese and olives."

The narrator in *Much Ado About a Gothic Labyrinth* provides a modern rewriting. Tamratag, one of the two "owners", lists, mostly in Egyptian vernacular, more than fifty items all belonging to the realm of modern popular culture; ranging from lipstick to a Yamaha drum set. Wardatag, the other "owner", uses high standard Arabic and prose rhyme to enumerate items belonging to the realm of classical heritage; ranging from two robes to "one thousand castles, the biggest as huge as Egypt and a part of Syria." When caliph Harun al-Rashid appears, the bag is opened. It contains the curse of a witch condemning Wardatag, Tamratag and the judge to repeat their descriptions until the witch's death.

It is obvious that the detailed and exaggerated descriptions do not describe the bag's contents; instead they provide a "change of codes", as Barthes has called it, that regards details as "lexicographic artefacts". In this context, writing no longer has the purpose of telling the reader a reliable story, but turns towards the radical aesthetic of *l'art pour l'art* – or at least of *l'art pour l'auteur*. The narrator celebrates his pleasure of enumeration and thereby achieves his goal of "increasing the number of pages" while proving that he is a masterful author.

This change of code – from illustrating a situation prior to writing to writing an artifact – is reminiscent of Barthes' elaboration on the word "to write" as an intransitive verb and its impact on the writer:

> I would say that we should no longer say today "*j'ai écrit*" but rather "*je suis écrit*", just as we say "*je suis né*" ... In the modern verb ... to write, however, the subject is immediately contemporary with the writing, being effected and affected by it. The case of the Proustian narrator is exemplary: he exists only in writing.

Limitations of self-assertion: body and emotion

> As for expression and feelings or emotions, the liberation, in contemporary society, from the older *anomie* of the centred subject may also mean not merely a liberation from anxiety but a liberation from every other kind of feeling as well, since there is no longer a self present to do the feeling.
>
> *Fredric Jameson*

Fredric Jameson describes the "waning of effects" as constitutive for western Postmodernism, "since there is no longer a self present to do the feeling." *Much Ado About a Gothic Labyrinth* may be considered for several reasons as a postmodern work; it includes metafiction, deconstruction, fragmentation and playfulness. Unlike in Jameson's elaboration, the subject or self in *Much Ado About a Gothic Labyrinth* is not dead, however, but decentered; it retains both its body and its feelings, which sometimes antagonize the narrating self and frustrate its tricky purposes.

When the narrator rearranges the order of the labyrinth, he suddenly feels trapped in the center, which he has created to confuse Borges. It is a dark room with clouded mirrors on the wall. This reminds him of the saying: "He who looks in the deep-black darkness at his reflection in the mirror becomes insane." In the darkness, of course, he cannot see his reflection; he therefore has no visual proof of his existence. Trapped in his own fiction, the narrator raises his hands in fear, gets goose pimples, and flees his fictional labyrinth. While the narrator takes advantage of the fictionality of the labyrinths on the one hand, he is disturbed and disquieted by the possible fictionality of his own self on the other. Writing fiction not only offers the freedom to act; it sometimes causes fear.

The infinite rewriting of the *Arabian Nights* finally comes to an end when the narrator imagines 'Amm Diyab entering the room and defending him from all harm, like a father would his daughter. A never-ending repetition of all the details may be considered as a curse not only for the characters in the story, but also for the narrator, who suffers the fatigue of telling his tales even after the allotted one thousand and one nights – until the witch's death.

In another story, the body and sexual desire play a major role. After the nurse Ragawat has rejected the narrator sexually, he wants to take revenge. He decides to listen to Ragawat's life-stories *ad infinitum* and not any longer with sexual desire, but like a priest taking someone's confession. While the priest, the narrator's alter ego, hears the confession of Ragawat's attractive alter ego, he feels suddenly aroused. Consequently, he betrays the beautiful woman to a Nazi who orders her immediate execution. In this allegory, the narrator's sexual desire re-emerges in the allegorical figure of the priest and unintentionally causes his quite unpriestly behavior. Ultimately, the narrator cannot deny his body or his sexual feelings in the narrative, not even in the allegorical figure of a priest.

Writing in this intransitive form gives birth not only to a self that is "being written" rationally, but also to an emotionally and physically written self. This emotionally written self cannot celebrate its complete fictionality, since it is overcome by fear. It cannot celebrate the infinite telling of the story, since 'Amm Diyab's parental feelings cut the story short. It cannot re-invent itself as a priest, since its sexual longings turn the allegory upside down. Thus, the narrative self is not only rational, but also emotional and physical. Body and feelings have a deep impact on the decentered self. *Much Ado About a Gothic Labyrinth* – and other autobiographic metafiction of the 1990s – has little in common with the kind of postmodern literature that deals only with surfaces. Although the self is decentered, it has a deep structure that influences and limits the struggle for self-assertion.

Therefore, emotional self-assertion must sometimes take place in a realm beyond writing. In Nora Amin's *An Empty Pink Shirt*, for example, the female protagonist gets emotionally trapped in her narration so that she finally ceases to write in the manner she was used to. And in *Much Ado About a Gothic Labyrinth*, the protagonist finds his *dénouement* in a kind of topographical vision of the Japanese Garden.

The Japanese Garden in Helwan: a sexual heterotopia

And also a totally different androgen appearance was on my mind in Japan, an appearance that drives the thinking mind (...) to contemplate the problem of hermaphroditism: the form of the Buddha. Is it imagined as asexual, monosexual or bisexual?

Magnus Hirschfeld

The Japanese Garden in Helwan is of great importance to the protagonist. In school days, he and his friends went to a prostitute in the garden's toilet. Waiting outside for their turn, they sat on the statues of the Buddha and imitated sexual intercourse by touching the Buddha's belly. The Japanese Garden, which is home to a large number of plants and trees from the Far East as well as about forty statues of Buddha, is an extraordinary place within the urban fabric of Helwan. It is a "cultural translation" of the Far Eastern Buddhism that preaches chastity as embodied by Buddha. But in the surrounding of Helwan, it becomes a brothel for minor clients located in dirty toilets.

The protagonist recognizes the peculiarity of this place when he contemplates the Buddha's "effeminate-looking and arousing body with soft folds of fat, one over another, and above a thin blanket uncovering the fleshy chest and the *thuwwa* of the round belly." This sexualized shape seems to him to have nothing in common with the demands of chastity. At the end of the novel, he believes that he will one day sit in the Buddha's lap while Ragawat sits in his lap and that the streetlamp's light will hit them "as if we were three images of the god Buddha." This sexual ambivalence, similar to that described by the German sexologist Magnus Hirschfeld at the beginning of the last century, neither accurately reflects Helwan's frivolous sexual identity, nor the uptight sexual identity of Cairo; much less the celibacy espoused in the sayings of the Buddha. Instead, the ambivalent Buddha embodies a kind of sexuality "in-between" these identities, entities and places. The presence of the statues of the Buddha renders the Japanese Garden in Helwan a "contestation of all other places", similar to Michel Foucault's concept of heterotopia – at least with regard to sexuality.

Like Amin, the protagonist of *What Amin Knows*, the narrator cannot find his place in greater Cairo. But while the Japanese Garden renders scene to Amin's humiliation, the narrator of *Much Ado About a Gothic Labyrinth* finds refuge in the garden – its statue of the Buddha serves him as neither center nor periphery, but as a counter-place. Becoming itself the "Buddha of Helwan" in his vision, the narrator finally finds a "room of his own". It is not a room of writing, but a room of sexuality. The narrator imagines his self-assertion beyond the "white sheet of paper" and the act of writing.

Conclusion

Who says that I want the normal reader? The normal looks for the normal.
The great is great. And the text is text, text, text.
Mustafa Dhikri

The "Generation of the 90s" often deals with life as a "fictional account". Terms like identity and self are no longer prior to the act of writing. Therefore, metafiction facilitates reflection not only upon the text, but also upon the texture of the self and its identity. Leaving grand narratives aside, this literature often depicts the struggle of the individual or self within the text: within its own texture and that of society. In the case of Mustafa Dhikri's *Much Ado About a Gothic Labyrinth* metafiction becomes a powerful method of achieving self-assertion, it foregrounds the shift from passive documentation to assertive writing. The double play of the narrated and the narrating self, carnivalization, the *riwaya qasira*, the change of codes – all these strategies fathom out the possibilities and limitations of the narrative textures. The ability to write becomes the *sine qua non* of the narrative self: I write, therefore I am. As consequence, self-assertion can be interpreted as control over the texture of the self, as the case of Amin in *What Amin Knows* illustrates: since he can neither narrate nor express his own point of view emphatically, he suffers from the humiliating speech of the others without either "writing back" to them or "being written" differently.

Despite all its disillusionment, the autobiographic metafiction of the 1990s – or at least Dhikri's *Much Ado About a Gothic Labyrinth* – does, at times, employ an idealistic concept of writing. The page serves as a place *besides* or sometimes even *beyond* the narrative constraints of society, allowing a somewhat idealistic texture of the self to appear. But at the same time, this literature narrates the limitations and failures of self-narrations; they are set and uncovered by the body and the feelings. Thus, this idealistic inclination does not necessarily produce an idealistic text. In fact, these narratives give evidence of the sometimes joyful, sometimes bitter existential *Geworfenheit*: the thrownness of the artist into writing. Since the self cannot exist apart from writing, it can only act within the possibilities and limitations of writing. In this context, writing is no longer the result of careful reflection, but becomes as spontaneous as life itself, erroneous sometimes, frightening, and also surprising and hopeful.

WORKS

Tadribat 'ala al-jumla al-i'tiradiyya (Practices of Parenthesis), Cairo: al-Majlis al-A'la li-l-Thaqafa 1995

Hura' mataha qutiyya (Much Ado About a Gothic Labyrinth), Cairo: Dar Sharqiyyat 1997

al-Khawf ya'kulu al-ruh (Fear Eats the Soul), Cairo: Dar Sharqiyyat 1998

Lamsa min 'alam gharib (Touch From a Strange World), Cairo: Dar Sharqiyyat 2000

Mir'at 202 (Mirror 202), Cairo: Dar Mirit 2003

Rasa'il (Letters), Cairo: Dar Mirit 2006

"Shahadat al-shakl wa-laysa al-madmun" ("A Statement of Form, Not of Content"), http://www.smartwebonline.com/New Culture/cont/018100070017.asp (access September 11, 2007)

'Ala atraf al-asabi'. Yawmiyyat (On the Tips of the Fingers. A Diary), Cairo: Dar al-'Ayn 2009

TRANSLATIONS

"Four Tales", transl. Waiel Ashry, in: *Banipal* 26 (2006), pp. 110–113

FURTHER READING

Sabry Hafez: "Jamaliyyat al-riwaya al-jadida. al-Qati'a al-ma'rifiyya wa-l-naz'a l-mudadd li-l-ghina'iyya", in: *Alif. Journal of Comparative Poetics* 21 (2001), pp. 184–246

Ismael Hissu: "Aswat adabiyya shabba tu'lin al-infisal. 'al-Kitaba al-jadida fi Misr' milaffan fi 'Banipal'", in: *al-Hayat*, May 3, 2006

May Telmissany: "al-Zaman ka-mataha fi adab al-tis'inat. Muntasir al-Qaffash wa-Mustafa Dhikri namudhajan", in: *Nizwa* 39 (2004), pp. 272–76

OTHER WORKS CITED

Alif laila. Book of the Thousand Nights and one Night, commonly known as the "Arabian Nights Entertainments", ed. William H. Macnaghten, Calcutta: Thacker 1839–42

Mikhail M. Bakhtin: *Problemy poetiki Dostoevskogo* [= *Problemy tvorčestva Dostoevskogo*], Leningrad: Priboj 1929

Roland Barthes: *Le plaisir du texte*, Paris: Seuil 1973

Roland Barthes: "Ecrire, verbe intransitif?", in: *Œuvres complètes. 1966–1973*, vol. 2, ed. Eric Marty, Paris: Seuil 1994, pp. 973–80

Karl Heinz Bohrer: "Zeit und Imagination. Das absolute Präsens der Literatur", in: Karl Heinz Boher, *Das absolute Präsens. Die Semantik ästhetischer Zeit*, Frankfurt/M.: Suhrkamp 1994, pp. 143–83

Wayne Booth: "The Self-Conscious Narrator in Comic Fiction Before Tristram Shandy", in: *Publication of the Modern Language Association of America* 67 (1952), pp. 163–85

Jorge Luis Borges: *Ficciones 1935–1944*, Buenos Aires: Sur 1944

Michel Foucault: "Les hétérotopies" [radio lecture, December 7, 1966], in: Michel Foucault: *Die Heterotopien. Der utopische Körper. Les hétérotopies. Le corps utopique*, Frankfurt/M.: Suhrkamp 2005, pp. 37–52 (bilingual, with Audio-CD)

Stephan Guth: "Why Novels – Not Autobiographies?", in: Robin Ostle, Ed de Moor, Stefan Wild (eds.), *Writing the Self. Autobiographical Writing in Modern Arabic Literature*, London: Saqi 1998, pp. 139–47

Magnus Hirschfeld: *Weltreise eines Sexualforschers im Jahre 1931/32*, Frankfurt/M.: Eichborn 2006

Linda Hutcheon: *Narcissistic Narrative. The Metafictional Paradox*, New York, London: Methuen 1984

Fredric Jameson: *Postmodernism, or, the Cultural Logic of Late Capitalism*, Durham: Duke University Press 1991

Edwar al-Kharrat: "The Mashriq", in: Robin Ostle (ed.), *Modern Literature in the Near and Middle East 1950–1970*, London, New York: Routledge 1991, pp. 180–92

Wolfgang Kraus: "Falsche Freunde. Radikale Pluralisierung und der Ansatz einer narrativen Identität", in: Jürgen Straub, Joachim Renn (eds.), *Transitorische Identität. Der Prozesscharakter des modernen Selbst*, Frankfurt/M., New York: Campus 2002, pp. 159–86

Thomas Mann: "Tonio Kröger" [1903], in: Thomas Mann, *Große kommentierte Frankfurter Ausgabe. Werke – Briefe – Tagebücher*, ed. Heinrich Detering et al., vol. 2 (Frühe Erzählungen, 1893–1912), Frankfurt/M.: Fischer 2004

Frank C. Maatje: *Der Doppelroman. Eine literatursystematische Studie über duplikative Erzählstrukturen*, Groningen: Wolters-Noordhoff 1968

Muhsin Jassim al-Musawi: *The Postcolonial Arabic Novel. Debating Ambivalence*, Leiden: Brill 2003

Somaya Ramadan: *Awraq al-Narjis*, Cairo: Dar Sharqiyyat 2001 (English translation: *Leaves of Narcissus*, trans. Marilyn Booth, Cairo, New York: The American University in Cairo Press 2004)

Leo Spitzer: "Zum Stil Marcel Prousts", in: Leo Spitzer, *Stilstudien*, vol. 2, Darmstadt: Wissenschaftliche Buchgesellschaft 1961, pp. 365–497

Transgressions, or the Logic of the Body
Mohamed Choukri's Work: A Fusing of Eros, Logos and Politics

Özkan Ezli

Literature as action

Diogenes of Sinope, who lived in the fourth century BC, used to masturbate right in the middle of the Athenian agora. He was neither pathologically disconnected from his community, psychotic, or simple-minded, nor did his society find itself at the beginning of what Norbert Elias has called the "process of civilization". Nevertheless, Athenians objected to his way of life in general and to this kind of behavior specifically. They regarded him as a public nuisance, for the phenomenon of privacy in the Greek *polis* related to bodily acts that were considered inappropriate to be performed in public. In this vein, Diogenes was also reproached for having eaten in the marketplace. He deliberately violated the principle of discreet behavior adhered to in the Greek *polis*, which refused to condone the concentration of collective attention on a single individual, while connecting his bodily acts to a specific issue: confronted about his act of public masturbation, he declared that he wished it were as easy to satisfy one's hunger as it was to satisfy one's sexual needs, by simply stroking one's belly. The transgressive dimension in Diogenes' actions resided primarily in countering the political and social foundations of the *polis*; flouting the rules governing the collective, concentrating on satisfying the needs of his body, putting it on show and thus turning his private self – his body – into a political issue.

As a result of a very similar dynamic, Mohamed Choukri's autobiographical novel *For Bread Alone* was considered highly political when it was first published in English, translated by Paul Bowles, in 1973. The Arabic original was not published until a decade later, only to be banned the following year. It was claimed that the novel, which traces Choukri's struggle for survival in Morocco between 1935 and 1956 in intense, extraordinarily blunt language, was nothing but "pornography" that showed a "lack of respect towards parents and religion". It remained banned in Morocco for the following twenty years, and Choukri was only officially rehabilitated as a Moroccan author after the enthronement of Mohammed VI in 1999, a monarch who represented a far more liberal political line than his rigid, dictatorial father Hasan II. In the preface to the 1980 French edition of Choukri's novel, Tahar Ben Jelloun remarks that while Moroccan society tolerates the prevailing wretched reality, it deems that literature should remain silent about it. The literary critic Salah Natij explains why the representation of misery is more destabilizing for a society than the actual existence of such misery:

> We accept that there is prostitution on the streets, but we do not accept that a literary character prostitutes him- or herself. Prostitution on the streets is simply a fact, prostitution in literature becomes a cause.

Whereas in the European tradition, from Gustave Flaubert's *Madame Bovary* through to Michel Houellebecq's pornographic novel *Les particules élémentaires* (1998), literature has evolved into an institution of transgression, used as a medium for breaking social taboos, this aspect still seems to be in its infancy in the Arab-speaking world. At the same time, it should be noted that, paradoxically, transgression and scandal in European literature no longer genuinely breach taboos. Scandal and transgression have appointed roles and strategic functions to play within an aesthetic repertoire and are described and generally accepted as artistic and literary forms. In contrast, in the Arab public sphere literary transgressions are clearly branded as such and dealt with as a political issue. Moreover, Islamic-Arab societies consider the shame associated with the body and the self of a person to be intricately entwined. This interdependence has played an important role in modern Arab autobiographies. In his autobiography *My Life* (1952), Ahmad Amin remarks:

> I have not told the whole truth ... there are truths that are too disgraceful and repulsive to be told and to be heard. Since we do not approve of the complete nakedness of the human body, why should we approve of the complete naked-ness of the human self?

A person's self-understanding and thus his identity are more strongly linked to the actions and abuses of his body than is the case in modern European cultures. Thus, the central private space in the Islamic-Arab world, the *haram* (harem), is one of physical intimacy, a space of very different actions from those primarily of language and psychology, which we encounter in Western cultures. The story of Choukri's life in *For Bread Alone*, told in a mode of complete exposure and profound irritation, radically transgresses the dividing line between the narrator's personal intimacy and the public space in two ways: through the nakedness of his body and the nakedness of his self. In this way, Choukri – much like Diogenes – manages to deconstruct the social superstructure by exposing his body and reducing his self to this body. Via the body, literature becomes a political, public act.

Logic of the body

"A consciousness of bodily desires and the will to pleasure, sooner or later, always turn themselves against oppression," Choukri once remarked, thus characterizing his writing as inherently political. He was an author of the oppressed, of the oppressed body, and of public space. In *Streetwise* (1992), the second part of his autobiography, Choukri characterizes himself as a political writer of the streets, in direct contrast to the Moroccan author Mohamed al-Sabbagh:

> I accompanied Mohamed el Sabbagh to his flat in the old part of town. The ambience of a person devoted to his art. Grapes, apples and pears in a large metal bowl; a subdued light that deepened the effect of the poetic silence. Chopin: "The Nights of Majorca", and reading letters by Michael Nu'imah [*sic*]. I came out from his house wishing that I had a refuge like that. He went through my writings and corrected them, using words that were finely sculpted, transparent—but *he was clay of one kind and I was clay of another*. He didn't have to eat the garbage of the rich. He didn't have lice like me. His ankles weren't all sore and bleeding. I don't know how to write about the touches of angelic beauty, the grapes of dew, and the paralysis of hunting dogs, and the songs of nightingales. I don't know how to write with a broom of crystal in my head. A broom is protest and not decoration.

Choukri was indeed "at home" in boarding houses, hotels, bars and street cafés. It was there that he read and wrote; it is there that his protagonists move about; and it was there that he met exiled writers. In the 1960s Choukri became immersed in the world of the post-beatniks and hippies who had been washed ashore in Morocco on their oriental journey from the uneventful prosperity of the West, whose world Choukri depicts in lurid colors in his novel *Zoco Chico* (1985). It was during these years that he met Jean Genet, who would remain one of his closest friends until Genet's death in 1986, as well as Tennessee Williams, Samuel Beckett, Tahar Ben Jelloun and Paul Bowles. They supported his decision to become a writer. Paul Bowles and Tahar Ben Jelloun went on to translate the first part of his autobiography into English (1973) and French (1980) respectively.

Acquaintanceships with exiled authors shaped Choukri's own understanding of literature, in the sense that the task of literature is to depict the abject aspects of life in its unique aesthetic. Here his long friendship with Jean Genet was of particular importance. Despite the stimulating influence of exile writers, Choukri was critical of some of them. In his book about the circle of literati around Paul Bowles, Choukri claims the city of Tangier, in which he has spent most of his life, as his own, shielding the reality of its hardships as well as its mythical, cryptic secrets against the widespread Orientalist representations of it, which reduce it to an exotic postcard image:

> They all came to Tangier to make their exotic dreams come true. They did not want to have anything to do with Morocco, but only used it as a colorful backdrop, and the Moroccans were only the objects of their mostly sexual desires.

Here, Choukri criticizes the Western perception of the "Orient" as a world dominated by the physical and sensual – despite his own debts to Western views and influences. Although Choukri engages with the Western perception of Morocco, his main interest remains the Islamic-Arab society itself. He was blacklisted by the Islamists because he openly wrote about his sexuality and called into question the institution of the family. A professed atheist, Choukri worried little about the threatening situation, saying in an interview: "There is no reason to be afraid. If it happens, it just happens." Meanwhile, *For Bread Alone* has been translated into thirty-nine languages, and Choukri is, next to Naguib Mahfouz, the most widely read author of the Arab world. He died of cancer on 16 November 2003 in a military hospital in Rabat.

Mohamed Choukri once remarked that not one but three swords of Damocles dangle over the Arab writer: the sword of religion, the sword of politics, and the sword of sexuality. The task of the writer is to challenge this triad. Like no other author, Choukri has fulfilled his own demand in his prose. Sexuality is the central concern of his autobiographical works *For Bread Alone* and *Streetwise*; this issue is transgressive on two levels: on a social level, through the intense and irritating representation of sexuality and the description of the father as a murderous tyrant in a society that considers the status of the family and in particular that of the father to be sacred; on the other hand, there is his literary style, which was new for Arab literature and can be understood as postmodernist. A brief digression shall elaborate to what extent Choukri's writing moves within a postmodern field.

"The novel is a private matter but at the same time an imitation of creation," wrote Christian Friedrich von Blankenburg in 1774. In the context of the Enlightenment, literary creation was understood to be subject to a causal nexus, a linear movement analogous to processes in the natural world and in history. Blankenburg characterized the genre as an individual story of "becoming", but also as a public, didactic text through which the reader could vicariously experience *Bildung* (a formative development) and thus educate and perfect him- or herself. The development of the protagonist in a novel is by no means open-ended but rather teleological. Above all, phenomena like the body and sexuality obey an economy of causality, the logic of the spirit, and an ultimate purpose. This conception found its expression in the *Bildungsroman* and the incipient novelistic autobiographies of Goethe and Rousseau.

Almost two hundred years after Blankenburg's *Notes*, Roland Barthes published his groundbreaking essay *Le Plaisir du texte*, which, in this context, can be read as a kind of counter-text. Central concepts in Barthes' essay are *plaisir* (pleasure) and *jouissance* (bliss). Barthes sweeps literary texts into two basic categories: the first comprises *textes du plaisir*, which employ classical, affirmative narrative modes; while the second is made up of *textes de jouissance*, which irritate, create scandal, and self-reflexively draw attention to language instead of focusing on telling a coherent and complete "story". Texts of this latter type are to be found in both modernism and postmodernism. Barthes characterizes the usual practice of classical modernist texts as: "Classics. Culture ... Intelligence. Irony. Delicacy. Euphoria. Mastery. Security ... House, countryside, near mealtime, the lamp, family where it should be ..." As a counter-model Barthes proposes tapping into the critical potential that inheres to text in contrast to other forms of expression based on language: the literary text is capable of deconstructing the unity of so-called morality; of undermining its own discursive category; and in contrast to the stereotype and the hierarchically-structured sentence, it is untrammelled. One prerequisite for an unbridled *plaisir du texte* contrary to the centering of thinking and argumentation, a *jouissance*, is a synchronous thinking of text and body. Barthes proposes apprehending the text as a body, as its anagram, and argues for a sensual perception of the text permitting *jouissance*, the inclusion of which enables textual practice to develop as an erotic and critical activity. In sum, Barthes puts forward a consequential aesthetics of *plaisir* which is to supersede more traditional aesthetic modes. In addition to the atopia of the text, Barthes develops the utopia of a so-called "sounding text", which he conceives in terms of a voice belonging to the body and embodying the text, fusing eros and logos. Mohamed Choukri's autobiographical writing can be characterized as exactly this kind of fusion of text and sensuality, as "sounding texts" in Barthes' sense.

Choukri's literary work, or an identity-free logic of intensities

In his picaresque autobiographical novel *For Bread Alone* Choukri tells the story of his life between 1935 and 1956 in a language of poetic brutality and obscenity. Hunger forced his Berber family to migrate from the Rif Mountains to the city of Tangier. While the father serves a prison sentence for black marketeering, the mother must ensure the family's survival on her own. The family's misery escalates, however, once the brutalized and tyrannical father returns. The son flees and struggles through with odd jobs, including working as a shoeshine. He experiences the friendship and enmity of other young men living on the street, as well as the sympathy and hatred of the adults from whom he steals. He loses his virginity to the famous prostitute Lalla Harrouda, who is also the central character in Tahar Ben Jelloun's novel *Harrouda* (1973). He learns Arabic and Spanish on the streets and in the brothels of the city; with his family he speaks a Berber dialect. When he is hired as a farmhand by some relatives, the mistress of the house chooses him as her houseboy but bored by his job, he seduces a beautiful boy of the neighborhood; as a consequence, he is sent back home to his family. From then on the narrator aimlessly roams the streets of the city, always on the lookout for a piece of bread, pot, a swig of wine and a roof over his head. He lives among peddlers, prostitutes, and smugglers, who share the little they have with him – or steal from him. He feels safest at the cemetery.

On 30 March 1952, the day street fighting breaks out in the struggle for Moroccan independence, he observes from a hideout a boy being shot by a policeman. At similarly close quarters, he takes part in one of the most important events in Morocco's contemporary history: on a boat loaded with Jewish emigrants he sells scarves and watches at excessive prices. Why they are emigrating to Palestine is something he consciously does not want to think about. He is only interested in wheeling and dealing. Having landed in prison, there he undergoes a "conversion": in order to be able to read the wonderful verses by the Tunisian poet Abu al-Qasim al-Shabbi that a cellmate has written on the wall, he decides to learn the Arabic alphabet. Al-Shabbi's reference to the "will to live" in the verse has stirred the "will to write" in the young man.

Conversions and turning points in the life of an author, perhaps the most important motifs in an autobiographical text, are generally bound to a teleological narration. Typical examples would be classical autobiographies from Augustine and Goethe through to Elias Canetti. Choukri's autobiographical text, however, cannot be read as teleological. There is no set goal; coincidence and chance reign. Choukri describes the decisive "conversion" in prison in passing, just like his good fortune when stumbling across some money. His literary style is too intricately bound up with the presence of the body, with life, and with the need to survive in the moment even to hint at possibilities in the future or where life is leading him. In *For Bread Alone*, he writes:

> But what does it mean, a man who was alive and now isn't? What does it mean that I should be sleeping here in this corner of a family grave? From the tiles and the well-kept plot I can see that the family was a rich one. What does it mean to allow a man sixty or seventy years old to suck on me and then give me fifty pesetas? There must be answers to these questions, but I don't know them yet. The questions come easily, but I am not sure of the answer to any one of them. I thought the meaning of life was in living it.

Choukri's texts do not generate reflexive meanings; they draw their momentum from their simplicity and intensity, which nullify any moral or ideological superstructure. The text employs a chain of intensities which bypasses, or has no bearings on, any kind of identity formation. It thus hardly surprising or confusing when the narrator, without much ado, describes his sexual desire for both the beautiful boy as well as the mistress of the house in one narrative breath:

> The wine ran through me, and I found myself trembling. My hand stroked his. He pulled away and sat up, looking at me with an expression of fear. What do you want? He demanded.
>
> Nothing. What's the matter? Lie down. I was joking.
>
> I don't like that sort of joke.
>
> With my eyes I said: I do, with you.
>
> He made as if to rise. I seized his hand. I was still trembling. He wrenched his hand away and got to his feet. Before he could take his first step, I wrapped my arms around his legs, so that he fell. I fell partially on top of him.
>
> I'm going to tell my mother! he cried. And my father too! First he bites my hand, and then he bites the earth.

Just a page later the mistress of the house wants to send him home for a holiday to see his family. The protagonist, who finds her physically attractive, thinks: "I said to myself, give me your haunches and I give you my whole family."

As Choukri does not connect these scenes causally, the events seem to be a string of unrelated incidents, where one intensive experience gives way to another without even the slightest hint that what happened before might have any bearing. Besides the obvious transgression of moral ideas about (homo)sexuality and the sacred institution of the family, Choukri also transgresses any coherent form of identity formation, in particular that of sexual identity. The text is not concerned with the idea of self but notions of the body, and this implies a different logic from that of the genesis and representation of a self-reliant subject who has mastery over his body and environment. The narrative technique of stringing physical intensities together like individually disconnected beads of a necklace is applied throughout. His ongoing struggle for survival, the stilling of his hunger, and his constant need for alcohol and hashish as a way of briefly escaping the harsh reality of life on the streets, are described in the same fashion:

> My life is not worth even one peseta now. After a few minutes of walking in the strong sun I began to feel sharp pains in my stomach. This sun will drive me crazy. I picked up a small fish that lay on the pavement, and smelled it.
>
> The odor was overpowering, unbearable. I peeled off the skin. Then with

disgust, with great disgust, I began to chew it. A taste of decay, decay. I chew it and chew it but I can't swallow it. I can't.

From time to time the small sharp stones hurt the soles of my feet. They hurt. I went on chewing the fish as if it were a wad of gum. It was like chewing gum. I spat it out. Its stink was still in my mouth. I looked down with rage at the mass I had spat out. With rage. I ground it into the pavement with my bare feet. I stepped on it. I ground it under my feet. Now I chew on the emptiness in my mouth. I chew and chew. My insides are growling and bubbling. Growling and bubbling. I feel dizzy. Yellow water came up and filled my mouth and nostrils. I breathed deeply, deeply, and my head felt a little clearer. Sweat ran down my face. Running, running.

The logic of intensities, crystallizing around the experiences of the body, breaks up any sense of causal motivational links inhering to a subject and thus any kind of *telos* in the text. Choukri draws on the reality of events he goes through. His prose is characterized by dispassionate sobriety and tempo: childhood and adolescent memories are described one after the other. There is neither time nor space for any kind of interpretation or reflection. The text functions like a body that, suffering hardship and want, is always driven towards gratifying its physical needs. This novel is thus not a text concerned with a sovereign subject who, drawing on its formative experiences, has secured the position of a detached observer and now looks back on his life. Rather, it is postmodern in the Barthesian sense: it deconstructs the aforementioned classical novelistic modes of reflection, mastery, security, house, meals or family by substituting them with the logic of the body. "The subversion of the intellect through the body will always be my pathological, but victorious madness."

What remains, ultimately holding text and body together, is the will to live, which is transformed in the second part of his autobiography into a will to read and write. Written twenty years after the first part, here we encounter a twenty-year-old first-person narrator whose world is still populated with drinkers, thugs, petty thieves, and prostitutes. But now the narrator has decided to learn how to read and write – a powerful caesura in the life of a drifter. What initially reads like the taming of the wild urge to life through culture and literature and perhaps even recalls an autobiographical *Bildungsroman* like Taha Husayn's *The Days* (1929), a classic of Arab modernism, gradually reveals itself to be a pathological obsession with reading and writing:

At that time I was reading anything I could lay my hands on: books that I'd bought or borrowed; and any item of printed matter that I happened to find on the ground. Mostly in Spanish. I developed a passion for reading. I'd even copy down the signs over shops and cafés. I'd write them on scraps of paper or in my notebook. They were mostly in Spanish too. I was more than ready to learn, even though I could have wished for better circumstances. Rimbaud was right when he said:

"It's not healthy to go wearing out your trousers on a school bench, studying." Wise words!

Reading and writing had become a sleeping and waking obsession with me. Sometimes I imagined myself as a big letter or as a pen.

Writing opens up a new world. Writing makes poetry possible, and it fosters a forgetting of the miseries of the present and the painful past. A self-portrait in *Streetwise* shows the narrator sleeping in a house entrance, his head resting on two books. While the chronological thread of Choukri's adult life is clearly plotted at the beginning of the text, the more the narrator penetrates into the world of texts and signs, the more this thread frays; the more the self becomes de-centered. The book even closes with a cryptic hymn to the city of Tangier:

But how to leave ... when you are my maze?
I am not of Ariadne's body, and not of Penelope's.
The waves have washed me up your shores,
Up towards the end of the coral reefs,
And when I met you with my gaze
The helpful thread of my search got tangled.

Choukri explains this loss of self by relating it to his desires – and recalls Roland Barthes' essay:

My desires are the secret that I live with. Possibly, they are the crime which no one will punish me for. I cannot drive desire from my body. A promise is an erroneous pledge. I will not wait to be paid by anyone. Rice: moderation. Bread: patience. Love: the salt – but always the madness of nature, never that of the temple.

A consistent, radical form of immanence characterizes the writing of Mohamed Choukri, an immanence that continuously subverts the autobiographical subject and allows the body, bound to sexuality, to follow its own logic. The unswerving exposure of life, of the body to a life without any moral, religious or metaphysical reference, is the fundamental motive in Choukri's writing, one that makes his work truly subversive both socially and with respect to the literary tradition.

SELECTED WORKS

Paul Bowles wa-l-ʿuzla fi Tanja (Paul Bowles and the Recluse of Tangier), Tangier 1972
Majnun al-ward (The Fool of the Rose), Beirut 1979
al-Khubz al-hafi. Sira dhatiya riwyaʾiyya 1935–1956 (For Bread Alone), Casablanca 1982

al-Suq al-dakhili (Zoco Chico), Tanger 1985
Zaman al-akhta'. Sira dhatiya riwa'iyya (Streetwise), Casablanca 1992
Wujuh. Sira dhatiya riwa'iyya (Faces), Tanger 2000

TRANSLATIONS

For Bread Alone, trans. Paul Bowles, London: Saqi 1993 (first published 1973)
Streetwise, trans. Ed Emery, London: Saqi 1996
In Tangier [*Paul Bowles in Tangier, Jean Genet in Tangier, Tennessee Williams in Tangier*],
     trans. Paul Bowles, Gretchen Head, John Garrett, London: Telegram 2009

FURTHER READING

Hartmut Fähndrich: "Fathers and Husbands: Tyrants and Victims in some Autobio-
     graphical and Semi-Autobiographical Works from the Arab World", in: Roger Allen,
     Hilary Kilpatrick, Ed de Moor (eds.), *Love and Sexuality in Modern Arabic Literature*,
     London: Saqi 1995, pp. 106–15
Stefan Wild: "Muhammad Shukri's *For Bread Alone*. A Hijra and a Book", in: Boutros
     Hallaq, Robin Ostle, Stefan Wild (eds.), *La poétique de l'espace dans la littérature arabe
     moderne*, Paris: Presses Sorbonne Nouvelle 2002, pp. 143–52
Salah Natij: *Comparatisme et réception interlittéraire. Présence du roman arabe en France.
     Le cas de Mohamed Choukri et de Tayeb Salih*, Montpellier 1990
Barbara Sigge: *Entbehrung und Lebenskampf. Die Autobiographie des marokkanischen
     Autors Mohamed Choukri*, Berlin: Schwarz 1997
Nirvana Tanoukhi: "Rewriting Political Commitment for an International Canon. Paul
     Bowles' *For Bread Alone* as Translation of Mohamed Choukri's *Al-Khubz Al-Hafi*", in:
     Research in African Literatures 34 (2003), pp. 127–44

OTHER WORKS CITED

Ahmad Amin: *Hayati*, Cairo: Lajnat al-Ta'lif wa-l-Tarjama wa-l-Nashr 1950 (English
     translation: *My Life*, Leiden: Brill 1978)
Roland Barthes: *Le plaisir du texte*, Paris: Seuil 1973
Tahar Ben Jelloun: *Harrouda*, Paris: Denoël 1973
Christian Friedrich von Blankenburg: *Versuch über den Roman*, Leipzig, Liegnitz: Bey
     David Siegerts Wittwe 1774
Gustave Flaubert: *Madame Bovary* [1857], in: Œuvres, vol. 1, Paris: Gallimard 2001
Michel Houellebecq: *Les particules élémentaires*, Paris: Flammarion 1998
Taha Husayn: *al-Ayyam I*, Cairo: Matba'at Amin 'Abd al-Rahman 1929 (English transla-
     tion: *The Days. His Autobiography in Three Parts*, trans. E.H. Paxton, Hilary Wayment
     and Kenneth Cragg, Cairo: The American University in Cairo Press 1997)
Stefan Wild: "A Tale of Two Redemptions. A Comparative Analysis of Taha Husayn's *The
     Days* and Muhammad Shukri's *For Bread Alone*", in: Angelika Neuwirth et al. (eds.),
     *Myths, Historical Archetypes and Symbolic Figures in Arabic Literature. Towards a New
     Hermeneutic Approach*, Beirut, Stuttgart: Steiner 1999, pp. 349–61

A New Trojan War?

Vénus Khoury-Ghata on Sexuality and War

Monika Moster-Eichberger

We are used to seeing war scenes in films, video games and clips, interactive games and on the internet. We are used to seeing valiant and victorious men revered, their ruses of war celebrated. The novels of Vénus Khoury-Ghata are also concerned with wars: like the war fought over Troy they are provoked by women, who are acclaimed for their resilience and daring, and who exploit the chaos of war to liberate themselves from traditional roles. In contrast, the men are depicted as pathetic creatures, helpless bystanders. Khoury-Ghata's female characters are strong women who take what they want, regardless of the consequences. Reversing conventional clichéd notions, it is the women who are presented as sex-craving monsters. The men are mostly submissive toys the women play with, ridiculous and "unmanly"; either they are pathetic lovers utterly subordinate to the women, unable to provide sexual satisfaction, or they go insane. War, violence and sexuality are interwoven in a remarkable way. For the author, it would seem that they are inseparable. Sexuality is presented as a violent act performed to satisfy basic drives, while the violence of war is sexualized and documented with images garnered from sexuality. Women live in a society that has become unhinged by the war conducted by men. In the unbridled living out of their sexuality these women seek to cast off the chains of their traditional role. They conduct their (gender) war sexually and thus shed the victim role.

Vénus Khoury-Ghata, born in Lebanon in 1937 and resident of Paris for the last thirty years, is one of the most famous Lebanese authors writing in French. She has established her reputation in France, where all of her numerous works have been published, as well as in Lebanon, her works being awarded several literary prizes. In 1980 she received the first of her numerous French literary prizes, the *Prix Apollinaire*. At the Frankfurt Book Fair of 1995 she was awarded the *LiBeraturpreis*, demonstrating her recognition outside of France and Lebanon. She is a member of various literature prize juries in France and Lebanon and co-editor of the journal *Europe*. Despite this acclaim, she is a controversial figure, her work defying firm categorization both thematically and stylistically: she writes both prose and poetry, and shows no restraint in facing up to and breaking taboos. The spectrum of her writing ranges from historical novels through to surreal experimental texts.

Madness

Her novels *Trouble about a Dead Moon* (1983) and *Deaths Have No Shadow* (1984), which form a thematic unity, are deeply provocative. They depict the story of Sarah, an Italian Jew who returns to the fictive country of her husband's family, which has been ravaged and torn by the turmoil of war: "la Nabilie", an anagram of "Liban" (Lebanon). In an allegorical and at the same time fantastic manner, the civil war in Lebanon and its impact on society and the individual are addressed, revealing how violence has penetrated into all areas of life, even the most private and intimate spheres.

The novels express the chaos of the war, the perversion of all norms on several levels. It is not only the thematic and configuration of the characters that mirror the bedlam of a society in war; a coherent plot capable of transporting a story is discarded in favor of a string of surreal and fantastic images – a technique later adopted by the Francophone author Ghassan Fawaz in his novel *The Wizzling Egos of Lost Wars* (1996). A family saga is only ostensibly narrated in snatches of plot and images. The actual thrust is to reveal a society in malaise. Just as Cubist paintings at first glance seem to be nothing other than accumulated details and fragments, refusing to merge readily into a composed picture, the narrative elements in Khoury-Ghata's work only come together to form a whole when looked at more closely. The whole is nothing other than the utter madness of war, which spares nothing and nobody.

In her novels Khoury-Ghata depicts a city that is "deranged" in the double sense of the word: dream and reality are as difficult to tell apart as truth and lies, life and death. Emotions degenerate into instincts, which in turn unleash violence. Hate, voracious lust, and violence rule instead of love. Perversion has become normality. It is therefore no wonder that people go mad in this atmosphere, as Sarah's husband does in *Trouble about a Dead Moon*. While it is the affair his wife lives out with the Hungarian violinist Max that first drives him insane, the bombs will later intensify his insanity.

In *Deaths Have No Shadow* the madness takes on epidemic traits. The unstable president, his nervous system worn out by ten years of war, finally succumbs to mental illness and with him the whole nation seems to go mad. Even the powerful head of the Christian militia, Sarah's brother-in-law Chérubin, can no longer always distinguish between delusion and reality.

War and the loss of norms

Not only people but also values, norms and gender roles are "deranged" in war. Women are torn out of their passivity within the patriarchal system and become active, whether as the new head of the family during the man's absence; as voluntary helpers, dispensing medical services, for example; or, in a few isolated cases, as fighters in the militias. In each and every case this radical shift brings about a change in their sex lives, over which they now have control in the chaos of war.

None of the characters in these novels obey the established norms and patterns of behavior; they are all "abnormal" in some way, due to their own personal histories and environments. Sarah, for example, flagrantly contradicts the conventional image of women: she picks out the men with whom she wants to have sex, even though she is vainly seeking genuine love; she decides when a relationship begins and when it ends; and she, not the men, sets the rules of the game. The war brings conventions into disarray, opening new paths and possibilities, not least in sexual relations. It is the war that seems to provide women like Sarah with the opportunity to transgress entrenched gender boundaries.

Gender relationships, in particular sexual relationships, which serve solely to satiate the obsessive need for sexual gratification, reflect the violent situation of a society shaken by civil war. All moral conceptions and codes of honor are overridden. Faithfulness between partners has become invalid, obsolete.

A new Trojan War?

In contrast to both of the aforementioned novels, which consist solely of isolated set pieces involving the protagonist Sarah, a story in the classical sense is told in *The Lover of the Notable* (1992). It is the story of Flora, a Christian of Polish heritage, who leaves her husband and children immediately after the birth of her last child to go and live on the other side of the Green Line with her lover, a Muslim notable. Although the novel is set after the civil war has come to an end, the peace is so fragile that a new war ignites between Christians and Muslims over this woman. A tug of war ensues, the Muslims wanting to keep Flora at any price, the Christians bent on winning her back. Losing sight of everything else, the fight for this woman becomes an obsession. The situation is perverse; at no point in time does anyone speak to Flora. Forces are mobilized to regain or defend a woman because both sides are possessed by the belief that Flora – or women in general – is at their disposal. Flora bucks against this, not feeling committed to any party.

In the same way as a new Trojan War flares up over Flora, in the aforementioned novels Sarah becomes the contested Helen. Sarah does not divide her suitors into two camps; what emerges instead is a war in which everybody fights each other, much like the Lebanese civil war with its frequently blurred and ever-shifting lines of conflict. When Sarah's husband is once more beckoned to share her bed after a long abstinence, his younger brother, Sarah's lover, decides to take action. He is not ashamed to drive through the city streets with a military jeep adorned with a portrait of his lover, a quasi declaration of war. At least he gains a partial success: shocked by the action, his rival loses his virility.

In revenge, Sarah accosts the first man she comes across to gain her daily sexual satisfaction. Like a cat on heat, she, "the hot Jewess", leaves the house night after night to find sexual gratification on the street, causing furor throughout the neighborhood. Every man now wants to have slept with the nymphomaniac at least once in his life. The men sleep daytime to go on the hunt for Sarah at night. But sleeping with Sarah is dangerous: besides branding them with a stamp to ensure that she does not sleep with the same man twice, she leaves serious burns and scratches on her "lovers'" genitals. One man comes away with second-degree burns to his penis; another is badly scratched by her fingernails. As the number of victims tops the one hundred mark, a lorry convoy filled with holy water is called in to fight her as if she were a vampire or the devil. Sarah has freed herself from the role of the passive Helen over whom men fight and become a predator. She now has men at her disposal; treating them like cattle, injuring and maiming their genitals: it is only a short step to castration. In an obsessive manner, she has turned the bestial male world upside down, her cruelty fully matching theirs.

Sexuality and war

Khoury-Ghata writes in the tradition of erotic Arabic literature, as exemplified by *The Thousand and One Nights*. But she goes far beyond this tradition: her presentation of sexuality is not playful; it is brutal, repelling, in parts also ridiculous and absurd, all in all provocative. The brutality of sexuality corresponds to the brutality of war and thus represents a means of starkly depicting the unimaginable violence unleashed by the civil war in Lebanon, a violence that strips away all social and moral norms. For her, civil war and the "battle of the sexes" are one and the same. The armed conflict gestates into a symbol for the inner conflicts of each and every individual and the conflicts between the sexes, hitherto concealed beneath the veneer of propriety.

In the novels of Vénus Khoury-Ghata incidents of war are given a sexual connotation, recognizable even on the microscopic level of the vocabulary employed, so that ultimately war and sexuality are equated. The advance of the "Hittite" fighters – the name given to Syrian troops in the novel – is announced as a "penetration in the south". Any lingering doubts as to the sexual connotation are dispelled when even Mme Alpha, Sarah's mother-in-law, can barely hold back her laughter at the "sexual resonance in the war terminology". Edmée, the gossip monger, who is briefly tempted into spying for the "Hebrews" (meaning the Israelis), depicts the events in Nabilie around the word "fuck". It has become irrelevant which words are chosen to describe what's going on. If war is sex and sex is war, then why not simplify language as well and reduce it to a single verb that covers both?

But the logic of a reductive equivalence goes even beyond vocabulary. With the war a real sex wave does in fact engulf the country:

> Following to the shellfire an orgiastic storm brushed over the city ... Sex became the currency ... A sexual fury lay over all districts ... Everywhere but in the houses, which where immobile targets, they made love. Crawling on all fours in the fosses, bestriding on the panzers, the sex in prolongation of the barrel of a cannon, or stooping behind the barricades.

The obsession with exerting power and the irresistible propensity towards destruction, of both the self and others, which are revealed in the conduct of war as in the uninhibited living out of sexuality, are not anchored in the individuals but in society as a whole. Everybody is afflicted.

As is customary in war literature, the phallic nature of weapons is emphasized, the penis at times replaced by a rifle. Because peace is not even secure in ceasefire periods, men never sleep without having a rifle at the ready between their legs. Their wives are so scared that the birth rate drops dramatically. Even everyday tools turn into phallic symbols: "The strong and regular hits of his hammer reminded of the hits of a male sex to find its way into the flesh of the woman." Weapons, tools and the penis are equated, becoming one soulless thing, serving the imposition of male domination and wielding violence. Sexuality is decoupled from love; the body becomes a battlefield.

Chérubin literally slugs out a battle on and in Sarah's body: "He surrounded her with his tenderness, attacked her with his kisses, conquered her flesh which he screamingly brandished like a trophy after having finished his victorious sex." He reduces her and her body to a sex object. Raging with jealousy and out of fear that she will leave him, he cripples her, makes love to her, or rather rapes her, until she cannot even move: Chérubin "imprisoned his lover in his bed and made love to her for such a long time that her legs broke down and made it impossible for her to go from one room to another." But Sarah is by no means depicted as a victim of male violence: she craves this brutal sexuality and seems to need it.

Eros and Thanatos

The physical attraction of heralds of death, like snipers and militiamen, represents a topos of civil war literature – doubtlessly because violence and sexuality come together here in a unique way. For the most part, these men are portrayed in deeply ambivalent terms. On the one hand they are merciless bearers of death; but they also display moments of touching kindness and are capable of being warm and caring, as in the relationship between the female first-person narrator and a sniper in *The Lover of the Notable*. The relationship that develops between the woman and Michel goes beyond sexual dependency; something akin to love arises out of what is initially purely sexual lust. It is Michel with whom she experiences her first orgasm, and he is the only person who steps out of the gray anonymity of the descriptive level and is addressed as an intimate counterpart with the familiar *tu*. He tells her about his ill-fated love for a Muslim girl, who was killed by her own brother because of his attention. To revenge this murder, he decided to become a sniper and kill all Muslims. For the first-person narrator, Michel is less a murderer than a sensitive young man: "You can say what you want, a sniper is so sensitive and so easy to destroy, just like the lives he sets an end to." By setting this relationship within the gender problematic, Khoury-Ghata goes beyond classical feminism, which views women as the victims of men. Men are also victims of the images and ideas foisted upon them by others, or indeed of those they create of themselves, and suffer under the weight of expectations.

In an environment marked by hate and violence, the relationship between Michel and the woman represents an isle of happiness – a theme previously taken up by Hanan al-Shaykh in her novel *The Story of Sahra* (1980). Despite this, both novels draw on the vocabulary of violence when depicting the sexuality between their respective snipers and first-person narrators. For all the affection she feels towards the sniper, the narrator is often seized by fear: "You hide behind your gun and point the barrel to the sky. You shoot everything which gets into your way. Every bird that falls down is welcomed with a howling of joy. Suddenly I am afraid of you and this roar of a savage." The ambivalence of their relationship, torn between closeness and cruelty, is only apparently a contradiction. In a society ravaged by war there is no enduring harmony and tenderness – the wounds inflicted upon every individual by the years of fear are too deep.

The violence becomes endemic just as the woman, convinced she is pregnant, asks the sniper to marry her. Beside himself with rage, he points his gun at her supposedly pregnant belly. Only at the very last minute does he yank the rifle butt upwards and shoot into the sky. As she hysterically screams that everyone is scared of him, he lunges at her throat, strangling her. But then the violent scene suddenly changes: to silence the girl the sniper kisses her, stifling her shouts until they turn into moans of pleasure. She begs him to enter her, but he breaks off, punishing her with contempt, turning cynical and cold: "Hook it or I will pierce you, crack your shell and slurp you like an egg." Slowly she realizes that he does not really love her. And yet he cannot live without her. He calls out her name incessantly in his despair, but is incapable of leaving his position on the roof of a residential block to go and see her. He remains trapped in his clichéd image of how a man should be; an image that prevents him from admitting any weakness and seeking solace with a woman. Ultimately, the girl is less of a victim than the sniper imprisoned in his understanding of the male role, for she has, of her own accord, used the war and her relationship with Michel to gain sexual initiation, satisfaction, and liberation.

The naïve Lucia, a former nun who previously lived in a lesbian relationship with a fellow nun, Anunciad, uses the war and its heralds of death to gain heterosexual initiation. She indulges in her first sexual experiences with men and hangs around the streets with militiamen. Once she is even raped by five of them at once but nevertheless, or perhaps precisely because of this pack rape, she is overcome with lust. The description of this rape covers the ambivalence she feels, the raw violence inflicted on her by the men as well as her cries of lust: "She did not show the least resistance. The five crossed her as quick as a train on rails. The idiot chuckled with joy ... She leaned herself far forward to make it easier for her rapists to rape her."

Bloodlust

Sarah also seeks physical contact with the militia in *Trouble about a Dead Moon*. She is impressed by the authority and aggressiveness of the militia chief Sabbab and lives out an exceptional erotic relationship with him: they spend twenty-eight days, a whole lunar phase, in bed. All the residents within a kilometer are evacuated, partly because "her orgasmic screams woke up everybody in the Muslim quarters of the west", and also because Sabbad ordered it so that he could "ejaculate everywhere." Their affair comes to an abrupt end with Sarah's menstruation. Sabbab, responsible for numerous bloodbaths during the war, cannot and will not see the menstrual blood: "Again blood, he shouted in a rage. Will we never get rid of this red shit." He turns into a raging animal, completely losing his mind:

> Sabbab crunched the mattresses, frazzled the slatted frame, cut the windows with his golden teeth, twisted the lusters with his hands and finally pissed from the balcony of his room in the 27th floor of the palace down on the heads of his sentries.

As he calms down again, Sabbab re-converts his militia headquarters into a hotel, which only girls before their first period and women in their menopause may enter.

It is not always possible to assuage the sex drive while at the same time fulfilling duties as a militiaman. Sabbab is so busy at his roadblock that he has no idea how he is going to cope with controlling the ID passes of those passing through the roadblock while fulfilling his "duty" to satisfy every girl; "the arrival of girls who need attention could coincide with that of men who have to be killed." Thus from time to time he has to let a girl pass without performing his duty, so as to attend his second duty as a militiaman, with his trousers around his ankles. Irritated by this "double burden", he shouts: "Can't I just fuck in peace? ... Is the war a good enough reason to let everything slide?"

Meanwhile Sarah has returned to Max, the Hungarian violinist who she had once loved so deeply. But his sensitivity and empathy, which once gave her so much pleasure, cannot satisfy her anymore. She demands that he become a replica of Sabbab, stating that he can sleep with her only when wearing his boots and that he should substitute his incisors with glinting gold-capped teeth. In order not to lose her he fulfils all her wishes. His obedience turns him into "a neurotic, a psychopath, and a hypochondriac". The responsive violinist is at once the caricature and cliché of a sensitive man. He is as ridiculous as Sabbab, except for the fact that sex with him is in no way as satisfying. This is the swansong for the loving, non-violent man who has deteriorated into a psychological wreck.

The sex and violence addictions of women

The sexuality described by Vénus Khoury-Ghata resembles rape and has nothing to do with love and erotic lust; one might say that the author allows her female characters to live out a violent sexuality, releasing them from the clichéd victim role.

The other residents in the building hold Flora responsible for the evil engulfing their lives; she is equated in their minds with moral decay, destruction, illness, war and death: "She has destroyed everyone"; "she brings misfortune, you can read it from her colorless eyes which have been washed out by tears." "Bad wife, bad mother, bad lover." It was not love that drove her to the Notable, which explains the repellant description of sex with him: she lies motionless under the weight of her lover, who "climbs" her as if she were a mare, "belabors" her for hours on end in the hope of bringing her to orgasm, and shouts: "Leave your power, leave your juice in my hand." Her refusal to submit or show her lust to the man is an act of revolt, a kind of castration by other means.

Sarah is also demonized, seen as the epitome of all ribaldry. She wants sex and is very direct in expressing this desire. Khoury-Ghata endows Sarah with a language that is consciously provocative and crude, such as when she shouts in *Deaths Have No Shadow*:

> I'm fed up with justifying myself ... Every guy who wants to mount me claims the CV of my ass and the timetable of my shanks. And what if I only want to whore around freely without justifying how my lower abdomen works?

Love never played a role in Sarah's earlier relationships either. She is fully focused on living out her sexual desires: displays of affection and expressions of love are alien to her. She spends the nights "aligning her body besides her lover's without ever having said the words 'I love you.'" For Sarah, sex is a possibility of achieving her aims. Consequently, her motto for life is: "Sex is the shortest way from one point to another." When fighting an influential man there is only one thing to do, to take the "childish solution" and "slink into his bed, sleep with him thirty times in a row, which makes his heart break into thirty parts." For Sarah, sex is the answer to everything and *the* means of solving problems, a means which in times of war even doctors praise as the panacea against the madness raging through the city.

Sex with the Jewess Sarah is life threatening, as a bar owner tells Max: "She didn't experience Auschwitz but she has it in her ... It is not because of profligacy that she changes her lovers so often but of mistrustfulness ... Let me warn you, she is an adventurer ... Diabolical." Here, a man at another table enters the conversation, remarking that she is more than diabolical, she is destructive. The bar owner takes up the remark and goes even further: Sarah is just like Hitler. In fact, Sarah does display a partiality to blood. She explains her habit of ordering a Bloody Mary each evening, which she then does not drink, as follows: "It's due to the florid name. It is bloody." She drives her lovers to suicide, or at the very least plays with them and makes fools out of them. She only sleeps with a banker according to a special "script": they are sailing the waves on a pirate ship and she dictates their course with commands like "hoist the sail", "turn to portside", "drop anchor" and finally "climb the mast" – the call for penetration. She reduces the enslaved man to a toy of her lust, making him and the whole sexual act ridiculous.

Without a doubt, Khoury-Ghata is once more seeking to provoke with this outrageous Nazi comparison, equating Sarah at once with Holocaust victims and Hitler. But the author cannot be reproached for anti-Semitism; Flora, a Christian, is also demonized. These diabolical comparisons should be seen as yet another way of exposing the absurdity of everything, while emphasizing that all religions harbor destructiveness. The characters of her novels are not realistically depicted everyday persons but allegorical figures.

Strong women – weak men

Khoury-Ghata's female protagonists are looking to change things in their own lives, in their relationships to men and their families. They are searching for self-realization, identity and sexual satisfaction. They wander between worlds, crossing borders; not only by crossing the demarcation line dividing the city of Beirut, but also in how they transgress the boundaries of their society: those of gender roles, decency, morality and good taste.

Fully preoccupied with herself, Flora discovers possibilities of transgression that are inconceivable for the other inhabitants of her apartment block, who represent the various groups in Lebanese society. In defiance of all religious and social constraints, she simply follows her own needs. Crossing the demarcation line – which Sarah also does – has a far deeper meaning in Khoury-Ghata's novels than the mere act of crossing a roadblock. Searching for love and self-determination, these characters dare to leave the world that is familiar to them and move into an environment that is alien and indeed hostile towards them.

The cliché of the strong man is disproved mercilessly. Women are the only ones who dare to explore other territories and conquer the terrain reputed to be solely that of men. Men are pathetic and helpless figures, a reversal of the omnipotence of machismo. They are incapable of coping with the fear which reigns in a war situation. In *The Lover of the Notable* Flora's son Frédéric tries to deal with his fear by writing poems or numb it by taking drugs. Only Flora, who experienced the Second World War in Warsaw, seems oblivious to fear. She is always the last one to seek shelter in the basement when shelling commences, because she prefers to stay in the apartment and calmly observe herself in the mirror. After she leaves him, her husband flees into a dream world, envisioning her return to the family. In another passage, he imagines a dialogue with her in front of the house of her lover. The distinction between reality and dreams becomes blurred and indistinguishable – a state the reader shares with him.

The only way of saving oneself from the influence of these strong women seems to reside in homosexuality. Vénus Khoury-Ghata explores the theme of homosexuality in both sexes as another form of sexual transgression, thus breaking yet another Arab taboo. Pining for protection, Frédéric seeks to find a sense of security as a girl. He does not want to endure this war as a man. After sharing friendship with a girl, he soon feels attracted to the militiaman Georges, lets his hair grow, and dyes some strands blonde. In this way he manages to keep out of the war primarily conducted by men. The moment he ceases to play the strong, courageous man, the men engaged in fighting lose all interest in attacking him. But homosexual love is also presented as soulless, inhuman and mechanic. The physical act of love between Frédéric and Georges is described as a horrible spectacle: "One crushes the other with his weight." Homosexuality is not presented as a freely chosen possibility; it appears rather as a flight from reality and from the female sphere of influence, and thus as an expression of weakness.

The family as the microcosm of a society at war

Stories of morbid families are also told in *The Mad Son* (1980) and *A House at the Edge of Tears* (1998). Both works must be approached and understood as literary attempts by Khoury-Ghata to work through her own childhood. At the same time, they give expression to the drama of the Lebanese conflict.

Both novels revolve around a violent father-son conflict that destroys the family. Hateful, ruthless and unpredictable, the fathers are isolated. At the same time, the portrayal of family life clearly implies the conflict in Lebanon; the brutality and potential for violence of the protagonists inherent to this constellation mirror as a microcosm the larger crisis of the civil war. As in the war, violence is a daily occurrence in the family. The battlefield here is not the streets of Beirut but the living room, which becomes a "place of oppression" and "theater of war". The son is beaten for every trifle; for a poem he writes or a stained sheet, the telltale sign of his masturbation. Blinded by rage, the father bashes the son. He does not care if the furniture is also smashed in the process and the blood of the battered son soaks the floor of the parental apartment. The family goes on living with these pools of blood in their living room just as the Lebanese people live with the pools of blood dotting the streets. As the Lebanese civil war is often seen as a proxy war, the war between father and son is also to be seen in these terms. The contempt and hate the father feels for his son, the beatings he metes out, are in fact directed against himself. Bitterly disaffected with his situation and displeased with himself, he needs a "scapegoat", and his son, deviating from preconceived norms, seems like the obvious object: he lives out his physical desire by masturbating and his sensitivity by writing poems, provoking the rage of his father.

Khoury-Ghata describes the monstrosity of the father, life with him as a "daily descent into hell"; a hell that is even worse than that of the civil war. For everyone else in the family, the father is the "hangman" and they his victims. This reality is so horrific that they all wish for nothing other than his death. The family members destroy one another, just as the Lebanese people are caught in a self-annihilating deadlock. The death of the father coincides with the end of the civil war – the end of violence across the whole country – and this in turn brings an end to violence in the family.

In contrast to the female characters of her other novels, the women here are incapable of becoming active. They remain passive, unable to free themselves from the situation and recognize that the war in fact offers them a chance. For them, war means suffering and so they decide to suffer. The women remain on the margins, mute, at the most weeping bystanders. Their scope for action is practically nil, whether in the family or in the civil war. Like the civil war, the familial war is one fought by men, where the women are powerless to do anything. This shows how Khoury-Ghata's female characters here, drawn from reality and therefore victims of male violence, differ from those of the aforementioned works, fictive characters rendered allegorically. What remains as a constant is the portrayal of weak, ridiculous men; even here the seemingly strong, despotic father is ultimately a pathetic figure, stripped of dignity, whose actions belie any earnest empathy on the part of the reader.

Smashed to smithereens

The war has broken the people, alienated them from themselves. Humans have turned into *hommes fragmentés*, people smashed to smithereens who are no longer at one with themselves; nothing more than patched-together limbs. The destruction that has taken place all around them is mirrored in their inner brokenness, the self maimed, relationships crippled. The soul that could give sense and cohesion to everything has gone missing in action.

In the novels of Vénus Khoury-Ghata, which plumb the depths of the civil war, there are only tragic figures. Even the end of the war is not enough to bring about a change in attitudes towards life. The wounds that this war, with all its hate and violence, has left behind are too deep. All of the characters are searching for their identity; as a man, as a woman, as a person. Their search never comes to an end; their questions are never answered.

WORKS

Le Fils empaillé (The Mad Son), Paris: Belfond 1980
Vacarme pour une lune morte (Trouble About a Dead Moon), Paris: Flammarion 1983
Les Morts n'ont pas d'ombre (Deaths Have No Shadow), Paris: Flammarion 1984
La Maîtresse du Notable (The Lover of the Notable), Paris: Seghers 1992
Mon Anthologie (Here There Was once a Country), Beirut: Dar an-Nahar 1993
Une Maison au bord des larmes (A House at the Edge of Tears), Paris: Balland 1998
Elle dit (She Says), Paris: Balland 1999

TRANSLATIONS

Here There Was once a Country, trans. Marilyn Hacker, Oberlin: Oberlin College Press 2001
She Says, trans. Marilyn Hacker, Saint Paul: Graywolf Press 2003
A House at the Edge of Tears, trans. Marilyn Hacker, Saint Paul: Graywolf Press 2005
Nettles. Poems, trans. by Marilyn Hacker, Saint Paul: Graywolf Press 2008

FURTHER READING

Carmen Boustani: *Effets du féminin. Variations narratives francophones*, Paris: Karthala 2003, pp. 77–89
Carmen Boustani: "La parole féminine dans les enjeux de l'arabité et de l'africanité: Vénus Khoury-Ghata et Mariama Bâ", in: *Phares-Manarat* 1/2 (2003), pp. 241–53

Zahida Darwiche Jabbour: *Parcours en Francophonie(s)*, Beirut: Dar an-Nahar 2002, pp. 67–87

Nelda Lateef: "Vénus Khoury-Ghata. Poet and Novelist", in: id., *Women of Lebanon. Interviews with Champions of Peace*, Jefferson: McFarland 1997, pp. 37–42

Monika Moster: "Chaos im Land, Chaos der Seele, Chaos im Kopf. Zur Darstellung des libanesischen Bürgerkrieges im Romanwerk von Vénus Khoury-Ghata", in: *Beiruter Blätter* 8/9 (2000–2001), pp. 111–15

Monika Moster: "Vénus Khoury-Ghata. Lärm um einen toten Mond. Ein Haus am Rande der Tränen", in: Angelika Neuwirth, Andreas Pflitsch, *Agonie und Aufbruch. Neue libanesische Prosa*, Beirut: Dergham 2000, pp. 129–33

Bahjat Rizk: "Les multiples vies et visages de Vénus Khoury-Ghata", in: Edmond Jouve et al. (eds.), *La Francophonie au Liban*, Paris: ADELF 1997, pp. 381–87

OTHER WORKS CITED

Ghassan Fawaz: *Les moi volatils des guerres perdues*, Paris: Seuil 1996

Hanan al-Shaykh: *Hikayat Zahra*, Beirut: Author's Edition 1980 (English translation: *The Story of Zahra*, trans. Peter Ford, London: Quartet 1986)

Beyond Autobiography

Under the Sign of Destruction: the First-Person Narrator in Alia Mamdouh's novel *Naphtalene*

Verena Klemm

> Umm Suturi emptied the bowls of hot water over my head, and soap went from hand to hand among my aunts. They rubbed and twisted my braids. I died among these women's fingers; my eyes were blinded by the soap lather. Aunt Najia clutched my thigh as if she were holding a chicken leg. My aunt sighed and leaned over her knee, her breasts putting me into a stupor. The soap, steam, and all that noise; I was an egg thrown into the ocean. I was moved from one lap to another and I saw.

In *Napthalene*, the Iraqi author Alia Mamdouh describes life in 1950s Baghdad, as seen through the eyes of a young girl called Huda. With tremendous poetic vividness, the novel follows her through childhood until she is about fourteen, amidst her extended family and neighbors in a traditional residential district in the heart of the city. A number of graphic scenes reveal the tyrannical nature of her father, a choleric police officer who is addicted to alcohol. Despite this destructive atmosphere, powerful episodes of female sensuality, passion and aggression abound. Relationships between the women, but also those between the children in the family and the neighborhood, are shown to be intensive and often tender and erotic. At times they even transgress the boundary to the illicit.

Huda tells of the people and spaces of her childhood, which she has harbored deep in her memory, as if she wanted to preserve them from annihilation and corrosion with "mothballs". The title *Naphtalene* – a hydrocarbon whose vapor is used as a household fumigant, as in mothballs protecting textiles – names the function of the novel, as a medium for protecting personal remembrance from being consigned to oblivion. It simultaneously evokes the association of the sweet and artificial odor whose small round pellets are a product of the petroleum industry. And so the title also refers to Iraq, which for the author is inseparably tied to the intense, often sensual, emotional experiences of her childhood in Baghdad. *Naphtalene* is not, however, an autobiography: beyond the biographical parallels, the figure of Huda, who tells of love, hate and great pain, is a mirror image for many girls in this city. This is a novel in which the personal merges with the collective.

Multiple partings from Baghdad

Alia Mamdouh was born in Baghdad in 1944. Like numerous other Arab writers of her generation, her biography reveals a "broken line": frequent breaks and new departures; a nomadic existence characterized by migration; loss of her home country and exile. In the 1960s, still full of idealism, she shared the values implied by "literary commitment" with a loose movement of progressive Arab writers and intellectuals. They sought to show the young nations that were emerging from colonial domination a path towards political freedom, modernity and a pluralistic and humane society. Many gradually lost even the semblance of idealism as the Middle East slid into violence. Losing all hope in the oppressive climate of violence, repression and censorship, Alia Mamdouh eventually left the Middle East; to the present day she does not know if she will ever return.

Her first parting from Baghdad was motivated by personal rather than political reasons. Aged twenty, she defied the wishes of her family to follow her lover, a much older, married journalist, to Beirut. She had already published a small novel under a pseudonym. Her father, like Huda's a police officer, had died a few years before. A well-read man with an extensive library of his own, he had sparked in his daughter an interest in both Oriental and Western literature. He also sought to prevent her from writing, even resorting to threats of violence. Alia Mamdouh had been separated from her mother early in life. After her husband divorced her, she was forced to return to her Syrian hometown of Aleppo without her two children and seriously ill with tuberculosis. She died there just a few years later. After the death of her father, Mamdouh managed to persuade her conservative grandmother that she could finance her school education by taking a job, and started to work for a newspaper.

After she had begun a new life in Beirut with her lover, who was a supporter of the pan-Arab Ba'th Party that was being persecuted by the Communist regime in Iraq, she had a sobering, harrowing experience: just like her father before him, her new husband now tried to prevent her from writing by threatening violence.

They returned to Baghdad with their son in 1968 when the Ba'thists seized power in a putsch. There, she worked at a newspaper founded by her husband and completed a degree in psychology. During these years her husband married a third and then a fourth woman. He allowed her to move back to Beirut with their son at the beginning of the 1970s. Shortly before, Saddam Hussein had claimed the leadership of the Ba'thist regime in Iraq.

In the Lebanese capital, a bastion of freedom and vitality that attracted journalists and intellectuals from all over the Arab world, the young Iraqi was at last able to nurture and express her creativity. She wrote for the feuilletons of various renowned newspapers and cultural magazines and published two collections of short stories. She remained politically independent amidst the ideological hothouse atmosphere of these years, and left the country upon the outbreak of the civil war in 1975. Returning to Baghdad, she became the editor-in-chief of the journal *al-Rasid*. She was finally able to divorce during this period.

In 1982 she left Baghdad once again – this time perhaps forever. Her position under the unrelenting pressure exerted by the censorship authorities in Saddam Hussein's regime was awkward and difficult, but this was not the immediate reason for her departure. What concerned her most was her son's impending drafting into active military service during the Iran-Iraq War. She chose to move with her son to Rabat in Morocco. Although she soon gained a reputation there for her work as a cultural journalist and was networked with critically minded intellectuals and writers throughout the Arab world, at the beginning of the 1990s she moved to Europe, settling first in London and then in Paris. There she was a Guest Fellow in 2001 and 2002 at the Centre George Pompidou as part of the "Cities of Asylum" program for persecuted and exiled writers, run by the European Parliament of Writers. Alia Mamdouh continues to live and work in the French capital, which is one of the main centers of exiled journalists and writers from the Arab world.

As a journalist and editor, Mamdouh has always been critical of any form of ideology and authority. She is well known for her intelligent and blunt observations of Arab intellectual and literary life as well as of East-West relations in culture and politics. Since 1981 she has published four novels, in which she presents her critical stance on power and culture, interwoven with an appeal for human creativity and freedom.

Huda and her world

Naphtalene is Alia Mamdouh's second autobiographically inspired novel, a work that established her literary reputation in the Arab world and a little later in Europe. Woven into a closely meshed and dynamic network of relationships made up of women and children, Huda is known locally as a "little monster". She relates her experiences of how the overriding patriarchal system seeks to dominate life in family and neighborhood circles. The main representative of the powerful and violent male authority is the father. At the end of the novel, the state assumes his destructive role.

The novel describes the old town neighborhood from Huda's eyes, which slowly widens as she gets older: her first, small world is the multi-storied building with a seemingly vast inner courtyard at its center. Nearby are other courtyards, the coffeehouse, the butcher shop, the bakery and cook-shop; a bit further away the Abu-Hanifa mosque, the local primary school and the broad Tigris, with promenades and parks along its banks. The alleyways and narrow streets between the apartment blocks and the souk are the stamping ground of the men who go about their business, drink tea, and play tricktrack. Women move in between this male activity and its terrain, some walking briskly, some ponderously, cloaked in their *abayas* (an over-garment covering the whole body). Many of the younger women appear chic and colorful, while scores of older women, obviously trying hard to seem chaste and virtuous or even invisible, wear dark, nondescript colors and yashmaks. Girls and boys are on the move in their school uniforms, sent on errands to do the shopping, or playing in the Tigris gardens in small mixed gangs.

The family sphere is in the apartment building, the inner courtyard and the roof terrace. This is where Huda lives, with her younger brother Adil; her mother, who suffers from a lung disease; Aunty Farida, a beauty who hopes to get married soon; and Aunty Najia, who may have been "passed over" and remained single but is nonetheless a strong female character in her best years. Whenever the male head, Huda's father, is absent, the grandmother is the mistress of the family. As his mother, she is the only woman whose opinion he listens to and at times respects.

> This grandmother was the center of the circle. I do not know where she concealed her strength. When she walked her footsteps were light and hardly audible. When she spoke, her voice was clothed in caution and patience, and when she was silent everyone was bewildered by her unannounced plans. She was strong without showing signs of it, mighty without raising her voice, beautiful without finery. She was beautiful from her modest hem to her silver braids. She was slim, of medium height, a narrow black band round her head, whose ends dangled by her thin braids. She was light-skinned. I never saw anyone with a white complexion like hers. It was a white between bubbly milk and thick cream. Her eyes were gray with dark blue, wild green, and pure honey-colored rays.
>
> When we saw her in the morning as we got ready for school, they were honey-colored, and by the time we came home in the afternoon they were blue. But at night they were gray. She was a well-organized woman; she loved justice and set great store by it. She rebuked my father and scolded him behind our backs, suddenly setting upon him, taking all her time, scattering him and tearing him apart, exposing him anew to us.

A career-driven police officer stationed in Kerbala prison, at first Huda's father returns regularly to the family in Baghdad. The visits soon become sporadic though: he has married another woman and moved in with her and their newborn son. When he does return to Baghdad, the whole family is exposed to his domineering whims. Even the grandmother's influence dwindlees. No amount of begging can help as the patriarch casts out his first wife, Huda's mother, due to her debilitating illness and sends her back to distant Syria, all alone. She dies there soon after, far away from her two children.

At this stage the old town quarter is still Huda's only world; a life elsewhere is unimaginable. As an adolescent, restrictions are imposed on what she is allowed to do; she is controlled by a strict traditional family and conventions. Despite this authoritarian upbringing, in the eyes of many people in the neighborhood she is a beastly little rascal, cheeky with an unseemly tendency towards impertinence and obstinacy. These characteristics seem to be nourished by a still subconscious need for self-preservation within the constrictive grip of a collective entity. But in many respects Huda is a young girl like any other in Baghdad at that time: she goes to school, gladly skips it and does so often, is always involved when her gang meets to play or there is a quarrel. She develops a crush on a boy called Mahmoud. Her father beats her in a fit of temper whenever he has even the faintest inkling of glances and contact. Sometimes a dramatic event ruptures the continuum of everyday life: the cruel disowning of the mother; later on, the news of her death during Aunty Farida's wedding celebrations and the panic it triggers in Huda, who then runs off to the Abu-Hanifa mosque. There, the traumatized child tries to disappear into the anonymous crowd solemnly celebrating the twenty-seventh night of Ramadan, hoping never to have to return home. Another episode that breaks the routine is the trip to the Shiite pilgrim site of Kerbala with her brother, grandmother and aunties. While the women circle the shrine of the martyr Husayn fervently wailing, praying, and beseeching, the two children are sent to the nearby prison, where the father, decorated with service medals but increasingly wrecked by alcohol and self-pity, works as a senior officer. Once there they plead with him on behalf of their grandmother to come back home. Towards the end of the novel, his ambitions to gain promotion having come to nothing, the father is seized by a fit of rage. Consumed by anger and frustration, he burns his uniform and medals and is immediately suspended from state service.

From I to you

The narrative voice in *Naphtalene* describes Huda's narrow world in a sober, objective tone. Neither concern nor emotion are aroused despite the lasting pain caused by the father's cold-heartedness and brutality; nor is there any sense of nostalgia when describing the tiny perishing neighborhood, whose residents are ultimately forced by the government to move out of the old buildings and relocate to other areas of the city. Throughout the novel, the distance between the narrator (now, of course, far older) and the young Huda is discernible only occasionally, for instance when the narrative voice switches subtly from "I" to "you", as if entering into an intimate soliloquy:

My tears did not flow. They found a different way of expressing themselves, and they held themselves back.

I did not stay long. When they left, when they took their suitcases and dreams, when they took all the streets, those things would be the only things that had power over you. I slammed the door behind me and went out.

It thus seems that Huda, the narrator, faces herself as a child and, at the very same moment, looks out at the world through the eyes of this same child. Perhaps with this contradictory narrative situation she is tracing the shifting counters of her own relationship to the protagonist: at times the original unity of self, space and time, which the novel strives to recapture through intensive acts of memory, is disturbed by an awareness of the unbridgeable gap to her present, cleaved open by the march of time and the disappearance of the world of her childhood.

The sensual and ambivalent female spaces

Huda's inner strength is nurtured by her untamable emotional and erotic needs in a milieu that is set on social and physical domestication. Her need for love and affection from her closest relatives, in particular her younger brother, is reflected in scenes of complete mutual trust, tenderness and care. Her awakening sexuality leads her to observe and experience with enormous curiosity the form, texture and functions of the female body when it is briefly liberated from social and religious constraints in the hammam. The homoerotic scenes between the young aunties are observed with the same detailed interest and impartiality as Aunty Farida's outburst of sexualized fury: having waited vainly for her husband since their wedding day, upon his entering unexpectedly she rips off his trousers and proceeds to thrash, berate and sexually humiliate him, full of pent-up anger and frustration.

Alia Mamdouh once characterized herself as a "writer of the sensual." In early life, caught in the oppressive confines of her family, her own body was her only refuge and her imagination the power capable of overcoming such hurdles and penetrating to the prohibited and tabooed: "That was where I placed my reliance as I moved toward maturity." For Mamdouh, the sensual is a "secret language" within Arabic; sensuality and poetic language extend and amplify inner worlds, bring people together, surmount their limits and antagonisms. The act of formulating this language overcomes the literary dictates and straitjackets which often characterized the didactic style of the social realism of the 1960s and 1970s.

In *Naphtalene*, Mamdouh's "secret language" leads into spaces that are the domain of women. These are not only the exotic and erotic realms conjured by the Western imagination: violence and suffering are very prevalent. Huda's narrative shows that these spaces occupied by women are in fact interstices, spaces limited and dominated by the male sphere of power. They have a double character: men have no permanent place there, because they do not live together with the women and children; they are sporadic intruders who continually and lastingly demonstrate their authority. The patriarchal order, represented by the grandmother, is mirrored in the female hierarchy as well as in the roles and status assigned to boys and girls. The grandmother undertakes nothing fundamental to challenge the authority of her son, whereby she ultimately stabilizes his role, as is evident in Huda's description quoted above. At the same time, she responds to his neurotic outbreaks of violence, consoling and protecting the family. She tells stories and so nurtures Huda's and Adil's fantasy lives. And while she incessantly recites religious phrases of forgiveness and repelling evil, she turns a blind eye to the erotic playfulness and escapades of the sensual aunties whose deepest desires remain unsatisfied. These women's spaces can be spheres of feminine personalities and bodies as well as sites of sensuality, sexuality and subversion. Symbolically, and sometimes in reality, male violence is nonetheless present in these spaces. Its impact on the bodies and psyches of the women and children is devastating.

A postmodern "secret language"

Alia Mamdouh's "secret language" of sensuality is part of a polyphonic literary current that seeks to shake the foundations of patriarchal and nationalist chauvinism in Arab states, societies and families through postmodernist and deconstructionist writing strategies. The authors who have set in motion this current are of the same generation. Like her, they have lived through the wars and the social upheaval and fragmentation that punctuate the history of the Middle East. After many years of postcolonial hope and literary commitment, they have learnt to distrust all ideology and official rhetoric. They also reject authoritarian Arab-Islamic traditions reverting to either open or veiled violence. The failure of earlier political and human hope and goals is shocking and painful for all those who shared these ideals and actively supported their realization during the climate of a new beginning that gripped the young Arab states. Their disillusionment, their profound distrust towards the nation and its dominant culture are something they share with numerous younger authors, who have themselves experienced political and social upheaval, violence, alienation and exile.

One particular characteristic of postmodern Arab literature is its humanist orientation. For this reason, the writers belonging to this current are known as the "new Arab humanists", a category that helps to distinguish them from the social realists of the postcolonial phase. Amidst the violent and authoritarian reality of the Middle East, these authors link their literary practice to approaches critical of society and culture, which they position and express beyond the framework of political ideologies. Their work often focuses on a powerless, isolated individual. What they reveal and analyze are the sources and destructive impact of the authoritarian forces and structures as embodied in the subject. The unrivalled forerunner of this literary focus was the Lebanese author Layla Ba'albaki. Fascinated by Simone de Beauvoir, as early as 1958 she portrayed the existential foundering of a female protagonist in conflict with family and social constraints in her novel *I Live*. Ba'albaki and her literary successors exposed in a single move that both the fathers and other male heroes – such as the leftwing nationalist committed intellectuals of the 1950s and 1960s, who were idealized and paid court to by progressive circles – were no more than loudmouthed weaklings with a propensity to violence.

The first-person narrator in the Arab context

The deconstruction of hegemonic political and social values often entails the use of the first-person narrator in Arab literature. Interweaving autobiographical with fictional strands, the first-person narrator has become a popular narrative form amongst critical female and male authors. In the Arab and Islamic contexts, focusing on the individual is itself a statement challenging the idealized collective entity of the religious community, the modern nation or the family. It is precisely in this sense that the first-person narrator is for Mamdouh a narrative device,

> a manner of putting myself in opposition to all, in the face of unjust ideas and iniquitous laws that were threatening my individuality – and my very existence – first and foremost as a female who was trying to undo and redo her relationship to the self, and then pushing it to the ultimate endpoint, to exercise a will that still has not diminished, the will to rebel.

Because the first person form concentrates on the individual's inward ponderings and any emotional damage that has been suffered, it is linked with an analysis of the open and veiled potentials for violence in religion, tradition, society and politics. This is characteristic of a number of novels written during or after the civil war in Lebanon, which in their retelling of first-hand experiences reveal a "history imprinted on the body." Of particular importance here are the authors Hanan al-Shaykh, Elias Khoury and Rashid al-Daif. Taking the ambivalent world of women as the central narrative space, the strategy pursued in *Naphtalene* and similar novels by the young Egyptian writer Miral al-Tahawi explore the slow but relentless process whereby the body and soul of a woman are tamed by structural and physical patriarchal violence, a repression that extends to mutilation. In al-Tahawi's work women are the hub of the world. More radical than Mamdouh, she breaks the conventional mould that was used to represent gender conflict in the 1960s and 1970s in committed Arab "feminist literature". In their efforts to achieve a credible "realism", these authors had mirrored the unjust divisions fissuring the social world, inadvertently bypassing any disclosure of the structural and symbolic centers of power. In al-Tahawi's novel *The Tent* (1996), set among Bedouins who have settled down in mainstream society, the outside world dominated by men is complemented by an autonomous female cosmos organized around a matriarch. As in *Naphtalene*, the grandmother, in the shadow of the mostly absent father, possesses the unchallenged authority. However, through maliciousness, envy and superstition al-Tahawi's grandmother figure drives her daughter-in-law, who gives birth to only "jinxing" girls, to social and psychological ruin. At the same time, the old Bedouin woman avenges the patriarchal society, for herself at least, by gaining autarchy over the female members of the family, which she wields mercilessly.

Beyond autobiography

With this concentration on the damaged self, which goes hand in hand with disclosing veiled sources and centers of power, the aforementioned authors move in a terrain that is far from the genre of autobiography, which has been a popular form of literary self-expression in the Arab world for decades.

Mamdouh's novel thus lacks the element decisive for an autobiography – credible, unmistakable authenticity and identity. Undoubtedly her protagonist Huda reflects the young girl growing up that she once was. Traits evident in other characters, too, are most likely gleaned from key persons of her own childhood world. Nonetheless, it seems that the real merges fluidly with the fictive in the literary rendering of Huda and all the people of her neighborhood; there are no autobiographical references to the depiction of concrete characters in the novel.

Another aspect running counter to what could be expected from an autobiography by Alia Mamdouh is that *Naphtalene* eschews plotting a continuous and ultimately successful path to an autonomous self. The novel leaves in abeyance the question of whether the narrator's will to assert herself, which saves her from total submission in her childhood and adolescent years, in fact leads to this goal. At the end of the novel, as the truck, loaded with household and personal effects, the grandmother, aunties and children, is leaving the neighborhood (which is about to be demolished), Huda knows of no-one whom she could wave goodbye to. The union between the families of the old town quarter, in whose female and childhood spheres she was protected and loved, has dissolved forever. As the truck moves from the old to the new district, Huda compares the lives of the people riding on the loading area to a trail of blood that stretches back behind them relentlessly.

This metaphor suggests an understanding of the figures as a community of fate and thus displaces an autobiographical historical outlook on what the future might hold for Huda and her family.

In Huda, Mamdouh develops a literary figure that moves beyond autobiographical congruity with herself. "The personal pronoun 'I'," the author once said, "is not an autobiographical confession for me. It is a convergence of the self with the other." In this sense, Huda's "I" does not harbor or express a distinctive, singular individual but is rather fashioned out of a synthesis of various, tightly interwoven life stories. The literary individual is a connecting "I" in whom the life and stories of a myriad of other people living in the Baghdad of the 1950s are captured – "women who suffered like I did," as the author confirms. Through this integrating and unifying usage of the first-person form *Naphtalene* may be understood as a "poly-biography" of victims in the face of violence.

In Alia Mamdouh's "secret language", a vision unfolds for writing a new self. This new self has surmounted the fixed limits of an autobiographically constituted identity. In this way, the painful failure of solidarity that the author has experienced in the course of her life within the social, political, and cultural spheres of the Arab world can be set in relationship to her literary search for the self, which itself interconnects people. In *Naphtalene* Mamdouh configures the community of the individual with others under the foreboding sign of omnipresent and powerful forces of destruction. The literary creation of the narrator's poly-biographical "I" leads the isolated, exiled individual back into a symbolic form of community that it has lost amidst the social and political reality of the Middle East.

WORKS

Layla wa-l-dhi'b (Layla and the Wolf), Baghdad: Dar al-Hurriyya 1981

Habbat al-naftalin (Naphtalene), Cairo: al-Hai'a al-Misriyya li-l-Kitab 1986; Beirut: Dar al-Adab 2000

al-Wala' (The Passion), Beirut: Dar al-Adab 1995

al-Ghulama (The Girl Who Lived Like a Boy), Beirut: Dar al-Saqi 2000

al-Mahbubat (The Loved Ones), Beirut: Dar al-Saqi 2003

TRANSLATIONS

The Loved Ones, trans. Marilyn Booth, London, Beirut: Saqi 2003

Napthalene. A Novel of Baghdad, trans. Peter Theroux, foreword by Hélène Cixous, afterword by F.A. Haidar, New York: Feminist Press at CUNY 2005

FURTHER READING

Farida Abu-Haidar: "A Voice from Iraq: The Fiction of Alia Mamdouh", in: *Women. A Cultural Review* 9 (1998), pp. 305–11

Abir Hamda: "Marriage, Madness and Murder in Alia Mamdouh's Mothballs and Salwa Bakr's Golden Chariot", in: *Raida* 18/19 (2001), pp. 47–9

Alia Mamdouh: "Creatures of Arab Fear", in: Fadia Faqir (ed.), *In the House of Silence. Autobiographical Texts by Arab Women Writers*, Reading: Garnet 1998, pp. 63–71

"A secret language has formed inside of the Arabic language. Conversation between Alia Mamdouh and Mona Chollet", in: *Autodafe* 2 (autumn 2001) (publication of the International Parliament of Writers)

Alia Mamdouh: "Baghdad: These Cities Dying in our Arms," in: Jocelyn Burell (ed.), *Word. On Being a [Woman] Writer*, New York: Feminist Press 2004, 5. 38–48

Alia Mamdouh: "Interview", in: European Cultural Foundation (ed.), *Remembering for tomorrow*, pp. 55–58, http://www.uclm.es/escueladetraductores/pdf/bookingles.pdf (access June 9, 2007)

OTHER WORKS CITED

Layla Ba'albaki: *Ana ahya*, Beirut: Dar Majallat Shi'r 1958

Miral al-Tahawi: *al-Khiba'*. Cairo: Dar Sharqiyyat 1996 (English translation: *The Tent*, trans. Anthony Calderbank, Cairo: The American University in Cairo Press 1998)

Contributors

Susanne Enderwitz is Professor of Arabic and Islamic Studies at Heidelberg University. She holds a PhD and habilitation from the Free University of Berlin. She was a Fellow at the Maison des Sciences de l'Homme in Paris 1992–3, and a Fellow at the Van Leer-Institute in Jerusalem from 1996–8.

Özkan Ezli studied German Literature, Sociology and Islamic Studies at Freiburg University, and earned his PhD from Tübingen University. He is a Research Fellow at the Center of Excellence "Cultural Foundations of Integration" at the University of Konstanz and teaches German Literature.

Hartmut Fähndrich studied Semitic Philology, Islamic Studies, Philosophy, Arabic and Comparative Literature at the universities of Tübingen, Münster and Los Angeles, and earned his MA in Comparative Literature and his PhD in Islamic Studies from UCLA. He has taught Arabic Language and Civilization at the Federal Polytechnical University of Zürich (ETH), and at the universities of Freiburg, Amsterdam, Naples and Lyon and is a distinguished translator of Arabic literature into German.

Stephan Guth is Professor of Arabic and Middle Eastern Literatures at the Department of Culture Studies and Oriental Languages (IKOS), University of Oslo. He studied Islamic and Middle Eastern Studies at the universities of Bonn, Cairo and Tübingen and earned his PhD from Bonn University and his habilitation from the University of Bern in 2003. He was a Research Fellow at the German Institute for Oriental Studies in Istanbul and Beirut and has been teaching at the universities of Berlin, Munich and Bern.

Andrea Haist studied Islamic and Arabic Studies, German Literature and Linguistics at the universities of Tübingen and Bamberg. She earned her PhD from Bamberg University and has taught Modern Arabic Literature at Bonn University.

Osman Hajjar studied Arabic Literature and Ethnomusicology at the Free University of Berlin. He is working on a research project entitled the "Experience of Aesthetics" at the Free University of Berlin.

Christian Junge studied Comparative Literature, Philosophy and Arabic Literature at the Free University of Berlin. He is a Junior Lecturer of Arabic Studies at the Free University of Berlin.

Ines Kappert obtained her PhD from the University of Hamburg, where she was also teaching contemporary literary theory. She is now an editor and heads the opinion department at the German daily *taz – die tageszeitung*.

Regina Keil-Sagawe studied Romance, German and Oriental studies at the universities of Bonn, Heidelberg and Paris and is a translator of literature from North Africa.

Verena Klemm is Chair of Arabic Studies at the University of Leipzig. She holds a doctorate in Islamic Studies from the University of Tübingen and a habilitation from the University of Hamburg.

Sibylla Krainick studied Romance and Islamic Studies at the universities of Tübingen and Freiburg and earned her MA from Freiburg University. She is a writer and translator.

Sonja Mejcher-Atassi is Assistant Professor at the American University of Beirut. She holds an MA in Comparative and Arabic Literature from the Free University of Berlin and a DPhil. in Oriental Studies from Oxford University.

Monika Moster-Eichberger studied Romance, Islamic Studies and Comparative Literature in Bonn and Paris. She earned her PhD from the University of Bonn and currently teaches French at a college.

Angelika Neuwirth is Chair of Arabic Studies at the Free University of Berlin and co-director of the Center for Literary and Cultural Studies. She earned her PhD from Göttingen University and her habilitation from Munich University, and has taught in Amman, Cairo and Jerusalem. She is also the director of the research project "Corpus Coranicum – a documented edition and a historical-literary commentary of the Qur'an" at the Berlin Brandenburg Academy of Science.

Friederike Pannewick is Chair of Arabic Studies at Marburg University. She studied Arabic, Oriental and Turkic Studies in Bamberg, Paris, Damascus and Berlin and earned her MA and PhD from the Free University of Berlin. She has taught in Berlin and Oslo.

Andreas Pflitsch is Research Fellow at the Center for Literary and Cultural Studies in Berlin and has taught Arabic Studies at Bamberg University and the Free University of Berlin. He holds an MA in Islamic Studies from Bonn University, a PhD in Arabic Studies from the Free University of Berlin and is a member of the EURAMAL (European Association for Modern Arabic Literature) Committee.

Doris Ruhe studied Romance and German Studies and Philosophy at the universities of Frankfurt/M., Gießen and Konstanz. She earned her PhD from Konstanz University and her habilitation from the University of Frankfurt/M. She has taught in Oran, Algeria, and has been Chair of Romance Languages and Literatures at Greifswald University since 1994.

Roland Spiller is Chair of Francophone and Latin-American Literature at Frankfurt University. He studied Romance and Islamic Studies in Erlangen, Granada and Buenos Aires and earned his PhD and habilitation from the University of Erlangen-Nürnberg.

Ulrike Stehli-Werbeck teaches Arabic and Islamic Studies at the universities of Münster, Bochum and Bayreuth, where she was Professor of Arabic Studies from 2005–8. She studied Arabic and Islamic Studies, Semitic Philology, Old History, and Literary Criticism at the universities of Münster and Damascus and holds a PhD from Münster University. She was a member of the EURAMAL (European Association for Modern Arabic Literature) Committee from 1999–2005.

Christian Szyska studied Islamic Studies at Bonn University. He has published on Modern Arabic, Hebrew and Turkish Literatures.

Stefan Weidner studied Islamic and German Studies and Philosophy at the universities of Göttingen, Damascus, Berkeley and Bonn. He is the author of numerous books and a distinguished translator of modern Arabic poetry. Since 2001 he has been Editor-in-Chief of the cultural journal *Fikrun wa Fann* (Art & Thought).

Barbara Winckler is a Research Fellow at the Center for Literary and Cultural Studies in Berlin and teaches Modern Arabic Literature at the Free University of Berlin where she earned her MA in Islamic Studies, French Literature and Anthropology, as well as her PhD in Arabic Studies.

Index

Abd al-Sabur, Salah 43, 44, 45, 410–428
Abdeljaouad, Hédi 246
Abdul Aziz ibn Saud 139
Abou-Haidar, Elias 308, 328
Abraham 53, 129, 130, 206, 337
Abu Nuwas 171
Abu Tammam 171
Aciman, André 309, 326
Adam 180, 225, 277, 305
Adnan, Etel 113, 240, 311–320, 328, 383
Adonis 58, 65–75, 90, 106, 173, 239, 318,
    342, 344
Adorno, Theodor W. 343
Afghani, Jalaladdin al- 88
Aghacy, Samira 131
Alameddine, Rabih 61, 242, 304, 308,
    321–330
Allende, Isabel 370
Amichai, Yehuda 266, 268
Amin, Ahmad 462
Amin, Nora 445, 447, 456
Amiralay, Omar 97, 99
Anderson, Benedict 238
Andrukhovych, Yuri 25, 239, 240
Antze, Paul 41
Anzaldúa, Gloria 316
Aquinas, Thomas 119
Arafat, Yassir 322
Aragon, Louis 172, 185, 246, 294, 295
Arkoun, Mohammed 26
Arnaud, Jacqueline 248
Asad, Hafez al- 221
Aslan, Ibrahim 29
Asma'i, al- 70
Assaf, Roger 91
Assmann, Jan 41
Auden, Wystan Hugh 410
Augustine 71, 440, 466
Avnery, Uri 183

Awwad, Tawfiq Yusuf 60
Azm, Sadiq al- 31, 42, 43, 197
Azoulay, Ariella 49
Azzam, Abdallah 125

Ba'albaki, Layla 60, 362, 363, 491
Bach, Johann Sebastian 307
Badawi, M. M. 415
Bakhtin, Mikhail M. 92, 298, 364, 451
Barak, Ehud 193
Barakat, Hoda 61, 328, 366, 382–396
Barakat, Najwa 61
Barthes, Roland 48, 89, 307, 372, 412, 454,
    455, 465, 468, 469
Bartol, Vladimir 253
Baudelaire, Charles 246
Beauvoir, Simone de 491
Bechara, Souha 125, 126
Beck, Ulrich 233, 234
Becker, Boris 307
Beckett, Samuel 237, 259, 463
Beethoven, Ludwig van 307
Begin, Menachim 322
Bel, Alfred 105
Benjamin, Walter 192
Ben Jelloun, Tahar 35, 366, 367, 369–381,
    462, 463, 466
Benlazhar, Abderrahmane 250
Bernhardt, Sarah 325
Berque, Jacques 426
Beydoun, Abbas 34, 35
Bhabha, Homi K. 51, 239, 298, 313, 316
Biller, Maxim 76
Bin Laden, Usama 247
Blanchot, Maurice 89
Blankenburg, Christian Friedrich von
    464, 465
Böll, Heinrich 27, 295
Borchert, Wolfgang 295, 296

Borges, Jorge Luis 33, 76, 321, 322, 372, 375, 376, 377, 452, 453, 455
Bosch, Hieronymus 276
Boudjedra, Rachid 366, 397–409, 432
Boullata, Issa 183
Boumedienne, Houari 250
Bouteflika, Abd al-Aziz 406, 407
Bowles, Paul 461, 463
Bradshaw, John 374
Brecht, Bertolt 98, 122
Breton, André 244, 343, 349
Britten, Benjamin 130
Bryar, Gavin 311
Buero Vallejo, Antonio 101
Bush, George W. 34
Butler, Judith 17, 364, 369, 370

Camus, Albert 113
Canetti, Elias 466
Castoriadis, Cornélius 373
Celan, Paul 173, 185, 188, 189, 190, 192, 254, 343, 351, 352, 353
Cervantes, Miguel de 322
Cézanne, Paul 315
Chanel, Coco 236
Charlemagne 238
Chedid, Andrée 240
Chopin, Frédéric 463
Choukri, Mohamed 367, 461–470
Cixous, Hélène 17
Cocteau, Jean 397
Colla, Elliott 332
Cook, Thomas 307
Crémieux, Francis 295
Cruise, Tom 322

Daif, Rashid al- 30, 61, 110–133, 306, 383, 387, 491
Daoud, Hassan 61, 113
Darraj, Faysal 108
Darwish, Mahmoud 35, 44, 47, 48, 51, 52, 53, 54, 55, 56, 60, 90, 123, 124, 126, 128, 129, 130, 171–196, 198, 200, 203, 207, 208, 209, 210, 213, 216, 259, 318, 414, 416
Daumier, Honoré 417
Debord, Guy 347
DeKoven Ezrahi, Sidra 47
Deleuze, Gilles 20, 21, 22
Demirkan, Renan 236
Derrida, Jacques 16, 18, 19, 20, 78, 80
Descartes, René 226, 228
Dhikri, Mustafa 46, 444–460
Dib, Mohammed 243
Diderot, Denis 256
Diner, Dan 50, 131
Diogenes of Sinope 461
Djebar, Assia 362, 368, 370, 397, 429–443
Domin, Hilde 253
Dostoyevsky, Fedor 332
Dugas, Gaetan 322
Dunqul, Amal 42
Durrell, Lawrence 84, 267, 268, 270

Eco, Umberto 13
Eddé, Dominique 328
Elias, Mari 102, 103, 108
Elias, Norbert 461
Eliot, T. S. 44, 199, 410, 411
Ellis, Bret Easton 22, 23
Enzensberger, Hans Magnus 35
Ette, Ottmar 329
Eugene, Prince 34
Eugenides, Jeffrey 235, 241
Eve 225, 305
Ezekiel 282, 283
Ezrahi, Yaron 266

Faiz, Faiz Ahmad 43
Farghali, Ibrahim 445
Fattal, Simone 313
Faulkner, William 398
Fawaz, Ghassan 115, 472
Fayrouz 60
Federman, Raymond 31
Feldhay Brenner, Rachel 51
Fisch, Harold 414

Flaubert, Gustave 398, 462
Fo, Dario 259
Forster, Edward Morgan 84
Foucault, Michel 15, 20, 89, 184, 372, 373, 375, 376, 378, 457
Frank, Anne 322
Frank, Manfred 17
Franz Joseph I 240
Freud, Sigmund 378, 379
Frisch, Max 305

Gable, Clark 448
Gaddafi, Muammar al- 152
Gagarin, Yuri 121, 122
Galiev, Sultan 251, 253
Galileo 278
García Lorca, Federico 172
Geary, Patrick J. 238
Genet, Jean 372, 463
Gertz, Nurith 56
Ghanayim, Muhammad Hamza 193
Ghitani, Gamal al- 31, 42, 46, 146–157, 225
Gibran, Kahlil 90, 132, 311, 325, 410
Glissant, Edouard 92, 316
Goethe, Johann Wolfgang von 77, 78, 238, 307, 465, 466
Goetz, Rainald 13, 14
Gosh, Amitav 236
Grass, Günter 398
Greenberg, Clement 318
Grünbein, Durs 35
Gruša, Jirí 309
Guattari, Félix 20, 21, 22

Habash, Georges 88, 306
Habermas, Jürgen 16, 234
Habibi, Emile 30, 53, 54, 55, 56, 126, 173, 197–219, 259, 415
Habshi al-Ashqar, Yusuf 61
Hafez, Sabry 223, 444, 447
Hagar 206, 337
Hajj, Unsi al- 342
Hakim, Tawfiq al- 138

Halbwachs, Maurice 46
Hammoud, Hani 241, 242, 308, 328
Hanania, Tony, 242, 302–310, 328
Handke, Peter 27, 79, 239
Hariri, Abu Muhammad al-Qassim b. 'Ali al- 200, 201
Harun al-Rashid 238, 454
Hasan II (Morocco) 461
Hassan, Husni 445
Hassan-i Sabbah 251
Hatoum, Milton 329
Hawi, Khalil 60, 111
Hawraniyya, Said 222
Heath, Peter 201, 203, 206, 207
Hegel, Georg Wilhelm Friedrich
Heidegger, Martin 244, 290
Heine, Heinrich 192, 237, 307
Henein, Georges 343
Hever, Hanan 266
Hikmet, Nazim 172
Himmish, Bin Salim 225
Hirschfeld, Magnus 457
Hitler, Adolf 479
Hölderlin, Friedrich 256
Hosea 282, 283
Houellebecq, Michel 462
Husayn, Rashid 56
Husayn, Taha 29, 138, 155, 468
Hussein, Saddam 137, 152, 485, 486
Hutcheon, Linda 446

Ibn 'Arabi 93, 149
Ibn Iyas 148
Ibn Khaldoun 102, 104, 105, 244, 440
Ibn al-Muqaffa' 58, 226
Ibn Qutayba 413
Ibn Saud see Abdul Aziz ibn Saud
Ibn Sina 311
Ibrahim, Sonallah 29, 42, 46, 114, 115, 158–170, 448
'Id, Yumna al- 317
Idlibi, Ulfat al- 222
Idris, Yusuf 42

Imalayène, Fatima-Zohra *see* Assia
   Djebar
Isaac 129, 206, 263
Isfahani, Abu l-Faraj al- 68
Ishmael 31, 206
Ismat, Adil 445

Jabra, Jabra Ibrahim 28, 48, 53, 56, 111
Jacob 201
Jahin, Salah 42, 416
Jalal al-Din Rumi 311
Jameson, Fredric 13, 14, 21, 455
Janabi, Abdalqadir al- 342–358
Jarrar, Maher 117, 118
Jarrar, Nada Awar 328
Jauß, Hans Robert 82
Jehoschua, Abraham B.
Jesus 322
Jibril, Ahmad 306
Job 267
Johnson-Davies, Denys 161
Jong, Erica 236
Joris, Pierre 244, 248, 254, 256
Joseph 261, 390
Joyce, James 115, 197, 237, 254, 377, 398
Judas 322
Jung, Carl Gustav 414

Kafka, Franz 115
Kanafani, Ghassan 53, 56, 59, 60, 174
Karasholi, Adel 237
Kateb Yacine 397, 429
Kavafis, Konstantinos 84
Kawabata, Yasunari 111, 120, 128, 131
Kerouac, Jack 342
Khadija 355, 356
Khairallah, As'ad 414, 415
Khal, Yusuf al- 57, 318
Khalaf, Samir 59, 118
Kharrat, Edwar al- 32, 33, 45, 76–85, 222,
   241, 444, 446, 452
Khashaba, Sami 415
Khater, Akram 58, 202
Khatibi, Abdelkebir 316

Khayyam, Omar al- 227, 251
Khleifi, George 56
Khleifi, Michel 56, 217
Khodr, Georges 88
Khoury, Elias 30, 32, 33, 61, 62, 87–96, 107,
   113, 115, 123, 124, 127, 173, 186, 187, 193,
   318, 382, 383, 491
Khoury-Ghata, Vénus 113, 115, 367, 383,
   471–483
Kleeberg, Michael 34, 35
Koni, Ibrahim al- 237, 331–341
Kotzwinkle, William 115
Kraus, Karl 343
Kraus, Wolfgang 446
Krishnamurti 322
Kristeva, Julia 17, 379
Krochmalnik, Daniel 49
Kundera, Milan 237, 309
Kureishi, Hanif 236

Laâbi, Abdellatif 416
Labib, Tahir 107
Lahad, Antoine 125
Lahiri, Jumpha 236
Lambek, Michael 41
Lautréamont, Comte de 344
Leeuwen, Richard van 175, 177, 178
Leibniz, Gottfried Wilhelm 200
Lejeune, Philippe 82
Lenin 253
Le Va, Britta 149
Levin, Hanoch 129
Levinas, Emmanuel 23
Lionnet, Françoise 316
Lorca, García *see* García Lorca, Federico
Lotman, Yuri 371
Lowenfels, Walter 314
Lukács, Georg 327
Lyotard, Jean-François 15, 16, 20

Maalouf, Amin 241, 253
Maghut, Muhammad al- 57
Mahfouz, Naguib 9, 30, 45, 57, 61, 87, 134,
   136, 138, 149, 150, 155, 464

Mahmud, Abdelrahim 182
Mailer, Norman 342
Mallarmé, Stéphane 316
Mamdouh, Alia 367, 484–494
Mann, Thomas 76, 237, 448, 449
Manson, Marilyn 236
Maqrizi, Taqi al-Din Ahmad al- 148
Marcuse, Herbert 342
Marquis de Sade see Sade, Donatien
    Alphonse François
Marx, Karl 200, 206
Masalha, Salman 193
Meir, Golda 297
Meyer, Stefan G. 87, 90, 391
Meyer, Thomas 306
Michelangelo 162
Midas 277
Mikhael, Sami 211
Milich, Stephan 186, 189, 190
Miller, Henry 236
Mina, Hanna 57, 222
Mohammed VI (Morocco) 461
Montesquieu 247
Morissette, Alanis 236
Mortimer, Mildred 434
Moses 244, 245, 277
Mouillaud-Fraisse, Geneviève 248
Mozany, Hussain Al- 238
Mozart, Wolfgang Amadeus 307
Mroué, Rabih 62, 91, 126, 127
Mubarak, Hosni 148, 165, 167, 168
Muhammad 214, 216, 226, 355, 356, 377
Munif, Abdelrahman 28, 108, 134–145,
    334
Murakami, Haruki 80
Musa, Salama 342
Musawi, Muhsin Jassim al- 447
Mutanabbi, al- 171, 227

Nabokov, Vladimir 237
Nabulsi, Shakir al- 416
Naguib, Nagi 43, 412, 414, 415
Naimy, Mikhail 60, 114, 132, 463
Najm, Ahmad Fuad 42

Nancy, Jean-Luc 123
Napoleon Bonaparte 225
Naqqash, Samir 272–286
Nasrallah, Emily 60, 132, 362, 363
Nasrallah, Yusri 90
Nasser, Gamal Abd al- 41, 42, 43, 80,
    146, 147, 148, 149, 150, 153, 161, 162,
    166, 297
Nassib, Sélim 61, 115, 234, 287–301, 328,
    385, 415
Nastase, Ilie 307
Natij, Salah 462
Negel, Joachim 118, 119
Neruda, Pablo 172
Nietzsche, Friedrich 20, 129, 410
Niffari, al- 70, 246
Nizam al-Mulk 251
Nizon, Paul 80
Noah 227
Novalis 175, 256, 327
Nu'ayma, Mikha'il see Naimy, Mikhail

Obenzinger, Hilton 176
Ortega y Gasset, José 335
Orwell, George 115
Owen, Wilfred 130
Oz, Amos 30, 31, 266
Özakin, Aysel 236
Özdamar, Emine Sevgi 235
Özdogan, Selim 236

Pascal, Blaise 364
Peled, Mattityahu 183
Pharaon, Albert 297
Picasso, Pablo 315
Piscator, Erwin 98
Plato 365, 392
Pontius Pilate 295
Portman, John 14
Pound, Ezra 316
Prose, Francine 141
Proust, Marcel 82, 326, 398, 450, 455

Qabbani, Nizar 57

Qaffash, Muntassir al- 445
Qasim, Samih al- 56, 198
Qays ibn al-Mulawwah 413

Raad, Walid 62
Rabikovitch, Dahlia 53
Rahbani, 'Asi and Mansur 60
Ramadan, Somaya 445, 446, 453
Rami, Ahmad 296, 297
Ramses II 161, 162
Raz-Krakotzkin, Amnon 54, 217
Reagan, Ronald 322, 324
Revel, Jean-François 398
Ricardou, Jean 398, 450
Ricœur, Paul 444
Rilke, Rainer Maria 410
Rimbaud, Arthur 244, 256, 344, 469
Robbe-Grillet, Alain 28
Roosevelt, Eleanor 322
Rosenzweig, Franz 176
Rothschild, Jacob 201, 209
Rousseau, Jean-Jacques 465
Roy, Arundhati 236
Rumi see Jalal al-Din Rumi
Rushdie, Salman 197, 236

Sa'adawi, Nawal al- 362, 363
Sabbag, Elie-Pierre 328
Sabbagh, Mohamed al- 463
Sadat, Anwar al- 80, 100, 148, 149, 150,
    153, 162, 165, 166, 411
Sade, Donatien Alphonse François
    Marquis de 344
Safranski, Rüdiger 34, 233
Said, Ali Ahmad see Adonis
Said, Edward 30, 55, 61, 87, 107, 111, 141,
    177
Said, Khalida al- 90
Said Makdisi, Jean 304
Saneh, Lina 62
Sarid, Yossi 193
Sartre, Jean Paul 29
Saussure, Ferdinand de 20
Sayf al-Dawla 227

Sayyab, Badr Shakir al- 44, 180, 185, 318
Schiller, Friedrich 77, 307
Schleichert, Hubert 31
Schumann, Robert 307
Seferis, Georges 250
Seigneurie, Ken 110, 119, 130, 131, 383
Serreau, Jean-Marie 97
Shabbi, Abu al-Qasim al- 466
Shakespeare, William 322
Shammas, Anton 54, 55, 202, 203, 234,
    259–271, 415
Sharawi 167, 168
Sharif, Mahir al- 108
Sharuni, Yusuf al- 222
Shawish, Fayza al- 108
Shawqi, Ahmad 413, 417, 422, 426
Shaykh, Hanan al- 113, 328, 391, 476, 491
Shehadeh, Raja 111
Shukri, Ghali 42
Siddiq, Muhammad 106
Silberstein, Laurence 50
Simon, Claude 29, 398
Sloterdijk, Peter 26
Snir, Reuven 55
Solomon 390
Spitzer, Leo 450
Stalin 253
Stein, Gertrude 90
Stendhal 141, 246
Stich, Michael 307
Strauß, Botho 33, 34

Taha, Ibrahim 202, 203
Tahawi, Miral al- 445, 447, 491, 492
Talbi, Mohammad 105
Tamerlane see Timur Lenk
Tamir, Zakariyya 58, 220–230
Tan, Amy 322, 326
Tàpies, Antoni 315
Tarafa 256
Tariq Ibn Ziyad 226, 244
Tawada, Yoko 235, 236
Telmissany, May 445, 447, 453
Tengour, Habib 33, 234, 239, 243–258

Timur Lenk 103, 104, 226, 244
Trakl, Georg 307
Tuqan, Fadwa 48, 56
Turner, Victor 365
Tuschick, Jamal 237

Ujayli, Abd al-Salam al- 222
'Umar ibn al-Khattab 68, 69
Umm Kulthum 296, 297, 307, 327
Updike, John 141

Valk, Thorsten 175
Virilio, Paul 15
Vivaldi, Antonio 307
Voltaire 200

Wallace, David Foster 23
Wannous, Saadallah 57, 97–109

Wei Hui 236, 241
Williams, Tennessee 463
Wilson, Robert 311
Wilson, Woodrow 238
Wollschläger, Hans 197

Yacine, Kateb *see* Kateb Yacine
Yeats, William Butler 410
Yehoshua, A. B. 54, 267
Yesenin, Sergei 253
Yunan, Ramsis 343

Zaimoglu, Feridun 236
Zayyad, Tawfiq 198
Zetnik, K. 259
Zuleikha 390